ISBN 978-0-364-28022-5
PIBN 11338758

1 MONTH OF
FREE
READING

at

www.ForgottenBooks.com

By purchasing this book you are
eligible for one month membership to
ForgottenBooks.com, giving you
unlimited access to our entire
collection of over 1,000,000 titles via
our web site and mobile apps.

To claim your free month visit:
www.forgottenbooks.com/free1338758

English
Français
Deutsche
Italiano
Español
Português

www.forgottenbooks.com

Mythology Photography **Fiction**
Fishing Christianity **Art** Cooking
Essays Buddhism Freemasonry
Medicine **Biology** Music **Ancient
Egypt** Evolution Carpentry Physics
Dance Geology **Mathematics** Fitness
Shakespeare **Folklore** Yoga Marketing
Confidence Immortality Biographies
Poetry **Psychology** Witchcraft
Electronics Chemistry History **Law**
Accounting **Philosophy** Anthropology
Alchemy Drama Quantum Mechanics
Atheism Sexual Health **Ancient History**
Entrepreneurship Languages Sport
Paleontology Needlework Islam
Metaphysics Investment Archaeology
Parenting Statistics Criminology
Motivational

From
A Surgeon's Journal

1915–1918

By

HARVEY CUSHING

With Illustrations and Maps

BOSTON

LITTLE, BROWN, AND COMPANY

1936

THE ATLANTIC MONTHLY PRESS BOOKS
ARE PUBLISHED BY
LITTLE, BROWN, AND COMPANY
IN ASSOCIATION WITH
THE ATLANTIC MONTHLY COMPANY

To

K. C.

for her sympathy
and understanding
through all this

287412

The marrow of the tragedy is concentrated in the hospitals. . . . Well it is their mothers and sisters cannot see them—cannot conceive and never conceived these things. . . . Much of a Race depends on what it thinks of death and how it stands personal anguish and sickness. . . .

—WALT WHITMAN, *Memoranda During the War*

EDITOR'S FOREWORD

IT is seldom realized how few of our contemporaries possess or seek to cultivate the diarist's habit. The tension of modern living, with its inevitable physical fatigue by nightfall; the availability of telephone, telegraph, and typewriter, which so facilitate our transaction of business and our communication of family affairs —fast living and ready service have between them curbed the impulse to jot down those personal records which so often illuminate our knowledge of the past. People to-day lack the incentive to rise as early as Pepys, or the persistence to write as late as Boswell. Good diarists are few and far between, and their paucity will be felt in the future.

There are of course exceptions, as this volume goes to show. Of the various arms of the service engaged in the Great War, the Medical Corps was surely the most humane and probably the best capable of "a long and dispassionate view." Army regulations did not encourage the keeping of diaries, but we know that the staff officers at headquarters set down their daily impressions, while in small dog-eared volumes many men in the front lines made penciled notes of their experiences. Those that have been preserved, in so far as they give an intimate picture of the war, are of utmost importance in strengthening our minds against the suicide of such another conflict. But no record of the war is complete until we have heard from those skillful and tireless noncombatants, the surgeons and nurses who fought for life in the hospitals behind the lines, taxing their skill and their pity to repair what the guns had done.

Dr. Cushing saw the war on the Western Front at close quarters. His first duty was in the early spring of 1915 when he served with a Harvard Unit in the American Ambulance at Neuilly,

France. At that time he became familiar with the French Service de Santé. From Paris he went on a visit to the Royal Army Med_ ical Corps and saw at first hand their work in Flanders. On his return to this country, as part of the preparedness campaign, he set about organizing one of the Base Hospital Units which were recruited from the professional staff of a number of university medical schools. As director of one of these units, known as Base Hospital No. 5—the second military organization of any kind officially sent overseas—he sailed for France again in May 1917. Throughout that year he served as an operating surgeon with the B.E.F., being detached from the Unit for special duty dur_ ing the battles for the Messines and Passchendaele ridges. In June 1918 he was transferred to the Medical Headquarters of the A.E.F. as senior consultant in neurosurgery, and participated in the three major engagements at Château-Thierry, St. Mihiel, and the Argonne.

In between these major offensives, Dr. Cushing was perform-ing a hundred different duties: he visited with the Canadians and the Anzacs; he attended the medical conferences in Paris; he crossed the Channel to be with Osler and to confer with the medi-cos in Oxford and London; he visited the front lines; he knew about the *postes de secours* and the ambulance trains and casualty clearing stations; his operations on wounded men were critical and prolonged, and during times of pressure he was sometimes on duty sixteen hours at a stretch.

Throughout these periods of incredible industry, working un-der a strain to which doctors are seldom exposed in times of peace, he still managed to keep, with few intermissions, a day-to-day record, not only of his surgery but of the extraordinary soldiers, scientists, poets, and philosophers whom he encountered in his tours of the lines. Bits of comedy, acts of uncommon heroism, the everlasting conflict of nationalities, snatches of history, thumb-nail sketches of the Flanders countryside, of night bombing, of the Hindenburg Line, of Paris in ferment—all this was written down with the sensitive and observant eye of a scientist. The journal was kept in longhand, on the backs of used temperature charts, X-ray reports, or such other scraps when paper was scarce; it was written often at night—sometimes as late as two in the morning

—but written down when the emotions were alert and before the day's events had been erased by sleep.

The author almost never alludes to the actual business of keeping such a record. Once he remarks *sotto voce,* "The ambulance is jiggling so I find it hard to write"—evidence that his chronicle was sometimes set down as he motored from hospital to hospital. And in September 1917 he utters this brief expostulation, the truth of which will be instantly recognized by anyone who has ever kept a diary in the past:—

I have neglected this diary for a week and find myself somewhat weary of it. It is costly in time, in paper and ink—three things of which there is no superfluity hereabouts. I have, too, been having a mental let-down —probably subdiaphragmatic in origin, and writing at such times is not easy. The writing centre is not in the angular gyrus, it's in the gastric mucosa.

Dr. Cushing's journal, complete with the maps, illustrations, letters, and orders, to-day fills nine bound volumes in his library. From its bulk of a million words this single and arresting volume has been culled, representing, as the editor believes, material of lasting interest to physicians, veterans, and the discriminating reader.

CONTENTS

EDITOR'S FOREWORD ix

GLOSSARY xix

I THE HARVARD UNIT AT THE AMBULANCE AMÉRICAINE   3
     The Journey to Paris 3
     Breaking in at Neuilly 12
     A Visit to the 2ème Armée . . . 18
     Hôpital Complémentaire 21, Compiègne . 30
     With the Blessés at Neuilly . . . 40

II WITH THE R.A.M.C. IN FLANDERS 56
     No. 13 General during "the Second Ypres" . 56
     The Battle from Scherpenberg Hill . . 69
     England in War Time 73

III THE BATTLE OF BOSTON COMMON 79
     An Episode of the Preparedness Movement . 79

IV WITH THE BRITISH EXPEDITIONARY FORCE . . . 102
     From New York to Camiers . . . 102
     Introduction to No. 11 General . . 111
     The Battle of Messines Ridge . . . 115
     A Visit to Vimy Ridge 135
     Camp Life at Camiers 142

V THE PASSCHENDAELE BATTLES 160
     Awaiting Zero Hour at 46 C.C.S. . . 160
     The First Battle in a Deluge . . . 175
     The Second Attack: Westhoek . . . 180
     The Third Attack: Langemarck . . 185
     The Fourth Attack: Menin Road . . 190
     The Fifth Attack: Inverness Copse . . 193

Bombing of Base Hospital No. 5 . . 200
The Sixth Battle: Menin Road . . . 207
The Seventh Attack: Zonnebeke . . . 212
The Eighth Attack: Broodseinde . . . 218
The Ninth Battle: Poelcappelle . . 221
The Tenth Battle: Again Poelcappelle . . 223
The Eleventh Attack: Encore Poelcappelle . 231
Corps Dressing Stations and the Twelfth Battle 234
A Glimpse of the Salient 240
The Thirteenth Battle: Passchendaele Village 247
Farewell to "Wipers" 249

VI IN WINTER QUARTERS: BOULOGNE 254
Taking Over No. 13 General . . . 254
Research Committee Meetings . . . 266
The Death of a Soldier-Poet . . . 280
The Army School at Bruay . . . 283
Fourth Research Committee Meeting . . 287
Five Days in Blighty 292
A Glimpse of the A.E.F. . . . 301

VII THE GERMAN SPRING OFFENSIVE 308
First Phase: The Advance on Amiens . . 308
Awaiting News at the Casino . . . 312
The Second Phase: Battle of the Lys . . 323
Switched Off for a Lecture! . . . 342
An Unwelcome Interruption . . . 351
Neurosurgical Organization in England . 356
Dublin in War Time 358

VIII THE GERMAN OFFENSIVE CONTINUES 364
Third Phase: The Second Marne . . 364
Marking Time in Boulogne . . . 372
A Transfer to the A.E.F. . . . 384

IX STEMMING THE TIDE 392
The Abortive Thrust at Reims . . . 398
The Offensive Changes Hands . . . 410
Office Work at Neufchâteau . . . 418

X REDUCING THE ST. MIHIEL SALIENT 430
Preparing for Casualties 430
The St. Mihiel Battle 439
A Look within the Salient . . . 443

XI THE ARGONNE OFFENSIVE 450
    Noncombatant Preparations . . . 451
    The Battle Opens 455
    An Enforced Change of Scene . . . 466
    Occupying a Bed in Person . . . 474
    A Combatant's Case History . . . 481
    The Last Few Days 492

EDITOR'S AFTERWORD 502

INDEX 513

ILLUSTRATIONS

SNAPSHOT OF AUTHOR IN ABBEVILLE, 1918 . . *Frontispiece*

THE LYCÉE PASTEUR AT NEUILLY 12

MEDICAL OFFICERS AND HOSPITALS AT COMPIÈGNE . . 32

THE HARVARD UNIT AT THE AMBULANCE AMÉRICAINE . 42

THE BATTLEFIELDS OF MEAUX IN EARLY DAYS . . . 54

OVERSEAS MEDICAL OFFICERS AND TRAFALGAR SQUARE IN 1915 76

PROPOSED HOSPITAL MOBILIZATION ON BOSTON COMMON . 94

ENLISTED PERSONNEL AND OFFICERS OF BASE HOSPITAL NO. 5 102

SNAPSHOTS ON THE CANOPIC, MAY 1917 106

SNAPSHOTS OF NO. 13 GENERAL, DANNES-CAMIERS . . . 110

SIR DOUGLAS HAIG AND PRISONERS AFTER MESSINES . . . 124

EXTREMES IN THE R.A.M.C. 132

THE PETITE PLACE AT ARRAS BEFORE AND AFTER . . 140

PARIS, JULY 4, 1917 146

BASE HOSPITAL NO. 5 AND THE QUEEN'S VISIT 152

THE OLD AND THE NEW FROM CAPTAIN TELFER'S HUT . 165

STRETCHERS MOVING UP AND COMING BACK 184

BOMBING BASE HOSPITAL NO. 5 203

THE SCOTTISH AT DAWN AND LATER ON 230

DUCKBOARDS AND DUGOUTS IN THE SALIENT 234

AN A.D.S. AND WALKING WOUNDED AT POTIJZE . . . 242

SKETCH OF YPRES, OCTOBER 28, 1917 245

POELCAPPELLE FROM THE AIR AFTER BOMBARDMENT . . 248

THE HUSKS OF YPRES AND THE DANCE MACABRE . . . 252

THE LAST DAY AT 46 C.C.S. 254

THE PLAGE AND CASINO AT BOULOGNE 260

Seeing Humor in Familiar Aspects of the War . . 270

Christmas at the Casino 272

Avenue du Président-Wilson, July 4, 1918 . . . 394

Arriving Troops and Medical Consultants . . . 398

A General and a Poilu of 1918 406

The Station Neurologique No. 42 at Salins . . . 422

A Main Figée before and after Treatment . . . 424

Conférence Interalliée and Research Committee Groups 468

Snapshots of Neufchâteau 472

GLOSSARY OF SOME OF THE MORE COMMON CRYPTICS

For the Convenience of the Reader

BRITISH

A.A.M.C.	Australian Army Medical Corps
A.D.C.	Aide-de-Camp
A.D.M.S.	Assistant Director Medical Services (chief M.O. of division)
A.D.S.	Advanced Dressing Station
A.M.S.	Army Medical Service
A.P.M.	Assistant Provost Marshal
A.S.C.	Army Service Corps (S.O.S. in A.E.F.)
A.T.S.	Antitetanic Serum
A.W.O.L.	Absent without Official Leave
B.E.F.	British Expeditionary Force
B.R.C.S.	British Red Cross Society
C.A.M.C.	Canadian Army Medical Corps
C.C.S.	Casualty Clearing Station
C.D.S.	Corps Dressing Station
C. in C.	Commander-in-Chief
C.O.	Commanding Officer
D.A.D.M.S.	Deputy Assistant Director Medical Services
D.D.M.S.	Deputy Director Medical Services (chief M.O. of corps)
D.G.A.M.S.	Director General of Army Medical Services (Keogh in London; Sloggett in France)—commonly spoken of as "the D.G."
D.I.L.	Dangerously Ill List
D.M.S.	Director Medical Services (for each army)—reports to D.G.A.M.S.
D.R.L.S.	Dispatch Rider Letter Service
D.S.O.	Distinguished Service Order
E.M.O.	Embarkation Medical Officer
F.A.	Field Ambulance
F.A.N.Y.	First Aid Nursing Yeomanry ("Fannies")
G.H.Q.	General Headquarters
G.O.C.	General Officer Commanding

G.S.W.	Gunshot wound
H.S.	Hospital Ship
I.M.S.	Indian Medical Service
K.O.S.B.	King's Own Scottish Borderers
L. of C.	Lines of Communication
M.A.C.	Motor Ambulance Corps
M.C.	Military Cross
M.D.S.	Main Dressing Station
M.O.	Medical Officer: battalion, etc.
M.P.	Military Police
N.C.O.	Noncommissioned · Officer
N.T.O.	Naval Transport Officer
N.Y.D.	Not yet diagnosed
O.P.	Observation Post (Signalers' "o-pip")
O.R.	Other Ranks
P.B.	Permanent Base—unfit for more active service
P.O.W.	Prisoner of War
P.U.O.	Pyrexia (*i.e.* fever, often "trench fever") of Uncertain Origin
Q.A.I.M.N.S.	Queen Alexandra's Imperial Military Nursing Service
Q.M.	Quartermaster
Q.M.A.A.C.	Queen Mary's Auxiliary Army Corps (later W.A.A.C.)
Q.M.G.	Quartermaster General
R.A.F.	Royal Air Force
R.A.M.C.	Royal Army Medical Corps
R.A.P.	Regimental Aid Post
R.E.	Royal Engineers
R.F.A.	Royal Field Artillery
R.F.C.	Royal Flying Corps
R.G.A.	Royal Garrison Artillery
R.M.O.	Regimental Medical Officer
R.T.O.	Railway Transport Officer
S.M.O.	Senior Medical Officer
T.A.T.	Temporary Ambulance Train
"Toc H"	Signalers for T.H. (Talbot House)
V.A.D.	Voluntary Aid Detachment (female)
V.A.D.G.S.	Voluntary Aid Detachment General Service (waitresses, etc.)
W.A.A.C.	Women's Army Auxiliary Corps ("Wacks")
W.R.N.S.	Women's Royal Naval Service ("Wrens")

AMERICAN

A.E.F.	American Expeditionary Force
A.G.O.	Adjutant General's Office

GLOSSARY

A.W.O.L.	Absent without Official Leave
C.S.	Chief Surgeon
G.H.Q.	General Headquarters
G.M.C.	General Motors Company
G.O.	General Orders
G-1	Personnel (G-2, Military Information; G-3, Military Operations; G-4, Supply, Evacuation, Hospitalization, etc.; G-5, Training)
L. of C.	Lines of Communication
M.O.R.C.	Medical Officers Reserve Corps
M.P.	Military Police
M.R.C.	Medical Reserve Corps
P.C.	Post Command
P.M.	Provost Marshal. Head of police detachment
Q.M.C.	Quartermaster Corps
R.C.M.H.	Red Cross Military Hospital
S.D.C.	Surgical Dressings Committee
S.O.S.	Service of Supply
U.S.R.	United States Reserves

FRENCH

Auto-chir	*Ambulance Chirurgicale Automobile*
G.Q.G.	*Grand Quartier Général* (General Headquarters)
H.O.E.	*Hôpital d'Observation et Évacuation*—the "Hashoway" of American Field Ambulance drivers

FROM A SURGEON'S JOURNAL

I

THE HARVARD UNIT AT THE AMBULANCE AMÉRICAINE

In August 1914, a group of Americans resident in Paris, under the leader-ship of Ambassador Herrick and his predecessor, Mr. Robert Bacon, under-took the organization of a military hospital and motor-ambulance service in connection with the existent American Hospital at Neuilly-sur-Seine of which Dr. G. W. du Bouchet and Dr. E. L. Gros were the well-known surgical attendants. For the purpose of this "Ambulance"—the usual name for a French military hospital—the French Government put at their dis-posal the Lycée Pasteur, a school building in process of erection at Neuilly which was altered and equipped to provide beds for some five or six hundred patients.

A staff of *auxiliaires*, orderlies and helpers who volunteered their services, was soon recruited, and on September 7 the first wounded were received. The expenses of this American Ambulance were met by voluntary sub-scriptions, and a subsidiary 200-bed hospital at Juilly, northwest of Meaux and nearer the line, was later established through the generosity of Mrs. Harry Payne Whitney. It had a rotating professional staff supplied chiefly by the College of Physicians, New York.

Certain universities in the States were subsequently asked to participate in the project by successively supplying the professional personnel capable of caring for a certain number of wards in this Ambulance Américaine at Neuilly for a three-months period. The first of these units, from Western Reserve University, under the direction of Dr. G. W. Crile and financed by Mr. Samuel Mather of Cleveland, began its three-months term of service in January of 1915. A Harvard unit organized by Drs. Cushing and R. B. Greenough and financed by Mr. William Lindsey of Boston followed in April 1915. [The Editor]

The Journey to Paris

Thursday, March 18, 1915

She seemed very low in the water—the *Canopic*—when we found her hidden behind the new Commonwealth Pier yesterday afternoon, with two interned Hamburg-American ships on the opposite side. Strange company! And when, after our false start at 4.15 we returned again at eight for the sailing, she was still lower. Ammunition for the Allies, it is said. What a temptation it must have been to *die Leute* across the dock! A stowaway with a bomb would do it—and there seemed to be no precautions such as one would perhaps expect on an English ship under existing circumstances.

It was a cold blowy March night by the time our pilot was dropped outside of Boston Light, and though the merrymakers, Benet and Barton, marched the decks with tin flutes tuned to "Tipperary," blue noses soon drove us in and to bed. There are only fifty first-cabin passengers, seventeen of them constituting our immediate party, to which three or four others are *c'est à dire* allied. So there's plenty of room, though no place to go but out, and no place to stay but in—with one's overcoat on in either case.

Friday, 4 p.m.

It still blows hard from the N.W. quarter. These people who talk about getting one's sea legs make me ill. Greenough says it's all in your head, but I know better: it lives just under your diaphragm, halfway in, and is intensified by culinary odours—Englished with a *u*.

March 20th, Saturday

We seem to be a musical "unit"—at least the average is high, with Barton and Benet together at the piano. The orchestra grows apace and last evening Osgood appeared with a fine bass drum made of an amputated barrel with canvas stretched over the ends for drumheads—improvised by the cook. I'm told it's the kind of drum sailors are accustomed to take ashore when they want to smuggle tobacco and other forbidden things aboard. Then two tin plates with some adhesive-plaster handles make useful cymbals; a large tin pan and a soup spoon; a kettledrum ingeniously fabricated out of a huge tin candy box by Osgood; and finally the steward, who summons us brazenly to meals six or eight times a day, could stand it no longer and appeared with his cornet and an old mandolin which it was found Strong was able to pick. With the two B.'s as ringleaders, it was carried off with the true music-hall touch.

Sunday, the first day of Spring

Overcast and dirty. A boat drill this a.m., and such a lot of pirates you never saw—shanghaied, I judge, from anywhere and everywhere. Transatlantic voyages just now are not too popular with deck hands. They were too funny in their cork life belts and we were not permitted to look on from the upper deck. I doubt if the ship's officers cared to have us see them. It was our unanimous decision to commandeer a lifeboat or two for ourselves rather than trust to any such aggregation, individually or collectively. Some of them would have made fine models for Howard Pyle.

We have been in Marconi communication both with Cape Cod and with the Azores, so it is rumored, but the Captain keeps mum. 'T is at his discretion, we 're told, that the sending of messages lies. They say he does not wish to be located—but by what? The *Karlsruhe* is in the South Atlantic. Perhaps by the auxiliary cruiser which is reported to have slipped out of her internment in the Azores the day before we sailed. Our lights have been fully blanketed every night since sailing—the storm canvases are stretched along the promenade deck and towels tacked over our cabin windows.

The service this morning was conducted by the Purser—a companionable chap named O'Hegan. He read from Psalm CV: "O give thanks unto the Lord . . . he increased his people exceedingly, and made them stronger than their enemies, whose heart turned so that they hated his people." One wonders to-day who are *his* people—if perchance He still takes sides—the hated or the hating. Doubtless the one of the combatants that would do the most after peace for the betterment of mankind and his abiding place. But which would?

Such thoughts were aroused by O'Hegan's reading; nor was his mind solely on his text, for, having interrupted his prayer to send a steward to stop the noise of a creaking timber, he could n't find his place again.

Monday, the 22nd March

Our steward's announcement that the glass was falling and that we are likely to find it damp in these parts comes true. There is a hurricane—*they* call it "a half gale"—out of the southwest which is tearing things up considerably—a veritable "white squall" which only lacks the scratching Jews to larboard.

4 p.m. Though it was enough to wipe out our wireless apparatus, the old boat has held surprisingly steady in the trough of the big seas. Most of the party also hold out well.

Tuesday, March 23rd: noon

We are still feeling the effect of yesterday's blow and the wind holds in the same quarter. . . . We have had a conference under Strong's direction on *les infections gazeuses,* and he went over *seriatim* the various organisms which have been known to be productive of emphysematous lesions. We had many therapeutic proposals to make and wonder what they may be doing for these cases in Paris. Strong has blossomed out in his olive-drab Red Cross uniform. A Dr. Metcalf aboard, who is conducting a group of seasick nurses bound for Hungary on a Red Cross mission, referred to him respectfully as a "five striper," for he wears on his sleeves the insignia of a Director in the R.C. With his broad-brimmed hat he looks like Oom Paul.

Wednesday the 24th. Off the Azores

8 a.m. We were called at an early hour this morning expecting to land, but find ourselves wallowing in the trough of a high rolling sea a few miles off the open roadstead of Ponta Delgada. We have been told various things—we 're to wait for calmer seas; we 're to go around to the north of St. Michael's and land our 160 second-class passengers there; we 're to try and put them ashore here and take their baggage on to Gibraltar.

The wind has held in the s.w. for three days and it 's still lowering. Certainly they will not let *us* land and I doubt if the "Portugees" we are to put off can like the looks of it, for the waves are breaking over an ugly-looking coast and sending up great puffs of white spray.

1 p.m. "At Flores in the Azores Sir Richard Grenville lay," and "the water continued to heave and the weather to moan." We 've been drifting broadside the length of São Miguel all the morning in rain and mist and now have turned our nose toward home—no one knows why. . . .

I have come in to get warm and dry in the library and find Mr. Souli here attentively studying some coins of the Empire which he pulls out of his various pockets wrapped in much handled bits of tissue paper. He explains his satisfaction by saying they are rare. Mrs. Souli is limp alongside of him. They are Americans who have lived years abroad and have just come from San Francisco, her home, and the opening of the Exposition which they say is quite wonderful; but the new America seems to them a place inhabited by foreigners. We think of consulting the barometer or of asking the Captain what the prospects are. Mr. Souli says from his coins—"You might as well ask the lob-lolly-boy as the Captain."

6 p.m. Golly! It's sure enough the real thing. The glass is still going down and at 45 miles an hour it's blowing, Billy be damned, from the same old quarter. We are barely holding our own—our nose pointed into the west. A great sight it is, to stand up on the hurricane deck in the lee of the bridge and see the steady *Canopic* actually poke her bows into a solid green wave and toss it in spray up to the crow's nest.

11 p.m. Sixty miles an hour and as dirty a night as one can imagine. We are hanging on with the Ponta Delgada flashlight about 10 miles off our starboard quarter and our nose pointing into the gale. O'Hegan says someone forgot to pay his washerwoman.

Sunday, March 28

6 p.m. Such a gloomy landing! In a perfect downpour we had a hazy glimpse of the African shore, were bespoken by a destroyer and told to go ahead, and then were carried down far beyond Gibraltar so that when it came dimly into view it was off the starboard bow, which was very confusing. But after all, the rock of which so much is said and written was mantled by a heavy cloud. Damp, cold, forlorn, and huddled together on deck, we finally, about ten o'clock, steamed into the Bay of Algeciras and came to anchor. In a wretched little boat we were then put ashore on the north mole—our luggage likewise.

After fiddling about for some time and learning that we must wait for a 2.20 boat to Algeciras, we clambered into strange little *fiacres* holding four on a pinch, and with flapping wet curtains and such individual protection as each of us had—'t was not much —we started to see Gibraltar. There was a long delay at the end of the wharf while our passports were viséed, and in return we were presented with a *water-port* pass. Meanwhile a fine Welsh bobby who stood in the downpour told us, as did others, that there had been nothing but rain—fifty-two inches for the season instead of the usual fourteen, according to his calculation. We could see up on the Rock only as far as the old Moorish castle.

The converted Cunarder *Carmania*, in her gray war paint, was lying alongside the south mole in the British harbor. It was she who sank the *Cap Trafalgar*. On the whole, there seemed fewer men-of-war than one would expect, even in times of peace. We rode along Church and Southport streets, rubbering at what we could see of the Rock in the rain and mist—enough to assure us of its fascination and interest in better weather—past the sad and dripping little Trafalgar cemetery as far as the Alameda, a park laid out a century ago. At its far end is a flight of steps surmounted by a bronze bust of General (or was it Admiral?) Elliot—hero of the great siege of 1780 or thereabouts.

Our later arrival at Algeciras, across the Bay, was the worst of all—simply drenched, we were landed on a long pier without cover and walked into the customhouse, our soaking baggage following after us. The jabbering officials finally satisfied, Strong, Boothby, and I, being about the only ones with overshoes, started out bravely for a promenade in the town. We were soon joined by a fascinating boy named Diego who attached himself to us for the rest of the afternoon. He took us first to a high point from which we had a lovely view of the distant hills—the Sierra de los Gazúles—with the winding Miel between us and the town itself. The clouds were breaking, and the light on the roofs of the houses crowning the opposite hill made a stunning picture. It was good to see and feel the sun again. Next—and most important to Diego —was the bull ring, where there was to have been a fight this afternoon, postponed owing to the rain, for the seats are without shelter. As we were strolling through the narrow cobbled streets lined by little, close-packed, unpretentious Spanish houses with their barred windows, there was an approaching sound of an excited rabble. Soon a crowd of small boys appeared, then a carriage, and then a mob of people shouting, "Belmonte! Belmonte!" It was the local hero—the bullfighter.

Tuesday, March 30. Madrid

6.30 p.m. Impressions of Madrid consist largely of trips to and fro Cook's central office and this Hotel with an occasional sidestep to the local hospital, the American Ambassador, the Prado, the French Consul, and an antiquariat. But Cook's and the Consul were the most time-consuming.

We got in about 9 a.m. and had the usual palaver with officials at the station—Strong coming in as usual most handily and politely for he has the gracious manners as well as the tongue, cultivated by his long stay in the Philippines and Spanish America. . . . At the American Embassy, which did not open till 10, we were informed that a new order was issued two days ago by the French Government—to wit, that no one may cross the border without a new passport issued by the French Consul here; and this required newly made duplicate photographs—all to-day!! Our Washington papers from Jusserand, etc., mean nothing, as some official at the border will have to pass on our things, not the Foreign Office itself. . . .

After lunch Strong and I managed to look in at the Prado for a short hour and I rather liked the Antonio Moros the best. Then at 3 to the Consul's where he made out a blanket passport for us—a formidable document with all our signatures and photos, with seals and stamps on a single sheet.

8.30 p.m. At the station—an hour ahead of time to make sure of our large collection of baggage. We 've had a horrid time with bad infectious colds—apparently the *Canopic* was infected for the Captain and the Doctor had had influenzal colds on their westward crossing. One after another of the party has come down and the amount of barking is distressing. Only a few so far have escaped. Strong is filling himself up with aspirin to-night.

Wednesday. March 31st

The Basque provinces. Cold and rainy—but early spring betrayed by fruit trees in blossom. Rugged, semi-mountainous country for we are in the foothills of the Cantabrian range of the Pyrenees. From Vitoria, founded in 581 by the King of the Visigoths, on to Irún-Hendaye. Prosperous country—good roads —cultivated hillsides, covered in spots with brilliant yellow gorse. Orchards, beech groves, great ivy-colored walls, deep valleys with terraced sides, trim gardens, stone walls, rows of poplars in their yellow spring dress, dwarfed buttonwoods, limestone cliffs, deep rocky gorges, white stucco or square-built stone houses with red tiled roofs.

Irún and Hendaye. Our elaborate passport *pour tout ensemble* obtained at Madrid let us through not only without scrutiny but with bows of welcome. A telegram from the Paris Government also helped some. Luncheon at the Restaurant de la Gare heartily enjoyed in view of our scanty breakfast.

4 p.m. After luncheon, despite the cold lowering weather and our various degrees of bronchitis and coughs, we started off in parties to see the little border town of Hendaye—the objective point of some being a *Sanatorium pour les Enfants* (550 of them) off on the northern shore of the Bidassoa looking out on the Bay of Biscay, where we saw the smoke of what we took to be a row of some 30-odd battleships on the horizon.

It was an interesting though muddy walk of 3 or 4 kilometres but the Sanatorium at the end made it well worth while—a place of convalescence for the children, boys and girls, up to 13, from the various Paris hospitals. Clean pavilions with neat gardens, vines, trained buttonwoods for shade, hedges, etc., and a lovely view over the bay. Also a superb beach. No wonder the children looked ruddy and well. *M. le Directeur,* when he learned who we were, had us shown through many of the playrooms, the kitchen, etc. The children were really too cunning—a *much* better-looking lot than one could easily find in a children's con- valescent hospital at home where our mongrel make-up shows itself plainly. All with their heads closely cropped except the girls old enough to braid their own—their little shoes lined up under the wall benches, their napkins in individual boxes, etc. The girls wore red and white circular caps and one roomful of them we took into the garden, to their great glee, for a chance photo, but it was dark and overcast. Such big, yellow, clean ome- lettes were being made for them in the neat kitchen as one rarely sees—boxes of eggs by the hundreds. The place itself looked like a regular incubator for a new French race—*post bellum.*

7 p.m., Bayonne. Encampments for the convalescent wounded

and soldiers returning to the line begin to appear. At every station are girls with tricolor buttons and money boxes *"pour les blessés."* We are going into France by the military back door. The men are still in their blue and red uniforms.

11.30 p.m., Bordeaux. Here they are—soldiers by the number. They look just like the pictures of our old Civil War veterans with their long blue coats and visored *képis.* Zouaves also, and occasionally a man in a blue-gray uniform, but all with red caps and trousers. They have put on many more cars, and the forward ones are packed with soldiers. They look very small and forlorn— not much *élan* here. We have wangled a few pillows and rugs and will try to sleep.

April 1, Paris

It was a poor night, and a most bedraggled group of people made some tea in one of our baskets about 6 a.m. But despite the cold, our first bright clear day brought us cheer; and we finally slid into the Gare d'Orléans, where was breakfast, and a chance to pull ourselves together. Very exciting to look out on the streets of war-time Paris—officers speeding by in motor cars—an armored car with machine guns—ambulances and all else—all in gray war paint except for the red crosses and the red splashes of the old French uniforms.

Greenough commandeered three big buses into which we clambered, bag and baggage, and set out across the river, through the Place de la Concorde, where Alsace and Lorraine are still draped in black, out along the Élysées, under the Arc to the Porte Maillot, and through it into Neuilly. A very interesting ride on a crisp, clear, spring morning. But the streets seemed very empty for Paris—children playing whip top on the Élysées paths as usual, showing that it was really not Sunday, though it looked it. Everyone not in uniform seems to be garbed in black.

The converted Lycée Pasteur, now the Ambulance Américaine, is not far from the Porte Maillot, and as we approached it along the Boulevard d'Inkermann it was immediately recognizable: the handsome school building with its courtyard full of Ford motor ambulances, over which a bevy of uniformed drivers—youngsters from home, for the most part—were tinkering, some freshly arrived *châssis* being newly assembled. A row of patients and nurses waved a welcome from the upper terraces; Blake and others of the permanent staff, most of them in khaki, greeted us below.

BREAKING IN AT NEUILLY

The hospital was quite a revelation, and we met so many people and saw so many familiar faces it's impossible to set it all down. They have admitted no new cases to our 164 beds—indeed, have emptied them as far as they were able, so that we may have a fairly fresh start.

The first man we saw had a dreadful paraplegia, with a huge bedsore, due to a section of the spinal cord. He'd been shot in the back by a pointed French bullet—recognizable in the X-ray. In a Frenchman, too! So war is doubly dangerous for the soldier— from behind as well as before. Many other minor cases—none of them very bad—we hurriedly glanced at as we were ushered through the several rooms. No Germans. They would require a guard, and the few they have had in the past did not make them very popular.

Good Friday, April 2

It is difficult to say just what are one's most vivid impressions: the amazing patience of the seriously wounded, some of them hanging on for months; the dreadful deformities (not so much in the way of amputations, but broken jaws and twisted, scarred faces); the tedious healing of the infected wounds, with discharg_ ing sinuses, tubes, irrigations, and repeated dressings—so much so that grating and painful fractures are simply abandoned to wait for wounds to heal, which they don't seem to do; the risks under apparently favorable circumstances of attempting clean operations, most of which seem to have broken down—a vari_ cocele, an appendix, and, worst of all, a thoracotomy for a bullet in the pericardium which apparently was doing no harm.

Some of this miscellaneous work savors of "souvenir surgery," and doubtless pressure may oftentimes be brought to bear by the wounded, for they are very proud of these trophies. From the man in question the unoffending bullet, which he wanted as an exhibit to show his visitors, was removed from the pericardial sac; but he got a collapsed left lung, a right pneumonia, then in turn a left pneumonia, and now a bad empyema, with a tube in his side which

The Lycée Pasteur (Ambulance Américaine) at Neuilly

Decoration of a Convalescent Officer at a Ceremony in the Court

may or may not close some day. Still he seemed very proud and happy.

The histories are all interesting, citing, as they do, the man's name, regiment, the place where he received the injury and under what circumstances, how long he had had on his clothes without changing them, where he got his first, second, and possibly third dressing before reaching our ambulance, and so on—each item full of horrible, though fascinating, possibilities. No doubt this will all seem very commonplace after we have been here a few days.

I was going over a man this afternoon with a facial paralysis from a bullet wound in the mastoid. He got hit during an engagement on September 7 at a place called Croult, and, with a field full of other wounded, was left for dead. The enemy came over them a day or so later; a soldier poked at him and, finding him alive, swung at his head with the butt end of his musket, breaking his jaw. He was finally picked up during a counter-attack and, after a bad otitis media and erysipelas, is now ready—after seven months!—for a nerve anastomosis. It seems hardly worth while, under present circumstances, to attempt cosmetic operations. What's a simple facial paralysis, after all?

Then, too, there are those not badly hurt who simulate worse things. For example, one strapping minor officer, a gymnasium instructor in peace time, threw out his chest and made a great fuss about a trifling crackle in his shoulder which Osgood immediately identified as a subacromial bursitis.

Many of the men have deformed toes (possibly from *sabots?*) and they complain that their military shoes are bad, though those we saw seemed sensible enough. But there are other bizarre troubles with the men's feet of really serious nature. There are erythromelalgia-like feet—painful, blue, cold, macerated-looking extremities; and indeed the whole circulatory condition of many of the *blessés* is very bad. It is presumable that the worst of this is over, with the return of not only dry but warm weather. The standing in cold water, even though above the freezing point—one cause of the so-called water-bite—is as bad as frostbite itself, especially when helped by the too-tight application of puttees which may shrink. Some of these poor devils must have so stood for days in hastily dug trenches without a chance of getting off their boots.

Al_{most} from the start, the majority of the men have been admitted with bronchitis, and many with influenza-like colds. Then, too, the African troops may have brought with them underlying tropical disorders of which we know little. One of them was a fine Turco in a gay Zouave uniform, with a through-and-through thoracic wound made by a German "ball," the wound of entrance so small it could hardly be found.

Can you picture him, with no one around he can understand or who can understand him, industriously putting together the biggest and most intricate jig-saw puzzle "made in America" you ever saw, on a table in an American hospital in France, with Americans taking care of him? What can his thoughts of us be? They tell us the Germans don't take the blacks prisoners; but then, what may or may not we believe about all this business? Here we are as near the worst affair in history as Boston is to Worcester, and everyone appears to take it as though it had always been so, and always would be, and meanwhile goes about his own little business unconcernedly.

April 3rd

A continuous rain. Morning passed at the Ambulance combing out and indexing the neurological cases. As a matter of fact, few of the wounded escape from a nerve lesion of one sort or another. Although we have been discharging rapidly (20 out of 81 in Cutler's division), so that some of the rooms contain only two or three patients, a partial list even now shows:—

Eleven upper-limb nerve injuries varying from wounds of the brachial plexus to minor ones of the hand; five of them musculospinal paralyses with compound fractures of the humerus.

Two painful nerve injuries of the leg; operated on by Tauer with suture.

Three facial paralyses. One of them had had *"un morceau d'obus"* as big as the palm of the hand driven into his cheek which he proudly exhibited—i.e., the *morceau*.

A cervical sympathetic paralysis in a man shot through the open mouth.

Two fractures of the spine, one dying, the other recovering. A beam supporting the *"tranchées d'abri"* had fallen on him when a shell landing near by blew up the section where he was stationed.

Only one serious head injury; this in the case of Jean Ponysigne, wounded five days ago in the Vosges and brought in here to the Am¯bulance in some mysterious fashion.

All the wounded from the s.e. part of the lines are supposedly routed to Lyon and the South of France—those from the centre come here; those from the North, including the British, go to Dunkerque, etc. There are very few Tommies in our wards. One of them to-day was playing checkers with a Turco and said his black friend had learned the game so quickly he could now almost always beat him—but he thought he had him this time.

One of the hospital attendants told me at lunch that on passing the Invalides the other day he saw an old veteran of 1870 in his long blue coat balancing on his two wooden pegs with the aid of two crutches, in order to salute a victim of the present war—45 years younger, but in the same condition.

A visit to the dental department this afternoon with Dr. Hayes —doubtless the most impressive work we have thus far seen— new, ingenious, effective. It is remarkable what they are able to do in aligning the jaws and teeth of an unfortunate with a large part of his face shot away; and there must be as many of them in the wards as there are neurological cases. It 's a pity that we could not have brought a capable dentist with us.

Easter Sunday, April 4

Our first batch of newly wounded received to-day—only seven in all. We saw them brought in and bathed, an interesting performance. They were not so terribly filthy, this lot, as I had expected, though one of them, a beautiful creature, a French peasant, had not had his clothes off for a month. He had come all the way from Flanders, wounded last Friday in the leg—only forty-eight hours from the firing line—to a hot bath, a shampoo, and a universal lather in a comfortable hospital.

Lunch at the Ambulance and a visit from Roger Merriman, who has had an interesting time over here helping in the Embassy while giving his French lectures. He has recently visited the Front at Nancy, watching the 75's in action, and dodging under an *abri* when a German shell gave warning, by its whistle, of near approach. He has first-hand information of atrocities—of which there may be something to say on both sides—stories about a few wild German regiments in particular whose course can be traced through Belgium. But M. Marty has just told me at tea of the Turcos who broke loose one night in Versailles and made away with some German officers who were there; also of the Turco in hospital at the College who presented a little girl, to whom he had taken a fancy, with the ear of a German soldier. But there are always points in these stories where they don't quite hold to_gether.

Monday, April 5, a holiday

10.30 p.m. At the Ambulance, working on histories all the afternoon. Some of our recent cases have appeared tagged with pink cards, which are tied on at a *poste de pansement* or at the *poste de secours*, and I gather that there are two zones of these first-aid stations, primary and secondary, the wounded being gathered up from the battlefields or trenches usually at night and taken to the primary line. There are several kinds of labels—pink (those capable of transportation), yellow, blue, and so forth. From the *postes de secours* they are taken in peasants' carts or ambulances to an evacuation centre (*ambulance de tri*) which may be anywhere, preferably some railroad station, and there the sitting and lying cases are separated, the serious from the minor cases, the medical from the surgical. The *petits blessés* remain and ere long go back to the Front; the bad cases—chest, abdomen, head, spine, and so forth—are sent to the nearest base hospitals. The attempt is already being made to concentrate particular kinds of wounds —as might well be the case here for fractures of the jaw. This programme will doubtless become perfected in time, and more efficient work will then be done.

In the early days things were badly disorganized, and the conditions were shocking. The wounded were all rushed south as rapidly as possible and the more seriously ill were put off whenever and wherever the trains stopped. They were picked up in any way chance might favor—luckily if by an ambulance, but more often by a cattle or provision train returning from the Front. One of these trains had dumped about five hundred badly wounded men and left them lying between the tracks in the rain, with no cover whatsoever. Blake spoke of one English officer who had been six days thus in transport, with a musket for a splint tied to a compound

fracture of the femur, no dressing whatsoever, almost no f
drink; he was in delirium when he arrived. Fortunat/
wounded were young and in the pink of physical condition; ι⌐
would otherwise have pulled through.

Thursday, April 8

Our admitting day brings in only ten cases, though there were
about two hundred at La Chapelle station last night. Still, this
must have been more than our proportion, for there are many
hospitals strung along the Champs-Élysées alone, and in all Paris
heaven only knows how many.

One of these men had had his spinal cord divided by a piece of
metal driven off by a German bullet from the bayonet case at his
hip. The vagaries of the foreign bodies are many. Not only may
one find the projectiles themselves, but often pieces of equipment
which have been detached, and which acquire the full velocity of
the bullet itself and are really more dangerous. Sometimes these
secondary missiles may have come from someone other than the
person actually hit, even a piece of the skeleton of a neighboring
soldier, or a bit of stone or wood.

The actual surgery itself, it would seem, is not very difficult,
but the judgment of knowing what and how much to do, and the
wheres and whens of intervention—these are the important things,
only to be learned by experience. First or last, most of the missiles
apparently must come out.

Some of to-day's wounded were very dirty, with the mud of
the trenches on them, and though they acknowledged some pain
and great fatigue they were cheerful and uncomplaining—even
gay. "*C'est la guerre,*" is all they say. It's a great sight to see
them get their hot bath and fall into a deep sleep the moment they
strike their beds—but not so deep either, for they are wide
awake at any call or noise. A temporary restful sleep is a desirable thing before X-rays, dressings, and ether anæsthesia—should
th last be necessary, as it was for two bad shoulder cases to-
day.

Everyone, of course, tells us that we know nothing yet of what
it can really be like. After the battle of the Marne the wounded
came in sixty at a time, with the operating room in continuous performance and not enough beds to go around.

Friday, April 9

One comes upon many examples of hairbreadth escapes. In our wards is a man who got off with a slight burn of the forearm when a German contact shell exploded near him, and yet many of his companions were killed. Another man had both bones of his forearm broken in similar fashion without being actually hit, and yet his more distant companions suffered heavily from shrapnel. One man was blown into a tree and hung there for a long time by his trouser leg. Another was blown out of a trench and found the timing piece (*fusée*) of a shell in the seat of his trousers. Many have barely escaped because they happened to be stooping when a shell exploded near by. One artillery officer was knocked down three times in succession by shells landing only a metre or two away from him; he suffers from a severe nervous concussion —what the British call "shell shock."

A Visit to the 2ᵉᵐᵉ Armée

Sunday night, April 11th

Strong somehow secured from the *Ministère de la Guerre* a coveted pink paper "good for three days" permitting him and a companion to visit the Amiens sector on a *mission spéciale itinéraire facultatif*. Before leaving for Serbia to-morrow, what he wished particularly to see were the provisions for the wounded near the Front and the methods of disinfecting for lice, scabies, etc. Parasites, human and otherwise, play an important rôle in the war.

He attributes the privileges partly to the five stripes on his sleeve and partly to the effectiveness, when making an unusual request in a foreign tongue, of demanding an interpreter. This conveys the impression that one knows what he is about and adds dignity to the scene. Preserve therefore your Parisian small talk for shopkeepers and waiters, but express your compliments and desires to officials through someone conversant with *les verbes irréguliers et défectifs*—and you may get a "pink paper" and visit the *2ᵉᵐᵉ Armée.*

After endless days of rain and influenzal colds, we were given a Sunday, raw though it was, for the most part in sunshine and without a shower. With the aid of a *pension* alarm clock I tumbled out at dawn and climbed into a brand-new ambulance uniform, well padded out with an extra sweater, two pairs of socks, and me, heavily armed with two kodaks and appropriate rolls of ammunition. Luckily, considering the hour, a taxi was encountered and I was delivered at the Crillon at the appointed time.

There had been difficulty at the Ambulance in regard to the military number of our car, which on our *permis* read 21243, whereas its actual number was 22060; but fortunately most of the sentries simply bowed before the magic paper without wasting time in scrutinizing it. At the suggestion of Alan Muhr, our Ambulance Corps driver, we stopped to fill the bottom of the car with cigarettes and should have bought more—a few hundred packages of 10-centime Caporals don't go far among a thousand men. Showing our paper at the Porte de la Villette, we took the Route Flandre toward Senlis, past the new aviation field at Le Bourget where there are hangars for innumerable planes, some of which were up—enough easily to defend Paris were it not, according to Muhr, that the Taubes can circle all around them; and when Zeppelins come on a Saturday night the flying men are likely to be at their club dinner!

A cool hazy morning and, as the spring is late, we were glad to be well wrapped up. Soon signs of neatly made trenches and entanglements were seen on either side of the road—unoccupied and never to be, let's hope—prepared doubtless to protect Paris long after they were needed. At Survilliers, only 15 miles out, Muhr waves at the little cluster of buildings—the nearest point to Paris reached by the *uhlan* cavalry. Then on across open farming country and through the Forêt de Chantilly until Senlis—or what is left of it—with its graceful twelfth-century spire comes in sight. A little town of importance in mediæval history and until last autumn a pleasant place in which to have a country home.

On the evening of September 3rd, the German right wing had reached the line of Creil–Senlis–Nanteuil, fully expecting to enter Paris on the following day. On the memorable 4th, however, it was learned that von Kluck for some unaccountable reason was swinging to the east, possibly to outflank the British or because he had come too far and too fast from his base of supplies, or because he was misinformed about the strength of the French in Paris—

who knows? At all events, it was on the 5th that Galliéni's taxicab-delivered troops crumpled up this turning movement by suddenly landing on its flank with the result which one *does* know—the subsequent battle of the Marne and the German retreat to the present—or approximately the present—impregnable line of trenches. It was apparently on this high-water line of von Kluck's advance that the looting and burning took place from which Amiens,

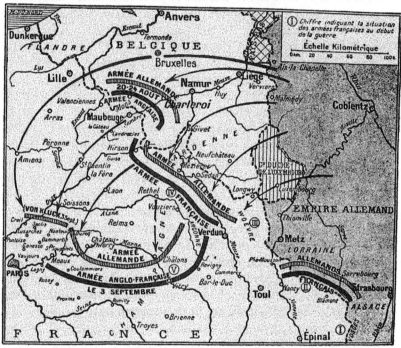

Showing the German Advance at the Outbreak of the War between August 20 and September 3, 1914

Montdidier, and places farther in the rear seemingly escaped—places the Germans expected to retain? or places where they met with no resistance or sniping? or where the troops were kept in better control? Someone better informed must answer.

Senlis at least shows what can be done in a short time. All the descriptions and photographs I have seen of pillaged villages fail to give any conception of what it all meant; and here seven months have elapsed—ample time to clear the streets of the débris.

At a little shop where some picture postcards were on display, an old woman wiping her hands on her apron finally answered to Muhr's bangings and let us in. Yes, she had three sons in the army —all good boys—one of them dead and another reported missing. She told us excitedly how the wine cellars were promptly broken into and the soldiers got very drunk on champagne. With the Eiffel Tower in sight from Senlis, they were as good as in Paris and demanded the names of the best restaurants, where they expected to be dining in a day or two. Then came the systematic burning—incendiary pellets carried by the soldiers being thrown in through the broken windows as they departed. This at least was Madame's belief.

They had time to wreck the Senlis railroad station, which was not the case farther west at Creil—but then, were these not Sherman's methods? The Allies have not had a chance to show what the Turcos and Cossacks might do under similar circumstances if let loose in Germany. . . .

On through Creil, an important railroad junction on the Oise, much knocked about by the German artillery; but the turning movement from here appears to have been too rapidly executed to give time for the sort of systematic demolition from which Senlis suffered. Only one street on the northern bank—the rue Gambetta, I believe—was badly gutted. The iron bridge, presumably destroyed by the French when first driven out, has been replaced by a makeshift structure and we crossed by a guarded wooden footbridge, finding the town full of soldier people—old reservists doing sentry duty, not a few cripples, others possibly home on sick leave—surrounded by their women and children. The Oise is quite a sizable stream here, and from the northern bank one gets a lovely view in the bright sun—for it grows warmer —of St. Médard, another old church of an early century. It has known other wars. Happily these were the last we saw of demolished towns, until we passed through them again like carcasses in the night on our return.

From Creil on to Clermont over roads in excellent repair in spite of what they 've been put to. And such beautiful country! From the appearance of the well-cultivated fields there have been plenty of hands, even though old or female, to do the work. Some of the fields are newly ploughed and some even show a few inches of early spring wheat. It looked more like our Middle West so far as the wide unbroken stretches were concerned—but far better groomed and intersected by good roads lined by double avenues of buttonwood or elm. A great shooting country, too, when harvests are in, says Muhr, who explains that the frequent copses of trees and undergrowth are left as coverts for sportsmen to whom the owners let out their places. For good reason there was no hunting last autumn and game is plentiful—pheasants fly across · the way—we see countless partridges—and a rabbit now and then barely gets across the road in front of us in time to save his skin. Another evidence of a war last Christmas is shown by the great nest-like tufts of mistletoe on the roadside trees, much of which would have been gathered in normal times and sold in the Paris markets.

It seems strange that the French did not remove their road signs as the Belgians are said to have done. They are at every crossroad, and what with a stone marker every kilometre giving the distance to Paris or to the nearest large town in the other direction, small chance that an invading force would lose its way, especially with a Taride motor map easily purchased at any shop and in every German officer's pocket. We passed what Muhr—whom I will cease quoting, as most of our information may be taken as coming from him—called a company of "Rats"—i.e., *Réserves de l'Armée Territoriale;* but otherwise, apart from a gray military car or two that whizzed by with some officers on the way to Paris, we had the road to ourselves and kept on through a far-flung, pastoral region in utter peace, with not a soul in sight except an occasional lone worker in some distant field. Larks and song sparrows could be heard even above the noise of the car, and innumerable crows and magpies were scared up from the fields as we chased by.

Through Clermont-de-l'Oise, a beautiful town on a hill slope, also with old churches and a mediæval Hôtel de Ville. The Germans were here also and indeed reached a point 17 miles to the west—at Beauvais on the other side of the Forêt de Hez. On through St. Just, and then Breteuil fairly eating up the road— the towns full of reservists in their long blue coat-like mantles with the corners buttoned back, red trousers, and military caps, looking for all the world, were it not for the red splashes, like our veterans of 1865 as they appear in Brady's old photographs of that time.

There are said to be 2,500,000 men on the Western Front with a million and a half reservists; and the 1916 class with another half million boys has been called up to-day. Then on through Flers-sur-Noye and other places, breathlessly passing mile on mile, as far away as one can see, of newly ploughed fields—prepared for planting beet-root, according to M.—till we finally reach Dury and the headquarters of the *2ᵉᵐᵉ Armée,* a little town just short of Amiens, where begin our real adventures.

The 2nd Army holds the line from Thiépval to Tracy, i.e., to a point about opposite Compiègne, and consists of three corps, each of them an army in itself. It is in command of Général Castelnau, who, in his shirt sleeves, did n't much resemble the pictures of him shown in the Paris windows. At the battle of Charleroi one of his sons, a junior officer, had been killed by a shell before his eyes. News of the death of a second son was brought to him during a recent council of war at these Dury headquarters, and without showing the slightest recoil he quietly said, "Gentlemen, we will continue with our business." There 's still another son—a football friend of Muhr's, which doubtless helped us some. . . .

Strong had a letter from the recent Surgeon General of the 2nd Army to a Col. La Bade, his successor, asking that he accompany us wherever we wished to go and extend to us all courtesies, etc., etc. Col. La Bade, alas, was away for the day in Compiègne, and we were confronted at the office of the Service de Santé by a not very cordial medical officer gorgeously attired in one of the new horizon-blue uniforms, who suggested that we look for Col. La Bade in Compiègne. Sizing him up as not caring to act as a cicerone for us on this pleasant Sunday, in La Bade's absence, Strong suggested that we be escorted to the local commanding officer. This to my surprise was promptly acted upon, the M.D. meanwhile muttering things about the uselessness of going to headquarters and our not having *le mot*—though what *le mot* had to do with it I could n't imagine, unless it was that our French was highly defective; but this was the last thing that bothered Strong.

Well, we got by several sentries and arrived at a little house further down the village street full of soldiers and soldiers' things, and were ushered into a room where was a billiard table covered with big envelopes, maps, and documents, while the walls were lined with the greatcoats and military caps of the staff officers. Strong requested an interpreter, a rôle Muhr was asked to play, and the next thing I knew we were being ushered upstairs and being greeted by a pleasant old man—Castelnau himself—who seemed really glad to see us and asked many questions of how we happened to be over here, which Muhr told him, and what we wanted, which Muhr told him also, adding that he had played on the French football team with his son. And before it was over—and it did n't take long—we were wringing each other's hands, *bonne chancing*, and so on, while the *Médecin Major* downstairs was let know that he was to take us to see everything that we wished to see. Whereupon we were given *le mot*—which password for the day was "Franceville"—whispered to us as though somebody might steal it. Strong later insisted that *le mot* by any other name would have served as well and been easier to remember, but we Franceville'd our way along until 6 p.m., when we got another.

Our guide—the reluctant M.O.—wanted us to go first to Amiens, apparently as a convenient place for *déjeuner*, which we did, and at the Hôtel du Rhin he was provided with a copious one. We were meanwhile informed that the medical situation which had promised to be most serious was rapidly improving. In the 4000 beds at Amiens there were now only 2000 sick and only (*sic*) about 500 cases of typhoid. At one time there had been 9000 cases!! in the 2nd Army alone, and some 70,000 in all the armies with about the usual 13 per cent mortality. During November and December cases were being brought in to Amiens at the rate of 300 a day, but since vaccination of the troops had become compulsory their number was rapidly diminishing. It might otherwise have been disastrous. Meanwhile, the British Army had been almost entirely exempt—only an occasional case among those unvaccinated.

He wanted us to stop long enough to see the Amiens Base Hospital and disinfecting plant, but as Strong had already been there (and says they were very bad) we begged to move along. So, having wasted considerable time over food, we got away about 2 p.m. and took the straight road which, almost without a kink, leads due east all the way to St. Quentin—or once did. To-day one can go scarcely half the way, some 50-odd km., before coming to the Boche.[1]

Some ten miles out we stop at Villers-Bretonneux to inspect an *ambulance de première ligne* in a medium-sized two-story house where a pleasant upstanding young officer was directed by our guide to show us things. The place was utterly makeshift but there were barely 50 wounded, whereas their accommodations were for 150—it's this way everywhere during the present lull. The 50 were mostly head and chest cases—apparently doing well. Head injuries are frequent from imprudent peering over the trenches, and that's why the Algerian Zouaves are not sent into the line as much as formerly, for they "want to see." The doctor, recognizing my uniform, said the wounded men all beg to go to the Ambulance Américaine, where *on dit* they are pampered and spoiled. Some cigarettes were distributed and one poor chap raised up on his elbow and said, "I tank you." *Bonne chance, mes amis.*

Then, with Muhr touching it up to 90 km., on to a small hamlet called Warfusée, where we began to see rows of trenches and entanglements and at one place, for at least a kilometre, an intersecting (communication) trench zigzagged beside the road, a clean-cut ditch five or six feet deep, the soft earth held up by coarse wire netting and scarcely wide enough for a man's shoulders—certainly no stretcher could traverse it.

Soldiers were gathering sod and stripping bark from the trees for the trench arbors and concealments; and alongside of them old men and women were working in the fields at their peaceful occupations, as unconcerned as though the sound of cannonading and the drone of aeroplanes were a normal accompaniment of their day's work. Warfusée had seen serious fighting in Septem_

---

[1] This term of derision which we have heard our *blessés* at the Ambulance apply to the Germans—like Yanks and Rebs of the 60's—I'm told is a contraction of "caboche"—a hob_ nail for shoes or the square head on a horseshoe nail—and has reference to the shape of the Teuton's head (*grosse tête*), which amuses the oval-faced and oval-headed Gaul.

ber; great ditches had been dug for the dead behind the little church burying plot—too small to hold them all; and scattered along the road and through the fields were little mounds with a wooden cross at the head—too many to count.

We got out to investigate the empty trenches, which appeared to be newly made and prepared as a second line of defense in this sector. They connected directly under the highway and were of a rectangular pattern to prevent enfilading, with shelters at frequent intervals, and in front of them were some crude entanglements (*chevaux de frise*). It 's amazing to think that these ditches extend all the way from Flanders to Switzerland, and not only one but several successive lines of them probably on both sides. Strange warfare, fit only for weasles, moles, or rats. . . .

At a place called Foucaucourt a sentry held us up, saying it was the limit of motor traffic, and we found ourselves under cover of some trees where the road runs along a slight ridge with a declivity on each side. On the right, drawn up before a shed, well protected in the arms of an old limestone quarry, was a company of soldiers who filed into the makeshift barrack and disappeared. We climbed out of the car and descended the sharp slope to find, running under the road, an old bricked-in tunnel which had once served as a *poste de premier secours* but was now being used for officers' quarters. A most engaging young officer stepped up, saluted, introduced himself as Lieutenant Woerner, and asked in perfect English if we wished to see his men, with whom he had just come out of the trenches after an eight days' period—for in this comparatively quiet area they are alternating eight days in and eight days out.

The moment we entered the door every man jumped to his feet at salute from the straw mattresses on which they 'd been sprawling. They seemed well fed and husky, but looked rather done up, and we were told that, owing to frequent alarms, they had had a sleepless 48 hours. They were of varied ages—one a boy of 20 and the others ranging up to 40—all in the 23rd Infantry. It was pleasant to see and feel the camaraderie, with each in his own place, which evidently existed between the men and their young officer, whom they addressed possessively but deferentially. This characterizes the French Army throughout, one is led to believe. Lt. Woerner was obviously proud of them and seemed well pleased when Muhr scrambled back to the car and returned with an armful of Caporals.

I confess that the sight of numerous freshly made shell holes in the field near by was disconcerting, and no less so the discharge of a cannon every few minutes on the other side of the road. Woerner asked if we would like to see the battery—they were shelling the Germans in Belloy, four kilometres away. Of course. So we climbed over the road and down the slope on that side, where the ground was literally pocked with holes, some of them big enough to bury an ox, while here and there was a wooden cross with a soldier's cap on it. We were reassured with a shrug that *ces sales Boches* were not wasting the ammunition and these *trous d'obus* were made a few days ago in an effort to locate the battery. Well camouflaged, it was hidden in a little copse about 150 yards from the road and partly protected by an embankment that was honeycombed with dugouts for the gunners' quarters—like cave men's holes.

Our host routed out a business-like young artillery officer who said his commander was away making observations. Would he mind our watching the guns?—not at all—and kodaking them?— not in the least—and he scampered off and disappeared in a hole somewhere in the bank.

The guns were well concealed—the third, for there were three side by side, I never made out at all, and the nearest one at the edge of the copse looked just like a fallen tree, for its long muzzle had been carefully wrapped with bark. They were 120-mm. guns, I believe, firing in rotation and meanwhile receiving signals from an observation post somewhere on the embankment a hundred yards away correcting their angulation. The target was said to be the church steeple in Belloy, which was too useful to the Boches to leave standing. I learned that kodaking a heavy gun in action and protecting both ears at the same moment offered an insoluble problem.

We subsequently found Woerner's platoon up on the road getting their mail, for the soldiers' post had just come in, and refus_ ing a Boche helmet which was offered us, and promising to send them a football to amuse themselves with when *en repos*, we again got aboard—and, everyone at salute, started back for Amiens. It was a wonderful afternoon, with sun and clouds, several aeroplanes up, farmers getting in hay between the lines of rear trenches; and finally the Amiens Cathedral loomed up on the distant horizon, kilometres away in the clear air.

It was about 4 p.m. when we finally dropped our cicerone at Dury, and as Strong had expected to reach Montdidier, then some 40 km. away, by 4.30, we had to make haste. This was not so easy, for we were frequently stopped by armed sentries who would unexpectedly pop out in the middle of the road, and if our "Franceville" did not satisfy them would hold us up while they scrutinized our pink *permis* in detail. Thus to Rossignol, then across country to Ailly and through Grivesnes—a lovely valley, town, and château—Cantigny—and finally—while going at about 90 km. with Montdidier prettily situated on a hill just before us—we suddenly have a blowout. It fortunately was a rear tire—soon replaced by a new demountable wheel; but what was worse than this, in trying to make up for lost time we bounced over a railroad track just before entering the town, catching our muffler on one of the rails, and the whole pipe was ripped off from the bottom of the car. Such a racket as we subsequently made beggars description, and with the noise of an aeroplane we drew up at the Montdidier station.

Hermann Harjes had told Strong that we would be met by a member of his ambulance corps, but being fully an hour late it was no surprise to find no one was there. The place serves in military parlance as a *gare régulatrice par le chemin de fer* and the station yard was full of French *ambulances mobiles de premier secours* which gather the *blessés* at the forward areas and deposit them in canvas-covered shacks on the station platform to be sorted before further distribution by train to points west and south. There was much bowing and scraping on the part of a robust Dr. Munie, the officer in charge, who finally gave us directions to the Harjes château—*Château d'Agincourt*—some ten miles further on; and without waiting for an escort we decided to push along by ourselves. We passed on the way large numbers of African troops— Moroccans—"going in," and could plainly hear heavy cannonading from French batteries on our left said to be at Guerbigny.

Though late for our engagement we were given a pot of tea by some friendly young ambulance drivers—one of them Major Higginson's nephew—while Muhr undertook to see what he could do to repair our muffler—and he could do nothing. One of the ambulance corps—a Mr. Goode from Iowa—then took us out in the dusk to a place called Grivillers only a half hour's walk behind the first line of trenches. It was a little hamlet fairly alive with troops, where, interrupting a game of cards in the officers' mess, one of the players, a young M.O. named Viallet, was told off to show us to the local aid station which he described as practically a *poste de deuxième secours*. It was in a partly ruined two-storied stone house where straw bags in lieu of mattresses were laid on gabion frames like camping-out beds—doubtless comfortable enough, in view of what the men must put up with when in the line.

There were some recently wounded—head and chest cases—and the corner for emergency operations was in a dark narrow passageway. Dr. Viallet was particularly pleased with a hammock-stretcher he had devised in which seriously wounded men can be promptly evacuated from the trenches without having to wait till dark as has heretofore been necessary. They can be carried through the winding passages, only the hands of the bearers and poles of the stretchers being above the level of the trench when they come to a turn. (In other areas, I believe, canvas chair-like litters are made to serve the same purpose.) In some such way the *blessés*, after receiving their first-aid dressings, can get back to Grivillers in two hours after being wounded and can sometimes be delivered at Montdidier on the same day.

There were some 3000 troops in this reserve station and they looked double the number as they crowded around our car reaching out for the remaining packages of cigarettes which, alas! did n't go very far. The 16th, 4th, 7th, and 103rd Territorials, the 17th Regiment, and others. Seasoned troops they were, and platoons of them were in formation preparing to move up into the trenches. Viallet urged us to go out with him to see the *poste de premier secours* in the front lines which by a devious *boyau* was perhaps a half hour's walk, though only a kilometre away; but it was getting pretty late—too dark to see much of anything—and we were far from Paris.

So we return to the Montdidier station *"pour demander le mot,"* for the password changes at six, and we 're told it is "Has_brouck." Thus protected, we set off via St. Just, Clermont, Creil, Chantilly, where is Joffre's headquarters, the town dark as a pocket with sentries holding us up about every 100 yards—a bad place to get through—then the ghostly Forest of Chantilly, Euzarches, Écouen, and St. Denis—making a terrific noise all the way like a *mitrailleuse.* We crept into Paris at the Porte de la Chapelle— and friend Muhr, fearing arrest should he go snorting unmuffled through the city, put us in a taxi somewhere in Montmartre. So home and to bed with a burning face and a bronchitis almost completely blown away.

Hôpital Complémentaire 21: Compiègne

Monday, April 12

A visit this a.m. from Carrel, who extracts a promise that I pay him a visit at Compiègne for a day or two and, as things are quiet, why not to-morrow. He looks like a little bear in a great fur coat over his light blue uniform. We lunch at a quiet restaurant frequented by the War Office people and are joined there by Madame Carrel. In the p.m. saw Strong off with his teeth grimly set for an adventure in Serbia which sounds like a large order.

April 13. Compiègne

Alexis Carrel, an Americanized Frenchman, is not to be confused with a Gallicized Marylander, M. Charles Carroll de Carrollton—as he appears in the *Social Register*—who arrives at 7.45 driving his own militarized car and announces that, taking advantage of my request for transportation to Compiègne, he is to do an unneutral thing, namely, to carry a French officer back to his station not far from there. His friend the French officer, who calls him "Charlie," proves to be the Duc de Rohan, whom we soon pick up together with his pet terrier "Vicky" and innumerable bags, which leaves room for but one behind—*viz.*, me. A handsome person is the Duc—a member of the Chamber of Deputies —one of the fourteen who preferred active military service to sitting behind a civilian desk—a lieutenant in the 27th Infantry.

Another cool misty morning with promise of a clear day as we leave again by the Porte de Villette, or should have done had not Charlie lost his way in Aubervilliers, over whose atrocious *pavés* we wandered about for some time before finally locating the Route de Flandre. This time I counted the lines of trenches defending Paris as we whisked by, for Charlie drives about as fast as Muhr. The first two at 19 and 21 km. and then Louvres, a picturesque place which marks the farthest point south reached by the German column along this road. At 28 km. another carefully constructed trench elaborately faced with interlacing wattles or gabion revetments; another at 32 km. with a network of entanglements before it. An aviator down in a field and a crowd gathering from nowhere and everywhere. At 15 km. beyond Louvres, the Duc points out where his regiment captured 15 German guns. On through Pontarmé and the delightful *forêt* of the same name: Senlis again, but this time out of it to the N.E. at high speed through lovely country and pretty villages—a beautiful view of Verberie from the side of a hill, and then through the Forest of Compiègne.

Nothing could be more peaceful and lovely than a well-groomed French forest in the early spring, its floor for miles on a stretch carpeted with flowers—lilies of the valley, anemones, and low-growing narcissus, the latter in such profusion as to give a yellow tone in among the trees as far as one could see—magnificent stands of beeches intersected by paths and formal *allées* of alluring kind. But our road lay *tout à droit* through it all.

Having a French officer aboard, our *laissez-passer* has rarely been called for, but the Oise divides the 2nd, to which the Duc belongs, from the 6th Army and we are frequently held up. Compiègne finally comes into view as we wind around a hillside road —a beautifully situated town—no wonder Nap.I picked it out for a residence. He would have felt at home there to-day. On through the town and across the Oise on a one-way temporary bridge, the old stone Pont de Compiègne having been destroyed by the English, I believe, during the retreat.

Once across, we climb the hill to Margny-lès-Compiègne, getting views across the river valley behind us almost as fine as that we had on approaching Verberie. Then in a northwesterly direction on the road to Montdidier which parallels the front in this

sector, only seven or eight miles away—a neglected cobbly road
lined by trees much shattered by shellfire and in process of being
stripped of their lower branches, presumably for trench gabions.
The Duc points out the line of hills which his division is holding
as we arrive at the little crossroads village of Cuvilly, where he
says he has been quartered the past three months.

Having been *en permission* 8 days, he was astonished to find
Cuvilly deserted and to learn from some stragglers that the regiment had moved away to get a better water supply for the *tirail-
leurs*. So on we go in search of them, and after winding around
interminably over atrocious back-country roads and asking many
questions—the region was seething with troops and lines of artillery and convoys—we end up via Moyenneville at a place called
Wacquemoulin where, surrounded by an eager crowd of his
brother officers, the Duc distributes a bundle of papers purchased
as we were leaving Paris, together with a huge box of *confitures*
and a "bale" of cigarettes—a present from friend Charlie.

They were all eager to know what was going on, for, as we
have found, the farther one gets from home and the nearer the
seat of war, the less you hear about it and the less frightful it
seems. As I was skirmishing for a favorable snapshot one of the
officers came up and asked in English if I could give him any news
of the war! I could have done so had I been in Boston. He told
me they were training dogs to work in the trenches.

And so we left M. le Duc in the arms of his friends and turned
back via Gournay and Monchy to Compiègne again, reaching our
destination fully two hours late—an embarrassment, as it proved,
for Carrel had expected us by 10 o'clock and, cherishing an idea
that my transfer to Compiègne for some work might be requisi-
tioned, had asked Gen. Nimier to meet us at that hour. We repaired to lunch promptly and I did the best I could to be polite to
M. le Médecin Inspecteur Général de la Sixième Armée and
his five colonels and to thank him for the inscribed copy of his
Blessures du Crâne et de l'Encéphale which he presented to me.
Having arrived two hours late and by mischance having excused
myself for a moment to say good-bye to Mr. Carroll, which moment happened to coincide with the General's own departure, I
could not have impressed him favorably. We then paid a visit to

away—a neglected cobbly road
shellfire and in process of being
presumably for trench gabions.
hills which his division is holding
ads village of Cuvilly, where he
ast three months.
days, he was astonished to find
rom some stragglers that the regi-
better water supply for the tirail-
f them, and after winding around
d-country roads and asking many
ng with troops and lines of artil-
M. venneville at a place called
by an eager crowd of his
s a bundle of papers purchased
a huge box of confitures
from friend Charlie.
was going on, for, as we
home and the nearer the
and the less frightful it
able snapshot one of the
I could give him any news
I been in Boston. He told
the trenches.
of his friends and turned
again, reaching our
embarrassment, as it proved,
and, cherishing an idea
some work might be requisi-
meet us at that hour. We re-
the best I could to be polite to
de la Sixième Armée and
for the inscribed copy of his
which he presented to me.
by mischance having excused
to Mr. Carroll, which mo-
General's own departure, I
We then paid a visit to

Henry D. Dakin and Alexis Carrel
at Compiègne

Hôpital Comp
(Rond R

Rossignol, and the Zeppelin *Trous*
in the Park

The Salle des Fê
as a Typhoid

the large ward where Dr. Dehelly did a number of dressings—
very badly I thought—unnecessary pain and bleeding from the
extraction of adherent gauze. It was awful—wicked indeed—to
see the poor devils, one of whom chewed a hole in his coverlet
rather than utter a groan. The time will come when they will
learn better methods, but meanwhile there will be much needless
suffering.

What is known as *Hôpital Complémentaire 21* is in a once
fashionable hotel—the Rond Royal—on the very edge of the
Forêt de Compiègne—an ideal spot and one which Carrel chose
for his purposes on careful survey after he got free from his miserable detail, first in the Lyon hospital and then at the War Office.
Here, backed by Rockefeller money and with an admirable staff,
a great opportunity lies open for special studies of wound treatment. The lines along which they have started to work include
the suction treatment of suppurating wounds without dressings;
the employment of irrigation with bactericidal fluids which are
being worked out by Henry Dakin; methods of increasing resistance to pathogenic organisms by turpentine injections, etc., etc.

There are at present 51 beds with 86 attendants, including
slaveys of all kinds—11 scientific, medical, and administrative
officers; 13 experienced Swiss nurses supplied by Theodor
Kocher; numerous secretaries, laboratory technicians, linen-room
people, scrub women, ambulance men; and 47 soldier orderlies
who do everything from boots to waiting on table and keeping up
the gardens. It is indeed a research hospital *de luxe* with running
water in all the rooms, which are large, most of them having baths,
comfortable beds, electricity, and all modern improvements. Over
the *dramatis personæ* Madame Carrel rules as housekeeper and
"general tyrant," according to her husband.

There are also stables and four chauffeurs whom I had forgotten to mention—one of them a professional racing driver who has
figured in international events—another Sarah Bernhardt's leading man on her last tour of the U.S.A.—the third an equally
celebrated actor from the Odéon—the fourth an underling. These
deserve special mention because late in the afternoon behind
chauffeurs 1 and 4 in an open car we went on an expedition, meanwhile clutching everything that was detachable and only coming

up for breath when stopped by a sentry, gun on high. Thus for some 10 km. to the west, where, in the château of the Duchesse de Quelquechose, an English lady of title has well-meaningly estab‑ lished an Ambulance under the direction of a most unprepossessing English surgeon, with a rachitic build and bad teeth, who has a single amateur nurse to help him—neither of them speaks a word of French, and they appear to have a comparable familiarity with surgery. We are plied with tea and English marmalade while he bitterly complains that the French don't send him the kind of wounded that make it worth while for him to remain—only minor injuries and few of those. In short, M. l'Inspecteur must have sized up the situation.

Then back in the other direction along the north bank of the Oise to Janville, where the Spahis—the Chasseurs d'Afrique— are quartered. Picturesque, fine-looking fellows who made an ef‑ fective color scheme against the stone houses of the village with their black and white turbans, dusky faces, and scarlet cloaks or bernous reaching to their heels. Some of them were in their work‑ ing uniforms, a jacket made of some sort of coarse brown cloth like overall material with the black baggy corduroy trousers of Zouaves drawn tight around the ankles. These daring horsemen have had little chance to show what they are good for—scarcely since the Marne—and like the French dragoons they now take their trick in the trenches on foot, I am given to understand.

Then farther on until we finally turn into a side road which leads us through groves uphill to the handsome Château d'Annel at Longueil, with the line at Ribécourt in German hands only six km. distant. Here we found quite a different sort of place from that we had just seen. Shortly before we arrived six badly wounded men had been brought in from Montmacq, a short distance away. Half the château is still occupied by the family and the staff— Mr. and Mrs. Depew and a daughter, Stanley, a nice-looking Bart's man of recent years in a British uniform, a Dr. Eaton of Albany who acts as his assistant and is soon to leave, Dr. Frere, one of Henry Head's London Hospital pupils, nurses and others. The other half of the building has been dismantled to provide beds for about 40 soldiers and 10 officers, together with operating rooms and a satisfactory X-ray equipment to which one of the pa‑

tients was taken and fluoroscoped for me, showing a shrapnel ball in the left frontal lobe. Another of the men was dying from a ball which had entered over the right kidney and was palpable under the skin in the pectoral region, where was a huge hæmatoma. It is quite possible that a transfusion might have saved him had there been provision for such.

In spite of the severe character of the wounds they receive, they have done reasonably well with 20 per cent fatalities, a large number of which occur soon after the patients are admitted. Their beds are full most of the time and they evacuate promptly to Compiègne. It would seem to be an ideal place for some young man of skill and quick judgment, for it is the sort of work a mobile Ambulance might do, indeed what the Ambulance at Neuilly practically was doing in September and October. It is possible here because the château happens to be near the present rather stationary line and was spared by the Germans supposedly because a U.S. flag was flying.

Mrs. Depew, an energetic American fifteen years resident here, got Joffre's ear early enough to secure a *permis* which lets her do about as she chooses, and she says the place was equipped by August 7th, before the Ambulance at Neuilly was started. She was then driven out and did not get back until September 27th after the retreat, to find the château undamaged—only some wine looted. Since that time they have been continuously busy. There are 7 nurses for the 40 patients, an ambulance corps consisting of 4 Ford cars; the large soldiers' ward is in a handsome hall with timbered ceiling—I presume the banqueting hall of better days. Just where this château, with its privileged Anglo-French-American staff, comes in on the scheme of things I fail to see, but I suppose it may function as an *ambulance de première ligne*. Nine acute cases yesterday; seven so far to-day.

April 14. 2nd day at Compiègne

A beautiful warm spring morning—buds swelling perceptibly—birds singing melodiously—artillery horses exercising in the open space in the *forêt* outside my window. Meanwhile distant cannonading recalls the more serious matters of the day and place. From the experience of yesterday afternoon it is apparent that society dotes on the excitement of war and loves to provide—however badly—for the wounded, particularly if they are presentable and can be wheeled in to afternoon tea—neither of which they ordi_ narily are.

So confused have I become as to where these privately run château-hospitals stand in the strictly military organization that Lieut. Rossignoli—a member of the French Ambulance Corps stationed here at the Rond Royal and one-time director of a chain of hotels spread from Paris to the Riviera—has taken the trouble this a.m. to give me such details of the Service de Santé as may some day be useful:—

It is divided into two sections—the *service de l'avant* and the *service de l'arrière*, which have naturally somewhat different functions. He has drawn a diagram to show how those unsung heroes of the war, the *brancardiers régimentaires* (musicians, tailors, shoemakers, barbers, etc., without rank), bring the wounded from the *champ de bataille* to a *refuge pour blessés* or *poste de secours* located in a comparatively protected spot or in an artificial *abri* actually underground. There the regimental *médecin chef* or one of his aides applies an emergency dressing, gives an injection of antitetanic serum, and attaches to the man's clothing a sort of baggage tag—pink for transportable cases and white for the more seriously injured. Then the *brancardiers divisionnaires*—actual *infirmiers* for the purpose—take those fit to be evacuated, by night, on stretchers or litters or two-wheeled push carts (*brouettes*), to the *ambulance divisionnaire*, i.e., *ambulance de première ligne*, where, unless actually under fire, they may remain for a few hours or even days until they can safely be picked up by the *section sanitaire automobile divisionnaire* (each army corps has 60 motor ambulances for the purpose) and transported (the farthest practical distance being 30 km.) either (1) to a *centre d'hospitalization* or (2) to a *gare d'évacuation* from which they are finally forwarded to a *gare régulatrice* (such as we saw Sunday at Montdidier) for further distribution either by *trains sanitaires* to distant points or, as in Paris at La Chapelle, by motor ambulance among the several hospitals there. A *gare d'évacuation* and *centre d'hospitalization* may of course be in the same place, as at Amiens and here in Compiègne, where in the hospital centre the severely wounded and critically ill—like the typhoid cases—may necessarily remain for weeks.

During the battle of the Marne, Rossignoli was in charge of 50 motor ambulances which were running day and night—oftentimes direct from the *postes de secours* to a *gare d'évacuation* either at St. Mord or at Nanteuil. There were two men to a car and they covered from 300 to 350 km. daily. The drivers took turns sleeping en route and had to carry their benzine in tins. The chief difficulty was in finding water, as the pumps and wells had been destroyed.

To see Compiègne as a hospital centre we then go off in a car behind one of the actor-chauffeurs, first to Royallieu, where some recently erected barracks have been turned into a hospital with accommodations for 1200—chiefly for the sort of minor injuries we are unaccustomed to see at Neuilly. There Dr. Landolt, a celebrated Paris ophthalmologist, conducts a huge clinic for diseases (chiefly trachoma) and injuries of the eye. He was in process of enucleating the eyeball of a man who had been shot from behind while in the attitude of aiming his rifle. The ball, having passed through the right shoulder, had entered the mastoid process to emerge through the very centre of the cornea, completely destroying the eye.

A no less distinguished aurist was hard at it in another room full of minor ear cases, a great many of them ruptured drums from the near explosion of bombs. The men are apt to be "batty" for a day or two after such an experience even when they have not actually been hit. We were shown a mobile bacteriological outfit ready to be moved at a moment's notice wherever it might be needed. Then back to Compiègne and to the palace, which from the time of Louis XV has been a favorite residence for the rulers of France.

It would have surprised them to see the famous *Salle des Fêtes* as it is to-day, lined with beds containing African troops laid low by typhoid, malaria, and other fevers. Edouard Rist, "the best doctor in Paris," Hartmann's medical colleague at the Laennec whom we met at the London Congress two years ago, is in charge —a delightful person who in appearance and speech is more English than French. He showed us several other beautiful rooms with their walls covered by historic paintings and similarly utilized for bed patients; but of the makeshifts for water and baths and toilets for the sick, the less said the better. Louis Quinze did n't put in much plumbing—especially with the present state of things in mind.

Then lunch at the Rond Royal with Babinski's assistant from

La Pitié, and some *médecins majors* of the district, one of whom subsequently, behind the racing chauffeur and Rossignoli, takes me to inspect a first-line Ambulance at Offemont, some 15 km. to the east in the direction of Soissons. We crossed the Aisne at Rethondes and then in a northeasterly direction toward the line along a road which winds through a valley to the east of the Forêt de Laigue, flanked with hills held by the French. It was about as busy a valley as one can imagine, with the road undergoing repairs by Territorial reserves, and the whole district alive with soldiers of all kinds in all sorts of uniforms, going or coming, of officers on horseback, of convoys taking up supplies or ammunition, and an occasional ambulance taking back something else. Across the fields there were batches of soldiers in groups or pairs making their way to the rear for their period of rest. They were very quiet—only one body of men, whom we passed later on, were singing, and they were merely keeping step with a sort of grunting chant. There is no martial music heard these days—at least on this side of the line.

We finally get into a more wooded part of the road and begin to see the dugouts and huts—*grottes*—that the officers and men have built for themselves. Every imaginable kind of structure of every possible form and size, from mere earthen excavations to quite pretentious arborized huts half underground. One cluster was labeled "Indian Village," and many of the huts were given individual names, Villa this or that, some even in English— "House of Hope," for example, printed on a bit of cardboard over a rustic door. A place to fascinate children!

The side of the hill at the edge of the large park surrounding the *Château d'Offemont* was literally honeycombed with these rustic coverings of holes dug in the hillside where the men live. Little roadways concealed by gabion mats have been built, and there are paths or streets which wind in and out and up and down the side of the hill between them. These primitive abodes must seem palatial in comparison to life in the trenches. Finally at the end both of the road and of the valley, we come to a small cluster of four or five stone farm buildings where doubtless tenants of the landowners once lived and where now the *ambulance de première ligne* of Offemont is quartered.

We were cordially received by the *médecin chef*, a Dr. Marie, who turned us over to his *aide-major*, Ferras by name· He, to expedite matters further, sent for one of the *brancardiers*—a young fellow called Hanon, lately a Catholic missionary in Natal, S.A., who speaks English and German like a native—wants an official position as an interpreter and begs me! of all people! to intercede for him.[1]

Well, we are shown through the buildings where are some recently wounded men, one badly hit—a serious head wound received this morning and just operated on by Ferras, who says that in their present quiet stage they get an average of about 20 wounded a day. Very crude surroundings without question—just bags of straw for beds. There was one large tent which I surmise is not unlike our own American Army hospital tents, with double canvas walls and six or eight little windows 2 feet square on each side with a stove in the middle. It has kept them comfortable during the winter, we 're told—for they 've been in this place several months. I try to take a time exposure inside of the tent, for they are willing that pictures be taken—many of the officers and not a few soldiers indeed carry cameras.

On a bench outside we are shown a large German shell the men have just put together—a shell which fell yesterday near by and buried itself fully a metre in the ground, as proved by Mr. Hanon, who climbs in to be kodaked. It was a *cent cinquante-cinq obus* which did nothing more than make a loud noise—and the men, having recovered every fragment by scratching about in the hole, had put the pieces together with as great delight as children would have in making a picture puzzle. I was requested to take a snapshot of it, and one jovial Arab rushes off and gets a rifle, turns up his moustachios, and imitates the Kaiser to the entertainment of his fellows.

There are other *obus* holes in the adjacent field; but most of the holes have been made for another purpose, for there is a sizable burying ground in which the graves are about equally divided between those with Christian and those with Mohammedan markers. Near by is a rustic altar for religious services, and at the far end of the field a *stake for executions*. There have been three, of men who

[1] This I did some days later in Paris, only to find that there is a waiting list of eligibles a mile long.

purposely shot themselves through the hand and were found out —not a difficult kind of wound to recognize, one would think. However, it is not always easy to spot a malingerer whether or not he bears a self-inflicted wound, and it is always possible that injustice may be done to one who gets sick or injured in some justifiable way.

On the way back from the château we stopped at "Indian Village" to visit the regimental surgeon, who had been there, he says, for six months without shift. His little cabin he shows with pride —an arbored front room with a big shell fragment as a weight to keep the rustic door to—and he is particularly delighted with a wash basin moulded out of some cement which had been brought up for use in the trenches and which has a hollow for his soap, and above hangs a tin petrol can from which he siphons off his water by means of a rubber tube. Then a little back sleeping room actually dug out of the hill and lined by gabion mats; and right alongside was his horse in another larger dugout. He has just equipped a little place where, now that the weather is moderating, the men, provided they carry up the water, may get a makeshift shower bath at least every 14 days when they are out for a rest. Regular camping out! And they all—the wounded—look very well and chipper and hopeful. . . .

An offer to go and see some 75's which we could hear at work was refused as it was growing late. And so we leave these modern cave dwellers and their fascinating huts and depart with the impression that they are cordial, patient, companionable, brave fellows who deserve the evident affection their troops have for them. May the victory be theirs!

With the Blessés at Neuilly

Saturday, April 17. Paris

Morning, in the wards at the Ambulance—in the X-ray, dental, and photographic departments. The Unit—both doctors and nurses—are all doing excellent work, and the condition of the patients and their wounds could not be better. Much telephoning in the evening from the *Château d'Annel*, where they wished to borrow someone from our group; but Greenough rather thinks complications would ensue. If this keeps up we are likely to get fined and may even have our telephone taken out, for talking English over the lines is forbidden—queer, this being the language of an ally.

Tuesday, April 20

Our admitting day, and last night 25 wounded were brought in —all recent cases from the 2nd Regt. Zouaves and curiously enough from the line at Tracy-le-Val where we were last Wednesday. There had been an unsuccessful German surprise attack Sunday evening—a hand-to-hand affair—*armes blanches*. They had come via Offemont and Compiègne, *évacués assis* as their tags indicate. Quick work. . . .

There is a strange medley of unassorted people working here. The orderly in No. 28, for example, I chanced to meet at dinner. He turns out to be an Englishman of widely traveled sort; has a home in Naples and another villa in Florence; seems to know everyone, and is attractive, informed, and modest. We talked of the early days when the Ambulance was sending cars to the Marne battlefields and getting patients from Meaux—when dead and wounded lay all along the roadsides. The disgraceful motor parties from Paris to see the gruesome sights were soon stopped by the authorities. It was easy then to get passes—*pendant la guerre*.

Wednesday, April 21

Autopsy on a poor fellow from Mignon's ward with a spinal paralysis. He had been hit while lying face down awaiting an attack, gun in hand. The ball had passed through the right scapula and on into the spinal column, dividing the cord. . . . In the afternoon while waiting for Jougeas to fluoroscope a man with a shrapnel ball in his cerebellum, a person appears in the garb of an ambulance driver who asks loudly for me, and, on my being presented, says, "Oh yes, of course, I'm Washington Lopp, you know; it was I put the salt in the water—ha, ha!—and I'm going to make up for it; and here are some wives of the cabinet ministers who will make it all right with you." And sure enough, he was followed by four females in black who might well enough have been wives of cabinet ministers. I was much mystified and did the best I could with "*heureusements*" and "*avec plaisirs*" and "*vos connaissances*" —all this while the corridor was thick with patients and nurses and stretchers and waiting attendants.

Well, they finally left without removing any salt from the wa_ ter, so far as I could see. Not until later did I learn that M. Lopp is a terpsichorean person who teaches, or once taught, the high life of Paris to tango—cabinet ministers' wives being his specialty, and possibly their husbands, also. He, having retired well-to-do, now keeps (or kept in *ante bellum* days) a large establishment where balls and dinners and dances and other social affairs are held. It is called, I believe, Washington Palace, which is better than Lopp Palace—a little. He is now an active and busy ambulance driver, but has many ears to whisper into; and learning through his wife, an *auxiliaire*, that a member of the Harvard Unit, newly arrived, wanted "head cases," he went about it. So this accounts for the twenty-five shattered jaws with which we were swamped the day Cutler and I went to Gare d'Orléans for *blessés*. M. Lopp and the cabinet ladies will have this all changed—the salt in the water, ha, ha! Of such is the Ambulance Américaine.

Thursday, April 22

The morning passed with Tuffier, and now waiting for him for a moment at his private hospital. Here at this place are several officers, one a general with half his face blown off and quite blind. T. says most of the officers have been killed, and that is why the men are so brave! It puts courage into them. Queer idea; but possibly I don't quite understand.

He tells me of peculiar wounds that he has seen. An officer, hit in the trenches by an explosion of an enemy hand grenade, had a small wound of entrance near the inner canthus of the right eye, without special symptoms. An X-ray showed an undeformed cartridge in the frontal lobe of the brain. This was extracted and it proved to be an intact French Lebel cartridge! I give it up. He explains that the captured French ammunition, which of course does not fit the German Mauser rifles, is used with whatever else may be handy to fill the hand grenades, now so murderously thrown about in the trench fighting.

Another instance was that of a woman who had been injured in the thigh by a fragment of the first of the aeroplane bombs dropped on Paris. There was in addition a trifling wound of the scapular region, and a point of tenderness low down in the back, where subsequently an X-ray showed the presence of a French rifle

removing any salt from the water did I learn that M. Lopp is
... at once taught, the high life of
... being his specialty, and
having retired well-to-do, now
... a large establishment where
... social affairs are held. It is
... which is better than Lopp
... and busy ambulance driver,
... and learning through his wife,
... Harvard Unit, newly arrived,
... So this accounts for the
... we were swamped the day
... M. Lopp and the
... the salt in the water, ha,
...

Thursday, April 22
... waiting for him for
... this place are several
... own off and quite blind.
... killed, and that is why the
... them. Queer idea; but

... he has seen. An officer, hit
... hand grenade, had a
... canthus of the right eye,
... showed an undeformed car-
... This was extracted and it
... cartridge! I give it up. He
... ammunition, which of course
... is used with whatever else
... grenades, now so murderously

... who had been injured in
... of the aeroplane bombs
... a trifling wound of the
... low down in the back,
... the presence of a French rifle

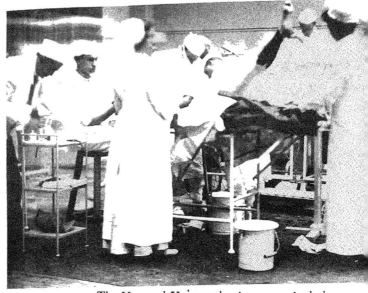

The Harvard Unit at the American Ambulance

Standing: Wilson, Benet, Barton, Rogers, Coller, Cutler, Smith
Nurses: Wilson, Cox, Martin, Parks. *Seated:* Boothby
Greenough, Cushing, Strong, Osgood

bullet! She had been hit by a falling ball that had been fired from a *mitrailleuse* ("devil's coffee mill") at the aeroplane. Strange coincidence that she should have got both injuries at one and the same instant.

Lunch with T. and a Belgian officer, who constitute a committee to supply artificial limbs to the *amputés*. A month ago 7000 were needed and the French can only make 400 a month at the best—the American manufacturers 500. Hence it will take the better part of a year to supply those already wanted. Many more will be needed before we 're through. Later to see a review at the Invalides of the 29th and 30th Regiments (territorial) of infantry—very moving. There is something about French troops on the march that dims one's eyes.

Saturday, April 24

This afternoon, in response to a call to the Ambulance for all of its many cars, Boothby and I went in one of them to La Chapelle, which is the present single distributing station—*gare régulatrice*—for all the wounded forwarded to Paris.

Red Cross ambulances of every pattern, and from a great many hospitals, were being picked up from all sides as we neared our destination—a rather unusual sight here at midday, for the authorities do not like to have the recent wounded carted through the streets by day even though it be in closed cars. As a matter of fact the larger number of our admissions occur in the late hours or at night.

A large, high building, once a freight shed, I presume, possibly 250 feet long, has been transformed for the present purpose. The train runs in on a single track behind a curtained-off side of the building—curtained off by a huge heavy black canvas which opens at one place through which the wounded successively come—first the *petits blessés* on foot, then the men in chairs, then the *grands blessés* on stretchers.

The impressive thing about it is that it is all so quiet. People talk in low voices; there is no hurry, no shouting, no gesticulating, no giving of directions—nothing Latin about it whatsoever. And the line of wounded—tired, grimy, muddy, stolid, uncomplaining, bloody. It would make you weep. Through the opening in the curtain, beyond which one of the cars of the train could be seen, they slowly emerged one by one—cast a dull look around—saw where they were to go—and then doggedly went, one after the other, each hanging on to his little bundle of possessions. Many of them were Moroccans, though for the most part they were downright French types. Those with legs to walk on had heads or bodies or arms in bandages or slings, in the hurried applying of which, day before yesterday, uniforms and sleeves had been ruthlessly slit open. Not a murmur, not a grunt—limping, shuffling, hobbling —in all kinds of bedraggled uniforms, the new gray-blue as well as the old dark blue with red trousers—home troops and African Zouaves, and occasionally a Marine, for they too have been in the trenches of late.

The procession wound directly by us, for the American Ambulance drivers are privileged to go into this part of the shed, owing to their known willingness to lend a hand. They were sitting in a quiet group, evidently moved, though many of them had been through the Marne days when cattle trains would come in with the wounded on straw, without food or water for two or more days, stinking and gangrenous. Things of course are very different now, and here at La Chapelle Dr. Quénu, of Hôpital Cochin reputation, has finally got a perfect system arranged to replace the utter confusion of those early weeks.

It has been only two days since these fellows were hit, and many of them, regarded as sitting cases, have stuck it out, believing they could walk off the train. But not all could. One poor boy, who collapsed before us, they put on a stretcher and took to the emergency booth. Others had to be helped as they walked on between the two rows of booths to the farther end of the building, where were two large squares of benches arranged in a double row about an iron brazier in which a warm charcoal fire was glowing; for it was a cold, raw, and drizzly afternoon. There was a separate place for the slightly wounded officers, of whom there were some six or eight.

The wounded all have their tags dangling from a button somewhere—a tag from the *poste de secours*, another from the *ambulance de première ligne*, and possibly one or two more indicating where they had stopped for a dressing; and in addition, on the train, to save trouble, each has been chalked somewhere on his coat with a big B (*blessé*) or an M (*malade*), so that they can be sorted readily.

It was soon whispered about that this lot had come from Ypres and that they had all suffered greatly from some German *gaz asphyxiant;* but I hardly believed the tale, or thought I had misunderstood, until this evening's *communiqué* bears it out. Many of them were coughing; but then, as I 've said, most of the wounded still come in with a bronchitis. We have heard rumors for some days of a movement of German troops in the direction of Ypres, and this attack is apparently the result.

By the time the wounded were all congregated, many Red Cross nurses were serving them hot soup and other things, ending up with the inevitable cigarette. The men were quiet, immovable, sitting where and how they first slumped down on their benches. No conversation—just a stunned acceptance of the kindly efforts to comfort them.

Meanwhile Quénu and his assistants were going about listing the men and distributing them as they saw fit among the hospitals in accordance with the empty beds at the disposal of each. Our drivers had handed in the number their cars could take and the number of patients the Ambulance Hospital could receive—possibly fifty, I 'm not quite sure—and we finally went away with our due proportion of the 250 that the train had brought in.

Quénu, though busy, was very polite—they all are—pretended he knew me and asked if I should like to see the room where the *petits pansements* were being made. Among the several who had been singled out as needing immediate dressings because of pain, dislodged bandages, or recent bleedings, was the poor boy we had seen collapse as he walked out of the train. He had a high fever and a trifling first-aid dressing on his badly fractured left arm. This was surely enough, but when the young doctor cut off his *circa* six layers of clothing an undressed chest wound in his right pectoral region was disclosed. We then sat him up and found the wound of exit near the shoulder blade—at which the boy said, "*C'est bon, je guérirai.*" He was in our lot and I saw him landed later at Neuilly spitting blood.

When we got back to the Ambulance, the air was full of tales of the asphyxiating gas which the Germans had turned loose on

Thursday—but it is difficult to get a straight story. A huge, low-lying greenish cloud of smoke with a yellowish top began to roll down from the German trenches, fanned by a steady easterly wind. At the same time there was a terrifically heavy bombardment. The smoke was suffocating and smelled to some like ether and sulphur, to another like a thousand sulphur matches, to still another like burning rosin. One man said that there were about a thousand Zouaves of the *Bataillon d'Afrique* in the lines and only sixty got back—either suffocated or shot as they clambered out of the trenches to escape. Another of the men was *en repos* five kilometres away and says he could smell the gas there. He with his fellows was among those of the reserves who were called on to support the line, but by the time they got up the Germans were across the canal, having effectively followed up their smudge. They seem to have been driven out later, or at least these men thought they had been. We 'll have to await the official *communiqués*, and perhaps not know even then. In any event, there 's devil's work going on around Ypres, and the heralded "spring drive" seems to have been initiated by the Germans.

Sunday, April 25

It has apparently been a large affair at Ypres, with the Germans the aggressors. Several hundred more wounded at La Chapelle this morning—all the ambulance men out—all our beds full. . . . We fluoroscoped two of yesterday's head cases this morning and operated on one of them—a young lieutenant named Daumale who was looking through his field glasses when a Mauser bullet made a direct hit of the lens in front of his right eye, exploding the cylinder and producing an ugly wound not only of his hand but of his right orbital region and cheek. Some metal fragments could be seen by X-ray, driven back into the base of the skull. The eye had been immediately enucleated by the regimental surgeon, but the whole region had become badly infected—an ugly affair. It was necessary to open and drain the antrum. The other man proved to have a fragment of *obus* deep down in his right hemisphere. . . .

Invited by Madame Benet to a supposedly informal Sunday supper in their apartment. Quite unsuspecting, I went "as was," direct from the Ambulance, and to my embarrassment found a large party all in full evening dress—the Ambassador and Mrs. Sharp, Poincaré and his wife, Mrs. George Munroe, and some others. There were no introductions and I was seated at a long narrow table opposite an unprepossessing-looking man who if possible said less than I did during the course of an elaborate dinner. All ears were turned to the end of the table where a woman was holding forth, indiscreetly I thought, about her impressions of Berlin, including a recent visit and conversation with the Kaiser.

After dinner I made myself scarce and retreated to a corner divan, where I was soon joined by my *vis-à-vis* of the dinner table, who evidently had taken pity on me. We sat and smoked silently for a while, when he finally said without looking round: "I understand your name is Cushing." This I admitted. After a puff or two he added laconically: "Brother named Harry?" At this I sat up and said, "Yes; how did you know?" "Roomed with him at Cornell," he replied. "May I ask your name?" said I. "House," said he. That was about all; but I may add that I liked him.

Monday, April 26th

Operation on a knee this a.m. to extract a shrapnel ball which had traversed the joint and lodged in the inner condyle of the femur—a case inherited from our predecessors and here several weeks. Osgood and I agreed on the procedure—*contra* the others. It was very simple by using a perforator and burr. The ball had carried a piece of cloth in with it. (After a 48-hours culture— rather slow—it had fractured the media—gas bacillus!! Why no serious infection?) Many more wounded being brought in from Ypres, where the Canadian-Scottish have been distinguishing themselves—by holding the line last Thursday after the French Colonials gave way. Everyone singing their praises. . . .

Inevitable that ructions should from time to time occur among the volunteer personnel at a place like this—all emotionally keyed up and working long hours under considerable strain. Oil occasionally has to be poured on the waters, and no one better able to do this than Robert Bacon, who turns up at the right moment wearing a British Red Cross uniform.

He is full of plans regarding the cluster of 1040-bed British Hospital Units now being erected near the coast south of Boulogne. He and Osler eager to have some of them taken over and officered by American doctors recruited from the several university medical schools, much as we are acting here, but for six-month periods. According to terms of Geneva Convention, Germany must be notified of the intention. Gives me a dossier of documents and letters on the subject to present to the Harvard authorities and thinks it desirable that I should stop at Boulogne on the way home to get first-hand information. We dine with the Charles Carrolls at their home, and there is more about this novel project during the evening.

Tuesday the 27th

Our first warm summery day and full of work. With misgivings I operated on poor Jean Cesare, one of the several long-time derelicts in Mignon's ward—and I fear M. did not fully approve, but all the others did. He has been paralyzed for six months or more from the effects of a ball which had passed (October 29th) directly through the spinal canal. Complete paraplegia below the lumbar level with a huge bedsore—and latterly such awful pain that he has been going downhill fast. It was a long and difficult three-hour job to section all of the spinal roots at the level where they passed into a dense and snarled scar around a piece of bone that had been driven into the canal.

Then after lunch another operation on the man we had X-rayed yesterday, disclosing a foreign body about 5 cm. in and forward from a small defect at a *plaie d'entrée* in the cranial vault, which had been promptly trephined at a *poste de secours*.

There were a lot of indriven bone fragments evidently infected, and at the bottom of the track the fragment of shell or whatever it was could be detected, but it would have taken a lot of manipulation with consequent damage to the brain to get it out. So we packed up and lugged the man down three flights to the first floor, where Chaveau happened to be operating, and there I tried the famous magnet. I missed the fragment the first time and feared that after all it was lead and a piece of shrapnel ball—but on the second try, out it came, hanging to the end of the large probe. It was the more satisfactory because they have had little or no success heretofore with the extraction of missiles from the brain in this manner.

Then some dressings for several visitors, chiefly to demonstrate the use of gutta-percha "protective" for painless and bloodless dressings—among them Lt. Daumale, he of the exploded field glass. He's doing well and presents me with the empty envelope of his *pansement individuel,* which he had attempted to apply on the field—it must have done about as much good as a postage stamp to stop a faucet. It had been picked up, together with the fragments of his field glasses, by the *infirmier* who led him to the *poste de secours.*

Dinner with Nicholas Roosevelt and a Mr. Orr, another of the young men at the Embassy—also Major Logan. At Ciro's. Very interesting to hear Logan talk, for he is full of valuable information, and this disheveled envelope—with "War Department" and "Official" carefully torn off the corner, when I asked for it as a memorandum—indicates that it was with a pencil in his hand.

It was a good dinner, but largely forgotten with Logan's illuminating description of the tactics of trench warfare, gunnery, sanitary corps, and the like—as well as his views of why von Kluck did not enter Paris—a proper thing to do from a strategic standpoint. He has been here since early August—one of the very few military observers permitted by our government to remain. Not a West Pointer, he broke into the army through Spanish War service, and is a most valuable man for us to have over here. What's more, he's an ardent admirer of Leonard Wood.

Wednesday, April 28

Still very busy and the hospital is crowded. I had a strange time operating for du Bouchet on one of his patients—Lafourcode in No. 77—supposed to have a *gouttière* bullet wound of the skull, which I did not question, though murmuring something about the desirability of an X-ray.

At all events, I was persuaded to take the case in hand and it proved to be

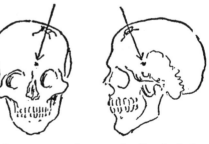

not a gutter wound at all, the presumed wound of exit being merely where the man had fallen and cut his head on some sharp object. The track of the missile, along which an aluminum probe could be passed, led directly downward toward the base of the brain. This afternoon an X-ray showed a fragment of *obus* just over the sella—not a bullet at all. . . . Letter from Osler that arrangements made through Generals Keogh and Sloggett for me to be shown the overseas hospital organization of the R.A.M.C., with the possibility of Harvard's supplying officers and nurses for a 1040-bed hospital. He admits it to be a large contract. . . . The British have launched a Dardanelles expedition and troops are said to have landed at Gallipoli. It seems very far away.

Thursday, April 29

Several unsuccessful trials this morning to extract the shell fragment by the aid of the magnet from the brain of poor Lafour-code. I was afraid to use the huge probe which they have and so determined to make, or have made, another—of which later. We had tried every possible thing in our own cabinet and in those on the lower floors without success. Finally, while I was at lunch, Boothby hit upon precisely what was needed in the shape of a large wire nail about six inches long, the point of which he had carefully rounded off.

Well, there was the usual crowd in the X-ray room and approaching corridor, and much excitement when we let the nail slide by gravity into the central mechanism of smiling Lafourcode; for at no time did he have any pressure symptoms, and all of these procedures were of course without an anæsthetic. While the X-ray plate was being developed to see whether the nail and missile were in contact, who should drop in but Albert Kocher with a friend from Berne; and then shortly a card was sent in by Tom Perry's friend, Salomon Reinach, *Membre de l'Institut*, author of the *History of Religions*, and much else.

So all together we finally traipsed into the first-floor operating room, where Cutler mightily brings up the magnet and slowly we extract the nail—and—there was nothing on it! Suppressed sighs and groans. I tried again, very carefully—with the same result. More sighs, and people began to go out. A third time—nothing. By this time I began to grumble: "Never saw anything of this kind pulled off with such a crowd. Hoodooed ourselves from the start. Should have had an X-ray made when the man first entered the hospital." The usual thing, as when one begins to scold his golf ball.

I had taken off my gloves and put the nail down; but then—let's try just once more! So I slipped the brutal thing again down the track, 3½ inches to the base of the brain, and again Cutler gingerly swung the big magnet down and made contact. The current was switched on and as before we slowly drew out the nail—and there it was, the little fragment of rough steel hanging on to its tip! Much emotion on all sides —especially on the part of A. Kocher and Salomon Reinach, both of whom could hardly bear it.

April 30, 1915

The Ambulance is chockablock and they are at last putting in more beds. A thousand wounded last night at La Chapelle, from which friend Lopp deliberately picked out a lot of head cases before the very eyes of the attendants—thus getting the salt out of the water, I presume. Too late for me, however, for Boothby's and my time is about up and there has been much to-do about getting our passports from the *Préfecture de Police*, permitting us to enter England—a most complicated business which took all the morning. Then a quick lunch and two urgent cranial operations— one of them a young Arab with a through-and-through occipital wound, causing complete central blindness.

Saturday, May 1st

My last operation this morning on a man with multiple shell wounds, one in the left temporal region—aphasic and with a right facial palsy—supposed on X-ray to have no cranial fracture. There *was* one, however, with a *very* wet brain, and a completely softened and disorganized area near Broca's convolution, without great extravasation of blood.

This over, they begin to bring in patients from various parts of the hospital, expecting snap diagnoses—cases which need a week for study—*e.g.*, a man probably shot through the splanchnic area, greatly distended, with a remarkable tremor, possibly an adrenal injury. Finally G. W. Lopp appears with the attending surgeons at La Chapelle, one of whom from his card seems to know more about *accouchements et maladies des femmes* than gunshot wounds of the head—and in some unaccountable fashion they are soon whisking me in a military ambulance down to Hottinguer's, where at one minute before twelve I succeed in drawing out the small residue of my funds. Then back to find de Martel lunching at the Ambulance with Heitz-Boyer and du Bouchet, and after a hurried bite we show them some of our cases—de Martel much taken with the wounds, some of which *are* pretty good, and he wants to know the secret of making "invisible" scars.

With them at 2.30 in another military car way across Paris to the great supply depot of the Service de Santé at Bercy, to see the new mobile-ambulance unit—"Auto-chir"—of the French Army [1] —a bit late it is, but admirable now that they have it. Evidently this is the first exhibit and there are many people on hand—perhaps 50 besides ourselves—officers mostly: Toussaint, the old director of the Service, Quénu, of the *triage* at La Chapelle, Dumont, who gave the demonstration, Gosset, Joe Blake, Carrel, and many others.

In addition to four motor ambulances of a new model to accommodate four stretcher cases, there were perhaps five or six other cars, the most important part of the whole equipment being the operating pavilion—quite perfect for its purpose—capable of being completely dismantled and packed for transshipment in two and a half hours, and of being set up in three hours. It has a receiving compartment; an operating room large enough for four tables; a room with four tables for dressings, into which opens the autoclave—big enough to sterilize four outfits at once—and alongside is the car with the furnace and boilers to run it. Then a good X-ray room, and little steam radiators!! and electric lights! provided by another car in which are two large dynamos run by the motor.

This car also carries all necessary supplies, admirably put up in cases and baskets—catgut, ether, drugs, bandages, etc., in ample amounts. This is roughly the story—what they should have had,

---

[1] *Ambulance Chirurgicale Automobile* subsequently used in the A.E.F. (*Cf.* p. 402.)

and the Germans possibly did have, in the beginning. It makes the little group of American Army field ambulances staked out at Bagatelle for a demonstration look silly. There are, or are to be, fifty of these units, one for each army corps, largely paid for by private subscription at 100,000 francs per unit.

Very good indeed, but I don't see where the personnel is going to sleep and eat. It would not be bad if our U.S.A. tent outfit could accompany such a motor caravan; and they might engage some of Ringling Brothers' employees, who could set it all up after a night's move in a twinkling. There is much talk of my coming back on a government invitation (!!) to do neurological work for three or four months in one of these things, with Craig and Martel and others. It would be interesting.

The late afternoon was a scramble, getting *sauf conduit* for to-morrow's outing; making necessary changes at the War Office in our *laissez-passer* for Monday owing to altered plans for transportation; paying final *adieus* to the many friends we have made at the Ambulance; gathering samples of the convalescents' work tagged with the *blessé's* name and photo to take home for sale— an excellent job Mlle. du Bouchet is organizing; and paying a final visit to the wards, where Cesare asks to be scratched under his plaster cast and Lt. Daumale, who has been decorated with the *Légion d'Honneur*, presents me with his damaged field glasses as a souvenir. In the midst of all this, Cutler's classmate, Norman Prince, appears in a jaunty blue French aviator's uniform and gets pumped about the new speedy "Baby" Nieuports, the Caudrons with wireless installation, the old Voisins, the first machines to be armed, the Maurice Farmans for air raids, the still older Morane "parasols" which carry a passenger armed with a carbine, etc., etc.[1] We 've just had our last supper at the *pension*. Our landlady, Mme. Marty, has secured a job giving ether for Tuffier at the Beaujon; a long letter from our spirited companion, Helen Homans, is read about her work as a V.A.D. probationer nursing English Tommies at Yvetot in Normandy.

---

[1] This was fully a year before the American (later Lafayette) Escadrille came into being through the energy and daring of Prince, Cowdin, and Thaw Cf *The Story of the Lafayette Escadrille*, by Georges Thenault (translated by Walter Duranty). Boston, Small, Maynard, 1921.

A farewell outing to-day for the hard-working juniors of the Unit. They stay on for another two months and have been cooped up in the Ambulance since our arrival, with no opportunity for sight-seeing. *Sauf conduit* to Meaux had been secured at the *Préfecture de Police* and we find the early train from the Gare de l'Est full of sight-seers like ourselves, souvenir hunters, soldiers *en permission,* and mourners—all bound for the Marne battle-fields—evidently a favorite Sunday trip.

Eight months have passed since that eventful sunrise of the 6th of September when the German tide was checked in this very region north of Meaux, but it might almost have been yesterday. A battle leaves enduring scars. The dead still lie in shallow graves where they fell—the fields and roadsides are dotted with crosses; and every haymow of last autumn's harvest shows by the grim evidence about it how its futile protection had been sought against the scythe of another reaper.

The roads leading north from Meaux had to be held if the Germans were to extricate themselves, and evidences of the bitter struggle of those first three or four days between Nanteuil and the Ourcq are clearly apparent. The roadside poplars show the effects of the cross-artillery fire from the French 75's on the west and from the British guns on the south as they turned to recross the Marne. The hastily excavated stances made by the German infantry on the west side of the road to Vareddes and Etrepilly are as fresh as though newly dug. So on to Puisieux and then back by another road through Barcy—much knocked about —and Chambry, with its tragic cemetery wall, and thus back to Meaux, whose ancient bridge the British had blown up in their retreat.

The towns had all been severely damaged by shellfire and the débris of battle still litters the fields—a lure for curio hunters. Because of the risk of detonating unexploded and half-buried shells, they have not yet been ploughed for planting and were dotted with boys carrying duffel bags to fill with souvenirs for sale on the streets of Paris. One urchin in the field near Barcy emptied out his pack to show us his plunder—caps of German and French shells, cartridges, buckles, a battered canteen, a blood-

Sunday, May 2nd

ie hard-working juniors of the
o months and have been cooped
rival, with no opportunity for
ix had been secured at the Pré-
: early train from the Gare de
:lves, souvenir hunters, soldiers
l bound for the Marne battle-
lay trip.

: that eventful sunrise of the 6th
ide was checked in this very re-
:ht almost have been yesterday.
:e dead still lie in shallow graves
oadsides are dotted with crosses;
nn's harvest shows by the grim
···:ection had been sought against

: Meaux had to be held if the
se!ves, and evidences of the bit-
- four days between Nanteuil
···· The roadside poplars show
··· from the French 75's on the
··· the south as they turned to
excavated stances made by the
··· of the road to Vareddes and
:ewly dug. So on to Puisieux and
··i Barcy—much knocked about
·emetery wall, and thus back to
c British had blown up in their

ly damaged by shellfire and the
;elds—a lure for curio hunters.
g unexploded and half-buried
oughed for planting and were
bags to fill with souvenirs for
urchin in the field near Barcy
his plunder—caps of German
:les, a battered canteen, a blood-

"En Avant." The *Piou-pious* of the Early Marne

The Road from Meaux to Vareddes, Showing German "St.
Embankment

stained gray-green cap and piece of tunic. If the picking is good to-day, what must it have been after the opposing armies had swept by to dig in ten days later at the Aisne!

We managed to engage for the day two decrepit one-horse *fiacres* driven by still more decrepit *cochers* of an ancient vintage.

Ours was stone-deaf and talked a toothless French, so communication by speech was limited; but his actions were unmistakable and spoke loud enough. He drew up at every *estaminet* and would disappear—ostensibly to get a pail of water for the horse, but it always took him a long time to return the pail, and before the day was over succussion sounds were plainly audible in both *cheval* and *cocher*.

II

WITH THE R.A.M.C. IN FLANDERS

No. 13 General during "the Second Ypres"

Boulogne. Monday, May 3, 1915

THE companionable Muhr motored us up from Paris this lovely
spring day. We had the road between towns practically to ourselves all the way from St. Denis to our destination. Through
Presles, Beaumont-sur-Oise, Beauvais, Poix, where we stopped for
lunch, Abbeville, where the Tommy and *poilu* join hands, and
where England now governs by courtesy as long ago, under
Henry the Second, she came to rule by force. We began to get a
smell of the sea at Nouvion, and thence on through Montreuil—
once *sur-mer* though now ten miles inland. As we crossed the wee
Canche River a row of French veterans of 1870, wearing their
medals with the green and black ribbons on their old frock coats,
were sitting sunning themselves on a log—doubtless talking of
Sedan, as another lot 45 years hence will probably be in the same
spot talking of the Marne. Then through Samer, and about four
we purred into busy Boulogne.

We were directed to No. 13 General Hospital, which occupies
the large casino by the Avant Port at the edge of the bathing
beach. There Gordon Holmes was encountered, and he escorted
us up the narrow path to the château on the cliff where Sir George
Makins, Colonel Sargent, Colonel Wallace, and he have their
quarters. A room was provided for me, and we were promptly
furnished with the inevitable tea, after which I was obliged to part
from my gentleman chauffeur and companion, over whom there
was some embarrassment. They appear to be much more strict
here than in the French zones, and permission to visit the hospitals
with us, which he would have been very glad to do, could not be
granted without consulting officialdom.

Different armies, different customs, no doubt—even among the several French armies, as I have observed. They were aghast at the kodak with which I was armed and had freely used elsewhere, though I fired it from time to time openly and without being warned. There were no mysterious passwords such as we had been given in the sectors of the 2nd and 6th Armies. Road sentries were comparatively few, and most of them French except near the G.H.Q., where not only was there an alert, clean-shaven Tommy, but a stolid *poilu* alongside of him, each with his different manner of saluting.

But, in place of all this, one must learn to use at least some of the cryptic initials which the Britisher habitually has on the tongue's end: e.g., the G.H.Q. for General Headquarters; the R.A.M.C., Royal Army Medical Corps; a C.C.S. is a casualty clearing station; A.S.C. means Army Service Corps; the D.G.M.S., or Director-General of the Medical Services, is familiarly known as "the D.G.," of whom there are two, Sir Alfred Keogh in the War Office at London and Sir Arthur Sloggett, the overseas director, both of whom have their A.D.M.S.'s, namely, assistant directors—and so on down the line through other combinations of letters to the many M.O.'s, the regimental medical officers.

After tea, Holmes and Sargent took me back to No. 13, where I saw an amazing number of head and spinal wounds, for they often receive daily convoys of 300 recently wounded. With the proper backing these two men have an unparalleled opportunity, not only to be of service to the individual wounded, but, when this is all over, to make a contribution to physiology, neurology, and surgery which will be epochal. The things chiefly dwelt upon this afternoon were the group of longitudinal-sinus injuries, mostly from gutter wounds across the vault of the skull, which are characterized by a striking rigidity of all four extremities. The condition resembles the spastic paraplegia following birth injuries, and they attribute the clinical picture to a vascular injury of the sinus. However this may be, the condition is quite recoverable spontaneously, and they therefore no longer operate on wounds of this type unless there are some complications compelling them to do so. Though recognized and described in isolated cases, as in Osler's recent report, nowhere, so far as I am aware, has anyone observed and studied such a large group as these men have had. We must have seen ten or twelve examples this very afternoon, all of whom will be evacuated in a day or two, for these hospitals must endeavor to keep empty.

Another group of injuries that were new to me were the transections of the spinal cord in the lower neck, which show, in addition to the total paralysis, an extraordinary lowering of body temperature—sometimes as low as 93° F.—with suppression of urine and death in two or three days, consciousness being retained to the end. They already have full notes of one or more spinal transections for every segment of the cord, with the specimens preserved for future study—a life's work. Such of the cases as recover sufficiently to be evacuated are sent to Henry Head at the London Hospital, by whom they are subsequently followed.

On the whole, I take No. 13 to be a good example of the large overseas hospitals of the R.A.M.C. The comforts are slight, the attendance insufficient, the work, though it naturally varies, is from time to time, as at present during this second Ypres affair, simply overwhelming—perhaps as many admissions a day as the American Ambulance might get in a month. And the wounded, bear in mind, are seriously and acutely hit, rushed on from one and all of the casualty clearing stations a few miles behind the lines as soon as transportation is possible. Records, if kept at all, must necessarily be utterly inadequate, so that such clinical notes as Holmes manages to jot down are purely personal ones. Indeed, in rushes no notes whatever can be made, and the wretched tags, insecurely attached to a button of the wounded soldier's uniform, are often lost or become rumpled and completely illegible—far less practical than the French tags with which we have become so familiar. There were two poor aphasic chaps from some Scotch regiment who were necessarily listed as "unknown" since all identification marks had been lost in transit.

The wounded to-day at the casino number 520, not counting the 200 who are under canvas; but occasionally in active times they run up to 900, with an attending staff which varies in number from ten to sixteen. There were none but very ill men, all bed patients, and in the huge restaurants, which contained about

200 closely packed cots, there may have been three or four nurses and as many orderlies. Compared with this our leisurely job at Neuilly with 162 beds filled with subacute or chronic *blessés* and an *auxiliaire* or orderly for every 10 to 12 patients seems child's play. This is truly a man-sized job, in the midst of which the Britisher stops for tea, and everyone—even down to the Tommy—has time to shave; and it's this taking-it-quietly that possibly enables them to see things through with some measure of composure.

And so, at seven, back to dinner at the château, where there was a pleasant mess with pleasant guests, among them Sir Almroth Wright, as amusing and chatty as he was iconoclastic. A good deal about wounds, antiseptics, infections, and several digs at Wright, which he parried with his customary cleverness. Much about the Indian troops, who seem to have been disappointing on the whole, and who broke last Thursday before the gas at Ypres, so that the Germans might have got through to the sea but for the rally of the Canadians. Still, the poor things are in a cold season, in a strange land far from home, and they are paralyzed by this artillery business, to which kind of warfare they cannot grow accustomed. More, too, about self-inflicted wounds, of which there are many; for, as Sir George says, the skulkers in an ordinary war such as that in South Africa simply lag behind, whereas here the men must go into the trenches where a panic may seize them and where there is no officer's back to keep your eye on and to follow where he may lead. These wounds appear to be particularly common among the Indians. In a recent large convoy there were, say, 50 wounds of the left hand, five of them among the white and 45 among the Indian troops—a disproportion too great to be a mere accident of figures.

The men, when questioned, explain that the top of the trench gets shot away by the enemy's fire and that they have to push the earth and sandbags back with their left hands. Powder stains, of course, would tell; but they have learned to interpose something—formerly a piece of wood, until the splinters found in the palm were recognized as a telltale. It is not always possible to be sure; and the Indian sergeants would hardly peach on their own men. And then more about asphyxiating gas and the question of retaliation and the difficulty of making the common soldier appreciate the moral reason for not fighting the enemy with his own and terrifying new weapon, even were the materials at hand.

As an example of how little the Tommy knows of what is going on around him in the larger field, and of the uselessness of questioning him, Wallace told of a man who had been brought in from a trench the other day with a minor head wound. He was trying to get some information as to what was taking place, particularly as the man was covered with tar. "Well, you see," says the Tommy, "my pal, 'e 'd bought a pack of cigarettes an' 'e 'd paid five francs for 'em and along comes a bloomin' shell and knocks 'is 'ead off afore 'e 'd ever smoked a one of 'em!" "Yes, but tell me something about the tar and what you were doing at the time you got hit," said Wallace. "I tells you, sir, 'e 'd never smoked a one of 'em when it knocked 'is bloomin' 'ead off." And that 's all Wallace could get out of him, and it 's the story of the fighting around "Wipers" he 'll tell to his grandchildren, and nothing more.

It is a drizzling night when we turn in with our shutters carefully closed. The town below is as dark as a pocket except for the four or five powerful searchlights which are burning holes in the low-lying clouds, for, as my hosts say, it 's a good night for a Zeppelin raid.

Tuesday, May 4

After breakfast, with Sir George to pay our compliments to Col. Carr, the local A.D.M.S.; and this informal introduction will apparently suffice without the necessity of my carrying such papers as would have been required by the French.

We expected to visit not only the evacuation trains but the hospital ships as well, there being two at the moment in the port, but there was no time for the latter. One hospital train was just pulling out, and another was in preparation for leaving—French rolling stock, pretty well gutted, but mostly composed of the usual second-class cars, which, owing to their lateral doors and undivided compartment seats, take stretcher cases very well. It 's disconcerting to think, in the case of our having a war, that none of our passenger coaches could be used for other than sitting cases, and that stretchers could only be put in the baggage cars or through windows after a train was made up.

Colonel Gallie, an effective and vigorous Irishman, was in charge of the transportation, and said that he had carried 184,000 people up to the end of March. In the past week alone, about 10,000 wounded have been brought back to Boulogne. I do not know how many trains they can keep moving, but at the moment there were nine at the Front—that is, I suppose, at the railheads near the clearing stations scattered along behind the thirty-odd miles of British Front, from just north of Ypres through Armentières to the neighborhood of La Bassée. And a pretty short line it appears on my Taride map in view of the munitions one sees going up and the destruction that comes back. Each one of Colonel Gallie's trains is about 300 metres long, this being the limit, and is composed of 23 cars, and can carry 250 stretchers and about 150 sitting cases—the *couchés* and *assis* of the French.

On each train, too, there are 45 attendants with three doctors and three nurses; and it takes as a rule from four to eight hours to get back from one of the clearing hospitals. There is a cross rail from Dunkerque south, which often ties them up, and, of course, food for guns and men has the right of way. Each train has a kitchen capable of cooking for 300 people, a supply car, and so on; but in view of the fact that one can pass from compartment to compartment, and, worse, from car to car, only on the outside footrail, it must require considerable dexterity on the part of the attendant, particularly if he happens to be dispensing soup. I hardly think this system is quite as impressive as at La Chapelle; but then I did not see any unloading, and as the army and Red Cross stretcher-bearers do it all, it is more simple than in Paris, where every small hospital has its car and its own drivers at the station.

So, after our long inspection, back to No. 13, where Sargent is finishing up his morning's operations, and afterward I saw a number of the recently "gassed" cases—two of them still conscious, but gasping, livid, and about to die, and I hope they did n't have to wait long, poor chaps.

And so to lunch, from which I escape for the proposed visit to the hospital base at Étaples, on the coast some fifteen miles south of Boulogne, where in course of preparation are seven large hospital units, each of which will accommodate 1040 wounded. These units correspond with those which the War Office is planning to turn over to contingents recruited from Harvard, Rush, the Johns Hopkins Hospital, and Columbia; and I gather that the first comers are destined to work here. With the available beds already in and about Boulogne, these seven hospitals will bring the number up to nearly 20,000. Sir William Leishman, the sanitary "boss" of the army, was there—pleasant and agreeable as ever; but Colonel Carr did the honors and we thoroughly inspected the place. For business only, unadorned and unattractive, and some day the heat reflected from these sand dunes on these corrugated iron buildings will make them nigh intolerable. Some of the wards were bad—so narrow that one row of cots must be placed end on; and the doors, wide enough for a stretcher, were too narrow to transmit a cot. But criticism is cheap, and there was much to commend.

We saw, too, many encampments of recruits in and about the neighborhood, and an aviation field, and we finally return by another route along a very pretty road where are peaceful hamlets and little of war in evidence. And so about five, as planned, we pull up at the Meerut Hospital for wounded Indians on the heights behind Boulogne. It was becoming overcast and cool, but tea had been set out for us in the woods behind the hospital buildings—once an old ruined convent—where there were numberless songbirds and wild flowers in profusion, which for the moment interested Colonel Wall, the C.O., and Sir George far more than wounds and gunnery. Most attractive persons, these men of the Indian Medical Service. It may be that only a certain type of Britisher applies for foreign service, or possibly the contact with the natives, and the patience this requires, is a character-making experience.

It was fascinating to see the Indians close at hand, and I was agog over them, from the first glimpse of the cooks squatting over their little outdoor open ovens, patting and roasting their bread cakes or "chuputty," to seeing them stroll about with their variegated turbans, as nonchalant as though they were at home. They are congenital thieves, I judge, and only a day or two ago a cache in the woods had been unearthed where an Indian orderly had buried eight pairs of riding breeches—what disposition the magpie had expected to make of them I can't imagine. There are said to be about 40,000 Indian troops in France, and an ethnological tangle they certainly make—great, lank, bearded Sikhs, mostly six feet and over, moving along with a glide like a camel, and alongside the little slant-eyed Mongolian Gurkhas. It's tough for the little fellows when they have to go into trenches prepared by Sikhs or Coldstream Guardsmen, out of which they can hardly climb; and I presume it may work the other way, too, for there can't be much protection for a Sikh pulled off his horse and made to take his turn in a recent trench which sufficed to protect a Gurkha. The varied religious tenets, particularly those which apply to food, must try the souls of the I.M.S. commissariat.

In the hospital, where many except the attendants were without their turbans, one learned to distinguish some of these strange fellows. The tall Sikhs and Jats with their fuzzy crimped beards and long hair are unmistakable anywhere after a first introduction; the Dogras, hillmen from between the Punjab and Kashmir, wear a distinctive little moustache and a queer little tuft of hair at the crown of the head. The little Gurkhas and the Garhwals are Mongolian in type and wear a pigtail, and are like enough, I observed, to make Colonel Wall occasionally ask of a man whether he was Gurkha or Garhwal. One Gurkha had a badly wounded hand, which he will never use again for much, and he was begging to get back to the line; for two of his brothers had been killed, and he wanted to revenge them even if he lost his own life—but what matter, since they will all be transfigured! Because of this belief, I may add, they will rarely permit an amputation. Can one imagine a future life on one leg, or, if the case may be, on no legs at all?

And so back to the *Château Marie Louise* for dinner, with other guests, and more talk about the casualties, which to April were estimated at 180,000; about the changed site and character of the wounds, many of which, early in the war, when the trenches were shallow, were foot and lower leg wounds, whereas now with the deeper and squared trenches it's mostly heads; about the scarcity of bayonet wounds which are seen—for in these days of close fighting little if any quarter can be given, and not many prisoners can be brought back, horrible as this may seem; about the mediævalism of the war, not only going back to the bayonet but beyond, to the grenade and bomb-throwing devices like the Roman ballista, to casques and armor, to burning oil and the "stinkpot" of the Chinese, and, stranger still, to the belief in the legend of the Angel of Mons and the Agincourt bowmen. And finally Holmes, Sargent, and I slip away and have a powwow until midnight over neurological matters.

Meanwhile, I learned something about the medical consultants and their status in the army. The regular officers of the Army Medical Corps inevitably become swamped in administrative work at such times as this, and the actual treatment of patients is taken over by doctors who have enlisted as M.O.'s in the service. The character of their work is supervised by distinguished physicians or surgeons appointed by the D.G. as colonels with a ca. £1000 salary, many of them being "in for duration." Sir George Makins was among the first to be selected, and he oversees the surgical work in the base hospitals, or at least part of them, whereas Sir Anthony Bowlby does the same for the forward hospitals or part of them.

Bowlby's lifelong friend and colleague at St. Bartholomew's, Sir Wilmot Herringham, supervises the medical work in the forward areas, and Sir John Rose Bradford and Sir Bertrand Dawson at the Base. A number of these men had seen active service in the Boer War. There are also consultants, both medical and surgical, for each army and possibly for each division, beside numerous physicians and surgeons on special duty like the group I am visiting—Wright, who is a colonel, in charge of a laboratory, here at the casino, Sargent a lieutenant colonel, and Holmes a major. Since all of these consultants have heavy responsibilities and more or less roaming commissions, each is provided with a motor car and an orderly-chauffeur.

Wednesday, May 5

Sir George and I got away a little later than expected, headed for G.H.Q., fifty kilometres or so to the eastward, and through quite a different country from what I have heretofore seen. Hedges and willows line a busy roadside, where soldiers are at work trimming, cutting, and piling fagots and brushwood; and the road itself, which is undergoing repairs, is crowded with A.S.C. people and their horses and wagons. Past camps of recently landed boys in fresh khaki, past an aerodrome, and on into country which begins to have a Flemish tone, with windmills and canals, though we are still in France. The G.H.Q. is in a lovely old town (St. Omer), the occasional glimpses of whose handsome towers as we approach along the road are very fine.

We finally park somewhere on a side street, pass many sentinels, and mount the narrow dark stairs to the busy and crowded offices of that important person, the overseas D.G., General Sir Arthur Sloggett. He had heard from General Keogh, and we were to be shown everything. Indeed Herringham—who, poor man, has just lost his son in the trenches—was to accompany us. Meanwhile we were told something about the poison-gas attacks and ways of protection by hoods, with which the men are being provided through the prompt efforts of Haldane. Whether they will answer the purpose, no one yet knows—the general feeling distinctly gloomy—a dastardly business—protests useless.

Under Colonel Herringham's guidance and in company with Robert Bacon, who meanwhile had turned up, we then went to Malassise to visit the camp set up by the Society of Friends for the Belgian refugees.[1] An epidemic of typhoid fever had broken out among these unfortunates, large numbers of whom, after the bombardment of Poperinghe, crossed the border from the remaining tiny corner of free Belgium where, according to Mr. Bacon, there are only about 50,000 people left. The several hundred men and children, largely convalescent, were wandering in the grove where the many rows of hospital tents were pitched, or were working on the roadways—all wearing the familiar blue convalescent uniform.

After this, with Colonels Herringham and Makins in one car and Mr. Bacon and myself in another, we moved on into Flanders, through a country where were great hop fields and fascinating canals. Passing Cassel Hill, the present French forward headquarters on the British left, we turn off from the main road

---

[1] For an account of this camp and much else concerning the R A.M.C. and its organization, cf. Sir Wilmot Herringham's *A Physician in France*. London, Edward Arnold, 1919.

at Le Nieppe and cut across the country, where it becomes less easy going because of the huge A.S.C. lorries—miles of them —all the way from Caestre through Flêtre and Meteren till we reach Bailleul, situated some fifteen miles southwest of Ypres and an important casualty clearing station for the British sector.

In normal times Bailleul—a typical old Flemish town—is a peaceful lace-making place of some 13,000 inhabitants with two old picturesque churches. But to-day it is a bedlam, packed with motor cars of all kinds, though ambulances predominate, since, owing to the recent evacuation of the clearing station at Pope-ringhe, the burden has fallen heavily on this place. We visit only one of the several hospitals—an old monastery, where a long line of ambulances at the moment were being unloaded. Many of the field ambulances and stations have recently been targets for Ger-man shells, and there has been a very heavy "take in," as they say, for several days.

A most effective young officer, Captain Leek, is found methodi-cally going over the cases which are being packed in the large receiving room—examining wounds, doing the necessary emer-gency operations, removing tourniquets, ligating vessels, giving antitetanic injections, and so on. Extraordinary how rapidly it is all done. Through this single hospital 43,000 wounded have gone, and there are three other clearing hospitals in Bailleul! No wonder Colonel Gallie is busy with his trains to and from Boulogne. I looked at the men's tags to see where they had come from—that is, from what field hospital—and was again disturbed to see how flimsy, insecure, and illegible the labels were—attached to a button merely by a slit in the tag. There have been 300 "gassed" victims admitted here in the past twenty-four hours, and all told they have received about 1000 cases since this business began, with about 30 deaths—not so bad after all—at least for those who manage to get back this far. Sir Anthony Bowlby joins us, also Col. Atkins, Sir John French's personal physician, and we are taken off to lunch at a mess where were a lot of overworked R.A.M.C. people. Bowlby has been in this forward area since Oct. 14th, following the German retreat to the Aisne, while Makins has held on at Boulogne; and he would like it better if they could rotate, each following a fresh batch of wounded to the

Base; but there would have to be a dozen of them to do that effectively.

I gather that the English system of evacuating the wounded, not unlike the French, corresponds with the printed regulations prepared before the war, except that at present there is no need of stationary intermediate hospitals between the clearing hospital and the temporary overseas base hospitals at Boulogne and Rouen. The wounded are either brought off the fields by the regimental stretcher-bearers, or else they make their own way at nightfall as best they can to a regimental aid post, which, like the *poste de secours* of the French, is merely a place of temporary refuge in a copse, a dugout, or the cellar of a ruined building somewhere. Here their first dressings are usually applied, or first aid, such as in rare instances may have been given on the field or in the trenches, is supplemented. Thence by hand cart, or some horse-drawn vehicle, or possibly even by motor, they reach a field ambulance or dressing station which, like the one we are to visit at la Clytte, corresponds to the *ambulance de première ligne of* the French and is in the zone of battle.

From there the wounded are taken in turn by motor ambulances to such a clearing hospital as this at Bailleul; thence by a hospital train to one of the temporary base hospitals near Boulogne; then via Boulogne–Folkestone by hospital ship to "dear old Blighty," to a hospital train again, to a general hospital somewhere, to a convalescent home, whence comes a final discharge, or back into service, as the case may be. This is all very fluctuating as the local character of the war changes, and to-day the bearers from the field ambulance often work up to the aid posts, and the duties of the two may so overlap that the bearer party, which goes out every day from the field ambulance, may even camp near the trenches. And remember, too, that the wounded man may sometimes never leave his original stretcher in exchange for sheets and a bed until he reaches England.

The R.A.M.C. officers and men figure high in the casualty lists. It's dangerous business to-day near the Front, and much of the work must be done at night and without lights, for the Red Cross in this war does not serve as much of a protection. The main aim, of course, is rapid evacuation of the wounded from France, and

I am told that wounded have been known to reach St. Thomas's Hospital in London eighteen hours after they have been in action. Yet in this particular sector in which we are, it is a variable three miles or so from the aid station to the field ambulance, another six or seven to this clearing hospital, and about fifty-five from here to Boulogne. Of course, the character of work of a clearing hospital such as we have seen is largely one of classification and proper distribution, and though its capacity may be small, say 200 beds, 1500 wounded may easily pass through in a day.

There is further talk at lunch of the gas attacks and possible ways of combating them without giving in to the Tommies' demand for retaliation, but the general feeling is distinctly discouraging; for if things keep on this way and the wind does n't change, Calais may soon be in the enemy's hands. In the emergency the troops are being supplied with makeshift respirators. Haldane thinks the gas is cheap commercial chlorine, which always contains some bromine. It is blown through long tubes passed out of the loopholes of the trenches. It must have been long prepared for, and the recent German claim that the Allies had been using asphyxiating gas was probably the usual ruse to prepare the public mind. Undoubtedly in the high-explosive shells of the Allies, in melanite, lyddite, and so forth, there are gases which have asphyxiating qualities, but these effects are evanescent and subsidiary to the explosive quality of the agent.

Well, we 've more than gobbled our simple lunch by this time and go back for another look at the station. The entire convoy of cases has been sorted over, relabeled, and passed on, and the great room is empty except for a few men who need immediate attention; a brachial artery is being tied for a secondary hemorrhage by a junior M.O. It is all very simple—nothing so elaborate as an X-ray machine and no beds except the few for officers. In one large room, under a new wooden roof—for a Taube dropped a bomb on the old one ten days ago—there were closely packed rows of wounded awaiting further transport, lying on their stretchers with their muddy boots protruding from under heavy blankets. In one row were seventeen head cases—men in every possible stage of intracranial injury, many of them needing the immediate attention of Percy Sargent or someone like him in a fully equipped hospital, and they 'll reach Boulogne to-night, I trust.

Then we saw many of the severely "gassed" men who had come in this morning—a terrible business—one man, blue as a sailor's serge, simply pouring out with every cough a thick albuminous secretion, and too busy fighting for air to bother much about anything else—a most horrible form of death for a strong man. Others seemed to be pulling through, though they looked bad enough. We went on into the officers' building, where were a lot of little cubicles and real beds, simple iron cots though they were, and here, too, were some queer things. One officer, also a victim of the gas and happily recovering, must have ruptured something in his mediastinum, for he was blown up with a surgical emphysema of astounding degree—cheeks, neck, thorax, abdomen, and thighs. It felt as though there were a layer of air between skin and chest wall about two inches thick. We saw, too, with John McNee, the young pathologist, some recent autopsy specimens which showed the extreme subpleural emphysema and the solidified lung which characterizes the terminal process. The fairly constant N.E. winds of late have greatly helped the Germans in this disgraceful business.

THE BATTLE FROM SCHERPENBERG HILL

It 's getting on toward three o'clock and, Bowlby taking Col. Atkins and me in his car while Sir George and Mr. Bacon follow, we proceed through Locre with windmills and hop fields on all sides. Dodging lorries and ambulances, and with the sound of continuous gunfire constantly drawing nearer, we finally reach No. 8 Field Ambulance at la Clytte, where I 'm surprised to find Henry Bazett the physiologist in charge. Almost as we dismount, an aeroplane circles up from this side of the line, and as it rises— we judge to about 5000 feet—it sails out to the eastward in the direction of the Ypres salient, and we hear the guns and see the white puffs of German shrapnel, all of the shells appearing to explode behind and below. And then another machine—a Taube —ascends from far beyond, and it looks like an engagement; but the Britisher appears satisfied with his reconnaissance and sails away to the north to disappear from sight.

The abandoned house serving as an Ambulance is about three miles from Ypres at the foot of a low hill near Mt. Kemmel. There were a number of desperately ill men, mostly with abdominal and cranial wounds, too ill to be evacuated; and we were shown some adjoining sheds where were other equally bad cases; but we do not care to examine them in any detail—it's too harrowing.

And so we finally leave friend Bazett to his forlorn job and take our way to the bottom of the hill, where we are to get a glimpse of Ypres and its surroundings, whence all the sounds of firing emanate. Up a short winding road, past a line of newly made English trenches, and then out on to a little cleared space. It would have been interesting enough as a simple, lovely, pastoral view across Belgian countryside; but here we were watching a distant struggle for a city—one of the most desperate as yet in this world's war. Col. Atkins says that from this same point on Scherpenberg Hill, King George, when here, watched the bombardment of Ypres—happening to have a cloudless day.

To-day is somewhat misty, but this may possibly after all add a little to the spectacle. On the horizon line, we can clearly see the cathedral clock tower and what remains of the Cloth Hall, and farther to the right the elevation of Hill 60, which has figured so much in the *communiqués* of late—and which this very afternoon is said to be again falling into German hands. The lines have been drawing in on the Ypres salient since the 22nd, when this desperate battle began, and the Germans are only about a mile and a half away instead of three miles as before, despite the heroic counter-attacks of the Canadians.

Then we go up a little higher for a still better view, wondering whether we are to be permitted, as this is an important observation hill. But there are no sentries, and we see nothing of any observers except for a single engineer who is heliographing to some distant point. On the very top are a little stone farmhouse and an old mill and some women squabbling over a flock of geese. From the foot of the windmill a wonderful panorama is unfolded, and the cannonading continues, and one can see the line of battle by the smoke on the horizon encircling Ypres and running up on Hill 60. A most impressive sight. There was heavy firing from some big guns somewhere just to the right of us— Canadians, they said—and finally two aeroplanes appeared again

and got fired at; and the tension was only relieved for me when, after about an hour, Sir George slowly straightened up and strolled over to the edge of the little clearing, and, picking a violet, put it in his buttonhole.

We finally wandered down another path through a wood to the road where our motors were awaiting us. And so we started back via Locre and Bailleul, through the crowds of soldiers and their officers dressed so much alike that the latter wear a patch of some

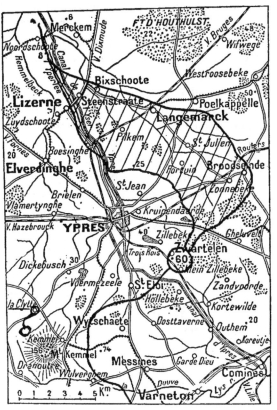

The Environs of Ypres. Shaded Area Showing the Ground Lost during the "Second Ypres" and the Pivot at Hill 60

bright cloth sewed high up on the back of their tunics so the men can identify them in attacks—for officers still lead and soldiers after all merely follow—past lorries and ambulances and A.S.C. horses and men, and an aerodrome from which a biplane starts out drumming and throbbing just over our heads.

And so through Bailleul and back to St. Omer, where we were

to meet Herringham in Bowlby's billet for tea. Again, there was rather indignant talk about German atrocities—the treatment of Belgium—of Belgian women—the holding of hostages and shooting them for feigned or actual sniping—the shielding of advancing troops behind civilian men and women—the submarine activity—asphyxiating gas—the bombardment of churches under pretense of their use for observation posts—treachery under a flag of truce, under which circumstances Bowlby's friend of the Black Watch was killed—the shooting of officers by captives after they had surrendered—all told, a serious arraignment.

Meanwhile, just across the way, sentries were pacing up and down in front of General French's quarters, and Col. Atkins proposed taking me over to meet him—good heavens! Refusing an invitation to dine at Gen. Sloggett's mess, Sir George and I start back in the hope of getting in by dark; but at a little place called Wizernes his driver, disregarding a sign pointing south which says "To Boulogne," continues on for several miles until an obdurate French sentry holds us up—"Nothing allowed to proceed west over this road to-night." A movement of troops, we presume, and we must retrace our steps. It begins to grow dark, and the orderly finds he can't light his acetylene lamps; so we have to feel our way in the dim reflected light of the road slowly to Clety and thence westward along an interminable and lonesome detour to Desvres and finally to Boulogne, long after nightfall.

After a pick-up supper, learning that Sargent was winding up a busy operative day at No. 13, Holmes guides me down there —literally so, for it is black as tar and he has to count the steps as we descend the twisting path down the hillside. And we are in time to see his final case, a bad shell wound of the right parietal region with a big piece of *obus* and countless fragments of bone, and a definite though well-localized infection. It was a very careful, neat, and expeditious performance. And so back again through the pitch-black town we grope our way up to our lodgings; and this was plenty enough for the day, and making these heavy-eyed notes before turning in has been an effort.

Later; under the date of *Wednesday, May 5, 10.40 p.m.*, Sir

John French's laconic report states: "The general situation remains unchanged. Fighting is in progress on Hill 60 southeast of Ypres on which the Germans attained a footing this morning, under cover of poisonous gases which were extensively used and favored by weather conditions."

ENGLAND IN WAR TIME

Thursday, May 6

The Boulogne–Folkestone packet was much less crowded than usual with furloughed officers, owing doubtless to the present activity at the Front; still there was a goodly number, and also many Red Cross nurses, some Tommies, and several aviators. Any idea that Boothby and I may have entertained concerning the hazards of this crossing was soon dispelled. At the end of the jetty there were mounted two rapid-fire six-inch guns; but the French guards basking in the sun were far more interested in fish than submarines, and every one of them had a line out.

It was warm; there was a sunny haze; the Channel was almost unruffled, with not a living thing anywhere except some wild ducks, at which the officers pulled out their field glasses as they would not have bothered to do for a man-of-war. Convoyed? Dear me! There was not a vessel of any kind in sight until we neared Folkestone, where in addition to a destroyer there was a peculiar-looking lot of mammoth floats for about a half mile, said to be a submarine net. Rumor has it that most of the German submarines have been trapped. Doubtless there is a mine field too, for we took a devious course into the Folkestone harbor, running down the coast a little distance and then backing in.

We landed about 12.30, passing the officials without difficulty, though every paper was scrutinized and there was particular inquiry as to whether anyone was bringing in uncensored letters, which I trust did not include this journal. The Tommies, of course, were fed as usual at the station in a Red Cross booth, and I procured a tea basket and some papers and subsequently slept most of the way to London, where we arrived at three. Then to the Metropole, where we get into civies just in time for me to catch the 4.45 from Paddington, where I became so engrossed with a new issue of *Land and Water* I failed to see Sir William with the Merrimans and did not know they were on the train until we met on the platform at Oxford.

A warm greeting at 13 Norham Gardens, where Lady Osler's sister is staying, and a quiet family dinner, after which delightful glimpses of Sir William's wonderful collection of books and manuscripts, for which he is planning to have a new sort of catalogue made. Also talk of Revere's growing interest in bibliography and the recent hoax which he, with his friend Bobby Emmons as an accomplice, played on his father—the fictitious sale of a valuable library in the hands of a hermit book collector in Norwich.

W.O. finally turns in, only to be aroused by news that Poynton's son has been killed—news which he must transmit to the family. And then Lady O. and her sister and I sit up long, talking the sort of gossip of the war to which W.O. never will listen, for he says he hears all he can bear during the day, being perforce in London most of the time. Also talk of the Belgians and their enormous families quartered in Oxford—Lady Osler's original scheme which has brought with it so many difficulties. So different, France and England! In Paris, everyone who has the remotest excuse wears black; in London, a ban has been put on the exhibition of any evidences of mourning.

Friday, May 7

London seems to all outward appearances no different from the London of ordinary times. People are leisurely and there are quantities of them in the streets. The men have time to shave and read the papers, the last page of which is full of racing and football, and they arrive at their places of business about 9.30 or 10 a.m. Disappointed is he who tries to get into a shop before that hour, as I have had occasion to learn. Then, too, there is abundant time for tea in the afternoon. All this shows itself down the line, even to Tommy Atkins, who is clean-shaven (by regulation, I doubt not), whereas *piou-piou*—or, as he is now commonly called, *poilu* ("shaggy" or "hairy")—either does n't have time or just does n't. Paris is empty and serious; London by ten wakes up to its customary crowded roar and is outwardly carefree.

Around the Nelson Monument are huge signs which conceal

the lions and call upon Englishmen to do their duty, while windows and signboards and buildings are plastered with posters which imply, "Come in, boys, the water's fine"—and if you don't, what will your children say—and similar themes. Meanwhile, the cockney stands with his pipe in his mouth, hands in his pockets, cap on one side, and looks on, listening to the recruiting band while the educated pick of the country, like young Poynton, are enlisting. Many windows display service uniforms "to be fitted in 24 hours," and the cinema signs read "Men in uniform admitted free." These of course are straws to indicate an overseas war. Still, one might be here without being especially struck with them. In spite of all Kitchener's appeals for volunteers there is scarcely a smattering of khaki to be seen in the streets—so different from uniformed Paris.

To the American Line office for my tickets on the *St. Paul* tentatively reserved in Paris, followed by a series of calls and errands. Then lunch at the Automobile Club with Sir William and Walter Morley Fletcher, the physiologist. He is secretary of the National Research Committee and has been appointed, in conjunction with Osler and Adami, to make preparations for a Medical History of the War. A colossal undertaking it will be, unless records can be more carefully kept than seems possible under present circumstances in France. This they hope to rectify.

Fletcher has been looking into the psychopathic ("shell shock") cases, of which there must be many—as I gathered from Pierre Janet to be true also in France—men who have broken down nervously under the terrific strain of trench warfare and the frightful bombardments. One story he told of an officer who, following the near-by explosion of a shell which did not injure him, has now a completely changed personality. He is at a hospital somewhere in Wiltshire, I believe, and has had to be reëducated to read and write and speak; he now uses a Wiltshire dialect whereas he came from an educated class in another part of England. He has absolutely no recollection of a previous existence, but when put in an hypnotic state he is his former self in every respect and perfectly clear on all events up to the moment of the explosion of the shell.

At 3 p.m. an appointment with Sir Alfred Keogh at the War

Office, where a pink pass must be filled out to explain my business. An interesting and rather prolonged visit, with much about the American university project; and he has to-day received an acceptance from Rush for July 1st, I believe, with 33 surgeons and 75 nurses. Then about my views of the Service de Santé and how it compares with the R.A.M.C. I feebly criticized the flimsy tags such as I had seen Bazett hooking on to men's buttons; whereupon he produces this new one with an envelope, which does not seem so very practical either. He points out on the huge map hanging on the wall where all the hospitals—military and Red Cross, both at home and overseas—are located.

The map is thickly flagged with different colors for each type of hospital, and there are evident preparations for an amazing number of wounded—certainly a good thing. I hint on departing that I should like to have one or two samples of their recruiting posters and had asked in vain for them at the recruiting station in Cockspur Street. Of course; but I must ask Major General Lorn Campbell, the director of recruiting, which I subsequently do; and he suggests that I see a Mr. Davies of 12 Downing Street; and he in turn is very pleasant and telephones to the office at 42 Parliament Street, where not only am I presented with a complete new set, but they insist on mailing them home for me.

After some hurried shopping, I go at five to Brown's to see Mrs. Emmons, who has come up for an appointment made at Lady Osler's request. On my return, while making some purchases in the Burlington Arcade, an agitated bobby pokes his head in the door and loudly announces: "They've got the *Lusitania!*"

There can be no doubt about it, for by the time I get back to Trafalgar Square sandwich men appear bearing the news—nothing more than the bare fact, however, and there is a huge crowd gathered before the Cunard office with policemen holding them back. "Wot'll they do next?" says my taxi man. "When will England wake up?" say I. This may arouse them—and us!

A few hours later I stop again at the Cunard office. On the street there is the same gathering craning to read the bulletin boards, which give no additional news other than that some of the survivors are being taken to Queenstown and that lists will

be filled out to explain my busi-
prolonged visit, with much about
, and he has to-day received an
st, I believe, with 33 surgeons
views of the Service de Santé and
A.M.C. I feebly criticized the flimsy
Bazett hooking on to men's buttons;
one with an envelope, which
her. He points out on the huge
where all the hospitals—military and
overseas—are located.
with different colors for each type
dent preparations for an amazing
a good thing. I hint on depart-
have one or two samples of their re-
vain for them at the recruiting
se, but I must ask Major Gen-
of recruiting, which I subse-
I see a Mr. Davies of 12 Down-
, pleasant and telephones to the
, where not only am I presented
y insist on mailing them home for

, I go at five to Brown's to see
up for an appointment made at
return, while making some pur-
, an agitated bobby pokes his head
: "They 're got the *Lusitania!*"
it, for by the time I get back to
man appear bearing the news—noth-
however, and there is a huge crowd
with policemen holding them
my taxi man. "When will Eng-
says my taxi man. "When will Eng-
may arouse them—and us!
at the Cunard office. On the
gathering craning to read the bulletin
ews other than that some of
Queenstown and that lists will

Sir George Makins with Holmes, Wallace, and Sargent in Boulogne, 1915

MEN OF
LONDON
OUR
BRAVE
SOLDIERS
AT THE
FRONT
NEED
YOUR HELP.

The Nelson Monument, Trafalgar Square

be published later. The office evidently will remain open all night; within is another crowd, with haggard, anxious, and tear-stained faces—waiting.

Saturday, May 8

There is little to be learned from the morning papers except the simple announcement—the *Lusitania* has been sunk. Boothby and I take the train from Euston at 10.30 and share a compartment with a lady who is traveling with a parrot in a huge cage; the bird tries vainly to sleep and can't. About three we pull into Liverpool and are packed, bird cage and all, into a bus and have a long rattly ride to some remote wharf far up the Mersey where lies the *St. Paul,* and there we find many people in trouble. . . . We and the parrot were almost at the end of the long line of prospective passengers, all of whom, one by one, were obliged to produce passports properly viséd before they could go aboard.

None of the usual business of baskets of fruit and flowers and friends skylarking aboard, I can tell you. It was a serious matter. People enraged and trying to "put it over" the consular officer until gently removed by a burly bobby who stood alongside —people in tears—or people simply stunned. One hysterical woman, whose papers were faulty, broke through and ran up the gangplank to the deck, where she was held by a couple of sailors until the policeman went aboard and started to pick her up bodily —they've had practice in England of late. At this point she became good, but we left her an hour later on the dock still protesting or wailing or fuming as the mood struck her.

Doubtless the *Lusitania* was a little on everyone's nerves. And doubtless, too, there had been a great many shifts of plans in the past twelve hours, both to go and not to go—and the "to go's" have had scant time to get their papers in order.

Well, we finally left some fifty despairing people on the dock and pulled out into the stream. We were locked down the Mersey and there, at the last stage, pulled up alongside of the mammoth *Mauretania,* in gray and black as though in mourning for her sister whose dangerous place she now must take. Some hours late, we are at last moving out into the Irish Sea between long rows of floating red and white flash buoys which mew at us disconsolately.

We sat at dinner with the Gifford Pinchots, who have just been turned out of Belgium by the Germans. They and others are wearing inflatable waistcoats such as are being distributed in the navy, I 'm told. There was much indignant and wildly belligerent talk in the smoking room afterward on the part of certain fire-eaters, of whom we seem to have a goodly sprinkling.

Sunday, May 9, 11 a.m.

The *St. Paul*, once a cruiser herself in the Spanish War, has been hitting it up very fast, so that we are off the Old Head of Kinsale an hour earlier than the passengers expected. It is a bright sunny day with just a little sea, and we have passed a destroyer or two, but nothing else.

Most of the passengers were at morning service and I was writing here when Boothby looked in and said I had better come on the forward deck. This I did, but rather wish I had not. We were going through the *Lusitania* wreckage—had been, indeed, for the past half hour. Steamer chairs, oars, boxes, overturned boats—and bodies. As I came out we passed quite near a collapsible boat which was bottom side up, with the body of a woman and a child floating alongside; they must have been tied to it in some way, else with the easterly wind the boat would have drifted from them.

All told, I believe some fifteen bodies were counted, and this was only in our immediate lane; the wreckage must have been strewn for some twenty miles or more—we at least were passing through it for considerably over an hour. Once we veered off to get a nearer view of the only boat which was seen to be right side up; but the officers, all of whom were on the bridge scrutinizing everything with their glasses, appeared satisfied and we went back on our course.

That was about all. No, there was something else: a single little trawler a long way off on our port quarter, evidently patrolling for corpses—at a guinea each—on this sunny Sabbath morning.

III

THE BATTLE OF BOSTON COMMON

An Episode of the Preparedness Movement

DURING the two years following Dr. Cushing's return from Paris, he kept no diary; but, prefacing a bound volume of correspondence covering that period, the following note occurs which will serve to fill the interval before the journal is resumed. [THE EDITOR]

THE letters herein are samples of the correspondence that passed over my desk subsequent to our return from Paris in 1915 and until we left for France again two years later. Largely through Leonard Wood's herculean efforts, "Preparedness" came to be a national issue, the Plattsburg Officers' Training Camps were established, and our reluctant President and his Cabinet had to take cognizance of the movement, though Mr. Wilson was re-elected in the autumn of 1916 largely on the platform of his having kept us out of war.

Even though the government would not permit any Army Medical Officers to go abroad to gain experience, some steps toward medical preparedness were being taken. In September 1915, General Gorgas proposed to Crile and me that we set about recruiting from the Medical Reserve Corps two surgical units similar to those we had taken to Neuilly. He suggested that such units might be useful—say at San Antonio—in case of war with Mexico. This plan was soon expanded into the idea of our enrolling the officers and personnel for two Army Base Hospitals to be called No. 1 and No. 2—each with a university-medical-school background.

How these plans were frustrated by objections from the Red Cross officials will appear in the letters here selected for preservation. They also indicate some of the difficulties subsequently experienced in organizing these units under any auspices whatsoever.

A university president who did not wish to be dictated to by Washington, who preferred an army to a Red Cross organization and expected to make his own appointments—Brigham Hospital trustees who could not see why, if the Massachusetts General and the City Hospitals were to have the credit of a Base Hospital Unit, they could not have one as well—the want of any definite plan of organization other than that based upon our brief experience abroad—the great difficulty of getting the requisite number of persons to enroll in the so-called minor personnel: these were but a few of the unexpected obstacles encountered.

We unfortunately in the end were not permitted to take undergraduate medical students, as did the Johns Hopkins Unit and one or two others. Fifty students had at one time been enrolled, but most of them were scared off by the University Committee when our probable entry into the war was threatened. The Hopkins students who went over as orderlies, after a profitable service under their accredited teachers, were graduated at Bazoilles, received commissions, and had the great satisfaction of seeing foreign service.

New England, from the time of the torpedoing of the *Lusitania*, had been in a more or less bellicose mood, with a strong undercurrent of insistence upon war. But the country as a whole showed small interest in the conflict, neutrality and pacifism representing the general attitude. This was partly traceable to the Bernstorffs, von Papens, and others, who openly preached the gospel of peace while secretly subsidizing plots to embroil us with Mexico and to undermine our legitimate commerce with the Allies. So at least it was generally believed.

In unofficial ways, meanwhile, noncombatant aid was being given to the Allied cause. Along the lines proposed by Sir Wm. Osler and Robert Bacon (cf. letters Apr. 3–May 5, 1915), a few medical units had gone to take charge of hospitals in France under the R.A.M.C. The service was not wholly satisfactory for a number of reasons. The rotation was too rapid, and with all good will on both sides unforeseen difficulties arose when a group of noncommissioned Americans attempted to work under a retired British Army officer as C.O. with British nurses and orderlies in the wards.

Harvard, from September 1915, continued to keep No. 22 General at Camiers supplied with medical officers, but in April 1916, after Cheever's return, Mr. Lowell could not decide upon or find a successor, and the plan almost fell through. Hugh Cabot finally offered to go and he stoutly held on for the duration of the war. A Chicago unit was given up after an unsatisfactory record, and the Johns Hopkins for some unaccountable reason failed to send any unit at all.

At Neuilly our unit was succeeded by a University of Pennsylvania group under J. William White and James Hutchinson, which with replacements remained until our entry into the war, when the Ambulance was taken over officially as a Red Cross hospital, despite the fact that in 1915 Mabel Boardman and R. U. Patterson had felt unable to give our small expedition even a semiofficial sanction.

Their insistence on neutrality to the very letter (cf. report of the October 28, 1915, meeting) had led to a general feeling that the Red Cross was pro-German; and the knowledge that more supplies were being shipped to the Central Powers than to the Allies—due undoubtedly to the fact that the German-Americans could only get their donations into Germany under Red Cross auspices—gave support to this idea. Nevertheless, in October 1916, Crile's Base Hospital Unit, having been the first to approximate requirements, was given a two-day trial mobilization in Philadelphia under Red Cross auspices, army tents being used for the purpose; and the two hospitals originally proposed were finally expanded to six, all of which were nearly enough ready to be sent overseas soon after our entry into the war. By that time plans were on foot to organize 27 more of them.

The New England Surgical Dressings Committee under Mrs. Mead's leadership, from its small beginnings in the Infants' Hospital, whence sterilized supplies were forwarded to Neuilly for us in 1915, had grown to a large organization that sent out millions of carefully prepared and sterilized dressings sealed in tins, which were distributed widely over France. This work ere long was transferred to a room in the Brigham Hospital, and though efforts were made from time to time to oust the committee from these quarters, the hospital superintendent finally came to appreciate and sympathize with the work whose good repute more than repaid the institution for the space given up to it.

Unfortunately this splendid pre-war organization, whose history should be written, was finally broken up and disbanded by the American Red Cross; there may possibly have been faults of misunderstanding on both sides. However this may be, No. 22 General as well as Base Hospital No. 5, throughout their period with the R.A.M.C., relied entirely on these incomparable dressings, and without the "Boston tins" Horrax and I could have done little during our long stay at No. 46 C.C.S. in 1917.

The Field Ambulance Service [1] under Piatt Andrew, thanks largely to Harry Sleeper's activities over here, had grown apace (cf. March 30, 1917) and become an integral part of the Service de Santé; the comparable Norton-Harjes Field Service had also become firmly established and likewise provided an outlet for many young college men who wished to serve the Allied cause in some capacity overseas.

Meanwhile not a few individuals entered the war as actual combatants. One notable group, small though it was in number, composed the Lafayette Escadrille which Norman Prince helped organize; and the vivid description of the life of these French aviators in the early months of the war, which he gave us at the Tavern Club when home on a brief *permission* during Christmas week of 1915, remains unforgettable. Many of the young ambulance drivers finally went into this corps, and a number of them, like Douglas MacMonagle, died a glorious death. There were others, too, one should not forget, who as individuals enlisted with the British or Canadians or entered the *Légion Étrangère*. But this was about all our country of 100 millions, most of whom were making money and were too proud to fight, really did.

In looking back on this period through the light of these letters it is interesting to see how far short of the final actualities we fell in our imaginings of any possible service our Base Hospital might render. They amounted to nothing more than a possible call to duty for a time on "the Border." References to San Antonio kept cropping up, and that we should ever come to work

---

[1] For the story of this organization, see *The History of the American Field Service in France*, "Friends of France," *1914–1917: Told by Its Members.* Boston and New York; Houghton Mifflin, 1920, 3 vols.

under canvas, rather than in an old building of some sort, was smiled upon when we attempted to inject life into our organization by an actual trial mobilization on the Common; this, it was believed, would not only lay bare our weak spots, but would give us some experience with army forms and incidentally arouse local interest and support in the general preparedness movement.

By March 1917, our possible participation in the conflict, in view of the German submarine programme, began to take on an increasingly serious aspect; and in the middle of the month I began to make some daily notes, which are scattered among the documents in this volume.

At the present day, June 29th, 1919, when I have been sorting over these papers, the Peace Treaty is being signed by unwilling frock-coated representatives of the unscrupulous Prussian swashbucklers who, under other circumstances—and it was unquestionably a close call—would have had the upper hand. In this case our fat country would have had to pay the piper in full.

Boston, Monday, March 19, 1917

Saw Mayor Curley this morning at 12.30 by appointment. Put before him the possibility of temporarily mobilizing the three local Red Cross Base Hospitals on the Common, partly to give them needed experience, partly to help on the Red Cross, interest in which might thereby be stimulated. He took the fly eagerly, but favored the Fenway—would look into it immediately and let me know.

A meeting of the Unit at 4.30 in my rooms—nearly all there. Officers' roster about completed—also the nurses—also fifty students enrolled. Took a typhoid inoculation No. 1, as an example to the others, much as I dislike being punctured for any purpose.

Tuesday, March 20

The Mayor is out with it in the papers this morning—unfortunately giving the impression that the encampment may be permanent. Pituitary operation. Executive Committee meeting. Dictating laboratory notes in afternoon. At 5 p.m. to a Red Cross organization meeting in Brookline.

Fever, backache, and herpes from my inoculation; so a milk-toast supper and then to the Medical School to persuade the artisans, who have volunteered for the Unit, formally to enroll on the Red Cross blanks. Most of them refused—only 36 signed up (to qualify we need 150). Others wanted to know about wages —and what if we should be called out? This is patriotism.

Thursday, March 22

Summoned at twelve to attend a meeting of the Park Commission to discuss the best place for the hospital mobilization. Mayor Curley has acted quickly. This means letters to Washington for advice and information. Long conferences during the afternoon with various committee representatives—Algernon Coolidge in to say that, though sanction had been given for their enrollment, the University has now formally advised all students not to sign any papers!

Friday, March 23

Usual morning's struggle with a pile of mail, followed by a tumor operation. Conference with Burlingham over the adjutant matter. He is going to St. Louis as superintendent of the Barnes Hospital and so is obliged to withdraw. Captain Reynolds, our volunteer quartermaster, here at 4.30. A long powwow followed with the second-year students who have enrolled, but now have cold feet. "Can they not serve their country best by continuing with their courses?" I am to strike off all the names and take those who *re*-apply—desire only men who are *sure* they know what they want to do. I am taking the same gamble they are. They took it very well.

The Germans seem to be making a stand on the so-called New Hindenburg Line, destroying everything in their wake on retiring from the Somme.

Monday, March 26

Afternoon in the wards till five, when a meeting at Colonel Peabody's office with the directors of the other two local Base Hospital Units, who do not look favorably upon a practice mobilization. Even a week's tour of duty would demoralize their hospitals and be an unnecessary drain on Red Cross resources.

We decide to buy the perishable goods for our three outfits— even though the specifications advise waiting till the last minute. The three "mother" hospitals can draw on them for their everyday needs and thus keep the supply for the units freshly replaced.

Seems a simple solution of the problem, but the administrative mind does not take kindly to it.

Telegram from Washington asking if we can send muster-in rolls on or before March 30. Kean strongly favorable to proposed mobilization. To an evening gathering at Opera House under auspices of Greater Boston Ambulance Committee, with music, speeches, and French war films. An appeal for more cars for use in France.

Leonard Wood appears to have been demoted to the Department of the Southeast, with headquarters at Charleston. New England is likely to be pretty mad. The *St. Louis* is reported as having reached England—our first armed merchantman. Her sailing was kept secret. "Armed neutrality."

Saturday, March 31

After two operations, to lunch with the Saturday Club. Much war talk and passing of resolutions, on the nature of which it took us long to agree—also, it may be added, on the value of them. Mr. Lowell from his end of the table: "If you wish to drive him [the President] to Dublin, he will try to go to Cork," and so on. However, there was a final compromise and the document was worded at the end according to Mr. Storey's version—"a state of war exists and should be prosecuted with vigor. . . ." Cameron Forbes, James Rhodes, President Eliot, Edward Forbes, Wm. Roscoe Thayer (who was ill satisfied with our compromise version), Major Higginson (who read letters just received both from Mr. Wilson and from his silent partner, Colonel House), Farlow, Howe, Professor Pickering, Dr. Walcott, George F. Moore (who left after giving his vote to Mr. Storey), and a few others perhaps. Doubtless the same thing is being done over the entire country. What Mr. Wilson will do, he alone knows.

Back to the hospital for a busy afternoon with Captain Reynolds over our enrollment blanks, which we finally got off to Washington lacking the minor personnel. The students have been advised to withdraw, and I am ashamed to send the lists with so many scratched names. It is "difficult to secure the cohesion of important mediocrities" at a time like this, and we are going to see a lot of pulling crossways before we are through.

So far as I can see, one must fix his eye on what Washington desires and keep to that whether one likes it or not. While *theo-retically* people in this community are bubbling with patriotism, *practically* many of them spend their time scolding the government because they think it is n't doing what they want—while it may be. After all, it 's their government. They laid the egg and now are doing their best to addle it.

Late home. Asked Gus on the way if there was any news. He said: "No, but it looks as though they might monopolize [*sic*] the militia any minute." In the evening another patriotic mass meeting at Opera House under auspices of the National Security League and sixteen other organizations—including Mayflower Descendants, Sons of the Revolution, Colonial Dames, and so on. Of all the speakers Paul Revere Frothingham alone was inspiring. He should be used oftener.

Monday, April 2

Meeting of the local Committee on Public Safety called at eleven at the City Hall. Stirring speech by the Mayor and then by the various chairmen of the eleven subcommittees. Resolutions to the President and to Congress. Rumor that Senator Lodge and a pacifist have had an altercation—that Mr. Lodge "has put the fist in pacifist." We parade to the Common, where pundits in tall hats on a platform wave flags and utter voiceless addresses to some 25,000 people. Strong and I escape with difficulty in the wake of a burly policeman and go to the Harvard Club for a meeting of the Committee on Hygiene. Base Hospital trial mobilization brought up. Colonel Williams alone supports me. Telegram received from Washington offering to detail officer and detachment to assist the project.

Tuesday, April 3

The President asked Congress yesterday to declare that a *state of war exists with Germany*—the message a great document! He has said effectively what we have all long felt. It is to be hoped that the German people may be given a chance to read it.

Letter from Red Cross Headquarters promising tents, but advising portable structures for operating room, mess, and administrative offices. States that there will be plenty of time: "the creation of an army will have to go on in a leisurely way." They are now making plans for 33 base hospitals like our own. Many of the directors already writing here to ask advice. Learn from Baltimore that the Hopkins Unit is enrolling students.

Wednesday, April 4

Held my usual clinic at noon. Appeared before the Administrative Board at the School to protest their action concerning the students who had reënrolled with the Unit. Find that someone has privately misquoted the action of the Board, causing about half of them to withdraw their names.

The Senate has voted for war, 82 to 6. The group of "willful men" has held out.

Friday, April 6

Left the meeting of the Committee on Hygiene, Medicine, and Sanitation early to attend faculty meeting. Succeeded in getting the Administrative Board vote, as recorded, rescinded.

The House of Representatives has overwhelmingly voted for war—373 to 50. Wilson has signed the declaration!!

To "The Club" at seven without time for dressing. Full gathering—even George Moore. Sat between him and Mr. Crafts. Free talk about war—the coming one, and the one of a half century ago, which is only too well remembered by all of them. A long talk with Mr. Higginson and Dr. Walcott about the Base Hospital mobilization. "The Major," as usual, is fired with a spirit of coöperation, and Dr. Walcott will see what he can do at the Massachusetts General.

Easter Sunday, April 8

Much telephoning in regard to a meeting with Eliot Wadsworth at the Mayor's office to-morrow at ten. The Mayor calls off a funeral for the sake of it—rather, his attendance at the funeral. Colonel Peabody, C. F. Weed, the three Base Hospital directors, Colonel Williams, Commissioner Dillon, and John Saltonstall. Chief arguments for the plan were outlined briefly as follows:—

"The Red Cross has already raised *circa* $100,000 for the equipment of three local base hospitals which are to revert to the army when called upon. As yet they are paper organizations wholly unfamiliar with army formalities. They need the experience of a mobilization no less than raw troops need it. Only in this way can imperfections and omissions in their equipment be disclosed. Their emergency requirements can meanwhile be supplied by the local 'mother' hospitals. A further object is to attract public interest and thus to facilitate the enrollment of the 150 minor personnel each hospital must have to meet army regulations.

"Of the several sites suggested, the parade ground of the Common is strongly favored. It is central and convenient to the source of most of the accidents cared for by the city. Moreover, it is associated in people's minds with patriotic demonstrations of all kinds. It is turfed, has a good slope for drainage, and could be easily policed. Gas, water, and sewer connections could be installed with but little expense.

"Apart from a few portable houses for operating room, administrative office, and kitchen, the hospital would be in tents. These could be floored by using the winter board walks taken from the public parks. The encampment would cover only six to eight acres of the Common. It could be made attractive and interesting with its flags, military guard, bugle calls, drills, Sunday service—and perhaps once a week a concert by a military band.

"It is proposed that the city accident cases be reported by the police to the Red Cross, whose ambulances would route patients to the Common instead of the Relief Station. The question of legality of treating city patients under these circumstances could probably be easily met. They would doubtless receive better care than under existing conditions in view of the standing of the medical officers and nurses to be in charge. As soon as the patients are able to be moved, they, with their records, would be evacuated by Red Cross ambulances to the City Hospital or elsewhere.

"An estimate of expense for a two weeks' service for the first of the three hospitals would be *circa* $15,000. Many requirements such as uniforms, laundry, fuel, electric light, and so forth, might in all probability be donated. A continued service for the other hospitals using the same equipment would add little to the cost."

Monday, April 9

To the City Hall at ten after getting through the morning's mail and many interviews. The programme was again outlined and Major Higginson warmly supported me. After he and Eliot Wadsworth had left, the Mayor came in, whereupon strong opposition to the proposal was voiced by the directors of the other two hospitals. I finally offered to go it alone. It will be a big job. Many will be glad to see it fail.

Tuesday, April 10

Ward visit at Children's Hospital. Laminectomy for spinal tumor. Busy with preparations to go to Washington by Federal Express to attend a meeting of the recently organized Standardization Committee for Medical Supplies.

Wednesday and Thursday, April 11–12

Two very busy days in Washington. Much shocked to find regular army officers in civies. "Not the thing for the officers to wear uniforms." How can they expect people to enlist? Called on Colonel Kean at the Red Cross Building and General Gorgas in the War Office. Visit to latter interrupted by entry of Senator B——, from a side door, with a young lady. The General bows and scrapes. The Senator's young woman would like a secretarial position. I escape. However, it appears that both these men—that is, Kean and Gorgas—will help in so far as they can. But *are* there any tents to be had?

Meeting of Committee. The standard medical chests are antiquated, with instruments dating from the Civil War. Much work to do in passing on army and navy and base-hospital kits. Instrument manufacturers in trouble. Men have long since left to enter munition shops, where better paid. By Wednesday night most of the Committee had faded away, leaving a few of us to make the final decisions—not so easy.

Friday, April 13

Busy all day over the proposed mobilization. Mr. George Cutler, Jacob Peabody of the Red Cross, Colonel Chamberlain of the army, and young Kettell, the architect. Plans for portable houses, and conspiracies to raise money. Mr. Rice in after luncheon, and we find he has made similar plans for a hospital at Quincy. At it until late in afternoon.

Evening spent in writing letters for Richard Strong, who sails to-morrow on the *Chicago,* with some physicists and chemists, to study conditions abroad. Joe Ames to be one of them.

Saturday, April 14

The Mayor to see me at his request at 9.15—does not come. Fear there is some legal entanglement about taking patients.

Brain-tumor operation—took longer than expected—missed lunch with Messrs. Cutler, Peabody, and Chamberlain, but joined them later to see portable houses at Dover. Mr. Hodgson guarantees to have four 22-foot-wide buildings by May 15. All his other work to be put off. Depressing dinner with a friend who says, "What's the use of all this hysteria about preparedness? We'll never be invaded."

Monday, April 16

The usual morning rush before operating. Ward visit and then Captain Reynolds about his commission. To the City Hall to see Corporation Counsel Sullivan. The legal mind! Fears we may have someone get out an injunction against us for putting up structures on the Common! Necessary to go to the legislature. Our conference interrupted by an urgent telephone from his wife that their house was burning down. So I took him home. It was n't.

Evening spent in arranging for our next step—Kettell and Colonel Chamberlain to plan out the encampment so we can have something to show on paper at least. I feel to-night that we have bitten off more than we can chew. People say, "There is n't going to be any war for us."

Tuesday, April 17

General Wood and a commission are in town—appointed to meet Balfour, Joffre, and others, "when and where they may land." The idea occurred to me that he might settle all doubts as to the base hospital, and, though these people are incommunicado, I found where he was at lunch and pursued him there. He will be glad to do anything we ask—would have liked to get one of the hospital units mobilized at Plattsburg. Long talk with him about his demotion.

To the City Hall, where Mayor Curley sends out 150 invitations to people to come to-morrow at eleven. I finally ran down poor Major Higginson at 1 Ashburton Place—looking very tired and showing his eighty-three years for the first time I have ever seen him. He gives me suggestions in the way of names, and I go back to help the Mayor's secretaries get out their list—women included.

Tea at Guy Murchie's with L.W., "Jimmie" Williams, and the two young army officers who are training the students at Harvard.

The General says he has ordered all officers to appear in uniform. High time. Discussion about the so-called "Commission" to meet the foreign guests and the absurdity of its having no high official to represent the government. Wood the only real figure. Lucky they have him. Says he knows Balfour—met him at dinner first in 1902, when he came back from the Philippines and after his Cuban governorship. Balfour asked him what the United States would do for him on his return—mentioning what England had done for Kitchener and Cromer. Wood replied that he would be lucky even to retain his commission in the army.

Evening spent in telephoning people to come to-morrow; most of my friends and supporters, alas, are out of town.

Wednesday, April 18

Rainy day and unfavorable for our meeting. Called at the Copley Plaza for General Wood. They denied his existence. The carriage flunkey finally told me that he had gone off "for a ride." I bribed him to put the General in a taxi and send him to the Mayor's office the moment he showed up. A small group finally gathered from out of the rain—practically those alone to whom I had written or telephoned. Good old Mr. Cochrane, Major Higginson and his brother, Allston Burr, Mrs. Sears, Robert Winsor, Mrs. Blake, John Saltonstall, Cameron Forbes, and a few others—perhaps thirty in all.

We were ushered into the Mayor's office and, General Wood not being there, I had to make the appeal myself. General Wood and Jacob Peabody finally came in—had been detained by Mr. Lowell in Cambridge. The General in his straight-from-the-shoulder manner said some very appropriate things. Mr. George Cutler was made treasurer and said he hoped the necessary sum could be raised on the spot. I estimated it would cost $20,000 for the four buildings and completed equipment and said that I would give $1000. Mr. Curley followed suit. The amount was promptly underwritten.

Unhappily we were then captured by the Mayor, who insisted on a photograph—Mr. Higginson, Admiral Bowles, General Wood, the Mayor, and I! The man had difficulty with his apparatus and I hope it was a failure. Apart from this episode it was a satisfactory and rather exciting meeting.

In the evening to hear Gerard speak at the National Defense dinner at the South Armory. Much smoke (tobacco) and little fire. The presiding officer worked himself into a fervor in answering the question (several times repeated), "What can we do?" Answer, with outstretched arms and eyes on the rafters: "We can only watch—and stand—and pray—while our great leader . . ." and so forth. L.W. spoke briefly, emphatically, and much to the point as usual.

Thursday, April 19 (Patriots' Day)

Much business *varia* at hospital until ten. Numerous visitors. Account of yesterday's meeting in morning papers brings many telephone calls—for example, from Miss Curtis expostulating on the proposed use of the Common; and finally a Mrs. Brown of the Boston Common Committee (!!) was announced, a little old lady who said she had given birth—in other words—to the Common Committee when there was a question many years ago of putting a pump on it. The Common would be preserved with her blood if need be. To have people "operated" (*sic*) in public on the sacred Common was a sacrilege, and so forth.

I have read about such people, but have never seen anyone quite like her, and equally misinformed, except at the antivivisection hearings. She said it was an advertising dodge of Mayor Curley's —or mine! But we parted the best of friends—"I must see the Common Committee and tell them just what I had told her—in the same way—so nice of me—busy man—give her so much time —come and have tea with her." An experience out of a novel.

Later, messages galore from other people who don't like our project. Cutler and Kettell here working on plans. Washington is growing dubious about tents. May need all they have themselves.

"The Auxiliary Medical Committee for National Defense of Boston, Massachusetts"—all that—met this p.m. to appoint a new chairman to take Strong's place. Meanwhile it gives origin to eight subcommittees! Committees breed like rabbits. We're digging up our front lawn to plant potatoes.

Saturday, April 21

Busy day—tumor operation—felt ill afterward—hope I can pull through the next few weeks. Captain Reynolds, Kettell, Cutler, Roger Lee, and others in at 3 p.m. Allston Burr with a letter to Mr. O'Brien anent the unfavorable *Herald* editorials. A telephone from the Mayor's office saying that he was going to put an appeal for more funds in the papers to-morrow. Lucky thing his secretary read it, for it contained statements that would, I fear, have ended the project. Begged the secretary to cut them out and hope he understood. Late afternoon spent over plans and specifications at the portable-house place in Dover.

Sunday, April 22

More telephoning from people—evidently "sicked on"—who do not want to see the parade ground desecrated and who fear that the Mayor has ulterior motives. Attempt to answer letters of protest requiring a personal reply: for example, "The building of a hospital on Boston Common would be a menace to the health of the hundreds of children of the vicinity who throng the ball fields and parade ground all summer and on every holiday. Last Thursday, April 19, there were ten games of ball going on and crowds watching. . . ." Streeter comes in and donates $500 plus a Ford car (on demand) for the hospital's use!

Monday, April 23

Meeting of the Unit in my rooms this afternoon. A discouraging letter from Washington that no tents can be had for this or any purpose. All looms in country called upon to manufacture duck for Quartermaster's Department. They suggest trying the state militia. So to Colonel Williams, who says no tents available here. So much for promises and our fine bird's-eye view of the encampment—just completed by Mr. Kettell.

Wednesday, April 25

Meeting with the uncommon Common Committee at 4.30 in Mr. James A. Lowell's office. Finally persuaded them—I think—that this is to be a purely military procedure in strict accordance with the Common's best traditions. Very funny—if it had not been so serious. Individually they stepped outside and wrung my hand —"Good thing"—"Push it along"—"I 'm with you, though did not like to say so in there." Just why I can't imagine, but this is Boston. It took nearly two hours. Mrs. Brown wanted to know why we could not have our encampment stretched along the mall on Commonwealth Avenue.

Stopped at Mrs. Thayer's to ask how she'd like it—also for a late cup of tea. Base Hospital No. 5's plans evidently the talk of the town—particularly of "sewing circles." Comment mostly unfavorable through misunderstanding of our objectives.

Thursday, April 26

Feeling the need of stemming opposition, to the Thursday Evening Club at James J. Minot's, and heard Osterhout "On the Biologist's Interpretation of War." Also Mr. Eliot, informally, on the good things that are showing up through the war—they seemed somewhat microscopic; and finally Chadwick and a group of young musicians gave some delightful seventeenth-century music accompanied by a harpsichord!

Then I began to get it. "You the fellow who is talking about putting a hospital on Boston Common?" I finally began to make some progress with William Thayer, Wallace Goodrich, and one or two others. Hope it will do some good. We plan for a meeting of the N.E. Surgical Dressings Committee in the Brigham amphitheatre next Wednesday in the hope of getting some tongues to wag in our favor. An encouraging telegram comes from Colonel Kean, saying don't be downhearted.

Friday, April 27

To J. C. Warren's to see, from his Beacon Street balcony, the Harvard Regiment march by, escorting the French officers who have come to train them. A fine sight, but the bystanders showed little enthusiasm. People interested, of course, but no cheering or waving; and I saw no one salute the flags. Fifty-odd years ago, from those same windows overlooking the Common, anxious eyes saw troops pass by to something that was real.

Back to the hospital, where Kettell is a little dubious over his bird's-eye drawing of the encampment about to be released for to-morrow's papers—it will do, I'm sure. Remainder of the day spent in trying to turn the current of public opinion. To the Tavern for tea, where they all said "a fine idea" after they learned what had been done and of our real purposes. "Had the French officers seen a military hospital on the Common this morning, they'd have thought we meant business."

Then to the Doctors' Club dinner at Taylor's, where it came up

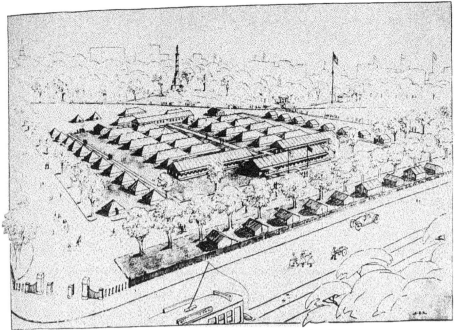

Sketch of the Proposed Mobilization on the Common

The Portable Huts in Process of Construction at Dover, Massachusetts

again, and I think I temporarily convinced most of them—best of all, Fred Shattuck, the last I had expected to come around. Mr. Lowell had telephoned me in the afternoon to say that the matter had been brought up before the Corporation—that they were unanimous in saying they could not give the movement their support—that it was not their project!

Saturday, April 28

My dander has been up like Dr. John Brown's little mongrel when a bigger dog exhumed his buried bone, and I 've been hitting out at these stand-pat Bostonians and their Common. A Mid-Westerner's traditions of the old parade ground and its noble history need be no less patriotic than theirs. Boston for two years past has been 75 per cent talk and kick, and 25 per cent action. Massachusetts is the thirty-third state to complete her quota of militia, instead of the first—as she once would have been. Curiously enough, they don't seem disturbed about it.

A busy morning; started a pituitary transfrontal operation an hour late. Good case—congenital suprasellar cyst—best operation of the kind I have ever done. Councilman joins me, and so to the Saturday Club luncheon—for more work as a publicity agent. On the way let off some steam on him and easily aroused his indignation at the opposition. An unusually large gathering—Haskins, William Thayer, Mark Howe, Ellery Sedgwick, Pickering, Dr. Walcott, President Lowell, Dr. Emerson, Sturgis Bigelow, Richards, and several more, with one or two guests—one of them Major Azan in his *horizon-bleu* uniform, a fine type of young French officer such as I remember two years ago.

Before we took our places Mr. Eliot quite unexpectedly said, "I should like to have you sit by me to-day." This I did—where some guest usually sits. We began with the oysters, when he turned, saying: "A friend telephoned to me this morning to use my influence to have this hospital of yours kept off the Common."

With that I was off with the familiar story. "Have as much respect for the Common as anyone—the Harvard Regiment parades down the principal streets behind a band—if they mean business a good many of them are going to get hurt, and someone had better begin to learn how to take care of them in an army hospital under something like field conditions—hospitals as necessary in war as troops—we don't propose to be put somewhere on a back street— deserve the most prominent place for the mobilization that the city can find—seeing some people in uniform actually at work will increase Red Cross subscriptions and encourage enlistments. More important than all, will give us invaluable training with army pro_ cedures and forms. Anyhow it's only for a matter of six weeks, even should the other two hospitals join in." Well, he got inter- ested and finally indignant. . . .

(*Later. Written on May 3*)

Too bad I could not have finished the above while I was warmed up to it. It was an extraordinary occasion. I saw no food after the oysters—only something red. Told them I thought little of their regard for an historically dead instead of a living Boston Common. Got Major Azan with his splinted arm to explain what military hospitals were for, which he did movingly; slammed out at some- one who wanted to bet there would be a stone annex of the City Hospital on the Common before the summer was over; chided Henry Higginson and Dr. Walcott for not having stood by me at the Corporation meeting.

Jim Curtis, who has been in Washington long enough to under- stand that we are supposedly at war, quietly remarked, "Funny, when I got to New York this morning the first thing I heard was: 'Boston has the jump on us at last; they are going to get one of their base hospitals out on Boston Common, and we are only talk- ing about ours.' " This provided a glimmer of hope. But someone bustled up saying he would personally defend the parade ground (on which his bedroom windows look down) against this sacrilege; and I, that he typified those who, to protect a plot of grass, would ignore the country's unpreparedness—the Common could be re- seeded.

Well, in the midst of it all—getting more and more "het up" —I was called downstairs to the telephone: telegram from War Department, Washington—"*Wire this office earliest possible date your unit can be mobilized for duty abroad. All expenses borne by Government. (Signed) Gorgas.*"

The grass will continue to grow on Boston's famous parade ground.

Sunday, April 29

Yesterday afternoon and evening a whirlwind trying to get in touch with members of the Unit scattered for the week-end. At it again all to-day in the endeavor to complete our enrollment. Many changes necessary. Frequent exchange of telegrams with Washington. Wonder what they will say about these eleventh-hour withdrawals. May lose us our chance. Decide to go on to-night with Cutler for inside information and authority to advertise for personnel.

Visit in p.m. with General Edwards for a few minutes. Will do anything—everything—for us. "First thing Leonard Wood told me was to get behind your base-hospital mobilization." He and Mrs. Edwards both very cordial—very cosmopolitan—very unprovincial. Just what is it? They will shock Boston. Fine to see him in his uniform, though he is not to be officially in charge till Tuesday a.m. Encounter Mr. Storrow on the train—much interested. Offers us, for the Committee of Public Safety, $5000 for incidental expenses.

Monday eve., April 30 (Federal Express)

A good thing to be "Johnny on the spot." After a snatch at breakfast we got to the Red Cross Building about 8.30, before anyone was there. As we were planning our campaign and reviewing the countless questions we wished to ask, Eliot Wadsworth came in and, knowing our mission, planted us in Colonel Kean's office. There we overheard much telephoning from all parts of the country, though the Washington exchange is poor and the lines overbusy—people wanting to know if they can be guaranteed against submarines, and so forth.

Meanwhile we gather information regarding the other five units that have been approached, Crile evidently the only one approximately ready, thanks to his mobilization last autumn. We finally learn who the other four are to be. Much business also on our own account. "How much luggage? Nurses' aids? Secretaries? Commissions? Passports? Can we draw on the other Boston units for personnel? What shall we do with our portable houses? What with our Red Cross equipment?" And I don't know what else.

Finally we were sent for from the War Office—Colonel Goodwin, the R.A.M.C. representative on the Balfour Commission there, also Kean and Gorgas. Everyone was pleasant. Joke me on being a Major. Congratulate us on our selection. Due solely to the Common mobilization activity—looked as though we meant business. Two immediate urgent needs of the British Army are more medical officers and more engineers.

Long talk with Colonel Goodwin—very fine in his staff officer's uniform, with its red facings, such as I saw in St. Omer two years ago. Whole thing his idea. Thinks we shall go to England first and later to France to join our first Expeditionary Force when it goes over. Knows Percy Sargent, Herringham, and the rest. Was on duty in France when summoned to join the Commission. Left his horse standing by the road, got a motor, fifty miles to Boulogne, barely caught the boat. Not a moment to outfit.

General Gorgas evidently tired, but cordial as always. Piles of unopened mail on his desk and still answering his own telephone, which is not even in reach of his chair.

Back to the Red Cross Building for further conferences. Major Patterson to go with us as our commanding officer. Very lucky, and he is delighted. Capt. Reynolds, alas, can't qualify—need a trained army quartermaster and one will be sent with us—terrific job. Lunch with Kean at the Army and Navy Club. Joffre and Balfour have stirred things up. People at last getting into uniform. A very different Washington from two weeks ago. An occasional French officer on the streets. Goodwin said we shall have much in store for us when we get over under the American flag.

A lively afternoon at the Red Cross Headquarters—finally given permission to send messages through to Boston with carefully worded advertisement for morning papers: "Wanted: 100 volunteers—cooks, orderlies, clerks, carpenters, electricians—to enlist in Medical Corps for early service overseas. Report to-day Harvard Medical School between 4 and 9 p.m."

Sunday, May 6, 6.45 p.m.

Quiet for the first moment since we got back Tuesday morning. Such a week! We feared the attempt to get ready for the Common by May 15 might break us down, with three weeks' time and a chance to borrow needed things; but to do it all in seven days! Well, we turned loose. Cutler was indefatigable. Captain Reynolds worked like a dog. The tailors put off all other work to make our uniforms; the Committee of Public Safety sent cars; the Special Aid Society, food. Secretaries appeared out of a clear sky. Mrs. Wendell presented us with our flags. Additional telephones installed and going all day long. Towne and some others giving physical examinations and inoculations for the volunteers, who began to appear in large numbers in answer to the advertisement in the newspapers. Lieutenant Villaret—a snappy young artillery officer from Fort Banks—put at our disposal by General Edwards. Helped us greatly, and with the aid of Sergeant Hepburn even began to whip the motley crew into shape by daily drills in the lane outside my rooms. Contradictory orders from Washington— one day one thing, the next another. Poor Patterson in a panic there about our commissions. Last-minute shifts in personnel and even officers! New physical-examination papers requested for deposit in Adjutant General's Office. Harry Forbes's glass eye was a stickler, but we assured P. he could see through it. Gracious, how we need universal training!

Every morning at 8.30 things would begin with a rush, ease up a little by late afternoon, and by evening some fearful problem would present itself to disentangle—usually on the job till midnight with Reynolds; very little food, very little sleep, and incessant cigarettes. A bad combination, but somehow it went along.

Went out twice for a change of scene—Tuesday to the Tavern annual dinner. Could n't bear it, though "the Major" gave them a straight talk about alcohol. W.L. at the close, raising his glass to me: "God Almighty intervened to keep you from putting a hospital on Boston Common." Ah, well! This at least an admission that we might have got there.

Friday night at "The Club" dinner was much better. Tom Perry, Morse, Storey, James Rhodes, Bigelow, Duncan, "the Major," and George Moore, and we talked freely. But not this time, as so often, about the bloody corner at Gettysburg and just what happened there. It was largely about prohibition—Sturgis Bigelow protesting that it would be very injurious for men, long accustomed to alcohol with their meals, to give it up. He was effectively slain. Sturgis's whiskers have had a sort of surprised look ever since I lashed out at him at the Saturday Club—only a week ago, though it seems a year. They were all very nice to me, however, and when I got up to leave before the usual hour were a little teary in their good-byes. I knew well enough what they were thinking of.

Endicott Peabody dropped in—Friday afternoon, I think it was —-to see me about Malcolm. My mind was racing, and before he had had a chance to say anything I fired him with the idea that we must have a service on Sunday so the Chaplain could talk to the enlisted men on their responsibilities abroad. He rushed off to see Bishop Lawrence, and the Bishop·cordially took to it.

Late Saturday evening our sailing orders came—"from an unknown port to an unknown destination"; and this morning our C.O., Major Patterson, with Capt. Harmon, the adjutant, and Capt. Rund, the quartermaster—to supplant good old Reynolds, who would so dearly love to go—all arrived from Washington in time for the service.

The enlisted men, with our big sergeant carrying the flag, marched across the Common to the Cathedral in the cold rain. A pew for K.C. and me with the children. Curious, our reactions. Most of the people were teary. We, stony. We have just been expressing our surprise, and believe it was because we were praying that the audience would feel it—that the people would wake up—and had little thought of our small affairs.

The French officers were there, General Edwards and his staff, the Governor and his—and Mayor Curley came, though late. Very decent of him to come at all, and I think he has played a generous and unpolitical rôle in all this, despite what people say of him. I'm beginning to believe those say the most who know the least and are least to be believed. Malcolm Peabody was a fine boyish Chaplain. The Bishop did himself proud. The singing was excellent. And our flags were blessed. My only moment of distress came when one of the children reached over and put a little warm hand in mine, while "America" was being sung just before we filed out.

Then back to my rooms at the Brigham. Orders issued to entrain to-morrow at 9 a.m.—everything—everybody. Enlisted men to be outfitted and mustered in at Fort Hamilton—nurses ditto by the Red Cross in New York City. Such meagre operating equipment as we have had time to get together boxed, labeled, and carted off. A last-minute flurry on learning that the Chaplain and the five "civilian employees"—secretaries and dietitians—*must* have properly executed passports accompanied by birth certificates! Many will have had no time for farewells—so be it. Better than to drag along in Boston for another five days before we embark. Patterson, Harmon, and Villaret for Sunday dinner, and then to the Hospital once more for a final afternoon's work.

So here we now are, as nearly ready as circumstances permit, and for almost the first evening in weeks really alone and in peace.

IV

WITH THE BRITISH EXPEDITIONARY FORCE

From New York to Camiers

Friday, May 11. 4 p.m.

ABOARD *S.S. Saxonia*, waiting at anchor in the Narrows while some new firemen are secured to take the places of six who vanished shortly before we left the dock—evidently preferring none to a salt-water job just now. It has been a hectic week. Word came from Washington Monday afternoon of a sudden shift in orders from Fort Hamilton to Fort Totten—some 30 miles apart—necessitating much telephoning and telegraphing to redirect our supplies already en route. Our rabble has been fully equipped and Lt. Villaret in five days of intensive drilling has transformed them. Fort Totten a busy place with our Unit leaving this morning and the Columbia outfit under Brewer moving in.

Getting accustomed to a uniform easier than expected. Cannon says when he first appeared in one his small boy called out: "Mamma, look, here comes Father dressed up like a Boy Scout!" One of Peabody's parishioners congratulated him on his "union suit"—indicating some confusion between the advertisements for underwear in the backs of magazines, "The Union forever," and *E pluribus unum.*

Getting accustomed to army ways less easy. Was informed yesterday that I must go ("proceed" is the word) to Governor's Island for my "ordnance"—not quite sure what that meant or how to get there, but saluted and obeyed. Found an old Col. Mitchem in the Quartermaster's Department who provided me with cavalry spurs—without horse—a villainous-looking, greasy automatic with holster to tie on my leg—also a woven belt, with the laconic remark, "Leather belts no longer worn." This was

Enlisted Personnel and Officers at Fort Totten the Day before Embarkation. *Top Row:* Ober, Goethals, Towne, Bock, Forbes, Robertson, Morton. *Second Row:* Denny, Brown, Cannon, Cutler, Stoddard, Horrax. *Third Row:* Villaret, Fitz, Derby, Boothby, Peabody, Lyman, Binney. *Fourth Row:* Reynolds, Cushing, Patterson, C. O., Lee, Osgood

disconcerting as the C.O. had instructed me to *get* a leather belt like his. Peculiar.

Crile's Unit was bundled Tuesday on the *Orduna*—undrilled and without uniforms or flags. They were permitted by Washington to rob us of five carefully chosen army sergeants—now replaced by somewhat questionable ones. The Columbia outfit sails to-morrow on the *St. Louis*—a faster ship than ours.

New York meanwhile was going mad over "Papa" Joffre—a $50,000 display and entertainment. He would probably have preferred to see our little band drilling at Fort Totten. They were brought up to the pier this afternoon in a government tender. Two hundred men look quite a lot. Soon the nurses appeared, miraculously changed in their street costumes of dark blue with red facing—a quick job by the New York Red Cross chapter.

It was quite a stirring departure. Eliot Wadsworth and the Drapers, General and Mrs. Goethals, Robert de Forest, and Mrs. Leonard Wood, who said the General would have given up his West Point visit with Joffre had he known we were sailing. The enlisted men called for Lt. Villaret, and then for Capt. Reynolds, whom they cheered wildly. Good old Reynolds—squaring his shoulders and pretending his eyes were not wet. They had given him a loving cup yesterday at Fort Totten. Our sailing was supposed to be "secret"; yet everyone in the N.Y. Harbor must have known the *Saxonia* was loaded with ammunition, have seen us go aboard, and have heard our whistles blowing when we left the dock.

Saturday, May 12

We passed out of the Narrows last evening with searchlights wigwagging and boring into the clouds. Patterson called a meeting in the saloon and introduced himself to officers and nurses, and this morning we started on a purely military basis with "Orders of the Day" posted—an office set up in the library—men on guard mount in the passageways, over the ammunition, etc. Calisthenics for the officers on the upper deck in the morning—the hour carefully arranged to coincide with that given over to the first-aid talks to the men, who, being indoors, are removed from the sight of our abdominous and awkward selves as we are put through.

First boat drill this p.m.—rather a gruesome performance—all

kinds of life preservers hanging on all kinds of people in all sorts
of ways. The Captain, being the proud possessor of an inflatable
waistcoat, finally appears and blows himself up for us. His name
is Vennison, a bantam Englishman recently on the *Alaunia*, which
was torpedoed in the Channel. He and Patterson swapped naval
and military yarns at dinner. An extraordinary monochrome eve‚
ning, all bluish-gray—the ship, the sea, the clouds.

Sunday, May 13th

Overcast with a brisk northwest wind. Enough sea running to
affect many of us—more especially the officers detailed to give
typhoid inoculations and smallpox vaccinations below decks. An
hour this morning with some of the enlisted men, trying to learn
from their past records who can most profitably be put to special
tasks. A very good lot; all kinds of surprises, such as a man listed
as a chauffeur who is an expert laboratory technician—can make
media, cut and stain sections. Malcolm conducted the services.
"They that go down to the sea in ships."

There are about a dozen meagre-looking civilians aboard—most
of them born within the sound of Bow bells—cockney traveling
salesmen, we had surmised. One of them approached me this
afternoon as I was watching the storm—spoke pleasantly of our
mission, and we fell awkwardly into speech. He was a Tommy—
had been in the Boer War—was one of the original British Army
—at the retreat from Mons—called home soon after the Marne,
being in the Engineers—at the Woolwich Arsenal for the next
six months while Zeppelins were trying to feel it out—then to the
U.S.A. at Pittsburgh supervising munition making. An English
drummer indeed! He believes fully in the Angel of Mons—indeed says he saw the apparition himself.

Sunday a.m., the 20th

Wet, foggy, and blowing. One can somehow sleep fully dressed
and wearing a cork life preserver, even with a snoring bunkie.
Orders issued yesterday that life belts must be continuously worn.

11 p.m. The weather moderated this afternoon and we had our
usual daily excitement over a sail—first on the starboard and then
on the port bow. Not quite sure just when the Captain began zigzagging, but we surmised he did not like the looks of her and was
turning to get our stern rifle to bear. She was on the horizon about

eleven miles away perhaps. I went aft and found the gunner rubbing up the mechanism, with Patterson's gun crew, organized from our own men, on hand. The Captain finally announced that she was "a Frenchman," signals were run up and we could soon see hers with our glasses—those who still have them, for mine are in use by the guard. We soon zigzagged up to her and she made a beautiful sight—a barque, under full canvas. Bound for Havre from China, out 90 days—knows nothing of the war since sailing, or of the recent submarine activity. One wonders what possible chance she can have. We finally crossed her bows about half a mile away. George Derby and I walked the afternoon out and timed our zigzags—a 90-degree turn every twenty minutes.

We learned that there were four life suits in the party; Peabody has one and William Potter's wife had insisted he take one. We turned them over to the four members of the Unit on the civil list —-the three secretaries and the dietitian. In the privacy of their cabins they practised getting into the suits—not too easy. With one or two exceptions everyone is outwardly calm. Stoddard slept on the deck last night armed to the teeth, and Percy Brown says "the deck for him to-night also."

Continuous wearing of life preservers is no joke and most of us have taken them off—but dragging them about is scarcely less irksome. The wireless to-day announces the arrival of the *Orduna* with Crile's outfit, and we are promised a convoy by to-morrow noon. It will be a welcome sight. Meeting with the inbound "Frenchman" this afternoon makes it reasonably certain that we are in the Bay of Biscay. A shore bird—some kind of snipe—came aboard and made itself very much at home.

Monday a.m. May 21st

Sunshine and a calm sea lift our spirits. Still, one becomes accustomed to anything, even to sleeping in one's boots in an unventilated stateroom. Our average course points N.E. There are gulls about and we have been passing wreckage—a hatch and some spars, a life belt, and nondescript pieces of wood. Still nothing to compare with the *Lusitania* experience of two years ago. That was a concentration of wreckage and emotions. To-day there is less intensity in our feelings just as there is in the scattered drift.

The matter of convoys has interested and disturbed us more or less from the start. There has been every sort of rumor—that 12 American destroyers went over with the *Orduna*—that the *St. Louis* (carrying Base Hospital No. 2) is armed fore, aft, and amidships, and is also to be convoyed. Meanwhile, poor we have been zigzagging across alone with a periscope behind every wave. The Captain, who told us at breakfast that we should have protection by noon, has been outwardly cheerful—largely put on, as was evident when at 5.30 he shouted excitedly down from the bridge: "There she is—our escort!!"

Everyone scrambled forward, soon making out a small dot on the horizon—and it seemed scarcely 15 minutes before she piled up on us with a huge bone in her teeth, swept around our stern, and took her place about half a mile off the port bow. We of course all cheered and waved; but the few dirty-looking sailors aboard stood motionless except for a lone figure on the low pilothouse who was going through a wigwagging performance at an astonishing speed. This small and probably antiquated destroyer has a large "29" painted on the seat of her pants. It hardly seems possible that she can make much difference, but her moral support is unquestionably large. There will be less sleeping on the deck to-night.

In the early afternoon we had an elaborate litter drill on the upper deck with stretchers, and were made to go through all the evolutions for both No. 1's and No. 2's. At one point the No. 2's had to stand for about half an hour holding the blooming things at shoulder arms while the C.O. gave us a long dissertation "from the book" on the theory and practice of litter drills. I happened to be a No. 2. The thing weighs at the outset 23 pounds—and considerably more after 30 minutes. Walter Cannon, another No. 2, remarked: "Mother never meant that I should be a soldier."

We expect to reach Falmouth to-morrow at 6 a.m. Our army trunks are packed and assembled on the forward deck.

Falmouth, May 22nd

Ca. 10 p.m. Waiting in a cold station for our train to start, with good prospect of sitting up all night. Enlisted men are to go to the R.A.M.C. training centre at Blackpool—officers and nurses to London. It's been a long day. Aroused early, we passed the Scilly Islands at 6 a.m. and soon ran into a cold fog. In the late afternoon picked our way slowly through mine fields into Falmouth

Calisthenics for Officers   Drills for Other Ranks

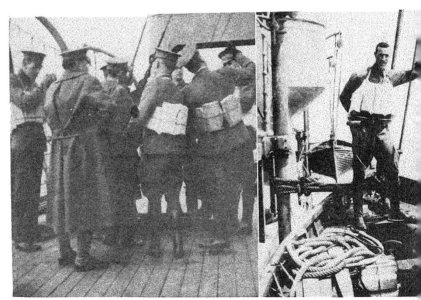

The Life-Belt Period   Boat Drill: Skipper of No

Harbor, passing tankers, trawlers, destroyers, a Dane painted white with big red polka dots, two Dutchmen—tramps—with "Rotterdam" painted on their sides in letters six feet high and the alternate eight-foot-wide red and white stripes prescribed by the Germans at the time we were told we might send one ship a week to Falmouth.

The British Commodore in charge of the patrol here has just told me we had a close call. The *City of Corinth*, an 8000-ton freighter loaded with rice from Singapore, was torpedoed off the Scillys just before we got there and two other ships escaped by a close margin. It's a bad place off the Lizard just now, and, being worried about us, he went out in a scout boat about 1 a.m. and spoke with our destroyer-escort without signaling the *Saxonia*, fearing a pot shot.

Wednesday, May 23rd

A fatigued and disheveled crowd reached London in the early a.m.—poor transport to our hotels: officers to the Curzon; nurses to the York. To the Embassy after breakfast for passports, etc. Mr. Page and "Irv" Laughlin very cordial—must do something for us. In the late evening an hour in the Royal Officers' Overseas Club, where we have been put up. Long talk with a British Columbia man, Col. Worsnap—with the Canadians when they took Vimy Ridge a month ago.

Thursday, May 24th

A Zeppelin raid over London did not waken us between our luxurious sheets. Sir William Osler for breakfast—wants us all to go to Oxford. Passports and much shopping. Cleveland Unit leaves for France. Luncheon at the Curzon with our monitor, Col. Bigbee, after which a scrabble for taxis, which are scarce; to the York Hotel, where we pick up four nurses with whom Patterson, Lee, Osgood, Cannon, and I to Clarence House to be received by the Duke of Connaught. He is a past master at this sort of thing—better than his nephew, I doubt not. The latter received and reviewed the Lakeside outfit at Buckingham Palace yesterday; and speeches were made. It did not last long with us to-day. There was a person in an official red cape—a Miss Bixby—who naïvely remarked to the Duke, evidently an old friend of hers: "I finally got rid of the first lot yesterday."

Then with Roger Lee to the Officers' Club, where we were to

meet Armour. There was a reception going on with the King and Queen in attendance; also the Princess—very pretty. It was given for the Canadian officers under the lead of Col. Godson. We slipped around behind the crowd, much embarrassed by the diver_sion our entrance occasioned. Finally, when royalty moved on, the Canadians gathered about—jubilantly cordial. Col. Godson, his wife, and daughter came up and we were introduced all round. A less formal and much more agreeable party than the one we had inadvertently stumbled upon. Col. G. speaks with a bare whisper —an ugly scar through his jaw, throat, and larynx.

Friday evening, May 25

A quiet dinner with the Godlees—iron rations, which I shared. Found them depressed but very cordial. A row of photographs on the mantel of fine-looking young people they will never see again. Sir Rickman has resumed his hospital work after several years of retirement. Yesterday he operated upon the surviving one of his nephews, who has lost an eye and one leg. Reamputation followed by serious erysipelas—ample reason for his anxiety.

Sunday, May 27th. En route to London

8.30 p.m. Just leaving Oxford after a good night's rest and a memorable day at 13 Norham Gardens. Fitz, Derby, Cutler, and I at the Oslers'; Cannon at the Sherringtons'; Boothby at Haldane's. England in May! Some of us never here before; few if any of us at this most wonderful season. The roadsides abloom— hawthorns, yellow-tasseled laburnums, lilacs, red and white chestnuts—rock gardens with every imaginable flowering plant, iris, tulips, wallflowers, and flowering vines of all kinds. It takes a gray wall to show off wisteria properly.

Before dinner we walked down to see the young cadets having supper at Magdalen—the streets full of them with their white cap bands taking the officers' training course. One young lad who showed us the way and walked with us for a bit was just back from France, and had been through Gallipoli. Now rising from the ranks to become a lieutenant and have about one chance in four of not getting killed within a year. The Isis was covered with boats holding convalescents.

This morning a visit to the hospital in the examination halls— Col. Parker and Capt. Gurdleston. The hospital overflows into

New College, of which Capt. G. is a fellow, and we went through the gardens, bounded on two sides by the old Oxford wall. There were shacks along the walls for the outdoor treatment of shell-shock cases—many of them there. M'Dougall, whom I saw later at lunch, told of one of them: a Tommy of the original army—through Mons, the Marne, and many later battles, including the Somme; had been over the parapet 19 times and finally, two months ago, was in an attack when they ran into their own barrage and many of his pals were killed around him; they were in the open and the fire from both sides was very intense.

He got safely through, had taken some prisoners in a dugout, and was searching them preparatory to sending them back, when an officer came up and shot all of them—"No prisoners to be taken." He went on a little bit, became tremulous; his left arm and shoulder began to twitch; then he broke down and wept. M'Dougall (who by the way was visiting us at the opening of the Phipps Clinic) says it 's often very wise to let these men talk and weep themselves out. This particular man had been rapidly im-proving; had lost his tremor; the twitching had become less and he was less lachrymose. Things looked promising till last night, when a bit of plaster from the old wall fell down near the head of his bed. His earlier symptoms are all back again to-day.

A pleasant dinner at the Sherringtons' with some undergradu-ates just back from the Front—one of them with his second wound stripe on his sleeve. S. talked much of the delayed tetanus which is showing up, and of his experiments to determine the best way of giving antitetanus serum. They now advocate four doses of 500 units, one every week after the reception of a wound. Sir David Bruce, whom we saw yesterday at the Medical War College, has kept a chart of the tetanus cases developing at home. Soon after the war they rose to terrifying numbers, but when serum had been supplied in sufficient amounts to be given at all first-aid stations tetanus practically disappeared. This was when we were first in France. Now what they call chronic tetanus is showing up—often involving one limb, or one side of the face alone.

We had an interesting visit at the War College Saturday morn_ ing. Capt. Roper, a Toronto man who works there, showed us the gas experiments—how the box helmet is adjusted and tested, and

also the less effective hood—like the one young Levick brought
me a year ago. These men making poison-gas experiments and test-
ing out devices to protect against them are unknown workers—
hidden cogs in the huge machine. Roper said they had now issued
2,000,000 masks of the recent box-respirator pattern, very quickly
applied, three seconds, I believe—time for "Rifleman Brown" to
have acted before ringing his gong.

Tuesday, May 29th

6 *p.m.* After the dull London bank holiday, to-day again a
lively one. Osgood blew in late last night announcing the arrival
of Joe Goldthwait and 20 orthopædists, free from any regular
army tangle, though commissioned. They are to do "reconstruction" work in various depots here under Robert Jones, who has
been overwhelmed with orthopædic problems, as may be imagined.
They are now here at the Curzon; also the St. Louis and Philadelphia Base Hospital Units have arrived. Col. Bigbee says we
are to have a further respite until 2.30 to-morrow, and then to
Folkestone. Apparently the aeroplane raid of Sunday and the
many lives lost have so tangled things up that the Channel must
be swept.

Luncheon with *the* Lady Randolph Churchill and a daughter-
in-law, at 8 Westbourne St. Much about "Winston" and the Dardanelles affair which he wanted to pull off in 1914, but was prevented; also his possible reinstatement in the government, his
relations to Lloyd George, etc. Afterward to the American Wom-
en's Hospital for Officers at 99 Lancaster Gate, to meet the King
and Queen. Mrs. Reid there, and Lady Ward, her daughter;
Lady Paget; Lady Harcourt; Mrs. Laughlin; Lady Astor; and
some other women, with Penhallow and myself. Mary very un-
bending. George very otherwise: quite chatty, in fact, and very
likable. Talked about our units and the accident to the Chicago
group, for which he had his own nautical explanation—gun badly
placed, etc.

Then to Henry Head's for an illuminating talk on the organization (or lack of it) of the neurological work of the war, and bad
it has been. As poor as the opportunities are great. How under
Walter Fletcher and T. R. Elliott the Research Council grew out
of—or grew into—its present relation with the War Office. Start-

Snapshots within No. 13 General's Compound
Above: Looking toward the Cement Works
Below: Looking toward the Ridges

ing as the Research Committee—an outcome of the National In-
surance Act—just before the war; then taking over the project of
a Medical History of the War, thus necessitating reports of cases,
without which such a history would be impossible. But no one
seems to use their sheets, and Head says if we will send back
"green tickets" with our neurological cases and accompany them
with notes, we will be doing more than anyone else has so far
done.

Wednesday, the 30th

To the War Office with the C.O. for an appointment with the
two D.G.'s—Keogh and Sloggett. Very much disturbed at our
prospect—a down-at-the-heels hospital at Camiers under canvas.
A most undesirable and badly drained camp, according to Strong,
who has just been there with the U.S.A. Sanitary Commission. A
short visit with Walter Fletcher at the Research Committee Room,
and he takes me to St. Paul's, where a service for the deposition
of the flag of the "American Legion"—Americans who have
served in the Canadian Corps.

Then a hurried lunch and we depart from Charing Cross at
1.30, together with a solemn crowd of British officers returning to
the Front. A gloomy crossing on the packet from Folkestone to
Boulogne—cold, foggy, crowded. In life belts again and most
everyone standing. We were surrounded by destroyers, which in
the fog were invisible, but which growled and screamed and
scolded at one another with their sirens all the way across. On disembarking our kodaks were taken from us and, packed in huge
charabanc affairs, we were carried some 15 miles down the coast
to our destination. A late frugal supper in a cold mess hall, and
now to bed on a cot in a small conical tent, without undressing.

INTRODUCTION TO No. 11 GENERAL

Thursday, May 31st. Camiers

Beginning to take over. A shockingly dirty, unkempt camp.
Luckily about half of the patients have been evacuated before our
arrival, leaving only 600 or so. Our first convoy of 200 wounded
at 1 a.m., half of them "sitters" and half "stretchers".—systemati-
cally disposed of by members of the outgoing unit, with whom,
naturally, we are not very popular. Each of our officers will have

charge of about 100 beds. What can they possibly do with daily notes of the cases?

Sunday, June 4th

4 p.m. I have just parted from young Graham, pathologist of the group we are supplanting, who is going to turn over his tent to me. He hates to leave this place—forlorn as it is and though he is going to a new billet where there is a good laboratory—chiefly because he has planted a few pitiful flowers in the hard-baked clay on the border of the drainage ditch about his tent and some of them are coming up. There are to be some Scotch marigolds, D.V., and in the corners are some ragged bamboo poles on which a little cluster of sweet peas may some day climb. Graham has been in since Mons, was wounded, has a shortened arm, and wears a D.S.O. ribbon.

We are having glorious weather—the first, according to all accounts, since last year. Lucky for us, as this particular "No. 11 General" is under water in wet weather. We are effectually swallowed up in the British Army Machine, and already Base Hospital No. 5 has completely lost its identity. Communication anywhere is nearly impossible: succeeded three days ago in sending home a cable requesting supplies and asking for an acknowledgment. None has come and there seems to be no way to get anything done—even to buy food for the mess—except through cumbersome channels. Little wonder people become inert and careless.

Our young officers have taken hold valiantly, and the wards, with the nurses' help, are already improved in appearance. The men too have been redding up and Osgood has some kind of shop emerging from the chaotic place called a carpenter's shop which was in a tent in a remote corner of our crowded encampment. I say crowded because on one side, behind barbed wire, is a camp of Kaffirs of the "South African Labor Corps"—black as the traditional ace; beyond that one of the huge Portland Cement works which infest this valley of the clay dunes; then comes a railroad embankment prohibiting drainage of any sort.

Yesterday afternoon after our first convoy of the previous night had been straightened out, Patterson, Lee, Osgood, Cannon, and I went to Wimereux, where another hospital group is emerging, similar to that of which we make a part here in the Camiers-

Étaples region. It seems small when compared to the 70,000-bed capacity of this district. We had been invited to a meeting (the second) of the Med. Soc'y of the Boulogne District, at No. 8 Stationary Hospital (Col. Simpson, C.O.) and, since we have no form of transport, a huge ambulance, commandeered from the Étaples Station and driven by two women, took us over. The dust covered us an inch deep by the time we arrived, but the meeting was well worth it.

Major Sinclair of the regular army—an orthopædic genius of the Robert Jones type—had the whole afternoon to himself demonstrating the treatment of gunshot fractures of the thigh with improved Thomas hip splints, Balkan frames, hammocks, etc. He put up four of them, for high, median, and low fractures, and showed the proper kinds of apparatus to be used in the first-line hospital, the C.C.S., and the Base. It was a remarkable demonstration—his manner of presenting the subject altogether admirable, and a man with a gunshot fracture of the femur is lucky to come under his care.

There was a large gathering of officers from everywhere, and Sargent, promising to bring me back in the morning, persuaded me to stay and dine at the Australian mess and spend the night with him at No. 32 Stationary. Like most of the evenings in this strange land, it grew cold, and I nearly perished in my thin American Army uniform, for they insisted on sitting out both before and after dinner. It is a famous mess in what was the Wimereux Golf Club. From the porch one can see the cliffs of Dover on a clear day, and alongshore the point of Ambleteuse projects out into the sea. This was Napoleon's naval base for his planned invasion of England—the old supports for the piers still visible.

10 p.m. There are many interruptions in this life. Canadians from Étaples ("Eat apples") here for dinner; a man had to be seen in one of the wards, from which I have kept pretty much away to give the younger men free swing. Then poor Col. Campbell, the displaced C.O., stopped me out in the cold and for half an hour unburdened himself regarding the work they had been forced to do, which largely accounts for the run-down condition of No. 11. Undermanned—often only eight medical officers and these frequently shifted—he and Wolfenden have faced the music for

the past few months, having had 8000!! patients pass through
their hands since the Somme offensive; most of them serious cases,
night work, secondary hemorrhages and major infections, and yet
they have found time to do some careful work with Carrel-Dakin
treatment. No wonder they have broken down and are to leave for
Blighty this coming morning at 3 a.m.

I am now returned to our untidy messroom wrapped in an overcoat, the remaining British officers drinking whiskey here, the dry
Americans writing home in the next room. This going "dry" needs
constant explanations and must seem quixotic to these people,
though we are doing it for them. Possibly we cannot stick it without seeming too peculiar and making people we really wish to see
avoid our camp.

But to go back to Wimereux. There was a large gathering for
dinner: Col. Eames, the Australian C.O.; Col. Pike, D.M.S. of the
1st Army just back from the Front; the Consultants, Fullerton,
Sargent, and Wallace; two French officers, one of them the old
Commandant at Boulogne wearing on his breast the black and
green ribbon of the Franco-Prussian War—black for sorrow and
green for hope.

The most striking figure of all was a Captain (Sir Beachcroft)
Towse, wearing the uniform of the Gordon Highlanders with a
V.C. ribbon—slim, dapper, erect, precise—and blind! One of the
most promising officers of the regular army, a great polo player,
shot through both orbits in the Boer War. He is now writing letters home for Tommies on a typewriter, and spends his days in the
hospitals, except when playing golf (actually!) on what is left of
the course, and entertaining people at the mess. He kept me up,
shivering with cold, long after the others had gone to bed. He
made his way about the room like a cat, smoked his cigarettes—
though his olfactory sense is also gone, as Sargent told me—with
precision, and handled his glass of whiskey as though he could
see as well as taste. I slept in a cot at No. 32 in some borrowed
woolen pyjamas about an inch thick—the pyjamas—which taught
me a lesson, for it was the first night I 've been really warm.

Thursday, June 14th. Camiers

Just back from an extraordinarily informing week—the week
of the Messines Ridge, taken by General Plumer and the 2nd

Army. The story, as near as I can recall it from some scarcely legible notes, may best be told day by day.

THE BATTLE OF MESSINES RIDGE

Wednesday, June 6th. Hazebrouck

An unexpected order came last evening to report to the D.M.S. of the 2nd Army at Hazebrouck. No explanation accompanied it and our C.O. was somewhat peeved thereby—"dictating to a United States Army Officer," etc. It was stated that a car would call for me at 9 a.m. and sure enough it did, in the shape of a large ambulance for four lying cases, as usual driven by two females. No knowledge of what to take, or for how long, but a compromise was made with a bedding roll—which was not needed—and a few instruments, which distinctly were.

We made our way via Étaples, through the crowded camps of this district, full of men rushing about like so many ants and all the color of the soil; drilling in the sand, practising with machine guns, throwing bombs, having bayonet exercise, digging trenches, and I know not what all. Skirting Montreuil, the G.H.Q. of the First Échelon, and by way of Aire, we crossed the great undulating pastoral district which goes on for miles and miles in this part of France. To my escorts almost everything was either "ripping" or "topping," and not a few things—like the great clover fields—were really "top hole"—everything except about five miles of impenetrable dust behind some Portuguese lorries that would not permit us to pass.

It took about four hours to make the run and I was deposited at the office of the D.M.S., General Porter, and from there was directed to the mess, which I entered looking like a dustpan. I was brushed off and introduced to the gathering: Colonel Arthur Chopping, the A.D.M.S., Colonel Soltau, Captain Stirling, D.A.D.M.S. of Sanitation, Sir Anthony Bowlby, Colonel Gordon-Watson (consultant of the 2nd Army just as Wallace is of the 3rd), and one or two others.

It was soon apparent that an important attack was impending— probably to be launched within the next twenty-four hours. Preparations had been made for heavy casualties—possibly 30,000— and for the first time some intermediary corps dressing stations

(C.D.S.'s) had been provided for in the zone between the field ambulances (F.A.'s) and the regularly established casualty clearing stations (C.C.S.'s).

Naturally, the Boches were fully cognizant of what was on foot but, not knowing just where or when the thrust was to be made, their artillery was attempting to feel out the strongest points and to locate concealed batteries by drawing their fire. A shell could scarcely be dropped anywhere in the area without hitting something important, particularly if it landed near one of the main roads, which were lined with ammunition dumps and crowded with men, guns, and trucks, both corps and divisional, of every conceivable kind and for every possible purpose.

As I came gradually to learn during the next few days, the five British Armies lay disposed from north to south in the following order: 2, 1, 3, 5, and 4; and the D.M.S.'s of each army in the same order were Generals Porter, Pike, Murray Irwin (Robertson's uncle), Skinner, and O'Keeffe. The 2nd Army, which alone concerns us, and which had not been given of late a serious trial, held the line from Boesinghe nearly to Armentières. It was made up of four corps: the 8th on the north, then the 2nd, next the 10th and 9th opposite the salient made by the Messines Ridge, and finally the Anzac Corps below. Each corps comprised four divisions, engaged or in reserve, the 10th corps having the 41st, 47th, and 23rd—the 24th came into the battle later. The 9th corps had the 11th, 16th, 36th (Ulster: the divisional emblem of the Red Hand of Ulster being a familiar symbol on many of the A.S.C. wagons), and the 19th in reserve. The 2nd Anzac Corps included also the 25th British, and the wounded from this division naturally congregated at the Anzac Corps Dressing Station, of which something later on.

For the four army corps with twelve divisions engaged and four in reserve, eleven casualty clearing stations were provided and also three corps dressing stations, for which officers and men had been drawn from some of the field ambulances as well as base hospitals. These eleven C.C.S.'s were disposed: two at Proven or "Mendinghem"; four just south of Poperinghe at a place called Rémy Siding; four at Bailleul—the Tommies' "Balloo," a town founded by Jean de Bailleul, an ancestor, I believe, of the founder of Balliol College; and one at Steenwerck. In addition to these, there are three so-called "stationary hospitals": No. 12 at Hazebrouck supposedly for head cases; No. 15 at Mont des Cats, where the slight wounds, and cases of shell shock also, I believe, were routed; and the third, No. 10, at St. Omer, where a large number of casualties of all kinds could be handled.

How many persons, in addition to the native population, were congregated in the sector in preparation for the battle I cannot say, but I was told that daily rations were issued for 520,000, which of course included noncombatants as well as the fighting units which probably represented scarcely more than half the

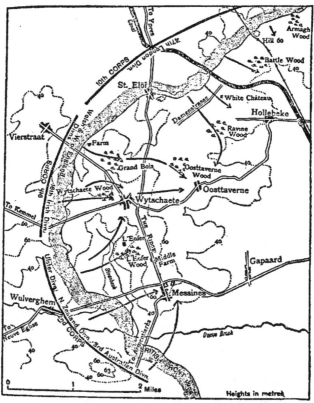

Sketch (from Nelson's *History*) Showing Scheme of the Attack by General Plumer's 2nd Army on the Messines-Wytschaete Ridge

number. The area was so teeming with people that an enemy shell, as I have said, could scarcely fail to hit someone somewhere; and already some 3000 casualties had occurred and the hospitals were busy long before the actual engagement.

After lunch Bowlby took me off on his final round-up of the hospitals and we began with No. 12 Stationary, now given over to the New Zealanders under Colonel O'Neil. There I found Stout, an Australian, who a short time ago was a visitor in Boston. The hospital was in an old parochial Catholic school, and one was as likely to stumble into a schoolroom of French children under the tutelage of a priest as to enter the ward which he had expected to visit; and school children would file out, stepping over stretch- ers of a recent convoy, or could be heard from the operating room singing or chanting their prayers. It is here that Bowlby wants me to lend a hand during the coming days.

Next on to Bailleul, where we stop briefly at the old convent, No. 2, under Colonel Leake, the place I visited two years ago and where we find them hard at work. Then No. 1 Australian (Colonel Dick, C.O.), also in an old building where they are busy with their rotation—"take in"—of cases; and I may add that the C.C.S.'s of a district take cases in relays of 150, when the next in the neighborhood has its turn; so that the usual first question is either "Who is taking in?" or "When do you switch off?"

Then on to No. 53, in another old building (Colonel Peake, C.O.), where we have tea with a number of very nice men. Meanwhile heavy firing going on—too much for comfort; only a few hours before C.C.S. No. 11, near the station at Bailleul, had been hit, and yesterday an ammunition train standing in the yard ditto, and car by car it went off during the course of the next half hour like a bunch of firecrackers. Col. Peake called my at- tention to a hole in the roof of the building made two or three days ago by a shell just as a medical case, brought in on a stretcher, had been deposited on the landing platform. Two of the man's toes were cut off by a fragment of the shell, making a "battle casualty" of him, much to his surprise and delight, for it probably would take him back to Blighty.

Bowlby thought No. 11 too unhealthy a place for us to visit this afternoon, so on to Rémy Siding, where are four C.C.S.'s in a row along the railroad, most convenient for evacuating cases. At No. 17 (Colonel Wingate, C.O.) we were shown about by Captain Meyer, and there I found Forbes Fraser, seen in Paris- Plage with Makins a few days ago. Then the 2nd and 3rd Cana- dian; and finally No. 10, where the brothers Henry and Adrian

Stokes were encountered. Adrian showed us some spirochetes in cases of jaundice in men and horses, more or less prevalent at this time; he showed us, too, some astounding pathological specimens from men who have died of their wounds—an aneurysm of the vertebral artery, and another of the heart.

Then back to Hazebrouck, with Kemmel Hill to one side and the Trappist Monastery of Mont des Cats to the other, through hop country with the vines now halfway up the poles—the fields stewing with soldiers—the roads packed with guns and lorries, and everywhere a prevailing sense of something serious impending. Captain Stirling had secured for me a *billet de logement* with a French family on the Square, where a bantam batman named Cholmondeley provides hot water, shines my American leather—unaccustomed to such attentions—and informs me that "zero time," from which everything is calculated, has not as yet been given out, but will be to-night.

The weather looks threatening, and a heavy rain would spoil the whole show as it has done more than once before. On our way back this afternoon we passed some huge 15-inch howitzers slowly moving up on their huge caterpillar tractors. A heavy rain would make it almost impossible to move them, one would suppose, even though the roads hereabouts have been vastly improved and widened during the two years since I first saw them, when there was a central strip of furrowed *pavés* barely wide enough for a farmer's cart.

Thursday the 7th. Hazebrouck

Zero time proved to be at 3.10 a.m. and I remember being awakened, probably by the great mine explosions—600 tons of explosives in 19 blasts—and of hearing the tremendous barrage which went on for half an hour or more and suddenly ceased— or else I went to sleep. Some of these great mines had been placed under the Boche lines, as I subsequently learned, as long as 18 months ago, at which time they had first planned for the attack. Warfare under the ground is almost as novel as warfare in the air—digging, listening with auscultatory devices—out-manœu_ vring enemy sappers by going below or to the side—and finally getting below with every chance that your tunnel will be dug into any minute.

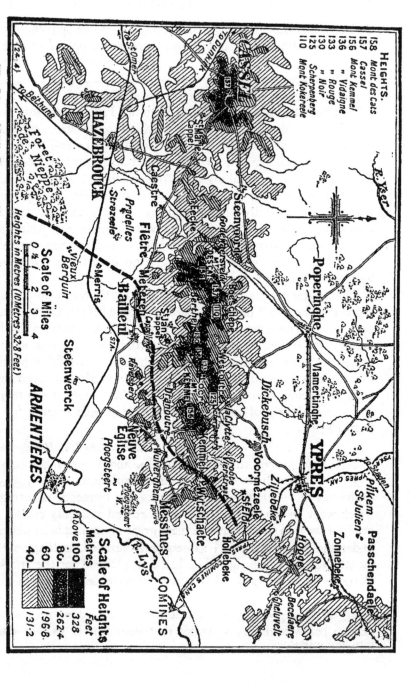

The Line of Hills Running East from Cassel and beyond the Messines Ridge Northeast to Passchendaele

As two years ago we found our way—the hard-worked Stirling, Sir Anthony Bowlby, and I—from Hazebrouck eastward, with the range of low hills on our left, extending from Cassel to Kemmel, just north of which is the Scherpenberg, where we stood on that occasion. Between this landmark and Kemmel lies Mont Noir —almost leveled for its product of sand to fill bags, to make road beds and concrete; this we cross and find our way to the top of Mont Rouge, where from a little knoll one gets a great sweep of the ridge. Even so it is difficult to get a clear idea of what is going on, particularly when one does not know the plays, and, being somewhat hazy, the visibility is not of the best. But we can see the long rows of observation balloons—unusually high and looking like curled-up slugs—probably 20 of them, whereas beyond the ridge we can make out only two German balloons. Aeroplanes of course were working everywhere and the artillery fire was very heavy—directed over the ridge by now, for the German stronghold on the crest perfected during two years' occupancy had been taken almost at the first rush.

There were many lines of guns along the near slope, though it was impossible to detect them except by the flashes, and heavier guns were being fired from our right and rear. Doubtless field pieces had been moved up over the ridge by this time. There were some A.S.C. men and gunners at the summit of Mont Rouge, which like the Scherpenberg is surmounted by a windmill, and we gather that the operation has been a great success—the troops are still advancing and likely to wipe out the salient from Ypres to Ploegsteert ("Plug Street") Wood. Returning wounded report that they were over the third line by 4 a.m.—as good as the Canadians at Vimy who ate the breakfast prepared for the Bavarians. The view, if not so good as from Scherpenberg, is nevertheless very fine and one could just make out Ypres in the more northerly distance.

There was little if any appreciable artillery firing in our direction and, as a contrast to what at the moment was going on across the exposed valley to which the British have tenaciously clung so long, not ten yards from us on the slope below was a little old man in a sort of garden, busily mending two long brown windmill sails which were spread out on the grass—either uninterested or unaware. There also was an old church near by, a sort of Lourdes with a famous healing spring. It will be visited by more cripples than ever before in times to come, no doubt.

Resisting the temptation to linger, we take our way back to Bailleul, where is a heavy intake of wounded, and Bowlby makes sure that the rotation between the several C.C.S.'s is going on properly. Fewer casualties than expected, however, and the men for the most part are elated and proud of themselves. Those at No. 53 that have reached the wards and are non-evacuable already have their Smith-Dorrien (Dolly, Dorothy, Comfort, etc.) bags and are happy to be in bed.

And so in all the C.C.S.'s. A great tent for reception, with rapid recording of patients—some to go on, some to remain, and of these a large quota to the preoperation room for their turn, and others with chest wounds to their proper ward, or still others in critical shape to another place; and meanwhile an equally rapid evacuation takes place and a train is ready for 600 cases, and before they are off in come another 150, and why can't No. 11 take these, and No. 2 is overcrowded or another behind in its work.

Then over to No. 1 Australian, which is groaning with its job and can hardly keep clear. The large receiving room still full and another convoy already coming in. To save time the men have been branded like cattle, at the F.A.'s, on the forehead— or arm if there's a head bandage—or anywhere it can be seen— with a *T* by an aniline pencil—tetanus antitoxin. I stopped to speak to one poor boy who was evidently dying—a stretcher-bearer, hit while carrying back a wounded Boche—a large piece of his pelvis carried away. Quite conscious. "I'm doing not so bad, sir, but I know I've got it this time." Terrific.

The usual quick lunch taken at No. 2 with Col. Leake, Shaw, Stevenson, and the big padre—and I learn that in these attacks about one out of every five who are hit is killed, while about 2 per cent of those who reach a C.C.S. die there. After lunch to Steenwerck (Col. Webb, C.O.), where is the 2nd Australian C.C.S. Many Anzac wounded—very pleased with themselves. Capt. Oliver, whom I met at Wright's mess two years ago, operating —also Craig and Barton. Excellent system of taking in, thanks to the husky bearers all over six feet. Also convenient evacuation on narrow-gauge tracks as at Rémy. Talked with some wounded Germans.

Then back another way to Bailleul and to No. 11, which for sufficient reasons we did not visit yesterday, but the Boches are not shelling to-day—for equally good reasons. Col. Humphries, the C.O., a cordial man, showed us about and told how they had tried to get the R.E.'s to put a ventilating roof on their operating hut, and showed us where yesterday a big piece of shell had made a suitable opening, just over one of the tables. Quite a new place —-in tents—in a field alongside the railroad, recently moved up from the Somme for this fight. Bowlby makes his usual compliments and we tea before moving on to No. 22, where I wait for Col. Chopping and learn meanwhile that they have taken in between seven and eight hundred already, and a convoy is just coming in, and the wearied bearers go out for them.

The long-legged padre has been attending burials and tells me of the officer just in who was saved from a chest wound by a Bible in the upper pocket of his tunic. Moral. The wounded on the crowded stretchers all over the big court invariably say, "Not so bad, sir," however bad it may be. And they all have very good news from the ridge: Messines and Wytschaete taken, and still going on. So Hill 60 which I saw lost two years ago has probably been recaptured to-day.

Chopping appears and takes me back to No. 12 at Hazebrouck, meanwhile informing me that Messines Ridge was far more impregnable than Vimy. We run into a cloudburst with hailstones large as marbles and get sopping wet from outside in. Later the same from inside out, for, with Stout assisting, I did my first head case, wrapped in a rubber apron and in my boots. A man with the name of Dark; and it was. No X-rays, a poor light and a bullet in the knee, which I did n't get, and another likewise in his side which had reached his lower spine and caused retention. All this incidental to his cranial wound which we repaired and closed.

Crile arrives from his base at Rouen and we learn that some of the great problems of the war are lice and scabies, which a bath and disinfection every ten days keep only moderately down. Mumps and measles too have been serious among the newcomers, especially the New Zealanders. Then, too, forms of albuminuria occur, and there are many fevers like trench fever that are poorly understood, together with a variety of febrile disorders commonly designated P.U.O.[1] for want of a more precise designation.

Friday the 8th

Wytschaete, Messines, and Hollebecke in British hands—a great victory. Capt. Myer Coplans at breakfast—water expert— just back from the Front—has been at Messines itself—water supply pumped there from tanks on Kemmel in five hours after the troops got in. Story of arsenic found in wells doubtless false. Water in this zone a serious problem, but there has been extraordinarily good health—no cases of typhoid or paratyphoid reported for three weeks. They have fear of typhus from the combination of omnipresent lice and possible Hungarian "carriers" among the P.O.W.'s. The same is true of dysentery among the men back from Mesopotamia and Gallipoli, 5 per cent of whom are "carriers," and the disease lights up on the slightest provocation. Coplans says the triumphs of the campaign are the duckboards and the incinerators.

At 9.30 to the New Zealand Stationary again, where Major Baigeant gathers in more head cases for me than I can possibly do. The unusual experience for me of operating alone on heads with a strange anæsthetist using chloroform and a so-called "cleaned-up" sister. Of course much too great loss of blood, poor if any X-rays, practically no neurological study. Luckily most of the cases went well with flaps and closure. Most of them really favorable. Captain Acton, a New Zealander with a badly lacerated shoulder and a left parietal lesion, giving him a pure right astereognosis, was one of them.

The wounds in most cases of course are multiple. "Multiple" indeed may hardly convey the impression. Mostly shell explosion effects—very few bullet wounds in a game like yesterday's. Indeed the more trifling the wound appears to be, the more serious it may prove on investigation. Or the reverse may be true—an ugly-looking wound that proved relatively trifling. One boy had a small temporal wound and stated that there was a hole in his tin hat. The operation showed that a strip of his helmet about

[1] Pyrexia of uncertain origin.

The C. in C.

P.O.W.'s after Messines

two inches long and half an inch wide had been cut out as though by a can opener. This metal sliver had curled in through the temporal bone over his ear, passed through the brain, and its point emerged just behind the external angular process. Not a pleasant thing to dislodge, particularly as it had divided his meningeal artery, which began to bleed after the bone was removed and the missile loosened.

Dinner at the mess with General Sloggett and his "Bobby"— Major Black. Many tales of the army and the struggle to perfect the R.A.M.C. during the early days.

Saturday the 9th

More operations at the N.Z. Stationary in the morning. More cases than we can handle and 50 are sent on to the Base. Those of yesterday seem to be doing very well and Capt. Acton is already gaining power in his arm. One can't tell much about these wounded soldiers. A man might have his whole face blown off and, if he could talk at all, he'd be "doing very well, sir." While I was attempting to switch a large flap of scalp over a lacerated wound —and none too happy about it—a red-tabbed staff officer appeared and looked on. I could n't very well salute and so smiled a Bazett smile. "You don't know me?" "No, sir." "I 'm General Macpherson." "Tiger?" "Yes, how did you know?"—and it was his turn to smile. "Blanchard Randall saw us off on the boat and said he hoped I might meet you."

At noon to Bailleul via Strazeele to meet Bowlby at No. 2— arrive just in time to see the Field Marshal visiting the wounded and congratulating the C.O. Best-looking man I ever saw—admirable to his very boots, which I may add were a sort of undressed kid, not the polished leather other British officers cultivate. A shy man, I judge, but very friendly. Col. Leake made us sign his visitors' book, where therefore the name of a Major, U.S.R., appears under D. Haig, F.M., and S. Kiggell, Lt. Gen. Sir Douglas seemed well satisfied with the past two days—said in fact that it was the most satisfactory operation in which he had ever participated. Everything had gone like clockwork—already 7000 to 8000 prisoners. Afterward lunch at No. 2 again with Col. Leake and all very chipper.

Then to 53 once more—passing the prisoners' compound.

Clever thoracic operation by Lockwood with closure of hole in diaphragm. Thoraco-abdominal wounds especially difficult, and on the left side a visceral herniation into the chest is likely to occur. At an adjoining table someone removed an *iron* shrapnel ball! First one I have seen. Scarcity of lead? At the third table was a man with a through-and-through wound of his left thigh, the piece of shell having lodged in the other thigh, breaking the femur without actually reaching it.

Talk with an intelligence officer who has been combing the prisoners. They are big, strong, cheerful, and well-fed, though very lousy. Extraordinary the details of information which opposing armies have of one another's forces. There were maps in General Porter's office the day before the battle, not only giving every German trench of every kind but the names of the trenches and just what troops under what officers occupied them, and what troops were in reserve. This of course is the main purpose of the raids and bombing parties.

Then a visit to the series of corps dressing stations—a new venture, as I have said—established for this particular battle. Ordinarily there is a field ambulance for each brigade, or twelve for each corps, and as these F.A.'s are in two sections, one nearer the Front than the other, the latter can be fused in time of anticipated stress into a large corps dressing station. This was first tried out at the Somme. I judge that it will not be repeated if a sufficient number of casualty clearing stations to make one for each division can in the future be provided. It would have required 16 for the 2nd Army instead of the 11 whose disposition I have given.

And so to the most southerly of the corps dressing stations at Pont d'Achelles, an Anzac place, comprising among other field ambulances the 9th Australian. An enthusiastic and energetic C.O., Col. McGuire, showed us about. Far better than our base hospitals—neat as a pin—extensive use of oilcloth. Many makeshifts of course, such as beef-tin covers for the bowls, but within, everything in order, and without, duckboards everywhere.

One would not have believed that 2000 cases had passed through their hands in the past 24 hours. The station, mostly in Nisson huts with monitor roofs—better ventilation therefore

than the usual Esquimau-like Nissons provide. McGuire estimated that the Boches sent over 20,000 gas shells during the few
hours before the attack, so their early intake was chiefly gassed
cases. For them oxygen (though useless in chlorine-gas poisoning)
had proved beneficial and there was ample provision for its administration—even for giving it to men while wearing the recent
type of box respirator.

Saw a convoy brought in—most of them hit within the hour—
splendidly handled by the husky Australian bearers and quickly
sorted. McG. emphasized again that the first duty is to record,
the second to clear the case through, and dressing of the wound
comes third. There were a lot of Mauris among the wounded—
wonderful big chaps! Bowlby told me of last winter's tree-felling
contest in which the Mauris beat all comers, Scotch, French,
Canadians, Australians, and English. The French were second,
and protested because the Mauris had cut the trees a foot higher
than they. The Mauris took them on again and beat them at their
own level. Rules: three men and three trees, I believe, and they
could help one another in any way they chose.

Then to the 2nd Dressing Station at a place called Westhof, not
far from Neuve-Église, where a shy Irishman named Kelly was
the C.O.—a Boche prisoner for a year and badly treated. Here
I saw the first cases, in unwounded men, of genuine shell shock in
the acute stages—just brought in. Very pitiful. One with pronounced general tremor, an anguished expression, and semi-
conscious; the other still more stuporous and jerking about, every
few minutes—as though falling in his sleep or having a strong
electric current passed through him. When some near-by Archies
went off, fired at a passing Boche plane, it was horrifying to see
them convulse.

Colonel Kelly's figures of their intake were: 4999 cases from
5.10 a.m. the 7th to 12 noon the 9th, i.e., to-day. They evacuated
during the main rush four cases a minute. From 3 a.m. the 7th
to midnight of the same day there were 1254 lying and 1581
walking cases, 2835 in all. Here, too, the reception as well as
the operating pavilion was as clean and tidy—even to the rows
of safety pins laid out—as though they were merely ready for
the rush instead of just getting through with it. The third C.D.S.,

at Dranoutre, just behind Mt. Kemmel, was more primitive, more recently established, and in a more exposed position. On our way back we overtook the Ulster Division—coming out—strung along for a good many miles; and there have been red hands elsewhere than those painted on the lorries these past three days, one may be sure.

Sunday, June 10th

Stirling, who has been up all night, brings to breakfast the "daily intelligence summary" of the 2nd Army—and remarkably detailed documents they are. Prisoners so far reported, 138 officers and 6377 other ranks, of which only 31 officers and 1231 O.R. are reported from C.C.S.'s. Also the translation of a secret order to German officers, telling them among other things that they would receive ample artillery support—which they did not, though several guns from the *Barbarossa* had been brought up— also that the ridge must be held at any cost.

Dressing of my cases at the N.Z. Stationary. So far all appear to be doing well. Back to the office of the Army D.M.S., whom I have come to like very much. He shows me a complimentary telegram from Gen. Plumer, "to be transmitted to all Hospital C.O.'s." Also explains his elaborate plotted chart of sick and wounded for the past year—the sick have long been about 0.5 per cent lower than in ordinary civil life. As usual for a few days before a great advance, no sick were reported at all, and then on the 7th and 8th came the peak in the red line—recording the 17,000 wounded of these past days.

Then with Bowlby once more on his rounds of the C.C.S.'s. First to Proven, where we have not been before, by way of Steenvoorde with its striking old fenestrated steeple, across the Belgian frontier at Watou—"What Ho" of T. Atkins. The road leads straight away north into parts of Belgium where new C.C.S.'s are now being established. B. says I may draw my own conclusions. It is quite evident that preparations are being made for the next thrust, which is to be north of Ypres, and I gather from various things seen later in the south that the 5th Army under General Gough is being slowly moved around from its present place near Albert, up into this sector, at the left wing of the British line. Indeed we passed, going north, a lot of the

38th Welsh Division, with their dragon symbol—and I do not identify them as part of the 2nd Army. The two "Mending'em" C.C.S.'s lie alongside a new British-built double-track railroad—built with the aid of German prisoners. No. 46 under Col. Ellis and No. 12 under Col. Hamerton, who was moved from the N.Z. Stationary in Hazebrouck only two weeks ago. We saw some excellent abdominal work being done in a Nisson hut. No. 12 is set up in a field, in marquees which can accommodate 1200 cases.

Next to Rémy Siding once more, passing on the way about 30 huge guns with caterpillar tractors. Some long naval guns were among them, asleep under the trees at the side of the road—their muzzles pointing south, so I presume their destination was north. Their habits of course are essentially nocturnal. Lunch in the mess at No. 10 with the Stokes brothers and Col. Marriott the C.O., a nice man; also G. W. Crile, who has been operating here for a few days.

Back to Bailleul again; first to No. 53 where Lockwood, Thomas, and Gordon-Taylor were at work; then to No. 1 Australian, where I was prevailed upon to do a laminectomy on a poor man with extreme radiating pains down his legs from a G.S.W. of the lower thoracic spine. They tried an 8-minute X-ray exposure! This proved a failure; and with misgivings I started in, only to find that the missile had skirted from the thorax down somewhere toward his pelvis. Probably a hematorrhachis.

At all of these places visited to-day the wounded were still coming in in large numbers. The tail end of the battle. Yet heavy firing keeps up and an occasional Boche shell comes even into Bailleul. The windshield of General Haig's car is said to have been broken yesterday by shell fragments as he was leaving No. 11, which has finally been evacuated to-day as too "unhealthy" even for a C.C.S. Some of the men brought in have been lying out for 48 hours—one poor chap for a double amputation. The Boches too have put a barrage over in the "Plug Street" area—using up their ammunition, it is rumored, before withdrawing their guns.

The German *communiqués* via Amsterdam make very light of the three days' battle, saying that they have merely straightened

their line. The papers announce the arrival of General Pershing
and his staff in London.

Monday, June 11th

A month since we left home. Rain last night and cooler. Again
with Bowlby on his rounds. First to Bailleul, passing an outcoming
division. The hopvines have nearly reached the tops of their
poles during the past week. At No. 2 we went through the abdominal ward with Col. Leake—very excellent results, particularly when compared with the early days.

There was one man I especially remember— Collaran, by name,
Sergeant Major of the 3rd Battalion Worcesters—has seen 16
years' service—came out with the original army on August 12th,
1914—in the 3rd Division with General Hamilton who was
killed—was at Mons, the Marne, in the thin line at Ypres; first
wounded November 1914, and twice since—back in England for
only thirteen days in the ten months. He was shot in the abdomen
on the 7th, early in the attack, crawled back to his original trench,
where an M.O. said he could do nothing and he must wait for
bearers. Collaran said he knew this might be many hours, so he
made his way back alone to an advanced dressing station, where
he got transport here. He had 19 intestinal perforations!! and is
the man I saw Shaw operating upon the first day we came up.
What's more, he's recovering, and wants to know when he can
get back—not to Blighty but to his battalion.

And so to No. 1 Australian again; then to No. 53, and from
there to Steenwerck, past the shell hole by the wall near No. 11
that just missed the Field Marshal. Colonel Webb says it dropped
between the C. in C.'s car and one of the hospital lorries. We lunch
while some big naval guns fire their screeching shells overhead.
Three padres at the table: Church of England, Catholic, and
Conjoint Board. The last named, a nonconformist, is called "the
Maconochie" after the ration of that name—a kind of Irish stew
which includes almost everything that is left over.

Bowlby wishes me to see some research work in the 1st Army
area on the early closure of infected wounds—so to Estaires
across a great alluvial plain—a huge market garden—to C.C.S.
No. 54—a sort of advanced stationary hospital with only 25 beds
and four M.O.'s on the staff who are experimenting with the new

antiseptic "flavine." The wounds have a remarkable appearance _–B. likens them to "cold storage wounds"—and though they do not become bacteria-free as under Dakin's fluid, they nevertheless may be closed after a few days.

The wounds were covered by a layer of fibrin which looked to me much like the thin layer made by Zenker fixation. They showed us some promising results; but sharing Sir Almroth Wright's views on the subject of the antiseptic treatment of these lacerated wounds, I don't feel enthusiastic. Certainly it will not do for penetrating cranial wounds, in which primary closure of the scalp after *débridement* seems to me imperative. I greatly doubt whether reliance on any known antiseptic will aid the average surgeon in accelerating the return of wounded men to active duty —which of course is the purpose of these studies.

We were joined by McNee, whom I met two years ago at Bailleul—now pathologist for five C.C.S.'s and the F.A.'s of the 1st Army—and with him to the 2nd London at Merville, where trenches are still to be seen, and a church considerably knocked about. There McNee has a large laboratory, and his co-worker Capt. Dunn showed us the brain from a fatal shell-shock case with its remarkable punctate hemorrhages—gas poisoning or shell shock? We were shown other examples of secondary wound closure under flavine; and then tea with the sisters and a pet kid (*sic*) called "Muriel." Ours at Camiers is "Percival."

Then via Haverskerque, along a road lined with ammunition embankments, to St. Venant and over the Canal. Lillers, Bourecq, to the chalk hills which run across the Pas de Calais from Vimy Ridge to the Coast—over the same table-land we crossed last Wednesday. Clover fields spotted with poppies, *luzerne* fields, corn just coming to ear, sheep browsing by the roadsides with a sheep dog on watch to keep them from the grain—also a nanny goat along to give the dog milk! An expanse of lovely farms with lines of old men and women slowly advancing on their knees as they weed between the rows—even back here there are miles of lorries and London busses along the roads. Through Heuchin, Anvin, and Erin—the "Tankville" of the British soldiers—fully 100 of the beasts, one or two of them ambling about like great prehistoric turtles.

Then past a region of thorn hedgerows—into more rolling country—the Fôret d'Hesdin, and my destination in an attractive château, in a park full of birds, with a batman named Ringwood to get me a bath and clean my boots, while some nightingales out-side are singing madly.

A pleasant dinner with the D.G. and his staff of A.D.M.S. officers—Col. Morgan, Majors Black, Martin, and Bulkley—with much not necessarily intended for my ears about preparations for the coming offensive farther north. This was all very restful and enjoyable until there unexpectedly blew in, late for dinner, a colonel of the 9th Lancers who is a British liaison officer at Compiègne, the present French G.Q.G., where he certainly has become tinged with pessimism. He finally let loose about the re-cent Champagne offensive something to this effect:—

Everyone in Paris knew all about it in January, especially the women, chiefly those other than respectable. Germans of course ditto. No effort to change plans. Was to be a big affair—to break the stalemate and end the war. Corps d'Élite of the French brought in. Became known that Germans had brought up 50 divisions instead of the 30 in the area when the plans were begun in January. French Cabinet goes out to Compiègne in a special train to bless the attack, which is a miserable failure, 150,000 casualties. Later no reserve troops brought up, no *repos* given. Finally about five divisions mutinied—very respectfully of course, no rioting and breaking of windows; they simply did n't care to go in again. Considerable drunkenness among French soldiers who are now getting four sous instead of one a day, therefore can buy more wine. New officers have little control of men, no more *camaraderie* —-women of Midi actually hiding men when in rest billets, and are firmly opposed to a continuance of the war. France indeed in an impossible state—fizzling out. Necessary to make someone a scapegoat, therefore not only Nivelle but his whole staff demoted. French never stand by one another: Briand tried frequently to oust Joffre and finally succeeded—same thing with Nivelle. Italy all through. The Portuguese a terrible lot—worse than useless. The only glimmer of hope is that Russia is not entirely eliminated and that Brussilof will put on a show in July.

The Frenchman of course a brave fellow—gets worked up

Extremes in the R.A.M.C.

Above: Two Battalion M.O.'s Giving First Aid in an Elephant Shelter
Below: The Headquarters Staff at Hesdin, Sir William Macpherson and Sir
Arthur Sloggett in Centre

to a flame heat for a few moments and is then irresistible; but the flame soon goes out and it takes an exceptional man to kindle it again. British soldiers never flame—only a steady glow all the time—indeed it 's up to the English to finish the job alone—with the possible help, in time, of America. We shall see. Disconcerted by all this, I was glad to escape to bed. Of course he was just letting off steam; but the first principle for allies is to keep the lid on.

Tuesday the 12th

With Bowlby to visit some of the 3rd Army hospitals. From Hesdin to St. Pol and Aubigny over the broad highway which was the chief line of communication during the Vimy Ridge battles. So to Agnez-les-Duisans, about four miles west of Arras and approximately seven from the present line, where some C.C.S.'s (Nos. 8, 14, and 19) have been set up for the past three months—admirably arranged in the fields between a railroad siding for evacuation and a roadway for ambulances. Not a particularly healthy place. No. 41 near by was blown up a few days ago and No. 19 had a close shave, for a "dud" landed by the C.O.'s tent and buried itself there. It was carefully exhumed and taken to a near-by field to be exploded.

After visiting the other two stations we stopped at No. 19 for lunch; and just as we were sitting down at the mess a disheveled and muddy young staff officer rushed in and said General Congreve had just been hit by a shell in the outskirts of Arras. We went over to the preoperation ward where he was being put through like anyone else—a badly lacerated hand, and the side of his face scraped a good deal. None of the staff officers with him had been touched.

A lean, scholarly looking, imperturbable person, he realized that an amputation was necessary; wished to have it over soon; did not want to give up the command of his Corps—what was the mere loss of an arm! B. knew all about him physically— long ill-health—nearly died at the Somme from dysentery—chronic asthma. Captain Samson did a quick amputation under light chloroform and the General, who wears a V.C. ribbon I may add, came out promptly and said he saw no reason why he should be relieved from duty for such a trifle.

Bowlby had expected to go into Arras, but this episode dis-couraged us and we merely skirted the town, with its ruined cathedral looming up, for a glimpse of the recent battlefields and the evacuated territory in a more quiet area. Through Warlus, Dainville, and on to Wailly at the margin of the old line—and there 's little of the village left to tell the tale; and so along parallel to the lines, to Agny, equally leveled, and where we cross the old trenches to the recently captured strip. This was not so very long ago—a short two months in fact since that snowy Easter Monday when, after a preliminary bombardment the like of which the war had not yet seen, the Canadians on the first rush reached the crest of the ridge; and a scant three weeks since the great battle drew to a close after the capture of Bullecourt.

We then followed a road leading south toward Boisleux-au-Mont—all the roadside trees for the three miles having been cut nearly through about three feet from the ground and broken back by the Boches in their retreat from the Somme to the Siegfried line. Near by was an advanced dressing station, which was being dismantled as no longer sufficiently far forward; and the C.O. was sending on his last abdominal cases—90 had been operated upon here during the fight—with 50 recoveries—not so bad. We walked across the open country, picking our way between shell holes and avoiding thistles and pieces of barbed wire and "duds" and unexploded grenades.

Near Boisleux station is a deep railroad cut which must once have been in French hands, for on the eastern side were old French dugouts in the protection of the bank, while on the western side were German machine-gun emplacements pointing to the west and down the slope we had ascended. How troops ever faced machine guns so protected is beyond me. To be sure, the one we particularly investigated had been destroyed by a chance hit, but it was encased in heavily reënforced concrete, and was so covered with earth and sod that it must have been practically invisible. The fire-opening was a narrow slit between heavy steel rails and the entrance was through a tunnel from the bottom of the embankment. In many places the great zones of German barbed wire were still in place and seemed impenetrable. We could look over to Monchy-le-Preux, where the afternoon "hate" was going on in lively fashion.

Then back to Hesdin via Doullens, Frévent, and the valley of the Canche—very lovely. A simple fireside dinner with Bowlby and Herringham in the library of the French billet which they share, and to which they endeavor always to return for the night if they possibly can. Sir Wilmot is reading with enthusiasm Thiers's "sublime" history of France under Napoleon, which he found on the shelves. There is not much that either of these men misses. They are steeped in the history of the Pas de Calais, once a part of the Spanish Netherlands—the château of Charles Vth's sister is one of the landmarks in Hesdin.

A Visit to Vimy Ridge

Wednesday, June 13th

I 've about had my fill of sight-seeing. The D.G., however, is not to be refused and he announced last night he was going to give me a "joy ride"—that Col. Morgan was going along and that we were to be joined by one "Davy," the nicest man in the army —"a dear boy in fact." Everyone below the rank of colonel is a "dear boy" to the General. And so we started out about nine for our rendezvous with Major Davidson (D.A.D.M.S. to General Pike of the 1st Army) at the Camblain-l'Abbé crossroads, north of Aubigny.

Joined by him who may, for convenience, henceforth be "Davy," we proceed through Villers-au-Bois to Carency—much destroyed—with the ruined towers of Mt. St. Eloi to the south and those of Notre-Dame-de-Lorette to the north—on to Souchez, absolutely flattened out—not even a piece of wall remaining as a landmark. Two big 15″ howitzers, knocked out by a lucky German shot, stood about as high as anything in the ruins, for Souchez with its little salient has been in the very thick of it since September 1914. It was about time to put on our tin hats and adjust our gas masks, which we wore for the rest of the day. Surprising how comfortable the helmets are—no worse than our standard U.S. officer's caps—but the box respirator around my neck weighed on me with unpleasant reminders of life-belt days.

And so across the lines to the ridge, where words fail to give any conception of the desolation. No convulsion of Nature could have done what man and man's machines have done. We bumped our way along a partly repaired road which led through "Zouave Valley," in which the Canadians had been desperately floundering for so long in the wet and cold, and up toward the ridge—passing craters from those 10 to those 30 feet across, and some almost as deep; passing rows and rows of old wire entanglements, communication trenches, line upon line of fighting trenches, all more or less obliterated. Finally past the German first line, barely recognizable except for the fact that the entrances to the dugouts now faced east instead of west.

It was an upheaval of sandbags, accoutrements, broken rifles not worth salvaging, entrenching tools, cartridge clips and machine-gun ribbons, food tins, water bottles, helmets, trench mortars, unexploded shells of every size, hand grenades, to which we give a wide berth, a human tibia exhumed from somewhere, bits of clothing—and often smells, though two months have given ample time for burials. What may be in the bottom of the pits, however, one can only guess. Salvage corps were still at work, and the whole western side of the slope was seething with people making new roads and engaging in the ant-like activity of man when he too burrows and builds and carries up food and takes away grains of sand.

We got as far forward with the car as was safe, and then on foot to the top overlooking the great plains to the eastward. The Boche was kind and all the firing was over our heads, indeed this was so all day, and we had no uncomfortable moments, though on the margin of the treeless ridge one could be as easily seen against the sky line as if standing on the hill crests behind Camiers. The visibility was low so that Lens was just to be made out in the haze. Everything between Souchez and Givenchy—for the long-fought-over line ran about halfway between them—has been absolutely wiped out a blot of ruins—nothing standing—and we could look down on Givenchy en Gohelle with "the Pimple" beyond it, on Petit-Vimy and Vimy itself, with what we took to be the husks of Avion and Mericourt beyond.

Fascinated, we stayed for about an hour—picking out the present line of German trenches by the puffs of the shell explosions, and trying to identify the distant towns through our glasses. The shelling from our side, as near as we could tell, was directed toward Fresnoy or Oppy. It recalled the view over Messines Ridge on Thursday, and that two years ago from Scherpenberg Hill out over Ypres—too vast to comprehend. Impossible to contract anything on such a scale down to one's own experiences; it is far easier to magnify small things in the imagination and thus get some conception of what had been going on.

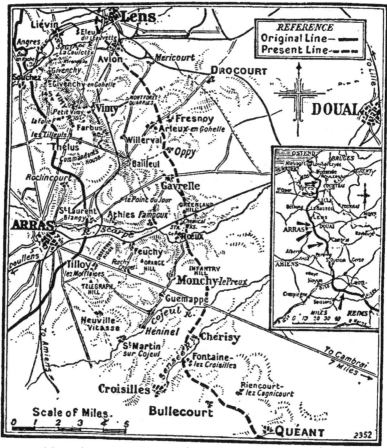

The British Salient at Arras and the Lines before and after the Spring Battles
of April 9 to June 5

Scattered everywhere was the litter I 've feebly described, with openings into dugouts which are not safe to investigate, for they may contain anything from bodies to traps as yet unexploded. Most of the craters had standing water in them, but some were dry, and into one of these I climbed down. Among the canteens and food tins and fragments of tools and weapons was a broken stretcher, and alongside of it a British helmet with a through-and-through rifle shot—also stains on the band within to show what happened to the poor chap who now lies buried and unknown in the bottom of the crater in which he had fallen—in all likelihood with the load he was helping to carry. At one place we came upon some rough graves marked C.D. 24, probably the 24th Canadians, but burials for the most part must have been shallow—often enough in holes already made.

We finally picked our way back over the long slope to our car, and then south along the former Lens–Arras road to the old line near Écurie, where we crossed the famous labyrinth and worked our way back toward Neuville-St. Vaast, of which, needless to say, little remains standing—for it too was in the path of the cyclone. Among the ruins we came on a field ambulance, in front of which flower beds had been planted with the "9th Canadian" outlined among them in whitewashed stones.

They were "taking in," and when we asked for the C.O. someone pointed to a hole in the ground among the ruins embanked by sandbags. Down this we went through a cellar, once part of an old brewery, and into a subcellar, where by the light of a candle a cheery person was found who said he was Charles N. Vipond, a McGill classmate of Patterson's. He showed us about through the amazing subterranean chambers constructed by the Boches before the battle of the Somme, I believe. Here in the dark the stretcher cases are stored on shelves, layer by layer, until they can be evacuated after a bad "strafing."

We finally got back to the road roughly parallel to the line and retraced our steps from La Targette toward Souchez, to pick up "Davy's" car, which was to meet us there. And such a road! There were entrances of dugouts everywhere along the eastern bank, many of course still inhabited, also rows of 9.2″ gun emplacements with the beasts in position, camouflaged with paint, and partly concealed under loosely woven wire screens entangled with shreds of cloth the color of the soil. Hollow observation towers stood among fallen trees, and not until they were pointed out did I recognize them for what they were. From the stumps of such splintered roadside trees as were still standing, shreds of brown burlap fluttered—relics of a screen to conceal the movement of troops or lorries along this important road which was in plain sight from the ridge.

In a thistle field we ate our lunch of oranges and sandwiches, and then up on the ridge again—this time through Thélus, of which no stone stands on another, and where we saw more big British guns badly damaged and not yet removed. We soon stumbled on a No. 3 Field Ambulance flag in front of an embanked and sand-bagged hole with precipitous steps leading down—I counted 40 to the first landing—Lord help the stretcher-bearers!—and we felt our way in with lighted matches and discovered a sleepy orderly, who showed us the chamber where first-aid is given—also the old Boche diverticula not yet investigated, and more or less fallen in or blown up—perhaps not very safe, for they had a way of leaving mine traps in these places when driven out.

And so on to the Thélus part of the ridge, where we expected to find the great underground caverns. First we came to the openings of some large, heavily concreted German gun emplacements, with their dugouts and ammunition pits behind them in what once was a beech wood stretching down the eastern slope. On the stump of an old gray beech with about a three-foot bole, initials and hearts had been cut, as on beech trees everywhere, but there were different kinds of scars now—and in one of them was wedged irremovably the round top of a German food tin with the label still adherent.

The British artillery must have located these guns, for the massive emplacements, heavily sodded over, were badly smashed up, and the piles of ammunition behind were tumbled about in every direction. They were evidently field pieces—77's—for the shells were all in the familiar baskets we used to see in Paris on people's mantels—three shells to a basket. There were hundreds of them sheltered behind each emplacement—their paper tags still on them: "Kleine Ladung" in pink and "Nur Az" in larger letters

on a larger label. A little farther down the slope, 50 yards perhaps behind the guns, were the German dugouts with some dirty
uniforms lying about as though they were still inhabited—and so
they were, for suddenly a Tommy gunner's head popped out of
one of the holes where he had come in turn to make his own nest.

The view was even better than in the morning, and beyond
ruined Farbus we could see Willerval, where the line now is, and
what we took for Fresnoy in the plain beyond. The plateau of the
ridge was pocked with craters and we chanced upon the dugout of
a lean gunner colonel, the color of the earth—an Irishman—very
voluble—very glad to have a chance to talk to someone—and particularly to grouse, which he did cheerily. Did n't want to complain of course, but had n't been on a rest billet except for 13 days
for twelve months. Now living like a rat in a hole off an old German trench—very unhealthy place. "Lice?" "No, shells; they
strafe us every day. Come in and have a drink." We found one
small cave inhabited by a few British gunners, but did not locate
the larger ones, regarding the exact situation of which the Tommies showed their usual vagueness of place, distance, and direction. No one seemed to want to come above ground; and indeed
up on the plateau no one but ourselves was to be seen.

And so back across the labyrinth country, passing the largest
mine craters we had seen—fully 60 feet in diameter. One of them
had the remains of a sandbag parapet and trench on each side east
and west, with communication trenches leading up to them. The
combatants must have looked into one another's very faces across
the space.

At the famous "aux Rietz" corner we again picked up our car
and proceeded along the highway toward Arras, through a country
packed with everything conceivable pertaining to war, past every
kind of gun and lorry—some with wireless installations, others
with carrier-pigeon lofts on them; the eastern side of the road
lined again with the sandbagged entrances to dugouts, past huge
camps of soldiers and A.S.C. men—a jumble. At St. Catherine,
on the outskirts of Arras, we stopped at a field ambulance in an
old, much shelled maltery. Col. Bewley—the divisional A.D.M.S.,
and doing the best job in the army according to "Davy"—happened to be there and showed us about. It was he who brought

The Ancient Hôtel de Ville and Old Spanish Houses on the Petite Place at
Arras before the War and Three Years Later

Gen. Congreve over to No. 19 at Agnez last Tuesday to have his forearm amputated.

Col. Bewley insisted on showing us his ambulance, and then took us to tea at No. 39's mess, which we found after dropping into an unexpected cellar through a trapdoor on which was the following inscription:—

NO!!

WE DON'T KNOW

WHERE YOUR UNIT IS

BUT THE TOWN

MAYOR

DOES

This sign to keep off intruders had little effect, for at least three officers broke in while we were "teaing," to ask their way—and usually failed to close the trapdoor, which made the company grouse, for a cloud of dust blew in on the tea and least popular form of jam—apricot. In this subterranean messroom was a beautifully carved inlaid and gilded sideboard of about Louis XV time, and I recall, on passing openings in other dugouts along the road, seeing once-handsome sofas and upholstered chairs, usually with splinted and bandaged legs and arms, to be sure. Why not, for the houses they have come from have since vanished.

Having thus looked first behind the curtain, we then went through Arras itself—more badly damaged than one would surmise from a distance, though the massive cathedral with its collapsed roof and ruined tower—little more than a great mound of rubble—can be seen for miles. Heaven only knows how often Arras-on-the-Scarpe has been laid waste and ravaged by vandals in bygone times, or how many treaties have been signed here or how many elaborate tapestries—perhaps after Jean Foucquet's actual designs—were woven here in the fifteenth century and scattered throughout Europe. Certainly it could never have been so hard hit before, yet I suppose a new Arras will inevitably arise on the ruins, and that these two recent years of incessant bombard_ ment will simply fade into past history.

So back to Hesdin, dropping "Davy" with regrets at St. Pol on the way; and subsequently a luxurious hot bath in a rubber foot tub, a pleasant dinner in agreeable company, and early to bed.

Anxious to see for himself in what condition the wounded have reached the Base, Bowlby brought me back in his car this morning. We made a detour via the Abbeville road to get a glimpse of Crécy, with the Fôret de Crécy beyond. In the little town itself we saw the old unexplained Spanish monument and one or two newer shafts; and finally with the aid of two sous and a small boy, who climbed on the running board, we drove off to the south for a kilometre or so and found the old weather-beaten granite cross with some lines from Froissart cut in below, and this inscription:—

> *Cette Croix rappelle la fin héroique de Jean*
> *de Luxembourg Roi de Bohème mort pour la*
> *France. Le 26 Aout* 1346

The blind John of Bohemia was one of eleven princes killed on that day, and it was his feathers that Edward the Black Prince, who commanded a division of the English, adopted as the Prince of Wales's emblem.

Then on to Douriez and along the valley of the Authie to Roussent, whence, by a lovely, little traveled road east of the main highway, north to Montreuil and to Étaples, where fresh vegetables are purchased for the mess; and so home—for my tent in our shabby old camp really has become "home." The 1000 or so admissions during the week have been well cared for by the Unit, and Sir Anthony is gratified with the appearance of the men and their dressings as sent down from the forward C.C.S.'s which he supervises.

CAMP LIFE AT CAMIERS

Friday, June 15, 1917. Camiers

A convoy early this morning—as usual, about 1 a.m. Fitz handled them well. It's been very hot—a good thing we have no thermometer. Fortunately the nights are better. It's also very dry. Young Captain Graham has just been here from his present quarters at No. 26 General, near Étaples. Wanted to see how the flowers he'd planted last spring around the ditch encircling his— now my—conical tent were getting on.

There is quite a showing of bright blossoms which he calls Virginia stock, among them some little blue nemophilas. Just behind these a few patches of scarlet Linum, if that 's the way to spell it, and a few ditto of dwarf (very) nasturtiums. Then come in turn a row of scarlet godetias, a few Shirley poppies, a thin line of mignonette, and at each corner some sweet peas now about eight inches high, but which (he assures me) are to be very wonderful —Queen Alexandra, Duke of Westminster, Lord Nelson in flesh tints, and some other lord or lady I disremember. All this from a circular mound of clay a foot wide around the tent, with occasional bamboo poles awaiting the peas.

We Americans are too new at soldiering to see the importance of such things, and poor Graham looked sadly at the little market garden beside the mess hut which had not been weeded since we took it over, and where parsnips, radishes, and carrots about two inches high are concealed by weeds of six. This is the way races overgrow one another—the more undesirable, the deeper they root —and I wonder what will happen here at the end of this blooming war. Talk of our American melting pot! For here are Annamites and Egyptians, Zulus and Kaffir laborers, Chinese coolies, Algerians and Indians—at least there once were. The labor battalions must far outnumber the male natives—certainly the breeding natives—and the women, it seems, are none too moral or fastidious. Well! I 'd rather think of Graham and his flowers. Scarlet pimpernels grow everywhere hereabouts. They, at least, breed true.

Sunday p.m., and stifling hot. The larks like it, however, and they are singing madly. Been tacking some oilcloth, which Harry Lyman has procured, on my packing-box washstand and dresser. Very fine. The Boston tins, too, are well adapted for compartments in one's dresser. Butler, my batman, seems to take an interest, though just why I do not know, except that these Britishers of the lower classes make extraordinarily good servants. He came out with the 2nd Army in 1915, was wounded at Loos, in hospital eight months with a badly shattered arm—fortunately left. Now he is P.B., which, opened out, means "Permanent Base"—in other words, unfit for any other duties than at the Base. He might have been T.B. ("Temporary Base") or even P.I. or dead. So Butler, after all, is lucky—so am I.

Our neighbors at No. 22 under Hugh Cabot are a festive lot

and, having unoccupied territory in their environs, play baseball vigorously once or twice a week—an open challenge. Yesterday some gunners from the training camp (infantry) at Hardelot, between here and Boulogne, accepted the challenge and were sadly beaten.

Monday, June 18

Disciplinary court session—wards—operating. Private Ford- ham and his brain abscess. Much about delayed tetanus, of which we have four cases. Some of the boys skeptical. Colonel Lister, the eye specialist, to tea. Says there are an immense number (2000?) totally blind among the Italian troops—shells dropping on hard rock send off myriads of fine particles. Sandbags, of course, have the same effect everywhere. Sand blown right through lids—and the globes are burst.

Wednesday, the 20th

Difficulties with the electric current, which we can only use by courtesy of No. 18. It went off duty just as I had a nail in Ford- ham's abscess and was about to connect with the magnet.

Thursday, the 21st

Succeeded in getting the piece of shell three inches deep in Fordham's brain. Hope the principle of "fixing" the abscess cav- ity a possible one. Rose Bradford—the Base Medical Consultant —here in p.m., and cheered the internists greatly. This old en- campment is infested with rats. Accordingly the gunners—they seem to be the most resourceful people hereabouts—appear with three yellow ferrets, a sheep dog, and many clubs. One rat secured, I believe. The British soldier dotes on a sporting event.

Friday, the 22nd

One of the many things I have to learn is how to get out of a tightly buttoned-up bell tent when the ropes are soggy and shrunken after a night's rain. I can manage the underwear, but the outer layer from inside beats me after one's batman has but- toned and laced it up securely from outside during the storm. Ligation of vertebral artery for traumatic aneurysm.

Wednesday, June 27

6 *p.m.* Hot. S.I.T.[1] Major Goodwill, U.S.R., here to-day in a large motor car talking copiously of "reconstruction"—must or-

[1]Sulking in tent.

ganize our American medical forces on the basis of reconstruction —going home Saturday to see Gorgas about it before be gets organized on some other basis. G. is a fine chap, though visionary. He came down to earth for a moment, in order to enter the slit in my palatial abode. In this process he observed that my garden needed weeding, and, stooping casually, pulled three varieties of weeds. I have long known it needed weeding, but as I could n't tell the dwarf nasturtiums from French weeds (though I am studying "French self-taught with phonetic pronunciation" while I shave in the morning) I did n't dare try any reconstruction business on my own hook. This is bad, too, because Graham cycles over twice a week from Étaples to see how "they" are getting on, and looks rather sad.

I therefore surreptitiously preserved the three samples of G.'s weeding and put them away where "P.B." Butler could n't find them. With the aid of these specimens, I have just weeded my southeast quadrant and it 's quite wonderful. To-morrow for the northeast; and I hope Graham will come over in the evening. I shall pretend that it was the first opportunity I have had to do any redding up. There 's nothing but clay southwest and north-west—not even weeds.

We have a new D.O.R.E. in our district—Colonel Kitto. The R.E. is easy—*viz.*, Royal Engineers—but D.O. beats me as yet. Anyhow, he is an important person to cultivate, particularly when you want to get the roof of the mess hut retarred, some linoleum on the floor, another electric light, and the kitchen made dust- and water-tight.

To No. 26 with Graham—a fine new layout all in huts! A special ward with a laboratory—heavy accent on the first *o*, please —in charge of Bashford. Great opportunity for work. B. doing some interesting things with Carrel-Dakin fluid on pollywogs. Very simple way of determining the relative bactericidal powers of different fluids.

.   *Sunday, July 1*

Much rain the past few days, leaving us in a sea of mud, which possibly accounts for my state of mind. We have learned from the Canadians that we have been given the poorest place for a hospital in France. So bad it was, even two years ago, that the McGill

Unit, who were then here, refused to "carry on" and were removed to the heights above Boulogne. It has since led a hand-to-
mouth existence and become much deteriorated. It was offered to
the Engineers, who said it might do for a hospital, but not for
them. We 've been at it a month now, and aside from the C.O.'s
justifiable grumbles about the water and milk and sump pits and
sanitation in general, I 've heard no complaints.

We were organized by the Red Cross for a 500-bed base hospital. We at this date have 1876 patients in our marquees, and during
the month 3000 have passed through our hands. Our Red Cross
equipment has never been received [it was subsequently sent off
to Halifax after the disaster there] and we are obliged to borrow
a motor ambulance to do our marketing.

All this has been taken in the day's work, but it seems time now
to find out what we are to look forward to—either remaining here
with the B.E.F. for "duration" and spending our company fund
to make the place habitable, or carrying on as best we can "as is,"
with the expectation of being transferred to the A.E.F. Meanwhile
our flags, so movingly consecrated by Bishop Lawrence, have
scarcely been out of their rubber cases since we left Fort Totten.
I wish the nurses and men were equally well protected from the
cold and wet.

Tuesday, July 3rd

George Denny, Chairman of the Laundry Committee, squares
himself by pinning notices on our bulletin board. I regret not having copied the earlier ones. To-day as follows—with an empty
match box tacked on below:—

LAUNDRY. Persons receiving articles in their wash of unknown origin
will kindly place them in this box. Honesty is the best policy, and by means
of the box method all hard feelings will be wiped out and each can receive
his own goods through an excellent clearing house system. I am counting
on the purity of soul of the command to make the idea efficient.

G. P. DENNY, L.C.

To-night a sock with many holes was draped over the box.

Yesterday a visit from Colonel Leishman on my solicitation,
concerning a mortuary; he brought with him a high-up sanitary
officer with many service ribbons and much gold braid. The belligerent Patterson was away, taking a French lesson, which was per-

July 4, 1917. In the Court of Les Invalides after the Desce
Officers Who Had Served with Lafayette Had Presented General
with the "Guidons de Commandement"

A Few Decorated Doughboys on Guard Outside the Picpus Cemetery
during the Ceremonies

haps just as well, for though I did not know the whereabouts of the sump pits—old and new—I *could* tell the general story of our unsanitary compound. Was it worth while, in short, to spend more money on an admittedly poor camp? We had tea, and I atoned later, I hope, for plain speech. As a result the local D.D.M.S. spent most of this morning here with our C.O. looking the ground over.

July 4, 1917

Vive l'Amérique! An historic day to have arrived in Paris— though a bad one for my particular quest on this very account. After a real bath at the Crillon, I met the Strongs hustling about —must go immediately to Les Invalides—they have tickets— special seats—Pershing—American troops—Fourth of July— punctually at nine—great doings, and so forth. So, breakfastless, I joined them and we rushed off in a decrepit taxi, but soon became so mixed up in the crowd we never got to our seats—merely saw between people's heads the bayonets of our boys squared up in the inner court. The corridors were jammed with *poilus* and others, frantically cheering while General Pershing received two banners from the descendants of men who had fought with La-fayette.

I escaped back to breakfast and was just opening an egg when they came marching across the Place de la Concorde—about a battalion, I should think, of not especially well-set-up or well-drilled troops—newly enlisted men of the 16th Infantry, I believe —marching in squads.

I left the egg and joined the excited populace, which was fairly mobbing the men, covering them with flowers—quite thrilling. In the midst of it all a daring aviator swooped into the square— down, it seemed, almost to the people's heads, certainly below the level of the obelisk—turned corners standing on one wing, then on the other—rose again, dived down and up once more—looped the loop once or twice—then climbed up and was away to the south. A most daredevil, Gallic performance. Guynemer, they said it was—an ace—many German planes to his credit—in a new His-pano-Suiza machine capable of 200 km. an hour. Sounds fast— especially the Suiza.

I walked back to the Crillon wondering about my egg, when

some American Ambulance people were encountered—a Mr. Williams, an *auxiliaire* named Mrs. Rhodes, and a newly arrived Mr. Turnbull of New York—who insisted that I go with them to the ceremony at the Picpus. The cemetery where Lafayette is buried is in a remote part of Paris, and we reached there some half hour before the battalion arrived. Though allowed in the churchyard, we were held up at the entrance to the small enclosure where is Lafayette's tomb, surrounded by an old crumbling wall about ten feet or so in height.

We waited while many pundits were shown through the gate; and, having had our offer to go through in company with them politely refused once or twice, we stood wondering what to do. Others, many of them in fact, were in the same boat, and we kept encountering folks like Major Parsons of the Engineers and his wife who shared our ambition. At this juncture various kinds of people—newspaper photographers, some *blessés* (not very *blessé*), and some French people of neither military age nor military sex —began to scale the wall with the aid of a ladder procured from somewhere.

A Frenchwoman, well astride, beckoned to Mrs. Rhodes that there was room beside her, and up she went without a moment's hesitation. So I followed and straddled the wall between a Moroccan *petit-officier* covered with medals and an oldish man who said he was a Belgian from Dixmude. This was a Humpty-Dumpty performance, but we had the best possible view of the ceremonies below us and hope we were not in range of the movie cameras going off like a barrage on all sides.

Many dignitaries were grouped about the tomb, "Papa" Joffre among them, and I may add that he had to be pushed forward into the front row, for, though he has been kicked upstairs by an unappreciative government, the people still adore him. Mr. Sharp spoke at length. Brand Whitlock read at still greater length many pages about civilization and humanity—very immaculate, in eyeglasses with a heavy black braid and in spats—both the speech and B.W. Then Colonel Stanton, U.S.A., brief and to the point. Finally *le Général* Pershing *s'avance à la tribune* "without the intention of speaking"; but he did, briefly—a fine-looking man with a square chin and proper shoulders. He may have said, *"Lafayette, nous voici,"* but if so we did n't hear it on the wall. Then followed more in French by M. Painlevé, Minister of War, concerning *"les deux peuples unis par le même idéal"*; and finally the Mayor of Puy wound up with an *hommage* or something of the sort to Lafayette. Thereupon we climbed down, or rather fell off, into the cabbage garden on the side we had ascended, and took our way back to the Crillon, seeing the flower-bedecked battalion pass by with their escort of French cavalry.

Then lunch and to business—my two Paris quests being (1) to find out what, if anything, the U.S. Army Medical Corps has in store for us, and (2) to secure a motor car of whatsoever sort for the use of Base Hospital No. 5. On the way to quest 1, met Robert Bacon by chance. Long talk with him about the general situation, on our way to the temporary U.S.A. headquarters; but 27 rue Constantine proves no place for a major—crowd there already—everyone trying to get something he wants—most of them out-ranking me.

Quiet dinner with the Blisses. They have had a strenuous time these past two years. It 's fortunate two people so popular and so conversant with French should have been at the Embassy. R.B. tells an interesting story of the two Wilson notes of last December. The first of them transmitted the German proposal for peace, and, the Ambassador being away, R.B. had to present it himself. A few days later came Wilson's famous communication to both combatants asking what they meant by the war anyway and what their objectives were—so far as he could see they were very much alike on both sides—or something of this sort. So it at least sounded to most of us at home.

Mrs. B. had been at the Chambres des Députés in the afternoon to hear the discussion regarding the German proposals, and the statement had been made there that the Allies would transmit their terms on the following day to the Central Powers through Mr. Wilson. This news she promptly telephoned to the Embassy, where they were in process of decoding the President's second note, which threw an entirely different light on the matter. Consequently R.B. thought it was absolutely essential—as soon as they got the drift of the note late in the afternoon—that the fact of its reception and general tenor should promptly be made known to the Foreign Office. In the Ambassador's absence he had to make this decision himself, and so he took it to Cambon. Cambon was quite thunderstruck and called in Briand. Both of them purple in the face—simply furious. Wilson on the side of the Germans —playing into their hands from the outset—Wilson a *mufle*. The only way they could be pacified was to explain that, while the message had not as yet been fully decoded, it seemed necessary that they should be made aware of its having been received. All told, a very trying time, and truly we had no friends anywhere.

Mrs. B. a trump—will help us get our needed transportation in the shape of a Ford ambulance with French trimmings—in fact through Richard Norton has already taken steps in this direction; and if she succeeds we had better be prepared to motor it back to Camiers instanter, before someone else gets hold of it.

Paris, July 6

People simply running around in circles here. Newly appointed officials arriving and the old volunteer organizations wholly disregarded. American Ambulance and Field Service people in a predicament—much agitated to know what will happen to them and rather inclined to remain with the Service de Santé. Found I could do nothing at 21 rue Raynouard in Passy;[1] but at the Ambulance later Mrs. Vanderbilt said she would give us one of her own cars if necessary. Col. Kean, late military director of the Red Cross, now in charge of U.S.A. motor ambulance services in France and the Norton-Harjes Formation (Section Sanitaire No. 5), likely to be disbanded. Richard Norton's despair over this was what gave us our chance. In another 24 hours we would never have squeezed a car out of the American Army. Telegraphed the D.D.M.S. at Étaples begging him to dispatch someone from No. 11 General to help bring back a motor ambulance.

American Red Cross at 5 rue François Premier getting a vast organization started under Jim Perkins, who was very kind; but the place was full of people, all of whom want something. Find I can do much better at the soon-to-be-abandoned American Clearing House, where Geoffrey Dodge and Russell Greeley promise to load our car with all manner of things we greatly need—from

[1] This was the private park of the Hottinguer family where, after July 1916, the American Field Ambulance had its headquarters.

needles and thread to warm woollies and matador stoves, cached in the Distributing Service Warehouse. George Derby arrives, and together we go to the garage at 79 rue Longier, where—we can hardly believe our eyes!—was a *ciel-bleu* Ford ambulance of latest model—the French Army number 44970 painted on its side with the usual "*4 assis: 3 couchés*"—also "*U.S. Army Base Hospital No. 5,*" black on a white background, and "*American Red Cross Ambulance*" along the bottom—heavy studded tires already on, her tank full of *essence*. And when we were then given, not only an official *Ordre de Mission* signed and dated, but also four booklets marked, "*Livret Matricule de Véhicule Automobile,*" on which we could draw for "*Essence et Ingrédients, Pneumatiques et Chambres à Air, Aménagements, Accessoires, Outillage et Rechange,*" at any French Military Park—our sensations were indescribable! We had been in the nick of time. What a welcome awaits us when we reach No. 11 General actually in our own car packed solid with much needed supplies. . . .

Wednesday, July 11th

Very busy two days. Evident wholesale evacuation of C.C.S.'s. A number of bad cases sent down. To my lot fell an aneurysm of the right carotid with left hemiplegia and pressure signs. A ligation under local anæsthesia stopped the aneurysm but did not improve his intracranial condition, and he died in the night.

Many official visitors. They are becoming concerned about us. "Tiger" Macpherson from G.H.Q. here with Colonel Carr. Tells us we can be transferred to No. 13 General in Boulogne if we so desire. The D.O.R.E. came in person to discuss our repeated request for repairs—three husky Tommies have taken a week to cover part of the messroom with burlap, with no underlying tar paper, so the dust comes in just the same. Another pair have taken two days in the attempt to cover a filthy screen, and finally gave it up.

An embarrassing episode in regard to our quixotic pledge which many men, and one officer, alas! have broken. We face it, and publicly call off the pledge before the men, though the mess is to remain dry, and I think most of us in it. The Kaffirs have been moved, and we are to be given their small compound—I hoped for a playground, but the Padre has already planted a recreation tent in the middle of the small lot.

Thursday the 12th

The pessimistic liaison officer's expectation of the Russians has come true. Halicz has fallen to General Korniloff in the course of a surprising advance of fifteen miles, with many prisoners and guns. Meanwhile it is rumored that the British in their new territory by the sea have had a mishap and been driven back to and across the Yser.[1] Strategic positions lost; and a whole battalion that was cut off by destruction of the bridges with shellfire was captured. A British officer tells me this is merely a tap on the nose received early in the bout.

Towne and I, with Miss Gerrard the anæsthetist and Pte. Clifford, constituting a "team," have been ordered to get our gas masks and helmets. We were put through the gas chamber this afternoon at the machine gunners' camp, while some tear gas was tried on us. Very disagreeable and suffocating. How anyone can sleep in the things beats me.

Sunday, July 15

Yesterday morning largely passed at Étaples, getting some peculiar supplies from the Medical Stores: e.g., asphalt, tar, beeswax (flav. and alb.), paraffin, and from No. 51 two guinea pigs. Guinea pigs are scarcer than rabbits, and Robertson, who has found some spirochetes in the urine of two trench-fever cases, simply *must* have them. They cost—approximately—a guinea apiece in the London market. At No. 51 they use two a week for their Wassermann reactions. They have about three left, and Robertson accepts from Major Wetherell the best two, with thanks, and they get covered with tar on the way home, having been put in the same receptacle with this substance. Robby transfers most of it to his uniform in the process of rescue.

To-day a visit at No. 26 to see Bashford about Dakin's dichloramine T preparations. Some very encouraging results by Morrison, with closure of large wounds by secondary suture. Explain my plans of combined paraffin treatment. Try a case with Harvey this afternoon—very septic compound fracture of lower leg. Serious air raids over London of late—the full details just coming out—together with an unrivaled specimen of the new sacred poetry of the Boche:—

---

[1] Fritz apparently struck just as the French were withdrawing and before the British had brought up their guns—rather poor teamwork—the first of the ill-luck series of events which subsequently hampered the British operations at Passchendaele.

Base Hospital No. 5 (No. 11 General, B.E.F.)   Portland Cement Works   No 22 General, B E F

Looking down from the Chalk Ridges on the Dannes-Camiers Hospital Groups.   View toward the Sea

The Queen and "the D.G." Leaving No. 22 General to Visit Base Hospital No. 5.   View toward the Ridges

Du der über Cherubinen,
Seraphinen, Zeppelinen,
In der höchsten Höhe tronest.

Monday, July 16th

10 p.m. R.B.O. and I have just climbed the hill to see the sunset over the distant sea. Very beautiful it was. Some Tommies up there shooting rabbits: also a few V.A.D.'s and gunner officers somewhat more interested in themselves than in the color of the sky or the rabbits. This at the end of a long day's trip in company with Roger Lee, Harmon, and the piratical D.D.M.S. of Étaples —to visit the camp site near St. Omer, offered to us as an alternative to No. 13 at Boulogne.

We reached Hesdin in time to lunch with General Sloggett and his staff, including "Tiger Mac." The D.G. described his recent tour with the Queen and her party—very enjoyable—"they like people to *be* like people." He says she is shy: so I retract what I said about her stiffness. They took all their meals together like ordinary folk. "Mary" very much gratified with the reception given her everywhere by the French people. Sir Arthur adds that the Prince is a little brick—"dear boy"—alert, interesting, lovable —wants to get into the trenches with the others. "Why not?" says he. "I have plenty of brothers." They evidently struck up a warm friendship.

I gathered that the D.G. and General Macpherson would like us to take on this new project—St. Omer to become a large hospital centre—ours, if we accept the offer, to be geographically the most advanced general hospital in France—largely for acute sick, cranial wounds, and fractured femurs. Also such other cases as we wish to work upon. Three other hospitals already there—No. 7 for shell shock, etc., Nos. 58 and 59, which are new territorial hospitals; also three stationary hospitals—No. 4 for eye, dental, cutaneous, etc., cases, No. 10 General and No. 7 Canadian, where wounded and sick prisoners are taken.

On reaching St. Omer we picked up Major Prynne, recently D.O.R.E. at Camiers, who took us out to the site—alas, nothing yet *but* a site—with a few Boche prisoners carrying some pipes across a field preparatory to laying a drain. Still, it 's a lovely spot —-an unpretentious French château in a small but charming park— an old wall covered with roses, a pretty wood with big trees, ferns, birds, and flowers, and a large field beyond. Very fine on a sunny day like to-day. But it would take six months at least to do anything with it; and the prospect of a winter passed in tents, even if better than what we now have, does not strike Roger or Harmon very favorably. For myself I should have liked to tackle the job and spend some of our company fund on it. After all, what 's a few months? The alternative is to turn No. 13 out, and they will have to find some other place. "Cuckoos" is a name given to an Irish Medical Unit that kept turning people out of their nests.

We stopped for a brief spell at the large aerodrome near St. Omer and saw a veritable flock of planes in the air. Then back home via Desvres and Samer—the country beautiful beyond words and the crops all very fine—just enough rain for them to swell before ripening. Harmon was greatly excited by our trip—his first away from Camiers—but had no idea where we were until we reached Neufchâtel and came in sight of the C.H.D.A.V.C.— Convalescent Horse Depot of the Army Veterinary Corps. Of course if this should ever become known to the enemy it might be serious, for war is a matter of secrecy and concealment, and no German could possibly have guessed what all these initials stood for unless I wrote it out.

Tuesday, July 17th

It 's extraordinary that our Harvard juniors at No. 22 General across the way, being enrolled as an R.A.M.C. unit, are using volunteer Americans as V.A.D.'s, whereas we, an undermanned U.S. Army outfit, must use British V.A.D.'s, of whom we have about 50, and are neither permitted to send for our officially enrolled Nurses' Aids from Boston, nor to gather in those who happen to apply to us. Wm. R. Castle of the Red Cross has just been here on his way home, and we have been urging him to plead with Washington that they be sent over.

This morning at No. 26 in Étaples trying out some wax moulds on a large recent through-and-through wound of the buttock. A great deal to learn about it yet. Bashford much interested—a good man, but a little too fond of scotching persons and things. He has scotched Sir Almroth, for example, and says the only difference between Wright and wrong lies in the matter of the *W*. He is now busily scotching flavine, and this ought to be an easier job. As I surmised, the stuff seems to act by merely necrosing the surface of the wound like any fixative.

Our first weekly lecture to the enlisted men fell to my lot—a general talk on the story of military medicine—the earlier wars on our present "terrain"—the existing medico-military problems and how they are being met.

Wednesday, July 18th

A strange lot of people one sees about here. Last evening as I was talking to the men in their mess hut at the back of the camp, a passing train gave its peculiar penetrating French squeal, and I looked out to see a long line of slowly moving boxcars of the cattle variety simply packed with grinning and gesticulating Chinese coolies—big fellows with their blue shirts open, showing their naked chests—going north, I may add.

To-day at lunch a shy, unprepossessing young New Zealander lieutenant—sent down here to see the N.Z. wounded, of whom we have a number. I was talking with Roger about the mysterious new gas cases and paid little attention to him, I fear, leaving this to the Adjutant, who had brought him in. I 'm sorry I missed any of it, for it was a story beyond any of Boyd Cable's I 've happened to read. I got in only at the end—very simply and quietly told. The Australians had had a disastrous bombing raid planned on an extensive scale—when they got over their parapet and near enough to do business with their bombs none of them exploded—they had been dealt out to them without detonators! Well, they left 1500 dead in No Man's Land before they got back. The New Zea_ landers had to take over their sector, and here our young friend enters in. He was selected to take out a patrol the next night to get information—his first experience of the sort. You can imagine the rest—crawling about in the mud among the wires—the impos_ sibility of telling whether a body was a dead Australian or a live Hun out on the same mission as yourself. Rather got on their nerves. I remember his saying that even the barbed-wire posts came to look so much like men if you stared at them long enough that they would appear to line up in columns of four. Another aneurysm operation this morning—anterior tibial. Also Summary Court after lunch. I personally have more bench than table work. Harry Forbes back from Paris with eight guinea pigs, so Robby

returns the two tarry ones and proffers one of our handsome eight.
This they refuse, though appreciating our generosity.

Friday, July 20th. 10 p.m.

Friends at home are laboring under the delusion that we are
subjected to all manner of privations out here, and quote an article
in the *N. Y. Times* which states that we are enduring hardships
untold. Life is simple, to be sure. Some of the rations, like the
Maconochie stew, are not particularly appetizing, and sugar as such
—on the ear, so to speak—is scarce. There is plenty of it, however,
in other forms. For example, in addition to marmalade, there is a
ration outwardly resembling honey, but which is n't, and goes by
the name of "the golden goo." Some take it on their porridge in
the morning. Others go without porridge. If anyone reaches out
for the sugar bowl unconsciously, H. Lyman, our economical mess
officer, sets up a howl. Indeed he went so far this morning as to
use it—the goo—in his coffee, and assumed a sort of "the water 's
fine" expression—indeed took two cups. No one followed suit.

Said the Tommy to his corporal, making a wry face, "That tea
tastes funny." "Then why don't you laugh?" comes the peevish
retort.

Still, our coffee is good, though expensive, for we import it from
London, and cans of condensed milk occasionally reach us from
home in precious individual boxes holding a miscellany from tooth
paste and a much needed cake of soap to blocks of maple sugar—
which we might use on our porridge. Then when it 's pleasant, as
it has been to-day, living in a bell tent and working in open
marquees is a tolerable kind of summer outing. And when it grows
damp and cold in the evening, there is a large gray *"robe de
chambre chaude"* brought back from Paris, some warm Jaeger bed
socks and pyjamas sent by Lady Osler, three heavy army blankets
from Mrs. Slater, a folding candle lantern from another unfail-
ing source of supplies, yesterday's London *Times,* some sweet-
smelling Virginia stock planted by your predecessor around your
tent, soaring larks trilling overhead—and what more could you
want?

Meanwhile a tennis tournament is going on, in which Horrax
and Miss Cunningham promise to carry off the Camiers honors,
ball games are frequent, lectures still more so. This week, for

example, at 8.30 at the Camiers Y.M.C.A. hut (I copy from our bulletin board):—

Tuesday—The 19th Ordnance Depot Concert Party
Wednesday—Lecture by J. Holland Rose, on "The Crisis of 1914"
Thursday—Dramatic Performance: "Waterloo" and "Phipps"
Friday—Lecture by Prof. Perkins: "The Story of Bagdad"

All this "for Sisters and Officers," and those who managed to attend were doubtless edified. For the men there are entertainments equally plentiful, and our Padre has things going on in our newly established recreation tent. Then, too, there are places to go and dine if you care to walk or cycle to them—at Hardelot, Camiers, Paris-Plage, and elsewhere. But even for those who mostly spend their days uninterruptedly in camp there is no chance for boredom. Indeed, I have never seen time go so rapidly, never found it more difficult to go to bed, never slept more soundly when once there.

We had our regular weekly Medical Meeting this afternoon— I have never attended a better one anywhere. Our patients are down to about 900, the lowest they have been, but there is a constant succession of new and interesting things. Osgood showed some ingenious splints he had devised, by bending the standard Thomas units which are supplied to us; Derby, some rare eye conditions; Denny, some examples of contralateral collapse of the lungs after thoracic wounds; Binney an interesting functional disturbance, involving movements and speech, in a man who had been buried. Towne, on gas-bacillus infections; and finally Lee on his original observations upon the effects of the new and unknown gas which Fritz has been throwing over well back of our lines. A characteristic œdema of the larynx and conjunctivæ, which comes on late, and, most striking of all, the remarkable cutaneous manifestations with great patches of purple pigmentation, which seem to come out wherever there has been any external pressure, as from a belt. One boy, a Singhalese soldier by the way, had a most extraordinary widespread purpuric erythema. Quite a feather in Roger's cap for, in this district at least, he is the first to have observed these things and to have ascribed them to a new form of poison gas.[1] Even Sir John Rose Bradford had never seen them.

[1] This was "mustard gas," as we subsequently learned, first used in large amounts by the Germans on the night of July 13–14, when it caused 3000 casualties, and again on July 21st, when there were 4000.

Apparently the gas is comparatively odorless and sent over in shells; the symptoms do not appear until after quite an interval.

So much time was given to these things that Robertson's studies of P.U.O. had to hold over till next time. He has been finding spirochetes pretty regularly, and now with a generous supply of guinea pigs from our Red Cross and two ounces of glycerine— possibly the most difficult thing to find in Europe outside of munition plants—for Giemsa stains, he will soon be making progress. Three or four young M.O.R.C., U.S.A., casuals from Boulogne, have been stationed here, waiting to be sent to British battalions at the Front—a ticklish job for a young doctor.

Patterson is back from his examination in Paris, wearing his Lt. Colonel silver leaves, and full of gossip from the capital. Lee wants to know where the rumor factory is located—whether it 's under the regular army or the Red Cross—the *Kansas* sunk, our flotilla with Pershing attacked by submarines, some of which were destroyed by a new mine which is dropped on them and explodes at a great depth. Meantime Bethmann-Hollweg has been dropped by the Kaiser and is succeeded by a Dr. Michaelis, who is saying familiar-sounding things to the press. Our belated home papers read as though the war were nearly over; but it does n't look so to us, and this favorite topic of conversation in America we studiously avoid.

To-night we inaugurated a course of exercises for the orderlies. The Matron began by a simple and much needed demonstration of bed making—I wish my batman could have been there. She dissected and put together again one of these army-hospital iron cots. Unquestionably no expense spared in the materials. The three square hair mattresses are enclosed in a heavy unbleached linen bag. She estimated that they would cost in peace times at least $12 —*circa* $12,000 for this hospital, or $60,000 for the mattresses alone in the five hospitals of this Camiers district.

I began by speaking of our pseudo-privations. We can manage to circumvent the rats and the imperfect drainage and the dark tents; but we can't keep ahead of the holes in our socks. Roger says he favors a purse-string suture and subsequent trimming with curved scissors borrowed from the operating room. Malcolm we find has secretly been making use of the secretaries, but this is a privilege only for Padres. The British War Office should send over a battalion of suffragettes and penalize them with this task, inscribing on their "V. for W." banners something like "Damn the Votes; Darn the Socks"—*pendant la guerre.*

V

THE PASSCHENDAELE BATTLES

Awaiting Zero Hour at 46 C.C.S.

Sunday, July 22nd. Mendinghem

10 p.m. Unexpected things occur over here. My last entry, as I recall it, was about our simple doings at No. 11 General, to which we have become attached and which, according to hearsay, we were soon to leave. The "team" for service in a C.C.S. had been counter-manded and, as we were under orders to evacuate, the wards were growing empty and there was time to study French, play tennis, and to look about at one's neighbors before our transfer to Bou-logne—in a few days, as we supposed! I had been interested in making wax moulds as a soft-tissue splint for large infected wounds, and with Bashford, Morrison, and Hartley, was dressing a case daily at No. 26 in Étaples.

On getting back from there Saturday, I found Sir Anthony Bowlby lunching at our mess and he said our team was to be called on after all—at his special request to go to No. 46—wherever that might be—to help with the head cases during the coming battle. Probably Monday—he was not quite sure. Probably, too, our move to Boulogne would have to be postponed. The present was no time for us to be taking over a new hospital—all beds would be needed.

This did not sound very urgent, and after lunch we looked at cases that interested him in the wards—among them a man with an arteriovenous aneurysm apparently of the subclavian artery and vein, with a greatly dilated right heart; also some of the "new gas" cases, of which he had already seen many—several thousand in fact—and then we went over to see the finals of the tennis match being engineered by Colonel Steele, the C.O. of

No. 4. Miss Cunningham was in the process of mopping up the court with her opponent when one of our sergeants made his way through the crowd and handed me a message stating that our "team" must be ready to leave for the Front at 4 p.m. It was then three minutes to four!

Aware of what was in store for us, at Bowlby's suggestion a request for an extension of time was put through to the D.D.M.S. at Étaples, and after considerable palaver we were given until eight this morning. By that time we had managed to wangle an extra operating table and to assemble some special instruments, a cache of sterile "Boston tins," gas masks, helmets, and baggage rolls holding a folding bed, blankets, canvas bath, bucket, and such—and it 's lucky we stayed to gather them.

Again two females driving a large ambulance, on the side of which was inscribed:—

PRESENTED BY THE TOUNGOO AMBULANCE GIFT FUND
ZEYAWADDY
TOUNGOO DISTRICT BURMA AMBULANCE

This legend I have down accurately, because, on account of it, I was nearly taken up by an M.P. in Poperinghe at 1.30 as a suspicious character. We really should not have been in Poperinghe, for it is an unhealthy place—shelled every day—on the direct road to "Wipers" rather than to our destination. But the females had never been up here—it was only a mile or two out of the way and one of them had a brother in "Pop." So we went that way—had lunch in a Flemish café, Towne and I, Miss Gerrard, Clifford our orderly, and the females—and a good one it was. While they were watering their car in the busy Grande Place I caught sight of the above inscription and pulled out my notebook to copy it. Promptly up whips a British M.P. sergeant who wanted to know what I was writing down. . . .

11.30 p.m. There was good reason for interrupting this tale. The C.O. from No. 64, an energetic young person named Wolstenholme, whose C.C.S. lies beyond the railroad track, had just dropped in—there were two or three of us in the mess hut writing under a feeble lamp—all were newcomers like myself. He was telling how he had seen, this afternoon, a Boche plane attack and "sink" a captive balloon, and be in turn attacked and winged by one of our planes—a tale incited by our hearing some curious explosions which someone said were aeroplanes signaling to their base. Suddenly at this juncture an M.O. hustled in and said, "There 's a Fritz about; they are looking for him"—so we went out—all but our neighboring C.O., who stayed to finish his whiskey. Well, it was an amazing sight—the air simply alive with searchlight beams—then many explosions of Archies—soon the hum of our planes going up, and the Archies ceased—machine-gun fire began up in the air—rat-tat-tat—the wise men of this command all rushed for their helmets, and in about a minute! Well, it sounded as though it were at our very feet—*one, two, three,* and then a fourth shattering explosion, the last one simply ear-splitting, leaving your head humming. Then rat-tat-tat in the air again on all sides—seemingly scores of searchlights crossing and recrossing—the planes flashing signals—how can one possibly describe it at the tail end of such a day?

It was some time before I noticed that two or three of the new Australians and I were the only people left looking on, and that somehow all the lights of the hospital were out. We finally came back in the mess hut, lit a candle, and found the visiting C.O. crawling out from under the table—wise man! Others of the local officers then began to appear, admitting that they had dived under beds or whatever else was handy.

"How far away were those things—about half a mile?" I innocently asked. "Oh, a little closer than that," said the C.O. from No. 64, wiping the dirt from his clothes and mopping up the whiskey he had spilled. In a few minutes Padre Robinson came in with a fragment of the bomb, which he said was warm when he picked it up—notice that he is a Padre—the nearest hole lies just between us and 64, near the railroad track, about 100 yards away.

Midnight. One of the M.O. anæsthetists has just come in and says the explosion broke many windows in the operating room, and they had to finish up with candles. This is evidently a warm corner we 've come into. Word has been passed around that in a few days will come off the biggest battle in history—about half a million troops concentrated in this area. They are after a ridge called Pilkem, about three miles north of "Wipers" and due east of Boesinghe and here. So the major offensive is not to be confined to the coast after all.

I will try and tell to-morrow more of to-day—or rather later to-day more of yesterday. I doubt if I shall sleep much, there's too much noise.

Monday, the 23rd of July

8 a.m. I did n't—not because of the noise (though about three there was some violent strafing, and frequent low-flying planes were disturbing), but because of the cold. These thermic transitions I have not become accustomed to, and there was little under me but a piece of canvas, though plenty of blankets above. At 5 p.m., when we reached here, my tent was suffocatingly hot—at 1 a.m. freezing.

I 've just been over to see the hole—it 's gone—filled up completely, and the bent rail straightened. Just as ants repair a damage to their hill. One bomb fell between us and 64—near the mortuary. The next one fell about 500 yards beyond—on the other side of No. 64 to the disaster of an *estaminet* ("Rest-a-minute"), a house, and some trees. Quite possibly the hospitals were too well lighted and made a good target. Lt. Colonel Young, the Australian, being a souvenir hunter, brings me two large fragments of the beast as keepsakes. It was an interesting reception here, but I hardly care to have it repeated.

6.30 p.m. Somewhat revived by tea, though nearly "done in" after a day's operating. Getting started is very difficult—learning other people's ways, how they clean up, what sort of gowns are available, how many towels one may use, how dependable are the X-ray, the ether, etc. One very bad case this afternoon which I tried to do with about 50 people looking on. Horrid, this having to operate in one's clothes, encased in a rubber apron, in a Nisson hut with the temperature about 85°F.

To go back to yesterday's departure from Camiers:—

Our start was delayed, as the women drivers said they had to report to the D.D.M.S. at Étaples; so we did, and a corporal there said we need n't have done so and advised us to push along. As a matter of fact, we would have needed no papers whatsoever, had it not been for the Poperinghe episode, the full recital of which was broken off last night.

Étaples, Camiers, Neufchâtel, Samer, Desvres, by a northern road through Wierre-au-Bois and very lovely, north through Brunembert to the main highway from Boulogne to St. Omer. We thus cut off a large strip. From St. Omer through Cassel, which we were only permitted to skirt, as it is the present advanced G.H.Q., and wonderful the views are, even from the lower road which we took. As I recall it, Cassel was spared during the German advance—saved by some few veterans of '70 who barricaded the road and made a showing as though the place were strongly held. Only one church, so far as we could see, was damaged.

All the old familiar landmarks stand out from the plain— Mont des Cats, Mont Rouge, Kemmel, the steeples of Steenvoorde, Bailleul, and Hazebrouck. As we were coming down the eastern side of the hill we met and passed Richard Harte and some teams from the Philadelphia Unit—equally dust-covered with ourselves. They stayed at Steenvoorde for lunch, while we pushed across the Belgian border toward Poperinghe. We should have turned north at Abeele and so to Proven via Watou, but, as I have said, we did otherwise.

Poperinghe is certainly a lively place these days, especially in the Grande Place, where we had to leave the car while we got lunch at the only place in the town where officers go—a place run by some refugee innkeepers from Ypres. All of the buildings except the few facing west were badly peppered, and there were occasional houses down. On one of the buildings was a large sign saying WIND DANGEROUS, and there was a big brass siren alongside of it to be used as an *alerte* against gas. The place of course was infested with troops, and all the paraphernalia of war; and from the square led a narrow road with an arrow pointing east and a huge sign: TO YPRES.

The road from Poperinghe to Proven was scarcely less congested. Among other things about half a mile's worth of pontoons—French, I believe, for crossing the canal—the first I had seen. We reached No. 46 about 3.30, and a friendly R.C. Padre gave me things for a bath on a rubber sheet, and helped otherwise to make me presentable. There was really no hurry whatsoever in our getting here, for teams from everywhere are still coming in. I will enumerate them some day.

We could n't possibly be in a better place—simple, of course, but the whole equipment is far better than at our No. 11 in Camiers. Many of the officers in funny little canvas Armstrong huts—really very comfortable—a grass tennis court, flower beds, and vegetable gardens. It must have been a typical Flemish road-side farm two years ago. My tent is only twenty feet from a picturesque barn with thatched and moss-covered roof almost reaching to its knees. and chickens and an old cart. Near by are a

The Old and
the New
From Capt Telfair's Hut

Mendinghem 46 CCS
26/VII/17

My tent

cluster of bell tents for the officers of these new teams, of which we make one, then some Sawyer stoves, and some Nisson huts for enlisted men in a pear orchard—everything of course connected up with duckboards. The hospital proper is across the new four-track railroad which goes through us—in fact that's why we're here—to Proven, which is only a scant mile away, and thence I know not where.

The place, as I have said somewhere before, is called "Mendinghem." This was originally a joke and was to have been "Endinghem"; but this on second thought was changed as being too much even for the Tommy. The army has a professional name maker, I may add. Mendinghem is already on the printed maps, and there is in this district a "Bandagehem" and "Dosinghem" which I have not located as yet.

At Mendinghem No. 46 and No. 12 are side by side and No. 64

is just across the track. At Dosinghem, which is in the direction of
Crombeke, are C.C.S.'s Nos. 62 and 63. Sir Anthony told me that
there would be fifteen C.C.S.'s for the 5th Army: better than
eleven for the 2nd Army at the Messines affair. They are probably all more or less like our No. 46—200 actual beds which
may expand to 1200 or 1300, and may "take in" without a
struggle, as did No. 46 the day before I got here, 1000 mustard-
gas cases.

Poor devils! I 've seen too many of them since—new ones—
their eyes bandaged, led along by a man with a string while they
try to keep to the duckboards. Some of the after-effects are as
extraordinary as they are horrible—the sloughing of the genitals,
for example. They had about twenty fatalities out of the first 1000
cases, chiefly from bronchial troubles. Fortunately vision does not
appear to be often lost.

A privileged character at Messines, I was told what was going
on. Small chance of that here, and it 's futile to listen to mess-table
gossip. To have reliable information naturally adds to the interest,
but after all it is not our special noncombatant business. However,
it would seem from hearsay that there has been a radical change
in the disposition of the armies. The 5th Army, under General
Gough, to which we are attached and of which Bruce Skinner is
the D.M.S., has its present H.Q. at Watou, the 2nd Army having
been pushed somewhat south of its former sector. The 4th Army
is supposedly up on the coast; and the best of the French troops,
with men chiefly from the northern provinces, lie between with
the Belgians somewhere about opposite Dixmude.

It appears that the operation is to be on an unprecedented scale.
As I sit here just outside my tent I can see the row of captive
balloons (*saucisses*), possibly a quarter of a mile apart along the
line. I counted thirty of them at one time as we were coming up
here yesterday. Meanwhile the air is full of throbbing things
which are not captive, and to which one never quite becomes accustomed. About half an hour ago a flock of thirteen big battle
triplanes came over headed east, and I should think all told fully
thirty or forty have passed during the hour—some low from the
aerodrome near by, others flying very high, straightaway east or
west like bees to or from their hives.

Aside from the constant dull rumble there has been no sound of serious strafing to-day. At the moment it's so comparatively quiet that I can hear a faint hum, like a fading tuning fork near one's ear. It's hard to find this particular bird, but he's directly above, barely visible, going north, about as big as a mosquito. They say the Hun comes over at about this height, when he comes at all—unless perhaps at night.

11 p.m. The personnel of No. 46 is a good and loyal one: Colonel Ellis the C.O.; Capts. Roper, Adjt., who also takes the X-rays; Wright, the surgeon specialist, and Shelton, his anæsthetist; Richardson, a surgeon, and Coleridge, his anæsthetist; Welpley, a surgeon, 6 ft. 3.5 in. and therefore called "Tiny"; Telfer, the evacuation officer, an extraordinary man-of-all-work both day and night. These eight made the original territorial group, with Warren, Quartermaster; the three Padres, Coffey, R.C., Robinson the Maconochie, Perkitt, C. of E., and Wetherill in charge of the Church Army Hut.

Poor Telfer is all bunged up with a secondhand dose of this mustard-oil gas or whatever it is. Many more of these men were brought in last night; and as the orderlies were panicky, owing to the raid, he did a lot of handling of patients himself and to-night has a bad cough, swollen and lachrymating eyes—like the men themselves. One or two others who have handled and undressed gassed Tommies have got it too in mild form.

After lunch Col. Wolstenholme took me through No. 64— a new C.C.S. which has been thrown together recently and is wholly in tents. It looks to me more workable than No. 46' which has been here the better part of a year, and while picturesque is rather sprawled out, the officers' quarters being separated from the wards and operating room by the tracks. Wolstenholme says No. 64 represents General Skinner's plan for all future C.C.S.'s —tents to be lined up in columns of four, so to speak, so that any_ one can readily find his way about when transferred from one C.C.S. to another.

The place is laid out in a rectangle with a broad central duck_ board avenue, and A-lines to the right for lying cases and B-lines to the left for walkers, who should be able to find their own way. There are some C-lines, too, but W. says the less said about them the better; for slightly wounded men they want to keep about the place simply disappear in the "deep blue C-lines."

Tuesday, the 24th of July

1.30 p.m. Very hot. We've just finished lunch, one of the features of which is the daily censoring of the Tommies' letters, which are dealt out by one of the Padres to each plate. They are mostly to Annie or Allie and "hoping you are in the pink as I am the same." Sir Wilmot dropped in and asked about the gas—says they now know the composition—a pungent smell, hence the suggestion of mustard—a very dark oily fluid, a trace only of hydrocyanic acid. He did not say what it is. It's very bad on this side, but we hope Fritz is getting the worst of it and wishes he had never used gas. The C.O. says that in retaliation of the first day's use we sent over 70,000 shells containing 30 tons of the British gas— whatever they now use—phosgene, I believe.

8.30 p.m. We have been taking in since seven, instead of at ten to-morrow morning, and are likely to be busy, though so far they are mostly more mustard-gas cases—very pitiful. It really must be quite a setback, and it's interesting to hear these men comment on Fritz—chiefly to the effect that he's hard to beat.

I asked the C.O. to let me see the new C.C.S. plans and he gave me his set to read and copy. I was standing by the operating hut later on, looking them over, when along came a man in a brass hat who proved to be none other than the 5th Army D.M.S. himself. He appeared pleased—told of the opposition he had received in getting the plans introduced—gave me two sheets of them from his own pocket—took me into the C.O.'s office, where he had much to say about the new gas, and left some directions about the disposition of the men's clothes, to prevent reinfections. He was lamenting the fact that they had cut him short of teams, and I suggested drawing further from Base Hospital No. 5, and at the same time commandeering our magnet, together with Capt. Derby himself, who would be most useful here caring for the eyes of these mustard cases, and looking at eyegrounds for us.

The General stayed to tea, which sounds formal but lasts about five minutes. A delightful man named Lyle Cummins, A.D.M.S. of the 16th Irish, was also here.

11.30 p.m. An extraordinary flight of aeroplanes came over this afternoon, more notably two flocks of them very high, going east, in V formation, with their fast scout trailers behind still higher up —a marvelous sight for one unaccustomed, as I still am, to these creatures. One of the flocks were battle triplanes. A young flier from the aerodrome near by paid us a visit and said he had been showing General Pershing about yesterday. Extraordinary, the offhand way these lads have of discussing their particular business. He was talking of the change in the character of the country. Two weeks ago behind the German lines it was all green fields and farms. Now for five miles beyond it is a devastated brown waste from the mere shelling preliminary to the real battle. His chief grouse was in being strafed by one's own Archies, particularly since Fritz rarely ventures over here nowadays.

Burge, the Australian major attached here with Col. Young, is an amusing soul, and has picturesque expressions. He says that among the Anzacs the act of searching for lice is spoken of as "reading your shirt." One can easily visualize the posture.

Wednesday the 25th. 10 p.m.

The "Summary of Official Communiqués" for to-day, No. 317, like other documents of its kind, is remarkable for its discretion in saying nothing. Nevertheless it is brought to us by the D.R.L.S. —a special-delivery person on a motor cycle—the Dispatch Rider Letter Service. This document begins: "*Russian Theatre* (24th July). No report received." Likewise ditto for the *Rumanian Theatre*. The *Salonika Theatre* and the *Italian Theatre* vary this by saying simply: "No change." The *French Front* mentions some artillery activity on the Chemin des Dames. Mention of our own "Theatre" is only permitted via the "Enemy Official Communiqué and Wireless Press Service." Herein it says for the *Western Theatre:* "In Flanders the artillery duel continues with unprecedented intensity. British reconnaissances are increasing in frequency." As a matter of fact, it's been a comparatively quiet twenty-four hours; but I'm glad Fritz feels as he does. Certainly he's giving it to us, and a steady procession of big Scots Guards continues to come in with bandaged eyes.

Four bad heads in our last take-in of 200 cases. Our team is beginning to work more smoothly, and Towne and I managed to clean up our cases. We rotate with Nos. 64 and 12, and at present it takes about twelve hours to get around. There must now be over 2000 casualties a day and this number will mount hugely when the time comes. I have said that there are half a million of all ranks in this district—twice the number of the 2nd Army at Messines. But I was told to-night that this means 500,000 rifles and gunners, and does not include all the A.S.C., R.A.M.C., and other noncombatants.

New teams are being added to our numbers. Two more to-day—-brought up here from the Somme. They had spent the winter in Ypres, living in the old prison cells, these being the only safe places for regimental M.O.'s. We now number thirty. There was evidently no reason for haste last Saturday afternoon. I 'm told that a message "to proceed forthwith" means to the B.E.F. "in about twenty-four hours."

Thursday, July 26th

Yesterday's cases doing well. We are planning to organize the work with the purpose of making an official report should we get a sufficiently large number of "heads."

General Gough, the 5th Army G.O.C. and one of the most popular in France, with his A.D.C. and staff, was here to lunch. An Irishman, he had resigned his commission rather than lead a force from Dublin against Carson and his Ulstermen. He was agreeable and attractive like most of the regulars I have seen. Talked much of Pershing and his recent visit here to the 5th Army—also of the problems of the war, including America's problems—left for the Anglo-Saxon race to finish.

After lunch a young captain from No. 32 at Brandhoek legged it in. They have put up their advanced C.C.S. during the past five days, and are ready to "take in" to-morrow—being halfway between Poperinghe and Ypres, shells go over their heads both ways. If the coming push does not result in an advance in the first few hours, they will be heavily bombarded. No. 44 and the 3rd Australian are not as yet set up, but soon will be. He says there are thirteen teams at No. 32—officers and nurses have been pouring in for the past few days.

My telephoning of Tuesday night has borne fruit. Though Patterson our C.O. not enthusiastic, George Derby, George Denny, and Johnnie Morton have turned up with the precious magnet—also with surprised faces showing through the layer of dust which covered them.

Friday, July 27th

Operating late last night—till 1 a.m. A 48-hour-old case getting pressure symptoms. Except ourselves, no.one at No. 46 knows how to use an ophthalmoscope. Wolstenholme at 64 is the real live-wire about here. He has already modified and improved the "Skinner C.C.S. Plan." Would make a fine hospital superintendent. He does not wait for "brass hats" to tell him what to do with the mustard-oil cases—he's already making a thorough study and sending them down with record slips. Apparently a good many have been evacuated with supposedly mild or receding symptoms, and have died en route to the Base with dilated hearts.

5 p.m. Rumors are flying about thick and fast. We are evidently approaching zero time. Many men dropping in as the stage is set, and nothing to do but wait. To see Capt. Leitch with a specimen for examination—in a mobile laboratory attached to No. 12. Setting: a Flemish garden surrounded by hop vines and lettuce beds. Met General Skinner on the way back through No. 12. Hints that it will be day after to-morrow—wants an outline of what we may be able to do with the head cases. Says the rats have all been killed in the trenches by the gas—may stop trench fevers. Methinks it may do the contrary if the flea is concerned, unless he is gassed also. Captain Graham Jones to tea—is at No. 121 Field Ambulance, a sort of C.D.S., at a place called "Canada Farm." Says it's remarkable how the skin is protected by shoulder straps —by a notebook or New Testament in a man's pocket: the new gas therefore penetrates clothing.

Special orders concerning these cases are issued—among them one from Herringham, who mentions experiences at 91 F.A. (the main dressing station of the 15th Corps) with the subcutaneous injection of calcium chloride. Graham Jones says the Boches are moving back about six miles. Whether this is a good or bad omen no one seems to know. Certainly their shelling has diminished There were one or two Boche planes over to-day, being Archied. Conditions favored them, as they could dodge in and out of clouds.

Captains Morrison, Fraser, and several others also here to tea —and later on McNee with an A.D.M.S. from the 3rd Army to see the mustard-oil cases. Awful to see these big Scots Guards-men dying from fulminating pneumonia about two weeks after first being infected. The original chlorine business two years ago, though a surprise and different from this, was certainly no worse.

11.30 p.m. The rumors of the afternoon seem to be confirmed. Fritz has gone back—the Guards and the 38th Division have been following and are across the Ypres Canal. Three young Flying Corps men of our neighborhood brought in as casualties—others here to inquire about them. Mere kids. They have been flying over the evacuated zone at about 200 yards' height to see what is left; one of them said: "They could have hit us with a beer bottle." The three have been hit with something more serious, however. There are practically no guns to-night—an ominous silence. Fritz is a hard nut to crack. It's no joke going forward in a devastated country with every dugout a potential trap, and possible mines everywhere.

Saturday, July 28th

Operations—getting teams in order. A vigorous walk this p.m. with George Derby out toward Crombeke and the observation balloons; and after tea copied the ground plans of No. 46 from the diagram in Capt. Telfer's possession. Col. Maynard Smith, the surgical consultant, here to dinner, and a long talk with him afterward. The C.C.S.'s are growing to be regular base hospitals as far as equipment is concerned. That there should be fifteen of them in a single army area would have staggered the officials even a year ago. The chief difficulty lies in bringing up their supplies, for the combatants need every square inch of space on wheels for their own purposes.

Our teams have at last been made out—very tardily it seems. Our neighbors are already at work on the same schedules, sixteen hours on, eight hours off, that they will follow when the rush comes. No one can explain its postponement. Some say the French were not ready; but as Derby and I saw a lot of *Chasseurs Alpins* when we were near the French Army sector this afternoon, they at least have sent some of their best troops. The offensive when it comes off is evidently going to cover a large area—it is now said the objectives are Roulers and Bruges. One takes these rumors for what they are worth—and that's very little.

Sunday, July 29th. Midnight

Much like other days except that the peasants have on their Sunday best, and we had a cold snack for supper. More operations this morning, and our first try with the magnet—unsuccessful. Still, things are beginning to straighten out. Maynard Smith took me out to Brandhoek on the Poperinghe–Ypres road after lunch. Up there the country is simply swarming with men, munitions, and mud, for it rained hard this morning. A bad thing for the advance if it keeps on. I recognized, by their red-hand emblem, the Ulster Division, which I saw moving up after Messines. The story goes of a race between two rivals to reach Ireland, and The O'Neill—if it was he—cut off his hand and threw it ashore before his rival could land, thereby claiming the soil. Curiously enough the 16th Irish is fighting alongside the Ulsterites, and both under General Gough!—shades of Curragh Barracks!!

No. 32 at Brandhoek is ready for work, though the sisters have not come up as yet. Colonel Sutcliffe, a big-bodied soul, was tramping about in the mud fixing up his final duckboards. There are about nine teams of abdominal surgeons ready for work— Miles, Carling, Sampson, and Anderson among them. No. 44 is less ready, but still far enough along to give us tea. The 3rd Australian also was floundering in the mud and getting established —our old Baltimore acquaintance, Col. Newland, being the Chief Surgeon. These three C.C.S.'s are necessarily alongside both road and railway, for hospitals and ammunition dumps must compete for sites of the same kind—hence they are likely to be heavily shelled, but this afternoon was comparatively quiet.

Then back by the cut-off around Poperinghe to the "Pop"– Crombeke road, which was crowded with troops and ammunition columns, and field batteries going up with a long line of mules, each carrying twelve shells—six on a side—past an aerodrome– and so to Dosinghem, where are Richard Harte at No. 4, Garrod at No. 47, and George Brewer at No. 61. Brewer was on duty in the reception tent and seemed very fit and well. All three of these places are—so far as the lay of the land permits—put up on the Skinner plan, and very admirable it is—just like our neighbor No. 64, except that smaller marquees are used. Very attractive wards they make too—the sisters and matron in the officers' ward at No. 4 were even puzzling over the color scheme, and asked Maynard Smith if he did not think they had made it too green.

So back to Mendinghem, stopping on the way at *Château Lovie,* where is the army headquarters. A fine Belgian country house, not differing from the usual French type, in a large park with a big pond in front, where some Tommies were fishing. All of the offices, of which innumerable ones are necessary, were so effectively camouflaged that one had to look closely for them among the trees.

A battle has come to be an enormous business—even such a thing as the map department has to be on a huge scale, and turns out new detail maps almost daily from studies made of aviators' photographs. Snapshots are taken of certain suspected roads, for example, perhaps every day, and preferably in the late afternoon, at the same hour, so that the shadows of the embankments on the roadway can be accurately studied, measured, and compared. This afternoon the shadow shows some irregularities not there yesterday—indicating gun emplacements established after dark —and to-night this spot in a given square is heavily shelled and they are blown up or driven out, as indicated by to-morrow's pictures.

Back to find a lot of work going on, and the evening spent in a futile endeavor to resuscitate disconsolate Johnnie Morton's first patient, who had a respiratory failure from a spreading intracerebral hemorrhage.

Monday, July 30th. 2 p.m.

Overcast and unpromising weather for an offensive. Very quiet—practically no guns—nothing in the air. Still waiting for zero day and hour. The general feeling is expressed by one of Bruce Bairnsfather's sketches pinned on the wall of the mess—two uncouth Tommies, Ole Bill and a companion, cowering in a dug-out: " 'Ow long are you up for, Bill?" "Seven years." "Yer lucky —I 'm duration."

There is even an air of uncertainty and despondency about the recent issue of jam. The present batch is referred to as J.U.O.— "jam of uncertain origin." Marmalade, such as "Mother used to make," is only a memory. Here is Shilton's bill—for one week's messing—it somehow sounds very untidy:—

Dr. To Mess President C.C.S. 46	28/7/17
To messing for week ending	
Entrance fee	15 frcs.
1 week's messing	15 frcs.
To Major Cushing	30 frcs.

5 p.m. Bowlby here inspecting us, and to tea. With him to Nos. 64 and 12. On the quiet, it is to be early to-morrow. Let us hope there will be no more rain, for it adds enormously to the sepsis. Gordon-Watson, Consultant of the 2nd Army, also lurking about, gathering up some of the teams they had loaned the 5th. Apparently the pressure is to extend as far south as Arras. Bowlby said that thirty-one German planes were brought down in the great air fight of day before yesterday and only three British failed to return. He is an unmitigated optimist—his strong point.

The First Battle in a Deluge

Tuesday, July 31

What may go down in history as the third battle of Ypres opened to-day—zero time at 3.50 a.m. After a week of favorable weather came the deluge.

Wednesday, Aug. 1

1.30 a.m. One of the disadvantages of our picturesque camp just came home to me as I felt my way back to this soggy red tent. Pitch black, pouring rain, and has been, I believe, nearly all this fearful day—two ambulance trains of the new variety, about a mile long, vestibuled so you can't climb under or over the couplings, standing between the officers' quarters and the hospital encampment—your electric torch burned out—trying to stick to slippery duckboards about a foot wide. Depressing for a well man, but imagine what these poor wounded devils have had to go through to-day, and what the many not yet found are enduring. The preoperative hut is still packed with untouched cases, so caked in wet mud that it's a task even to strip them and find out what they've got.

Thursday, August 2

2.30 a.m. Pouring cats and dogs all day—also pouring cold and shivering wounded, covered with mud and blood. Some g.s.w.'s of the head, when the mud is scraped off, prove to be trifles— others of unsuspected gravity. The preoperation room is still crowded—one can't possibly keep up with them; and the un-systematic way things are run drives one frantic. The news, too, is

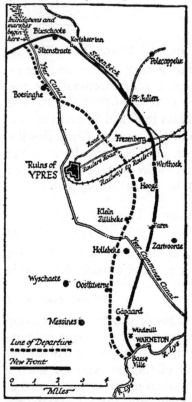

Approximate Advance in the First Battle. French on Left Reach Steenbeck; 5th Army in Centre; 2nd Army with Australians and New Zealanders on Right Opposite Messines. St. Julien and Westhoek Soon Lost in Counter-Attacks

very bad. The greatest battle of history is floundering up to its middle in a morass, and the guns have sunk even deeper than that. *Gott mit uns* was certainly true for the enemy this time.

Operating from 8.30 a.m. one day till 2.00 a.m. the next; standing in a pair of rubber boots, and periodically full of tea as a stimulant, is not healthy. It's an awful business, probably the worst possible training in surgery for a young man, and ruinous for the carefully acquired technique of an oldster. Something over 2000 wounded have passed, so far, through this one C.C.S. There are fifteen similar stations behind the battle front.

10.30 p.m. We're about through now with this particular episode. Around 30,000 casualties, I believe—a small advance here and there, and that's about all. Doubtless there are many prisoners—we've seen a lot of wounded ones, big husky Hun boys. But I do not believe it has

been other than a disappointment. Much ground has been lost (e.g., at St. Julien) in counter-attacks.

Operating again all day, and finished up an hour ago with an extraction of a large piece of shell from a man's badly infected ventricle with the magnet—then dinner, and now to bed. It still rains. A lot of wounded must have drowned in the mud. One of to-day's cases was a fine young Scot having frequent Jacksonian attacks from a glancing sniper's ball through his tin hat, a piece of which was driven into the brain. He had lain, he said, in the protection of a shell hole with one or two others—the water up to his waist—for twelve hours before they were found. But there has been scant time to talk to wounded, to prisoners, or to "brass hats," and I know little of what has gone on.

Friday, August 3

Continuous downpour for the fourth consecutive day. Expected to have an easy time to-day and to catch up on dressings, notes of cases, and statistics. The morning went somewhere. The D.G., Sir Arthur Sloggett, at the mess for lunch, together with Sir William Somebody, head of the British Red Cross and a friend of T.R.'s. I was half an hour late, which is not the thing—properly chided by the C.O.

In the early afternoon a large batch of wounded were unexpectedly brought in—mostly heads—men who have been lying out for four days in craters in the rain, without food. It is amazing what the human animal can endure. Some of them had maggots in their wounds. Then a long operation on a sergeant with things in his brain and ventricle like the man of last night—the magnet again useful—George Derby ditto. He has been helping me lately, while Towne makes records, and Johnnie Morton, with George Denny as his anæsthetist, is at another table. Many muddy bystanders from the adjacent hospitals looking on and fairly sitting on the instrument stands.

Saturday, August 4 (really 3.30 a.m. on the 5th)

Another night helping Johnnie and Blake as long as I could stand up. I think the teams do better work by night than by day, and it is noticeable that the night shifts are composed of the emergency teams. Urgent operations on more rotting men. One case I did had a gross gas infection of the brain. My particular grouse lies in the fact that no one protests against locking tight every door of a twenty-car ambulance train between the hospital and our camp. There are two alternatives—to feel your way around in a sea of mud or to crawl under. I crawled under to-night and nearly cracked my head. I 'll feel less peevish later.

Sunday, August 5

8.30 a.m. I do. Except for the fact that my ragged batman, Ashford by name, says there are orders not to provide us with our customary inch of bath water—that we must henceforth go to the bathing tent. This structure lies in the hospital grounds on the other side of the barricaded track. Lt. Zinkhan—a joyous American attached here as a "casual"—said at breakfast that he had thought it out fully. He told his particular batman to bring him some weak tea. He says it makes a fine lather.

Three years ago to-day England declared war against Germany. About four months ago we did.

7.30 p.m. Lieutenant Zinkhan is not only joyful but venturesome—a typical American—known as "Zink." He enjoys Mutt and Jeff, and quotes them often. The Britishers laugh, but don't entirely understand.

On Sunday last—it seems a year ago—among others a Scots Guard came down with a head wound, and on his No. 24 Field Ambulance card was the name "Lt. Zinkhan, U.S.R." We naturally supposed that our Zink had in some mysterious fashion found his way up to an F.A. and sent this man down. But not at all. When confronted with the fact later in the day he denied having been farther than Proven. When shown the card he exclaimed: "Good God! That's my brother. I've been looking for him for three months."

Late Monday evening there was delivered here in a large limousine our Zinkhan. He had been to see his brother—had started out about noon on foot to Poperinghe and been given a lift in a lorry—again on foot toward Ypres until he "hopped" another lorry. He finally got wind of where F.A. No. 24 roughly was situated and was put down at a point where it grows too hot for motor transport. At a remount station he wangled a horse, which he rode for two miles, until a 5.9 blew up a donkey engine near by—it simply disappeared in the air. At this juncture Zink dismounted and walked—a concealed naval gun nearly blew his head off—he got across the canal and up into the Ypres sector. There he somehow found his long-lost brother in a dugout near "Hellfire Corner." His brother said: "Zink, I'm scared to death." Said Zink: "So am I."

He stayed ten minutes and got back as fast as he could. No one questioned his going or coming. People were too busy getting themselves under cover and staying there. He made his way back to the Poperinghe road this side of Ypres. There he encountered some staff officers, one of them evidently an American, who wanted to know what he was doing up there. It turned out to be the American C. in C. being shown about by General Gough! General Pershing's curiosity had been aroused by the unfamiliar sight of an American uniform. "Zink" dined with them, and was sent home in the General's car.

That, he says, was the most trying part of his expedition, for, unaccustomed to a limousine, he was n't sure whether it was proper to loll back or sit forward upright. He decided to loll back. One essential difference between an American and a Britisher is that the former can hold up his trousers with a belt; the latter has to wear braces. Zink is an American. But turning up in the C. in C.'s car was about all that saved him from a court-martial for going A.W.O.L.

To-day Zink's brother was here for tea—out for two days' rest—very shaky, and well he might be. Browsing around Hellfire Corner and Hooge for four days looking for wounded under heavy fire, in his triangle between the railroad and the Menin Road. His battalion had missed their barrage and only got ahead a very short distance. He finally got ninety bearers, mostly oldish men. On their first trip twelve of them were killed. The next time there were volunteers—some N.C.O.'s and others—and they succeeded in getting in a batch of Devons who were in shell holes, wounded. It took twelve bearers to carry a two-man stretcher—eight at a time and four in reserve—often sinking in above their knees in this impossible mud. That was on the fourth day, and the wounded men had been without food all this time—they had to leave four of them behind, as they could not get back to them.

Some tank officers here also for tea. One of the tanks practically disappeared in the mud and they had to escape through the roof. There are three or four inches of pasty mud between us and C.C.S. No. 64, where the bearers have been carrying some of our overflow wounded—it is enough to suck off your rubber boots unless you curl up your toes. What another ten inches would be like can be imagined. It would take off everything below your waist, if you could pull yourself out at all. Perhaps that's why Britishers all wear braces.

Tuesday, August 7th

1 a.m. Another day of work—our "taking in" day, and almost as many head cases as during the rush. Very bad ones, many moribund. Swift and Zink came into our team and helped Johnnie and myself. Many visitors and onlookers. George Brewer and some men from Dosinghem; in the afternoon General Blackader of the 38th Division, which did so well on the right of the Guards. They have just moved out and are replaced by the 20th Division. Bruce here looking on most of the day. Our team really working very well, with a Sister Dunn, a Canadian, Miss Gerrard, the anæsthetist, Clifford, our orderly, who has a tough job lathering and shaving clotted hair from dirty scalps, and a helper loaned us by No. 46. . . . A muggy steaming day yesterday—neither sun nor rain.

THE SECOND ATTACK: WESTHOEK

Friday, August 10

2 p.m. A flying trip to Camiers in a downpour on Tuesday for supplies and information. Evidently the second battle scheduled for Wednesday was on a smaller scale or else was postponed. The *communiqués* have said little or nothing about it, though ground was recaptured at Westhoek and Glencorse Wood. It was not a large affair—a matter of 500 yards at some points.

11 p.m. My young friend the pilot, Turberville by name, just walked back with me from the aerodrome which lies the other side of Proven. He is scornful of searchlights, which are merely to encourage the populace. If a searchlight should catch you, which is most unlikely, when you are up at night, the thing to do is to fly down the beam and turn on your Vickers. This puts it out.

After nearly two weeks of either atrocious or unsettled weather, to-day has been perfect and it looks as though the bad spell might have passed—a favorable day for photography, and therefore ideal for the eyes of the army. After working all day on our statistics for the past few weeks I could not bear, after tea, to go back to the clerks' hut—the panorama of aerial activity was too

alluring. So I hied me across lots—this in Flanders means jumping ditches and circumnavigating turnip fields and hop entanglements—to the aerodrome a mile away.

It was about half after six, and from their field one gets an unbroken view of the long line of observation balloons, and above
and beyond them the sky full of planes and clusters of shrapnel
bursts—black ones from the Archies of the enemy, white ones
from our own. Turberville was in, having had his two flights
earlier in the day. I must stay to dinner, and so to his tent while
he shaves, and strops his razor on the palm of his hand, and talks.
One begins to learn by banking to the left, and subsequently always finds that easier—*viz.*, one climbs in a right-handed spiral,
which would certainly have interested the first of their clan,
Leonardo da Vinci. The infantry officer knows only his bit of
trench; the flying men know the whole field of operation and
what everyone is doing on both sides.

I dined with them, as I say—together with an officer of the
Scots Guards. Fifty in the squadron, though only forty-seven
to-night—one away and two killed yesterday in a collision in a
cloud. Cheerful boys, yet they know full well the seriousness, responsibilities, and risks of their job. Extraordinary tales passed
about—of the number of aircraft over this particular sector (one
of them said he counted forty planes while he was over the line
and got tired of it), of meeting high in the air Boche howitzer
shells en route for some point in our rear; we occasionally hear
them whistle over us toward Hazebrouck, which, I may add, has
been heavily shelled of late. But that one could see them pass
by, head-on in the air! Well, I'm not doubting anything the
Flying Corps tells me.

Saturday night, August 11th

1 *a.m.*—having just finished breakfast with the night shift.
More rain all day—clear streaks alternating with downpours.
Statistical study of our cases until tea time, when we began to
"take in." The 2/ Scots Guards are out at rest billet and I had
promised Ross to dine at 8 with the Transport mess. So began
work in the late "Pip-Emma" [1] on what promised to be a simple

[1] This was the signalers' term for p.m. (afternoon), just as Ack-Emma was their term
for a.m. (morning).

case—"G.S.W's neck, eyebrow, and lip (serious)." There was a minute puncture wound in the right temporal region which had evidently escaped notice, and as is so often the case this proved the more serious wound—a penetrating fracture with torn meningeal and cerebral arteries, and a small foreign body showing by the X-ray on the opposite side of the head. It came out with the magnet—the nail at its full length—on the first trial; but even with Johnnie's help it was 8.30 before I had finished up with the whole affair.

Ross has the reputation of being the best quartermaster in the British Army, and his directions were precise; but it was dark, raining hard, the roads impossible. So it was 9 before I found "Privet Camp," in an old farmhouse on the Camp P3 road near the railway—and then only after having butted into the G.O.C.'s mess far out of my way.

There were only five, Ross himself—an old soldier with many years' service—two young aviators, Pilkington and Bowen, a Padre, and Haywood-Farmer—a polo player of international fame. The Scots Guards deserve a rest, having done well in their particular sector—we saw many of them wounded and gassed. The Guards were on the left of the line adjoining the French; and they took their objective, the Steenbeek, and have since gone beyond, despite the mud.

All these things I have had no time to learn about; and being eager for information I pulled out my little map, at which they laugh and produce large-scale ones while I am being given my belated dinner—official maps—scale of 6 inches to the mile— which are subsequently presented to me, for, though much used during the past weeks, they are now obsolete, and the trenches so carefully recorded no longer exist.

In the midst of all this, sounds of a bagpipe came in out of the rain, and a person who stands six feet six appeared—a pipe major. He almost filled the little stone-floored room—his longest pipe a few inches from the beams of the ceiling—and what little of the room he left was more than filled with his music. They were all very silent—and at the end I was presented with a glass of whiskey—*full* of whiskey—which I had to give to Mr. Pipe Major—very seriously. I suppose it meant that the concert was given for me—and so I politely asked him for another and he blew up his bellows and gave what they said was a "Skye Boating Song"—very mournful, despite the whiskey.

A pouring rain outside, we six about a small table in an old Flemish farmhouse, this big kilted giant who, they say, is the World's Champion Piper—he must be—seriously squeezing his native airs out of a bag—a strange situation for me, even in this summer of strange situations.

Sunday, August 12

Very busy operating all day. Horrax and Forbes from our base appear in the afternoon, and Generals Skinner, Wallace, and Davidson here to tea. Extraordinary aerial activity. Four Boche planes over during the day, which was perfect for playing hide and seek in the white clouds. Archies going all the morning and afternoon. One Boche plane brought down by two opponents in sight of our camp. Zink has been out exploring and saw a Fritz make a direct hit on an observation balloon and the two observers come down safely in their parachutes.

Monday, August 13

Just two weeks ago to-night the final preparations for the third battle of Ypres were at their height, and the expectation in the minds of many was that the enemy would be blown out of his diggings from the sea to the Lys and driven back into open warfare. After a long spell of unusually fine weather the thirtieth was overcast and showery, and by noon of zero day—Tuesday, the thirty-first—Jupiter Pluvius had decided the matter by bogging the artillery and infantry and blinding the aeroplanes. Such papers as I have chanced to pick up make much of "substantially obtaining all the objectives laid down," but this, I am sure, is not the way people feel about it up here.

Tuesday, August 14, 7.00 p.m.

Orders to evacuate and a succession of "brass hats" and consulting surgeons indicate that events are impending. Rather discouraged, as we have been having a streak of bad luck—infections, and so on.

Walked over to the Scots Guards camp to pay my party call. The Padre had just returned from "Pop" and had seen a Boche plane fall out of the clouds and attack a row of balloons. The observers tumbled out of them in their parachutes, and Fritz was in turn dropped on by three of ours and driven to earth. He adds that it is a favorite trick to try and machine-gun the officers in the air as they are descending. This is war, I presume, but it seems particularly unsportsmanlike.

Find on my return that No. 46 is "taking in," and we are preparing to do two cases regardless of dinner and a concert by the Coldstream Guards military band. This won't be much anyway, as it's raining hard again. I am driven to distraction by the local dilatoriness, the everlasting stopping for meals. Someone is eating all day long—orderlies, sisters, noncoms, officers. As a result there is only about an hour between any two meals—breakfast, lunch, tea, dinner, late supper—when the team as a whole can work together. In the other operating room they stop also for broth and biscuits at 11 a.m. As most of these men breakfast at nine, this means quite a gastronomic day, and many of them eat more meals than they operate on patients. I shall try to drive our American team into eight head cases a day or bust.

Wednesday, August 15

We nearly "busted" on six cases in the twenty-four hours since yesterday's note. We began at 8 p.m. on "L/Cpl. Wiseman 392332; 1/9 Londons S.W. Frac. Skull," which interpreted means that a lance corporal of the 9th Londons had a shell wound. It went through his helmet in the parietal region, with indriven fragments to the ventricle. These cases take a long time if done carefully enough to forestall infection, and it was eleven o'clock before we got to "Sgt. Chave, C. 25912. M.G.C. 167—S.W. head and back—penet.," according to his field-ambulance card. This sergeant of the Machine Gunners had almost the whole of his right frontal lobe blown out, with a lodged piece of shell almost an inch square, and extensive radiating fractures, which meant taking off most of his frontal bone, including the frontal sinuses—an enormous operation done under local anæsthesia. We crawled home for some eggs in the mess and to bed at 2.30 a.m. —six hours for these two cases.

This man "Chave"—queer name—when roused from his semi-consciousness made it known that he had some precious false teeth.

"Moving Up." Reënforcements with Stretcher-Bearers

"Coming Back." Lying Cases at a Field Ambulance Ready for Convoy

They were removed, somewhat more easily than was his broken frontal bone. They must have been on his mind, for I remember when rongeuring out fragments of his skull he kept muttering that I was breaking his teeth. He was evidently familiar with this somewhat similar sound. Though he pulled out his Carrel-Dakin tubes, he seems to be all right to-day, and is wearing his teeth.

This morning a man named Ward, rifleman of the 10th Brigade, was ticketed for us in the Resuscitation Ward—hard to tell whether he or we were more unfit for the operation. We began at 9 a.m.—an hour earlier than we had ever succeeded in starting before, for there is always trouble in getting boiling water, owing to the scarcity of Primus stoves, so-called. A penetrating wound of the occiput, with complete central blindness, and lodgment of the missile in the right frontal lobe. Also with novocaine, lasting another three hours, with extraction of fragments driven into the ventricle. Then really a bad one—another rifleman, Saunders, with a mid-vertex wound, rigid extremities, unconscious, and two foreign bodies with many fragments of deeply embedded bone showing in the X-ray. This carried Morton and me up to 2.30— too late for lunch. I got what might be called a high tea, and Horrax, who had been recording cases and doing dressings, took Morton's place and we did two more penetrating cases, and then our more serious dressings, and managed to get to the mess for dinner nearly on time.

They shove the more serious cases on to us, which is what we want, but I 'm beginning to be a little doubtful about eight a day if they are all of this magnitude.

This has been an ordinary slack time with a "take in" of only 200 cases in rotation with our neighbors Nos. 64 and 12. The rush has not yet come—another postponement; perhaps due to the heavy rains to-day.

THE THIRD ATTACK: LANGEMARCK

Thursday, August 16 (really 2.15 a.m. on Friday)
They tell me that heavy firing, aeroplane raids, and some French naval guns to the north of us made much ado last night after three o'clock. I heard none of it. The zero hour, long de_

ferred, came at 5 a.m. Walking wounded began to come in to Nos. 12 and 64 in a few hours, and to us at ten o'clock. We began operating at twelve noon and had done seven cases, one better than yesterday, by midnight. Have our system running, with lunch and tea in the operating room instead of coming way over here to the mess. Two cases always waiting, so that we can go from case to case without delay. We ought to manage eight to-morrow—that is, to-day, which is Friday. Clear, cool, cloudless. No very startling news. Langemarck taken, possibly Poelcappelle, and the ridge beyond—the objective. The Boches are using an entirely new gas, which gives bad gastro-intestinal symptoms. They also are dotted about in concrete machine-gun emplacements and can enfilade the oncoming attack. Hence more bullet than shell wounds, it is said, are to be expected.

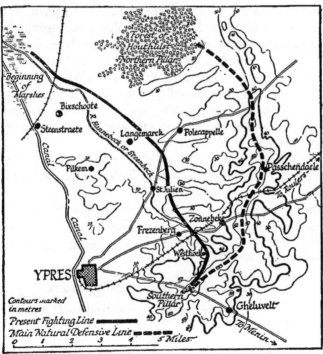

Contour Map from *Land & Water* Showing Crest of Ridges (Broken Line) and Advance in Third Battle (Solid Line) beyond Langemarck. Note the Southern Pivot or Pillar at X, "Clapham Junction" (Hill 60), on the Menin Road

Friday, August 17

We beat our record to-day with eight cases—all serious ones. A prompt start at 9 a.m. with two cases always in waiting—notes made, X-rays taken, and heads shaved. It 's amusing to think that at home I used to regard a single major cranial operation as a day's work. These eight averaged two hours apiece—one or two very interesting ones. One in particular—a sergeant, unconscious, with a small wound of entrance in the vertex and a foreign body just beside the sella turcica. We have learned a new way of doing these things—*viz.*, to encircle the penetrating wound in the skull with Montenovesi forceps, and to take the fractured area with the depressed bone fragments out in one piece—then to catheterize the tract and to wash it out with a Carrel syringe through the tube. In doing so the suction of the bulb is enough occasionally to bring out a small bone fragment clinging to the eye of the catheter. Indeed, one can usually detect fragments by the feel of the catheter; they are often driven in two or three inches.

In this particular man, however, after the tract was washed clear of blood and disorganized brain, the nail was inserted its full six inches and I tried twice unsuccessfully to draw out the fragment with the magnet. On the third attempt I found to my disgust that the current was switched off. There was nothing to do but make the best of it, and a small stomach tube was procured, cut off, boiled, inserted in the six-inch tract, suction put on, and a deformed shrapnel ball (not the expected piece of steel shell) was removed on the first trial—of course a non-magnetizable object.

To-night while operating on a Boche prisoner with a "g.s.w. head," about 11 p.m.—our seventh case—some Fritz planes came over on a bombing raid, as they do almost every night nowadays —-nowanights (which is it?). Of course all our lights were switched off, and we had to finish with candles. If we did n't do a very good job, it was Fritz's fault, not entirely ours.

The Boche prisoner, I may add, was a big fellow with a square head, badly punctured though it was. The case in waiting was a little eighteen-year-old Tommy from East London—scared, peaked, underfed, underdeveloped. He had been in training six months and was in the trenches for the first time during the pres_ ent show—*just ten minutes* when he was hit.

Saturday, Aug. 18

8 a.m. A rumor that the C.C.S.'s at Dosinghem and Rémy Siding were bombed in the raid last night; that there were thirty casualties at No. 17, where Crile is, among them some Boche wounded. Hazebrouck has also been so thoroughly bombed and shelled that the New Zealand Stationary where I worked a month ago has closed up after heavy casualties. General Porter and his staff have had to move out, together with most of the civil population, who have closed all the shops.

Poor little Harris, an R.A.M.C. captain who was here when I first arrived, was switched over to No. 3 Australian at Brandhoek three days ago. Last night at 10 p.m. he was in the mess tent with another officer—the rest of them operating, fortunately. A bomb was dropped, killing him outright. He had gone, unhurt, through a winter in Ypres and then through the Somme in advanced posts. How he hated the whole business!

Midnight. The C.O. and I have just dined with General Blackader and his staff at the Divisional H.Q. in Proven where the 38th are in rest billets. They somehow seem to feel obligated to us at No. 46—we certainly had a lot of the Royal Welsh Fusileers during the 31st and early August days. One of the officers confided to me that the 20th Division had taken their place, meanwhile securing Langemarck; also that they were going in again to-morrow without reënforcements, though they had lost 120 officers and 3000 men.

The Welsh Fusileers enjoy the unique distinction of wearing "the flash," a knot of black ribbon sewn to the back of the collars of the officers' tunics, representing the patch of black leather which, before the abolition of pigtails a hundred years ago, served to protect the uniform from this ornament. They came home, I believe, after a long detail in Bermuda and found pigtails no longer the fashion, and, being the last to wear them, "the flash" represents this historical fact of some interest.

I consequently expected to find everyone wearing "a flash," but not at all. Indeed there was not a Welshman among them, perhaps twenty in all—and many kinds of regimental tunics were represented—the only uniformity being in the staff officers' red facings on the collars and red arm band. As is usual there were no introductions, and we dined simply in a small Nisson hut. I sat between General B. and the divisional A.D.M.S., who had recently been C.O. of a C.C.S., and talked a good deal about it, while my rather fatigued brain puzzled more over the question of buttons than what he was saying.

The Brigadier on General B.'s left had—in contrast to the highly polished buttons of the others—black ones, which, as I learn from Burton, our sluggish operating-room orderly—who, however, is full of army lore—are peculiar to the King's Royal Rifles. They were organized in America in 1755 and lost an entire battalion at Quebec, for which these black buttons with a stringed bugle on them are a sign of perpetual mourning. Opposite were buttons characteristic of the Guards. Some in twos, some in threes, and I believe they go up to fives—Grenadiers, Coldstreams, Scots, Irish, and Welsh.

My intelligence, then and now, is about on the plane of buttons. Though variously buttoned up, and though not Welsh, these officers nevertheless were the executives of the 38th, which, to the right of the Guards, went over Pilkem Ridge to their objective, the Steenbeek, on the morning of the 31st. This is all the more remarkable in view of General Gough's "Routine Orders" of Aug. 16th, which contains a "Summary of Statements of Sergeant Phillips (Royal Welsh Fusileers), Captured by the German 23rd Reserve Division on 27th July." Sergeant Phillips in fact gave the whole show away, after his capture, as was evidenced by a "German Intelligence Summary" which in turn was recovered on the 31st.

I remember expressing some surprise at the dinner that the divisional officers of the R.W.F.'s were not wearing "the flash," and someone said that had all gone by, that the Guards are the only regiments which are still under their own officers; and there is something in their regulations to the effect that they *must* so be. One gossips and puts on a cheerful face at these regimental dinners the night before an attack—realizing all the time that many of his table companions at dawn will be leading his men behind a barrage into something than which the Inferno could be no worse. That is a subject of which we don't talk.

The Fourth Attack: Menin Road

Sunday, August 19

Morning. My prize patient, Baker, with the shrapnel ball re_ moved from near his sella, after doing well for three days sud_ denly shot up a temperature to 104 last night about midnight. I took him to the operating theatre, reopened the perfectly healed external wound, and found to my dismay a massive gas infection of the brain. I bribed two orderlies to stay up with him in the operating room, where he could have constant thorough irrigation over the brain and through the track of the missile. No light ex_ cept candles was permitted last night. We fortunately are not taking in, and I was dressing him this morning—for he still lives —when someone leaning out of the window cried out: "There's a falling plane!"

Nose down, spinning, wings laid back, like a dead bird. He fell just beyond No. 64, and the familiar, irresistible impulse made everyone run toward the spot—I too as soon as I could leave. I got across the track, past the post-mortem tent, as far as the rapidly growing cemetery on the other side of No. 64. Here were about a hundred grinning Chinese coolies, in their blue tunics—though some were stripped to the waist—digging two fresh ditches, about six by twenty feet. The Far East digging in the upstart West with its boasted civilization! This held me up, and I refrained from crossing the road to see the mangled machine and the dead thing under it.

Afternoon. Welpley has had the grass cut on the tennis court and the lines freshly marked out. He has arranged, too, for a tournament—mixed doubles. We are to have tea served there. I am contributing a box of Page and Shaw's chocolates from the usual source of home comforts and delicacies.

Night, 11 p.m. A baby crying in the operating theatre with a badly wounded arm; its mother on the next table with several small wounds and badly shocked. An unusual sight for a C.C.S. There had been the usual raid—one comes every evening. It's about our turn, and not a light is permitted. Rumor has it that these are reprisals—that one of our big naval guns fired into Roulers and hit a German hospital. Consequently Rémy has had it, also Brandhoek, and yesterday Dosinghem, where there were many casualties, I believe—one of Brewer's American nurses was slightly wounded, and some M.O.'s also.

At ten or thereabouts he came—a clear, cloudless, dark night with no moon—just right for him. We could get some idea of where he was by the focusing of the searchlights and where the Archies were bursting as they tried to pick him up. Twenty or more shafts, and in addition the two huge beams—from naval searchlights in Dunkerque, 't is said—which simply poured shafts of light down in this direction. Once we saw him picked up with all the shafts for miles around focusing on him, but he dodged away. This was to the east of us, then Archies to the south in three places, so that possibly there was more than one raider; then after a time to the north, Bandagehem way, apparently, where he dropped eight bombs. The big French searchlights got at him and one heard machine-gun fire—perhaps from Fritz himself. Finally we could hear his engine as he passed over us, then two more explosions, and the searchlights began to blink off. He'd gone.

Then the baby and its mother, a *poilu*, and an excited Belgian, in the reception hut. Weird sight it was—candlelight, bearers and M.O.'s in their tin hats—a wounded woman and her baby—the fruit of the raid.

Monday, August 20: midnight

A busy day. Six only, but one of them required three major operations—two cranial penetrations, one in the temporal, another in the vertex, and a bad shoulder wound as well. So this should count for our eight. It was not our rotation, but Miller thought I had better take him on. All three were done under local anæsthesia, and during their course I learned from the man, whose name is Atkins, that he is a collier at home—a stretcher-bearer here. He had gone out to get a wounded man they had seen lying out for six days in a bad spot. No one else would go and he finally volunteered, though the man did n't belong to his Division. That's all he remembers, though he was quite conscious to-night and can talk, for it's his right brain that's damaged. Hero? Not at all. It was only in the day's work, and probably no one will ever know or care. A simple coal miner. There are thousands of cases of this kind despite Ellen La Motte.

General Skinner came in while I was operating this afternoon

and had much to say about the casualties at Dosinghem, Brandhoek, and Rémy. He apologized for appearing in slacks—as
though one could not wear what he wants up here. A bee had
stung him! I asked if it was a battle casualty, and if it made a
P.B. man of him. He did n't get it at all. Still, it was very feeble.
I 'm about done in and had to put off an unconscious "unknown"
—a soldier with no identification tag hit by the raiders last night.

Tuesday, the 21st

Rather a depressing time. Letters and packages from his home
keep turning up for Capt. Harris, who was killed a day or two
ago at Brandhoek. Our C.O. seems averse to taking any precautions—thinks it will frighten the sisters! I found at No. 64
that Wolstenholme's people were lowering the floors of their
tents about a foot. He had even put a sandbag barricade about
his own tent and had provided a dugout for the sisters. Last night
they had taken refuge in the new ditches dug by the Chinese in
the adjacent cemetery.

Dressings and operations all the morning, and finally an attempt
to save the "unknown." A hopeless procedure, I fear. A late
lunch about three, thanks largely to some potted chicken from
home. The Coldstream Guards band came again to play and cheer
us up. Very fine.

Being a Consulting Surgeon for the Canadians, Bruce, who is
attached to No. 64, has a limousine at his disposal. In it he took
me this afternoon to Dosinghem. They have really had a shocking time. At No. 61 five bombs had been dropped, four with so
horizontal a spread—"daisy cutters"—that lying down did not
suffice to escape fragments. The fifth, a torpedo, was a dud; it was
dug up and exploded in a field to-day. There were three killed
and twenty wounded, all among the personnel. George Brewer
had gone down to the Base, taking the nurse wounded the other
day.

When I got home at six I found the officers here all digging
funk holes about two feet deep alongside of their tents, and most
of them have prepared to sleep in them. Only a direct hit can
catch them there. They were also, at last, digging a trench shelter
for the sisters. Four new ones have been transferred here from
Brandhoek. They 've had a bad time, under cover for the last

48 hours with no sleep, and of course impossible to do any work. Bombed by night and then shelled by day. Several casualties, I believe, on the staff since poor Harris was killed.

It's ugly business. Evidently the Hun is laying for the 5th Army C.C.S.'s—Brandhoek, Rémy, Dosinghem—only Bandage-hem and Mendinghem have escaped so far from actual losses. They were all much upset at Dosinghem because General Skinner had ordered an electric Red Cross to be shown at night—a good mark to shoot at.

Tuesday, the 21st

Shilton's brother here to-night, and showed me just where his Division, the 61st, the Oxford Bucks, is to go over to-morrow. He was up yesterday taping out the line in sight of the German trenches, behind which his men of the 184th Brigade are to get when the barrage starts at 5.45 a.m. The line runs from B of Border House about s.s.e. through Fortuin to the road by Capricorn Keep. The 48th are on their left, the 15th on their right, and they hope to take Pond Farm and a few other bad nests of concrete fortifications, and to get on a bit toward the German third line, which must still be intact.

One fifth of the Brigade remains behind as a nucleus for a new one in case the others are wiped out. Shilton is among them this time. He is both sorry and glad. No one likes to go over; no one likes to see his friends go over alone. The detail of the preparation is quite incredible. Every man carries three days' rations with him, and must live of course in the open in such a ditch as he can dig for himself, after moving up 30 yards behind his barrage.

THE FIFTH ATTACK: INVERNESS COPSE

Thursday, the 23rd

2.45 a.m. Yesterday morning just as we were getting to work, a Fritz came over flying very high. He was thoroughly Archied and we saw him brought down before he could get back—a lucky shot. It's difficult to tell, however, who actually has the air supremacy.

Wounded began to arrive at noon and we managed to do seven cases between then and 1 a.m. when we switched off, having previously sent our two exhausted sisters to bed. Morton, Horrax, and I cleaned up the theatre ourselves and have just had a pair of eggs apiece and a pot of tea in the mess before turning in.

Evening. I have learned from a participant in the 14th Di_ vision that they were supposed to take Polygon Wood but made no gains, and there were severe counter-attacks. It appears that some troops advanced far enough along the Menin Road beyond "Clapham Junction" to penetrate Herenthage Wood, which the troops have dubbed "Inverness Copse." The purpose of these desperate recent attacks has been to gain control of the southern end of the ridge. It would look as though the nibbling tactics of the 5th Army on a short front were impossible to carry out because of enfilading fire on the flanks.

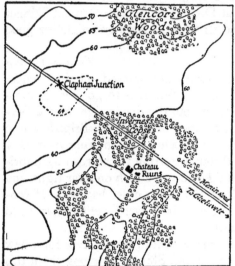

The Principal Terrain of the Battles of August 12, 22, and 25 for the Important High Ground Lying across the Menin Road in Contour 60

The three C.C.S.'s at Brandhoek have finally been abandoned as untenable. A sergeant and a boy who were left to clean up the mess were both killed to-day. I wonder how long Dosinghem will stand it. No further word from them.

Sunday, Aug. 26th

Back in Mendinghem again after two days at the Base for supplies. Horrax has done well with our cases and they look better, possibly as I am fresher after two good nights' sleep. Many dressings this morning, and after lunch Bruce took me first over to Rémy to see Crile, with whom a good talk. Says he does n't know the day of the week or month and does n't care: feels like a savage and is astonished to find he likes it. From there on to Mont des Cats, where a Colonel Slater is C.O. at the old monastery. Wonderful views of the country round about, with flashes of guns along the line to the north of Ypres. We took Colonel Blanchard, C.O. of No. 3 Canadian, back to his camp at Rémy and from there to a place I had always wished to see—one of the miniature maps laid out so the N.C.O.'s can familiarize themselves with the terrain before an attack. It was farther away than I thought, well to the s.e. of Poperinghe, somewhere on the Reninghelst–Dickebusch road, not far from la Clytte, which we visited in 1915.

The topographical ground map represented an area of some 2½ miles square beyond the July 31st line of trenches held by the 2nd Army with Hooge, Sanctuary Wood, and the Ypres–Menin Road to the right; and to the left the Ypres–Roulers railroad as far as Zonnebeke. Zonnebeke and Gheluvelt, lying somewhat beyond the map, were represented merely by signboards with the towns painted on them. On a scale of 1/50 horizontal and 1/12 vertical all the trenches were laid out by colored strips, almost every cottage, the woods, the little elevations—all very familiar names—some, like Westhoek, now ours, some not yet ours. "Inverness Copse," the Polygone de Zonnebeke, "Clapham Junction" on the Menin Road, and so on.

The present line of our trenches was in blue, and it plainly showed how Glencorse Wood proved a snag that held up a division, while that on the left, having gone well forward, was obliged to fall back as their right wing was in the air. And what a three years of war this particular region has seen! Gheluvelt, now in German hands and so far away! Yet there at the most critical moment of the first battle of Ypres, FitzClarence had the presence of mind to send the 2/ Worcesters in to stop the gap which kept the Germans from Calais and the coast—that fateful afternoon of October 31, 1914, when French and Haig thought the jig was up.

Some of the officers and N.C.O.'s who were studying the place like enough will be trying for their objectives to-morrow on the actual terrain itself. How the children would delight in construct. ing such a map on the sands at Little Boar's Head! Here it is a war game for the Engineers, but they nevertheless must enjoy it. . . .

To call things by improvised names is an essential part of the

game and deceives your opponent—supposedly. You must al_
ways speak in terms of concealment. You don't call a spade a spade
but "3946 Shovels G.S. earth." When, after mess, the C.O. walks
off to his hut with the only copy of yesterday's *Times*, he pretends
he has n't got it behind his back, and calls your attention to the
day's bulletin which he has put up on the door. The meaning of
this document is so well concealed it 's safe for *us* to read, but *he*
prefers the *Times*. As it was *my* copy of the *Times*, for which in
desperation I have subscribed, I think I am justified in walking
off to my tent with his bulletin. Here it is:—

2nd, 5th, 8th, 14th, 18th, 19th Corps, 5th Bdo. R.F.C., O.C., Spl. Coys R.E., 5th Army
A.A. Group, 1st Cav. Bde., 1st Cav. Div., Cav. Corps, and all concerned

G.794   26   A A A

Morning	Report	aaa	YAWL	reports
S.O.S.	sent	up	about	5
a.m.	this	morning	on	left
of	CABLE	and	right	of
LUCKS	front	Enemy	attacked	on
front	J.14.A.5.8	to	right	at
5	a.m.	Posts	at	J.14.A.7.4.
were	driven	in	Posts	at
J.14.A.8.8	are	still	maintained	aaa
Front	held	by	LATE	at
present	JARGON	Trench	J..4..A.5.8	J.4.A.55.60—
then	along	trench	running	S.W.
to	strong	point	at	J.14.A.25.25
Enemy	used	flammenwerfer	on	JARGON
Trench	successfully	driven	off	by
L.G.	fire	aaa	LAUNCH	reports [1]

Monday, the 27th August

An offensive was predicted for to-day. About midnight very
heavy firing began, followed by the customary deluge after a
week of good weather. The excessive bombardment all quieted
down before daybreak. Apparently the attack is to be postponed,
and our "take in" so far has been negligible. . . . Telfer tells me
that from his platform between July 23rd and Aug. 23rd, 17,299
cases were evacuated from these three Mendinghem hospitals.
There are twelve other C.C.S.'s in the 5th Army.

Tuesday the 28th

Atkins the stretcher-bearer was sent down to-day. He 's a fine
cheery fellow. After his last dressing this morning he gave me
a bit of ribbon to remember him by. He won his Military Medal
at the Somme and is to have another bar on it for this, I believe.

[1] It is needless to reproduce this 5th Army report in its entirety. Be it enough to say that
there were thirty-three additional lines, equally unintelligible.—The Editor

Wednesday, August 29th

Remarkable for the extraordinary storm of wind and rain, which blew down a lot of our tents and even took the roof from one of the cars of a waiting ambulance train. This lasted nearly twelve hours. We were busy on some desperate cases till 2.30 this [Thursday] morning, and though cold it was clear as a bell when I turned in. Now it is raining again. No wonder the British at another time swore horribly in Flanders.

Wilson's reply to the Pope's peace proposals "made in Germany" helps some.

Thursday, August the 30th

Last Sunday came a letter from Lady Osler telling me that Revere was somewhere near St. Julien and how dreadful it would be should he be brought in to me with a head wound, and yet how thankful they would be. I answered immediately, asking her to wire me the number of his unit so that I could try and locate him among the millions. Rather used up, I was preparing to turn in at 10 last night, when came this shocking message: "Sir Wm. Osler's son seriously wounded at 47 C.C.S. Can Major Cushing come immediately?" The C.O. let me have an ambulance, and in a pouring rain we reached Dosinghem in about half an hour. It could not have been much worse, though there was a bare chance—one traversing through the upper abdomen, another penetrating the chest just above the heart, two others in the thigh, fortunately without a fracture.

The local C.O. would not let me cable, and I finally insisted on phoning G.H.Q.—got General Macpherson on the wire and persuaded him to send to Oxford via the London War Office: "Revere seriously wounded: not hopelessly: conscious: comfortable."

Crile came over from Rémy with Eisenbrey, and after a transfusion, Darrach, assisted by Brewer, opened the abdomen about midnight. There had been bleeding from two holes—in the upper colon and the mesenteric vessels. His condition remained unaltered, and about seven this morning the world lost this fine boy, as it does many others every day.

We saw him buried in the early morning. A soggy Flanders field beside a little oak grove to the rear of the Dosinghem group —an overcast, windy, autumnal day—the long rows of simple

wooden crosses—the new ditches half full of water being dug
by Chinese coolies wearing tin helmets—the boy wrapped in an
army blanket and covered by a weather-worn Union Jack, carried
on their shoulders by four slipping stretcher-bearers. A strange
scene—the great-great-grandson of Paul Revere under a British
flag, and awaiting him a group of some six or eight American
Army medical officers—saddened with the thoughts of his father.
Happily it was fairly dry at this end of the trench, and some green
branches were thrown in for him to lie on. The Padre recited the
usual service—the bugler gave the "Last Post"—and we went
about our duties. Plot 4, Row F.

Major Batchelor, the C.O. of A Battery, 59th Brigade, and
seven men had been brought in at the same time, as I learned from
the records. I saw and talked with several of them during the
evening. They were just beyond Pilkem, between Langemarck
and St. Julien, two to three hundred yards this side of Hindenburg Trench, and were preparing to move the four batteries up
to-day. Major Batchelor, Revere, and eighteen men were bridg-
ing over a shell hole in preparation for the move of the guns in
their battery. It was about 4.30 in the afternoon and there had
been no shelling. They were so busy they did not even hear the
first shell—a direct hit which wounded eight out of the twenty.

It was difficult to get back, but they finally were brought to the
dressing station at Essex Farm on the canal—a 3000-yard carry,
then a short distance on a narrow-gauge ammunition track—the
advanced post of the 131st Field Ambulance in front of Canada
Farm, then by ambulance to No. 47, which was "taking in"—
a matter of four hours.

Sept. 2. Sunday evening

Marvel of marvels—a cloudless afternoon and evening, with
a full moon just appearing in the low east. This is fortunate, for
we have been going through a most depressing time. Much discouragement in the air, fostered doubtless by the long period of
wet and wind. These people are certainly "fed up," as they say,
with the war. The great offensive has been a dismal failure, which
we may justly attribute to the weather. In the words of the *communiqué* "our objectives were gained," but it's a good deal like
the farmer who said his "crops were not half as good as he ex-

pected and he never thought they would be." We are glad to make much of the recent French success in pushing the line a little back from Verdun, and the unexpected Italian advance on the Bainsizza plateau, which must have given the Austrians a jolt after many months of standstill.

I have been cooped up of late—too much so—and walked over before dinner to see the Boche plane which came down near us, bag and baggage, the other night. He began about midnight by dropping bombs in Proven, flew directly over us, very low, and suddenly his engine stopped. By that time those of us who have no funk holes were lying on our faces in the wet grass—but nothing happened and we did n't hear him start his engine again. Preferring a bomb to pneumonia, I took to my cot. It turned out that because of motor trouble he was obliged to coast to a landing, a mile or two from here. Such a different-looking country between No. 46 and the aerodrome! I could hardly find my path of two weeks ago, the landscape had so changed. The hops ripening, and many of them down; the hay all in and built up in stacks; the days are shortening: autumn is here.

Gerard's disclosures in his *Four Years in Germany* and Wilson's reply to the Peace proposals of the Pope are as good as battles won. The pen is mightier than the sword, especially when it rains in Flanders. There is no blotting paper to dry up mud. There is little doing according to the "canned" *communiqués* of Sept. 1st and 2nd, yet we seem to have plenty of work.

Tuesday, September 4th

7.30 p.m. A still, clear evening after a full day's work, with little sleep last night, for we operated till 2 a.m. The airmen are coming home, ten, twenty, thirty of them. Somersaulting, side_slipping, volplaning, cavorting, pretending to be engaged. Some, mere specks, tumble out of the sky; others almost in reach just overhead. Perfect children. Turberville goes home to-morrow to instruct somewhere. I shall miss his frequent "cheerio."

To see Gen. Skinner last evening at the *Château Lovie* in re_gard to a temporary leave, which he is loath to grant—says we must apply in the usual form. In two weeks' time we must be back. There is to be another "push"—weather permitting. I stayed to dine at his mess with a group of junior officers. There was a good deal of gentle banter which seemed to amuse him. He looks old to me and shows the strain. People with responsibilities have aged fast, I judge, in the past three years. I urged him to set apart a forward hospital to be restricted so far as possible to wounds of the head. We could easily train the teams to man it at our base and instruct them in the rudiments of neurosurgery. Our single team during the past month has knocked the mortality figures for pene_ trating wounds from 56 per cent to nearly 25 per cent. He will look into it and talk to the D.G., but foresees difficulties—e.g., no rotation with adjacent hospitals and therefore continuous and kill_ ing work. Thirty thousand wounded for the 5th Army from July 31st to August 2nd, and three thousand recorded "G.s.w. skull." Could any one hospital possibly cover it?

A lively night, the last, from Boche raiders—they seemed to be everywhere. Dunkerque severely bombed; also Boulogne, we hear. For the first time we saw our own planes up to meet them—carrying the lights to warn off our own Archies!! A good deal like looking for a burglar in the cellar with a lighted candle in your hand, and with the idea you 'd shoot first. Our flying men are a sort of day swallow; the enemy are more batlike and nocturnal.

BOMBING OF BASE HOSPITAL No. 5

Thursday, 6th Sept. En route Camiers

At about four this morning, this disconcerting message was put in my sleepy hand, and a match struck to read it by: "Hospital bombed last night. Fitzsimons and three men killed. Whidden, Smith, McGuire, wounded but in good shape. Since going on satisfactorily. (*Signed*) Patterson." Fitzsimons, Smith, and McGuire must be the new M.O.'s attached since my departure. So Base Hospital No. 5 has had its turn again—one of the first American units over—one of the first if not *the* first to suffer casualties. Almost too bad that newly attached men have had to take the full brunt of it rather than those of our own group.

I luckily got permission from the Army H.Q. to be away for a few days without the delay of a movement order through tortuous official channels; then to Dosinghem to see if the bribed corporal is properly caring for Revere's grave; then a hurriedly written report of our six weeks' experience for General Skinner to submit to the D.G.; then this rattly ambulance. An attempt to write is no joke—it will be better after St. Omer when we get off the *pavés*, but I shall then crawl inside and try to sleep.

The fields are much changed since my last trip. The hop pickers are at work; the last of the haystacks are being groomed, their headdress terminating in a wisp like that on the top of a mandarin's scalp; only the fields of mangoes are still green and untouched; some officers are exercising and jumping horses in the bare fields; more Tommies are playing football in others; and on the sides of the thatched or red-tiled cottages what looks like tobacco is hung up to dry. Beside the larger dome-shaped stacks are funny little spindly ones which my Tommy chauffeur says is a kind of French bean: "They calls 'em hurry-coverze." An anxious pig meets us head-on in the road wearing a triangular wooden collar on his neck; he thinks he's run against something and ludicrously tries to step over the crossbar, first one foot, then the other; we crowd him grunting into the ditch, where he's more at home. Arques, full of Australians; the cut-off south of St. Omer; rain.

Thursday evening. Camiers

It was worse than I had feared from the C.O.'s telegram. Five bombs of the daisy-cutting variety, about 10.30 Tuesday evening —direct hits in our camp, after two anticipatory ones beyond No. 18, and a torpedo dud in No. 4's compound. The first two hits were close together, just at the entrance of the hedge, behind which were the tents for the N.C.O.'s and for some of the overflow officers. McGuire, a Kansas City man recently attached to us, was in his cot and had a most providential escape, with his three or four wounds. His tent is riddled; a sergeant tells me he counted 400 holes and got tired; his tin bucket is full of horizontal perfora_ tions. Poor Fitzsimons was standing in the opening of his tent— or had been when last seen. The bomb must have dropped almost at his feet, and he fortunately could never have known what had happened. He was literally blown to pieces. Whidden was in the nearest tent on this side of the hedge and among other minor things has a penetrating chest wound.

The third bomb fell at the near end of C-V; the fourth directly through one of the marquees of the same ward, tearing things to pieces and killing Private Tugo, who was standing near Miss Par_ melee, though more actual damage was done in C-VI, the adjacent ward. The last went through the reception tent, where Rubino, Woods the bugler, MacLeod, and English were on duty. The first two were killed, and MacLeod badly injured. Sergeant English heard the bomb's whistle and, warning the others, made a rush for the opening. Thanking English for his seat, Woods got up from a bench and plumped himself in the chair he had just vacated. Details will doubtless be given in an official report. There were many narrow escapes; many holes through tents all over the compound, even as far as the mess hut, which is peppered at about four feet height, just at our end of the table. Many amusing episodes also. Jim Stoddard, he of the life preserver, automatic pistol, and night watches of the *Saxonia* days, was working in his laboratory making media. The window and its sash were broken; there were several through-and-through holes in the corner of the room. Thinking a local munition dump had blown up, he never stopped work.

But all this is not my story. I only wish it were. It was a bad night, and everyone seems to have behaved admirably. There were of course a number of critical and urgent operations. MacLeod, the nice young chap who brought over our last reënforcements, lost both legs, and the next day had a double thigh amputation, high up, for fulminating gas-bacillus infection. To Cutler's great credit he promises to recover. There has been a curious amount of rapid and severe infection from several of these wounds, perhaps due to our badly infected old encampment. Twenty-two Tommy patients were rewounded.

Camiers. Saturday, Sept. 8th

7 *p.m.* My old tent is somewhat the worse for wear, having been used as a receptacle for bicycles—bicycles no longer of much use, for fragments of the bombs went through most of them. Graham's little fringe of garden is a sad spectacle from neglect. A few dwarf nasturtiums are still ablaze in the tangle, and the mignonette shows a bold rear guard, but the front line is "na poo." Some German five-pfennig bits were picked up at our camp the morning after the raid. Was this an act of insolence on the part of the Hun, or an accident?

G. Bastianelli in his Italian uniform has been about all day. He

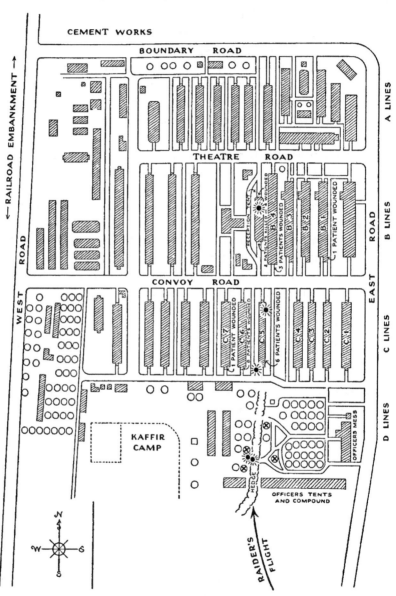

Ground Map of U.S. Army Base Hospital No. 5 Showing Where the Bombs Were Dropped in the Air Raid of September 4, 1917. The Five Stars Indicate Where the Bombs Fell, the Circles with Crosses Bell Tents Whose Occupants Were Killed or Seriously Wounded

and Foster Kennedy lunched here, and afterwards we went down to No. 26 at Étaples. There I encountered Major Lindsay, formerly of No. 11, more Scotch than ever, and equally observant. Recalling that our naturalist expedition had never come off, he said he had a new discovery—fossilized echinoderms—the hills full of them—had never noticed them before. Then Captain Yellowlees, who is in charge of the mental cases, showed us some Roman coins (*circa* A.D. 400) and some pottery which had been dug up in the sand dunes. Fifteen centuries since some Roman legionnaire dropped or buried his pieces of money on this strip of coast, and how many more since Lindsay's fossils were living things and these hills were below water, I do not presume to guess. But these are merely the straws of history—a fossilized sea urchin, Roman coppers, and Boche nickels from the same chalk hills. Probably neolithic man had his camp here; we know that Cæsar did, and Napoleon, and now the British—not for the first time either.

Yellowlees proceeded to show us some crazy men who thought there were bombs under their beds, and I went off to find Morrison, Bashford, and Hartley, to get some dichloramine-T for use on my return to Mendinghem. Then to see Miss Parmelee, our nurse, who had the closest kind of call; rather used up to-day after her antitoxin, but she deserves a Military Cross or whatever women are given for presence of mind, neglect of self, and thought of others, in time of possible panic. She was standing at the entrance of C-V, not twenty-five feet from the third bomb. She's rather frail and it knocked her down, but she heard the cries and groans of the patients, got right to work, and stayed on duty all night. In the morning she turned up in the operating room, where had been a *mêlée* all night, to get Morton to take a tiny shell fragment out of her eyelid. Her sweater had six good-sized holes in it and her heavy outer coat about as many. Her watch was picked off by a piece of the shell, leaving only the strap, and it has not yet been found.

Sunday, Sept. 16th. Mendinghem again

Meeting called by General Skinner at 11 with the C.O.'s and Surgeon Specialists of these three C.C.S.'s to discuss the question of head cases—possibly the outcome of my report. I suggest having a weekly conference and we agree on Tuesday afternoons. Commission[1] to investigate the wastage of M.O.'s here for lunch while visiting Mendinghem. They arrived about ten minutes past one— were fed abundantly—left at ten minutes of two. I asked the C.O. whether anything was said on the subject of their quest. He replied that the only question put to him was whether the ambulance train standing on the track—it had been parted for them—was bringing patients or taking them away. Since these trains are only for evacuating patients, this was evidently something off the Commission's beat. I had a chance for a few words with Stiles and asked him what it all meant; he admitted that they could do nothing more than send in a whitewashing report—"eye wash," in short. I told him the work done here could be covered by just half the M.O.'s if they would use sisters or orderlies, as our team was doing, to give anæsthesia.

As a matter of fact it seems to me that there *is* an enormous wastage, and much injustice, largely due to the professional arrangement of zones (Front, L. of C., and Base), rather than radially from Front to Base for each army. As things stand, an M.O. gets attached to a field ambulance and may stick there for two years without ever being exchanged; may be in constant danger; though busy, may have no medical work whatever to do and so rust out completely. On the other hand, vigorous young men who ought to be with a regiment or an F.A. at the Front get easy jobs at the Base and remain there for an equally long time. For example, Hallowes and Kennedy, capable young chaps who, after a year, one at the 17th, the other at the 18th F.A. of the 6th Division, finally succeeded in getting out and were attached here for a couple of weeks—they have never seen service at the Base.

Ere long, word comes from headquarters to the C.O. that two M.O.'s are wanted for F.A. positions "forthwith." He naturally selects men he does not know very well and therefore those who have been here the shortest time. Hence the C.O.'s Territorial friends remain while Hallowes and Kennedy are returned to the line. This I drag out of them after the Commission departed. They

[1] This committee was appointed by the British Secretary of War to proceed to France to inquire into the administration of the Army Medical Services. Its members were: Major General Sir Francis Howard (chairman), Sir Rickman Godlee, Sir Frederick Taylor, Sir W. Watson Cheyne, M.P., Lieutenant Colonel H. J. Stiles, Dr. Norman Walker, Dr. Charles Buttar, Dr. J. B. Christopherson (secretary).

naturally were itching to tell the Commission a few things. Another M.O. here from an ambulance train has had nothing what_
ever to do for six weeks. There are others who do nothing but ride
on motor ambulances.

The regimental M.O.'s—one for each battalion—likewise have
very little medical work to do, but there is no doubt from what
Miller tells me that they are absolutely essential to the morale of
the men. Having a doctor around when they go over the top is a
source of comfort, even though the M.O. knows there is little he
can do for them that an orderly cannot do. He is useful also in
looking after the sanitation of their billets, and I presume a good
M.O. of Miller's type is next in importance in many ways to the
colonel. Incidentally Miller wears a D.S.O. ribbon for "going
over" to get lying-out cases.

Tuesday, 18th

After a morning and afternoon spent in preparation, the first
clinic with demonstration of cases was held in the old operating
hut from four to five, General Skinner presiding. Many from
Nos. 12 and 64 there. It was possibly too good; no one would
speak: all glued to their seats until I moved an adjournment for
tea. They then discussed for a time whether future meetings had
better be at four or six owing to tea time. The D.M.S. was for
having a secretary, at which I protested, urging that the sessions
be kept informal.

Mr. Buttrick, G.E.B.,[1] told me Saturday when I saw him in
Camiers of his encountering in Liverpool a former friend—a
Canadian lumber merchant—who had drifted over with the first
contingent and was now in British service. Mr. B. asked him what
he was doing and he said he was a sort of magnified stevedore engaged in unloading lumber ships. He was given the job presumably because he owned lumber mills and therefore knew lumber
when he saw it. Being given it, he got to work and found them
unloading the heavy timber with an antiquated apparatus which
necessitated placing a chain on each end of every beam, and which
then deposited them in a huge pile on the dock. This pile subsequently had to be disentangled, like picking out jackstraws, and
sorted into some six or eight sizes—a performance which took

[1] General Education Board.

about ten days. He therefore installed an unloading device with a long swinging crane which could not only pick up a log in its middle, but deposit it on the dock in its appropriate pile according to size. It took about ten hours for the whole performance. "But," he added, "the curious thing is they dislike me for it."

Indeed the British—individuals of course excluded—look upon our restless activity as a failing, not as a virtue. It hurts their pride to read what Northcliffe has to say about the scale of preparations in the U.S.A. They say England can and will win the war alone on this Western Front, which is an admirable spirit—the trouble is they are *not* winning it and have no prospect of doing so. The interesting psychological part of all this is that the talk is all on one side; for surprisingly enough one meets little of the proverbial American boasting—over here at least.

After a period of good weather it is overcast and drizzling. We have rapidly followed No. 12 this evening in our rotation of 200 gassed cases. This sounds like the preliminaries of the offensive of July 31st.

The Sixth Battle: Menin Road

Wednesday, Sept. 19th

10 p.m. Three divisions are supposed to go over the top tomorrow to try once more for the high ground along the Menin Road—the 55th, the 9th, and one other on the 5th Corps (?) front. About an hour ago a steady downpour of rain set in.

Friday, 21 September, 1917

1 a.m. British, Australians, and South Africans went over on a wide front at 5.40 yesterday morning. Wounded began to come in about 10, giving us time to finish most of our morning's dressings, and to evacuate as many old cases as possible. Since then we have done seven, nearly all "multiples," so the total is about fifteen. Some unusual injuries—for example the lateral suture of a bra_ chial artery and vein, etc. We 've evacuated about 1500 cases__ three trainloads. The weather has not been bad—no rain, I be_ lieve, though overcast.

Difficult to tell what has happened: the morning *communiqué* says Pheasant Farm, Wurst Farm, Barry and Anzac Farms in our hands, and the 2nd Army, on the right, has reached its "red line" ⁻—their objective, I presume. It 's impossible to learn much from the Tommies, especially from these hit soon after going over. About 50 German wounded here, one cocky young lieutenant who admits the attack was *"ganz unerwartet."* No word of the airmen or the tanks.

10 p.m. Waiting for Gil to finish a case before I tackle this West-

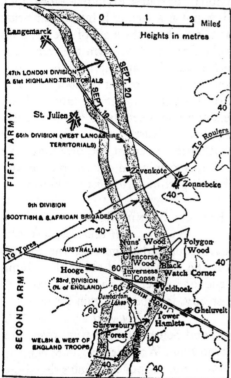

Approximate British Advance in the Battle of
September 20

phalian German boy lying here. He seems a nice lad; says they know it's all up, but no one is permitted to talk about it. He says, too, their officers never go over the top in an attack the way ours do, and the men dislike them. He's very glad to be here getting his head ready to be opened, and adds that he tried two years ago to get taken prisoner, but there is always an officer behind with a revolver. There's a German lieutenant here aged 22—with a wounded finger!! Says he will be court-martialed after the war—no officer without a very good excuse may surrender. He was in a blockhouse—one of the "pill boxes" so much talked of—with eight men, all of them either wounded or killed but himself. What was he to do?

It's been a sunny cool day—ideal for an advance. General Sloggett was here this morning with Bertrand Dawson to say the usual things to the M.O.'s and nurses in praise of their hard work. He said all was over, for a few days at least, and we need expect no more wounded. Nevertheless a batch of Liverpool Scottish and South Africans have just been brought in after lying out for thirty-six hours—many bad wound infections. Indeed, it seems to me that most of the wounds have been even worse than last time.

Telfer says we have evacuated 2719 cases in a little over 24 hours; also that since October 5, 1916, when No. 46 was set up, there will have been 20,000 cases through this one place by some time to-morrow. They then will shift to serial number 1 again. Twenty thousand cases—nearly a division—and the proper arrangement is one C.C.S. to a division. One may draw his own conclusions as to how long it takes before everyone in an army division may expect to suffer some form of casualty.

Fritz is "up" to-night, the first time I have seen him since returning from Camiers—also some of our own planes which quickly drop a Verey light if the big French searchlight happens to probe them out. Results of this last battle, according to hearsay, 2000 prisoners, six guns, 1000 yards over a ten-mile front. Nothing about our own casualties or counter-attacks. It certainly has gone better than the muddy affair of seven weeks ago.

Saturday, Sept. 22nd

11 p.m. Falling off to-day. It has not been so bad, though these late gas-bacillus infections are shocking. One of the afternoon's cases was a man named Traynor of the King's Liverpool Regt., with a huge 3-inch piece of shell, big as one's index finger, which had gone from his frontal eminence through the frontal lobe into the orbit. He must have been wounded sometime yesterday and came through the Wessex F.A. at 12.30—they are noting the hour as well as the date since our discussion of last Tuesday—was admitted here at 6.47 a.m., got lost somehow in the crowded wards, and was fired in at us unexpectedly this afternoon.

I was in the midst of this, under local anæsthesia, when General Skinner came in with some French officers—Ferraton of the Val-de-Grâce, now *Genl. Inspecteur* of the French Army up here, also the Liaison Officer of the 5th Army, a Major Romando I believe, and one or two others. They hung about, apparently interested, and when the stinking missile was finally dislodged and I got the gassy odor, I held it out to the D.M.S. to smell. He did, and did n't like it.

Sunday, the 23rd

7 p.m. We expected a rest to-day and a walk, but it has taken till now to do 18 dressings, most of them major ones, here in the

theatre; and then at the end a try at saving one of the resuscita-
tion-ward cases, a stretcher-bearer with a perforating wound from
the right temple and out the left eye, cutting both optic nerves.

There is a nice fellow from Devonshire named Killick, a subaltern of the 6th London Regiment (174th Brigade and so the
58th Division) with about ten wounds, who is doing well enough
to evacuate to-night. His objective was Wurst Farm and he is
cheered to learn that it was gained and hopes his platoon got
through the German barrage which caught him about at the concrete emplacements west of Hoppner Farm, quite early in the
morning. He says that they were swinging round from the north,
through the "triangle": Hoppner, von Tirpitz, to Wurst Farm,
and were to meet the 55th Division coming up from the south to
catch the place like a pair of nippers. Judging from the objective
map for the 55th, I rather doubt this.

While doing dressings this morning there was a sudden furious
Archie bombardment. We dropped everything and rushed out.
A great sight—twelve Boche planes in formation, very high, black
as larks against the gray clouds, and simply surrounded by dark
puffs of shrapnel; finally one of them dove and fell. It was almost
like shooting into a flock of ducks. Then a lot of our planes appeared and the flock scattered. The visibility has been extraordinarily good, and this afternoon the sky was fairly dotted with
high-flying planes.

Monday, Sept. 24th

8 p.m. I decided last night that I was fed up with the place and
its work, and suggested to Zink that we get up early and make our
way into "Wipers" to see the Cloth Hall before it is entirely gone.
So I was called at five by Thompson, who brought shaving water
and breakfast—an egg, bread and butter, and something which
might have been tea or coffee, I was not quite sure. A cold misty
morning, and we started to leg it toward Poperinghe in the dim
dawn. We finally hopped a lorry which carried us well through
"Pop" and to a certain corner, where the driver advised us to wait
for a lift. And sure enough, soon some big cars of the Salvage
Corps came along and one of them gathered us in—it was labeled
"Annie lorry."

A ghostly ride through a dense chilly mist, past camps, dumps,
and dugouts, with glimpses of morning parades and Tommies

stripped to the waist getting some sort of wash. Finally there appeared through the mist a faint greenish-yellow sun like the yolk of a hard-boiled egg, and on its surface a black spot! I thought at first it was a high-flying plane, or a bird, or something nearer— a fly or indeed a spot on my retina. But no, it stayed, and the driver said: "Looks like a bit o' shrapnel 's 'it 'im." It must have been a sun spot with some rare atmospheric conditions making it visible.

We were on the southerly detour to Ypres via Oudendom, Dickebusch, and Kruisstraat. At a devastated place called "Pioneer Dump" we picked up some Australians who were "going in" and who said that their people had made an attack in the Shrewsbury Forest region, which accounts for the early morning barrage we had heard. It was weird enough getting glimpses through the mist of the wreckage in this forward area. The Porte de Lille was reached almost before we knew it, with traces of the old moat and tumble-down ramparts of the ancient fortifications. We had committed a great breach in not bringing our tin hats and box respirators instead of our small pocket gas masks, and only got across the bridge and by the traffic police by borrowing helmets from the Australians.

The moated city covers only a small area and we were soon dropped in the *Grande Place* at the very entrance of the ruined Cloth Hall—still a noble ruin whose former proportions may easily be imagined from what remains. Of the Cathedral near by there is practically nothing but a great mound of rubble, and if this part of the town is like all the rest, the ruin is complete— much worse than I had thought possible, even after three years of more or less incessant shelling.

Ypres is a safe enough place, especially on a misty morning, and to-day there was no gunfire on either side. Still, at every corner —one of them is known as "Suicide Corner"—a traffic officer respectfully notified us that no one was permitted there without helmet and respirator. So we had to move along, finally getting a lift through Vlamertynghe on our way back to Proven, where we arrived at ten, in time for the day's work, which fortunately has not been heavy.

I find it impossible to do justice to the ghostly view we had of ruined Ypres. I recall the huge water tank near the Vlamertynghe Gate which has been torn from its roots and tilted on edge—not the ugly sort of gas or oil tank which offends one in our cities at home, but one which had been veneered with brick and Gothic stone tracery to match the architecture of the town. Beyond that, it's a blur, like a kodak film developed after overlapping exposures.

THE SEVENTH ATTACK: ZONNEBEKE

Wednesday the 26th Sept.

The attack came this morning with zero hour at 5.50. It was a minor affair of which we had received no notice, else we would not have ventured into Ypres. There have been low clouds all day on the verge of tears—fortunately unshed. We were off our guard as there were no walking wounded, Brandhoek having been reopened to care for them. Hence our first warning was when a lot of lying cases began to arrive about 1.30, and it took only two hours for our quota of 200. Apparently the attack has been a success, with comparatively few wounded.

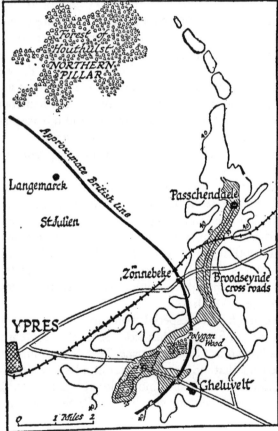

The September 26th Advance on the Southern End of the Ridges with Capture of Polygon Wood

The men quite elated. We have seen chiefly Suffolks, Welsh Fusiliers, and Gordons of the 3rd Divisions. They say they went beyond Zonnebeke, and believe the Polygon Wood has been taken. Wounded from the 59th Division were also very cheerful and a sergeant told me they had taken Gravenstafel. However, I saw some wounded this evening at No. 12, who say there were three very violent counter-attacks and that they had to give way, with loss of all the ground gained. We may pay for this to-morrow.

Friday, Sept. 28th

2 *a.m.* We 've had a day of it, and though it 's late I must put some of it down, lest the next twenty-four hours crowd it all out. We have covered since 9 a.m. yesterday twelve head cases, which owing to multiples constitute a total of about twenty more or less major wounds—our record so far.

It was a little hard "sticking" to-night for it sounded as though the world were exploding—almost noisy enough for a field ambulance. At one time a munition dump went off near by—at another a Fritz came over, was caught and held in the searchlights for three minutes by the watch—Zink timed him—and in the midst of Archie flashes one could see his tracer bullets as he methodically swept the road with his machine gun. Soon a lot of bombs were dropped near by—Proven perhaps—and every now and then the big French naval guns would go off and rattle the operating hut as though they were next door instead of a mile or so away. As I say, it was hard sticking while so much was going on outside in the clear moonlight night; but we had our work cut out for us. Just as we were leaving we saw brought in the victims of one of the bombs—from near Vlamertynghe—three officers among them.

All manner of stories are flying about and it is difficult to learn what really has happened. First we had all our objectives; then we were driven back all along the line; then, according to some, we were back again. It all depends on what a man happened to be doing or seeing when he was hit. A wounded officer told me this afternoon, with tears, that his men—new recruits—had actually run.

Blake has just come into the mess where I am writing, with the tale that the men are seeing red—that they were driven out of many places but regained them later to-day, and have found all the wounded they left behind bayoneted in the interval. There 'll be the devil to pay and not many prisoners will be seen. While

Gil was dressing his pet Boche officer this afternoon I asked him what he thought of the war. He looked scornfully at me and made no reply. I then asked him what he thought of the Kaiser. He rolled up his eyes, put his hand on his heart, and said solemnly: *"Unser Kaiser—Unser Kaiser."* These are hard people to beat.

There was a perfect succession of cases and we managed to turn them off more rapidly than ever before; no less carefully, I hope. I remember my surprise at one of them, a queer-looking chap named Rifleman O. Butler, from Banbury Tutwell (*sic*), where he works in a brick yard, peace times. He had an awful-looking, not to say evil-smelling, gutter wound. While novocainizing his scalp I as usual tried to make him talk, and asked him his division and regiment. "Oxford Bucks; 20th Division, sir." "How can that be, they went over on the 20th, a week ago?" "I went over with 'em, sir." He actually did, and has been lying for a week in a shell hole, until, during the attack of yesterday, someone found him. He said he had eaten nothing, for his bully beef went "agin" him and he was n't hungry—indeed thought he had been out of his head for two or three of the days. Then when it got dark he used to holler, but no one came.

A stolid soul is O. Butler from Banbury. He does n't seem to think his escapade anything out of the ordinary and I have n't a doubt he will recover from his ugly wound—his kind does. I asked him if he was in the barrage of yesterday morning and whether he knew there was an offensive under way. No, he just heard a terrible rattle and crawled up to the edge of his shell hole and waved his hand: some stretcher-bearers came along and took him away—that 's all he knows.

October 1st

2 p.m. They got the No. 29 aerodrome on the "Pop"–Proven road last night, about half an hour after Gil and I passed there. Seventeen wounded, the Squadron Major among them; he with four others died here during the night. One of the R.A.F. officers from No. 29, who came in to see the survivors this morning, said that some daredevil had gone up from No. 70, which is alongside of them, to meet the Hun—the first one over this area after sunset. They were showing a green flare to give him his bearings and the C.O. of 29 had stepped out of the dugout, where they were at mess with some guests, to protest, for it was an equally good guide to the Hun. He got a bad g.s.w. multiple with a torn spleen, and Alexander's effort to save him, when they got him in here, was too late.

In fact, it was such a bad night that our cases this morning are much agitated and upset—all begging to be sent down. No operations; dressings only. Some of the cranio-cerebro-facial cases are doing remarkably well under Dakin's dichloramine-T.

7.30 p.m. The transitions over here are quite unbelievable. This morning hell fire was loose—much worse than on the days preceding July 31st—the bombardment, though six miles away, was so heavy that the operating room shook with it—drum fire hardly describes it, for that suggests interruption of sound, whereas this was practically continuous from the time I awoke till about noon. Repelling a German counter, I judge—possibly our men going over. This evening by contrast is absolutely quiet except for the faint strumming of some M.O. in the mess, on an old piano wangled from Dunkerque, and the occasional clatter of someone's footsteps on our noisy duckboards which sound like a sort of muffled xylophone—if that's the name of the instrument. Mess call. . . .

Along the Proven road toward Dunkerque, two miles northwest of here, is a pretty village called Rousbrugge, stringing out along the usual main street, with its town hall, shops, church, and market place; then a fascinating canal with lazy barges and *poilus* in horizon-blue fishing from them. Others lean over the bridge which separates Rousbrugge from the next village, called Beveren, and watch a long-haired black dog plunge into the water to retrieve a stick thrown out for him. In the little market place plays a French military band to accompany a soldier with a fine baritone, who sings a spirited song.

All this is a scant two miles away from Mendinghem—and a Flanders as different from our khaki-colored area as the sky is from the soil. I had never been in this direction before, and this afternoon walked over with Fred Murphy, who is with a team next door at No. 64. We got our pictures taken by a little Belgian woman in Beveren. She has a brother living in Detroit and there-fore is proud to say a few words in English. So here on our im-mediate left is the 1st French Army, with their best fighting corps, the 36th and the *Chasseurs Alpins* (the "blue devils") under General Antoine, with headquarters at Rexpoede; and a fine-looking lot of men they are—every other one, it would seem, wearing a *Croix de Guerre.*

An *auxiliaire* who proved to be a Miss Tredwell of American Ambulance days breezed up saying she was at H.O.E. No. 34 over Crombeke way; also that in Rousbrugge was a Franco-American Ambulance supported by a Mrs. Burdon-Turner; and there she escorted us for tea. At this *Centre Chirurgical* they take only *grands blessés*—an interesting place, completely under cover in well-spaced Adrian huts and with ample room in contrast to our crowded British C.C.S.'s. This Burdon-Turner Ambulance No. 1 has attached to it an *Hôpital Chirurgical Mobile No. 1*—the identical mobile outfit originated by Marcille and perfected by Gosset that I saw in Paris in May 1915.

The *Médecin Chef*, Le Normant by name, showed us the chief features of the place, including his device for resuscitation tables and the splendid X-ray equipment and bacteriological laboratory. We hie ourselves home arguing over the comparative merits of the Tommy and the *poilu*, but agree that if Joe Flint's Yale Am-bulance is built on the lines of these mobile units of which the French now have eighty, he will have done a great service. I spoke about them with some enthusiasm at dinner, but my British neighbors showed faint interest. . . .

Col. Ellery, C.O. of No. 13 C.C.S., is a temporary guest here, as Elverdinghe proved too hot a place for them. He was in Gal-lipoli—at Anzac. Awful experience—the blizzard, the flies, the dysentery, and constant exposure to shellfire. His C.C.S. is shown in the picture in Masefield's book.

Wednesday, 3rd Oct.

11 p.m. It has been our "taking-in" day and we have been mod-erately busy with cases from bombs and shells, largely in back areas. Nevertheless, the information is abroad that there is to be an attack to-morrow in which only two 5th Army corps will participate. This, however, may be preliminary to a widespread engagement—weather permitting—from the sea to the Lys, for the 4th Army has become rejuvenated since its setback in July. Meanwhile the 5th Army is shortening its front and the 2nd on our right may participate in the effort to straighten the line south of Ypres, where, from the slowness of the advance, it is now so indented the enemy can enfilade our positions. . . .

Young Capt. Walker, the M.O. of the 2/ Scots Guards, came for me at seven to dine with Ross at their present billet in some field "a twenty minutes' walk" from here near Heydebeek. A dark cloudy night, we got lost in French territory and kept getting challenged; so it was 8.30 when we reached the camp, to find Ross and a Lieut. Menzies sitting under a queer little umbrella tent with dinner waiting for us. They are going in to-morrow for their part of the big push, and Ross said that the next two or three weeks will make it clear whether or not the British could have done it without America's participation. They and the French are to coöperate in an attack on Houthulst Forest, which is probably a badly infested spot.

Ross had just come from Calais, where he passed the night of the raid; more than 100 bombs dropped in the town, with much damage and many casualties despite the defensive preparations with 30 or more planes on patrol. The raiders came two or three at a time from varying directions, and only three of them were brought down, and the roads out of Calais were packed with refugees.

There was much talk of the war and the international situation; of England's refusal in 1914 to let a million and a half Japanese participate on this front; of the characteristics of the Hun, and hate, and the dead and their gruesome appearance—a skeleton in a uniform and helmet—the crows, the frogs, and the maggots make short work of a dead body. Gloomy talk for people the night before an attack. Meanwhile there were other dinners in various officers' huts, and Pipe Major Ross with two or three others played again. I asked the name of one particularly mournful tune and was told it was "The McIntosh Lament." Very appropriate to the evening, for it was blowing up cold and wet.

THE EIGHTH ATTACK: BROODSEINDE

Friday, Oct. 5th

2.30 a.m. Zero was 6 a.m. yesterday—cloudy and drizzly. Morning report of 5th Army addressed to 29th and 4th Guards, 11th, 48th, 18th, 9th, 63rd, and 58th Divisions. "Attack appears to be everywhere progressing satisfactorily."

R. Bastianelli turned up in the morning. With Soltau, took him after lunch to see the D.M.S. and then to Dosinghem, where very actively at work. Got back here at four, when lying cases began to come in. Operating till now—belated owing to necessity of re-opening the Anzac Padre's extensive temporal wound because of a secondary hemorrhage, which I finally secured. Bastianelli stuck it manfully to the end.

Poured cats and dogs all the late afternoon, but clearing now. Apparently the heavy rain held off until most of objectives gained. Second Army has sidestepped and with the 48th and 4th Divisions has taken over the area previously held at right of 5th Army by the 5th Corps. Rumor that the 29th Division has taken Poelcappelle—also that the attack opened just a few minutes after an extensive counter had been launched by two or three divisions of Boches who were caught in the open by our barrage and wiped out. Indeed they have been making successive counter-attacks during the past week with fresh divisions, which show how loath they are to give up these ridges.

10 p.m. I have just left the mess, where is going on, around a little stove with its first winter's fire, a lively discussion on religion between Bastianelli, the R. C. Padre Coffey, Wheeler, an Irishman, the C.O., Roper, and some others. Time for me to get out and make up for last night's short hours. We have been busy, but everything is cleaned up for the time being. No great numbers of wounded, at least in this 5th Army area. Rémy, however, now in the area of the 2nd Army, has had its hands full.

October 6th

Dressings all day long—this lot of cases doing exceptionally well. Only 2 or 3 thousand casualties in the 5th Army area, I believe; only 11,000 in the 2nd Army—very good considering the importance of the positions taken, for we are now astride of the ridge east of Broodseinde and can look off over a flat plain for thirty miles in which the enemy must now wallow.

All this much clearer to me after seeing the large topographical maps at the D.M.S. headquarters near Cassel, where Bastianelli and I dined and spent the night. Quite like old friends—General Porter, Capt. Stirling, Soltau, Gordon-Watson, Myer Coplans, a newly attached boy named Patterson, whose room we had, and Col. Chopping. It came out that Chopping was responsible for naming Mendinghem, Dosinghem, and Bandagehem; the latter was to have been Kuringhem; also Choppinghem was suggested but discarded.

A very delightful dinner with these 2nd Army people, in an old château at the foot of the small hill just east of Cassel, with much showing of maps and discussing of the Italian situation and our own. Coplans's stories of Ypres, of which he has made a close study, were particularly interesting to me—the place built on an alluvial plain where several streams meet and now run under the town—or did. All this with the building of the Cloth Hall in the 13th century when the place had some 400,000 people. Then the cloth trade shifted, I believe, to Bruges, and Ypres shrank greatly in size so that to-day's shells turn up and expose the foundations of buildings in a wide area outside its modern boundaries. The place, like others in the area, was walled and fortified in the 17th century by Vauban, who made the walls from the soil dug out of the moat—massive walls which have stood up against these three years of shelling—honeycombed with casemates in which thousands of civilians took shelter during the first winter, and in which thousands of Tommies now do likewise.

.   .   .   .   .   .

The operation of October 4th extended from Tower Hamlets, on the Menin Road, north to Langemarck, a distance of about eight miles. A long strip of the main ridge centring from Zonnebeke to Broodseinde, at the neck of the ridge, was taken by English, Australians, and New Zealanders. The Australians were in the centre and took Broodseinde; the New Zealanders on the left took Gravenstafel, the Abraham Heights, and possibly Poelcappelle.

This "battle of Broodseinde," if so it comes to be called, is prob_ ably the most important British victory of the year. A powerful

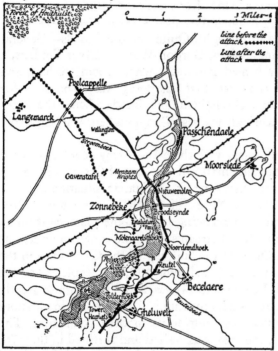 enemy counter-at- tack by fresh divi- sions from the east was nipped in the bud, and Bruges can now be seen from our positions on the western slope of the ridge. All the Gheluvelt region except the short spur on which ruined Gheluvelt stands, and the low spur with the vil- lage of Becelaere, are in the British hands, and they are within 2500 yards of Passchendaele village. Moreover, having Poelcap- pelle gives a good

Extent of Ground Gained in the Attack of October 4 (Solid Line). Poelcappelle Soon Retaken by Enemy in Counter-Attack. The 55-Metre Contour Shaded

footing toward the outflanking of Houthulst Forest. There are said to be over 4000 prisoners, and at Rémy alone there were 700 German wounded.

Monday, Oct. 8th. Mendinghem

10 p.m. I would never have believed that weather could be so atrocious. I have just returned to this forlorn camp after 24 hours in Camiers. A howling wind and rain all the way, and here every- thing is wet, sodden, and cold. At Proven just now we ran into a brigade of dripping troops going to the Front, and we were held up for half an hour while the poor fellows trudged past, followed by their kitchens and limbers. It was almost as bad going down on Sunday. This certainly is not a propitious time to hit the Germans again.

THE NINTH BATTLE: POELCAPPELLE

Wednesday, October 10th

2.30 a.m. They went over, despite the weather, at 5.20 (winter time) this (yesterday) morning. The bad weather has broken and to-night it is cold, still, and clear as a bell, with a waning moon. Col. Soltau, who came in this afternoon, said there was a powwow at G.H.Q. at midnight, some opposing any attempt to advance in such unpromising weather. The men have come in very cold and muddy, but highly elated at the success of the attack. The Boches seem to be on the run; many prisoners taken—one whole battalion surrendered in a body, it 's rumored.

Our cases mostly walking wounded again and the heads not particularly bad ones. We have just finished a Yorkshireman of the 4th W. Ridings, with two separate penetrating wounds, and it took a long time. He says he 's in the 49th Division, and we 've seen men from the Guards, the 29th, 48th, 11th, 9th, and 4th. Nevertheless this is not supposed to be the final big push over a twenty-one-mile front. The Guards and the 29th have been in together this time and a wounded officer of the 29th has given me his dirty barrage-map which shows their objectives and the times, with a six-minute wait almost every 50 yards, and from zero to the crest a six-and-a-half-hour continuous barrage. The French participated, and report taking Mangelaere.

Thursday, Oct. 11th

1 a.m. Not so late as last night, but done to a frazzle after our final case. Having made my notes on the man's field-medical card, I summoned the clerk, who did n't show any signs of intelligence until I called him "clark," when he shambled up and I asked him, "if he could read my notes, to please copy them in his operating-room book." He assumed an expression of going over the parapet and began: "Long gee tudinal sinews signdrome"—I gave it up and copied them myself.

This second day after a battle is always to be dreaded—bad cases, many of them after lying out a day or two. The news does not sound quite so good to-day—a German counter and the Guards driven back from Poelcappelle. We shall have to wait for a chance newspaper to learn what happened day before yesterday. To-day

Horrax gathered in from a Boche prisoner a copy of the *Frank-furter Zeitung* of October 8th!—the most recent news we 've had, for the C.O. as usual has taken the *Times* to his Armstrong hut.

It 's been a cold raw day with rain in spots. When I woke early this morning I heard the hum of a flock of planes, and getting up poked my head out of the tent and saw some eight fighting planes hovering over the aerodrome very high, and circling irregularly about. Suddenly first one and then another turned sideways and fluttered down, spinning like a leaf, for a thousand feet or more, and then flattened out. A most astounding spectacle, but one to which we shall doubtless all become more accustomed as time goes by. We sailed from New York five months ago to-day.

7 p.m. Another day of dressings. I recall asking one of the Parrys—we have two of them in adjoining beds—how he was feeling to-day. "Tray bong," says Parry. And this is the custom-ary reply, even when things don't look the best to us. All round, the Tommy is an amazing fellow and only grouses over trifles— particularly his food, which is exceptionally good. Mr. Wilson's high-sounding phrase, "To the last man and the last dollar, etc." is met by "Ole Bill," who wants to know who 'll take his rations up to the last man.

The wounded New Zealand Padre turns out to be the senior Chaplain of the corps, who has made it his practice always to go over with the men—but this time he happened to be back with the artillery! "There was a good deal of Fritz's 'heavy stuff' com-ing over; two or three batteries had been hit; the men were begin-ning to get the wind up; I was trying to keep them steady when something happened and I just settled down to the ground." That's all he can remember till yesterday, when he found himself in the officers' ward here and wondered why he could n't see out of his left eye.

Fred Murphy has just been in from 64. Wants to know how I manage to keep warm. I don't. The oil stove I wangled from Camiers Monday is defective according to my batman, who is per-haps better at polishing leather and brass buttons for the English than in coaxing an oil stove to burn for an American.

11 p.m. The Tuesday battle—the ninth or possibly the tenth since we came up here on July 24th—started in with the usual downpour, on waterlogged ground, over a front from s.e. of Broodseinde to St. Jansbeke, about a mile n.e. of Bixschoote. To the right, if I gather correctly, the Australians went over the crest of the ridge; in the centre the Lancashire Territorials moved toward Passchendaele and Poelcappelle, recapturing the latter; on the left, the 19th Division and the Guards, coöperating with the French, reached the outskirts of Houthulst Forest. Marlborough once said: "Whoever holds Houthulst Forest holds Flanders." In 1914 the Belgians flooded a vast area to save the last remnant of their country. It now makes the strongest defense against the Allies' efforts toward its liberation.

Word has come to expect a busy day to-morrow. It is again drizzling, though nothing like the evening before this last battle.

The Tenth Battle: Again Poelcappelle

October 12th, Friday

Imagine a brigade plodding toward the line in pitch-dark, a cold wind, a downpour of rain. They start to move up at six in the evening—a trip which should take three hours. Stumbling over impossible roads, in impossible mud, heavy with their packs, this trip takes eleven hours! Exhausted, they reach the broken area where a semblance of a line is held; and half an hour later, while still dark—at 5.25 to be exact—they go over behind their barrage toward the enemy and probable death.

Three of them get on together about 500 yards toward some obscure objective—they did n't quite know where or the name of it—nor care much. All three get wounded from the same shell and find a temporary refuge at the edge of one of the many craters. It was half full of water and the sloping banks were of sticky mud. One is drowned very soon. The survivor, who is now here, held the second, his chum, who was badly hit, out of the quicksand and water for three hours, and then from sheer fatigue had to let him go, and saw him drown before his eyes. This is not an exceptional story by any manner of means.

They went over again, in short, this morning—worse than any morning we have seen, if that is possible, and it is only three days since the last. I 've had a sergeant of the Irish Guards from Cork, with a skull thicker than a Baltimore darky's and no depression of the inner table despite my expectations. The Cork skull is mightier than the tin hat. Another sergeant of the 2nd Scots Guards—a machine gunner—who said they were on the edge of Houthulst

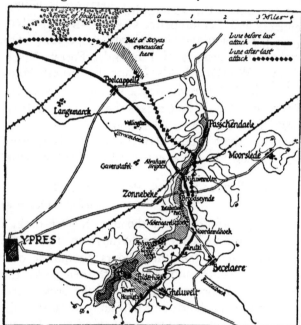

Forest where he saw my friend Captain Walker in the thick of it with his bearers. He had much praise for the regimental M.O.'s. Then there were some of the Household Battalion attached to the 4th Division, which therefore must have been in; ditto some of the Black Watch and I believe the 34th and 17th.

Dotted Line Shows Advance Made on October 12 with Poelcappelle Temporarily Reoccupied

It's hard to tell how well they have done. Certainly there must have been a setback after Tuesday's advance, for some of them spoke of *again* retaking Poelcappelle, which means that the Guards must have been pushed out of it. Others spoke of being near the ridge, but whether it was Passchendaele or not they were not clear. Apparently the Germans came out to meet them this time, and there was hell to pay—waist deep in mud. One wonders how men could long survive even were there no fighting. One of my morning's cases had been lying out since Tuesday's battle—and I thought it was damp and cold in my tent and under blankets last night!

Saturday, Oct. 13th

12 m. We have been busy through an encouraging surgical day, with three successful magnet extractions. Horrax is just finishing up the last case—a perforating wound through the left hemisphere. The casualties of this last battle must have been heavy, for the wounded keep coming in—so fast that we have been wondering whether there might not have been another attack to-day. The weather continues to be atrocious—certainly rain fifteen hours out of the last sixteen—and a gale of wind.

This morning the "pre-op" was full of cases for us. Here is my list starting the day:—

Winter, E. 860594. 7th Borderers, 17th Div.—penetrating cerebellar. Sitting down. Helmet on. Blown into the air. Unconscious for a time, does not know how long. Later crept back to a trench—legs wobbly—dizzy, etc.

Robinson, H. 14295. 1st So. African Inf., 9th Div.—penetrating rt. temporal. Wounded yesterday about 6 p.m. Knocked down but not unconscious. Helmet penetrated. Walked 20 yards—dizzy—vomited—numbness left arm, &c. No transport until this morning owing to mud.

Matthew, R. 202037. 8th Black Watch—penetrating right parietal; hernia cerebri. Thinks he was wounded three days ago, etc. A fine big Jock.

Hartley, J. 26th M.G.C., 8th Div. Wounded at 11 last night, not unconscious. Walked to dressing station. Thinks they had reached their objective, &c.

Bogus. 3rd N.Z. Rifle Brigade, 1st Anzac. Frontal gutter wound. In line for two nights before show began—awful conditions. Had gone 1000 yards when wounded, &c.

Beattie. 7th Seaforths, 9th Div. Stretcher-bearer, wounded while bringing out his third man—4 to a stretcher—300 yards from advanced line, &c. Occipital penetrating (?).

Medgurck. 11th Royal Scots, 9th Div. Multiple wounds, including head, &c.

Dobbie. Household Batt'n., 4th Div. Wounded near Poelcappelle sometime yesterday afternoon. Adm. here 7 p.m. In "resus" since. Severe. For X-ray, etc.

Very difficult to know what has been going on—no news to-day, no newspapers. It would appear that we have not done so well. This is about the fifth major battle within a month.

Sunday, Oct. 14th

6 p.m. I asked an officer of the Oxfords who was here to lunch why they did not postpone Friday's offensive owing to the storm. He said such a thing is impossible—it would take two days to check an attack of this magnitude. When once staged and the time set

the scale of the operation is so enormous it has to come off regard_
less of the weather—which certainly seems always to favor the
Hun.

Friday's battle was on a six-mile front, with the heaviest fight_
ing between Passchendaele and Poelcappelle, where the line had
been pushed back on Tuesday evening. The principal obstacles
to the advance are not so much the enemy and his elaborate
concrete defenses as the wet terrain. Men who are trying to
struggle on, waist deep, in a morass full of shell-hole ponds
into which they can slip and drown make an easy target for
machine guns.

11 p.m. To Sunday supper at 8.15 with Harris and the R.E.'s
in Proven, through much mud, but very pleasant while there.
They tell me another push is expected to-morrow. Fritz is panicky
about it and has been over here often this morning to see what is
going on, and often to-night to leave his card.

Monday, Oct. 15th

The raiders yesterday did much damage and got a lot of men—
200 of the Canadian labor battalion at one clip, so that our last
night's "take in" was mostly bombed cases. . . .

6 p.m. To-day's expected attack did not come off—unfortunately so in view of the favorable weather. It has been a cold but a
beautiful day, with great masses of billowy white cumulous clouds
about which many planes could be seen, and I have chanced to see
several squadrons of six or eight go over. The birds are migrating.
I never saw an actual swarm of them before—wheeling and
circling over a little wood just to the west of us—thousands of
them, like a flock of locusts. Suddenly another swarm would approach and join the main one, and so the swarm grew—mobilizing
for a flight south. Were I an aviator I would join them. I have
been in to No. 64 to tea with Carling and Briggs and asked
Wolstenholme what they were—field-fares, he said. Sampson at
our mess says starlings. . . .

The British papers contain very little about last Friday's battle
—possibly for a very good reason. The 5th Army as a "thrusting
army" seems to be "in rather bad," though we do not talk about it
much—the 16th and 36th and Guards so broken up and decimated
they have had to be sent out altogether. All this may account for

the gradual taking over of our area by the 2nd Army, with the resultant lessening of our work at No. 46.

A letter from the D.G. requesting me to lunch with him to-morrow regarding Base Hospital No. 5 affairs.

Tuesday, Oct. 16

6 p.m. En route, Hesdin–Paris. Some French civilians in the corridor vigorously discussing the American automobile industry —an English staff officer opposite, whose sandwiches and chocolate I have just shared—two Belgians asleep in the other corners. The light is too feeble for reading—one's fingers almost too cold for scribbling—a poor choice.

A cold ride this morning from No. 46 to Hesdin, where I arrived a half hour late. The roads so packed with troops till we neared St. Omer that it was slow going. Between Watou and Steenvoorde a continuous line of R.F.A. limbers going up; between Fruges and Hesdin a continuous line of cavalry—coming out, alas! They could not be used. Mostly Indian horsemen, many lancers, the Deccan Horse among them, from all parts of India.[1] I was in the back of the ambulance by this time to get out of the wind, and my impression of them was one of turbans and teeth. Riding into the wind and dust—for the roads have dried off back here—they curled back their upper lips into a sort of snarl such as a monkey makes. The Tommies with them had their mouths shut. There was a young American M.O. "casual" riding with the field-ambulance section, who eagerly saluted when he saw my uniform. A whole cavalry division covering twenty-five miles of road, according to their A.D.M.S., who took lunch with us at Hesdin.

General Sloggett very anxious to know whether we are to remain with the British or be transferred; so are we. If we are to remain, I am to take charge of all the cranial work of the B.E.F.,

[1] The Jodhpur Lancers also, as I have since learned, with their picturesque leader, an octogenarian, Sir Pertab Singh (Hon. Lt. Gen. His Highness Maharaja Bahodur Sir Pertab Singh, C.C.B., C.C.S.I., C.C.V.O., etc., etc., of Jodhpur). Every time the cavalry have been brought up with a chance of their being engaged, the old man puts on all of his decorations and appears ready for any fray; but he has had nothing but disappointments. King George has tried to send him home, but he refuses to go. He wishes to die in battle and in France.

The Lahore and the Meerut Divisions sailed for the European War in September 1914, undermanned, ill-equipped, though the best fighting material in India. They had no personal cause in the quarrel, came to a strange country, and fought, bled, and died out of their sense of duty in a very bad sector, from Neuve-Chapelle to Givenchy. Gurkhas, Garhwalis, Sikhs, Jats, Dogras, Pathans and Punjabis, all did their full share in the first winter of 1914–1915 and lost heavily in officers and men. Lord Roberts's visit to them in November of '14 resulting in his death two days later showed how he felt toward an army he had done so much to build up.

and go about from hospital to hospital, demonstrating and in_
structing and learning. If we are not to remain, it is not worth
while moving us to No. 13.

Thursday, Oct. 18

2 a.m. En route, Camiers. The man next me has wakened and
sneezed. So have I. The rest are dead to the world—a French
sous-lieutenant of the 10th Regiment wearing a *Croix de Guerre,*
a French colonial in khaki with a sphinx on his collar, a French
colonel, and a nondescript in black whom I take for a Padre,
curled up in a corner, and the sneezer. All the world has a coryza
—in Mendinghem, in Hesdin, in Paris. Paris again a confusion,
and after the first glow of their arrival the Americans show signs
of discontent and disagreement. Many of the people over here
really have n't enough to do, and as they are unaccustomed to
authority as the military sees it, they grouse. There is such a thing
as the soldier's cheerful grousing over trifles which is often amus_
ing and obscures greater miseries. This grumbling at the Base has
a different note.

Reached Paris in time to find a dinner being given for Colonel
—now General—Bradley, by a group composed largely of members of our old Clinical Society who are over here. I cannot believe
that he will long survive in his present difficult job as Chief Surgeon for the A.E.F. Just now a peculiar mix-up between the Red
Cross and the Army, made worse by Jim Perkins and Murphy
getting into U.S. instead of R.C. uniforms. No longer possible on
short notice to get such things as warm underwear for hospital
nurses by requisitioning the R.C., which has them in stock. Requests must go through regular army channels, with the goods possibly delivered sometime next spring.

The next morning to Tuffier's hospital on the rue de la Pompe,
where he demonstrated some thoracic cases; then an assistant told
of their studies of wound cicatrization and the laws that govern
it; and after this T. himself gave a most instructive account of the
present hospital organization in the Service de Santé.[1]

---

[1] The basis of Tuffier's talk was on the present French organization—the gist of it being:
if an attack is to come off, the commanding general merely informs the Service de Santé of
the number of divisions to be engaged. They will know within reasonable limits the number
of wounded, the character of the wounds, and the required number of beds, of surgeons, of
brancardiers, of trains. This was all carefully worked out at Verdun and a curve can be
plotted for every attack. E.g., of 12,000 men in a division there will be 400 wounded on the

October 19th, Mendinghem

6 p.m. It 's embarrassing to receive "thanks awfully for cheering us up" when you know that you are really not an optimist inside no matter what you may try to show outside. Ross, on the other hand, not only is a professional soldier with a longer service in the battalion than anyone else, but he is a professional optimist as well. He has had it from a staff officer, who told him straight from someone else who knows, that there would be Peace by Christmas, and so on.

Perhaps it 's his cows, for the 2/ Scots Guards, as I may have said before, have real milk, and hence it 's particularly pleasant to have tea with them. There are three cows which go everywhere _-except over the top—with the battalion; they were commandeered in this Ypres sector just three years ago this month, their owners having taken flight. Meanwhile, there have been two calves and another is expected, worth many gallons of petrol. To-morrow at 4 a.m. when the Guards move back to St. Omer for a rest, the cows go along in a boxcar attached to the officers' train, bearing the label—"horses, 3, officer's."

Capt. Walker (who after all was n't killed) and the Padre dropped in on me at four, saying they were out in a rest billet a couple of miles from here—near Bandagehem—and would n't I walk over and have tea with Ross. Moreover, the pipes were playing at No. 63 and we could stop and hear them, which we did. Very fine it was and stirring—Pipe Major Ross and eleven other strapping pipers, with five drummers in addition, all in their Royal Stuart tartan. They played while marching and going through simple manœuvres. The pipes for a march or a dance!

I had never visited No. 63 before (Col. Lyons, C.O.), though it is a scant two miles along the railroad track to the north. They

---

1st day, 400 on the 2nd, a drop to about half on the third, and on the fourth everyone exhausted and the numbers fall to 10 or 20. Then this is again repeated. If there are 10 divisions engaged, the numbers are simply × 10.

The important time is, therefore, the first two days when operating tables are going without rest night and day. One table can do 35 operations—20 major ones included. Therefore 350 for 10 tables. If 10 divisions are engaged, 8000 wounded the first two days; thus one can calculate the no. of tables, surgeons, etc, required.

The one vital thing is to close the wound when you can—1, 2, 7, 10, or 12 days. *"Tout blessé qui suppure a le droit d'en demander la raison à son chirurgien."*

A special place has just been established for fractures, where they can be closed in 1–2 days. One may close 50 per cent immediately, 30 per cent in 5–10 days, 20 per cent must wait. This for all fractures, except the femur, of which 20 per cent can be immediately closed take only the sick; and No. 62 near by takes the shell-shock cases. The Guards were encamped about a mile back straddling a cross-road, and Ross's umbrella tent was in a wet pasture—good for the cows—beside a pond, doubtless very pretty in summer.

There we had the milk in our tea and they told me about their part in the action, and reaching the edge of the wood. Walker lost eight out of his thirty-two bearers, which he thinks not so bad, and the battalion had 200 casualties—not so bad either—one *must* be an optimist. Pessimist me, knowing that they had gone in with only 500—for they leave 500 now in reserve as a nucleus in case they are all wiped out—adds "of course not so bad." Walker's bearers got along only four to a stretcher—two miles along the tape in what becomes a trench, with mud up to the knees before you get to the duckboards—after that it's fine going. They are to be replaced by the 35th Division—Sherwood Foresters, Lancs, Oxfords, and others—by "misgeeded Englishmen," in short.

Saturday, the 20th Oct. 10 p.m.

A full operating day, Briggs and Carling from No. 64 looking on. Five perforative cases, a Lancashire Fusilier, a Northumberland ditto; a man from the Tank Corps hit while on a salvage expedition trying to rescue a mired male tank; an artilleryman from a siege battery; also a boy hit while taking up rations across No Man's Land during the night—scattered cases therefore. Our "take in" was slow—less than the 200 in 24 hours. . . .

The Boches have taken the island of Oesel and with its capture now control the Gulf of Riga, the Baltic, and with it the Russian fleet; but there are rumors of mutinies in the German Navy, which is somewhat cheering.

Sunday the 21st

A beautiful autumnal Sunday. Clopton over in the morning from Rémy to look on at our dressings. In the afternoon to Dosinghem to see Revere's grave and meet the new sergeant who is caring for it. It's dreadful to see that place grow—a thousand burials in the past three weeks. A service going on—a Padre, a Tommy at attention at the foot of the grave, a body in a blanket barely showing above the surface of the muddy water in the bottom of the ditch.

A notice is posted to the effect that no one is to absent himself

The Scottish "Going Over" at Dawn, and Some That Remained to Be "Piped" Back Several Days Later to Rest Quarters

from the camp after 10 a.m. to-morrow—a new way of announcing an attack. There have been many rumors and heavy firing
every morning for the past three days, but less discussion than
usual concerning it—a good thing. It is said that a railroad has
been laid as far as St. Jean. May this weather hold!

THE ELEVENTH ATTACK: ENCORE POELCAPPELLE

Monday, Oct. 22

9 a.m. It did n't. A heavy downpour at 5 a.m. and now heavily
overcast.

Midnight. It cleared later and has been warm and pleasant.
Zero hour was 5.35. Not a very large affair apparently, though
had it been more successful it might have spread to the 2nd Army.
Anderson over from Nine Elms in the morning. They had not
even been warned of a possible push. Walking wounded began to
come in about 2 p.m.—very muddy but, as usual with walkers,
optimistic and jubilant at getting back with a prospect of Blighty.
The attack seems to have been in only two areas—in front of
Poelcappelle to get the brewery (so long an obstacle), and in the
direction of the forest to straighten the line there. So far as one
can judge, the 18th, 15th, 35th, and 31st Divisions participated.
I have seen men of Norfolk, Suffolk, Berks, and Essex regiments
from the 18th. One of their officers, who has a slight scalp wound,
says they were in the Poelcappelle area, and the artillery of an
entire army corps was concentrated behind their two brigades. The
35th has taken over from the Guards on the edge of the forest,
and some of the Sherwoods were also appropriately on the forest
end of the line.

The conditions must be appalling. An officer who is in here with
trench feet says that a messenger he had sent back lost the tape
and his sense of direction, wandered twenty feet away, and was
found the next morning in a quagmire nearly up to his neck. He
was still living when extracted, but died. The officer himself was in
a shell-hole lake for five days with two or three of his men. During
this time they had only three meals, and when they finally were
reached this morning during the advance, and he was carried back,
he could n't get his boots off. During the early attack in the mist,
dummy figures of cardboard were put up to draw the enemy's

machine-gun fire, and the barrage was timed to advance and recede so as to catch the Boche after he had come out of his dug-outs and pill boxes. A German threw away his gun and floundered up to one of the dummies shouting "Kamerad." . . .

The Mess President promised us a great treat for dinner—some Indian corn—on the cob! "They" simply did n't know what to do with it, and for that matter neither did we Americans. The objects were about the size of hen's eggs, boiled and tasting of paraffine oil, difficult to hold and particularly untidy when you are at a mess which boasts of no napkins.

Across the table from me is a new Padre—Wesleyan. This one wears the gold stripe on his sleeve signifying a wound. He came out with the First Hundred Thousand, served in the line two years, went home and completed his theological course, and is now back, able to talk the soldier's language to the living as well as to read a service over him dead.

Wednesday, Oct. 24th

Spells of cold rain all day. News that Bob Fitzsimmons, the pugilist, has died of pneumonia in Chicago arouses more interest than the results of Monday's battle. The attack was about as I had gathered—from Poelcappelle to Mangelaere. The French troops did particularly well in spite of the swamp, and got well into the forest. More important is the rumor that four or five Zeppelins got adrift in a raid over England and came down, or were brought down, somewhere in France the next morning.

Thursday, Oct. 25th

Flanders weather continues to be the topic of outstanding interest—and condemnation. Last night following a prolonged cold downpour it came on to blow a hurricane. My tent, after flapping like an unfurled topsail, began about 4 a.m. to settle down on top of me. Fishing for tent pegs in muddy darkness is no joke; fortunately a stray P.B. man secured a shovel, which was much more effective with loose tent pegs than the brick with which I was belaboring them. My tent was new when I came and has had only three months' wear. Though it grows leaky in spots, it did not rip asunder as did many others early this morning. So I got off lucky.

All this brings up the lavish employment of canvas by the

British. The cost of a marquee is 80 pounds and four to a ward make 320 pounds. They last about six months. A hut of the type of our Church Army hut costs 250 pounds and will hold more patients and take up less room than the marquees. · · · But the real waste is in smaller things. Our so-called platform some 200 yards long beside the tracks is built up of ashes and gravel. Suddenly a week ago the R.E.'s appeared with six-inch logs and have perpendicularized the edge bordering the tracks, where the platform slopes off. To-day this is all being torn up and a corrugated iron facing put in its place. No one seems to know why. The logs, having been once used, are thrown in the ditch.

And the wastage of food is prodigious. The waste bread from the ambulance trains is put in sacks and unloaded anywhere. Our own waste, which is enormous, goes to the pigs—not ours but those of the Belgian farmer, who still inhabits his buildings. He is growing wealthy on it beyond his dreams of avarice, for, once raised and fattened, he sells the pigs back to us. The men in the mess kitchen have had no instruction whatever concerning the saving of food. Such economy as a bread pudding is unknown. A woman housekeeper and a farmer could feed our mess, keep pigs, cows, and chickens, and make money. Telfer estimated at breakfast that the daily waste of our officers' mess alone would provide for a London family in the East End for a week.

Later. It's an ill wind, etc. Things have been drying rapidly and it feels less like rain than for some time. To the *Château Lovie* —haunt of the red fox—to get what information I could about our Base Hospital being moved. The red fox is the 5th Army emblem and the splotch of red color on caps and brassards at headquarters is a relief in the khaki-colored landscape. The leaves in this area are falling fast. Consequently many a building and ammunition dump is left scantily concealed. There are only two corps remaining in the 5th Army—the 14th and 18th. Even the 5th was crossed off on the Headquarters map; so that the 2nd Army comes well up to the St. Jean line.

Still later. Bandagehem I find is misnamed. They don't bandage at all. A walk over there along the tracks to tea at No. 62, where all the N.Y.D.N.[1] cases are congregated, in other words the shell-

[1] Not yet diagnosed nervous.

shock cases—very dismal. A dumping ground for M.O.'s who can't wriggle out—none of them appear at all interested in, or acquainted with, psychiatry. We are warned of another battle to-morrow. A clear cold still night for a change, and Fritz is up taking advantage of the returning moon. The conditions promise to favor us.

CORPS DRESSING STATIONS AND THE TWELFTH BATTLE

Oct. 26th. Friday

3 *p.m.*, while Sullivan is doing some scalps. To-day, according to my unofficial reckoning, was the *twelfth battle for the ridges.* Pouring as usual since an early hour this morning, despite the brilliant promise of yesterday.

Early breakfast on some G.W. coffee in my wet and shivering tent, and a get-away at seven with Maynard Smith to visit the C.D.S. for each of the two corps still in this army—one at Du- hallow for the 18th and the other at Solferino Farm for the 14th Corps. Good going at first, by the switch road around "Pop" to Vlamertynghe, which is far more damaged than when I first saw it a month ago. Then on to "Wipers," passing dripping Australians on the way out, for they were replaced last night by two divisions of the Canadians, one of them the 3rd from Toronto.[1] By the asylum—over the moat—the prison—the Grande Place, and on through the wreck of the town with its big sewers torn open and bared to view—an eviscerated as well as mangled city—to the Menin Gate.

Then St. Jean and the Junction Road; and so northwest to Boundary Road, which runs north and south behind Admiral's Road, and so to Irish Farm (C27a5.2)[2] where is the Collecting Station for Walking Wounded of the Corps—a desperate place

[1] This I believe was the first of the Passchendaele battles in which the Canadians participated, and they found it a full-sized man's job—five miles of devastated country, reduced by the unprecedented rains to a quagmire full of shell holes, lay between the old lines around Ypres and the new front. A wide zone of fire had to be crossed by advancing troops before they could make contact with the enemy, and the morass was swept from point after point by enfilading fire from the concrete pill boxes. Their objectives of the first day were Dad Trench, Bellevue Spur, and Wolfe Copse. After desperate fighting Bellevue Spur was gained, though the day was stormy and wet, and it was almost impossible to maintain contacts.
[2] Enumerations of this sort identify points on the variously enlarged official British military maps on which primary 6000-yard squares were indicated by the 24 capital letters from A to X. Each large square was subdivided into 36 secondary 1000-yard squares, each of which was again divided into four 250-yard squares, small a, b, c, and d. The final numbers represent the coordinates, horizontal and vertical, for a given point (Irish Farm in this instance) on one of the smaller squares measured from its southwest angle. Every landmark, even a ruined house, could thus be quickly located with great accuracy.

Laying Duckboards in the Salient

Sandbagged Dugouts on the Canal Bank

in a sea of mud and crater lakes. To be sure, there are still some fairly intact trees standing in this area, though most of them are broken and splintered past recall. The pollard willows, which encircle the little Flanders ponds, alone seem to have largely escaped, as though they had gradually become immune to wounds at the hand of man. Indeed, only by the fringe of willow stumps can one tell whether the pond is old or newly made by the rain filling a large crater. Every time a shell lands it of course makes a pond.

The C.O. at Irish Farm had established this advanced station by order, on the 21st, only five days ago; the leveling of the ground and partial filling of shell holes occupying the first day, and then after all was nearly ready the wind storm the other night blew every tent down. He now has wangled a lot of the crinkled iron posts designed for wire entanglements, and using them for tent pegs, with some wire for ropes, hopes he will outlive the next gale. There's no way, alas, to reef a tent—it must weather a storm under full canvas. In such a camp as this, too, one learns the absolutely essential rôle played by the duckboard. Crushed stone and the duckboard versus tea and jam. I wonder which Tommy would take if he had to choose between them.

We are early, and though they are busy enough all the time with bombed cases from the area, to-day's wounded have not yet begun to come in. They are to receive from the 18th Corps, where are the 63rd—the naval division—on the right, and the 58th on the left, to which division the C.O. belongs. In his outfit are four M.O.'s, fifty-six bearers, and thirty temporarily attached people. At a similar place during the last—i.e., Monday's—battle they passed on 1745 wounded and 246 walking-sick in twelve hours, between 9 a.m. and 9 p.m.

Irish Farm, as I have said, lies near Boundary Road about where Buff's Road joins it, and from all appearance it is thoroughly searched by shells. Just across the road were some huge howitzers sulking under their camouflage, and beyond, in a fringe of stumps marking a former wood, was a long row of naval guns whose snouts we could see and whose flashes and roars were too close for comfort. Certainly not all of the guns were blinded, and though it was raining and misty, the air was simply buzzing with planes like swallows, singly and in formations—there must have been fifty or sixty within the near radius of a mile.

The C.O. shows us what he can in the time he has; and while we wait for Kenzie to disentangle the car from ambulances and lorries and ammunition mules the wounded straggle in—one of them with a bloody bandaged leg being helped along on the narrow duckboards by two Boche prisoners, a sight which would be good for "the Hate" of both sides. A toy of a narrow-gauge Decauville with its little gasoline engine pulls into the camp with a load of liers from some forward area—a sopping Tommy rides by on a mule with its upper lip, nostrils, and part of one ear blown off, but still worthy of salvage—farther on a recently disem_ boweled horse lies at the side of the road, reddening the pools and the muddy water of the ditch for a hundred feet beyond—a large slug of an observation balloon begins to rear its carcass up from a wrecked copse just behind the camp.

So back to the canal, which we cross just north of Ypres, with the skeleton of the Cloth Hall and the stump of St. Martin's western tower still dominating the distant landscape despite their pulverized condition; and finally to a place called Duhallow where formerly was an advanced dressing station dug in the bank, and where the 18th C.D.S. is now placed.

In this part of the canal, south of Boesinghe, the English held both banks, so that the western slope of each bank is lined with quasi habitations, their entrances toward the west. Those on the western bank lie between the canal itself and the little tributary of the Yser—the Yperlée I believe—running parallel to it.

The C.O. ordinarily in command of F.A. 150 had been stationed here for only a week, but had erected his tents on a sea of mud and shell holes which had to be filled with whatever could be found. Indeed, more like the ancient lake dwellers in parts, for the Yperlée has expanded into a veritable lake, over which duckboards in many areas stand close together on piles. We found the C.O. in one of the dugouts— the so-called "elephants" which line the canal bank—corrugated steel frames like miniature Nissons about six feet high along the centre and ten feet long—comparatively safe in view of the very heavy additional sandbagging above and around; and advantage had been taken of a brick wall supporting the bank at this place. The only danger lies in the great air pressure in the enclosure, should a large shell happen to burst just behind.

The C.O. was by no means daunted by this sanitary problem, and, managing somehow to scrape together men and shovels, had dug a ditch from the stream through the bank, and in the bottom had laid a huge pipe three feet in diameter made of rolled-up corrugated iron sheets, through which the muddy water was pouring in a solid mass down into the canal below.

I had never realized before how high were the banks of the canal, or how wide it was—certainly a formidable military obstacle with either bank well fortified in defense of a crossing. We slipped and waded out on the canal bank, avoiding shell holes and German duds which abounded, to see this engineering feat of the C.O.'s, of which he was most proud; and despite the rain, the water under the wet part of his camp had fallen over a foot. How the D.G. must have raised his eyebrows when we complained that the lower part of No. 11 General at Camiers was occasionally under water!

Some young American M.O.'s were attached—everyone saying a good word for them. I saw one who said he was from Georgia— all he wanted was to know where he could get an officer's cord for his hat. The place is at C25d3.0, just east of what once was the Belgian town of Noordhofwijk; and when on the canal bank we could see better than at Irish Farm the ridges from whose low elevation the Boche so long looked down on this region which he could shell at his pleasure. Though it was 10.30 when we were there, only one wounded officer and ten other-ranks had as yet been admitted.

Then back to Salvation Corner on the way to Solferino Farm (B23a5.1), a name indicating, as do the occasional graves with their red and blue circle on the wooden cross, that the French long ago were holding this area—desolate beyond words—a ruined château—some derelict tanks—past the H.Q. of the naval division, where the white naval ensign flies over some scattered tents in a sea of mire—through the wreck of Brielen village, where from a niche in the remaining wall of the nave a stone saint looks down on the rubble of his church and the adjacent cemetery, topsy-turvy with barbed wire and headstones and opened graves, new and old—for a reserve line of abandoned trenches runs through it.

So on to Dawson's Corner and the new-laid Boesinghe road, where we should turn but for a traffic youth who holds us up and makes us retrace our steps—first left at the road leading to Essex Farm, then first left and first left again to Solferino Farm, which is but a little way down the road, but it 's a one-way road for all but horses and bicycles. Owing to this we got stalled for an hour.

The second "first left" was evidently a mistake, for it put us on to a narrow and badly broken road from which there was no turn_ ing; and after about a mile we ran up against two lorries. They completely blocked the narrow path of rough-laid cobbles on which we balanced, with ditches and unfathomed mud on each side. Two signs just beyond were labeled "Perth Road" and "Rum Road," though there was no recognizable track to be seen.

Each lorry held a dissected small Nisson, and the young officer in charge apologized; but there was nothing to do but for him to unload—which he would do as fast as possible. Incidentally it was pouring, and from somewhere a bedraggled group of mud_ colored Tommies appeared, picking their way through the mire, and began to carry away the sections. These poor devils were out on what is regarded as a temporary rest billet! From their strug_ gles I got an idea of what a stretcher-bearer must endure, only he carries a *man* on a stretcher and not a mere curved plate of rusty iron which minds not whether the bearer slips on his face or sinks into a hole halfway to his middle and has to let go. Low-flying planes were scudding over—mostly our familiar R.E. No. 8's. A continued hubbub of guns, meanwhile, their flashes showing against the fragments of a wood and the slight elevation of Pilkem Ridge beyond. And then from the east, cross country, sucking herself along through the mud like a prehistoric lizard, came slithering a tank—female of the species, for painted on her chest was DAME. I could think of nothing but "all mimsy were the borogoves," for she certainly "gyred and gimbled" in the mire, but came on nevertheless, ignoring crater pools, and finally down the ditch by the road she sank, then heaved herself over, then down the other side and on across the country beyond—doubtless home to feed her young. She crossed the road immediately in front of the first lorry and I was so dumbfounded I got out of our car and immediately sank in above my ankles, for alongside the narrow track of loose *pavés* there was no roadbed whatever. So I got aboard again and lit a cigarette as though I were quite accustomed to these things, having been in the army for a full five months.

But this was not all, for shortly Kenzie, the chauffeur, called out: "Here come some more of 'em!" and sure enough, from off our starboard quarter was a procession of the beasts. This time a male—DEATH'S HEAD his name—with guns sticking out of his side and a man on his back—like a bird on the back of a rhino—scratching the mud out of his claws as they passed by. DEATH'S HEAD barely negotiated the road. Then three more along the same slimy track: DRUID, a male, DRONE, a lady—then a final female misnamed DOMINIE, possibly escaping in female disguise.[1]

Well, the lorries were finally unloaded and moved on to the spot marked Rum Road where we could just squeeze by, and then came a succession of shell craters which seemed too much even for Kenzie—"worse than anything they'd seen on the Somme"—but we got through somehow, the car tilting over the fragments of muddy duckboards we had rescued from the roadside. Luckily I had rubber boots, but the well-groomed Smith was mud to his knees.

At Solferino Farm is the M.D.S. for the 14th Corps, and it would be good for all who only know the meagre discomforts of the Base to be detailed for a time in some such place. Col. Gowlland, the C.O., and a big red Scot of a young captain named Barclay, who wears an M.C. ribbon and has been with this 51st F.A. of the 17th Division for full three years—they two showed us around the station and the scattered structures of sandbags and railroad ties in an adjacent muddy copse, where they eat and sleep. It was 11.30 and the first real walkers from the battle were coming in, straggling along a rickety duckboard path labeled "Track to Pilkem," which led from nowhere in the direction of No Man's Land. It was 5.45 when they went over—this means nearly six hours—and these are the slightly wounded during the first few minutes of the attack.

So home through Elverdinghe, with the usual ruined church,

---

[1] So-called "male" tanks were armed with a cannon, "female" tanks only with Lewis machine guns.

and a sign on the sandbagged chapel door reading "To the bomb store." And we get back just as the first trainload of walkers is being dropped at our dripping platform.

And all this "carrying on" in the muck and mire of a back area is nothing to the condition further on. I have just been talking with a young subaltern of the 50th Division, who, shaking and trembling, is pretending to smoke a cigarette in his bed in the officers' ward. His battalion went in last night, following a muddy tape. They got absolutely scattered and lost—had no idea where they were—many wandered directly into the enemy's area—they tried to dig in where they thought was their objective, merely throwing up a little mud and lying in the puddles behind it— the wrong place and they were ordered away—this was repeated twice, the last time just before zero. Wet through and thoroughly chilled, they tried to follow a barrage which got ahead of them, and passed over their real objective: a line of concrete gun emplacements camouflaged as old frame buildings which opened up on them. Well, there was practically nobody left.

It's easy to play the game from the grandstand; but I can't help feeling that this show in view of the downpour ought to have been called off. It certainly could have been even at the last moment, by a system of prearranged rocket signals which could reach all the participants, even though wires might not, for wires are often cut and units thereby temporarily shut off from their communications.

Saturday the 27th Oct.

5 p.m. Only one penetrating wound out of this entire lot, and this a man wounded just going over. Almost all the wounds are minor ones—walking cases, and about 2000 have gone down from our platform. This means either that we were driven back and left our more serious wounded, or else only the walkers survived to get away and out of the mire. The papers said almost nothing of the attack of the 22nd, and they probably will say as little of this one.

A GLIMPSE OF THE SALIENT

Sunday, Oct. 28th

Little wonder that people have found it difficult to describe. Yet one has the sensation of vague familiarity, doubtless due to the official photographs—like seeing Niagara for the first time and being surprised it is so like the picture postcards. Apart from the wreck of the last remaining house, which the Canadians now use as an A.D.S., the salient is a waste unbelievably littered with débris of every kind, dead horses, derelict tanks, fallen and crumpled aeroplanes, cordite cans, shells, mortars, fish-tail bombs, broken and abandoned limbers, barbed wire, old trenches, water-filled craters, strips of old road camouflage, gravestones and tumbled cemeteries, sheet-iron fragments of old Nisson huts, fallen trees, frames of inverted A-shaped trench supports, and I can't remember at the moment more—except the gooey mud.

And on this particular day the road to Zonnebeke, which, like the Menin Road, is kept in some sort of repair, is alive with Canadians and ammunition mules and artillery and lorries; and from the tumbled surface of the country on all sides are flashes of guns, some of them silent flashes from Quaker guns to deceive the enemy's planes, others belching out a rushing and ripping shell with a thunder and roar to deafen you—8-inch "hows," naval guns, rows of field guns, and you have to look close to see them; and people the color of the mud that encases them are moving about on all sides, singly, in clusters, in columns, in bodies, waiting their chance or their orders to move up; and in the air are crowds of black planes at various heights and appearing the size of gnats, swallows, cranes, circling singly or in formations, some surrounded by black shrapnel puffs showing they are Huns, and the puffs cease as other flocks of gnats appear, and they engage and separate, leaving only scattered planes.

And before long there 's a bang! and black earth is thrown up like a geyser 200 yards away and another one nearer—in short, just like the picture postcards. And the savage in you makes you adore it with its squalor and wastefulness and danger and strife and glorious noise. You feel that, after all, this is what men were intended for rather than to sit in easy chairs with a cigarette and whiskey, the evening paper or the best-seller, and to pretend that such a veneer means civilization and that there is no barbarian behind your starched and studded shirt front. . . .

It came about through Myer Coplans, the sanitarian of the 2nd Army, who, as I 've said somewhere else, knows much about

Ypres, and told me some day he would take me there. We get away at eleven, leaving the capable Gil to do the two stray heads that have come in.

A cool misty day with thin clouds and visibility a little too good for safe journeying as far afield as was hoped for. A stop at the Canadian H.Q. off the Poperinghe switch road, where for politeness we register our intent of entering their area—even though M.C. is everywhere *persona grata* when strictly on business bound. Major Greer, the A.D.M.S. of the 4th Canadian, we find is away at Bridge House, which in fact is one of our objectives (C24a3.6) —and Col. Peters we will find at the Menin Gate. Our final point, the Hun permitting, will be the A.D.S. at Frost House (D25a1.2), from which we will have a complete survey of the ridge—no place for an officer's motor like Fullerton's, and we therefore proceed by ambulance.

So on by the usual road—the famous Poperinghe–Ypres plaisance of Chaucer, where we dodge lorries and artillery columns and dispatch riders and troops going up or coming out. Coplans is much distressed over the roadside drains, which are not well cleared, so that water is backing up, and there is much from him about road construction; the character of the soil which "puddles" when churned up and won't let the water get through easily— hence the mud produced by the footsteps of an army. Not really a great rainfall—only about 20 inches, and in this country, as in the case of dry farming with us, the farmer harrows and then rolls the soil to keep in the moisture. Also about the *limon*, the yellow sticky clay under the soil and the blue clay many feet below— and much more only indirectly relating to war. . . .

C. was in this area early, and knew Vlamertynghe when to its normal 3500 inhabitants 3000 refugees and 11,000 troops were added with no doctor, and typhoid in every house. But what I have heretofore thought was Vlamertynghe is only a part of the town; for beyond in what appears to be waste country beside the road were places he knew—here stood the town hall, here the station, here the blacksmith shop—now nothing—hardly a trace after these two years even of the grass-grown cellars. So along the crowded Chaussée de Poperinghe, past the brick ruins of the huge insane asylum, once Von Bissing's headquarters, into Ypres at the

n tough
ss bound.
s away
C.24a3.6)
Our final
st House
ey of the
, and we

se–Ypres
columns
. Coplans
not well
from him
"puddles"
n easily—
it really a
try, as in
hen rolls
e yellow
below—

ien to its
oops were
hat I have
the town;
e the road
he station,
trace after
along the
f the huge
pres at the

An Advanced Dressing Station in the Salient with Walking Wounded
German Prisoners

Moving Up Behind Tanks in the Battle Terrain

Poperinghe Gate, with the wreck of the Yser canal-lock on the right, the leaning water tower—the *Château d'Eau*—on the left. Then by the rue d'Elverdinghe and to what remains of the prison where No. 11 F.A. of the 4th Canadian Division has established itself.

Preparatory to the coming battle—whether to-morrow or the next day is not quite apparent—thirteen Canadian M.O.'s are gathered here under Major Moshier, their C.O., and he volunteers to accompany us to Potijze—to Bavaria House—and, if the roads are sufficiently clear, to Frost House, which he warns us is a hot place. So in tin hats and gas alert, out by the Menin Gate to the rue de Roulers, the shell-peppered signpost pointing to Zonnebeke, and on as far as Potijze, where, in the ruins of the last house standing this side of present and former strips of no man's lands, is located the A.D.S. so recently taken over by the 4th Canadians, who are on the right, astride the railway.

We turn in from the crowded road and get out in time to see a great aerial engagement, quite indescribable—there must have been 60 planes over our immediate vicinity—during which all traffic is stopped and the moving troops on the road fall back and scatter. In the heavily sandbagged cellars of this one remaining Potijze house, wrecked as it is, were the preparations for the coming event, and we are told that the Canadian bearers bring in their wounded in relays of four carriers who cover the 5000 yards from Frost House to this point rather than to have the same bearers bring one patient all the way, as is customary.

We start in from here over the muddy road, on foot, along with the limbers and lorries and miles of mules and men, well beyond the line of observation balloons, and get across the old line of fixed trenches a little beyond Verlorenhoek and toward Frezenberg, when some heavy German stuff begins to come over in answer to our batteries which are trying to draw them out. An explosion and a geyser of earth about 300 yards ahead, then another a little closer—the advancing column halts and begins to open out, and I can see by Major Moshier's behavior he does n't care to assume the responsibility, this afternoon at least, of taking us any further along this particular road.

We pick up our car again at Potijze and so back toward Ypres, whose ruins stand out against a brilliant red sky made by the sun setting in a haze. We turn off to the left past a tumbled cemetery and along the Menin Road, by the ruined *École de Bienfaisance,* where the 5th Division had its headquarters in 1914—a spot which will probably figure in many a diary kept in those days. We are now in the 1st Anzac Area, and here again we find our way to the cellars of the ruins, past piles of dirty stretchers to which occasional bloodstained first-aid dressings still adhere, past sandbag protections; and the C.O., Captain McCoy, does the honors of his A.D.S. and tells us incidentally what the Boche would like to know—probably does—at this moment, that the entire 1st Anzac Corps lies in the angle between the Menin and Potijze roads. A lot of howitzers are banging away in the neighborhood—loud-mouthed ones—8-inch I 'm told, though to me they sound 80 inches at least; and I am given to understand that when in a given sector an SOS. rocket is sent up—such as my friend Evans of the Proven R.E.'s spends his time in making— the batteries in the ensuing five minutes fire off 80,000 pounds' worth of ammunition. . . .

We drop Moshier at the Prison and C. goes to visit his pumping stations, securely hidden in the ramparts at a certain corner of the town. Rather than wallow after him through the mud of the embankment I choose to stay outside and watch the fading glow of light behind the cloven tower of the distant Cloth Hall—indeed endeavor to make a sketch of it while one of the big balloons is being lowered for the night and the Boche is sending over at regular intervals shrapnel shells which burst over the *Grande Place,* doubtless searching for the ration wagons which begin to move up at dusk.

Monday the 29th

11 p.m. "If he drops them now he 'll just about get us"— "Ripping, right on his tail"—"There he goes off"—"He 's turning back"—"Into the moon; now they 've lost him."

Thompson, the intelligence officer or "Brains" of Flying Squadron 7, 18th Corps, said it was a long time since I had visited them and I must come to dinner, so after holding forth for two hours at our weekly meeting while the M.O.'s of Nos. 12, 64, and 46 picked my lean brains for the last time on matters cranio-cerebral,

I hied me to their mess which is, "for safety," some 300 yards beyond the aerodrome.

A very festive dinner, and their new C.O., Sutton by name, transferred from No. 9 squadron, had invited a friend who brought a band with him—an enlivening guest. Before he went into the R.F.C., Sutton and this patron of music had been in the Earl of Lonsdale's Westmoreland Yeomanry—mounted troops. I had seen none of these fellows before, with their square buttons and white gorgets with a central red stripe. The band was near and

loud, and a band confined in a Nisson hut which opens out of another Nisson, where is the mess, can make quite a little noise. But not enough to blanket the sound of anti-aircraft guns and bombs falling in Proven.

During the meal no one even commented on them, but when we were through we crowded out for a moment and there he was, the usual illuminated moth sailing along almost overhead with every-thing let loose at him and, what's more, a good deal of it falling round about. He finally turned and passed almost across the orb of the full moon, when they either lost him or he got beyond the reach of the rays. Even these boys, familiar as they are with this sort of thing, were interested and excited.

They tell me it's positively blinding to be in the rays, and one is absolutely helpless unless he can slip out, for over the German lines you can't fly out of reach as the Hun can over here; for another picks you up immediately, and they have an uncomfortable kind of gun which fires in line of the light as soon as you are picked up. The Hun in fact, it 's admitted, does most things pretty well —and, "How many American troops are over here?" is the usual question which follows this train of thought.

Possibly the most lively and jovial of the lot was young Gardiner, who must do the contact patrol to-morrow, three hours after zero, when the troops should have reached their objectives. "A somewhat sticky job," says the Oregon youth, standing in a group of Canadians. "It 's the second time he 's had it and after the first he wound up in 46 C.C.S. with a bullet in his bottom." It means of course flying the length of the corps' final objective, at a low altitude, and identifying the position of the troops either by their sending off of flares or by actually seeing them, in case those carrying flares for various reasons never get there.

And this is not straightaway flying, but zigzagging, tumbling, falling, dodging, until one's observer often gets nauseated and maybe nearly jerked out of his seat, for countless machine guns are turned loose on you at close range. Then if he gets through he comes back and drops a bag containing notes of his observations at the army, the corps, and each of the two divisional headquarters, and brings still another home. If he does n't come home in about an hour, another goes out to tackle the job, and about this time most of the rest are out for counter-battery work. For such tasks, together with photographing, are the main duties of these fickle R.E. 8 machines.

I finally fled, but not before the yeomanry band played "Marching through Georgia," and Thompson as a parting gift presses on me some Poelcappelle pictures and accompanying maps. It 's a frosty clear moonlight night and Fritz abounds; but nevertheless two of these delightful youngsters, bareheaded, insisted on walking through Proven and nearly home with me—a way they have in the air corps. It certainly cannot rain to-morrow.

THE THIRTEENTH BATTLE: PASSCHENDAELE VILLAGE

Tuesday, Oct. 30th

8 a.m. I sat up so late last night shivering in my cold tent over Thompson's maps and photographs of Poelcappelle that they were afloat on the surface of my mind when, from Ashford: "Seven-thirty, sorr, and coffee up. Shall I close your tent, sorr, it's raining and gusty." I groan and look out, and, though a high wind, not an unpromising morning after all, and they've had a two-hour start. But the bad thing about it is that it's not decently "flyable" weather for those poor boys.

From these pockmarked photographs of Poelcappelle one can easily understand how units get lost, particularly when they go up at night, for the remaining landmarks of one day may be obliterated the next, and after a barrage such as must be going on this minute, roads and crossings and the rubble of remaining buildings are so tumbled about that even in daylight it must be nigh impossible to tell where one's objective really lies. A given area may even turn into a shallow lake overnight, for banks of swollen streams are broken down with the flooding of large areas which previously were relatively—though only relatively—dry.

Ashford, in reply to my question as to how, during the night, I may keep the moisture from condensing inside my ground sheet, and thus waking up on a saturated blanket, says: "I'll ask the quartermaster for a couple of biscuits for you, sorr." I look at him vaguely, and swallow my coffee. Ashford, I may add, is a Tommy from Limerick and belongs to the 2nd Royal Something Fusiliers. He has been out here for eighteen months, has never seen any fighting, and is going on a two weeks' leave to-morrow. His thoughts are probably concentrated on this.

  · · · · · ·

Some have acquired dogs to keep them warm, others favor cats. I have Beatrice. I found her at the canteen. Miller's dog is a small unintelligent-looking fox-terrier bitch of which he is very fond, though some wag long ago dipped her tail and caudal segment in a pan of picric acid. The Flying Squadron had a collection of cats which sat on their shoulders at dinner, and they make good muffs to warm one's head. "Beatrice" is a small kerosene-burning affair, distinctly feminine, and, lest you overlook the fact, her name is painted in gilt on each side of her bottom. She suffices to warm a basin of shaving water in the morning—for which I am

Broken Line Shows British Front Just Short of Passchendaele after the October 30th Battle. (For Squared Area in Upper Left Corner, Compare the R.F.C. Photograph on Opposite Page)

waiting—also, later on, the cold iron-clad soles of my issue boots. At least she does these things when Ashford remembers to fill her up. She has an insatiable appetite and Ashford a feeble memory.

Wednesday, Oct. 31st

1 a.m. Unquestionably it's been another disappointing show, like the last two—rain, mud, heavy casualties, a small advance difficult to hold. . . . The wounded have come from the 63rd Division with men of the Nelson Batt'n, Artists' Rifles, Hawkes' Batt'n, and Bedfords; the 58th also with London troops; the 57th with Lancs, King's Liverpool, etc., and the 50th with East Yorks. So four 5th Army divisions at least were engaged. It sounds as

The Poelcappelle Crossroads from the Air on October 2 after a Heavy Bombardment. The Ruins of the Church below and a Concrete "Pill Box" above the Direct Ypres-St. Julien-Poelcappelle Road. (*Cf.* Squared Area in Map on Opposite Page)

though they had done the King of France's trick; but if I know the Canadians, in the army on our right, there 'll be no marching back if they once get astride the ridge at Passchendaele before the downpour. . . .[1]

General Skinner summoned me to say good-bye—rather depressed, I thought, and after the mere statement that 140,000 casualties had occurred in this 5th Army area since June, we talked about other things—racial characteristics notably; he has great respect for the fighting quality of the Teuton—only the French and English can stand up against him. By English he means of course British. There is a story of a Scot who saw on a signboard a reference to "Gott strafe England." He took a black crayon, scratched the last word, and substituted "Britain."

Gil has held on till this late hour, while I have struggled with the loose ends after our three months of work. We have orders to leave for the Base and rejoin our unit to-morrow. Patterson has wired that we are to be transferred immediately to Boulogne.

FAREWELL TO "WIPERS"

Oct. 31st. Evening

Another beautiful clear morning. Yesterday's battle in the rain was sandwiched into this stretch of good weather by some Jonah. At 4 a.m. a raider dropped six torpedoes by the crossing at Proven about 400 yards from here, but it was n't enough to wake me. One of our bearers has brought me a fragment about eight inches long, and the thing must have had a circumference of between one and two feet. The big French mobile naval guns were browsing around this neighborhood and firing as I went to bed, and the Hun was possibly after their train—or else the R.E.'s dump which was near. No damage done, I believe.

To-day is the anniversary of the Gheluvelt day of three years ago, so fateful for the British, for the enemy were on the point of breaking through to the Channel Ports. It ends our period at No. 46, and we will be cut off from further close contact with this recent ghastly struggle for the very same ridges.

---

[1] Before the horror and misery endured by the British troops in these battles for the ridges were over, two more attacks were made on Nov. 4th and 10th, when the Canadians pushed forward beyond Passchendaele to Goudberg spur, thus gaining control of all the highland that had for so long permitted the enemy to dominate the salient.

After a morning's clean-up of dressings, of handing cases on to
our successors, and of packing our chattels, Horrax and I have had
a memorable final afternoon in what was once *Ypra opulenta;* for
Myer Coplans thought we might like to see for the last time what
for the British would ever remain the most hallowed spot of the
Great War. Again by the now familiar but always fascinating
causeway with its unending processions, one moving east and the
other west, and a chance for an ambulance occasionally to dodge
ahead. We make for the *Grande Place,* and spend the two hours of
remaining daylight among the ruins of St. Martin's and the Cloth
Hall—climbing over and around the piles of stone and rubbish
and fallen columns—picking up bits of white Carrara and marble
of other colors from the altar; of leaded glass from the great
windows; of gilded and painted stone decorations. What would
not a little digging bring forth! Much of the fallen stone is
weathering, and the piles of débris are beginning to be moss-
covered and grass-grown. There must have been a court or possibly a churchyard between the two buildings, for there are large
shell holes full of water, and though no recognizable gravestones
are seen, bits of human skeletons are exposed—a tibia and fibula,
part of a skull and humerus—possibly from a recent grave, it is
true; and many dud shells—some very large and quite rusty—
are lying about.

Despite what I felt before, the Cloth Hall tower is still a very
noble ruin; and on this rather cloudy late afternoon, with the
tottering pinnacles and arches between us and the reddish streaks
of light from the broken western sky, it was particularly effective
—sad and depressing as the spectacle is. For the mutilation is too
recent for us to forget its beauties of only three years ago. Coplans
knew it well at that time, and admits he is always much affected
—100 years to build and a few short months for man to destroy.

Most striking was the way in which the birds had taken possession. The ragged top of the Cloth Hall tower was literally alive
with them, and whenever a shell burst—for they were being
dropped on the distant side of the town—the birds would rise in
a cloud and twitter and settle down again, just as I have once seen
the birds rise off from Piercé Rock when the passing steamer blows
its whistle. Mostly starlings and a few doves, but there were

smaller birds too, some of them in song, and the conical-shaped
ruin of St. Martin's, as well as the square one of the Cloth Hall
with its dentated top, were covered with them. And beyond, in the
sky, was the row of ugly balloons, like partly curled-up black
maggots, and still higher were mechanical birds becoming apparently more numerous every day, and more sure and skillful in
their flight. Some day they too would be landing like these birds,
on towers of their own, to rest and prune their wings.

I wandered through the old basements of the Main Hall, with
their low arches supported by stone pillars, where some Tommies
are billeted and are making tea. Then out through the littered
court to the old Square—*die Groote Markt*—and around to the
Place Vandenpeereboom, alongside of which rushes the muddy
Yperlée in the broken-down conduit which once completely
covered it over.

Then we go on to see the pumping station, and even Coplans
has difficulty in finding the camouflaged entrance to the engine
rooms, where are two pumps, each capable of pumping 7000
gallons of water an hour from the moat. The water is first allowed
to settle, and then it is aerated, chlorinated, and stored in great
tanks—also camouflaged—though not as well as I should like to
see for a place so vital to an army's welfare—to be distributed
finally to the large force of thirsty men in this battle area.

We pass the old Vauban wall, which, though battered, still
stands despite the rain of shells, and one marvels at the strength
of brick and mortar which in the freshly scarred areas is almost as
solid as newly laid concrete. Indeed Coplans once had to make a
passage through the outer fortification to the east of the moat;
the mortar laid down in 1680 was hard as iron and proved nearly
too much for them. It's growing dark, and the old moat, with
the wall of the fortification beyond lined by the dead and fractured trees reflected in the still water, was a striking example
of war's desolation.

Then a visit to the cellar of an old brewery, where the personnel
of the R.E.'s are billeted and well barricaded by sandbags—necessary enough, for they said that fifteen Gothas had been over earlier
in the afternoon, dropping bombs on that part of the town. And
from there a painful scramble through mud and fallen trees and

old wire entanglements onto the ramparts, where we can look down, at the risk of our necks, onto the moat, and where one of us nearly falls into a hole leading down a precipitous flight of steps to a dugout some 30 feet below. And who should climb out and accost us in broken English but a Russian soldier! Just why he is here we are at a loss to know, but as the Canadians now occupy one half of Ypres and Anzac troops another, why may not a Russian or a Zulu or an Indian pop his head up from somewhere? One need not be surprised at anything in this war.

So across the darkening town by the rue de Lille, past the ruined Church of St. Pierre, and out through the Lille Gate, and Coplans explains to us the marvels of the ancient system of canals and gates and sluices whereby the streams flowing down from the low hills—the Zillebeek and Kemmelbeek and one or two others—are controlled. Remarkable, the management of these low-lying and crisscrossing streamlets which would flood the country if let loose. The Dickebuschbeek, for example, dips by syphonage under the Ypres–Comines Canal, and so the Yperlée, further north, dives back and forth under the Canal de l'Yser. The Dickebuschbeek empties into the moat on the western part of the town as does, I believe, the Zillebeek at the southeastern corner, while the Bollaartbeek flows along below this Ypres–Messines roadway directly under our feet, and at the Lille Gate becomes the Yperlée.

In the faint light we follow along the road—the Chaussée de Warneton—as far as Shrapnel Corner, where the Ypres–Comines railway crosses the road—a low country, pocked with shell holes which are full of water reflecting the sky. In the old defenses it was an easy matter to inundate all this area by the mere closure of one of the gates, which prevented the Bollaartbeek from emptying into the Yperlée. For the beginning of this stream is directly under the Lille Gate, a massive structure—I counted eighteen paces in going through. In short, by the system of gates one should be able to make the water flow, in these streams and the moat, in any given direction, or if desired flood the outlying marsh; and Coplans was disturbed to find, as he thought, that the current in the moat was in the wrong direction. He ought to know if anyone does, for he gets his water from there.

We went into the casemate just to the west of the gate and

The Husks of Ypres from the Air in October 1917

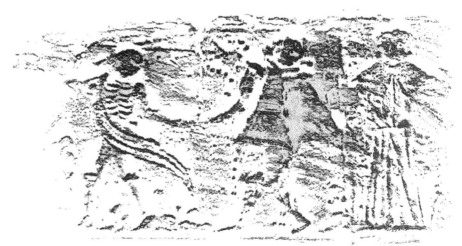

A Rubbing from the Totentanze Theme Encircling the Old Bell

could hear the rush of water under our feet. Meanwhile some New Zealanders who were lodged therein, cooking their supper with fuel which was as bad on the eyes as lachrymating gas, took an interest in us, and one of them showed us, by the light of a candle, the cathedral bell, which had been placed for safe-keeping in custody of the occupants of this particular casemate. A big bell standing about four feet six, and some four feet in diameter at the base, with a ragged hole through its thick side. It was partly buried in sandbags, and Gil and I took some rough rubbings of the figures round its top—evidently the *Totentanze* figures—Death beckoning to the bride—taking the old man by the arm, and the like. Probably an old bell, and doubtless with the date inscribed on the line of letters below, but with only a shaded candle, and even that not permitted to be shown at night in this area, we made no attempt to decipher the Latin inscription. So the bronze cathedral bell of St. Martin's has carried the ancient legend cast in its crown all these years; but it has now tumbled into a dance of death more horrible than any it has previously seen, and it doubtless has known many.

Then after a visit to a large T-shaped dugout in the ramparts, full of Australian R.A.M.C. people—two officers and seventy-eight bearers who are "in rest"!—we creep out of the black town and home again, very sad and very muddy, and in time for our last mess, when speeches and thanks and good-byes have to be said.[1]

---

[1] Criticism has been heaped on the British 5th Army for the heavy casualties sustained in the Passchendaele battles with so little to show for them in the way of gained ground. As a matter of fact, the German losses were no less heavy, and Ludendorff in his Memoirs confesses that it was a period of the greatest anxiety for them. It prevented the execution of their own plans for an offensive which might otherwise have been launched in 1917 before American troops became available. The failure of Neville's April offensive on the Aisne, leaving the French morale at a low ebb, and the Russian Revolution, permitting the withdrawal of German divisions from the Eastern Front, provided a favorable opportunity for the Germans to strike had they not been kept so busy by Haig in Flanders.

VI

IN WINTER QUARTERS: BOULOGNE

Taking Over No. 13 General

Sunday, Nov. 11th. Boulogne

Six months ago to-day our eager party sailed from New York. Eleven days ago we assembled—those still attached to the Unit —in Boulogne. The transfer has been in the air since June and we were promised at least ten days' notice, but the order came like a bolt from the blue. We may possibly have to thank Cadorna's weak 2nd Army for this; for the Boche, freed from the need of holding the Russian line, joined the Austrians and broke through, claiming almost 200,000 Italian prisoners and countless guns— the British got theirs away in time. All this meant urgent help from the French and British—the hurried sending of troops together with medical units. Here this large affair touches us, for our predecessors at No. 13 General were chosen to go on short notice and we must supplant them, which we managed to do in a two days' period.

On the morning of the first, after a parting snapshot at the 46 C.C.S. group, Gil, Miss Gerrard, Pte. Clifford, and I, with all our enlarging equipment—for one's personal possessions in some curious fashion grow apace—started by ambulance, as we anticipated to Camiers, stopping for lunch with the D.M.S. 2nd Army people at Quaestraete by Cassel—then on to Boulogne, which we reached after dark. By mere chance we found the Unit already moving up and taking over.

So we were dumped here; and though I went down to Camiers the next day to see if there were any loose ends I might pick up, the place was completely evacuated, a new British unit having taken over our supplies. Thus No. 11 General with all its interests and discomforts, its bombing and its sump pits, has become an

Our "Team" and End of the Operating Hut at 46 C. C. S. on Our Last
Day

The Staff of 46 C. C. S. with Attached Officers, at Mendinghem,
October 31, 1917

episode of the past, and I looked sadly on Graham's neglected little flower beds with patches of mignonette still bravely blossoming about the margin of my long-unoccupied tent.

The days since then have been full of a number of things—my chief concern being to keep the group together and have them continue to mess in company. Some had already broken loose and engaged rooms before I got here. To induce a collection of warweary individuals to live amicably together longer than six months is no light task; but the Unit and its *esprit de corps* come first. So, after rustling round, a small unoccupied villa named "Saint Joseph" was found on the water front a few minutes' walk from the Casino, and adjacent to a place where thirteen of our predecessors had lived. In the villa, Cutler, Horrax, Morton, William Potter, and I promptly deposited ourselves on a six months' lease; and then there was a struggle for the larger house, with interviews and inventories and papers to sign, and a new Mess President— George Denny this time—and a new range to buy, and I know not what all. But we have secured about twelve occupants, and our five—for we mess with them—mean a fair proportion of the officers. They had their first breakfast there this morning and should be reasonably happy.

Here we have engaged an old *bonne*—a "Goody" I presume, Élise, by name—who carts water for us, gives us breakfast, and tidies up. So far we have cooked our own suppers from the Campbell's soups, Libby's corned-beef hash, cocoa, etc., which come in our parcels—chiefly mine with the green string—from home. Meanwhile gas men have provided us with *les becs nouveaux,* if anyone knows what that means, so that we are becoming moderately well illuminated, and soon we 'll get sheets and pillow cases from the hospital supplies and have something between us and our blankets and be really civilized once more.

Meanwhile many people lend a hand: Sir Arthur Lawley, the Red Cross Commissioner who immediately purchases for us— at 450 pounds!—the Casino's second-rate X-ray outfit which Captain Gamlin had wholly dismantled; Col. Blaylock, the Canadian Commissioner, with Phœbe Wright in his office, through whom I got this house; Sir Almroth Wright, who takes me into his comfortable billet where, with Freeman, Colebrook, and

Fleming, his assistants, I stayed for three days until we got established, meanwhile using abundantly his expansive limousine for
errands. Col. Elliott and "the deaf one" at No. 7 General are
eager to help; also the McGill people at No. 3 Canadian in the
old Jesuit College at the top of the town on the Calais road, where
are old friends, Jack McCrae, Lewis Reford, Birkett the C.O., and
Elder, who is soon to succeed him; the Chief Ordnance officers'
place, where a D.A.Q.M.G. tells me how I can wangle this particular expansive "table, field service," I am writing on; the
Church Army Hut with some nice women in charge—Mrs. Dyson,
Miss Haldane, Mrs. Northcote, and some others who will permit
us to gather there for tea at 4.30 until we can get settled; also
very useful to us was Miss Fitzgerald, our Edith Cavell nurse,
long in service at the Casino. She, having a perfect knowledge of
the country and speaking Italian like a native, is the only one of the
outgoing unit who is not "to proceed forthwith to Italy."

The weather has been good, so different from Flanders, only
one rainy day, and that was Thursday the 6th, the day of a final
Flanders battle—I 've almost forgotten about them since leaving
No. 46. This Italian business with its second Hun invasion has
eclipsed all else; and the Russian situation is almost worse,
Kerensky now a fugitive and the Soviets in power with "an im-
mediate peace" their slogan. These are the darkest days for *Les
Alliés* certainly since the Marne.

Wednesday, Nov. 14th

10 a.m. *En route Paris à Boulogne.* On Monday afternoon,
Sargent, who has been anxious to see us operate before his departure for home, rushed in a poor Canadian from No. 8 Stationary
whom Nature had treated badly by giving him a cleft palate, and
the Boche had added insult by a penetrating wound of the skull.
One of the type of cases I fear Sargent and Holmes and I are going
to disagree about, for they favor leaving them alone. At all events
there was a large stinking abscess in the temporal lobe and under
local anæsthesia this was found and opened, and the missile easily
extracted with the magnet.

The same evening Sargent gave a farewell dinner at Foquet's
in Ambleteuse to "brass hats" and others. I was included—among
the others—and Sir Almroth took me out and also sent me in

again, for I had to leave early in order to get the 9.06 p.m. for
Paris. Very pleasant, but after the soup I pocketed an apple and
in Wright's car beat it for the train. It was a scramble; and I
passed an unbelievably shivery night—not having had the fore-
thought to take a pillow and a blanket.

One really should be an hour ahead of time for a train these
unhappy days. I tried to be when we changed this morning but,
even so, barely got a place, which I suspect may belong to the
Portuguese officer who is glowering in the corridor, though he
left nothing recognizable here to indicate his intended occupancy.
I should like to ask him, but as there are Russians—one with
enormous white whiskers down to his centre of gravity—Belgians,
with their silly little tassels hanging from the peak of their caps
—doubtless on the principle of dangling a wisp of straw before
a reluctant mule—a dark blue French aviator who, after reading
La Vie Parisienne, is now sunk in a novel entitled *Ma P'tite
Femme*—a middle-aged French lady and her husband encased
in a traveling shawl and the morning *journaux*—I 'm shy about
asking him. There are some more of his kind farther down the
corridor.

Traveling is a matter of *sauve qui peut* these days. But I wonder
what the Portuguese really is thinking about, and these Russians
too. They are over here, the Russians, several divisions of them
I believe, eating up food and doing nothing. The men won't fight
of course and, worse, won't work. Meanwhile Kerensky and Korniloff seem to have embraced again, probably with kisses, and together are marching on Petrograd and the Soviets.

One sometimes wonders what it 's all about and what indeed we
are all over here for. Some kaleidoscopic turn may alter our
destinies at any minute: what we want—we Allies—is unity of
purpose, and leaders, or, better still, one leader. An Allied War
Council of three is in the air, but Cadorna refuses to serve. Lloyd
George, who is about the only minister anywhere who has been in
the war from the beginning, talks plain when he says: "With the
whole united strength of our people we shall win—but we shall
only *just* win." And British troops are pouring over the Alps
and French are already there, while the Hun is known to be planning to break the Western Front before spring.

Meanwhile the Flemish farmer on whose land No. 46 C.C.S. was laid out—and I presume it 's true of other farmers elsewhere —does n't really care. He philosophizes that he and his forbears long before him have tilled the same acres, as will his progeny long after him. It has not made much difference to any of them, what governments have come and gone—now Roman, now Spanish, now French, now German, now Belgian, now English—nor what wars brought them; and for that matter he usually manages to make a little more money at such times—as in the case of the pigs at No. 46 fattening on crusts from the officers' mess. Is his the *vox populi*, or is Albert's? Julius Cæsar said the Belgæ are by far the bravest because they are most distant from the culture and civilization of Rome—furthermore they are neighbors to the Germans across the Rhine, with whom they constantly wage war.

My object in Paris was to attend a meeting of a newly appointed research committee called by Alex Lambert.[1] He unfortunately had gone on a trip to Italy. Also another meeting was scheduled for the earlier afternoon, of the Tuffier group, the subject for discussion I particularly desired to hear being cranio-cerebral injuries. Gibson and I were the only ones who turned up. It appeared that the meeting had been held the week before! in conjunction with the *Conférence Chirurgicale Interalliée.*

In Lambert's absence our Research Committee meeting was not much—vague like everything else in Paris, and lacking punch. We finally decided to recommend an intensive study of trench fever, alone or in conjunction with the British, who possibly can lend us an entomologist in the shape of Bacot of the Lister Institute. He has had a greater familiarity with the louse family than anyone of whom we know. He takes them as boarders—food and lodging both, as a matter of fact. Strong, Swift, and I were put on a special committee of action which convened immediately, and in general it seems best: (1) for Strong to organize the study; (2) for Dr. Welch to send a bacteriologist; (3) to use Bacot if we can, or get Brues from home as an entomologist; (4) Swift to direct the clinical work; (5) to use freshly landed personnel from the med-

---

[1] The organization and transactions of this Committee in its successive monthly meetings were published, together with *résumés* of other papers at various hands, by the American Red Cross, without printer's name or place, in two volumes under the title, *The Medical Bulletin: A Review of War Medicine, Surgery and Hygiene.*

ical corps as volunteer experimental material; (6) to shut them all up together where they will be free from the interventions of the devil and a C.O.; and (7) expect results as far as the louse is concerned in three months. Col. Elliott tells me there is never any difficulty getting volunteers; that when McNee tried his direct-transfusion experiments men came up like trout to a fly—one of them a baronet caught in the service as a private. He knew that if he got trench fever it meant Blighty and if he could only get home he might get a commission. He got the fever, the leave, *and* the commission.

Sunday, December 2nd. Boulogne

The "deaf one" came to lunch with us at the mess to-day—the food largely left over from our Thanksgiving feast—cold turkey, cider, nuts, and raisins. He was a little vague about Thanksgiving Day, said he had an idea we held it in July: Chinese firecrackers, tetanus, and the rest—had read about it in our papers. Indeed he had read a great deal of American literature—especially fond of the *Saturday "Morning" Post,* and of Charles, or was it James Fenimore Cooper who wrote stories about the blockade runners in the war between the North and South—or was it East and West. Never could really understand our geography very well nor our flag, haw, haw! the stripes—tried to count 'em the other day on the flag now over the Casino, but it was blowing so hard could n't tell whether there were nine or eighteen—I reckon—don't you always say "I reckon"?

Then, after some turkey, more of the same—always struck him as peculiar that Washington was situated where it is—saw it on the map the other day—just south of British Columbia. Has a niece living in a part of New York City—perhaps we might happen to know her—an idea that she is a trained nurse and may have come over with us; but perhaps she is n't, not quite sure of her name nor the place she lives in. We suggest Brooklyn, Harlem, Hoboken, Jersey City, Coney Island, Chicago. No, don't sound familiar; but she goes over the bridge that divides New York and uses the overhead—he "reckons," that 's it, the "overhead" —to get home.

And by the way, speaking of bonds, do any of us know what Ingersolls are? Watches, we suggest. No, does n't think so, but bought some once and made a lot of money—so much he was afraid there was something phony, so he sold out—always wondered what they were and had wanted to ask some Americans.

But we could n't be typical Americans as we did n't say "wahl neow" as they do in the *Saturday "Morning" Post*—great paper! Colonials always acquire a certain peculiar accent—not always disagreeable—for example, there was a Miss Fitzgerald at No. 13, an Englishwoman who was born in Florence—never lost it—could always tell she was a colonial. When we told him she was an American and our Edith Cavell nurse sent from Boston, Massachusetts, he said we must be talking about quite a different person, for his Miss Fitzgerald wore an English sister's uniform.

Then after some apple pie, which he recognizes as such from experiences with the *Saturday Post,* he produces his wonderful cigarette holder—which is so much a feature of his apparatus I have never commented on it before—and inserts therein an expensive "guest" cigarette proffered by Sgt. Wilson. This is too much for Cutler, who asks him to explain, which he does—it's really two cigarette holders, connected by a piece of red rubber tubing in which you put a piece of cotton—used to have a cough every year from October to May, but since using this, never. Would recommend it to anyone—makes every cigarette, good or bad, taste just alike. We hope he'll come again, and we guarantee really to teach him our language. Sometimes it's very difficult to know whether the "deaf one" is *wholly* an ass or just part.

. . . . . .

The meeting with the "deaf one" spurs me, after a three weeks' lapse, to resume this journal. I hesitate to say it's been P.U.O., for this malady stands under the shadow of the louse, with whom I have made no acquaintance, so far as I'm aware. Whatever the disorder may have been, its chief symptoms were shivery sensations, aches, and a weazened brain. The weather fortunately has been wonderful for a Picardy November—only one or two days of rain, quite warm at times, and with grass and shrubs still a brilliant green.

To-day for the first time there is a bite of winter in the air, and a half gale is driving in a pounding surf. It breaks high over

A Peace-Time View of the Plage at Boulogne as Seen from the Casino,
Showing Our Billets at 124 and 122

View of the Casino at Boulogne Taken from the Plage

the sea-wall roadway a hundred yards from here, and interrupts the traffic between Boulogne and Wimereux. We have no coal, find we are not permitted to buy kerosene in the local shops, and as the days are growing very short and the wind whistles in through the large cracks of the French windows of this summer residence there is little to encourage writing.

But it 's a great sight—the sea—from our front windows. They face due west, overlooking the jetties through which must pass all the multitudinous craft for this port: hospital ships, packets, fishing trawlers, small sailing craft of all descriptions, hydro-aeroplanes, gray ships, camouflaged ships of every description, ships indifferent to the U-boat. But when the convoys come out morning and afternoon, Blighty-bound, two or three low-lying destroyer hounds pick them up a mile or so out and race with them across to Folkestone and bring others back, and at times the sea from our outlook is fairly alive with boats.

Not so this afternoon. A mile beyond the jetties lies the breakwater, now simply smothered by huge waves, which explode into clouds of foam that run along and envelop the lighthouse and the mast of the latest wreck that lies close by—twice the height of the lighthouse they are. There will needs be some sweeping for floating mines before free communication is opened again. It 's half after three and the sun, which is getting very low, sends, through holes in the broken clouds as through the doors of a fiery furnace, shafts of light which play here and there on the spray over the sea wall, pick up a small tug which is cavorting in the open, or light up a patch on the sands beyond the road at our front.

.   .   .   .   .   .

We had quite a gay Thanksgiving Day, with a large feast for the men at two, another for the sergeants' mess at three, and in the evening at the officers' mess, where for the first time all were gathered as of old. In the afternoon the men issued a football challenge to the sergeants, which the latter did not accept, so they worked off the effects of their dinner on one another by having a strenuous game on the sands just beyond the Casino—so noisy a game, in fact, that the D.D.M.S. telephoned to the Casino to inquire the meaning of it. Capt. Wall—a Mississippian and a very good sort—was the officer of the day and received the message.

He endeavored to explain that it would not occur often, that the day merely happened to be one of our national festivals—and to make sure the D.D.M.S. would fully understand he added that it was in honor of our Declaration of Independence. The D.D.M.S. thereupon abruptly rang off.

.   .   .   .   .   .   "

The dull month somewhat enlivened by occasional visitors. Yesterday de Schweinitz and Mosher, majors in the M.O.R.C., over here in the interests of a "Section of Surgery of the Head," which has a subsection of Brain Surgery being organized by Charles Bagley, who has published a book "from the Office of the Surgeon General" on the *War Surgery of the Nervous System.* The Medical Department is to be divided into eight sections, each of which is to be represented in every hospital, and everyone is to be a Colonel, tra la—three Chiefs of Sections already appointed: Finney for Surgery, Young for Venereal Diseases, Goldthwait for Orthopædics.

To-day a visit from Archie Malloch from No. 3 Canadian, who brings a young M.O. from Hamilton, just back from a period at the Front where he was as horrified by the waste as all others seem to be—except those who can check it. A large dugout whose floor was paved with bully-beef tins—full ones—narrow side up—keeps the dugout quite dry, fine drainage between the tins. Another in which 250 pairs of rubber trench hip boots were found buried beneath a lot of litter—the men had simply found this a con_ venient place to take them off. And as for rifles which cost the army five pounds apiece—well, they simply lie about and rust— used as signposts, used as supports for sandbags to cover a dugout, thrown away if a man is tired—"lost" of course.

Then the everlasting question of rum; for the thrice weekly ration is only a fillip. Food becomes the medium of barter. Two drinks in an *estaminet* for one bully-beef tin. It had become so bad that a raid was made in two towns just as an example; and thou- sands of pounds' worth of canned food, and jam, and tins of bis- cuit, and soups, and blankets, and uniforms being cut over for the children, were exhumed from the Belgian attics and cellars—all very depressing. But worst of all are the numbers of valuable things the men discard before going into battle—poor fellows, one may well sympathize with them. If they come back at all they will be re-outfitted without a question, or else be bandaged, put in blue pyjamas, and given a Smith-Dorrien bag which will contain all they 'll need in hospital.

A few days ago dined with Blaylock, the Canadian Commis‾ sioner, Cuthbert, his house mate, Colonel Elder from No. 3 Canadian, and a bearded person—Sir Edw. Stewart with British Red Cross connections. From them I learned that poor Major Moshier who took us up to Potijze that memorable afternoon was killed the next day. We seem very far away from the war and the Passchendaele ridges where they are still grimly hanging on. Taylor Young, who dropped in later this afternoon to give me all the gossip of No. 46, shakes his aged head about it. Even No. 62 at Bandagehem had its turn of bombing a few days ago—some sixty casualties. Not a very helpful experience for shell-shock cases.

.   .   .   .   .   .

On Tuesday the 20th the British under General Byng, with the aid of a lot of tanks, gave the Boche a surprise wallop without preliminary barrage, and pushed through the Hindenburg Line toward Cambrai in a big salient, some of which they may be able to hold.[1] It was a brilliant affair—said to have been suggested by Pershing—and served to cheer everyone up after the slow progress of the summer through the Flanders mud, the Russian *débâcle*, and the Italian retreat. Russia we must now discount; but the Italians are holding, and winter has descended in the high Alps with necessary cessation of all activity on that front.

Sunday, Dec. 9

4 p.m. A rainy Sunday and growing dark already. Both sea and sky of the same dirty gray color, hanging like a curtain dragged in folds up onto the wet sands. On it are a few painted boats mistily showing. The full moon has gone and no recent raids—perhaps owing to the bad weather, for it blew steadily a half gale for some days. The raiders got over London once, and Calais several times, and though we had a single *alerte* one night given by the gun on the cliff-head behind us, there was nothing further.

Harvey and Goethals back from No. 46—their return an‾ nounced for Tuesday—they arrived Thursday. A characteristic

[1] It was only for ten days.

mix-up. They had had little to do during their first two or three weeks; many of the teams had been sent away; No. 12 was trans_ formed into a convalescent camp, and the new D.M.S., having ordered things put on a winter's basis, had gone on a vacation. Whereupon "things" began to get active. There was a final attack on the ridge, of which from the papers we have heard nothing, with an advance which was forcibly repulsed by the Boche. Many casualties followed. The two C.C.S.'s, still on duty at Mending-

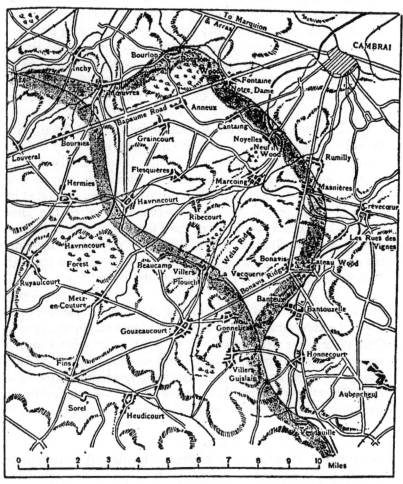

Map Showing the Front from Which the British Attack Was Made (Nov. 20, 1917), and the Greatest Extent of Ground Gained

hem, with rotations about every two hours, were swamped—cases lying on stretchers, untreated for hours, all over the place.

Our usual weekly meeting—Thursday this time—on wounds again—just ourselves with Wright and his people, though others have begun to come in—Fullerton, who speaks highly of the meetings, also two nice young captains from Charles Peck's unit at Chaumont were there. We are slowly learning something about wounds, and those we have to tackle here at the Base are very bad —old and suppurating.

Saturday afternoon Major Sinclair gave us an hour at No. 8 Stationary, and put up a fresh hip for our instruction in his fishnet frame; got another man with fractured femur on his feet in a caliper hip splint after union, and told us 80 per cent in his *circa* two hundred fractured femurs have thus "walked" home. He's a very clever person with a strong mechanical genius.

Subsequently to dinner—on dos Santos's invitation—at No. 32 Stationary, where I dined once before with the hospitable Colonel Eames. Their regular guest night, but this time in honor of the two new consultants, T. R. Elliott and Webb-Johnson, the latter having taken Sargent's place. Many speeches and toasts, with "He's a jolly good fellow" oft repeated and horribly sung—a deadly custom. Wright made an amusing speech, but General Sawyer slobbered over "our oldest allies the Portuguese" and "the representative of our newest ally—no, not ally, cousin, brother, etc., etc., all past differences to be wiped out, now arm in arm to march to victory forever, amen," or words to this effect. So dos Santos and the representative of the newest ally had to respond feebly, and modestly express their appreciation of being so warmly welcomed. Then after these tortures, two of Santos's boys—eight of them are attached there, all from the University of Lisbon— played duets on the piano and violin most delightfully, something the Anglo-Saxons, arm in arm stolidly awaiting victory over the enemy, never could have done, nor would have done so naturally and simply even could they.

On the way home Sir Almroth said there are three kinds of people in the world: those who offer you something because they desire you to have it; those who offer you something because they want it themselves; and those who never offer you anything at all. Just what the allusion was you 'll have to guess. You always do.

RESEARCH COMMITTEE MEETINGS

Thursday, Dec. 13, 1917. En route Paris à Boulogne

When the Tommy shouts to the farmer's wife: "Mama doolay promenade," she, understanding him perfectly, knows immediately that the cow has run away. When I say to a ferocious taxi driver: "Avenue du Bois du Boulogne, rue Piccini 6," he makes me repeat it with every variation of pronunciation I am capable of —and they are many—and then like as not refuses to go. The Tommy, in short, gets movement out of the farmer-wife which I with my cultivated French am incapable of getting out of the reluctant and bewhiskered chauffeur. Possibly he does n't propose to waste *d'essence*, as the cow was wasting *du lait*, for it 's some distance to rue Piccini, 6. All this because our sessions have been held at this old place of Doyen's, now Red Cross Military Hospital No. 2, under the care of Major Joseph Blake.

We have had our second meeting of the Research Committee and attendant gathering—very successful. We went down on the 2 p.m. train Monday—Lee, dos Santos, and I; dos Santos an altogether charming companion and very full of talk—of history, art, architecture, and the people of the Peninsula. He would have had a good excuse for being less companionable, for the papers say the revolutionary troops in Lisbon have barricaded the street at a point which S. says is just opposite his house, where are his wife and two children.

He will have words with the Portuguese Minister, an old friend and patient who has been through other revolutions—been in fact more or less shot up in them, exiled to Africa, escaped by being sent across the continent boxed up as mdse. to Mozambique. To him S. is carrying two bottles of port as a present. This for the reason that British and Allied officers have access to Portuguese wines through the army canteens—others can't get them. And so, as I say, to Paris and the Edouard VII and a luxurious hot bath and bed.

On Tuesday morning, after many commissions—more especially to get a wig and costume for Pte. Call, who 's the "Mimi" of our men's coming show—to the Strongs' for lunch with Warwick Greene, the Blisses, and Col. Elliott, who as representative of the British Research Committee has been invited to participate in our deliberations.

The afternoon meeting was given over to gas gangrene, and Colonel Wallace gave the clinical side very well; then Herbert Henry, leading up to the serum treatment. There were possibly sixty there—some French and English guests, McNee and Wallace from the 1st Army with their Gargantuan D.M.S. General Thompson, T. R. Elliott, and others.

Then our committee meeting. Much was accomplished and a few important points registered. Strong reported his experience with the B.E.F. Trench Fever Commission, who had gobbled the entomologists Bacot and Peacock as soon as word got about that we wanted to tackle the louse question. But it must have been clear to the Britishers who were present, as well as to Cols. Ireland and Kean and Siler, our regulars who also were there, that we wanted merely to get things attacked promptly, done thoroughly, and with mutual help, regardless of professional priorities, jealousies, and personal recognition—indeed that it would be far better to have contributions issued, unsigned, as official papers, and to wait for the end of the war for the distribution of credits. The great concession was made by Col. Ireland that our subcommitteee could get to work unfettered by army red-tape and channels, and that any men we wanted to select would be detached and put to work for stated periods on our problems.

So an Inter-Ally Gas Gangrene Committee was appointed with Wallace and Henry, Fred Murphy and Taylor, and a fifth to be named by Dr. Welch from home so as to keep in touch with the work being done at the Rockefeller Institute. And we are to comb our units over here for the proper men to work with Henry, who prefers the Lister Institute to the laboratories in Blake's hospital.

Sunday, Dec. 16th. Boulogne

Dinner last evening with some neighbors—a Captain and Mrs. Langridge, who once occupied this villa and are now a few doors above. *He* of the Red Cross, with the interesting job which he has organized of caring for the relatives of wounded men in the overseas bases on the D.I.L. It must be a satisfactory business, receiving, forwarding, making comfortable, cheering these grateful people who are soon to see their own, even though it be for the last time. Much more satisfactory than the doctors' business, which is accepted without thanks as merely a part of the day's necessary humdrum. Pathetic too, often enough, as in the case of the homely old washerwoman—never out of England before—who crossed in response to a call because her Joe was ill. Having been met and given tea at the Christol, she was taken in a limousine to Wimereux, and said to the M.O., "Wot's wrong with my boy Joe, 'as 'e a cold in 'is 'ead?" When told that Joe had lost both his legs and had a bad chest wound she said: " 'E never let on to me 'e was a-solgerin'. I thought 'e was doin' hoffice work."

She, of the Church Army Hut, works at No. 2 Australian and has come to think almost more of the Australian than the Tommy. They came out together in 1914, he a shipowner, their three children dead and buried. Soon came the rule that husbands and wives could not be here together, and he said to the Red Cross officials: "That 's too bad, I 'll have to go home, for my wife must stay." This was so unexpected that the matter was arranged somehow, and here they have been and have managed to dine together about once in ten days—as last night for example, he waiting on the table and managing the dishes which a high-tempered cook sent up from below on a dumb-waiter. Nice folks.

Robertson is back from the Front, where he has had an interesting period with his uncle, D.M.S. of the 3rd Army, and done some excellent work on blood transfusion. He knows the Cambrai performance at first hand. Someone blundered badly, and three Boche divisions poured through as far as Gouzeaucourt, almost before their presence was known. They nearly got a contingent of U.S. Engineers, who, armed with picks and shovels, helped the military police to check the rout.[1] The affair opened by the enemy sending over about 100 aeroplanes which bombed and machine-gunned the British out of their positions.

Robby thinks we are pessimistic at the Base. We are. From my small experience there is less grousing at the Front than the rear

[1] For a vivid account of this episode *cf. The American Engineers in France* by William Barclay Parsons. Appleton and Co., 1920.

_-the less perspective you have of the whole situation and the more you are concentrated on your own little job, the better for you. And people talk too much, particularly the pessimistic ones. There's a sign hanging in the Étaples station which says:—

> A wise old owl sat in an oak,
> The more he saw the less he spoke,
> The less he spoke the more he heard:
> We all should copy this wise old bird—

or words to this effect. General Scott, on refusing to speak at a public dinner in London, merely quoted the Spanish proverb which says: "A closed mouth catches no flies." During war time only optimists like Bowlby should have the privilege of speech.

Dec. 18th

Henry Stokes here for dinner on his way back to Rémy after two weeks' leave. Took him into the Casino to see a man with an amputation I was anxious about. He said, coming out: "I 've been in here often before, but this is the first time the place has n't smelled bad." Another compliment yesterday from Sir Almroth, who said that since we came they had either stopped sending patients to the Casino or else we did things differently somehow, for his work used to be interrupted by howls from below which he no longer hears.

Col. Alexander sends word that my dear young friend Gideon Walker, the M.O. of the 2/Scots Guards, was killed in the Cambrai counter-attack of the 30th November—a brave lad—I 've long expected it. Rumor has it that the Guards, who had been in the primary attack on the 20th, had been withdrawn and were suddenly called on to stem the onslaught on the southern side of the salient, where the Boche broke through, penetrating our original lines even to Gouzeaucourt and beyond.

Capt. Blake from 46 C.C.S. was stationed at Ytres, and he says it was an exciting ten days. The original objective was Cambrai, but one of the two bridges over the canal got crushed in by a tank so the cavalry were held up, and when they finally got over, they allowed themselves to be checked by a strip of barbed wire, so that by the end of the first day there were some bad jags in the penetrating salient. This gave the Boche time to bring up troops, which increased every day, and finally on the 30th he nearly bit off the entire salient. At the Ytres C.C.S. they were all very nervous about it for days—in fact had attempted to do no work and were packed up ready to evacuate. The planes came over in a flock, as I have said, and the Boches might have come right through if they had only known it.

Wed. the 19th Dec.

Robertson gave a talk this afternoon on his transfusion work at No. 3 C.C.S. in Grévillers near Bapaume; also at No. 46 in Ytres during the Cambrai affair. Very interesting. Made sufficient impression on Colonel Gray to cause him to volunteer as a donor, since they had few walking cases from whom they could get blood to store. Gray must be an A-1 man for the consultant's job.

Later Wright took me out to a hospital (Col. Rodway, C.O.) at Wimereux, to their weekly guest night, on Michael Foster's invitation. Very cold, particularly in a Boston-made uniform which is too small to cover the padding we all need. The usual "Mr. Vice —The King" and later "The President of the United States." This in water for me—and very difficult to get—a final compromise on a siphon of soda water, with the result that I would have gone off like a bottle of ginger pop if anyone had pulled my cork. Then snuff was passed about before the port had its turn. Foster took a large pinch and went through the usual motions. As nothing seemed to happen, I suggested that he had struck a dud.

Later we gathered round a red-hot stove where Foster told some amusing anecdotes, e.g., about Prince Christian, who was once under his care and called his attention to the fact that he wore a glass eye. "Never would have guessed it, Your Highness," from M.F. "And what's more I have two," solemnly continued the Prince, "one a trifle bloodshot to wear after I've been dining out."

We depart at ten. A hard frost for the past three nights—deep enough for the ground to stay solid. The new moon is coming and the Hun is taking advantage of it—a raid over London yesterday evening and probably another to-night, as our lights went out during Robby's talk in the afternoon, with the usual four signals. But Fritz probably had larger game than Boulogne.

She : We seem to have a lot more raitons now, Mr. Clibbit, then wot we did used to

The Cartoonists Help the British to See Humor Even in the Worst Aspects of the War.   An Echo of
the Air Raids, by George Belcher ;   and of the Duckboards, by Will Owen

Monday, Dec. 24th

Very raw and cold with mist and rain. For this we rejoice as it will keep Fritz away this Christmas Eve. He came Saturday about eight—from over the sea, so there were no warning signals—the lights went out suddenly and then the bombs, with practically no interval.

I was caught giving a dinner at the du Nord for Alexander Lambert—to meet the local Red Cross people and some others —Sir Arthur Lawley, Blaylock, Langridge, Cols. Elliott, Eames, Webb-Johnson; and Elliott brought Colonel Thorburn with him. Lambert barely back in time from a visit to the Front, and just as we were gathering at 7.30 in the small hotel packed with newly arrived Canadian nurses, who should turn up but Strong with Opie and Baetjer on the way to St. Pol for our trench-fever mission. Strong was persuaded to join us, and by climbing over the abundant luggage and blanket rolls of the blue-coated and brass-buttoned Canadian officer-nurses we managed to get into our room.

About at this juncture the lights went out. We heard what sounded to me like five distant bombs, and then the Archies. It was like being back in Mendinghem, but we went right on with our repast with the aid of a lamp—no one commenting particularly on the raid. At about ten, however, an orderly came for Blaylock, telling him that they had gotten the Canadian Stores and there were some casualties. I began to be uncomfortable about the Casino, but feeling that if there was trouble they would send for me, and having Lambert on my conscience, I stuck it until they broke up about eleven.

Langridge, learning that I was going to see Lambert off at 1.06 for Paris and had no conveyance, got one of his cars and we went over to see what the damage had been—a badly wiped-out street in a thickly populated part of town across the river—a lot of people caught in the open, as there was no chance to take cover —170 casualties and 50 deaths, a French soldier or guard told us—chiefly civilians and Tommies of the labor companies—mostly gone to 13 General!

They certainly had had their hands full—the faithful Cutler being first on the spot and taking matters in charge. The hospital already overcrowded and 50 of these bombed cases suddenly dropped on them. Very bad cases for the most part—21 deaths practically on admission—many others in too bad shape to touch until the next day.

On Sunday morning the cases were pretty well cleaned up, a penetrating abdomen from Goethals's ward falling to my share —had evidently been bleeding during the night—pulseless, but picked up after a transfusion and found to have a perforation of the large bowel with the abdomen full of blood. My first operation for some time, and I hope he may do better than the last, a poor fellow who died of a mediastinal abscess after transection of his œsophagus from a penetrating shell fragment low in the neck.

There is to be a clean sweep of officers approaching their 60th year, so we learn. Col. Morgan to succeed Gen. Sawyer here as D.D.M.S. and Capt. Stirling to remain here instead of going to Italy with Gen. Porter, who has been taken ill. General Skinner is probably one of the lot. Word came on Friday from the local D.D.M.S. that he—Gen. Skinner—was coming to Boulogne by train to arrive at 6.30—had telephoned to ask if I could put him up for the night and meet him with my car!! "Yes, most gladly, but what sort of an establishment do you suppose he thinks I keep?" "Oh, a château and a limousine." So they arranged to lend me a car which I could pass off as mine, and at 6.30 to the train, meanwhile having asked Webb-Johnson, with whom I was to dine in Wimereux, if I could bring the General with me.

How long an American major ought to wait for a British general, about to be retired, I do not know, but after three hours, cold and supperless, I told the R.T.O., who had encouraged me with "ought to be in any minute now," oft repeated, I'd be hanged if I'd wait any longer for the C. in C. himself. What happened to General Skinner I can't imagine, but I *can* imagine what happened to Webb-Johnson's dinner, to which he had invited some V.A.D.'s —Miss Sloggett and Miss Lawley—who were to be brought from No. 14 in his car *after* it had fetched me.

Dec. 25th

Our Christmas Day will probably be much written about, and great credit is due the committee who had the festivities in charge, with George Derby their chairman.

... the must part—21 deaths
... in too bad shape to touch

... were pretty well cleaned up, a
...'s ward falling to my share
... during the night—pulseless, but
... found to have a perforation of
... full of blood. My first opera-
... may do better than the last, a
... abscess after transection
... shell fragment low in the

... approaching their 60th
... Gen. Sawyer here as
... here instead of going to
... taken ill. General Skinner
... on Friday from the local
... coming to Boulogne by
... to ask if I could put him
... up!! "Yes, most gladly,
... do you suppose he thinks I
... So they arranged to lend
... mine, and at 6.30 to the train,
... Johnson, with whom I was to
... General with me.
... ought to wait for a British gen-
... know, but after three hours, cold
... who had encouraged me with
... oft repeated, I'd be hanged if
... C. himself. What happened to
... but I *can* imagine what happened
... he had invited some V.A.D.'s
... who were to be brought from
... me.   *Dec. 25th*

... be much written about, and
... had the festivities in charge.

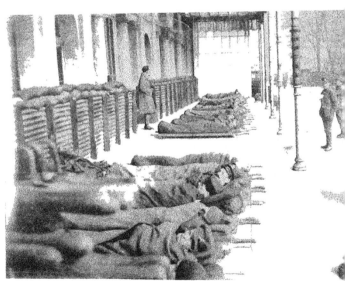

Christmas 1917 in the Baccarat Ward

Christmas Presents for Blighty — Awaiting Transportation
caded Casino Platform

Last evening our carols in the wards from 6 to 7.30; then a buffet supper at the sisters' mess, very abundant and good with a turkey pie and much else, followed by the tree and distribution of presents by H. Lyman in the guise of St. Nick. Most amusing, many of them, with very clever skits in verse perpetrated largely by Johnnie Morton, George Denny, and Miss Hawkins, who constituted the Joke Committee. "Carrie's On" was probably the best, and a close second the skit on the C.O. in his slacks meeting the Queen on her visit to Camiers.

This afternoon from four to six a procession through the wards, of people in costume and of others who had come to entertain the patients—the Frivolity people again—some Scotch performers piloted by Padre Jeffries—our own men's vaudeville with Clifford as an Irishman, McGann a Maine farmer, Call in Mrs. Bliss's wig and a few other things, McDonald as a negro minstrel, and so on.

There being many rings to the circus and only two pianos, it required much navigating to get all the events in all the wards, but it was very gay and the wards much decorated with a big Christmas tree in each—indeed three in the baccarat ward. Then at 7.30 more carols in the Church Army Hut for Mrs. Dyson and her Britishers: "O come, all ye Faithful," "Holy Night," and "The First Noël," which, in much diminished numbers, we struggled through before silent smoking Tommies, and were resuscitated subsequently by some powerful tea of no recent brew.

It's been a mixture of a day—clear, windy, snowy, rainy, in alternation, and to-night clear again as a bell, with the moon, alas! nearly full.[1]

December 26th

Boxing Day—just why I do not know, but the British find it useful as a day in which to recover from the effects of the day before—a sort of Sunday-Monday and it's-Tuesday-before-we-really-get-back-to-work idea. Wright says he hates Christmas. He appeared in his laboratory to-day to find "God Bless Our Colonel" in cotton and glue over his desk and the room festooned with papers daubed with fuchsin, gentian-violet, eosin, and methylene blue, which made him hate it worse than ever.

[1] Christmas packages from home addressed to us via the A.E.F. in Paris reached us sometime in May.

Saturday, Dec. 29

A farewell dinner to General Sawyer, the local D.D.M.S., who is being retired. Small and enjoyable. The Base Commandant, Wright, Eames, Fullerton, Elliott, Holmes, Taylor, Captain Towse, and myself. Wright was at his inscrutable best—on morals and the Decalogue—only four Commandments really to be considered and he believed in breaking them. Many British officers going on leave, Captain Towse among them. They say Queen Victoria wept when she pinned on him the V.C. which heads the two rows of his service ribbons. He is going to be sent on a talking tour of England to buck people up who are wobbly.

Jan. 6th. Sunday

The inarticulate Col. Hamerton, C.O. of No. 12 C.C.S.—our Mendinghem neighbor of last summer—in to lunch. They are to make over No. 12 into a Convalescent Camp. On water alone he managed to loose his tongue and talked most interestingly about Africa and the negroes. Like most English regulars of middle age he has lived in various out-of-the-way places and been for months on end in the interior of Africa, the only white man in his post. "All coons don't look alike to him" by any means, and the conversation turned on his chance remark that the Jamaica "niggers" out here are Ivory Coast "niggers" from the Congo.

He was in Uganda when T.R. went through with Selous. The natives wanted to know if he was a king. "No." "A governor?" "No." That was as far as they could get, for "President of the U.S.A." meant nothing to them till it was explained that it had something to do with *americani*, the name they give to their loincloths made of American calico—so "President Americani"—president of the loincloth—he became. They probably thought he owned a cotton plantation or mill.

A long tramp in rain and slush up to No. 3 Canadian by roundabout back roads. Tea with Elder and Rhea. John McCrae comes in late: back from giving a lecture in the Lens region. Does not appear to me at all like the "In Flanders Fields" person of former days. Silent, asthmatic, and moody. There are only seven of the original McGill Unit still attached.

Monday, Jan. 7th

Our coal is not only scant but atrocious, being largely dust, and flakes of soot fall all over our papers. This due in part, possibly, to the lack of draught in the chimney, which has certainly not been cleaned out in many a day and year. The only time the fireplace does not smoke is when the blower is on, but that burns up the dust in short order and we get no heat. The choice lies between warmth and smoke therefore. Cutler has concocted a sort of half blower out of two sides of a Boston Surgical Dressings Committee tin. It is quite handsome and promises much.

We can get no more petrol for our feeble lamps and the gas has gone bad. Élise has summoned the "Bec Auer" again, and this time he has come in the person of a *poilu* of the 1st Artillery just back from Nieuport. Jolly, smiling, quick, skillful. He has set us ablaze with new Welsbachs, and meanwhile told us all about himself and the war, which will last one year longer—then more *d'argent* and less *gloire*. He incidentally presented a bill to us for the last *réparation* and thought it a great joke when Elliott pulled out a receipted one for the amount. They 're wonders, the French.

Working here all day on the "penetrating wound" section of my paper.

Thursday, Jan. 10

The snow has vanished under a warm sun in a clear sky. A land of contrasts. "*Tous les saisons dans une journée,*" says old Élise, who staggers in with a bucket of coal dust she has wangled from *l'ordonnance,* as she calls the mess next door. Most of it will in the course of an hour precipitate itself as fine dust over these papers.

Wed., Jan. 16th

Once more en route Paris to Boulogne. We came down Sunday afternoon, Col. Elliott, Bock, Stoddard, and myself. B. and S. had not as yet been absent from the Unit for a single day these past eight months—and were never before in Paris. It was a joy showing them about the next morning in Alex Lambert's Cinderella R.C. car which he loaned me for the purpose. But I think two episodes that interested them most were these: (1) On leaving the Gare du Nord the night of our arrival, and while struggling to get into the Métro, an aged gentleman of military bearing, ahead of us, gave way, bowed—"*Les militaires!*"—and insisted on our getting into the train before him. (2) An hour before this at Amiens, we were crowding around the steps of the diner on which stood a French waiter in a white coat, holding back the push so that those with *billets de réservation* could get aboard first. In the crowd, though standing head and shoulders above it, was the D.M.S. of the 1st Army covered with service ribbons. He reached out, lifted the Frenchman by the scruff of his neck like a puppy dog, and, depositing him on the platform, majestically climbed aboard. The waiter, who, I may add, was also wearing decorations, never lost his equanimity or smile, but, remarking *"Les Anglais! !"* climbed back on the step and went on with his job as though nothing had happened.

To the Continental this time, hoping for a room overlooking the Jardin des Tuileries, a hot bath, and a long sleep between sheets—much needed, for it's been "to bed after midnight" these past ten days. Elliott promptly turned in—I around the corner to see the Lamberts and ask for a car. Their small room full of smoke and people—General Wood and his aide, Williams; Robert Bacon, now a colonel and going to the British G.H.Q. as our liaison officer; Henry Stimson, one-time Secretary of War, also a colonel in the artillery. L.W. just back from a visit to the British front and most enthusiastic about what he had seen.

Monday afternoon on tetanus. Leishman, who had to suffer from a wrong pronunciation of his name, was altogether satisfactory and there was a very good discussion. I plead for an initial dosage of 1500 units to be tried in a given sector and compared with the initial 500 units with repetitions. There was some sparring about local and delayed tetanus and methods of treatment and so on—all told, a much better meeting than we could have hoped for.

Tuesday devoted to the important subject of scabies and I.C.T. —which had to be explained [1]—and furunculosis and impetigo— in short to "the itch" and its sequelæ—its prevention and treatment; thus the louse and delousing were naturally dragged in. In due course a most handsome portrait-in-oil of Mr. Louse by Sgt. Maxwell was passed about—indeed a family group. This is always done.

No figures were brought out, but McCormick, who is with us on the train, estimates one hundred thousand cases a year and an average of 15 days out per case—some wastage indeed. This affection must well head the list, not only in numbers but in total

[1] Inflammation of Connective Tissues.

loss of days. Men must be glad when it's time to go over the top if it makes them forget to scratch.

Gen. Thompson—Wright calls him "Harry"—often rose in his majesty and to the delight of all would put his stamp of disapproval on some wild American project. "Squirting soldiers with cresol oil!—the Tommy simply won't do it—could n't go into an *estaminet* and talk to the girls stinking like that—he would make a tobacco container out of the squirt gun in 24 hours. As for flat-irons!—no coal or gas to heat 'em—no men available to use 'em—would n't spit on 'em to see if they were hot enough if they *were* available—tried it once myself—men gave 'em away to the French girls."

Lunch with John Finney, who has been ill and looks thin. He has a large job ahead as Director of the Surgical Services. The eight-section idea "made in Washington" apparently given up, and there are to be only three—Surgery (Finney) and Pathology (Siler). Who for Medicine? Thayer seems to be the natural choice, with Tommy Boggs as ballast for his sail. Looks a good deal like a transplanted Johns Hopkins, but after all the thing to do is to get the best men and let people criticize if they wish. Peck and Billy Fisher to be Finney's assistants. Wants me to take over and organize the neurological work. Young's and Goldthwait's appointments, made in Washington, will have to stand—but no others for a time. Lyster has been sent over from Washington to let the regulars know they are to coöperate thoroughly with the M.R.C. people—the Directors of Base Hospital Units henceforth to be actually in charge of the professional work and disposition of the staff.

Then in the afternoon Capt. Jacobs, another R.A.M.C. guest—on delousing, and a good deal of confusion occasioned by the difference between pants and trousers and breeches, for "drawers" by any such name are not worn by the British. Well, we got thoroughly deloused. Subsequently a Research Committee meeting, at which Sir William Leishman and Col. Elliott again sat in—and we made plans for our next meeting's programme, and the investigative problem to come out of this one, with reports from our trench-fever and gas-gangrene-serum committees, which are already at work.

We broke up in time for me to go, about six, to the Blisses', where I ran into a large tea party of French people—officers, aged philosophers, dames, and demoiselles—and in the middle of the room Pte. Call and Pte. Reed, our two nice, chubby enlisted men —perfectly at home! I had told Call in the a.m. to see Mrs. Bliss and thank her for the costume and wig. They went the first thing —were invited to lunch—back again for tea—enraptured!

Breakfast with Leonard Wood, Capt. Williams, and a Col. Somebody. L.W. to have a meeting with a man who at one time in his career was a school-teacher in Connecticut—Clemenceau; and then off for the French front. Wants me to go along, but I have business in Boulogne with my report.

There was an interesting episode at the committee meeting on Monday. Strong reported on our trench-fever progress and spoke of the volunteers for inoculation. Col. Ireland, who usually keeps wholly in the background, got up and said he wished to tell a story. It was in Cuba, during the occupation after the Spanish War. Walter Reed presented to the Governor—i.e., Leonard Wood— his proposal to use volunteers for an experiment in the transmission of yellow fever. He was told to go ahead with full authority. The Governor's then aide was a young lieutenant named McCoy. Mc-Coy is now colonel, and serves on Pershing's staff. Ireland's proposal for Strong to make experiments here went through his hands to the General—McCoy remembered and Pershing gave the order. Ireland only asked for six men: 100 promptly volunteered from the 26th Division.

Tuesday, Jan. 22nd. Boulogne

Dinner last night at the Anglo-American with Lady Hadfield to meet a home neighbor—Mrs. Larz Anderson, who is working over here in a French Ambulance and is soon going to join De-page in Belgium. Wright there—also Col. Kennard. Sir Almroth simply paralyzing. Does not believe in exercise—has not walked a mile since he can remember—told the War Office if he was to come out he must have a car, even though his billet and laboratory are only a half mile apart. Asked them if they wanted him over here to use his legs or his head. They gave him a car—we go to dinners in it at Wimereux. Col. K. was in the Boer War—got talking of Colenzo, Hart's Hill, etc., and told of going over the battle grounds at the end of the war with a friend. On Hart's Hill they met an old man in civies wandering about—he seemed to know a good deal of what had taken place and when they finally parted they ventured to ask his name—"General Hart."

This led to talk of battlefields, among them Gettysburg, and of Lincoln and the "Address." Wright had n't read it for years—tried to recall a passage—finally gave the entire Address with one or two word changes—an amazing person! The only things that interested him in America, for which Lady H. stands up warmly, were the colors of the autumn foliage in Canada and the fact that someone had discovered some good lines in Milton—saw them painted on the walls of the Congressional Library. Knows most of the two *Paradises* by heart but had missed these lines.

Much cheered to-night by the advent of Bull. He has evidently had a triumph in London and Capt. Henry behaved admirably. Bull says Henry could not have appeared more pleased and cordial if he had been the one first to get the gas-bacillus antitoxin. Evidently it is just as effective when *B. welchii* is mixed with *B. sporogenes, B. histolitica,* and the rest. Also it can be given together with A.T.S. without impairing the activity of either. In its specificity it is comparable to Behring's diphtheria antitoxin as a prophylactic as well as therapeutic agent. A really great discovery. If it is substantiated, amputations for gas gangrene ought to become as rare as tracheotomies for diphtheria.

Incidentally he says there are half a million of our troops over here—we think he's probably wrong, but it's pleasant to have someone believe it—and that they are coming at the rate of 30,000 a week. Pretty good.

Saturday, Jan. 26th

11 p.m. The Queen of the W.A.A.C.'s was at the nurses' tea— at least I took her for the Queen—name unknown—ought to be Mrs. Jarley—controls the Waacs works—chance for someone to evolve a joke. There are some new ones coming out—the "Wrens" —Women's Royal Naval Service or something of the kind, whereas the brown ones are "Women's Army Auxiliary Corps," I believe.[1] Soon as many women as men, almost enough to go one

[1] I should not forget the Fannys—the F.A.N.Y.—First Aid Nursing Yeomanry. They were the first on the field. Organized, I believe, before the war as a sort of Territorial group of "horsey" women—sporting females accustomed to ride and shoot and drive high-powered

apiece for the Australians, who are in rest hereabouts, and doubt_ less the sea makes them homesick. At least they sit out in front of here and gaze at it a good deal in pairs. Though not apparent on the surface, there must be some honey which can still be squeezed out of the Waacs.

.   .   .   .   .   .

Count Czernin for Austria and Count von Hertling for Ger_ many reply to-day to Lloyd George's and Wilson's terms. There's nothing for it but to push on.

THE DEATH OF A SOLDIER-POET

January 28th, 1918. Boulogne

I saw poor Jack McCrae with Elder at No. 14 General last night—the last time. A bright flame rapidly burning out. He died early this morning. Just made Consulting Physician to the 1st Army—the only Canadian so far to be thus honored. Never strong, he gave his all with the Canadian Artillery during the prolonged second battle of Ypres and after, at which time he wrote his im- perishable verses. Since those frightful days he has never been his old gay and companionable self, but has rather sought solitude. A soldier from top to toe—how he would have hated to die in a bed. A three days' illness—an atypical pneumonia with extensive pneumococcus meningitis, as we learned this afternoon—for Rhea came for me and we went out with Sir Bertrand Dawson. They will bury him to-morrow. Some of the older members of the McGill Unit who still remain here were scouring the fields this afternoon to try and find some chance winter poppies to put on his grave—to remind him of Flanders, where he would have pre- ferred to lie. Was anyone ever more respected and loved than he? Someone has said that "children and animals followed him as shadows follow other men."

---

motors. They applied to the War Office early, like other groups of people. The War Office was paralyzed at their effrontery. "Women—nurses—no possible use for them in France." They finally got over under the wing of the Red Cross, with whom they remain—in and about Calais from the beginning—at times a very hot place. Brought their own motors at the out- set, made over as ambulances, and they've done heroic work—better than men in some respects. There are about 40 of them there now and they've had numerous casualties.

Most of this from Captain Saxon Davies at the Red Cross. He was agent for the Reming- ton and other typewriter concerns in the Far East and uses the same method for looking after his cars and ambulance drivers that he once used to keep track of his machines of an- other type. The Red Cross has about 2000 vehicles to keep track of, some 1700 drivers, 400 of them women of the V.A.D. organization—like the ambulance drivers in the Étaples district.

Tuesday, the 29th

We saw him buried this afternoon at the cemetery on the hill-side at Wimereux with military honors—a tribute to Canada as well as to him. A large gathering of friends—all who could get there, even from a distance: the Canadian Corps Commander with his divisional generals; General Dodds, Jack's former Artillery Commander; General Sloggett and the D.D.M.S. of our district; the Base Commandant; we Americans, with some Portuguese M.O.'s from No. 3 Canadian; all the C.O.'s and Consultants of the neighborhood.

We met at No. 14 General—a brilliant sunny afternoon—and walked the mile or so to the cemetery. A company of North Staffords and many R.A.M.C. orderlies and Canadian sisters headed the procession—then "Bonfire," led by two grooms and carrying the regulation white ribbon, with his master's boots re-versed over the saddle—then the rest of us. Six sergeants bore the coffin from the gates, and as he was being lowered into his grave there was a distant sound of guns—as though called into voice by the occasion. An admirable prayer by one of the three Padres who officiated. The Staffords, from their reversed arms, fix bayonets, and instead of firing over the grave, as in time of peace, stand at salute during the Last Post with its final wailing note which brings a lump to our throats—and so we leave him.

　　　·　　·　　·　　·　　·　　·

Sometime early in January, Jack, looking much troubled, came to Col. Elder saying: "I wish you'd come and see Windy—something's wrong with the poor dog—had him in my tent for the past two days—been vomiting, refuses all nourishment." So Elder found them, Windy on the mat before Jack's little stove, licking his hands. Jack had already given him two or three hypos of morphia, and there was not much else one could do. So Windy died and was buried with military honors in the grounds of the old Jesuit College which became the Meerut Hospital, where, with Sir George Makins, I saw the Indians under Col. Wall's care in May 1915, and where No. 3 Canadian General has now for two long years been thoroughly dug in.

Windy adopted the 1/Lincolns—a large black mongrel dog. He came to be the pet as well as the mascot of the regiment and

knew the khaki and those who wore it for friends—more par_
ticularly one of them—his chosen master. Those who did n't wear
it were to Windy enemies or slackers, and this was the cause of his
undoing—but we will come to that—alas—anon.

Fortune of war first took the regiment to Gallipoli, and there
Windy was twice wounded, and he was wearing on his collar two
bits of narrow gold braid when No. 3 Canadian first came to know
him. This was in the early days of last August, after the first of the
many mad rushes toward Passchendaele in which the battalion
participated. Both Windy and his master were wounded—the one
with multiples, Windy with a compound fracture of the leg from
a fragment of the same shell that had his master's number. Bearers brought them in on the same stretcher. Windy, like his master,
got his A.T.S. and a proper medical card at the field ambulance.
Like hundreds of others, they were dressed at a C.C.S., and together were evacuated by hospital train to the Base. There chance
brought them to No. 3 Canadian on the Calais road skirting the
hills behind Boulogne.

Windy in a plaster cast went about on three legs, devoting himself chiefly to his master—when not with him, consoling himself
with Jack. Wounds, even multiples, recover in time, and so it
came about in the course of three or four weeks that Windy's
master was to be evacuated H.S. class B to England—but the
dog—no. Every manner of protest and appeal in vain. Even
Elder went himself to intercede with the E.M.O., who was
adamant—strict rules against dogs into the United Kingdom
without suitable quarantine and papers.

A conspiracy to smuggle him on the hospital ship between the
blankets of an empty stretcher was frustrated. So in tears Windy's
master was taken aboard alone, promises being made that the dog
would be well cared for until he came out again and they would
rejoin their battalion together. Windy, to pass the waiting time,
betook himself ardently to Jack. They had many an afternoon
run (for his leg was now well) beside Jack's spirited Bonfire, who
too had been wounded when Jack was in command of a battery at
Neuve-Chapelle.

But there was work to do at other times of day for a Lt. Col.
of the R.A.M.C. at the head of the medical service of a large

hospital. Windy could not always sit whining at the door of a hutted ward, when interesting things were going on in the world near by. And some of these things were being helped along by people who did not happen to be in khaki! So when Windy was alone and a French *ouvrier* or anyone else in civies went down the road or through the grounds he would be likely to continue minus portions of his clothes.

Thus in certain quarters Windy grew unpopular, and to make a long story short it was, as Lawrence Rhea found, probably poison that did it. So all that sorrowing Jack could do was to ease his pain and last hours with euthanasia, as I have told. And Windy, with three wound stripes on his collar, lies in a cross-marked grave like any other Tommy; and though it's now midwinter, this afternoon found crocuses budding on the grave of the mongrel mascot of the 1/Lincolns, who will never again go barking over the top with them as they follow their barrage.

THE ARMY SCHOOL AT BRUAY

Wednesday, Jan. 30th. Lillers

5 p.m. I came down here in the afternoon, after the ceremony —and much subdued. Gen. Thompson, 1st Army D.M.S., had sent his car for me and we went along by a new route from Boulogne through Desvres, Thérouanne, to Aire, and so down to this district behind Béthune. The countryside in an entirely new guise—winter wheat being planted and advantage being taken of the fine weather for ploughing, much of it by people in blue uniforms—the underbrush from the forests being cut out and timber being sawn (by hand: not by a buzzing and screaming saw as with us)—the pollard willows getting their winter haircut and the roads full of old women and girls staggering home bowed with bundled fagots.

A typical glimpse of Picardy in winter—as it has always been, I presume, and long will be—regardless of the fact that just now an Australian division on the move blocks the slippery highway; that there are squads of well-fed-looking Boche P.O.W.'s going back to their compounds after their day's work; and that most of the population around Aire seems to be Portuguese. But perhaps not so typical in one other respect, for it's warm enough to ride on the front seat with the chauffeur and sunny enough to have brought the green tassels out on the roadside alders.

I am put up in a billet where lives a small boy named Edouard, who has taken a fancy to me—as I to him—and who now sits here doing arithmetic—"getting his lesson too." Tea—of course —where were Soltau and Wallace; and later dinner of rabbit and cabbage and rice pudding—very good, though—perhaps I should say *because*—rations. I learn that Gen. Thompson, who came out with a division, was captured at Mons and spent five months in Germany, though how he got away was not made clear. Later he was D.D.M.S. of the 6th Corps before coming as D.M.S. to this army—and he's a good one.

This morning to the 1st Army School at Bruay, where is No. 22 C.C.S., whose C.O. is Col. Goodwin, brother of the successor to Keogh and a fine type of officer. I was quite terrified by the audience (the Army Commander, Gen. Horne and his staff, a lot of nurses, 50 N.C.O.'s, with innumerable stretcher-bearers and sanitary-corps people), a difficult one to interest in my topic of head injuries—the more so since I was preceded by some extraordinarily good things from these forward-area people. One in particular on the subject of clearing the battlefield was given by a young Irishman from Trinity College, Lieut. Col. Fletcher, C.O. of a field ambulance, wearing a D.S.O. ribbon and a bar to his Military Cross. There's no question about Fletcher's going out with his men into No Man's Land; and he told how they did their carrying, particularly around a broken traverse when in the trenches.

All this was illustrated by actual demonstration, even down to such details as concerned the disposition of the wounded man's box respirator and "tin hat"—the proper pads for the bearers' shoulders and neck—the numbers of bearers in a squad—all of the same height—should be pals—the M.O. must know men well enough to recognize their voices in the dark—the standardizing of the regimental aid posts—the placing of shaded lamps in obscure places and dugouts—the best way of carrying morphia. So much for everyday trench warfare; and then he went on to active operations—the using of German prisoners to carry wounded and the help often given by the R.E. people—the necessity of every man's bringing something back, cups, blankets, water, dressings, etc.—the ways of searching for wounded at night and the need of warning the infantry well to left and right of your own area that searchers are out—and if searching parties get lost and have no landmarks, go toward the heaviest firing, as it's probably British! Then the question of whether stretcher-bearers should bring back identification tags from the dead, encountered when looking for wounded—with this is tied up the whole question of the possibility of looting. What to do when you're out and Verey lights are shown—lie down? Not at all, merely stand absolutely still.

It was all very practical coming straight from such a man as Fletcher—and told to the bearers themselves. He added one thing about carrying in the field, and the difficulties due to the fact that the duckboards, though laid in pairs, were too narrow for four bearers carrying a stretcher on their shoulders; so he had persuaded the engineers to put the lines of duckboards about six inches apart so the bearers could keep on them.

When he was through, Gen. Thompson asked for comments and there were several, and finally to my delight a big Canadian sergeant arose and said he would like to show how they carried *their* wounded and could keep to duckboards while doing so. He and four bearers, all wearing M.C. ribbons, came forward—one of them got on a stretcher—the other four swung it up to their shoulders, but instead of its resting on their inner shoulders they put their heads and bodies close together and got the handlebars on the outer shoulders. Fletcher admitted he'd never thought of carrying in this way and he asked some other questions which brought out that the Canadians carry six men to the squad; and when someone asked about carrying in the trenches, the sergeant said: "We never uses a trench, sir, we takes over the top." This to the great delight of General Horne and the rest of us, and it's probably true.

Well, there was much more, and finally my feeble lecture, and then lunch, after which were visits to the hut, where McDonald, the X-ray man, was conducting the drill for the application of Thomas splints; to the area where the sanitary squads were getting instructed; to the field where riding exercises were going on under a sergeant riding master; and, much impressed with the school and its very democratic methods, we motor back to Lillers and to this French billet where in the tile-floored kitchen small Edouard and I, as I have said, are pretending to do our lessons.

Saturday, 9th Feb. Boulogne à Paris

Have just finished lunch in the dining car with two interesting people, a young tank officer and a major in the Intelligence Service. He of the tanks was led to tell of the Cambrai affair and the part played by his Battalion H, or 8 as it now is—how they gathered unobserved in the mist of the days preceding the attack, how they went out on the morning, a fine sight in battle formation—the crossing of the famous Hindenburg Line, which was a great disappointment—just ordinary trenches with very low wire that did not bother them at all—the green fields where astonished Boches were caught hoeing potatoes—the intact buildings with window boxes and flowers—the Boches scurrying away on bicycles or whatever else they could get aboard, most often their hind legs—the capture of two cows, some pianos and furniture, among other useful things—the long disappointing wait for the cavalry, which never came because one of the bridges was down and it did not occur to them to take the other two bridges only a mile up or down stream—Cambrai in front of them inviting entry and no opposition of any sort.

Life in a tank with its heaving and pitching a joyous frolic on such a day. His particular beast was a little faster than the others, and so drew away from them—luncheon in a farmhouse with a feast spread for some German officers who had beat a hasty retreat. They stayed up there some days and luckily were withdrawn before the Boche countered—otherwise he might have captured the whole fleet. As it was, British tanks are now an exhibit in Berlin, according to the papers.

Kept in bed for a few days by a bogus pneumonia, I missed the *Conférence Interalliée*, the Tuffier meeting where I was to give a paper, and also the surgical conference of the next two days. I was finally given a Paris leave, partly to see Finney about his organization plans and partly to see General Wood. He had had a close call—a Stokes mortar blown up—many fragments through his clothes, but only one flesh wound—this taking his biceps, grazing the median nerve, and just missing the artery—then on to kill the French officer with whom he was conversing. Three other French officers blown to bits—their arms and legs and brains and bowels over everybody. Colonel Kilbourne with a small fragment penetrating to the right brain.

I found him with his sick-room full of people—as Williams, his aide, says it has been from the moment he reached Paris—very fit, showing what he could do with his palsied hand. Very anxious I should see Kilbourne, which I did, and advised him to go on home, it being two weeks with no symptoms and he being rather shattered nervously. Not so L.W.—he showed not a sign —has been lunching out—expects to go to the Front again to finish his observations. A long drive with him in the afternoon— quite lovely. In an unfrequented part of the Bois we passed a closed carriage out of which stepped a heavy, oldish-looking man in a dark blue military cloak, who then tenderly helped out a little old lady in black—Madame Joffre and her forgotten husband.

FOURTH RESEARCH COMMITTEE MEETING

Feb. 14

4 p.m. W. B. Cannon, Michael Foster, and I are on the way to Paris for another Research Committee meeting. Cannon just back from England on his way to join the A.E.F. gas service. He remarked while breakfasting at our mess that we live well—we do. Practically unlimited toast instead of two half slices, and a communal bowl of granulated sugar staggered him after Blighty rations. In this connection he supplied the following:—

> My Tuesdays are meatless,
> My Wednesdays are wheatless,
> It is getting more eatless each day;
> My home it is heatless,
> My bed it is sheetless,—
> All are sent to the Y.M.C.A.
>
> The barrooms are treatless,
> My coffee is sweetless,
> Each day I get poorer and wiser;
> My stockings are feetless,
> My trousers are seatless,—
> My God, how I do hate the Kaiser!

This jingle, he says, on reaching Germany was taken as proof of the economic woes of the English and appeared *übersetzt* in the *Hamburger Nachrichten:*—

> *Am Dienstag fehlt mir Fleisch und Speck,*
> *Am Mittwoch ist das Weissbrot weg, etc., etc.*

Feb. 15–16. Paris

The meeting a great success—even better than the preceding ones, though we failed to get another piece of research started. A large crowd, overflowing the small room at 6 rue Piccini. Cannon presiding and very well.

On Friday afternoon—cerebrospinal fever. Two papers in French by Prof. Dopter of *Val-de-Grâce* and by M. Nicolle, which I missed because the U.S. Consul at Lyons fears he has a brain tumor. Then Col. M. H. Gordon—altogether admirable in substance and presentation. All about their intensive studies of the epidemics—and the poor results with serum—and finding out that there are four types of organisms which require different sera —and the carriers and contacts—studies of the throats of large groups of men show that contact studies are less important than determining the number of carriers throughout the command. When the percentage of carriers begins to rise, then look out, for outbreaks occur among those recently brought in, who may be unfit, tired, without resistance, or have acquired no immunity. Contact studies, in fact, little use.

Then the whole matter of spraying wholesale in a large building which is filled with spray, just as one fixes the surface of a crayon sketch, with sprayed shellac—the same principle, I mean, so far as the apparatus goes. Various substances used—zinc sulphate and dichlor. T. The latter somewhat irritating, and as soon as the spray gets thick enough so he can't be seen, Tommy puts up his handkerchief and breathes through his mouth. All depends, therefore, on whether there is a good sergeant present. The soldier's attitude is—"You can't fool me, this is some kind of experiment with a new gas." An enormous amount of work represented by swabs taken from thousands of throats.

Dinner with Finney, Yates, Crile, Tom Arbuthnot, and others, at some place near the Continental. Finney very amusing with tales of our colored labor battalion, told in his best style—"Get up, yo' black niggah, an' go to work; wha'd' you t'ink you is, a West Pointer?" sort of story; and "Boss, ah can't *tell* you wha' I'se gwine—we 's travelin' under sealed orders." None so good, however, as Walter Cannon's of the darky who said he 's always noticed that if he managed to get through March he 'd live the rest of the year.

Arbuthnot's single-handed capture of a Boche aviator while he was on temporary duty with a British F.A. was dragged out of him. Very funny and true. He ran two miles to the spot where the lame duck was seen coming down, and having outdistanced the field brought back the Iron-Cross-bedecked man, personally conducted.

Saturday proved a washout for antiseptics—in the morning the "primary" and "delayed-primary" closure of wounds. First Pierre Duval—an altogether A-1 paper read by Vaucher. The French certainly have the art of presentation—and what 's more, the material to present. Primary closures possible in from six to eight hours—after twelve hours a contaminated wound has become infected. In quiet times all so treated—in times of rush about 30 per cent. Delayed primary suture must be resorted to in times of great activity—3rd, 4th, 5th day.

Primary suture means three weeks out—66 per cent successful.

Delayed primary suture means two months out—36 per cent successful.

Secondary suture means three months or over—i.e., wounds closed on the 18th to the 20th day.

He showed a number of admirable color photographs, in the midst of which Gen. Sloggett comes in looking like a Christmas tree with his polished buttons and four rows of service and honor ribbons. Much stirring of chairs to make a place for him—and as he must go soon Cannon asks him to say a few words. He does— to the effect that he notices his old friend Harvey Cushing in the audience and that the matter of primary closure of wounds has long been close to his heart—his old friend H.C. much embarrassed, might have added—"Since Feb. 2nd when he first heard of it."

Exit the D.G. with more scraping of chairs; after which Dr. Vaucher on his own topic, *viz.,* the "bacteriological aspects of wound closures"—the wound soiled but not infected till six or eight hours, when bacteria begin to appear—cocci and especially bacilli—also methods of giving a quick answer to the surgeon by using five tubes—milk, broth, and agar slants—which suffice for an early report.

Then Le Maître with a very detailed paper presented by Joseph Blake, on a large series of successfully treated cases—emphasis laid on most careful technique with leaving of strands of horsehair in the depth to be withdrawn and tested culturally—an elaborate paper chiefly on technical methods with a long series of cases (2664 of primary suture) extending over the past two years. He advises following the track rather than to approach the missile by the shortest route. The average stay of his cases in hospital is 28 days.[1]

Finally Col. Gask, with a report from No. 10 C.C.S.—only 123 cases but with 82.9 per cent successes—the average interval being 10.2 hours—longest 28 hours—admits temptation in the B.E.F. to use antiseptics. Still the results of those using "Bipp," flavine, Carrel-Dakin, and *no antiseptic* whatever were precisely the same. Advocates Le Grand's coloring solutions as an aid in the *débridement* procedure. The Tommy is given a two weeks' leave after the wound is healed—the *poilu* only eight days. It keeps the men cheered up—"a Blighty one" means much to the British soldier. They found that 86.6 per cent of the wounds were already infected.

A lively committee meeting in the late afternoon with Edouard Rist present for the first time—we wish to publish the papers instanter and distribute them. Rist thinks it will be allowed by the French censor—Leishman does not think it will be by the British. So we decide to print and distribute the French papers only; whereat Leishman thinks pressure might possibly be brought to bear, etc., etc.

Siler and Gordon are to organize a study of the prophylaxis against carriers of throat infections—meningitis, influenza, infectious colds, etc.; but no work was planned as a result of the wound treatment papers. The obvious need is to find what anti-

[1] The primary suture of wounds after *débridement* was first successfully worked out and put in practice at the stationary H.O.E. at Bouleuse, south of Reims, by Le Maître and his co-workers, Leriche, Policard, and Tessier.

septic, if any, will shorten the period of time before the secondary suture of an infected wound is possible.

Dinner with the Britishers—a visit from Leonard Wood—the 11.40 to Boulogne with Michael Foster, by good luck in a *wagon-lit.*

Feb. 28th, Thursday. Boulogne

I feel as if I had emerged from a winter chrysalis to find the spring here, lilacs budding, bluebells and dandelions in the fields, M.O.'s playing golf at Wimereux, a hockey game here on the beach, the sea a wonderful blue, visibility such that the shore of England is in sight from the cliffs at Wimereux. Really a beautiful sight from these windows on such a day, now that one has time to think about it. · · ·

After three months' solid work, late hours, and much anguish of soul, a monograph on head wounds was finally delivered to the world night before last. It was, in fact, born triplets, two of them being immediately dispatched to the D.D.M.S., thence by D.R.L.S. to G.H.Q. 2nd Échelon, where Col. Martin in the D.G.'s absence assures me they will be quickly censored and sent to Adastral House, London, to be again censored, and then—poor things—to one Hey Groves, editor, in Bristol.[1] The third I retain to give a start in life myself. Meanwhile there has been much wastage of paper—also gas (illuminating), and much faithful clicking by hospital secretaries in copying and recopying in triplicate.

Having emerged from my winter state, as aforesaid, there have been things to do. Col. Elliott will send me to England via hospital ship—not so pleasant as he would lead me to think, as the *H. S. Glenart Castle* was torpedoed yesterday off Bristol—the seventh since they began with the *Asturias.* But it's the only way if I am to unload myself of a collection made for the Warren Museum, consisting of pathological specimens, clinical histories, souvenirs of Ypres, shell cases, helmets with holes in 'em, and I know not what else—in addition to McGuire's much perforated tent, which a search brought to light. All this means much time in packing and arranging with the help of Sgt. Campbell—five

---

[1] A study of a series of wounds involving the brain and its enveloping structures. *British J. Surg.,* 1918, V, 558–684.

.pieces in all. Then some repairs to myself—a tooth fixed by
Parker, eyes and my first pair of glasses by George Derby—a
haircut in a highly perfumed French shop—heels raised on
R.B.O.'s advice for slumping arches. Some day Barbara will
flatten her nose against a window on Walnut Street and say:
"Mother, who is that testy old man with specs hobbling up the
front walk?"

. . . . . .

Work at 13 General has been slack and many have gone on
leave. Cutler just back from ten days with Depage, at La Panne,
simply bursting with enthusiasm. Wall and Ober from the Riviera, in a similar condition, though for other reasons than seeing
military surgery. My first operation since the New Zealander—
who luckily is regaining his vision—was on Wright's ear, which
I've Darwinized with a fine tubercle—in fact, have pointed.
This for the removal of a small epithelioma. Wright's friend
B. Shaw should be similarly treated, though his may be pointed
already; and I suspect he's a goat below stairs and plays split
pipes cross-legged in his natural environment. He tells Wright,
however, he's less a faun than a jackdaw—picks up everything
he can find, particularly from other people's brains.

FIVE DAYS IN BLIGHTY

Friday, March 1st, 10 p.m. London

Another travelogue begins to-day, which has come in like a lion.
An early omelette and coffee—an ambulance sent by the E.M.O.
to the Casino for my five boxes and McGuire's tent and another
package added by Miss Haldane to bring over by hand—so, with
a haversack of French butter to make me welcome in England,
through a blizzard half snow and half rain, to the *Hospital Ship
St. Denis*. There coffee again with Major Bird, the C.O. of the
boat, a sister, and a V.A.D., the last being something of a "sister"
in her own right insofar as all the Barnum-Carters of the army
are her brothers. The sister and the V.A.D. are in attendance on
a poor Brigadier Gen. of the 5th Cavalry being sent home with
a bad cough, though he, poor man, does not yet know of the
malignant growth causing it. The attentive E.M.O. sees that my
papers are correct—the few wounded and many sick are gotten

aboard—and we slide out of the harbor between the jetties to take our place as the third in our convoyed procession.

A gorgeous day, with patches of blue sky which let the sun through to illuminate areas of brilliant green sea covered with cavorting white horses. But soon less interesting—no more sun coming through—the breeze stiffening to a half gale—the former green of the sea shifts to the face of the sister, who abandons her general to the V.A.D., who in turn abruptly departs to seek her mate, leaving their patient to me. I finally get him on a couch in one of the officers' cabins and, with threatening innards of my own, watch the seas sweep from stem to stern over our torpedo-boat companion while she first shows us her upper deck and then her keel. And *so* cold! Go in and get warm? Not I. Nor the Tommies. "Worst crossing in six months," says the Captain as we finally, after seeming hours, slide under the lee of the cliffs where our consorts put in to Folkestone and we proceed alongshore to Dover.

There a feint at lunch, aboard, with a cheery person named MacCreery, the Dover E.M.O., wearing an M.C. ribbon which I judge was won in Mesopotamia, where he endured the siege of Kut—in fact, he's none other than the optimistic Mac in the story of Kut which ran in *Blackwood's* during the summer. He showed me his arrangements for eight trains a day and as many boats, and where the men are fed and warmed and "dolly bagged." The dolly-bag woman said she presumed we'd had a poor crossing as the men were shy of cigarettes and only wanted chewing gum. An acute observer—she—I took gum myself.

Then the train—very comfortable—sitting with Gen. Campbell and a used-up aviator boy who finally talked: At No. 9 Aerodrome in Proven since the middle of November riding an R.E.8 bus—knew all my friends and adored Major Sutton—wounded while photographing—bad business in the morning as the Hun gets in between you and the sun where you can't see him —-the Huns rather scorned for they never engage in single combat—never unless three or more to one and then they turn tail if you show fight—but their anti-aircraft guns very bad—much more accurate than ours. He got caught by a group of twelve scouts, which was his final undoing, though twice wounded before, and a patient once in No. 12 and again in No. 46—not sleeping now nor eating much—living on cigarettes—six months in fact about one's limit, and three if you use alcohol—then home, and if there's anything left of you, you engage in instruction work. Their area covered the four miles from the forest to Poelcappelle, while my No. 7 friends covered the four miles further south. All this was punctuated with a good deal of zooming and banking and looping and spinning, though an R.E. 8 is not much good for stunts.

We finally pull in to the outskirts of London. There three or four cars, including ours, are switched off, and in due time, after the sick and wounded have been taken care of, I gather together my things. Then a person named Wolf, who is a jeweler (mornings) on Dover Street, takes me and mine to the College of Surgeons, where I finally dig out a caretaker who accepts the precious boxes. The College to take what they want—the rest to be forwarded by the Red Cross to the Harvard Medical School.[1]

Then to Brown's, where Prof. Chittenden and Graham Lusk are encountered and they press me to dine with them on the strength of their meat and bread cards, I having none as yet—and quite prepared by that time for something more nourishing than gum. I expected one 8-gram roll such as "Chitty" is supposed to live on, but instead a very fine dinner with tongue, which they said the British do not call meat, and a bottle of cider which I strongly suspect was a bit fortified. They are over here in the interests of nutrition, and when their influence becomes felt I will see myself growing thin again. Lusk says the Germans claim to be winning the war by using the Hindenburg offensive and the Chittenden defensive.

So to Mr. Burghard's on Harley Street to leave my manuscript; to the Sargents' to leave a present of butter; and finally here at the American Officers' Club in Chesterfield Gardens—to deposit myself for the night.

Saturday, March 2nd

Oxford and wintry cold, though things are growing and Prunus blossoms are out. Even the wall peaches in bud. The usual mis-

[1] They were so forwarded, but the boat was torpedoed in the Channel.

cellaneous gathering at the "Open Arms."[1] Sir James Fowler, who quickly gets in mufti—Miss Nutting's young nephew, a Canadian signaler convalescing from wounds—Susan Chapin and I. Tea and many appear, including the Robert Chapins; then much over books in the library, where enter a strange pair—the enthusiastic Charles Singer, he of the *Studies in the History and Method of Science* which begins with the visions of St. Hildegarde—and the other an aged and shriveled university professor of Spanish with some rare medical incunabula under his arm.

And W.O. sails through the interruptions as though they were the very things he cordially longed for, with no secretary and unfinished notes on his letter pad—papers everywhere—that is, everywhere there were no books. Meanwhile, he finds time among other things to write a review of Lucien Dorbon's *Essai de Bibliographie Hippique*, which happens to have crossed his path. But the poor man is a shadow of his former self.

Thaxter and Van Gorder in after dinner, and then more books till it's overlate. Much from Sir William about Thomas Bodley, who "concluded at the last to set up his Staffe at the Library doore in Oxford; being thoroughly perswaded that in his solitude and surcease from the Commonwealth affaires, he could busy himself to no better purpose, &c."—this at the end of his sixteen-page autobiography—one of the best ever written. He first got all his friends to bring books, and they would tell prelates who might be visiting Oxford to take an armful of books to Bodley—which they would do, pilfering them from their cathedral stores. Hence the Bodleian possesses rare manuscripts from Exeter and Cairo and elsewhere which these places have moved heaven and earth to get back.

So to bed reading an amazing privately printed and rather vitriolic volume called *Astarte; a Fragment of Truth Concerning George Gordon, 6th Lord Byron,* Recorded by his Grandson, Ralph Milbank, Earl of Lovelace.

Sunday, 3rd March. Oxford

A morning visit to the Cowley Hospital with Thaxter and Van Gorder; many here to lunch; more to tea—poor Collier, who has just lost a son, and Sir Charles Sherrington, who looks as

[1] Familiar name for the home of Sir William Osler.

though he expected to any minute—nevertheless friendly, bright, and cheerful as always. Mrs. Draper; Mrs. Wright and Marian, with many more. A choral service at six in New College chapel with Lady O. and Sue—old Spooner peeking out under his bristling white eyebrows giving the benediction.

W.O. and Sir James go to Christ Church for supper. Ours at home, and afterwards a long talk with Lady O. about Revere and their tragedy—the months of dread—of the telephone, the messenger boy, the postman. Whenever she saw the telegraph boy at a distance he would quickly shake his head—"not for you this time." In Revere's kit which finally came was his pocketbook in which W.O. had written the names and addresses of some old German friends—v. Müller, Ewald, and others—in case the boy should be taken prisoner—no thought that they might have gotten someone into trouble if found on this side of the wire.

March 4th. Oxford

A cold, still, leaden day—no rain or snow, but might have brought either. W.O. in his Lt. Col. uniform—entitled to a Colonel's but did n't know the difference—or care. With him on his weekly visit to No. 15 Canadian at Cliveden. By the old Oxford–London turnpike; the Harcourt place at Nuneham Park; Dorchester Abbey; the Chiltern Hills; Shillingford and the Thames; the Henley "mile," Henley and the hill over the river; Maidenhead; Taplow. Very beautiful—elms budding, gorse in yellow bloom, forests of magnificent beech trees.

Col. Mewburn from Calgary, in charge of the surgical division, meets us and, joined by the staff, we visit the neurological cases —some of them very interesting. We were at the far end of the pavilion gathered round a bed when Nancy Astor in her riding habit popped in the other end of the ward and began most vigorously to abuse one of the Tommies—a huge Yorkshireman— sitting forlornly beside his bed. "Get up," she said—"you have n't any guts." He does—and she belabors him with her crop. He roars with delight, and the others join in. She is doubtless the best psychotherapeutist in the establishment; they all adore her. Everyone thinks it is the best military hospital in England—I rather agree.

Lunch at the officers' mess, where I 'm called on for a speech.

We then escape with Harry Wright to the house and find Lady A. and two Englishwomen lunching—on American hash!—with her adorable children. She said that two of them were rowdies like herself.

Sunday, Mar. 10th. Boulogne

The crossing on Thursday was uneventful. During the run down to Folkestone, chief interest centred on two spick-and-span West Pointers—a colonel and a major—just out of a bandbox —tight-fitting, neatly pressed thin uniforms, paper-soled pointed riding boots—very alert and erect—also very complaining. Such a contrast to the civilian officers of the B.E.F. just returning from leave with all emotions buried behind the *Times* after a "So long, old girl," and "Bring back a D.S.O., Charlie," on the platform. Charlie, like most of the others, in heavy trench boots and enveloped in a soiled raincoat over a ragged "British warm"— many of them with wound stripes and the spectral Mons-Star ribbon in addition to others, indicating long as well as meritorious service.

"Rotten town, London—had to wait fifteen minutes for our hotel bill—almost missed breakfast and the train—never want to see the d——d place again. And they would n't give us a check for our luggage! Now in America you can check your trunk right from your room to your destination, etc., etc."

"Yes, just landed Tuesday; saw two 'subs,' think we got one of 'em; fine trip, brass bedsteads, bath, all to ourselves, twenty aeroplane squadrons on board. Going to send machines over in droves, engines not very fast, but so many of them we won't miss the few crashed by faster Hun planes. Training our men to shoot; British have been all-fired stupid; when we break through there'll be open warfare and the men'll know what to do; lots of niggers, great fighters, fine shots. Now if you had only done this at Cambrai, etc., etc."

The patient young captain to whom this was chiefly addressed showed wonderful restraint. "You see, we're very fed up with the war. That's the way *we* used to feel; but then we've made so many mistakes, and your country understands administration so much better and has no red tape and will show us the way, I'm sure."

"We certainly will, we 've got 600,000 over here already and they 're coming at the rate of 200,000 a month, all arrangements made for it—is n't that going some?" And so it went all the way to Folkestone. I saw them later shivering on the packet's deck— no one taking any notice of them. They have much to learn and they 're probably at bottom very brave and capable, though tactless, fellows. . . .

Yesterday afternoon with Col. Sir Henry Erskine and another A.S.C. officer to Calais. By the back road through pretty Wimille and other less attractive—indeed squalid—French towns. A wide expanse of fertile country being ploughed and planted by people dressed in fragments of old French uniforms—this fact, with the two huge aerodromes and anti-aircraft stations which we passed, alone indicating war. Off the direct road at Marquise and through Guînes near which was the Field of the Cloth of Gold, though there 's now no trace of Henry VIII or Francis I unless the relic of the old earthen fortifications can be such. This detour let us in to the south of Calais with its tangle of tracks and miles of enormous warehouses which line the canal, and we drop our companion at the offices of the Director of Supplies and go on into the town.

The old Notre-Dame like an English church—the Jardin Richelieu, where is Rodin's amazing group representing the six hostages demanded by Edward when, after the battle of Crécy, he starved Calais to surrender. It is difficult to understand the writhings of the group in whose centre stands Eustache de St. Pierre. Such feet!! The group is so high on its pedestal one has to look up at the figures and sees chiefly feet—enormous feet. Rodin was after shadow effects, I 'm told, and cared little for anatomy in proportions. Perhaps if placed somewhere on the ground among trees with an opening to give a silhouette effect, or even on the sands with nothing about—very good; but here by the highway on a pedestal—impossible.

To the market place with the market in full blast, and fat, red-cheeked children and well-fed dogs despite the war. Interesting, the ancient Hôtel de Ville, and especially the old watchtower near by—the Tour du Guet—which I understand goes back to the ninth century and was used as a *phare* (lighthouse). The buildings are a good deal peppered by bombing raids, many windows are boarded up, and by curious chance a direct hit has occurred on the high tower of the unfinished new Hôtel de Ville, which is modern and promised to be ugly.

March 13. Abbeville

An interesting change to be with the Australians, many of them wearing the divisional patch indicating service in Gallipoli—Col. Purdy the C.O., Fiaschi, who once visited us at the Johns Hopkins, Col. Powell, whose C.C.S. was about 250 yards from the Turks' line.

My lecture was scheduled for five, with officers from No. 2 Stationary and the South African hospital near by as the audience. Introduced by Col. Thurston, the A.D.M.S. of the district, cousin of the present D.D.M.S., Boulogne. Col. Thorburn there. Subsequently a formal mess dinner at which I sat by Col. Gallie, who in May 1915 was found dispatching ambulance trains from Boulogne—curious how I continue to run across the R.A.M.C. people I first met at that time. Charing Cross and Port Said no longer are supreme as places in which unexpectedly to encounter friends. . . .

"Mr. Vice; the King," of course, followed by the usual speeches —some very amusing. We then adjourned to the common room, a wheezy box melodeon was procured from the Y.M.C.A. hut, and much local talent was dragged out of the company, in all of which Col. Gallie entered with zest. Old songs—darky songs—college songs of ancient date—with Scotch, Irish, South African, or Australian variations. Captain Bryden a regular Harry Lauder with "Stop your tickling, Jock," and such. A South African named Drummond with many Biblical songs—a man named Chaplin, as good as his namesake, danced, another whistled—Col. Russell a song—and the old music box nearly jumped off the table under the Padre's enthusiastic handling of its short, tuneless keyboard.

Finally, all together, "A wee doch-an-dorris," then "Auld Lang Syne," and after "God Save the King," Col. Gallie scuttles off to do two hours' work which he has neglected, Eames and Powell get wrapped up to start back for Boulogne, the surgeons fortify themselves with coffee in preparation for a convoy—me for bed, where I nearly froze and longed for my bed socks.

A hospital visit and then with Taylor Young for a glimpse of Abbeville. Across lots to see the remaining bit of the Vauban wall, and by the stockade where No. 1 Punishment is still given for certain offenses in the British Army—tied to a stake for two hours a day and the rest of the time in unproductive work like digging trenches and immediately filling them again. Very mediæval and little better than the earlier whipping post or stocks, though the ordeal is no longer public.

Abbeville very interesting—the rendezvous for the first crusade —under English dominion from the time of Edw. I for about 200 years, i.e., the fourteenth and fifteenth centuries. The Somme runs through the town in a most picturesque way, while the splendid façade of the old unfinished church of St. Vulfran is the chief landmark. The whole region is surrounded by remains of Roman camps—Cæsar's defenses against invasions by the Belgians—the great Roman road from Lyon to Boulogne passed through the town, in whose local patois many Latin words are still used. Then in the fifth century came the Hun destroying as he went—after which the Dark Ages, from which we awake to find the House of Capet building St. Vulfran. And now in the whirligig of time the Hun tries to repeat the process.

A farewell visit to Col. Gallie, who was found chuckling over a bundle of official papers concerning the transportation of 800 Tommies, sent from the Italian front to Havre, under "Y-scheme" treatment for malaria. Before they could find out what the Y-scheme of treatment was—it took two months of inquiries "through proper channels"—the contingent had reached England.

Then the afternoon train to Paris for to-morrow's Research Committee meeting. A late supper with the Strongs, after which Wright (Sir Almroth) blows in and I drag out of Richard the story of the investigation at St. Pol, and Wright for once admits that someone has really done a good piece of work. Strong, as usual, overmodest, praising the Trench Fever Committee and the 150 enlisted men who have been subjected to the experiments.

Wright finally asked who was going to get the credit. "Damn the credit; we're trying to win the war; it's unnecessary to mention any names." All this he thinks very absurdly idealistic. Strong has done a fine job—thinks the army could easily be deloused, but whoever attempts it would need the authority of a major general. It's gratifying to have had this demonstration of the source of trench fever come out of our first discouraging meeting of the Research Committee back in October. · · ·

A GLIMPSE OF THE A.E.F.

Sunday, March 17. Neufchâteau

Here by train with Thayer, Bert Lee, and Allison—learning much meanwhile about the situation and activities—or inactivities _–of the A.E.F. Very beautiful along the Marne Valley through Meaux, Château-Thierry, Épernay, the Champagne country, its brown hills stubbly with the vine poles stacked like tepees for the winter—in regular rows like the prickly spines on a cactus leaf.

Through Châlons-sur-Marne, where Attila was turned back in the fifth century; Vitry-le-François; Revigny, where we pass some trainloads of U.S.A. troops—the 2nd Division, I'm told, just going to the Front for the first time; Bar-le-Duc; Ligny, and finally Gondrecourt, where Eben Finney—just graduated from the Hopkins Base Hospital—meets us, and in a rattly Ford takes us the 20 miles through Domremy, of Jeanne d'Arc memory; and so to Neufchâteau, where Finney, Fisher, and Yates are billeted in what Thayer calls a *Tour Babel*.

The unusual spectacle of American soldiers—many of them wearing green ribbons for St. Patrick—wandering around the streets interested me particularly; but it was too late to look about and we sat down hungrily to a dinner which turned out to be a feast, owing to the recent arrival from Baltimore of numerous packages "not to be opened till [last] Christmas," containing plum puddings, fruit cake, and the like. Eben says that the old lady in whose house Thayer is billeted eagerly asked, when they arrived with his abundant luggage, including an iron trunk full of books: "*Le monsieur, il est un général, n'est-ce pas?*"

Monday, March 18. Neufchâteau

After an early visit to the office of the "Consultants" where were Young, Keyes, Thayer, Boggs, and others, we went to Bazoilles sur Meuse about 10 km. away, near the place where the river disappears underground through the cracks in its bed. Here a good-sized hospital centre suddenly greets one's eye from the crest of a hill—the Johns Hopkins place (Base Hospital No. 18) dom_inating the valley landscape. There many friends, Cy Guthrie and Stone in charge, and many nurses of long remembrance. As good work being done as in the J.H.H. itself, and their 32 students are perhaps even better trained than they would have been at home. Would that we could have brought ours! In an attractive situation beside a pine hill—the whole hospital under wood—evidently a very fine spirit on all sides despite their most un_comfortable winter. They call the place "Bacillus on the Mess." But one forgets past rigors on a day like this.

In the afternoon to Sebastopol, north of Toul, where John Gibbon is struggling with Evacuation Hospital No. 1 behind the 1st Division, who are holding a part of the line north of there. Through Soulosse and Colombey, we then skirt Toul, a fascinating place with complete encirclement of walls, by Vauban of course, and a fine old cathedral within. It is a fortified area of the 1st class on the Moselle with the Marne–Rhine Canal passing like a moat on the northern side of the walls. Almost equal to Metz and Verdun in its military importance—the three heights near by, particularly the isolated cone of Mont St. Michel, dominating the great plain of the Woëvre.

A very busy area it appears—roads lined with big guns coming up—ammunition dumps innumerable, new railroads being laid in all directions by Annamites and Italian labor corps—the latter composed of soldiers who gave way last autumn before the Austrians and are now undergoing penance by breaking stones on French roads.

Pagny, where the old signpost to the east still reads "Strassburg"—-Ugny—Vaucouleurs—Maxey-sur-Vaise, where the stream wanders through the main street and is conveniently arranged for the washing in public of one's dirty linen—Goussaincourt—Greux—and Domremy-la-Pucelle again, where we stop for a few minutes at the wee cottage in which the Maid was born. Then home with a brilliant sunset to the west, outlining the huge château on the crest of the hill across the valley where lives an aged American woman, the Princesse d'Alsace—at least so says Eben, who like most "Sammies" picks up extraordinary bits of information.

Wednesday, March 20th

«Oh, we're wise guys, we are: there's a lot yet to learn," says a young major of Marines in his gray-green uniform. "They got on to our SOS. signal the first night and up went a lot of rockets along the line and, bang! our artillery sent over their barrage; and when they were through up went another lot of rockets and they went at it again. When things had finally quieted down we found that a million and a half dollars' worth of shells had landed beyond the wire where there were no Boches. Gimme a light.". . .

We got away yesterday about 8 a.m. from the *"Tour Babel"* —Finney, Allison, and I in one flivver, Fisher and Lee with his field equipment in another—Lee being bound for the H.Q. of our 2nd Division, who are just going into the line for their first experience.

It promises to be a fine day, though very dry, and the dust from the roadside has so settled over everything that the hedges and trees look as though covered by hoarfrost. On once more through the pine and beech forest to Domremy, Greux, and Gondrecourt. Thence along the valley to picturesquely situated Bar-le-Duc, a port on the Marne-to-Rhine Canal, where we stop to ask directions at a crossroads, one corner of which lies in ruins from an aviator's bomb, while the other carries a monument to the *"inventeurs de la pédale,"* MM. Michaux, *père et fils.* The town, an important centre, is often bombed and considerably scarred, not to say scared, for large *Cave de Secours* placards are on every side.

To reach our destination, at Ancemont, we are told to follow the road to Verdun by way of Souilly, and what a spectacle it is! The *voie sacrée*—the wide 50-mile causeway from Bar-le-Duc to Verdun that saved the day for the French, and over which, in lieu of a railroad to the fortress, an endless chain of 10,000 motor *camions* went up and down a few feet apart in those anxious weeks of last summer! What road builders the French are! Even now this great artery of traffic is so much traveled that the usual isolated piles of crushed stone do not suffice for repairs, but there is an uninterrupted wall of it ready for use, extending for miles along the roadside. How the British in Flanders would envy these people with limestone rock merely waiting to be blasted out and used for road building without the need of transportation.

We soon turn north and pass through numberless small towns of the mother-hen and chicken variety and proceed by Issoncourt to Souilly. Very dusty it becomes with our 2nd Division moving in and the French coming out. A mile or so of our Packard trucks looking more like motor-driven "prairie schooners" than the British lorries so familiar. And the boys! simply white with dust but cheerful to a degree; as Finney says, they look as though they were out for business.

Souilly, as I recall, was a wee town fairly blue with the French 7th Army there in billets, and in front of the Town Hall of the small place stood two captured German Minenwerfers and a huge unexploded 420 shell, five feet high. The valley of the Meuse opens out at Ancemont, and we cross on some new-laid wooden bridges, pass through Dieue and on to the divisional H.Q. under General Bundy at Sommedieue, a small hamlet full of our troops, including Marines. We lunch on coffee and a Hamburg steak (instead of tea and bully beef) with Col. Morrow, chief M.O. of the division on whose staff Richard Derby chances to be, so that Lee finds a friend and we leave him very happy and hopeful in his novel and squalid surroundings, with shell holes in the wall and an ominous ABRI DE BOMBARDEMENT in large letters before a dugout near by.

Finney's business done, we get away about two, it having come on to rain mildly so that the dusty roads promptly become miry and slippery—there's no halfway stage. It's impossible to give an idea of the signs of activity past and present as we proceed along the valley of the Meuse on this western side of the St. Mihiel salient.

Verdun is the nodal point of this area from which everything radiates, just as Ypres is the nodal point of the Flanders line, and there is the same concentration of material and the same evidence of determined resistance whatever the cost and sacrifice. But the way it is done is as different as horizon-blue is from khaki. *On ne passe pas* represents the spirit in both places, but no Britisher would have ventured to show the sentiment concealed in these four words. And the situations, too, are utterly different—Ypres on an alluvial plain with no modern fortifications; Verdun on a high escarpe in highlands, a fortress of the first rank with a circle of secondary fortresses all about.

Through Dugny and Belleray, and finally the town with its unmistakable twin towers and the distant circle of fortified hills came into view. We strike into the road from Clermont and approach from the west to enter by the Porte Neuve, which has been fairly well protected during these three years by the precipitous walls of the massive Vauban citadel. Still the upper part of the battlements even here is damaged, and there is an oblique crater in the middle of the southern wall from a direct hit at a time when the German lines had drawn in closely on each side.

The Territorial who bars the entrance to the citadel scrutinizes us, then turns us over to a sentry who takes us to a spiral stone staircase electrically lighted, and up we go—86 steps to a level still far underground, where are galleries on galleries, protected by masonry many metres thick. First to the great vaulted chambers where the État-Major has his office. He appears, greets us cordially, regrets that *M. le Col. Commandant d'Armes* is occupied and he himself too busy to accompany us, but he will detail someone for the purpose. Would we like to see some of the specimens which had fallen on the citadel during the customary morning's bombardment? There was a large table covered with big pieces of *obus*, mostly 380's, some of them with the pointed cap to overcome windage still in position—all carefully marked and labeled.

Our guide then takes us through more corridors, past great racks full of freshly baked loaves, some of them still warm to the touch—120,000 loaves a day, he says, made from a mixture of American and French flour with a proportion of rye, beans, and sago—"really a more palatable bread than that from pure flour" —but we are to see the baking later. Then into the open across a bridge leading from the top of the isolated citadel over to the walls of the town proper, and the *Esplanade de la Roche;* for this is the Haute Ville on the plateau of Verdun from which the Kaiser boasted he would review his troops in Feb. 1916. Even here are trenches and wire in preparation for a last stand for the citadel.

He takes us through the Porte Châtel, the oldest monument

of Verdun, to the Cathedral. "Yes, the 44th Territorials are the honorary guard for Verdun—been here since the outbreak of war —500,000 Germans and 350,000 French the estimated casualties of the 1916 offensive—not such a bad exchange, though it 's estimated to mean one dead for every square metre of Verdun—a good deal of the town still standing, but no house has escaped a hit from something or other: *tous les maisons, un obus.* They shell us every day—ought to begin again about 4 o'clock—100 *arrivées* were counted this morning—mostly 380's."

Such items we gather from our cicerone, who takes us first into the courtyard of the old *archevêché* dating from Louis XIV, and recalling the architecture of Versailles. A wonderful outlook over the town, but very sad in its present state. Then the Cathedral, which had a direct hit yesterday, making another large hole in the roof, and the place was full of workmen dismantling and boxing the organ, together with such architectural and sculptural treasures as can be removed and sent to the Petit Palais in Paris.

The Cathedral has been curiously spared, at least when compared with St. Martin's at Ypres; but there, to be sure, the enemy was firing down upon a town in a low plain from the encircling ridges, while here the town itself is on a height. Like ordinary tourists we are led down to the old crypt, evidently Roman, with low columns, having curious capitals on which are carved bearded faces upside down for some symbol or other; also some twelfth-century mural decorations. Then into the *sacristie,* where are the remains of beautiful woodwork, and from one large room through arched windows is a wonderful view of the remaining houses of the red-tiled town—ready to crumble at a touch. The sight of a cat makes me ask if there are any *civils* remaining—no, only the guard, this long time, and the *pompiers,* for almost every day there 's more or less of a conflagration.

We hear the scream of two *arrivées* and it 's about time to take cover, so back into the citadel where we 're shown the huge bakery, the kitchens, chambers on chambers, the electrical plant, depots of food to last a year for thousands of men, wireless telephone and telegraph stations, engine rooms, a chapel, a museum, the entertainment hall, where in Sept. 1915 the ceremony of decorating the town with the *Légion d'Honneur* and the *Croix de Guerre* was held, and where now a lively song is grinding out on a talking machine; the huge coöperative store in a corridor full of *poilus* making purchases—every provision for existence, defense, and entertainment in case of prolonged siege. *On ne passe pas.*

VII

THE GERMAN SPRING OFFENSIVE

First Phase: The Advance on Amiens

Thursday, 21st March. Boulogne

WAGSTAFFE down from St. Omer and here to lunch. Says the Hun has dropped big shells within three miles of No. 7 at Malassise—28 miles from the line. Something important evidently on foot. He expects to be transferred to Lillers to do head cases and was told a team would be called for from here. Prof. Chittenden and Graham Lusk at the Meurice—tried in vain to locate them for dinner at the mess—just as well, for they would have thought we had too much food—we probably have. They claim that people are more economical of food in the U.S.A. than some of our allies. When all cards were laid on the table as to stores, the French forgot to mention certain large reserves of barley. They favor a 2000–2400 calorie ration *per diem* whereas our army ration is 4000 or more. When this was brought to the attention of the Congressional Committee, it was stated that a ration established by George Washington should continue—like the Constitution, I presume.

11 p.m. Col. Fullerton just in—back from behind Bullecourt with the news that the Germans have opened up on a wide front south of Arras and that the British have given way in many places to a depth of three miles. This is an inappropriate time for a discussion of calories and basal metabolism.

Friday, March 22nd

Just dined with Sir Arthur Lawley to meet Sir Charles Russell, who failed to appear, though Gen. Wilberforce, the Base Commandant, came in his place and incidentally asked Sir Arthur how long it would take to evacuate the Red Cross office, and if all their preparations were made. It is rumored that Arras has been taken. Most disturbing talk about our present situation and the critical significance of these next few days. Calais has been badly bombed on successive nights; Dunkerque shelled from the sea; the gassing of back areas will come before long.

Saturday, 23rd

6 p.m. A dense fog for the past three days and no papers or mail. Very meagre news filters through and that discouraging. Saw Newton D. Baker for a few minutes this morning in his private car—sidetracked at the Boulogne station while awaiting safe transport to England. Looked very tired and serious. Twitted him about sending the Lakeside Unit over before ours—Crile and I both being Clevelanders, he might at least have flipped a coin. Convoys of gassed and wounded from the Armentières region were brought down in the afternoon.

12 p.m. Perfect weather for an air raid after the fog lifted— and we've just had a bad one.

Sunday, March 24

12 noon. This a.m. with General Wilberforce and his A.D.C., Bartholomew, to see the results of last night's raid. One big bomb right in the court of the Medical Stores—the largest in France— much damage—quite serious indeed—countless X-ray tubes ru- ined—glassware and dyes lost as well as other fragile laboratory stuff. All else is now exposed to the sky so a rain in the next day or two would play the very mischief. Another bomb had dropped on some cardboard French houses and demolished them com- pletely, the inmates being buried.

Then, joined by the officer in charge of the labor battalion of this area, we went to Wimereux to inspect the No. 94 P.O.W. camp. Most interesting. They were out of their wire stockades and lined up on parade in two groups of about 500 each. The General scru- tinized each man and was rather severe on the C.O., a poor decrepit Lt. Col. with two wound stripes. Some of the captives had ill-fitting heavy corduroy coats which he did n't like—he spotted every torn pocket, and picked out one man without the blue patch sewn in his trousers. Very little escaped him.

We then visited the two compounds and went through them with a fine-tooth comb—even poking into garbage cans and finding a few potato peels which should have been eaten and a bone which should have been in the soup. They are all fat, healthy, and well-treated—the French think *too well*. But they are an ill-assorted lot, few intelligent faces among them—far below the average of the Tommies in appearance and stature—undersized as some of the present-day Tommies actually are.

They are allowed to receive packages from home with goodies; and a number of N.C.O.'s have had uniforms sent out in which they attire themselves Sundays—many with the Iron Cross ribbon. Jägers in their green uniforms—guards with the white stripe on their collars—obedient animals with much heel clicking. After the inspection they paraded by us in columns of four with the goose step—many of them pretty poor at it—on their way to their compounds.

Their huts very spick-and-span—the prisoners indeed were hutted long before the British wounded were under anything but canvas. The place itself is an ideal one—a perfect summer resort. Some of these men came from the Somme; others from last fall's operations in Flanders; but even the ones captured earlier did not impress me greatly—certainly no big fellows such as I have seen elsewhere.

3 p.m. This is the third day of what our local paper calls the *Gigantesque Bataille sur le Front Britannique*. There is a strange feeling of something critical impending. Yet it 's a lovely spring day—warm—a little misty—with no horizon. Windows are open and the sun streams in. Across the curtain of calm sea merging into a cloudless sky three large destroyers are passing south—some absurdly camouflaged transports are anchored near the breakwater, and were it not for their stacks it would be difficult to tell which way they were pointed—numberless fishing schooners are lying idly, doubtless praying for a breeze. Above a half-dozen noisy French hydro-aeroplanes are circling around, and a big yellow "Lizzie" has just gone over—low enough to see her pilot's head. The tide is low and people are lazily scattered over the shoal sands, or the rocks beyond, picking up mussels. On some benches are a group of our officers playing with a little French child. Sailors and nursemaids and Australians and W.A.A.C.'s and Tommies and civilians are strolling about sunning themselves—blues and browns and blacks.

An hour ago a Gotha went over and the air was full of white shrapnel puffs. He was very high—20,000 feet perhaps. Early this morning there was another. It's unusual to have two a day. There was but one yesterday, and as is customary he returned at night. I had gone to the Casino to mail a letter after dinner, when the show began. It was midnight when I got back.

They were over for an hour. I don't know how many of them, nor how many eggs they dropped, but Keenan reports that a French Intelligence Officer says 55, which seems doubtful. They got some 30 or 40 civilians and a few French officers, I believe, in the Haute Ville. Only three cases came in to us—one abdominal— Tommies. This back-area business is merely a part of what's going on forward—to get our wind up. But most amazing is the announcement that they've been able to reach Paris!! with 240 mm. shells—one every quarter of an hour—from a point some 75 miles away. Incredible!

Doubtless Ludendorff's greatest effort. The question is, can we hold? The long-expected affair opened on Thursday with feints all along the line—at Nieuport, Merckem and Dixmude, Reims and Verdun, under gas and a smothering bombardment. The chief attack at 8 a.m., centring on the 5th Army (Gough), was over a front of approximately 60 miles, from the Scarpe near Monchy to the Oise near La Fère. Mass attacks—heavy fighting—gradual giving way before some 60 German divisions, about half a million men. All weather conditions favored them with a three days' mist —just what favored General Byng at Cambrai last November. They claimed 16,000 prisoners on the first day. On the second day Haig admitted a retirement to our reserve line, "our troops fighting with the greatest gallantry."

We've had practically no wounded, which is ominous. Word has been sent to Wallace that Cutler and I will go up to Lillers immediately if needed. Meanwhile there is nothing to do but sit in the sun and stroll on the sands—and wait. This is the hardest thing to do.

Monday, March 25th

They have broken clean through—there's no gainsaying that. The first real breach on Friday opposite St. Quentin, made by von Hutier. The whole line from the Scarpe to the Oise had to fall

back toward the old Somme line of July '16· Péronne and Ham
were the hot spots yesterday, both lost. Also ground lost at Ervil-
lers north of Bapaume.

Their objective is evidently to drive a wedge toward Amiens between the French and British armies. They may thus envelop this
northern area and again threaten the Channel Ports. The test is
yet to come; they already claim 30,000 prisoners and 600 guns.
Paris has had an especially lively week-end. There are all sorts of
speculations over the long-range bombardment. Many still doubt
it. Old Élise, with a shrug, says, *"Coup de théâtre."* Possibly she
is right.

Tuesday, March 26th

The wedge between the British and French armies widens out.
The chief drives of yesterday in the direction of Bapaume and
Nesle, with Péronne holding. Evidently a stubborn British resistance. The weather has been perfect for an offensive. What luck
for the Hun! There appear to be three German columns: (1) von
Bülow on the right from Cambrai in the direction of Bapaume
and Albert; (2) von der Marwitz in the centre from St. Quentin
to Péronne and along the Somme; (3) on their left von Hutier
in the direction of Noyon and Roye, and up to to-night they have
advanced to a depth of 36 km. These are all new German generals
on this front.

Wednesday, March 27th

Morning. The thrust clearly is being made toward Amiens—
perhaps Abbeville and Dieppe. This would cut the British off
from the rest of France, but no one seems in a panic about it.
Élise continues cheerful—*"Les Boches, ils ne sont pas encore ar-
rivés"*—this as she brings our morning coffee. She adds that all of
the French boys from fifteen to nineteen have been taken away to
a place of safety and all the men from forty to sixty are to be mobilized. We presume that they long *have* been, so don't argue
with her over the morsel which she enjoys.

AWAITING NEWS AT THE CASINO

Noon. "Does everyone get a coffin at the Base?" "Oh, yes, sir,
the officers very fine ones with planed tops. These are just thin
ones of unseasoned wood—green elm, but French elm, I 'm sure,

quite a different grain from ours." "How do you happen to know so much about wood?" "Oh, I 'm a house furnisher and under-taker too—they goes together with us."

While anxiously awaiting the news of the situation on the Somme one must do something to kill time; and this conversation was with a Tommy, Class B3 of the Devons, who was nailing up the boxes in the Autopsy Hut, where I spent a part of the morning examining brains of these poor devils. All too many, unoperated upon, have died soon after reaching here with bad 48-hour infec-tions—end-results of the kind of injuries we were seeing last sum-mer at No. 46 and usually could save.

House furnisher and undertaker! One thinks only of soldiers out here and forgets previous occupations. On going through the wards later to see dressings, I asked some of the men with ampu-tated arms or legs what they did peace times:—

That rascally red-headed Jock, Aikenhead of the Black Watch, was footman to the Duke of Atholl in Dundee; and only Harry Lauder could imitate him on the subject of poaching pheasants and taking them to the lassie who lives down the glen. The Duke has many other footmen; but Jock says he 's the "fast footman," whatever that may mean.

Next to him is Childrey of the Royal Berks, whom Frank Ober and I have been working over—both legs off at the knee—born on the estate of a Mr. Cranfield in Brampton, Huntingdonshire, and a groom in the stables. Both he and Jock are relics of Passchendaele and are being evacuated to-day to make room for these newer cases.

Coombs, aged 23, shifted just two years ago from polisher in a silver-smith's shop to B battery, 236 R.F.A.—the 18-pounders—wounded on the second day somewhere near Bapaume; and Ober had to take off his right arm yesterday near the shoulder for a gas infection.

Hendry, a youth of 20 from Toronto, apprentice in a machine shop, out for a year, through Passchendaele untouched, and got this one recently, before Lens.

Blondell is 34, a joiner, only out since March '18 with the 7th Bor-derers; was in the support line near the Cambrai road when he got "his," at 9 a.m. the first morning, March 21st. He never even saw the Boche. I fail to understand how he reached here.

Holland, an Edinburgh boy of 25 in the 3/ Grenadier G'ds, a brass polisher in a foundry. They had just come out of the line from near Arras on the morning of Mar. 21st for divisional rest—were on parade. He was the only man in his platoon hit—his right arm.

Heslop is 42, 23rd Middlesex, a hack-yard manager in Stockton, County Durham. Been out 9 months, part of the time in Italy. Sent up with hurried reënforcements—encamped at Achiet-le-Grand and he got "his" five minutes later.

Burdett is a husky young coal miner of 20 from Fifeshire—in the 1/6 Black Watch. Out 10 months—hit on the first day near Beaumetz to the left of the Cambrai road.

Thompson, a postman from Welburn, of the 7th East Yorks, 17th Division—out 18 months—back from leave only one day. They were re_tiring and on the third day—his birthday, March 22nd—were in bivouac behind Avrincourt on the top of a canal bank—a shell got him and killed seven out of eight of his pals.

George Clements says he 's a loco' driver in a cement works in North_fleet, Kent—had been in the home coast defense since last October in a battery of six-inch guns of the R.G.A. He and four others were taking up rations and had gone back to a lorry for a box of bully when they got it, he in the leg.

Another legless man is Joe Mason of the 9th W. Yorks, a "grease ex-tractor," peace times, in Bradford. He 's 47 years old and has a family; came out with the first Kitchener army—this his first wound.

Peter Bias, aged 20, with a strange dialect and a well-nigh toothless grin, comes from the Orkney Islands, which he never expected to leave and hopes he never will again. He 's a ploughboy—with one leg—a year in France with the 8/10 Gordons, 15th Division—hit on the 19th when his battalion was moving up between Monchy and the Cambrai road.

A. Brook, a Rifleman, in the 4/ Lincolns, a master painter, aged 38, with a family in Lindley, Ottersfield, Yorkshire. Wounded Mar. 23rd near Bullecourt—he, too, leaves a leg in France.

Sam Hemphill at 20 says he was a "killer and flesher" in Edinburgh; and aspired to become a butcher, I doubt not, before he lost his arm, hold_ing a strong point to the right of Armentières on the afternoon of Mar. 21st with the 7th Camerons. Out 22 months; this his second wound.

Davies is the youngest, a fine boy from Llanelly, South Wales, who says he was a mechanical fitter, and is now only 19. He joined up with "Kitchener's Mob" when 16 and came out with the Northumberland Fusiliers in April 1915. This is his first wound—on March 21st at 4.30 p.m. to the left of Bullecourt—a rear-guard action with machine guns and no artillery support. Luckily only an arm so he got out alone— "sorry—he wished he could have stuck it with the rest."

And this is by no means all, for there were an electric-crane driver, a lathe worker, a handkerchief packer, a musician (bassoon and strong bass), a stationer, and many other *mutilés* I did not happen to question, in addition to the two black boys from the Jamaica labor company—still in Ward 3 C with amputations after trench feet acquired last December—Esau Lemon and Samuel Hibbert. Esau says he "cultivates" and so does Sam—probably means they drive mules.

There are old army men, too, though they don't happen to have amputations. On Towne's ward is an old boy of 48—16 years in the regular army and worked up to sergeant in the Northumberland Fusiliers—in the Soudan, Crete, South African campaigns—came out here with 200 others from his old regiment who reënlisted as privates in Jan. of 1915; though three times wounded, he prefers this kind of warfare to South Africa— would sooner fight than march, which is what you did in S.A., from 3 a.m. till night, with nothing but a piece of bully at the end. "Here you fight and get plenty to eat." He's a well-nourished party, I may add.

Alongside of him is a Mons man—a "contemptible"—a young, clean-limbed Tommy 10 years in the regular army—came to France from India with the first native battalions who were thrown in the line, Sept. 14th, 1914—28 days in the trenches near Estaires and then a four days' march to Ypres—not a shave all the time!! Things must have been desperate for this to happen to a Tommy. He's very scornful of all these Mons ribbons being worn by people who were in offices at the Base—only three are alive in his regiment who deserved them. It was his company who took the sergeant down who had been crucified near St. Julien.

Later. The tension is somewhat relieved by a quiet dinner at Wright's with Col. Gage, once of the 14th Hussars, now Receiving Officer here for men; Mrs. Gardner, the Queen W.A.A.C., ditto for women; also Lady Algernon Gordon-Lennox. Last night at the Anglo-American Hospital with Lady Hadfield, Mrs. Kennard, the Base Commandant, and Sir Charles Russell,[1] the King's Councilor; very interesting talk—much self-criticism by the British—"Why are we such a damned stupid race?"—this from Sir Charles. Much about the Irish Question; the seriousness of the threatened strike of the A.S.E.; the opposition to Lloyd George, and would Asquith be any better; Kitchener's rough handling of the Irish Question so far as volunteers went; Redmond's successor; the King's colorlessness; the Prince of Wales here in Boulogne and "off on his own" somewhere—this last to the great

[1] Son of Lord Russell of Killowen, attended the Bering Sea Arbitration for the U.K.

anxiety of General Wilberforce. America as usual also a topic, and Sir Charles tells of the barmaid who served a mug of beer to a Sammy. Says he: "It's flat, this beer." "Naturally," says she, "it's been waiting for you three years."

Wednesday the 27th

p.m. S—— in to lunch, rather jumpy and tired. Most outspoken about the British and the fact that the French have had to bring up reserve divisions. He is in the Intelligence Office—one of the few men who know the French cipher, quite a different thing from the codes by which messages are sent. Other ciphers in reserve of course—a single letter sent out over the wires would shift to another cipher in a jiffy in case of suspicions that the cipher was known.

But the British—stupid, pig-headed! Been warned for two months by his Office just where the attack was to be and practically the exact day—and been told over and over again. They would do nothing—no reserves sent over—their chief ammunition dumps within three miles of the line—warned about this several times—would take no action. Now Lloyd George is saying, "Hold fast, my brave lads, we will send you reserves and guns"—from where? and the French have to move divisions up to stop the gap. France already nearly bled white, and holding a length of line two to one to the British, who are enjoying theatrical campaigns in Palestine.

There may be some truth in all of this, but it had better not be ventilated. And when I try to interject that they are dogged and courageous and one must take his allies for what they're worth, S—— gets excited and gesticulates.

Thursday, March 28th

A Boche salient thrown out yesterday between the Ancre and the Somme almost to Amiens—about 12 km. distant, I believe. Montdidier the crucial point as the railway needed to bring up French reserves. The French Colonials have come in and are helping the British to hold the line. Amiens, they say, is a mess— train service almost stopped and the city full of refugees. The weather gives promise of breaking—cold, rainy, and windy today—this will check our aeroplane activity but will hamper the enemy's getting up his guns.

p.m. Rumors fly thick and fast. Some 500 walking wounded day—detained cases, so-called—here merely for a meal and while awaiting a boat. Most of them should be sent to a convalescent camp on this side—but there seems to be no machinery to comb out those who ought not to go home in the present stress.

Good Friday, March 29th

"Les combats ont pris sur ce point—à l'ouest de Montdidier un caractère acharnement inouï!" This from *Le Télégramme* at breakfast announcing the loss of Montdidier. A busy day with all forward hospitals shooting cases at us and a large number of them recently wounded.

Lloyd George says the battle is only beginning and sends a public appeal to America to hurry reënforcements. General Wood has reached home at a crucial time and appears to have stirred people into renewed activity by some plain truths.

Saturday, March 30th

Cold and rainy. The news possibly a little better. At least they did not do so much yesterday. Their line north of Montdidier was straightened, but the heavy attacks before Arras on their right to regain Vimy Ridge appear to have been held up. It is rumored that in the emergency Foch has been made at least a temporary generalissimo for all the forces.[1] Everyone takes hope remembering how before Fère-Champenoise in 1914 he sent word to Joffre: *"Mon centre cède, ma droite recule, situation excellente, j'attaque!"* Pershing meanwhile has come up to the scratch and offered everything he has to the French. This has brought a sense of great relief to everyone. . . . A large convoy this afternoon of detained cases—all from the hospitals at St. Omer, which evidently are being evacuated. The men had all come from the Ypres salient and say there is feverish activity there in the construction of secondary defenses, including concrete pill boxes—high time.

Sunday the 31st

So far as one can tell, what has been going on the past critical ten days is about as follows: The valley of the Oise separated the

---

[1] It does not appear to have become known for four days that the supreme command had been given to Foch. The deal was apparently made in Pershing's absence on March 25th in Doullens at a conference between Lord Milner, Clemenceau, Sir Henry Wilson, Foch, Pétain, and Castelnau. The two latter were for withdrawing to protect Paris, leaving the British to shift for themselves. Foch insisted on keeping contact with them at all hazards. Haig was near by and when called in agreed to a supreme command.

British and French armies. The surprise attack of the 21st, which spread over a 50-mile front from Arras to the Oise, was mainly concentrated on the British right wing, held by the 5th Army under General Gough, which was in process of being reformed after its Passchendaele losses. It moreover was vulnerable, being furthest removed from its source of supplies, and also for the reason that it had recently taken over from the French a part of their line as far south as La Fère, with which it was unfamiliar.

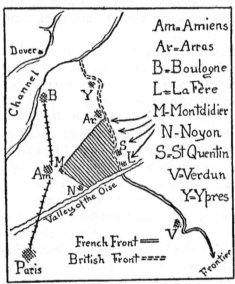

Am=Amiens
Ar=Arras
B=Boulogne
L=LaFère
M=Montdidier
N-Noyon
S=StQuentin
V=Verdun
Y=Ypres

French Front ===
British Front ====

First Phase of the German Spring Offensive. The Thrust toward Amiens

The purpose of the Boche apparently was to drive a wedge between British and French and to roll them back, if parted —the one on Boulogne, the other on Paris. Meanwhile the valley of the Oise would serve to protect their left flank (cf. sketch) as far as Noyon (N), on reaching which they hoped to complete the breach.

On the first day (Thursday, the 21st), judging from captured documents, they did not get as far as planned and this changed their entire programme. The chief pressure was on the Cambrai salient—or what we still had of it—and the line held fairly well, their deepest penetration being in the neighborhood of Croiselles.

On Friday the 22nd, things changed in their favor, and between 3 and 5 p.m. the main defensive positions west of St. Quentin were pierced and they poured through along the Omignon Valley, compelling a retirement during the night of the whole line from Vimy to the Crozat Canal.

In the course of this enforced retirement, as the British gave way the French extended their lines by throwing in reserves between Noyon and Montdidier. This place became a sort of German spearhead where for the past few days there has been severe fighting, which appears temporarily to have checked their advance. Meanwhile for the British from the Oise to Arras it 's been a case of *sauve qui peut* in a headlong retirement of army and refugees feebly protected by rear-guard action. By the fifth day all the ground gained in 1916 during the prolonged battle of the Somme and ultimate retirement of the Germans has again been lost.

Very little change in the past 24 hours. We were pushed back a little at Mézières, the rest of the line holding despite fierce attacks delivered against the French. The poor old 5th Army! Gough is said to have been withdrawn and Rawlinson put in his place.

B., who has been here, attributes the break-through to several elements (cf. sketch). St. Quentin lay in a small salient between the French and the British armies, and in deference to the French had not been shelled; for this reason the enemy, taking advantage of the mist, brought up large forces unobserved. What is more, on the insistence of the French the British had recently taken over 25 miles of line which took them down to La Fère, possibly to the Oise —the line necessarily very thinly held. When the break finally occurred at St.

How the Extension of the 5th Army Front toward La Fère Got Trapped by the Crozat Canal

Quentin the enemy poured through north of the Crozat Canal, and the British troops and supplies in the triangle made by St. Quentin, Ham, and La Fère were trapped, as the only bridges across the Canal were on its northern arm.

Few participants in all this have come our way and we consequently have no first-hand information. What has been going on in that new German salient bulging day by day closer to Amiens can readily be imagined. We have been chiefly concerned as to how we are to extricate ourselves should Amiens be taken and the Boulogne to Paris L. of C. thus be blocked. Even now all through traffic—and little is permitted—is being routed deviously via Abbeville.

Everything serene at No. 13 General, though we 're told the other hospitals of the district have been hard worked. The convalescent camps are overfull and the German prisoners at 94 P.O.W. have been removed to a place of greater safety and their place turned into another "Con. Camp."

Monday, April 1st

General Bradley, the Chief Surgeon for the A.E.F., here this morning, says Base Hospital No. 5 is to remain with the British but I am to be detached—sometime in the future—not a very important line of work—can wait until things are well organized. The General scarcely seems aware of the present desperate situation. Evidently I must find work here and Fullerton puts in a timely offer, namely, to see the head cases of this district, which we promptly do—good and bad—visiting most of the hospitals —No. 83, No. 55, No. 54, and No. 32 Stationary, where we had lunch.

Across the table sat two young American M.O.'s—Cameron and Osincup. From the latter: "I 've seen you before, sir. . . . You were sitting in the back of an ambulance on the road from St. Pol to Hesdin—I was riding with the Indian Cavalry Division; Col. McNab told me who you were." Small world this. They with about 1500 others were hustled over here as "casuals" about the time we were. Since then they 've been with British regiments in the thick of it and know more about the war and what it means to the foot soldier than anyone with the A.E.F.[1]

In the afternoon again to No. 83 to show them the tricks of a lumbar puncture, and there another encounter—Miss Duncan, the matron of No. 46 C.C.S. They certainly had a close shave— called from Proven to Noyon to rejoin the 5th Army—had taken over a French H.O.E. still containing French wounded, and on Monday, March 17th, were given full charge, regarding themselves as a sort of base hospital, of *circa* 1000 beds. By Saturday night they had 3500 patients, many very badly wounded. No. 61

---

[1] Not a few of them had by this time been recommended for the Military Cross, but our government long objected to these decorations which were so highly prized by our Allies. For an account of the experiences of some of these "casual" American medical officers, cf. *The Lost Legion*, by Dr. W.A.R. Chapin, privately printed, Springfield, Mass., 1926.

C.C.S., which was at Ham, had evacuated to them, and sisters began to arrive from forward areas. Also many wounded from a field
ambulance, among them a legless American M.O. from California.
A shell had landed on their party as they were withdrawing.

By Sunday night orders came for the nurses to leave on an
hour's notice—the order countermanded—on Monday morning
more conflicting orders, but they finally got away on a civilian
train, heartbroken at having to leave the wounded behind. The
M.O.'s and personnel stayed until the afternoon. They evacuated
about 1000 wounded, and then got away themselves. Telfer was
the last to leave just as the Germans were coming in—he would
be. Most of them had to walk 30 miles, the Sgt. Major and others
tramping way back to Amiens, where, to complete the story, they
got badly bombed that night. They expect to be brought together
again at a place called Picquigny, 10 km. west of Amiens. Miss D.
never wants to go through anything like it again, and, I judge,
would have preferred to stay with the wounded. Why should n't
they have stayed, some of them at least?

· · · · · ·

Yesterday's papers say we are holding all along the line, yet our
local, *Le Télégramme*, headlines that *"Dans un Splendide Élan
les Troupes Franco-Britanniques Reprennent Moreuil."* This
means a bulge of two or three miles nearer the Amiens–Paris railway than I had reckoned on. But the French remain serene and
confident in Clemenceau and Foch, whose praises fill the news
sheets—*"tout va bien,"* and *"ils ne passeront pas."* Paris continues
to be shelled from 75 miles away; on Good Friday they got a
church full of people—chiefly women and children—a chance
shot, having caught a pillar supporting the roof.

Tuesday, April 2nd

Despite the low ceiling an air raid aroused us early this morning.
I finally got up at 3 a.m. and went to the Casino, but all was quiet.
They dropped several in the fields out behind No. 83—no great
damage done. No marked change in the line the past 24 hours,
though "fierce encounters" continue in the Démuin–Hangard–
Moreuil area, and also north of Montdidier. This part of the line
is only five miles from the railroad. Foch says he is prepared to
guarantee Amiens—to whom? The Australians got in on Wednes-

day the 27th and relieved the hard-pressed English troops. It 's announced that the Americans are to be brigaded with the Allies until sufficiently trained to form their own divisions.

Thursday, April 4th

8 p.m. Busy with brains—other people's. Have been at No. 83 and at No. 2 Australian (Col. Powell, C.O.)—a good place and my first visit there. Very attractive blue and white wards, and about 90 femurs. Abbeville has been evacuated of its hospitals—to become an important military centre.

A drizzling rain. Things have been comparatively quiet for two days with only local fighting. We hope they 've shot their bolt. They are said to be digging in. Reserve troops continue to pour through here. At this moment a long line of shadowy Tommies, stretching from the Casino as far toward Wimereux as one can see in the dusk, are tramping by in column of fours—whistling and singing as they march. They must therefore be the new draft —boys out for the first time: older troops are less likely to sing going up. Old Élise was watching them at our door as I came in from the mess—*"C'est toujours triste, n'est-ce pas?"*

Friday, April 5th. Boulogne

Have just dined in a little cold room at the Criterion with Sir Arthur Lawley to meet Sir William Garstin. Jim Perkins and Snow expected from Paris, but they started by train this morning and heaven only knows when they may arrive. The D.D.M.S. there; also Maj. Collett and a man in civies named Anstruther, who, I believe, not long since was whip for one of the parties in the House of Commons.

Garstin a most interesting person—much traveled—great friend of Kitchener's, an engineer, indeed built the Assuan dam, possibly while K. of K. was in Egypt; on the Suez Commission which meets once a month in Paris. Much about another friend, Wingate, the present sirdar, who has just lost an only son; I was told later this has happened also to Garstin himself. He got on the subject of Kipling and said he thought "They" was his finest thing: one can easily understand why.

Lawley himself an old soldier, once captain of the 10th Hussars,[1] so that there was much talk of the British Army, chiefly

---

[1] Hon. Sir Arthur Lawley, G C.S.I., K.C.M.G., etc., son of Baron Wenlock, Sec'y. Duke of Westminster, Admin. of Matabeleland, Gov. Western Australia, Transvaal, Madras, etc.

reminiscent of Africa and India; but this not all. Many tales that will scarcely get told—how the native Indian officers from the Lancers led foward the Irish Guards at Cambrai after they had lost their own officers; tales of the Flying Corps in these recent battles; of General Sloggett's son, who has disappeared with his entire battalion.

Tales, also, of the Tommy by Col. Thurston—in dialect not always easy to follow. A sergeant of the North Lancs he had just been interviewing was telling him of their long-unavailing stand: "Then the hofficer, 'e sez 'ook it; so we 'ooks it with the L.F.'s" —which merely means they finally withdrew with the Lancashire Fusiliers. In regard to the full participation of the U.S.A., the D.D.M.S. said it's worth remembering that every man requires each year 2½ tons of supplies—about 15 pounds a day (for food, clothing, etc.) irrespective of his ammunition.

THE SECOND PHASE: BATTLE OF THE LYS

After a few days of quiet the enemy have opened a new phase of their offensive—this time farther north. Word has finally come through that I am to report to the D.M.S. 1st Army: an urgent telephone to Wallace to learn if I cannot bring a team with me.

Saturday, April 6th

A year ago to-day Congress declared us belligerents on the side of the Allies. We have not yet really met the enemy, though we are likely to do so soon with fragments of the small force now over here—the sooner the better.

Tuesday, April 9. The Casino

The local D.D.M.S. has suddenly decided that he wishes us to care for all head cases in this base area under his jurisdiction. He consequently has objected to our departure, though word came from G.H.Q. for us to proceed on Saturday. Having promised Wallace we would come, a preference was expressed in that direction and we were supposed to leave at nine this morning. It's now 3 p.m. and we have just learned that the 1st Army has been notified that if they want us they must send for us.

The landing platform and reception hall here are full of gassed men—stretcher cases—from Armentières just east of Lillers, where we were supposed to be going. Apparently a heavy bombardment there on Sunday night with an enormous number of gas shells thrown over. This presages unexpected trouble in that supposedly quiet sector—whether something real or only a diversion on the Boche's part, time alone will tell.

Wednesday, April 10th. Lillers

12.30 a.m. It certainly *did* presage trouble and Cutler and I have run into a second act in the present drama. Our ambulance finally arrived—was sent down with a sick M.O. for transshipment. We came up over the same roads as on January 30—through the Boulogne Forest, its floor now fairly purple with wild flowers —the blackthorn hedges everywhere white with blossoms. We soon began to meet straggling Portuguese—then more Portuguese —their whole corps in fact moving westward—strung out all the way from Aire—very bedraggled and downcast. We did not know until later that they had given way opposite La Bassée and let the Boche through, and that the Liverpools on their left had trained a machine gun on them as they broke.

Finally Lillers, about 6 p.m., where a very tired-looking D.M.S. is found; and under Wallace's guidance we are taken to No. 58 C.C.S., which has long occupied the grounds of a château on the edge of the town. The C.O., Col. Martin, has arranged for us, and we get unpacked and set up immediately in the operating hut. I am quartered not far away in the town itself —a ten minutes' walk—in the house of M. le Docteur L. Walloert, *ex-Interne des Hôpitaux*—a local practitioner.

Dinner with the D.M.S. at his mess in the *Château de Philiomel*, also on this edge of the town, where were: Wallace; Hume, the new Medical Consultant, who must have taken Jack McCrae's place; Col. Kennedy Shaw, a remount officer (taken in because his mess in the town was recently blown up by a bomb); Davidson the A.D.M.S., i.e., "Davy" of Vimy Ridge recollection; Parkinson, A.D.M.S. Sanitation; and two young D.A.D.M.S. people, Capts. Young and Gibb. The news was very disturbing. An attack in force this morning taking advantage of a thick mist—Portuguese bolted—the Boche came through—the 51st Scottish (Seaforths, Camerons, Black Watch, etc.), brought up here from the Somme supposedly for a rest, was thrown into the gap—the line to-night, over a twelve-mile front, has been driven back for a depth of five miles—possibly to Estaires and Sailly-sur-la-Lys; at the two ends Givenchy and Armentières are still holding. Very little news, however, is attainable. No one really knows where any units are actually located. Bethune badly shelled—

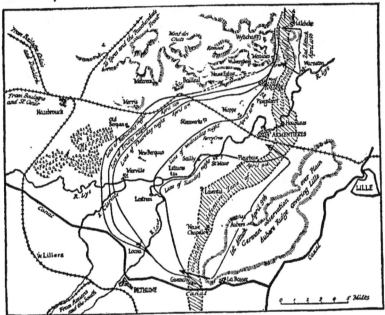

Map from *Land & Water* Showing German Advances in the Valley of the Lys, Tuesday, April 9th, to Saturday, April 13th. Note That This Offensive Was Directed against Important Railway Centres at Hazebrouck and Béthune

also Aire 10 miles from the line—we must have seen one drop there this afternoon as we came through, though we did not realize the cause of the commotion which we saw. One can't hear a shell explode when traveling in an ambulance over *pavés*.

The operating hut was closed for an hour to catch up on supplies, and we finally got to work at 9 p.m. They 've had an arduous day of it and the place was still full of wounded when we knocked off half an hour ago. There is a heavy continuous bombardment.

Later, April 10th. Getting acquainted with C.C.S. No. 58. An old French H.O.E. layout with ridged Faveron and round-roofed

Tarrant huts of generous size—big enough to hold the ordinary narrow British Nisson and room to spare. Seven such hutted wards to hold 26 beds and space for 1000 under canvas. The hospital huts not particularly well concentrated but the whole encampment is made very attractive with flower beds, which only the French seem disposed to lay out when time permits. All this in the Park, outside the walls of the château grounds proper. We alternate with three other C.C.S.'s in the First Corps: No. 23 at Lozinghem; No. 18 just set up under canvas alongside of us; and No. 4 Canadian at Pernes. No. 58 had three surgical teams of its own and five new ones are expected. It was providential, our getting here first scarcely aware that this new offensive was on. Yesterday 1600 cases were passed through and 600 were evacuated during the night, many of course surgically untreated—a few Portuguese but mostly Scottish of the 51st Division.

Still later, Apr. 10th. I've stood—on my crippled arches— the day's work better than I anticipated. The cases mostly Jocks, but also Tommies and quite a number of civilian wounded. Women and children lie in the Resuscitation Ward on stretchers alongside the grimy soldiers. At times such as this, how futile all one's fine talk about wastage and primary closure of wounds really seems! But these young surgeons of the C.C.S. type have learned their jobs well and do the finest sort of emergency surgical work for chest, knees, and abdominal wounds.

. . . .

The general situation is far from reassuring. The Boches across the Lys, north of Armentières, are in "Plug-street" and have a footing on Messines Ridge. At one time they got across the Lawe at Lestrem, but were finally ousted. Armentières seriously threatened, but it's an empty shell at best.

Thursday, April 11. Lillers

7.30 a.m. L/Cpl. Copstick is the most mild-mannered of men for the heavy artillery. He is a car conductor in Lancashire, peace times, and probably some lady has his job, which he will certainly never be able to get back by any force of character—but he makes a fair batman. His name is too much for me when he slinks in, and I can think of nothing but Chopsticks when I ask him what's the weather and if he will please close the window. "Very fine, sir, but cloudy and promises to rain." Moreover he seems unable to get hot water, for which at the moment I am waiting. There must be good reasons for the delay as the proprietor of this *maison* may be hesitating to give him any at all; he informs me that there are signs of trouble downstairs because my bath went through the floor yesterday morning and ruined the ceiling of the parlor. The Anglo-Saxon and his bath—so unnecessary to bathe thus—why more than hands and feet? My folding canvas tub after ten months' service suddenly sprang a leak at every pore, I think because Élise made frantic efforts to dry it before our hurried departure on Tuesday and probably put it in her gas stove. How I shall face the family belowstairs I don't know—but here comes Copstick with boots and shaving water.

11 p.m. We certainly have invited ourselves into a warm corner. The day crowded with work of all kinds, though only an occasional cranial operation. The Boche got a direct hit on a troop train and several lorries full of wounded were brought in—many of them dead on reaching us. Meanwhile the flow of men from the retreating Front keeps up. They shoved in on us, just before eight o'clock, a man bleeding from a gluteal artery, so we were an hour late for the mess; and while partaking of a pick-up meal in the château all the lights went out—but no Taubes have come over.

The last time a Taube came—not long before our arrival—he got an ammunition train or rather a large cache of alcohol near by, which set the train on fire—32 trucks of 9.5's, and as the siding is only a hundred yards from No. 58, things were lively for a while, unexploded as well as exploded shells dropping all over the place, and one sister was killed. No. 18 started to move away to-day and orders are issued for us to keep no lying cases—all to be sent on no matter what their condition. Most of the M.O.'s newly gathered here are from the Somme and have had recent experiences of similar sort in the area whence they came—mostly unpleasant. We left the night teams working by candles and torches—power shut off owing to the *alerte*.

This afternoon, refugees from Calonne-sur-la-Lys, this side of Merville, about six miles away, began to pour through—old men carrying packs, women pulling carts, and children pushing baby carriages. Where were they going—They did n't know—just away, that 's all. When I groped my way back to this billet I found a covered cart standing in the court and the old French doctor was anxiously sitting up—tried to press coffee on me and what was the news? Are they coming and how near?

He has gathered his movable possessions together, *pour pru-dence*, and his wife, with two little girls—grandchildren they must be—and the two dogs are ready to move at a moment's notice. Their first move, I may add. The Boche has never before been in Lillers. He has heard that two French divisions have been sent up here. Every little will help, certainly, for the Tommy has been badly cut up. Meanwhile the firing is getting uncomfortably close. Me for bed, nevertheless—anything better than an air raid.

Friday, April 12th

7 *a.m.* "They put a 17-inch shell into the T.D.O. just in front of Lagore and got most of the h'officers, and the Boche has five of our six batteries." This from Copstick of B. 276 who says he can't get any hot water—there is n't any fire. He 's now gone for cold, but the blinds open on to a fine sunny morning with the birds gayly chirping in the budding horse-chestnuts of *M. le Docteur's* little front yard. A toothache and need of dental care brought Copstick to No. 58 C.C.S. for renovation a day or two before this show opened; and he has just seen one of the survivors of his battery go by in an ambulance: hence his news of the shell landing in the Telephonists' Dugout.

Late last night just before coming home they were evacuating wounded to the train, and two bearers were carrying out a pretty little French girl of about nine summers who will never walk again without crutches, as she 's lost a leg at the hip. Behind her was her mother with her arm in a sling. Slumping along in the procession after them were two bearers carrying what appeared to be a stretcher loaded with folded blankets, out of which suddenly peeped a bright little face about as big as a fist—the girl's tiny brother—unwounded. I had seen him during the day playing about the camp with a dirty fox-terrier puppy and making friends with the bearers. They were smuggling him onto the train as a lying case.

Between operations at No. 58. There's a Tommy achondroplastic dwarf attached here—a great pet—too small to carry a stretcher of course, but an indefatigable worker at odd jobs. It's pitiful to see the Jocks come in—a kilt is picturesque but unserviceable. Many a Jock has been inextricably caught in the wire by his stout cloth skirt, and even gorse and brambles must be difficult enough for him to negotiate. I've never seen one in service boots. Imagine a pair of "Boots: gum: trench: G.S." under kilts! They wear a little gaiter over the top of their shoes, coming up just above the ankle—then stockings—then nothingness.

Later. Yesterday the Boches pushed on well toward Bailleul— some seven miles. Armentières was evacuated, being "full of gas." Estaires and Steenwerck taken and the enemy in the low country south of Messines and Mt. Kemmel. The Germans report Messines and Hollebeke captured Wednesday. They were long checked by the 9th Division, which, like the 55th, had just come up after participating in the Somme retreat.

10.30 p.m. In Gask's billet at Longuenesse in the outskirts of St. Omer near No. 7 General—and for the past hour sitting in the cellar with some French peasants, two children, and a pile of potatoes, while a Boche raider dropped about a dozen eggs unpleasantly near and Archies were going off furiously. We've jumped from the frying pan to the fire. Nor is this exactly the case, for it's very cold—particularly in a French cellar in April; but while it lasted I didn't quite feel like coming up to this level even for my overcoat.

It's been a lively day with flyable weather for a change and there's been plenty of both—change and flying. An early start with a lot of wounded—more Jocks from the 51st Division. A full morning's work. Then word came that we must evacuate everything—abandon the place in fact—teams to scatter to Nos. 23 and 22 in Lozinghem, others elsewhere—the lying cases to go first, and by 3 p.m. an M.A.C. convoy takes them away—then the sisters—tents going down—supplies of all sorts packed. Sad to see the lovely old place abandoned, with its gardens laid out for another summer, jonquils in bloom, sweet peas coming up. I shall long remember the wonderful avenue of elms—erect columns of 150 feet or more around the old château, once Haig's headquarters, with its brick-towered portal and patch of marshy woodland behind.

General Thompson came, in the afternoon, very distracted— giving severe orders right and left about trifles—must see about the sisters—what did *I* want to do—"Anything you wish, sir." Then I must come with him. The hard-pressed C.O. of No. 18 gets a scolding—only here since Monday and now everything again on the ground—lorries waiting to be loaded—but with no men in sight—"Why not?"— "Giving them two hours' rest, sir, as no sleep for four days."

Thus we fume away—to his French teacher in Lillers—the town packed with *réfugiés* streaming through—paraphernalia of war, with dusty and tired troops being herded by red-capped military police—and to the mêlée the inhabitants of Lillers are being added as they dump such of their possessions as they hope to carry away in front of their shops and houses. The "French teacher" has two old aunts aged 89 and 90!—he *must* send an ambulance for them, etc., etc.

So finally to the *Château de Philiomel*, where G.H.Q. 2nd Échelon gets on the line with orders that our team is to be sent to No. 7 General in St. Omer. Since this is not in the 1st Army area the D.M.S. expresses himself as "fed up" and wishes he were lying on the grass at Lord's watching a cricket match. Insists that before he leaves we must take a last walk in the garden, where are strawberries and a pond with goldfish and wild geese—and I with difficulty get away.

Back at No. 58 things have been moving fast. Most of the officers gone—but still possible to get tea, during which I learn that the Boche is about five miles away; and I may add that the D.M.S. in the course of our afternoon's meanderings casually produced from his capacious pocket a large revolver—no getting taken prisoner a second time—not he—there may be Uhlans about any minute. But there's no use getting the wind up even with an occasional burst of machine-gun fire all too near; and we wait around till about 6.30, when an ambulance appears for us.

The ride was an exciting one—St. Hilaire—Norrent—Aire— Arques—Longuenesse. The dusty road simply packed with lorries and Australians who have come in, and artillery limbers, and kitchens, and staff officers scurrying by, and devil dispatch-riders on motor cycles getting through somehow at breakneck pace. A beautiful cool evening with a glowing sunset, silhouetting on the low ridge to the west of us a long line of figures bent under packs and bundles—old men, women, and children—no room for them on the road. So to No. 7 General in the old monastery of Malassise, where a welcome by Col. Waring and by Gask, who feeds at their mess—and so do we.

. . . .

Merville taken; Bailleul threatened. Over 110 German divisions so far identified since March 21st, and over 40 of them thrown in more than once. They claim 20,000 prisoners.

Sunday, April the 14th

Overcast, with a chill penetrating wind, November-like, and as most of the glass has been blown out of the windows of this isolated farmhouse on the road through Longuenesse, one has to keep

Showing Allied Ground Lost in the First (March 21–28) and Second (April 9–18) Phases of the German Spring Offensive

wrapped up. Gask and I walked in to St. Omer after dinner last night to see Col. Shine and ask about our movements—whether our team had better stay with No. 7 or go on to Boulogne, where there is doubtless much work at present. He said "stay." Lady Victoria Someone-or-other was there, boss of the local V.A.D.G.S.'s, which is a new brand to me (Volunteer Aid Detachment General Service)—women who are doing all sorts of work from driving ambulances to waiting on table at No. 7 General. She had it that three American divisions were moving into this area, also French cavalry and a French Army.

All the serious cases retained at No. 7 General—femurs, chest and head cases—were evacuated yesterday afternoon by ambulances to St. Omer and thence by canal barge to Calais. No further cases to be admitted. No. 7 General to move and a C.C.S. to come in. Meanwhile the Christian Brothers and the Father Superior, who look as though they had stepped out of a mediæval picture, continue with their flower beds, planting and trimming the crucified fruit trees which encircle the huge garden behind the main building. Gask and I have decided to become experimental agriculturists after the war.

9 p.m. A disquieting day with no surgical work to take our minds off what is unquestionably a critical situation. They are packing up all the transportable property here and estimate 250 tons, which will require 300 lorries for the movable equipment of this single general hospital! Think of what it would take to evacuate Boulogne! Had the cards fallen differently last autumn, Base Hospital No. 5 might well enough have been set up in this area to share in the predicament that No. 7 General is facing. The place will probably be taken over by two C.C.S.'s, for there is a fine row of new Nissons and an operating suite as yet unused and suitable for casualty purposes.

Wallace and Gen. Thompson stopped here late for lunch—only time for a cup of tea—busy placing C.C.S.'s, which seem to be scattered all over the lot. The D.G. and Black hereabouts also; and late this afternoon Soltau, looking worn-out, came in to Gask's billet for a moment. Apparently only two clearing stations are left behind the 2nd Army, one of them still at Proven—Poperinghe practically evacuated—also the hospitals at Rémy. He himself at Blendecques, south of here.

In the afternoon to St. Omer again along the Boulevard Vauban which overlooks what remains of the old fortifications, now a botanical garden and park with a bastion in which is a large casemate capable of holding many hundred people, used at present as an *abri* for No. 58 (Scottish) near by. No. 58 is laid out on the old *champ de manœuvre* of the town, where are many jovial Scots who think they 've suffered badly. Col. Grahame, C.O., and a Major Scot-Skirving, most voluble. The place lies near the motor-lorry park which the Hun was after Friday night. Six months ago they were badly bombed, so that a large part of their compound was given over to a P.O.W. camp, and on Friday five big ones were dropped within 50 yards of the officers' quarters. We saw the craters—a huge elm was largely engulfed in one.

McGowan, the pathologist, took me over by the fish market and down the rue de Calais, where other bombs had fallen—direct hits on houses which were completely collapsed, with tumbled beds hanging by their hind legs from shelves of upper floors—the beds not occupied of course, for the people were in the cellars, in one of which eight *habitants* were entombed—so, at least, I 'm informed by a woman standing in the doorway of the windowless house just opposite—"*C'est abominable, cette guerre.*"

Haig's most disquieting Order to the Army appears in to-day's —that is, yesterday's—papers. It ends as follows:—

With our backs to the wall, and believing in the justice of our cause, each one of us must fight on to the end. The safety of our homes and the freedom of mankind depend alike upon the conduct of every one at this critical moment.

11 p.m. The officers of No. 7 General are sitting about reading, writing, playing bridge, and waiting, while an old boy is strumming the piano. The last news comes from the X-ray man of No. 10 C.C.S., formerly of Rémy, who is looking for his unit. He says the Ypres salient has been abandoned back to the canal. If this be so, all our last summer's work for the ridges—Messines and Passchendaele—has gone by the board in the space of six days.

Monday, April 15

Unseasonably cold, with a high wind blowing from the north. An occasional plane struggles against it, but not many. This standing by with nothing to do but await orders is the very devil. It affects everyone alike, for we know that somewhere there is overwhelming work under which surgical teams are struggling. Outwardly everyone is cheerful and brings in news such as the recapture of Armentières; the Padre even had the line back to Laventie shortly after breakfast—had seen someone who came from there who told someone who told him—quite authentic!

. . . . .

Both the first and this second phase of the German offensive concern chiefly the control of important railways. The object of the first was to put the Boulogne–Amiens–Paris line out of commission and this they have nearly accomplished. In this second phase the territory lies directly opposite Lille, which for the Boches is a great railway junction. On the Allied side, Hazebrouck and Béthune are the essential centres, the loss of which would seriously affect the lines of communication to the British front in the North.

Tuesday, April 16th

a.m. Still cold and overcast. No. 7 nearly evacuated—another 500 cases went down last night. Our orders to proceed to a C.C.S. in the 1st Army have finally come through. We are given an extra nurse, orderly, and a batman! Wagstaffe and a team from here are to go along with us.

10 p.m. No. 4 Canadian C.C.S. Pernes. We got away about 11 and came through Aire, passing French cavalry and reserves which have come up here about 100 miles in five days. The roads full—like the salient last summer at its worst, plus innumerable refugees. Still, many a farmer keeps on with his ploughing, scornful of war while crops are to be considered—even crops which may belong to the Boche to-morrow. On to Lillers, which has become practically deserted in the last three days; and our driver says the foundries near Lillers, where French 75's were made, were evacuated two days ago. Then the St. Pol road past Lozinghem and through several dirty French villages—for mill operatives, I take it—in sight of great pyramidal slag piles; and finally Pernes and our destination.

They've had a busy time, these Canadians who have been pitched here for only a few days, after leaving their comfortable site in Rouitz. Quite short-handed, too, but to-day teams have crowded in—from 44 C.C.S. under Munro; from No. 18 C.C.S., our former neighbor in Lillers, under Blake and Buck; from the 1st Canadian; two teams from 12 Stationary at St. Pol under

Maj. Anderson and Capt. Wilson; still another from 7 Can. Stationary under Capt. Fisher; from No. 58 C.C.S. under MacEwan; from No. 7 General at Malassise, Wagstaffe and ourselves. McNee also here looking after the Resuscitation Ward; Walker from Taplow after chests; and in the Unit proper, which hails from Winnipeg, Col. Campbell and nine officers, down to "Jimmy" Crawford, a dentist who is acting as E.M.O. We got to work immediately after lunch and kept on till the night teams came on duty. Six of us are at the moment crowded in a small Nisson preparing to turn in.

Wednesday, April 17th

A very heavy bombardment last night, shaking and rattling our hut—whether the Boche or our own artillery seems uncertain. The night shift—four of them—came in about 4 a.m., everything cleaned up. One of them proceeded promptly to snore—the crescendo kind prohibiting sleep. Then our batman, Pte. F. James Farnen, a one-eyed—and that wild—Lancastrian, unused to the finesse of being a batman, came in heavy-shod and woke us all at 6 a.m. looking for boots—ours—apparently thought they would come to him if he made a noise like another pair. Cutler bounced

up and demanded shaving water, and he shortly brought a small, porringer-like affair containing a few ounces. There are doubtless good batmen, but they have been captured by officers longer in the field.

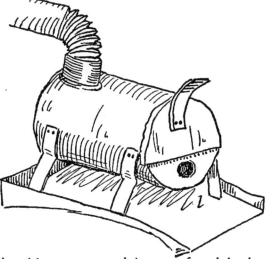

Evening. Cutler and I were permitted to shift our quarters this afternoon to a hut affair with a corrugated iron roof and burlap walls. On the door it says "Sports Hut: Closed from 12 to

12.30." This camp, I may add, was a Canadian Corps training ground before No. 4 took it over, and there are relics of their buildings—hence the small Nissons and hence the Sports Hut, about 12 feet square. In its centre sits an extraordinary homemade mongrel of most aggressive aspect—a cross between a stove and a petrol tin—an iron cross. If you try to lift the creature up by his tail you expose his—or her, as the case may be—insides where a fire can be built—or could be if Pte. F.J.F. were properly trained and knew how to procure wood or coal; but others more skilled in the art of "scrounging" and with two eyes seem to have beat him to it. Meanwhile he's scrubbed the floor and left it very wet, in the midst of which the iron pup stands on its tin raft with subnormal temperature.

Life at a C.C.S. alternates between pressure of work and no work at all. Both are killing. We had one hard case to-day—otherwise nothing. We wandered into Pernes this afternoon and found it full of cavalry people—a division of dragoons being quartered hereabouts. There is no news to-day—no papers—not even a *communiqué*. A wounded German officer in the ward says the war will be over this year—*their* way. He admits that they have little food except for the army; Lichnowsky merely a puppet—his letter means nothing.

One of the German wounded brought here the other day had a Tommy's uniform on under his own. They have been sending scouting parties out in kilts and in Portuguese uniforms. When they get near enough to be suspected they turn on a machine gun. This may be permissible in war, but it's not nice.

Thursday, April 18th

a.m. We were awakened early by Pte. Farnen falling over the iron pup which, with tail erect, was smoking furiously at both ends—doing everything but bark at Farnen, who was on his knees blowing at its rear elevation. "How's the weather, Farnen?" "Cauld and rough, sorr." This proved to be a good description and we've dressed in it, as usual without shaving water.

11 p.m. Work was turned loose on us to-day and it's been difficult to keep up with it. Back again to "shell wounds; multiple; severe." McNee has his hands full in the Resuscitation Ward. No X-ray plant set up as yet. Hence it's difficult to deal properly

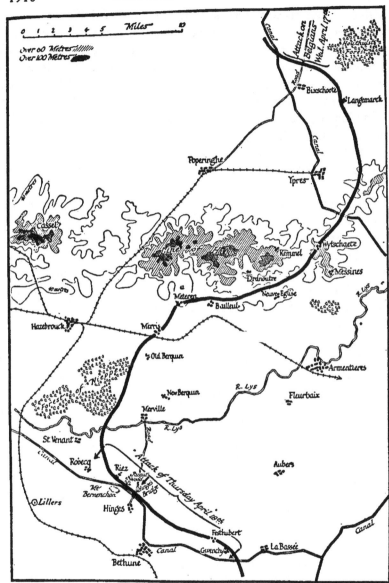

Map from *Land & Water* to Show Position of Critical Attack on April 18th
Threatening Hinges Bridge at Béthune

with the head cases. We are sending on many of the favorable ones, therefore, untouched. Our orderly had finished shaving an uncon_ scious man this afternoon with a huge wound and fungating brain. I thought him too far gone to touch and turned to the more likely case on the next table, a man named Dix—an old soldier 14 years in the army, who came out with the 4th Division. As I was novo- cainizing his scalp and asking him how he ,got hit, he said, "We was in a barn, a-holding on, when a heavy landed in on us—that's my pal on the next table." "Your particular pal?" "Yes, sir, my booze pal." There could be no greater degree of intimacy.

.   .   .   .   .   .

To-day's heavy fighting from Givenchy to Robecq was to hold the Hinges bridge, the loss of which would threaten Béthune. Apparently Bailleul, with the Messines and Passchendaele ridges, was taken Tuesday by new German divisions. Yesterday there was a thrust at the Belgian sector. This may mean giving up Calais should it succeed. It looks as though I may have to burn this diary some day. If I do, something better than this iron pup will have to be found for the purpose.

Friday, April 19

11 p.m. Major Moshier is far from having been killed at Pas- schendaele last November 1st. He 's now Lt. Col. and O.C. of No. 11 F.A. with the 4th Canadian Division, for the time being in the Canadian Corps rest camp. He came down here in an ambu- lance this afternoon and finding us finishing our last case took me back to dinner with his people. That last case, I may add, was a Boche P.O.W. with multiples, including a bad frontal gutter wound which looks as though someone must have made a success- ful counter-attack, else we should scarcely have been receiving enemy wounded.

After a strenuous day it was good to have a change. It was bitter cold, not to say "rough," in the morning with a heavy frost on the ground and flurries of snow alternating with rain and wind; but by the late afternoon came signs of clearing, the clouds breaking into great cumulous masses with wonderful coloring. Due south- east in the direction of the old Roman road from Boulogne to Arras—through Pernes—Camblain-Chatelain, which even the French now call "Charley Chaplin"—Divion, through a hilly

mining country with pyramidal *crassiers* here and there and unattractive barracks for houses—Houdain, from which one sees
the church on the edge of the hill commanding the valley—
Ranchicourt and Rebreuve—the old mediæval thirteenth-century
moated castle at Oblain where Dumas staged the *Three Musket-
eers*—and so to Fresnicourt, where is the rest camp in the grounds
surrounding an attractive château.

We motored up on the hill from which one can see far down
the wonderful Ranchicourt Valley we had traversed—the best
view in France according to Moshier. He knows about views as
he is accustomed to drive his car frequently the 300 miles into
Banff and has crossed "the Great Divide" in it more than once.
Particularly beautiful it was to-day looking west with the sun behind a huge isolated cumulus. Then on to Villers-au-Bois, 10 km.
due west of Vimy, where we find Col. Peters, once of the Montreal
General, now A.D.M.S. of the 4th Canadians.

Very cheering to see these people and to know how strongly
they are entrenched. Holding 25 miles of front with their four
divisions—and the Boche does not dare touch them—from Arras
nearly to La Bassée. The only way the enemy can recapture Vimy
is to cut them off by first pushing back the 5th Army on the south
and then by breaking through to Hazebrouck and Aire in this
new attack.

Here for the first time I saw secondary defenses which *are*
secondary defenses, back ten miles or more, and there are rows of
them with pill boxes in between; and nearly every roadside embankment is scarred by the recent passage of tanks like the trail of
some antediluvian monster. It would take all the Boche horses
and all the Boche men all summer to get through here.

They 're the boys—divisions at full strength, 12,000 in reserve
—and they wish the Americans could have been put in alongside
of them. No talk from them of falling back—of the end of the
war, etc., but rather of their famous box barrage and the tons of
cyanide gas projected into Lens on the pressure of a single electric
button.

Saturday, the 20th

A thick crust of ice on our waste bucket this morning. Private
Farnen has been removed from our midst—also the iron pup. It

probably followed him. He informed us yesterday that he came from St. Helens. "Didna we kno' where was?" This with a monocular expression of astonishment. "It's where they makes Beecham's Pills."

10.30 p.m. A good day's work to-day—from seven to seven—much easier than the 16 hours on and eight off during the No. 46 days. More Boche prisoners this afternoon with heads—they seem to be rather fed up with the war, which is encouraging.

Dinner in Pernes with a Captain Lance of the Imperial Corps Training School. A very formal mess and I was perforce late, which was not a good beginning; had no slacks, which was poor; wore a belt, which was worse; and took no alcohol—incomprehensible! We parted early.

Sunday, Apr. 21st

Awakened by a heavy barrage—almost like the drum fire of last summer, but it was of short duration. A beautiful quiet sunny Sunday. A walk with the C.O. after lunch through the woods—indescribably lovely. Spring much later here than near the coast—trees just coming into bud—blackthorn not fully blossomed out, but the ivy- and myrtle-covered floor of the wood was brilliant with a profusion of wild flowers—star anemones big as a shilling, periwinkles, cowslips, buttercups and dwarf daisies, wild hyacinths, and violets everywhere. On to the top of the ridge to the north of us where the training school has its trenches and exercising ground. A wonderful view from the top—of the country northeast and south—Lillers, St. Pol, and to the east all the little mining towns with their red roofs, chimneys, and pyramidal *crassiers*.

In the late p.m., Col. Peters and Moshier came with an invitation to dine at Aux Rietz corner with Sir David Watson, G.O.C. 4th Canadian Division. This sounds very swell but it was far from being swell—though exciting; for we were underground with occasional *arrivées* landing above us—but of this later on. In an 8-cylinder Cadillac we retraced our road of Thursday to Fresnicourt, where Moshier was dropped at his field ambulance—then up to the ridge at the N.E. end of the beautiful valley down beyond which the sun was brilliantly drinking water from behind a dark cloud—past the *estaminet* of the fairies and the large Druid stone table near by—past the headquarters of the 1st Army Commander, ditto of the Canadian Corps Commander, and soon the wooded top of the Lorette, from which the barren crest of Vimy Ridge came into view—and finally to the famous crossroads at La Targette.

The Béthune–Arras road was much as it appeared last June, with its countless dugouts. Peters asked if I cared to wash and if so would I go with him to his billet; and to my amazement he leads me down a breakneck flight of steps to a huge cave 60 feet underground where several hundred troops are quartered and where the officers have little curtained-off cubicles—as primitive lodgings as I have seen, but comfortable enough—and, of chief importance, safe.

At the General's mess were Col. Panet, a British General Staff Officer, attached; Col. Marshall, A.A. and Q.M.G.; Maj. Gavin, the one-time owner of Raeburn's "The McNab," recently sold for 30,000 pounds; Cap. MacLeod Moore, the General's A.D.C., whom I took one day to Revere's grave in Dosinghem, and Peters, the divisional A.D.M.S. They were most cordial and pleasant; and after exhausting that perennial topic of conversation, the louse, I learned that they are giving the Boche an unpleasant time, for Sir David seems to believe in an offensive defensive. On the preceding night, for example, they had projected 600 tons of gas shells into the enemy's back areas—or was it 6000 tons? I 'm not good at remembering figures.

So home by moonlight—with Boche raiders about, through dark villages, and I find Captain Fisher and Anderson operating on an emergency—an artillery sergeant who got someone's knee in the pit of his stomach during a Sunday afternoon football contest in the neighboring field. He had finished the game, gone to his billet, and had tea before he gave in. There was a rupture two inches long in the lower jejunum.

Monday, Apr. 22nd

Very busy day—our "take in." No news. We 're likely to have much work to-morrow judging by the bombardment, which has been particularly loud and continuous all the evening. Raining. The "Wireless Bulletin" issued from the Canadian Corps Signal Office at 2 a.m. daily quotes the German wireless of yesterday afternoon to this effect:—

Between the Meuse and Moselle, Lower Saxon battalions attacked the Americans in their trenches near Seicheprey. They stormed the position and broke into the enemy's lines to a depth of two kilometres. Weak counter-attacks from the enemy were driven off. Stronger efforts to attack were repulsed. In the night our assault troops, after destroying the enemy's positions, returned to their own lines. The losses of the Americans are extremely high, 183 men, including 5 officers, were taken prisoners, and 25 machine guns were captured.

Not much, this, other than that we 've at last been heard from; and this affair will probably be headlined at home. There has been a comparative lull in the fighting since Thursday, when Béthune was seriously threatened.

Tuesday the 23rd

Having finished our last 200 by 3 p.m., with Captains Walker and Cotton we walked over to Bours, some 5 km. to the south of here along the St. Pol road, to see the old feudal *donjon* there— the one remaining tower of the four which once stood at the corners of the enclosure.

We were particularly interested in the caretaker, a blind tabetic who has lived within for 43 years. He told his little tale and showed us the *oubliette*, a hole in the dungeon floor with a well which led down 30 metres to water; also the *souricière*, and it was some time before we understood. There was a small stone vestibule in the wall just within the point at which the portcullis was raised. An unwelcome guest, entering there to knock at the castle door, could be trapped by raising the draw. This small vestibule, though within the walls, had no ceiling, and from above with great convenience horrible things could be dropped on the guest's head— boiling oil, *cailloux*, and such. This the old man told with glee as he felt of the walls and rocked about in his efforts to balance on his wobbly legs.

SWITCHED OFF FOR A LECTURE!

Wednesday, April 24. Boulogne

While in the middle of a serious operation this afternoon the C.O., looking, for him, very disgruntled, appeared and read me this disconcerting and unwelcome message from the A.E.F. forwarded through No. 13 General by Roger Lee, who is now our C.O.

Following telegram received quote paragraph fifty-seven special orders forty-one these headquarters April twenty-second directs you to proceed to Neufchâteau and Langres for temporary duty you should arrive at Neufchâteau not later than April twenty-eighth acknowledge quote signed Bradley forwarded

"What's to do?" said I. "Nothing to do," said he, "except pack your duffel bag and beat it, but I say to hell with 'em." "Can you send that answer for me?" "Under the circumstances, no."

At 5 p.m. I was sent down in one of the ambulances they could ill spare—a cold, misty, and frightfully dusty afternoon. Instead of striking the old Roman road to Thérouanne, we got lost in a maze of crowded byways to the south around Coyecque and made very poor time. No one here at the Base knows what it's all about—or what "temporary duty" means—a few days or as many months.

No. 13 General has been very busy these two weeks. Horrax up to his neck in cranial wounds—many more than we have had. This probably due to prompt evacuation from all the forward areas to Boulogne—now the only available base with an open line of communication.

Tuesday, April 25. Hôtel de la Poste, Rouen

Midnight. "Owing to the mixed bag I've got in the back seat I think we'll not go through Montreuil." This from Major Langridge—the "mixed bag" consisting of Mrs. L. of the 2nd Australian Y.M.C.A. hut, and myself with a blanket roll, etc.— she in one of her husband's cars for the first time since coming out here and off to Rouen for a two weeks' rest—I being taken with them to avoid the present interminable and uncertain journey by rail to Paris via Eu. An R.C. official does not drive his wife through G.H.Q. by choice. . . .

We got away from Boulogne at 2.30, reaching here at seven— four hours on the road and very good going—most too fast when Langridge took the wheel from Sgt. Ruff at St. Valery and let her out—62 miles an hour at one spot and over 50 much of the time. Samer—Neuville—Nouvion with the Forêt de Crécy on our left—then out to St. Valery-sur-Somme with the widespread estuary of the river in view, down which William of Normandy set sail for his conquest of England. Then along the coast road—

Brutelles—Ault—Eu, with its very fine approach; then west again to the coast to take in Le Tréport with its big cliffs like small Towers of Hercules, on one of which is No. 3 General (Harte's Unit), in a large summer hotel.

Then Dieppe and the direct postroad to Rouen, the same that was taken by Jeanne d'Arc on her last journey, after her capture at Compiègne. A lovely part of the country—half-timbered farms and houses like those in old English villages, though which was the imitator I know not—the trees bursting into leaf, much further forward than about Pernes—the roadsides a profusion of primroses—fruit trees in bloom—past great country houses with wonderful avenues of elm and beech—all very fine with no reminder of war except the villages, which were full of Belgian soldiers whose rest area this has been since the early days.

We finally pulled up at Tôtes before a picturesque old coaching hotel, built in 1611—Hôtel du Cygne—with a wonderful great kitchen decorated on all four walls by a rare collection of blue plates and platters in racks reaching to the high ceiling, and with brassware and old prints and a carved clock eleven feet in height —a picturesque courtyard with a huge stable on one side capable of putting up at least 50 horses, solidly built with great beams two feet thick—a cordial host in a fancy embroidered waistcoat—also coffee with *confitures*. An ideal place for some future pilgrimage.

Rouen, in time for an hour of sight-seeing before dinner. Then Sgt. Ruff drove me out across the river to the race course, where, in No. 12 General, Fred Murphy and his St. Louis outfit have been comfortably quartered—the best situation I think of all of our original six base-hospital units. Near by in No. 9 General were G. W. Crile and the Lakeside people. They have been very busy —almost on a C.C.S. basis. From Crile, just caught turning in, I learn that he too has been ordered to report at Neufchâteau on the 28th inst.

Saturday the 27th. Paris

To Paris, our train an hour late in starting. Dinner with the Strongs—self-invited. Richard just back from a trip to Étaples to meet the British Research Committee, on which Col. Lyle Cummins has taken Leishman's place—in an open car—very wind-blown and tired—as tired as he ever gets. Came through

Amiens on the way down because the shortest way—the place
burning.

People here much discouraged about the general situation—the
army regulars keeping effective men down—General Bradley
openly stating that he had put Keller in as a buffer above Finney
as he did not propose to deal directly with "specialists" any longer.
Even worse in other services. Warwick Greene dropped in later—
his chief, Col. Bolling, recently killed by a shell while motoring
through Amiens—regulars now put in charge and most of the
good work of the past six months undone—utter demoralization
in the air service—not a single machine over here yet. All this
most depressing to hear.

Paris to-night very quiet and dark—despite the big yellow
moon low in the east. If the long-range gun has been at work
to-day I have n't heard it, though I found poor old Gentile, the
instrument maker on the *Rive Gauche,* very shaky, anxious, and
preparing to make a move; for their quarter of the city has suffered most. No unbridled street lights anywhere—merely occasional shaded bluish lamps on the thoroughfares to mark the
abris and the entrances to the *Métro.*

Monday 29th. Neufchâteau

Arrived with Crile at Gondrecourt in the rain at 5.30 p.m. Met
by Cannon, who brought us over here. Finney and his group have
moved from the *Tour Babel* to new quarters—a former loft which
they have had cleaned up—somewhat—though there are sus-
picious-looking places dried on the floors which are incompletely
scraped off. Swallows which formerly occupied the premises continue to flock in when a window is opened—the walls are pasteboard partitions supplied by the Red Cross—the guest bed has a
husk mattress—belowstairs dwell *poilus,* who are garrulous till
ten, after which they cough and snore; at 6 a.m. they become
garrulous again. Leastaways it was thus this morning as far as the
"guest room" is concerned. Finney, Peck, Thayer, Boggs, and a
young Philadelphian named Widener, who came over in Peck's
unit as a private. He has now been advanced to a stripe in the
Sanitary Corps and acts as housekeeper for the group.

Most disquieting accounts of the local situation. General
Bradley's letter about the reorganization of the professional serv-

ices makes me wonder whether it would not be better to remain with the B.E.F. The army is very lousy, but fortunately no trench fever as yet; the soldiers dirty and shabby, the death rate from preventable disease far higher per 1000 than at home or in the other armies out here. But what may we expect? The French shrug their shoulders at us and carefully guard everything we do —particularly the parts of the line they allow us to occupy. Goldthwait tells me that all winter neither *poilu* nor French officer bothered to salute an American in this area; they have only begun to do so of late since some of the divisions have been given a chance to show their mettle.

Still, it's a cheerful group here, and they try to see the amusing side of their troubles and the humiliations they are under. Walter Cannon said that while in a C.C.S. at Béthune working on "shock," he went into the ward one day to see a patient and asked the sister what she was giving the man. "What the surgeon tells me to," snapped she. Later on he happened to return with Capt. Fraser, and when she observed how much deference was shown him she asked the Matron who he was and confessed that she had snubbed him. The Matron then apologized to Walter, saying that the sister thought from the U.S.R. on his collar he was a United Service Reader. Imagine Walter's delight; but it's less funny here in the A.E.F. to be regarded about on this basis by our own regulars. . . .

This morning down the valley of the Meuse again—Bazoilles, Clefmont, Bourmont, lovely places on hilltops; but "distance lends" to the French villages in this cattle-raising part of France, where there is a highly developed passion for manure piles under your front windows—finally Langres, most charming from a distance and far more tolerable within its old walls from a sanitary standpoint than other towns round about.

We scrabbled lunch in a small restaurant crowded with young officers; and then to the Army School,[1] where I gave a lecture to some 50 of Col. Ashford's pupils who are undergoing preparation for line officers. Ashford appears to be a hustling good fellow, and very effective in his job. I intimated, however, that he would

---

[1] For an account of this Army School at Langres, cf. *A Soldier in Science* by Bailey K. Ashford. New York, Wm. Morrow, 1934.

get better lectures if those who received summonses out of a clear sky were warned as to the object of their call and given their subject—also that it would be embarrassing for me to let my friends in the B.E.F. know that just at this critical time I had taken a week off merely to give a lecture. This he admitted, but "it 's the way we have in the army." . . .

"The French don't care very much about it—they just make gestures and say nothing." This from Salmon, whose experiences are many and peculiar and who, like a pin, has a head which keeps him from going too far. Someone has expressed this better: I 've forgotten who. Nothing done about self-inflicted wounds as yet. One underdeveloped boy, feeble-minded, explained the small wound in his left hand by saying he was on sentry duty and fell asleep and his gun went off accidentally—not realizing that falling asleep was enough for a court-martial; but nothing was done.

In a recent German raid two Austrian-Americans from our troops were seen walking back with the raiding party. One of them was shot in the act and during a counter raid the other was captured, but no action was taken against him. The French shrug their shoulders with some reason. An officer makes advances to the daughter of the family with whom he is billeted—marries her —a public church wedding. It is learned that he has a wife at home. He is examined and it is brought out that this poor girl is his third wife—in other words he was a bigamist when he married No. 2 before he went into military service, making a complicated tangle for the A.G.'s department. Of course the man was insane.

Still more remarkable, the story of a youngster—born in Germany of American parents—finally brought back home—a queer stick always—enlisted on the outbreak of war—was observed to be full of pro-German talk—rebellious at restraint, discipline, disparity between privileges of officers and men. Finally made friends with a German P.O.W.—gave him his uniform, fixed up another for himself with officer's trappings—forged some papers requesting that they be privileged to look over the Belfort area to see if suitable for tank manœuvres.

They made their way on foot, by *camion*, etc., to the Front in the French area, where they were first suspected, and were caught in the act of getting across. The French dealt with the German prisoner. Our enlisted man, whom they would have shot without examination, was found by our board to have dementia præcox and sent home to an asylum to enjoy the remainder of his days at national expense.

Salmon says that the incidence of insanity in ordinary life is 1–1000; when people come under restraint as in an army, even in quiet times such as the Mexican border, it jumps to 3–1000; over here it has become about 12–1000. The slightly unbalanced man, bolstered up by his customary surroundings where his oddities pass without comment, goes to pieces when he has to conform to a common type.

Wednesday, May 1st

Major Finney's position here is comparable to that held by General Bowlby in the B.E.F. There is the same disparity in rank as in means of transportation. This morning we go off on a visit to the local hospitals in the last surviving car at the disposal of this group—a rattly flivver sounding, as someone remarked, like two skeletons wrestling on a tin roof.

A fine view of Neufchâteau perched on one hill as we climb the adjacent one to the east, with the winding Meuse threading its way through the valley between. On to Mirecourt, 40 km. away, through villages picturesque with blue-coated soldiers—a grazing country between, with cattle on a thousand hills. Finney, like others of us, seems to think he is through with surgery—55 his next birthday—after this is over, *he* for his Maryland farm in Ruxton, his grapes and his pet boys' schools.

Finally Baccarat on the Meurthe, much damaged in spots, with a church still standing and its bells still ringing, though a large hole shows through the belfry. Headquarters of the 42nd Division now in the line with a front of 10 km. just N.E. of and parallel to the Baccarat–Lunéville road—carefully flanked by a French division on each side.

Col. Grissinger, the Divisional A.D.M.S.—whatever he may be called here—is visited and a young Capt. Smith of Buffalo takes us to lunch in his mess. Smith is not such a rare name but that it's important to pick out your branch with care; and for a young M.O. the "Nathan" branch is a good one. We lunch largely on beans and bread—very good and white.

Then to Evacuation Hospital No. 2 with a band (U.S.A.) playing in front—the first I 've heard. Excellent music, but our men somehow look most untidy compared with the *poilu* or Tommy. The C.O. Major Lyle of the National Guard—very efficient and making much out of little. I left as a suitable motto: "Do what you can, with what you 've got, right where you are." Not a bad motto for all these places. The teams are headed by Lincoln Davis, who strikes me as looking worn, Major Morrow, and the aforementioned Smith, with Sanford, one of Young's men, in addition.

Along the Muerthe on the Lunéville–Nancy road—more graves, and near Vitremont stands the ruined farm on the hill which was the scene of captures and recaptures. A hop country with the pole forms of culture—along the canal connecting the Marne and Rhine—St. Nicolas with its fine towering church—Nancy, and through the Place Stanislas built by the last Duc de Lorraine, a patron of arts and architecture, once King of Poland—through the lovely Forêt de Haye, with Mont St. Michel and the Cathedral of Toul coming into view. Then the cut-off to Evacuation Hospital No. 1 for a glimpse of Heuer, Pool, and McWilliams, who are at work there. I hope to enlist Heuer for the Neurological Service. So via Toul, Colombey-les-Belles, and finally back home, where we arrive at 8 and dine. While I attempt to write this the others are playing reversible hearts very noisily.

.   .   .   .   .   .

They receive no daily *communiqués* here and have little interest in the situation on the British front, so I am without news since my sudden departure from Pernes a week ago to-day.

Thursday, May 2nd. Neufchâteau

A very handsome day—there are none too many in this part of France, I 'm told. To Vittel, some 25 km. southeast of here, a sort of French Saratoga-watering-place with large hotels, a golf course, and actually places to bathe. Here, and in the adjacent town of Contrexéville, are four hospital units which have passed a .qu^arrelsome winter until they became fused under the ad_ ministration of a regular named Col. Rukke.

One of them, under Major Shurly's guidance, is scattered in four great hotels. They were sent over shortly after the news reached home that we of the original units were undermanned and underequipped for hospitals of the standard British size. Consequently they came doubly manned and with equipment enough for several hospitals—five huge X-ray machines for example— $60,000 worth of material presented to them by the Knights Templars. They are called a "Head hospital," though there is no neurologist or neurosurgeon, no one with maxillofacial experience, no good ophthalmologist—only an otologist. Here they sit, and have sat all winter, an enormous daily expense to the government, with an equipment no one else can use—a personnel Finney does not dare use. Situations like this will be increasingly difficult to handle—and more are arriving every week, unannounced.

Friday, May 3rd

En route Gondrecourt à Paris. Two very polite and punctilious French officers occupy the seats by the door. At Vitry-le-François a noisy Y.M.C.A. damsel and three American Marine Corps officers with an excess of baggage crowd into the compartment without a polite word of by-your-leave or greeting. They are large-limbed fellows chewing cigars. One of them, after sitting down, scales his hat toward the rack, which it misses, and falls fortunately into my lap—not a Frenchman's. It is rescued without a word. They cross their legs with their muddy boots almost against the knees of their French neighbors, who shrink in the corners they occupy and exchange glances with the slightest possible lift of the eyebrows. Doubtless they are brave fellows, but, like d'Artagnan, they have things to learn.

At a conference yesterday of the Allied Premiers and Commanders at Abbeville it was agreed that British shipping was to transport 10 American divisions to the British Army area for training and equipment. The U.S. Senate institutes prosecution in alleged aircraft graft in which a billion dollars is involved.

Saturday, May 4th

2 *p.m.* We are creeping out of Camiers on the way to Boulogne —en route since 9.40 last evening—an 18-hour trip. Next time I shall fortify myself with food. We probably came via Eu, and got into Abbeville about 11, wending our way by the canal, on the

other side of which was a column of some 300 mules, easily keep‐
ing pace with us as we slowly felt our way along. It looked as
though all the rolling stock in France were in and about Abbeville.

Boulogne, 4 p.m. During the week that I have been away, as
I gather from accumulated copies of the *Times,* severe fighting
has taken place around Villers-Bretonneux in the Avre region,
which finally was retaken by Australian and County troops and is
still held, I believe.

In the French area the chief activity was around Hangard,
which also has changed hands many times.

On the 26th a severe attack was launched east of Bailleul, and
the British withdrew from Dranoutre, Kemmel, and Vierstraat,
losing Kemmel Hill after a desperate struggle to a finish on the
part of the French troops on the summit. Severe fighting followed
for days around Locre, Scherpenberg, and la Clytte, where the
French had been put in. They were forced out of Locre on the
29th, but it was later retaken. The same day the enemy pressed in
the Ypres salient to Verlorenhoek, Hooge, Zillebeke—practically
the old line.

On the 30th, 13 German divisions were thrown against the
Meteren–Voormezeele 10-mile front—also in other parts of the
line, with only temporary advantage gained in some places. Locre
was again lost and retaken—this of course means only a spot—
Locre as a town long since disappeared. Since the 30th there has
been no great change, though there is more or less activity all
along the line. Some American units of our 1st Division got into
action near Montdidier for the first time a day or two ago and are
well spoken of.

An Unwelcome Interruption

May 8. St. Omer-en-Chaussée

Midday. As there was no chance of returning to duty with the
1st Army, I was making arrangements to start in with neurological
work at No. 13 General when out of a clear sky yesterday came an
order from the A.E.F. that I was to report "at once" to Head‐
quarters Service of Supply to the Commanding General, etc., etc.
Got away from Boulogne at 8.30 p.m. and should have been in
Paris by 9 this morning, but here at this particular place, which is

somewhere between Eu and Beauvais, they are rapidly double-tracking the road and there are high dumps of supplies on every side. Chinks and Dagos at work on the road—one can hardly say feverishly. Meanwhile we simply creep along—stop for long periods—creep again.

May 9. Tours, 37 rue de l'Alma

10 p.m. I jokingly told the boys before leaving Boulogne that I was probably going to be reprimanded for some misdeed; I really thought that the U.S.A. Consultants were being summoned to be given examinations for advanced rank. As things stand, I may perhaps even be court-martialed for inadvertently enclosing some notes of this journal in a letter home—those in which S. says, in a moment of irritation, needlessly harsh things about the British.

How I came to do so I do not recall; but we were expecting orders to close up any day and all of us were sending home whatever lay loose on our desks. It's one of the reasons why it's dangerous out here to put one's thoughts too much on paper along with the things one hears. I have written a letter of apology and explanation and can but await the verdict with the greatest possible humiliation. Being my second offense with the British Censor makes matters worse; and they have passed the matter on to our Adjutant General. It took most of this afternoon to find out what my summons was for: no one had any record of it; and when the blow came I should have been glad to be *"spurlos versenkt."*

Tours, Saturday, May 11th

The anniversary of our sailing. We are privileged to wear two gold service chevrons, and Patterson, who happens to be here, also [now Cpl.] Call and [now Sgt.] Russell from our Unit, have blossomed out in theirs. Col. McCaw, who is in charge here as acting Chief Surgeon in the absence of both Bradley and Ireland, though very friendly, shakes his head over my sorry case and says: "Come in again to-morrow." I therefore sport no chevrons and keep as inconspicuous as possible.

Monday, May 13th

Bob Osgood here to-day for an orthopædic conference. He sails for home shortly to continue his excellent work in the States and to act as Goldthwait's representative there. Col. McCaw says so far as he can see I too will be sent home—though for different reasons. I go about with my tail between my legs and humbly report once a day to ask if there are any orders for me. None.

Wednesday, May 15th

Memorable for my first flight. We dined again last night upstairs at Pacquet's wee place. I knew none of the people but there were two vacant places beside me, and soon Stewart Forbes, now a liaison officer with the French, came in with a U.S.R. major whom he started to introduce to me—none other than Jim Barnes. He is with the aviation service and had much to say of his present and past jobs. As we broke up, the people at the other table, sitting under the busts of departed chefs, turn out to be the Marlborough-Churchills, and with them a tall young lieutenant, Raymond Noyes, an instructor in the local flying school. He pressed me to visit him, though I had little expectation of doing so.

However, after my usual morning disappointment, and having been refused a movement order to spend the day in Blois, I wandered out to the Pont de Tours, sat in a park at the foot of a statue of Rabelais, played with some French children there, and finally, seeing some young flying men standing on the bridge, asked them how to get to the aerodrome. They were going that way themselves—indeed were waiting for a bus, and would I not go along; only about 7 kilometres on the Route Nationale to Paris.

Thus it happened; and I found Noyes, who is in charge of the Observation School in this the 2nd Am. Aviation Centre. We had lunch, made an inspection, looked at photographs, and about 4 p.m., weather conditions being perfect, he asked: "Would I care to go up?" Of course. So I am put in appropriate togs, a pilot named Taylor appears, and in a Sopworth Type I A2 with the ominous number 13 on its side we are off before there is time to reconsider.

We were up an hour and flew over the beautiful country down the right bank at an average height of 1100 metres—almost down to where the Vienne empties into the Loire—then across the river, with Chinon in the distance; over the Forêt de Chinon, Azay-le-Rideau, then directly over Tours and so back to the camp. It was what Taylor called a bit bumpy in spots, but on the whole much the gentlest and most comfortable form of transport imaginable, and I came down tingling as though I 'd had a glass of cham_pagne. One experiences no sense of height at all and practically none of leaving the ground. The only moment of what might be called surprise was when we began to spiral down over the camp; but Captain Taylor, I 'm glad to say, is not a stunting pilot.

Thursday, May 16th. Tours

While at headquarters as usual the first thing this a.m., McKernon turns up en route to Paris with a blanket movement-order covering all Consultants. Though I have officially received no such appointment, on the basis of this order Col. McCaw gives me permission to accompany McKernon; and to atone, I presume, for having kept me on the rack these past two weeks, he invites me to lunch with other regulars of the Medical Corps at a luxurious billet hung with tapestries and with an outlying garden.

Friday evening. Paris

To-day's open meetings were held in the Hotel Continental as were those of a month ago when I was too busy at Pernes to attend. Morning sessions given over to military orthopædics (Goldthwait and Osgood and two French Médecins Majors). At our committee meeting in the late p.m., Rose Bradford, T. R. Elliott, and Cummins represented the B.E.F. No report from the "wound closure" subcommittee which, alas, had never been called together owing to some mix-up between ourselves and the British. I urged that the policy of the organization be formulated, for it has never been set down and there has been a good deal of misunderstanding about it; then, too, the antivivisectionists have openly protested against the prostitution (*sic*) of Red Cross funds for animal experimentation under such "celebrated vivisectors" as Crile, Cannon, and myself.

Saturday, the 18th

The "medical aspects of aviation" in the morning with papers by Col. Birley and Major Flack of the R.F.C., and remarks by Barcroft on polycythæmia—all very interesting. At noon Cannon, Taylor, Elliott, and I had a confab, as a result of which I missed not only lunch but most of the afternoon session in an effort to draw up a statement of the original unwritten policy of our meetings, from which we seem to be slipping away.

Participants in the gas session of the afternoon were Cols.

Elliott, Herringham, Barcroft, and Meakins, representing the British; then a French Colonel and Col. Fries of our Engineer Corps in charge of the Gas Service. Col. Fries indiscreetly described our losses at Seicheprey—indiscreetly, at least, from the British point of view, for all matters relating to gas warfare are "confidential" with the B.E.F. Barcroft, who I believe is a Quaker, appeared comfortably in civies; and though he may be a conscientious objector, he certainly, as contributor to the chemistry of gas warfare, is in a position to concoct more devilish ways of killing Boches than if he were actually in service.

There are, in Elliott's opinion, good reasons for military secrecy regarding gas. For example, the enemy sends over his gas in shells marked with a yellow (mustard gas), blue (the arsenical compounds), or green (phosgene) cross, as told by the investigation of duds. The British learned that after shelling with mustard gas the enemy never attacked for a few days because the gas lingers and his own troops would consequently suffer. Hence after a bombardment of yellow-cross shells the British used to move out their holding troops and substitute reserves in small numbers.

Now, mustard gas takes a day or two before showing its effects, and the Boche one day sent over a lot of yellow-cross shells which contained merely a fleeting lachrymatory gas. They gave the British time to move out their troops and then, attacking in force, gained all their objectives. Furthermore, the French perfected a new and supposedly deadly cyanide gas, which after expensive and elaborate study was put into use. They employed it for about a year, and the British also used it extensively; but they never received any information as to its effectiveness and finally gave it up altogether. So much for the value of secrecy.

A late Committee meeting held for the first time in the new library room of the Red Cross, where to my great relief Col. Ireland breaks it gently to me in a corner that the censorship matter will be dropped.

May 19th. Whitsunday

To Boulogne by motor with Col. Elliott, Meakins, and a Major Best, a regular in the R.A.M.C. long in Nigeria on the west coast of Africa. A hot cloudless summer day and we basked in the sun as we sped along over the same route I took with Alan Muhr in April 1915.

2 p.m. A stop in Beauvais for lunch and afterward a look at the gigantic but unfinished cathedral. The amazing height of the graceful arches in the choir is indescribable. This choir, together with the nave of Amiens, the portal of Reims, and the towers of Chartres, would have made the architectural marvel of all ages. Beauvais, being now the G.Q.G. of Foch, is likely to be bombarded. Consequently the tapestries are down and the glass is being removed from the windows where much of it has been untouched for 600 years.

11 p.m. Boulogne seems like home, though at the moment we are being bombed—the moon is bright and flying conditions perfect.

Neurosurgical Organization in England
Monday, May 20. Boulogne

A long-sustained raid here last night; and bad as it was, Étaples got it worse. In that area they tried repeatedly to get the single bridge over the Canche, which would have shut us off from the south. Meanwhile the neighboring hospitals, particularly No. 1 Canadian, suffered greatly, and it is rumored that the raiders swept the place with machine guns after dropping their bombs. Kipling says that mankind can be divided into two classes—human beings and Germans.

10 p.m. London. My being here is the result of a conversation this morning with the D.D.M.S. of Boulogne, who, with the understanding that certain American divisions are to come into the British area, favors unifying the neurosurgical service for the combined front. He will take the matter up with the D.G. and an answer should be forthcoming by the end of the week. The idea would be that the proposal made by General Sloggett last November to the Chief Surgeon of the A.E.F., but refused by the latter, be reopened, and that No. 13 General serve as a training ground for men capable of undertaking neurosurgical work not only for the British, but for the American Army as well.

While awaiting a decision, he suggested that I familiarize myself with the disposition and condition of the cranio-cerebral cases here in Blighty. It would give me time for a twice-postponed visit to Ireland—just now in a turmoil with the arrest, by order of Lord French, of about 100 Sinn Feiners.

I crossed with Meakins and Barcroft, feeling particularly safe, as Sir Eric Geddes was aboard—burly, thick-necked, smooth-shaven. He looks as though he were accustomed to having his own way and the devil take those who oppose. Doubtless the Admiralty needs a person of this particular type to-day.

Tuesday, May 21st. London

With Sargent and Buzzard to the Tooting Hill Hospital, getting a lead on the neurological cases there. Dinner with Henry Head, to meet Riddoch, who is at the Empire Hospital, and Fearnsides, who is at the shell-shock hospital on Golder's Green Road. Apparently the Neurological Home Service is all at cross-purposes with patients scattered at Tooting, King George's, Queen Square, Maida Vale, the London, and 200 incurables at the Star and Garter, Richmond; also officers in small batches at the Empire, Roehampton, Brighton, and elsewhere. I am to see General Goodwin and put the project of organization and unification before him.

Wednesday, May 22

The morning at the Empire seeing wounded officers with Riddoch—among them Capt. Hyam of No. 46 recollection. The spinal-cord transections, some 40 of them, are doubtless getting better care than would be possible anywhere else. Then at a penny lunch counter some cold tongue and ham on a meal ticket, the waitress putting a spoonful of brown sugar in my coffee when no one was looking.

This prior to a conference with Col. Delaney and General Goodwin at Adastral House, on their plans for looking after our wounded here in England. Tea with Capt. Trotter, and more ideas from him of neurological work, followed by an hour in the library of the Royal College of Medicine. Dinner with several neurologists and neurosurgeons, among whom there was little agreement about heads, spines, and peripheral nerves—except that there is an immense lot of work to be done on the incompletely treated cases which gravitate over here from France.

London is muggy and depressing—the streets full of cripples —people very tired of the war. They universally voice the feeling that all would shortly have been over if America had not come in when she did. Let us hope it may not have been too late. The expected third phase of the great German offensive gets put off from day to day.

Thursday, May 23rd

With Buzzard this a.m. to see poor "Micky" Bell-Irving at Lady Ridley's Officers' Hospital, 10 Carlton House Terrace. He only vaguely recalled me—suffering the tortures of hell from neuromata in the stump of his amputated leg which he sat nursing while propped up in bed. Still the same charming person, however, despite his thoroughly drugged condition. He was up in a scout machine—stunting. Had been looping and rolling when one wing gave way at 5000 feet—so said his flight commander, who had been watching him. Now a suffering wreck—death would have been less bad.

The only apparent food shortage in London—at least the only things one has difficulty in getting—is butter and sugar. Two little pats of a crumbly sort of fat are given with coffee and a roll at St. James's for breakfast, but no sugar. Still, at our Commissary Stores I subsequently bought for a few pennies two pounds of granulated sugar, which was presented to me in a yellow pasteboard box once occupied by Fatima cigarettes. I knew not what to do with this, so presented it to Susan Chapin to hand on to Lady O. for preserves. There is apparently no scarcity of anything if one knows how to find it and what to do with it when it's procured. I might except taxicabs. People therefore eat less and walk more. Their minds are probably the clearer.

Perhaps the most noticeable thing in London is the stripping off of the traditional British reserve. I presume that a dozen times people stopped me on the street or in the tube to ask if they could do anything for me—often going to unnecessary trouble to give me directions or explain situations. This is quite a different England.

DUBLIN IN WAR TIME

Friday the 24th

London to Dublin via Rugby, Holyhead, Kingstown. Very pleasant journey—two amiable Irish officers in the Regular Army, an Artillery Major wearing an M.C. ribbon, and a Lt. Col. of the Inniskilling Fusiliers bore me company. I learned from them something of Sinn Fein and the present situation in this inscrutable and incomprehensible country which the Irish, if possible, seem to understand even less well than anyone else.

French had been Viceroy only six days when he arrested and deported to England the Sinn Feiners' chief leaders—men and women—many of them implicated in the 1916 affair but liberated only to begin their nefarious plots anew. Parliament stopped short, as it usually does, and failed to reach the bottom of the matter—*viz.*, the priests, who have openly opposed Lloyd George's conscription legislation. So the situation hangs in the balance and the government has not yet even made public their justification of these arrests—far from having had the courage to arrest the priests. Recruiting is at a standstill. The Irish will follow a leader if he can be found, but they won't be driven.

Saturday, May 25th. Dublin

Breakfast again just as 10 years ago with the Royal Zoölogical Society in Phœnix Park—some 30 people who partook of their porridge standing and of salmon and eggs—yesterday's (the dates were on them)—and coffee and marmalade sitting. No shortage of food nor food restrictions in Ireland. I sat between the Pres. of the Soc., Sir Fredk. Moore, and the D.D.M.S., Dublin, Major Gen. Sir Jas. Maher, who was in charge of the L. of C. in the Gallipoli campaign. His stories of the conditions at Lemnos are about on a par with the printed tales concerning that ill-fated campaign—automobiles sent out instead of steam launches—plenty of stores in the holds of the ships, but no way to land them or any place to put them when once landed—much less any way to sort out ammunition from surgical supplies.

Luncheon at Friendly Brother House, an intimate club where people call each other by their Christian names, prefixed by "Friendly." The president is always "Sir John Friendly" and there are "Perfect" Brothers, and others less so, I presume. I asked if it had anything to do with Masonry, which it has n't, though Masonry is widespread in Ireland, my host being a 30th degree Mason—at two degrees more he should melt. I don't mean to imply by this that there is a chill about him—far from it, as he is very warmly Irish.

11 p.m. The Royal College of Surgeons in Ireland occupies a fine old Georgian building facing St. Stephen's Green. To-day it was flying an American flag, though I did not dare imagine why. It was there on that Easter Monday, 1916, that the Sinn Feiners, after first barricading themselves on the opposite green, broke in and held off the troops for a week. There are many marks of bullets in the woodwork and the canvas of the large painting of Victoria which hung in the front room was torn out of the frame and the portrait destroyed. The frame is still empty. Otherwise there is no evidence of the fighting and barricading which took place, though everything was in most disreputable shape when the rebels finally gave themselves up after a good many were killed—for the place was raked from the Shelbourne Hotel and other buildings in the neighborhood. They had made a mortuary chapel out of the dissecting room. So much for a half-baked rebellion under the Republican Army of Ireland, which chose as its fortress and chief scene of operations the one place in Dublin which boasts that neither politics nor religion concerns its affairs.

The ceremony in the afternoon was most elaborate, and amusingly disproportionate to the occasion—*viz.*, me. There was a guard of honor drawn up in the lower hall—the students' O.T.C., which I had to inspect. Then tea in the council room for the elect, and Viscount French appears with his Staff—very fine. He reminded me of a small edition of a much-decorated Leonard Wood.

Then they proceeded to the Hall above, and after the audience had been admitted, the President and the Viceroy, the Lord Chancellor, the Council, and the rest filed in while a military band did "God Save the King," and expecting me to follow immediately they quickly shifted to "The Star-Spangled Banner." I was put in a robe with blue stripes, surrounded by four proctors, male and female—it's a co-educational school—and some hitch occurred, for old Sir Chas. Cameron forgot that he was to escort me.

As he did n't appear we walked in rather belated—applause— and I sank alongside of the Field Marshal, Lord Lieutenant, Viscount, and Viceroy rolled into one—sank, I say, into a large carved chair in which, as I was told later, Daniel O'Connell once died or did something equally foolish. As a matter of fact, I should have stood, but too late now.

Then they began tormenting me—the Vice President read slowly the names of former Honorary Fellows—66 I believe— Abernethy, Benjamin Brodie, Syme, Pott, Astley Cooper, John Hunter, Lister, Huxley, Jonathan Hutchinson, Paget, Helmholtz, John Billings (this made me feel a little more at home), Robert Jones, Moynihan, Keogh, Sir Almroth Wright—perfectly at home. They then told other things about the College and finally, coming to me, read dates out of an ancient *Who's Who*, about someone I vaguely recognized as having met.

Then I arose and stood back to the audience before a large and threatening mace, while the President, between me and a background of intertwined American and Irish flags, uttered other things about painting the lily and such sentiments. Finally I was permitted to sit again in the lap of Daniel O'Connell's chair and wished I too might also die there—but no, I had to sign the roll—a slippery parchment containing signatures if anything less legible than mine—then was given a green box with a diploma, a book in green vellum containing the roll of honor of the College in this war, and Lord French was given a duplicate of it, which he will doubtless prize.

Then, horrors! I was given the opportunity of making a public acceptance!! It was pretty bad, but they cheered me along and I got through somehow with a kind of after-dinner-speech effect. Lord French was given a similar opportunity which he did not accept, but contented himself with shaking hands with me and indicating that it was high time to go.

So we filed out again with the help of the band and went down and had more tea—the elect, that is—his Lordship, Mr. Schott, M.P., "Chief Sec. to the Lord Lieutenant in Ireland," and his wife, who was very nice, Mr. Walter Long, who is in the Cabinet as Sec. to the Colonies, though he does n't look it, the Earl of Belmore, the Lord Chancellor, Sir Ignatius O'Brien, Sir Charles Cameron, and others both medical and lay. Meanwhile the students tea'd in the Library, where I should greatly have preferred to be.

Sunday, 26th May. Dublin

The morning paper says that with my most "pronounced American accent," I addressed the gathering, etc. . . .

At Taylor's dinner last night I sat by a delightful person dressed in clerical purple—the Most Rev. Dr. Bernard, Archbishop of Dublin. Something happened to be said about Dean Swift's friend Richard Helsham, who appears in the *Journal to Stella,* and His Grace suggested that before he got tied up with his Sunday duties he would like to show me around St. Patrick's.

So with him there at 10 a.m. and a most fascinating hour alone together. Snakes or no snakes, St. Patrick seems to have really existed, and near the site of the present building he had a well, marked by a stone on which was a Celtic cross dating from the ninth or tenth century. This was recently dug up and reposes on view among other relics. Along about 1191 a church appears; but it was in a bad place, for this well of St. Patrick's, being near the Poddle River, had a way of overflowing. So St. Patrick's Church and Cathedral in the succeeding ages acquired a habit of falling in in spots. . . .

The Archbishop loves the old place and when Dean became steeped in its lore. There was much to see in a short time. The huge monument to Richard Boyle of black marble and alabaster, with R.B. himself, Earl of Cork, in an upper berth, while some generations, down to an infant, the great Robert, kneel and pray below; the interesting old brasses; the tombs with amusing inscriptions like that of Dame Mary Sent Leger, who, after disposing of four husbands, died in childbed at 37 years of age, and "whose soule (noe doubt) resteth in all joyfull blessedness in ye heavens." His Grace dotes on the subtlety of the "noe doubt."

But chiefly of Swift—the black slabs he had put up, some with most sarcastic Latin inscriptions like that containing the dig at the Duke of Schomberg's family—and the wonderful bust of the great, though finally crazy, Dean, with his prominent eyes and amiable mouth—but a fine head it is! And in the nave below is the plain brass plate marking the spot of his burial, and beside it another for the mysterious Stella. . . .

This afternoon Taylor took me to the old Meath Hospital with its memories of Dease, Crampton, Whitley Stokes, Graves, Richard Helsham, Porter, Colles—and more I scarce remember. At the entrance I was accosted by a woman—a lady in much disrepair with a black eye who wanted to know, between hiccoughs, if I could get her boy back to her from the hospital in Scotland where he had been for the past two years missing one leg. This illicit pot-still whiskey must be the very devil—the three great industries of Ireland seem to be poteen, politics, and the priest-hood—and poverty is the inevitable consequence.

Monday, May 27. London, Charing Cross Hotel

A pleasant and uneventful crossing last night on the *Leinster* with Sir Arthur Chance. Civilians and military now carefully separated as has not heretofore been the custom. Indeed to-day some 450 aliens—Germans and Austrians—who have been interned in County Meath were deported from the Liffey by special steamer, while the large crowd of onlookers cheered, waved green flags, and sang Sinn Fein songs. Queer business!

I gather that there are many Irish boys in the small towns who would welcome conscription if only the government would insist with a firm hand and not shilly-shally about it. Independently to enlist practically means ostracism from their communities, in which the priests have such a strong hold; so they would be glad to be freed from the responsibility of making a decision themselves.

To all of this the government unconsciously gives aid, for to Maynooth College, where the priests are given such education as Rome permits, the government actually gives financial support. The supply of priests never fails, as every family aspires to have one of its sons take orders. Potatoes may have a bad year, but the crop of priests never. Meanwhile the population of Ireland has dwindled enormously—the most likable, hospitable, generous, and nimble-minded people in the world.

. . . . .

To-day's paper announces that Lieut. General Sir Arthur Slog-gett, K.C.B., etc., having reached the age limit of service on the active list, is being retired from his position as overseas D.G. and will be immediately succeeded by Major General Burtchaell. With this, the project of a neurosurgical training ground at No. 13 General probably goes up in smoke.

VIII

THE GERMAN OFFENSIVE CONTINUES

THIRD PHASE: THE SECOND MARNE

May 28. No. 13 General, Boulogne

WHAT appears to be another phase of Germany's determined effort opened yesterday on a 40-mile front between Soissons and Reims. An army group under the Crown Prince broke through at Craonne, took the Chemin des Dames ridge at the first rush, reached the Aisne by midday, and by midnight got across the river in masses. We must take our hats off to them—it was absolutely unsuspected—not even known that they had brought up tanks in that area.

Also yesterday our 1st Division, which had gone into the line of the Montdidier salient on April 26th, captured Cantigny in a brilliant local action which for the first time has demonstrated the fighting qualities of our troops.

May 29th. Boulogne

With Wright in the afternoon to hear his talk at St. John's Hospital in Étaples on "wound infection"—a further elaboration of this, his familiar, theme. Wonderfully well presented, but it aroused much opposition and criticism. . . .

Étaples has had a bad hit—much worse than we had supposed. On the night of our last Boulogne raid ten days ago, No. 1 Canadian General lost half their personnel with 158 casualties, 59 of them fatal, including 1 officer and 3 sisters, in addition to 8 patients. There was apparently no warning. The officers were playing cards in the mess when the first bomb dropped about 100 yards away. The next landed in the men's quarters and started a fire—possibly an incendiary bomb. Then for two hours the raiders kept it up, returning again and again like moths around a flame.

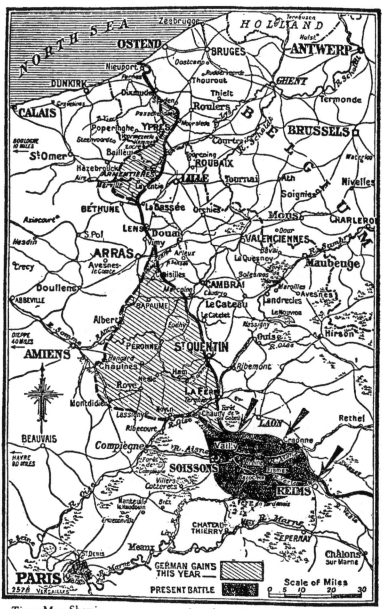

Times Map Showing the German Gains Since March 21st and the Status of the Present Third Phase on Friday, May 31st, with the Great Tardenois Bulge (in Black) Still Incomplete

Twenty-two bombs, large and small, were dropped in the Ca_nadians' compound, and about 160 in the neighborhood.

They were doubtless after the railroad and perhaps the bridge half a mile below. In this area the Camiers–Étaples road separates the hospital wards from the quarters for nurses, officers, and men, which for the most part are placed on the sand dunes between the road and the railway. . . .

There were many close calls. Col. Trimble, the jolly Irish C.O. of St. John's, had his clothes punctured by a bomb which fell close to him, and some of his people received slight wounds; but the Canadians were badly hit—two hours' lying on the ground with torpedoes falling and bursting about, followed by an effort to succor the wounded and collect the dead in one's camp, is nerve-racking to say the least. It 's bad enough to have a single raider cross over once and have it all over in a moment—but this was quite different. . . . They will all certainly be dug in after this. The Canadian Engineers have sent a tunneling company down to prepare shelters—meanwhile the nurses and orderlies are sleeping in the open on the back hills.

May 31st, Boulogne. Corpus Christi Day

Good weather continues. A raider—perhaps more than one— came over last night—dropped a bomb just in front of here on the edge of the sea, another (a dud) in the aerodrome just across from the hospital, and several others in the town. They also reappeared in Étaples and got one arch of the bridge over the Canche River, holding up traffic thereby for seven hours. This time the town was badly hit and many civilians suffered, but the hospitals escaped.

11 p.m. Our usual Friday medical meeting this afternoon— Fitz presiding, and very well. An *alerte* has just been sounded and raiders will soon be over. There has been heavy bombing and the sky is lit up, apparently in the direction of Étaples.

. . . . . .

This new German thrust which opened the day I got back is too far away to affect us and we 've had no wounded. The attack, however, appears to be in force, and if anything on a larger scale than those of March 21st and April 5th. The Chemin des Dames seems curiously remote—like Salonika or Mesopotamia. Four

British divisions—the 8th, 21st, 25th, and 50th—had been moved down to that supposedly quiet region for a rest, and the line must have been rather thin. The Hun, "employing an incredible number of tanks," came through with a wallop to a depth now, on the third day, of 20 miles on a 30-mile front. Soissons has fallen to the Brandenburgers, Reims is seriously threatened, and the Paris-Nancy line connecting our army nucleus with Paris lies scarcely more than seven miles farther on.

The Germans claim large amounts of booty and 35,000 prisoners—probably no exaggeration. The 50th Division, worn down by fighting first on the Somme and then on the Lys, made a gallant stand on the Craonne plateau, but were practically wiped out. The attack during the first day on the British front, between Locre and Voormezeele, was evidently only a diversion. It, however, gave an opportunity for the first long American *communiqué*. Our new divisions apparently did well.

Meanwhile another hospital bombed. At 1 a.m. on the night of the 30th, No. 3 Canadian Stationary at Doullens, halfway between Arras and Amiens, got a direct hit—absolutely in the centre of a red cross painted on the roof. A four-story building, the bomb went through to the ground floor, where one team was still at work operating on an officer; the three other teams were at supper. Lieut. Sage, an American M.O., was giving ether and there was practically nothing to be found of the team. The building caught fire and there was great loss of life—three sisters killed and two M.O.'s. The place stood on the citadel a mile from the railroad.

Saturday, June 1st. Boulogne

A send-off to General Sloggett—the most elaborate any retiring general has seen. Even French, when recalled, had nothing like it. It betrayed a very genuine affection for Sir Arthur. A guard of honor—some Americans, Canadians, Australians from Powell's place, and R.A.M.C. people of this base. Many officers: "Tiger Mac," who himself is to go in three days; Black, who crossed with the General; Burtchaell, his successor; all the C.O.'s of the Boulogne Base Hospitals; the Base Commandant; the D.D.M.S.; General Carr; the Red Cross people; the Consultants; and others I 've forgotten.

He did it very well; reviewed the guard; a pleasant word for everyone; kept his poise and dignity like the old soldier he is; went aboard, got on the bridge, and stood at salute as the packet pulled out, while a band played some lugubrious tune. It was quite moving. They hardly waited for him to get home to gazette him: his name was on the list in to-day's paper.

In the p.m. with Major Langridge to Étaples, for news had spread that St. John's and other hospitals there were again seriously hit last night, with much damage and many casualties. As we approached the hospital area we passed a burial party escorting the bodies of four sisters to add to the ever-widening forest of crosses. And then the hospitals! It was appalling—our first sight of St. John's, where we had so comfortably gathered two days before. The row of huts on the Camiers end were collapsed and splintered like so many card houses, with beds and blankets and ward furniture and letters home and torn books scattered broadcast. The X-ray plant, the laboratory, the chemist's shop, all demolished, and a smell of drugs in the air. The wrecking parties still at work, though bodies could hardly have been overlooked; still, they had had no time for a roll call. Col. Trimble worn out and in bed; he deserves a V.C., having called for volunteers to help extinguish a fire in one of the wards while bombs were falling on every side. The hospital entirely evacuated to Camiers; the few M.O.'s and orderlies that we saw obviously had quite shattered nerves. The northern side of the compound had suffered most; but the hospital as a hospital was ruined and topsy-turvy— a nightmare of a place!

The raiders came as before about 10.30, in squadrons from the north. There was no moon, but at the outset they dropped a blinding magnesium flare which lit up the country like day for miles around, and then the bombs—showers of them. And this kept up for two mortal hours. They could hardly have failed to know where they were. No damage of military significance was done, or could have been done, except the confusion of the area.

This may be their intent. If it is, and they come again to-night, the demoralization will certainly be complete. The time before, everyone thought they were after the railroad and excused them; the second time the bridge across the Canche a mile or so further on; but this time what? It is certainly staggering in view of the British agreement—on the Pope's request for a one-day truce—not to bomb German towns on Corpus Christi when the streets would be full of religious processions.

We went on to the Duchess of Westminster's hospital at Le Touquet, where they naturally had the wind up, though the place seems remote enough from danger. The wounded officers naturally don't much like this bombing business while in bed on their backs. I had to calm down one of our "casual" reserve corps M.O.'s, a young doctor from Pittsburgh who will in due course be taken home legless to his wife and three children.

Boulogne by day is like a summer resort: by night quite otherwise. As I came through the black town near midnight—apparently the only person stirring—I found the sidewalks near the *abris* strewn with the sleeping forms of women and children. So many of them on the broad walk by the fish market one had to go in the street to avoid tripping over them.

Sunday evening, June 2nd

No raiders last night, contrary to all prophecies. Another gorgeous day. Col. Webb-Johnson took me to Calais to see some spinal cases, and we made a day of it. To Audreselles, cutting across Cap Gris-Nez to Wissant—the villagers in their Sunday best; the villages decorated with gaudy bunting and flowers and the streets strewn with greens—the *Fête Dieu*, which, according to my *Histoire de France,* goes back to 1246 and was inaugurated in Liége.

But far more gorgeous were the hillsides with their rectangles of bright yellow mustard, others of brilliant scarlet—*luzerne,* I presume—and still others with a pinkish vetch, sewed in on the quilt of varied greens. The road bordered by a profusion of wild flowers, thrift and buttercups and the first of the red poppies, with other things I did not know. Across the bridge with its line of trenches dating back to 1915—then Sangatte, where stand the partly demolished brick buildings which some 15 years ago were erected by the company organized to tunnel under the English Channel—a project which was abandoned, alas!

There are three hospitals still in Calais. No. 35 (Col. Pinches, C.O.) lies in rather cramped quarters just behind the Casino.

This formerly was used as a ward for the more serious cases but, owing to the bombing of late, has been abandoned except for walkers. No. 30 has been on its present site for three years and they have made things grow on the sands—flowers as well as vegetables—even have a little rock garden and waterfall, fed by water carted by hand, I fear. The place was full of femurs very well cared for by Capt. Driver; and after Webb-Johnson had made his visit, Col. Pinches took us through the town for lunch at the Officers' Club, where were many Americans newly landed.

They are coming in here, I believe, at the rate of two to three thousand a day, and I saw men in hospital (sick) from our 30th, 47th, and 28th Divisions. Such a medley of people as occupy Calais by day—and, I may add, get largely underground at night—Americans, Belgians, French, British, Indians, Colonials, negroes, Chinese laborers—every uniform known to this front— except possibly that of the much-abused Portuguese—all out for a Sunday holiday.

·   ·   ·   ·   ·   ·

During the last six days the Boches have advanced 35 miles as the crow flies from the Chemin des Dames all the way to the Marne—phew! It must have been a near rout. This time at Château-Thierry, with Paris only 40 miles away. Should they get across the river they fortunately will not be as close as they were in 1914 when at Meaux.

Monday, June 3

We had a mild argument at the mess as to whether they purposely bombed hospitals, I having expressed the opinion that they did not. There being so many other things better worth hitting from a military standpoint, it would be a waste of expensive projectiles to drop them intentionally on hospitals. Nevertheless, while it seems most improbable, it is rumored that the whole Étaples district is to be moved—33,000 hospital beds in the area.

·   ·   ·   ·   ·   ·

The Boches by furious attacks are endeavoring to expand the west side of their huge salient, but it is said at a heavy price, for the French are now resisting stubbornly.

Tuesday, June 4

Leave from this base is reduced to one officer per day, but the consultants are taking advantage of it. Both T. R. Elliott and

Gordon Holmes going home to be married. A farewell dinner this evening to "Tiger" Macpherson, who follows his chief, the D.G., into retirement.

Friday, June 7th

This "third phase" seems to be slowing up. The German High Command claims 55,000 prisoners, including more than 1500 officers; and over 650 field guns and 2000 machine guns. The main effort slackened on the 5th, on which day, according to

Showing Counter-Attacks of June 7th against New German Salient by French W. of Soissons, Americans W. of Château-Thierry, and British S.W. of Rheims

the press, some American troops (2nd Division) made a mag-nificent counter-attack at Veuilly-la-Poterie, ten miles west by north at Château-Thierry. A German cruiser-submarine has ap-peared off New York!

MARKING TIME IN BOULOGNE

Saturday, June 8th. The Casino

Americans are suddenly growing numerous hereabouts and don't know what to do with themselves—nor the British with them. They are being given new Enfield rifles so they can use the ammunition of the B.E.F., and the storehouses at Calais are said to be filled with the excess luggage which their heavy packs contain.

There is a young fellow here—from the 59th Inf., a new-comer and already with a ball through his elbow, which picked out his radial nerve in its passage. He was one of a circle squat-ting on the ground near Calais while a British corporal demon-strated the workings of a Lewis gun. He incidentally succeeded in wounding several of the group.

Capt. Kelly of No. 30 General at Calais has brought down for operation the young American soldier with a presumptive brain tumor whom I saw the other day in consultation. Kelly has lived on the desert sands of Calais for a year or more without much change or, of late, much sleep. I loaned him a pair of shoes to replace his heavy rubber-soled boots, and took him to our Recrea-tion Hut, where he passed the evening, as did others, at a dance given for our nurses.

During the afternoon a Lt. Col. of the 80th Division, with a Major of the same, freshly arrived in France and spending the night in the Officers' Club, dropped in and asked to be shown the kitchen arrangements. "Certainly": and Sgt. Edwards escorts them while I continue to look after Capt. Kelly. A half hour later I encounter them again, Edwards much crestfallen. From the Lt. Col.: "The kitchen and all about it a disgrace to the American Army—very glad he saw it—important for him to know what kind of place the wounded from his Division would be brought to—once they get into the line and begin to break through —as they certainly will, for "they have the right punch." In re-

joinder—I was not the C.O., and had no recollection of ever having seen the kitchen. Thereupon he takes me by the arm and
shows it to me—in all its disgrace. It looked very good to me;
but I apologized for it, nevertheless, and admitted we probably
had grown very dilatory during the past 12 months—indeed
walked down to the club with him, where he was left fairly burning up with his importance.

Just now a Court of Investigation is being held here in our
rooms—military and civilians. A Portuguese stabbed an Australian
some time ago in the lower town and then licked it up the hill
with the world and its wife after him. They must have caught
him; and the present court is trying to decide, I presume, why
the Australian, who is a patient here, did not kill him outright.
Recently a street fight occurred in which several were taking a
hand when the A.P.M. appeared and was about to make arrests.
At this juncture a British Marine, who happened by with itching
knuckles, knocked down the A.P.M., then the Portuguese, as
well as his assailant, and vanished in the crowd.

This afternoon the Boulogne Medical Society met in the Consultants' Hut at No. 14 Stationary. McCormick dilated on scabies
and impetigo to make one itch—40 per cent of all losses from
sickness are due to these causes. Subsequently a number of us
dined at 32 Stationary—their regular mess night. Sir Bertrand
Dawson, Fullerton, Lister, and a number of others. Among them
the naval officer who is in charge of the anti-submarine activity
along this coast. He seems to think they are making headway—
six done for in the past week. The whole Channel is marked out
in squares—and when a "sub" is located in one of them a deep
mine is set off and that's the end.

A long powwow after dinner on the after-the-war problems of
medicine, and the urgent need of formulating plans to meet the
new situation which will doubtless arise. All agree that State
Medicine will come to play an increasingly important rôle and
the profession must anticipate legislation by formulating it themselves rather than having this done by politicians and lawyers.

Sir Bertrand is an interesting person with a lively mind. I
remember his saying that the two great disappointments of the
war were not medicine, but the Church of England and the Bur-

berry raincoat. He would be the last, however, to belittle what
"Tubby" Clayton—almost single-handed—at "Toc H" in Poperinghe had been doing for both British officers and men since
December 1915. For those who lived in continuous danger,
squalor, and misery, Talbot House ("Every man's club") opened
its door in a welcome spirit of laughter and prayer. To this the
10,000 and more, who meanwhile had gone with him to the upper
room, could testify. Clayton kept the house open in "Pop" from
December 1915 until only a few days ago. He was about the last
to leave—and then only on compulsion from H.Q.

Sunday, June 9th

This morning a cranial operation with Gil, for the benefit of
Capt. Kelly, who has managed to prolong his stay. A highly
nervous Jock with a 48-hour temporal penetration, very septic,
with a gassy abscess in the temporal lobe. It was not only *necessary* for the Scot, who abused us roundly during the process of
shaving, but was *good* for Kelly, who has been brought up in the
school advocating delay in cranial wounds.

Lunch with Michael Foster at No. 55 out beyond Wimereux,
and afterwards a walk with him and Captain Fletcher over the
sand dunes on a showery afternoon. Most charming companions
of the cult naturalist. They delighted in everything, from the
patches of pink sheep sorrel and cotton grass on the neglected golf
links beyond 32 Stationary, to the suckers on the feet of the tiny
green frogs which abounded in the rank growth underfoot.

Fascinating, this rolling seaside country with its mixture of
sand dunes and swamps and scraggy patches of trees—alders,
haws, scrub elms, and poplars, with an abundance of fragrant
elder just coming into flower.

Their particular objective was to see the nest of a water rail in
the long grass at the edge of one of the swamps—a nest they had
been watching; and to-day the last egg was found hatched and the
nest empty but for some broken bits of shell. The marshy places
are still showy with yellow flag, though its glory is past, marsh
marigold, which also is nearly over, and clusters of ragged robin,
of bog bean, and of purple orchids—which they don't bother to
pick, together Fletcher gathers samples of most everything else to
botanize with when off duty.

Countless flowers there were—pink and yellow rattle, speed-well, bittersweet, four or five kinds of forget-me-nots, comfrey, dog's tongue and the water variety, stitchwort, spearwort, violets in masses, and other things low on the ground, stonecrop or golden moss, beds of bluish-green dead nettle or bugle, an occasional wee scarlet pimpernel, patches of horseshoe or bird's-foot trefoil —"eggs and bacon" and "fingers and thumbs," according to Foster—herb Robert, festoons of bryony.

A cuckoo was announcing the hour (every few minutes) with a full June voice, and in one of the thickets a pair of nightingales —old friends of my companions—were merrily practising. Scattered everywhere between the swampy and grassy places, which had their individualities, and the actual thickets, which likewise had theirs, were the rolling dunes with their coarse grass and low privet, osier willows and grayish-green sea buckthorn—a wonderful place for a water colorist.

Finally a person of the French forester variety with a shotgun over his shoulder and a dog at his heels came up and announced that we were trespassing on a preserve; but seeing Fletcher's handful, he bade us follow him and, opening out a path through a thicket, he showed us some low bushes with three kinds of wild roses just coming into bloom, from which he picked branches to present to us before bowing us on our way. We came back across the links in a shower—soaking wet and did n't care. We 'd been far from the war and there was hot tea to welcome us.

Monday, June 10. Boulogne

No. 13 General is fast filling up with Americans who bear no relation to the present or any other battle—a mixed bag of "sick," some 250 in number—hammer-toes, hallux valgus, hemorrhoids, hernias, varicoceles, backaches—and, worse, tuberculous pleurisies, chronic heart disease, and the like. Very inefficient medical examinations at home this would seem to indicate. It 's difficult to know where to send them until American bases in England are opened—if there ever are to be any. I gather that there are about as many of our troops over now as we can digest, particularly if they have to be chewed over in this way before they are fit even to undergo training.

I saw a young chap this morning whose weight on enlistment

was 108 pounds; he now weighs about 90 pounds, and his pack
with rifle, ammunition, and all else weighs more than he does.
Another feeble soul—before his khaki days a few weeks ago—
was a combination of an Armenian and an undertaker's assistant
on the N.Y. East Side. A young Swede, a chauffeur at home and

The Thrust toward Compiègne—the Abortive Fourth Phase, an Attempt
to Straighten the German Front from the Oise to the Marne

machine gunner out here, had a hysterical anæsthesia of almost the entire body—associated I thought with a moderate flat foot. Another in Arlie Bock's ward—of German-Jew parentage—a tailor —had a mitral stenosis, with the apex in his axilla. He has not been able to run or climb stairs for many years. A young medical officer thought something was wrong and called his major's attention to it, but they sent him along nevertheless. He 'll have to be boarded Class C. All these people were in the 77th Division.

·   ·   ·   ·   ·   ·

News reaches us that on Saturday the Boches opened up again over a front of 22 miles on the south of their great Somme salient between Montdidier and Noyon, making a drive toward Compiègne. Supposedly to straighten their front by forcing the French to withdraw from between the Oise and the Aisne. If this was to be a new major phase in the great offensive, it appears to have been checked.

11 p.m. An extraordinary and depressing spectacle! Like prehistoric cave dwellers packed in for the night, but in this instance only women and little children, for the cave man is elsewhere carrying a gun. Still chattering and jabbering at 10 o'clock as they squatted or curled up on the hard hummocky dirt floors—some eating their supper of bread and wine by the aid of a bit of *bougie* —others wriggling to find a place that was not too crowded; and not only the floor but the air was full of humanity.

The unexpected advent of George Crile to spend the night led me to think of the caves under the citadel where, as I had heard, the poor people of the *haute ville* take shelter these nights. The old thirteenth-century citadel with its high massive walls and round towers lies detached from the walled city proper, and must have once had a moat, but this is filled in, the area at the moment being used as a city market garden.

At one of the lower portals a friendly *gendarme* is found, with a flickering square of lantern, who will gladly escort us; so down through long passages opening out into wide chambers, and then more passages with scant headroom till, some 10 metres underground, we begin to hear the echoing murmur of countless voices like a thousand nurseries settling down for the night—the two main casemates *"pour ceux qui dormirent."* Women and children all over the floor, still awake most of them, and the tots on seeing us get off their few English words: "Good morning," "cigarette," "pennee," "yesno," as we step around and over them.

We made our way through for a look into the farther vaulted chamber at a still lower level, doubtless packed with the first-comers. And in the distant corner one dimly makes out by the yellow glare of the *gendarme's* raised lantern the black hole representing the entrance into the cell where Louis Napoleon is said to have been incarcerated. Then we are led through other passages and chambers, which become crowded with those who are merely transients during an actual raid, unlike the night lodgers—room probably for some thousands of them. To such extremes are the populace driven—underground like moles, into subterranean chambers built for a similar purpose six centuries ago—then as now the only safe ultimate refuge.

Crile much affected—so affected he gives pennies as long as they last to all the little beggars who in the late evening are still playing about outside—this very bad for their morals. We agree that we 'd rather have our families take the chance of a hit in their own beds than the certainty of illness from repeated nights spent in the vitiated atmosphere of *les caves de la citadelle.*

Tuesday, June 11

Without doubt Hepburn is the most interesting character in our Unit. I shall never forget his first appearance in my rooms at the Brigham a few days before we sailed—bursting with the desire to get abroad and into the "circus": this, I 'm quite sure, largely from eagerness to see his old pals again. Had it not been for Villaret—and our recruits to drill—I should not have had the least idea what to do with him. Erect, massive, with sufficient breadth of shoulders to disguise his height, bristling waxed moustachios, prominent red eyes, full of energy and sometimes of alcohol. Well, he 's all kinds of person, is "Hep."

He became automatically our Master Hospital Sergeant, knowing more about paper work and the mysteries of channels and ways of getting out from under—certainly more than anyone in our Army, and at least as much as the most beribboned and sophisticated of British sergeants. He can quote verbatim paragraphs and sections from the Service Manual, Field Regulations, and other

black books—particularly those paragraphs useful to you when
you want to pass the buck. At least, so I 'm told.

I remember, the day we landed in Falmouth, his coming down
the gangplank to the lighter, the last of all, so full of business,
so unmistakably different from any of the rest of our men, that
the British officer who met us and was standing by me asked who
he might be, adding that he looked like an old British soldier.
Hepburn, when summoned, approached, saluted, and got rigid.
Yes, he had been in British service 14 years. "How old are you
now?" This was evaded. "How old were you when you enlisted
in the States?" "The same age as when I enlisted in the British
Army, sir." And he might easily pass for his enrolled 40 instead
of his probable 55.

We got on the subject of punishments, at lunch to-day; he
knows not a little about them from personal experience. It was
in 1884, I believe, that he became "a bloomin' 'ermaphrodite,
soldier and sailor too"—in short went into the Marine Corps.
There he suffered many vicissitudes, working up to an N.C.O.'s
stripes time after time, and then being reduced to the ranks again
to the tune of various and diverse penalties. "Hep" can talk
eighteen to the dozen—like a *mitrailleuse* in action—and I cannot
begin to tell all that sputtered out of him when we got on the
subject again to-night after dinner—about the cat, passing the
shot, picking oakum, or working the pumps for imaginary
leaks.

He finally managed to get transferred to the Navy and worked
in the sick bay, meanwhile learning, among other things, the
multitudinous ways of simulating diseases, ophthalmological, intestinal, orthopædic—diseases which would justify having the
Captain put the old *Victory* into port with some critically ill patient
who would promptly recover. Just the right drops to simulate
infectious conjunctivitis; just how long friction on one's under-
shirt will raise the mercury in a thermometer to about 102° and
no higher; just how to simulate scabies by jabbing a stiff scrubbing
brush on the tender skin of the groins and between the fingers.

Once he "licked it"; made his way up to Edinburgh and tried
to enlist in the Black Watch under the name of Charles Edward
Stuart—which was going some. Said he was a sailor off a private

yacht, the *Norman*, in Portsmouth Harbor. They kept him on for a day, giving him his shilling in advance, and then confronted him with a telegram from the *Norman's* captain that no hands were missing; but he said he was a sailor nevertheless and wanted to join the Black Watch.

His shilling a day as a prospective recruit was not discontinued, so he was quite happy, spending it in the canteen, the officials meanwhile making efforts to identify him with others in Her Majesty's service who chanced to be "missing." For example —a musician from the North Lancs had taken Scotch leave and "Hep" was suspect for some time of being the person in question. He a musician! Ha, Ha! Ultimately they identified him and he was sent back to Portsmouth under a guard of two. He finally reported for duty on the *Victory* with his handcuffs in his pocket and both guards speechless from certain fluids, for which "Hep" has a peculiar tolerance.

One thing you evidently had to learn in the old army was to decide quickly what religion you professed—whether a Catholic or "one of the fancy religions," Church of England, Wesleyan, or the like. It often made a great difference in the amount of oakum you had to pick in the hours of rest that followed the more severe periods of enforced activity. In the Marine Corps one was always tipped off to give a "fancy" religion, for Catholics had only one service a week, whereas the others had a daily service, and if you said "Catholic" you had to pick oakum six days in the week while the other more canny prisoners religiously attended service.

"Hep" seems to have made the wrong guess in this direction at least once. It was when he met the chaplain—you always have to see a chaplain—the time he not only was reduced to the ranks but served 90 days in a naval jail for having stretched his one-day leave to twelve. This was after 3½ years on the west coast of Africa and London looked good to him! Well, his sailor collar and chevrons were cut off before the ship's company; he was given a thing like a muff for a cap, and looking as though sewn up in a bag was marched off to clink through Brighton and other public places where people thought he was at least a murderer—while he'd really only taken 12 days off.

When they got to the place of confinement they first cropped his hair and then brought him to the chaplain. He took a chance and said "Catholic" and the chaplain just said: "Take him away." He finally served his term, and found his old father, a poor man, waiting for him with two pounds to put in his pocket, with which untold wealth he rejoined his former ship's company.

In due course, after some years' further service, he got dis‾ missed—with a pension—as a victim of "Mediterranean fever and rheumatism"—on crutches in fact. They brought him home from Malta, where he had learned to simulate this particular malady, and put him ashore. While still in sight he hobbled down the street, turned a corner and stopped in at a convenient "pub," where he left his crutches. The next day he joined up with the Liverpool police. They thought it a rather quick recovery, but were glad to get him, since the other 49 applicants did n't look like much.

Then at the outbreak of the Boer War he joined the Gren‾ adiers and subsequently got transferred to the Irish Guards, with whom he became a "Top" Sergeant, I believe. After the war he stayed on in the Natal Mounted Police, among whom his nick‾ name was "big moustache," and a long time was passed—was it another three years?—in Zululand—at least there was one time when he went that long without seeing a white man or white woman or a glass of beer! There follows a period of obscurity before he is located in the Philippines in the Medical Corps of the U.S. Army and *par hasard* lands at the Brigham Hospital in the days of Villaret.

Needless to say "Hep" has numerous acquaintances, in various walks of life, in various parts of the world, who could easily identify him even without his service ribbons—Ashanti, South African (both King's and Queen's), Zulu, and he has several still earlier ones which he cannot wear, for they represent Egyptian and Indian campaigns and would make it appear—at 40—that he had entered the army almost before he was born. So he finds him‾ self very much at home here with the British Army, for there are plenty old 'uns still about. To judge from him, his old pals, who have survived, have all become higher officers—colonels at the least. But he seems satisfied to have become a Second Lieu‾

tenant in the Sanitary Corps, attached to Base Hospital No. 5, and to be eating at the Officers' Mess, though it is doubtless much less elaborate and certainly much less wet than the Sergeants' Mess he has recently left.

Wednesday, June 12th

(1) An ulnar nerve suture this morning on an original Mons man of the 3rd Division—a clean section of the nerve two inches above the wrist. For want of an operation he has been all this time in a labor battalion. (2) A sciatic nerve divided and two inches removed in a *"débridement* operation" by an enthusiastic M.O. at a C.C.S. If any are needed, these are arguments for the establishment of a Neurological Service.

·   ·   ·   ·   ·   ·

The enemy claims 10,000 prisoners as a result of the recent offensive which has brought them near Compiègne. The French have countered and seem to be holding. Secretary Baker announces that 700,000 soldiers have now been sent to France. A visit from the "deaf one" to-night.

Friday, June 14. Boulogne

An A.E.F. "special order" No. 158, Par. 90, issued under the date of June 7, has just reached our C.O. (Roger Lee) stating that I am relieved from further duty with Base Hospital No. 5 and will proceed to Neufchâteau for duty as Senior Consultant in Neurological Survery. This is a final blow to any plans for a fused Neurological Service for the Anglo-American armies. Everyone seems to approve of the idea, and if I can manage to get the ear of the new D.G. before leaving, there is a bare chance it may still be put through.

Sunday, June 16th. Boulogne

"We were stationed at Portsmouth—a very cliquy lot of regular army officers, and as it was a dull time we took to cricket—got up a good team and played the people around about. There was a young surgeon practising there named Conan Doyle, who played on the local team, and we did n't think much of him or them or anyone but ourselves.

"Well, we finally arranged for a series of matches for a week on the Channel Islands and, just as we were to leave, some of the officers were called away, and to fill a vacant place on the team we had to go outside, and as Doyle was a good cricketer he was chosen. But no one paid any attention to him—he was merely a supernumerary. We ate together, stayed together on the boat, and permitted him to shift for himself.

"The day of the first scheduled game it simply poured. We sat around all the morning in a very dismal hotel and by afternoon someone said let's have some music. There was an old piano and all the well-known songs of the crowd were dragged out of our coterie, the man Doyle sitting unnoticed with a book in a far part of the room. Finally, as the afternoon wore on, somebody with a little more feeling than the rest called out, 'Oh, I say, Doyle, do you sing?' Doyle gathered himself up—it was the first time anyone had addressed him—came over to us, and said he was sorry he didn't sing, but if we liked he would try and recite a piece. Anticipating the worst, we said 'go ahead,' and he recited a poem called 'Waterloo'—this was many years before he ever published it. Well, after a few minutes first one and then another of us began to sit up and take notice, and before he got to the end—it took nearly an hour—we were all hanging on his words. From that time we paid Doyle a little more attention, and he really became a member of our party."

This story was told by the D.D.M.S. at lunch to-day in their billet high up in the old town near the Calais Gate. Col. Thurston, Major Best, Capts. Ferguson, Brandt, and Farquhar. A farewell lunch for me and hopes expressed for my return, which is entirely up to the D.D.M.S., who has gone so far as to have all the head cases of the area transferred to No. 13 General—this after six months' waiting. The wheels of the army like those of the gods, etc.

11 p.m. Sad saying good-bye to the boys. . . . Sir Almroth came in later on and stayed till our *alerte* was sounded, so I walked down with him past the crowd in front of the fish market as far as his billet. People don't like being bombed, but it's not a mournful or depressed crowd, nevertheless. I saw one woman lift a baby in the air and call out—*"Mais la guerre, ce n'est pas toujours."*

A Transfer to the A.E.F.

June 17th, Monday. Paris

To Paris in our Frenchified Ford ambulance—our sole means of transportation this past year—with MacDonald driving, and through to our destination without incident, reaching the Porte St. Denis at 5.30. I chiefly remember the dust, a very hard seat, an attempt to memorize some French verbs—*effrayer, égarer, égayer,* etc.—fields full of red poppies, and the first crop of clover being harvested. We averaged about 50 km. an hour—quite good for the old bus, which has seen hard usage. When we finally struck the *pavé* of the broad avenue leading in through St. Denis, Mac-Donald said: "Gee! Reminds me of Columbus Avenue"—the highest compliment he could pay, I presume.

A fortunate encounter at the Continental with Finney, Peck, Keller, and Blake, with whom I have dinner. Evidently things have not gone well with the care of our wounded during the past ten days—almost as bad as in 1914, according to Blake. All from lack of mobility of our medical personnel. Juilly, like Blake's and Hutchinson's hospitals here in Paris, overcrowded and full of gas bacillus infections. But however this may be, the Marines in their small area have been giving the Boche a serious jolt this past week, and we are beginning to be looked upon as having an army which at least has fighting potentialities.

The truth of the matter is that during the retreat the French lost heavily in hospital equipment—30,000 beds, I believe, which was worse than the 5th Army's loss in C.C.S.'s during the first phase of this spring's offensive. Owing to this, more pressure came on our few units than they would otherwise have had. There is always a great howl about hospitals being captured, just why I do not know. Much fuss about a few iron beds and some equipment easily replaced; whereas a lot of planes crash, tanks and heavy guns get captured by the hundred, each of which cost about as much as a field hospital—and not a word.

June 18th, Tuesday

At the old Am. Ambulance, Neuilly, in the a.m., seeing nerve cases with Jim Hutchinson and lunch with him. Then to No. 3 Red Cross Military Hospital—Mrs. Whitelaw Reid's place for officers in the rue Chevreuse—to see Archie Roosevelt, whose musculo-spiral paralysis has been the object of discussion and disagreement.

June 19, Wednesday

The morning at No. 2 R.C.M.H. with Blake, Heitz-Boyer, and others; Patterson, now a Colonel, to lunch and full of his experiences with our people behind Château-Thierry. Enthusiastic about our troops, but equally abusive of French hospitals. The chief reason for our breakdown, however, was due to Lee's inability to secure sufficient teams for the work, his efforts in this direction having been blocked by the Divisional Surgeon. These things will get straightened out some day, but only when the Consultants are given more authority.

Price and I then went to see young Roosevelt—a bad end-result of Pool's successful primary operation with closure over a fractured humerus. These privately run hospitals for officers are a pest, and it looks as though we may, in this respect, fall into the same error as did the British.

Dinner with the Strongs—he just back from Dijon. Tales of his chauffeur—he's lucky to have one at all. He got out on a rainy night to read a signpost halfway to Paris from Dijon; the man drove off and left him in the middle of the road and did not miss him till he reached Paris. R.'s philosophy is, "It might have been worse." More serious was the time, returning from H.Q. at Chaumont, when the same man left the portfolio containing his completed manuscript of the trench-fever report on the running board of the car, after having turned up the back seat to get out some tools. It wasn't missed till they reached Paris at dawn. It's too long a story to tell here—the immediate retracing of their steps—rewards—giving it up—going back the next day, and finally stumbling on the very farmer who had picked up the portfolio. He nearly passed away when presented with 200 francs.

Sunday, June 23rd. Neufchâteau

11 p.m. Three days of getting oriented and accustomed to work in an office where people are falling over each other. Finney, Fisher, Peck, Blair, Greenwood, and McKernon in one room—most of them trying to use their own typewriting machines. In another Thayer, Salmon, Cohn, Dexter, and a few more. In a third I have been given a table with Goldthwait, Baer, Allison, and others. Young and his trio in a fourth. One telephone for all in the entry—visitors every few minutes—reports of new divisions arriving that have to be fitted out with teams and officers. Some confusion!

I have a vague recollection of orders permitting some of us to assume silver leaves—of an Army Order G.O. 88 which left many things, such as the relation of Divisional Consultant to Divisional Surgeon, most uncertain—of a visit from Col. Keller—of a long night's powwow in Finney's room—of a call last night from General Ireland, who is the real thing, and straightened matters out in a jiffy—of our good friend General Thompson of the 1st Army, B.E.F., who is being shown around by Col. Ashford, and a dinner for him at the Red Cross Club—of getting accustomed to U.S. Army paper work—of preparing for a lecture—of visiting with Terhune the two local hospitals (No. 66 and the Red Cross Civil Hospital near which our new offices are being built)—of seeing Heuer, Norris, John Gibbon, Col. Brackett, fresh from the U.S.A., and Gerald Webb—of saluting Sammies —of cows, cats, pigs, and a French feather bolster under which I shall now endeavor to insert myself.

June 25

With Salmon to lecture at Langres before Ashford's school— Salmon in the p.m., Baer in the a.m., I in the evening. "A superfluity of lectures causeth ischial bursitis"—however, the pupils were attentive and apparently interested. Following Salmon's afternoon talk—he has been dubbed by the irrepressible Yates the "nut picker"—he and I gathered up dear William Potter, who is still a lieutenant and has worked unceasingly at his job here since leaving us in Boulogne eight months ago. He's a patient soul—a veritable Job—and to complete the picture he has had a succession of boils on his neck for the past two months which give him the attitude of a robin listening for a worm.

He took us to many interesting old corners of the town in the best of which—an old thirteenth-century residence used as a prophylactic station, alas!—were some wonderful mural carvings. Then a walk around the walls with lovely views of distant country —even Mont Blanc to the s.e.—and so supper with Ashford, my talk, and the 70-kilometre ride home with Salmon by moonlight, meanwhile discussing the past of peoples and governments.

June 27th, midnight

Due in Paris at 8 p.m., we arrived an hour ago, supperless, and as an *alerte* sounded just as we were getting into the Métro—stopping all trains, and no taxis of course—we decided to hoof it to the Continental—a long way. By the time we reached the Place Vendôme things were getting pretty lively, but as Col. Bell had never witnessed a raid we stood on the corner of the rue Castiglione for some minutes watching the anti-aircraft guns and searchlights and then walked on down to the hotel. We had to pound on the big iron doors before the *concierge* would let us in, and just as he did so the whistle of a torpedo and bang! bang!!—two of them uncomfortably near.

An attentive hall boy has conducted me to the balcony overlooking the Tuileries and we have seen the whole show for the last half hour—Gothas—lights—shrapnel—the explosion and flame of an occasional bomb—a small fire—a pitch-black Paris—the moon low and behind a cloud, intensifying the darkness. I wonder why they did n't drop a magnesium flare, as at Étaples, to see what they were doing.

Friday, June 28. Paris

The two we heard last night, so near by, got the Place Vendôme and fell about 50 feet from where we had stood. Moral: Don't be too curious about an air raid. The place is a sight—practically every window blown in and the façades much pockmarked. This a.m. the holes in the pavement were already being filled in and the place was full of curiosity seekers whom the *gendarmes* had to keep moving along. A pile of plate-glass fragments, about 4 feet high and 15 feet square, was stacked up near the Column. This is the second raid they 've had on consecutive nights, and I may add that the sirens at this moment are racing through the streets announcing another for to-night. Paris, however, does n't seem to have the wind up.

The Research Committee meeting to-day began with "Chest Wounds." Major Lockwood of No. 36 C.C.S. on the surgical aspects—very good. Then Col. Soltau, admirable. Next Rose Bradford, talking as to a class of third-year medical students—not

much. Then two French papers—very unfortunate—Cannon first
called on Tuffier, who should have come last. T. read from a man‐
uscript in an English no one could understand. At the end of 20
minutes Cannon rapped, T. paying no attention. After three min‐
utes C. rapped again—no attention. Finally C. got up to speak to
T., who kept turning just the wrong way so Walter was unob‐
served, and he finally announced from behind T.'s back that the
Professor had exceeded his time but we hoped he would continue
and finish his paper. He did. But he forgot to show about 100
photographs and to exhibit a row of *blessés* who, covered with
medals, were sitting before us in the care of numerous *auxiliaires*.
Well, it was all very funny as one thinks of it now—and Tuffier is
so dignified and effective in his own language!

11 p.m. The Strongs'. Things are pretty lively outside—diffi‐
cult to tell bombs from anti-aircraft guns—evidently a good deal
of both in this neighborhood—all the family and maids have gone
to the cellar. Col. Lyle Cummins, who is here, and I both prefer
to take to our beds.

Saturday, the 29th

Research meeting continues. Neuropsychiatry programme under
Salmon's guidance—rather disappointing. Salmon himself suffer‐
ing from an aphonia which he explains is not hysterical. Foster
Kennedy—excellent! Gordon Holmes urges more neurology;
and in the afternoon we got it—three more papers by Frenchmen
whom no one could understand as they undertook to read in Eng‐
lish. Leri spoke and Babinski, and also Pierre Marie—nice old
man! Later a meeting of the Committee with tea for the sake of
the British, though afternoon tea is *défendu* nowadays in Paris.
Alec Lambert reads a version of our policy as he sees it, with much
insertion of Red Cross, and we then have prolonged and various
discussions till seven.

Sunday, June 30th

A gorgeous June day in Paris. One looks on the monuments and
vistas of this incomparable city, wondering if it is to be destroyed
—and when. This must be continually in the minds of all. The
morning spent with Dean Lewis at the American Ambulance, as I
still incline to call it, though it is now officially, I believe, U.S.

Red Cross and Military Hospital No. 1, looking at peripheral nerve records.

5 p.m. Col. Cummins and I have been wandering the streets of Paris all the afternoon with a feeling that it may possibly be for the last time. He knows the place intimately and is a charming companion. We have just come from visiting a friend of his, Edouard Estaunié, author of *Les Choses Voient, La Vie Secrète, Solitudes,* and other serious romances. We found him in Passy— his wife and children sent away for safety because of the bombard¯ ment—sitting at his desk, writing with a robe over his knees. "One has to work."

I would give much for a record of his conversation during the hour we sat there—sad beyond degree—the end of France and her great monuments—first Reims, then Amiens, now Soissons, and soon Paris. Better go out against the enemy and lose 40,000 men than to lose them in a retreat like the last. "The army at all costs must be preserved?" No. Look at the Belgian Army, but where is Belgium—the Serbian Army preserved, but where is Serbia? France will go down fighting and die in the last ditch—very fine for future times to point to as glorious, but what of France? *C'est effroyable. . . .*

It's impossible to describe how he said all this and with what fervor. We think he's wrong, of course, especially about the right never having triumphed in the history of the world—always the barbarian. Nineveh, Athens, Rome, Alexandria. It was a torrent, crystal clear. We venture to suggest that the Americans may yet do something to help France. He doubts it. It's almost too late— they've been here a year and what's to show for it?

.   .   .   .   .   .

When the next offensive will come off no one knows. It probably won't be long postponed. I gather that the epidemic of grippe which hit us rather hard in Flanders also hit the Boche worse, and this may have caused the delay. Then too perhaps the Austrian retreat, which became a near rout on the swollen Piave, may have had some influence. Meanwhile our people are piling in—48 divisions, I believe, at present—750,000 or more, but they've kept the secret well.

July 1st, Monday

With Strong to the old American Hospital of Paris, where the final stages of the trench-fever problem are being worked out. One has to go there and see the volunteer victims fully to realize what they have been through, some of them to-day on the peak of a 104° fever from having sedimented urine or louse fæces rubbed in or injected under their skin two to three weeks ago. College men several of them—I ran across two Yale graduates. They certainly deserve the meritorious conduct medal for which Strong has recommended them to an unwilling Congress—or possibly President. I learned for the first time to-day that when they volunteered for these experiments last January they all expected that the work would have to be carried out *actually* in the trenches— one reason they were eager to volunteer—the quickest way to get there.[1]

To the rue Chevreuse again, and then Gentile's—poor old man; most of his instrument makers have left him for work elsewhere giving higher wages, and preferably outside of Paris. The exodus indeed, caused by the Big Bertha and the approach of the Boche, has been over one million—about a quarter of the population. Then to the Red Cross Library; lunch at the new mess of No. 1 in Neuilly; a séance with the neurologists there and plans for future coöperation.

In the afternoon to Juilly with Jim Hutchinson—my first visit to the old Jesuit College where Mrs. Whitney started the adjunct to the Am. Ambulance, which did such good work before our entry into the war. They had a bad time during the recent offensive, having been commandeered by Col. Wadhams, who really saved the day by persuading Hutchinson to send up his ambulance cars without authorization of the Paris office, by getting two evacuation hospitals set up, one at Juilly and the other at Coulommiers, and by starting to move up medical supplies.

Well, that's an old story now, as is the fact that the reserve officers Lee had asked for got there too late to be of real service. Hall, my old classmate, now has Evac'n Hospital No. 8 set up in the grounds, and it's difficult to know whether he, a regular Lt.

---

[1] Later on, when they were taken to Dijon, these brave lads were treated like lepers— shunned and avoided. "Dirty fellows—they've had a louse disease, better not go near 'em."

Colonel, or Charles Mixter, a reserve corps Captain, is really C.O. Mixter undoubtedly carried off the honors—1500 cases went through in one day and Lee jumped in himself and worked at a table before the teams could be brought up.

IX

STEMMING THE TIDE

11 p.m. "C'est ainsi que les américains ont brillamment enlevé le village de Vaux, à 4 kilomètres ouest de Château-Thierry, ainsi que les hauteurs à l'ouest du village." They certainly have, and our pessimistic friend of Sunday would have been cheered could he have been to-day with the 2nd Division, who are holding what they call the sector "Pas Fini," this side of Château-Thierry. They

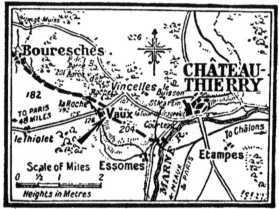

are the boys! As the Marines have been three times cited and the regulars only twice, the latter begged to have another show before going out for a much-needed rest period. They had it, and yesterday morning after a detailed preparation the 9th and the 23rd Infantry successfully stormed the strongly fortified town and took some 600 prisoners, to the amazement and delight of the French. What's more, the Boche prisoners confess they don't like it much on the other side, and many of them *"Kamerad"* for the asking.

After a reëxamination of young Roosevelt with Alec Lambert I went out in a Red Cross car to see Bert Lee, the Divisional Consultant, and to find out what they needed. Again via Claye, Meaux, and over *pavés* and bad roads, but through pretty country to La Ferté-sous-Jouarre, where in Field Hospital No. 103 he was found. They've had heavy work the past few days, with four teams working in 8-hour shifts—very cramped quarters in the grounds of an old convent; no field medical cards, merely slips of paper; four Bessonneau tents for wards; only the very severe cases detained—chests, heads, abdomens, compound thighs, occasional multiples—the rest all evacuated to Coulommiers; about 500 urgent cases handled in three weeks and of course a high mortality, as the transport has been difficult to manage.

Of the other three field ambulances of the division, No. 1 is at Bazu-le-Guéry, and acts as the divisional *triage*—an A.D.S., it would be called in the B.E.F.—about three miles behind the present line. We went there after lunch and found Richard Derby looking rather worn, unshaven and sleepless, with a boil on his neck to try his patience—but cheerful as ever and playing an important rôle as second to the Divisional Surgeon, Col. Morrow. The C.O. is Capt. Evans, a reserve officer from New Mexico and a daisy—moved up to this post because the regular could n't stand the strain.

From there we ran over to Villiers-sur-Marne, where is a Reserve Ambulance Co., No. 15, under command of a Lt. Bruce, occupying the *Huard Château*, made celebrated by *My Home in the Field of Honor*. The little old donkey is still there and the two grandchildren of Father Poupart, if that was his name. The other two field ambulances, Nos. 15 and 16, are at Luzancy, a little further back, where Derby had the foresight to establish a gas station in an old school building which has done timely and good work. They started with accommodations for only 250, but on June 14th, their second day, they had 756 cases from the region of Bouresches. Major Lavake, if that is his name, is proud of his unit and thinks they could handle 2000 cases a day without teams. Maj. Reynolds of Providence, one of Salmon's people, there and doing well, having already returned 150 shell-shock cases to the line.

Thence back through La Ferté-sous-Jouarre and so to Montanglaust, picturesquely overlooking Coulommiers. Here are two units functioning as a C.C.S.—Mobile Hospital No. 1 under Maj.

Macrae and Evac. Hosp. No. 7 under a regular named Col. Tefft. A beautiful park with wonderful trees—very damp, I fear, in bad weather. They are making headway and show a fine spirit—their chief source of complaint being the "Pershing dressings," which are pitiful compared to the S.D.C. products some of us have grown accustomed to. It 's C.C.S. work of a very good order, with Cutler's team perhaps doing as well as any. We dined in a large open tent, nurses, men, and M.O.'s, and then back with Lee to La Ferté buzzing with requests to hand on to Finney—enough to fill my notebook.

July 4, 1918. Paris

La Fête de l'Indépendance, and they were actually celebrating it in England! Here it has absorbed everything. Even Bastille Day has been fused with this our own national festival. An actual holiday for *tout Paris*—all the shops closed. The city began to be decked out yesterday with intertwined American and French flags, and Old Glory floats on the very tip of the Eiffel Tower. A beautiful day—everyone much cheered by the fighting qualities shown by our 2nd Division culminating in their recent attack at Vaux. Commanding generals, premiers, admirals, and presidents send telegrams of felicitation. In a note which is given wide publicity Secretary Baker lets out the actual number of troops that have come over—1,019,115 in all—six months ahead of schedule.

De Martel had sent word to say that the meeting of the Société de Neurologie was called off, and would I go with him and Major Jarvis, the C.O. of the Astoria Hospital, to see the review? No possibility of seats, but he had secured three tickets for standing room reserved in a balcony. Remembering the uncertainties of sitting astride a wall just a year ago, I accepted with alacrity. We joined the holiday crowd bound for the place of ceremonies, climbed the back stairs of a building on the corner of the rue Pierre-Charron and the Avenue du Trocadéro—after to-day to be the Avenue du Président-Wilson—and found ourselves on a narrow fourth-story ledge looking down on the Place d'Iéna. The broad thoroughfare down which the troops were to come stretched directly in front of us—the equestrian statue of Washington and reviewing stands past which they were to march lay just at our feet.

American Troops Passing through the Place d'Iéna on July 4 along the
Avenue du Trocadéro

Soon pundits began to arrive in shoals to fill the six large tribunes—diplomats, soldiers, sailors, ambassadors, politicians, in blue and khaki and black, with a dash of red here and there on British Staff Officers and on Joffre's legs, for he still sticks to his old uniform; Poincaré, Lord Derby, Mr. Sharp; Pau, with his empty sleeve; General Dubail, the Grand Chancellor of the Legion of Honor; General Guillaumat, the Military Governor of Paris; Lloyd George, who had just come from somewhere; Clemenceau (loud cheers for the idol of the people); the Diplomatic Corps, the Senate, the Deputies, the Municipal Council, Ministers of Commerce and of Affairs Interior and Exterior.

After some speeches (to us inaudible) by the President of the Senate, by the Minister of Foreign Affairs, by Mr. Sharp and some others, the Garde Municipale moved aside, their band struck up the *Chant du Départ,* and the troops began to pour down the Avenue toward us. First a few French dragoons, and then, after the bands of the 2nd and 4th Divisions, came samples of our American troops, perhaps 3000 of them, in service caps, very sturdy and marching superbly. They were followed by platoons from the various regiments that have been in the line—Marines and others from the 2nd Division only relieved yesterday by the 26th after nearly 40 days of continuous fighting—wearing tin hats, rather straggly, tired, and disheveled.

Next, after a contingent of American nurses, came more French dragoons, and then with gleaming bayonets waves of *poilus*— glorious in their *horizon-bleu.* For some reason they always make me tearful, but de Martel said he had never before appreciated how squatty they were, compared to the Americans.

While all this was going on, three daredevil airmen were swooping and cavorting and looping about, skimming over the housetops and roaring over the Place. Well, it was a great and stirring show! The procession continued down the Champs‐ Élysées and there were more speeches, I believe, before the Stras‐ bourg monument in the Place de la Concorde. *"Nous pouvons envisager l'avenir avec sûreté."* . . .

Sunday, July 7. Neufchâteau

Returned to this place yesterday with some officers of the 4th Corps, which also is to have its headquarters here. A hot, cloudless

day. Wonderful weather continues and yet no renewal of the
Boche offensive. Many theories—shortage of men? internal
troubles? an epidemic of the 3-day fever? preparation for some
sort of surprise? Meanwhile he's losing his most valuable ally—
Time. Our people are coming fast, though they are sadly without
means of transportation. We all suffer alike in this respect.

To La Fauche to see an unconscious sergeant this a.m.—for want
of transportation they had to send over an ambulance. Luncheon
with Schwab, who is doing excellent work and preparing to write
up the war neuroses· from the point of view of "over here." Most
of the texts on the subject seem to come from those still "at home."
He misses the chance to observe organic cases alongside of the
neuroses. Psychiatry is rather overemphasized, but there is no
chance to enlarge these hospitals now.

The 89th—Leonard Wood's division—is scattered between
Liffol-le-Grand and Rimaucourt on the road to Chaumont. Very
snappy fellows as all agree, but heartbroken to have lost their
leader at the last moment. It would have been a fine chance for
Mr. Wilson to square himself and do a magnanimous thing. They
say the Midnight Division is the "salutinest" division in France;
but the 89th is a close second.

Wednesday the 10th

Making plans for work at No. 18 on peripheral nerves. A trip
to Bazoilles in consequence. Orthopædists and urologists have a
way hereabouts of grabbing every available medical officer who
comes overseas. The spirit of *sauve qui peut* is not good teamwork.
John Finney back from his trip, and soon to leave for the U.S.A.
—ostensibly in relation to personnel—actually at the behest of
the regulars over here to support Ireland as Gorgas's successor.

July 13th, a.m. Saturday

On our short and crooked street is held weekly the pig market.
It has strange hours. From Friday afternoon till dark at about 10
p.m. they gather in carts and park outside our windows—the pigs
always of the same age, about 40-pounders, pink and with an enormous squeal. Pigs of any other age or squeal are apparently un-
salable. Their owners, dressed alike in long aprons—the uniform
of the pigster—have a penchant for *pinard* and there is a convenient place near by. *"Pas de pinard, pas de soldat."* During the eve-

ning they become most voluble and quarrelsome—both pigs and pigsters, for the latter have a way of exhibiting the former by holding them up to view by one hind leg and a tail, in which position the squeals run out.

But this is nothing to the morning, when barter really begins— at daybreak, which is about 3.30. I have only a faint idea of the destiny of these piglets, but they seem to be sold in pairs. This transaction accomplished, each is laid in turn on its back and while someone stands on its neck it is publicly emasculated—worse squeals! Then the two are taken, each by one hind leg, and squealing and clawing madly with their forefeet, which barely reach the ground, they are ignominiously marched down our street and around a corner. We do not sleep Saturday mornings after daybreak.

Neufchâteau: Sunday, July 14

Evening. Bastille Day and a gala day in consequence, with the weather still fine and the Boche quiet, though from all accounts he has been massed in a wide area north of Châlons ready for an offensive on a large scale for many days. So we proceed with our celebration with an arch over our office street on which *Hommage au Président Wilson* is inscribed in large letters amidst a flutter of tricolor bunting.

In the afternoon there are speeches from a platform in a field at the edge of the town—a platform covered by people resembling undertakers in silk hats and frock coats—the pundits of the village. Then a review of a company of ancient French Territorials and a contingent from our 36th Division, who have sent us a small band. In time the people surge into our rue de l'Hôpital, which becomes renamed in honor of Mr. Wilson. A noisy ball game follows between the men of No. 66 and some others.

Then dinner at the Club with E. L. Keyes and the Town Major, who are to make speeches, owing to the appeal of a Falstaffian person who bosses the local Y.M.C.A. hut. There was music by the 145th Inf'y band—ragtime music, to which the French have taken kindly—they have to, for it's all they get. An eloquent prayer by a Dominican priest in his white gown which was translated for us—the prayer—afterwards, and effectually spoiled by an Intelligence Officer gifted with poor English; then songs—

"Ninette et Rintintin" by *la classe enfantine du Collège de Jeunes Filles*—very cunning. Keyes followed—most eloquent with much about *"aux armes, citoyens,"* wholly in French; then Major Bluem in similar vein ditto; I with more of the same, much less effective in English; and finally a gent sang some baritone songs about "when we cross the Rhine, bohoys." It was altogether very hot and enthusiastic and I reached home to find my tunic covered with green paint and patriotism which I had absorbed from the freshly decorated walls of the hut. *Vive la France! Vive l'Amérique! Vive* everybody, particularly Prezydonc Veelsong!!!

On the way home to dinner I skirted the town along the Meuse tributary and had the gratification of seeing a large bull poke his head over the wire fence which enclosed him, in order to investigate the contents of a wheelbarrow evidently containing the Monday's wash of some family. He finally selected a succulent pair of long black stockings knotted together above the knee and, beginning at the knot, proceeded to swallow them. The two feet finally disappeared together—a dead heat—to the exquisite delight of some passing *poilus,* one of whom went to the door of the cottage and explained matters to an unbelieving female. She apparently suspected the *poilu* of some trickery—what had happened? Then such a tornado of abuse as that old beast got! But he stood calmly regarding the irate washerwoman, his head on one side, evidently enjoying his black cud and with an expression as much as to say, "What a peculiar female, this." The *poilus* nearly died—and I also.

The Abortive Thrust at Reims

Monday a.m., July 15th

Yesterday's atmosphere of festivity, which extended over all of France, was abruptly checked this morning by the news that another great German attack had been launched—from Château-Thierry to the Argonne—an 80-km. front. It will probably be their supreme effort. However, in our Neufchâteau billet at this particular moment Finney, with Bill Fisher's help, is wildly packing for his sudden departure home, meanwhile discovering strange bundles—from unopened boxes of candy to ophthalmoscopes—among his year's accumulations. I am supposed to substitute for

They Begin to Show Up on the French Landscape

Consultants Gathered at Rue Gohier before Dr. Finney's Departure.
Seated: Finney, Thayer. *Standing (Front Row):* Blair, Case, Young,
Cushing, Salmon, Fisher, Boggs. *Back Row:* Waters, Baer, Brickner,
Keyes, Allison, Dexter, Peck, Widener, Derby

him during his absence—not a particularly desirable job under present circumstances.

He, Thayer, and Salmon go to Chaumont as a committee of protest regarding a new draft of Circular No. 25 relating to General Orders 88. May they be successful! Col. McCaw probably will object to their "Ireland or Nothing" campaign—sounds like a Sinn Fein slogan. If Ireland for the U.S.A., Wadhams for the A.E.F. Efficiency first, last, and all the time! When the war is over, the regulars can do as they like about seniority and rank, for which we care little.

Meanwhile we hear next to nothing. Indeed our Medical H.Q. is permitted to have less news than we used to get as a.m. and p.m. bulletins posted at every British C.C.S. for all to read. It would appear that the Boches are after Châlons and Épernay, which would make Reims untenable. That they have been concentrating in this area has long been surmised. Brewer, who was here yesterday for lunch, hustled away as he had been given to understand the show might open any minute. It was therefore no surprise, unlike the Mar. 21st and May 27th affairs.

Later. The hospital in La Ferté-Gaucher got badly bombed, as did many others: Châlons, Coulommiers, La Ferté-s.-Jouarre. Apparently the enemy's zero hour was known to the French, whose artillery opened on them two hours before the attack, causing losses and confusion.

July 16, Tuesday. Châlons-sur-Marne

8 p.m. Under a cloudless sky, with the temperature well up in the 90's, I left Neufchâteau this morning to locate Geo. Brewer with the 42nd Division north of Châlons. In a borrowed National car behind Holbrook, who after leaving Gondrecourt missed the turn and we had to make our way cross-country through Monthiers and Chevillon before we struck the Joinville–St. Dizier road. At Chevillon a blow-out, as the tires got so hot the old patches melted. We nearly blew out, ourselves. A woman appears with three small children and expecting another. She protests that they have 100 grams of bread a day for all—her husband for four years in the war and now in hospital, and, *"M'sieur, voyez les légumes!"* They certainly need rain. Vitry-le-François, and on the road to Châlons another blow-out, so it is nearly nine when we get in. I learn that a Captain Mills, liaison officer with the French 4th Army, is the only person who can tell me where to find the Divisional Surgeon. Captain Mills unfortunately is at the General's mess, where I can pursue him if it is urgent; and it certainly is if we are to get under cover this night.

Wednesday, July 17th. Écury

Capt. Mills was an unconscionable time, but it was worth while as I met General Gouraud—one-armed and lame since Salonika days—who is in command of this sector. Capt. Mills, with apologies for his hour's delay, took me to his billet, where we found people preparing to get underground and where after a half hour's attempt to reach the H.Q. of the Divisional Surgeon by telephone I was told that Brewer had gone to the 1st Corps and was no longer here. Also that things were likely to be happening in Châlons any minute and perhaps I 'd better move along and try again to-morrow. He added the information that the French were jubilant over holding the Boche and attributed it all to us—as good as a victory! They were celebrating this at the General's mess and that was why he could not come out.

Holbrook and I debated whether to stick to the countryside for the night or try and find a hotel and some food; we chose the latter. We would n't have done so had we known what was coming —no food and a bombardment which lasted from 10.30 to 4.30 this a.m. With no expectation of guests at such a time, the hotel was not only empty but closed and barred. We finally roused a servant and were let in, given two rooms, and allowed to park the car in an open court. We were then hurried to the wine cave two flights underground, where was the wife of the *maître d'hôtel* with two aged women propped upon mattresses. There was no place to sit and they would n't let me smoke as "it would spoil the wine"! I stuck it till 12.30 and then went up to bed and finally slept—in my clothes—wondering whether bombs were actually dropping in the court or whether an anti-aircraft gun was firing from there—and not caring much which.

In the morning we tried Écury, some 9 km. south of Châlons, where Brewer said that Evac'n No. 4 was to be set up. And there they were in trouble enough, alongside a French H.O.E. Brewer had been operating much of the past 24 hours and I soon got to work with the rest. Golly, it was hot.

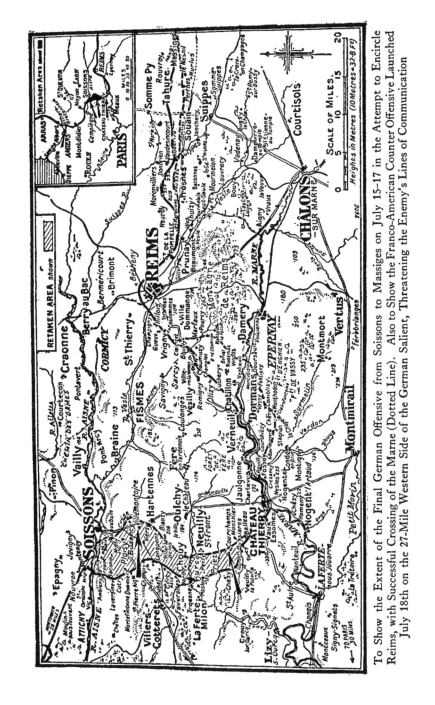

To Show the Extent of the Final German Offensive from Soissons to Massiges on July 15–17 in the Attempt to Encircle Reims, with Successful Crossing of the Marne (Dotted Line). Also to Show the Franco-American Counter Offensive Launched July 18th on the 27-Mile Western Side of the German Salient, Threatening the Enemy's Lines of Communication

7 p.m. We went on to Vatry in the afternoon, some 10 km. far_ ther on—where Mobile No. 2 (St. John's Unit) had just been moved. They had had a bad shelling at Bussy-le-Ch^au for the first six hours of the show and had to get out. Luckily no casualties and the nurses behaved splendidly, refusing to go and sticking to the work till the last minute. They 're a picked lot. Rose Peabody is with them as a Red Cross representative.

July 18th. Neufchâteau

11 p.m. We worked on at Evac'n No. 4 till about 11 last night winding up the last of the cases—some 1500 wounded, they esti- mated, had gone through. An awful rainstorm and hurricane in the middle of the evening—some tents down, but we all hung on to the Bessonneau in which we were operating while it flapped like a loose mainsail in a gale and shook out most of the lights.

A lot more might be told. I remember beans for supper with poor coffee, and rice for breakfast with poor coffee, and some weak pink lemonade passed about by the Y.M.C.A. folks. At midnight I crawled into the wounded officers' tent and lay down on an empty cot; but there were one or two noisy ones alongside and sleep was fitful. This morning—93 miles in 3.5 hours—back here to try and get some supplies and neurosurgical outfits for each of these groups.

News has come through that two of our four divisions with the French Foreign Legion under Mangin and Degoutte on a 25-mile front have walloped through on the Soissons–Château-Thierry side of the salient; that there are 18,000 prisoners, and a penetra- tion of 24 km. This from Col. Stark, whom I have just seen, hoping to get him to requisition the neurological tools cached in Cosnes, by phone. He passes the buck to Col. Keller. We 'll see in the morning what Keller will do. . . . The German *communiqué* this afternoon admitted great activity on their front *south* (*sic*) of the Marne. Those that got across at Dormans, if we have luck, may wish they had n't.

Saturday, July 20th. Coulommiers

11 p.m. In Macrae's tent at Mobile No. 1, the *"Auto-chir"* [1] which is set up in the park behind the *Château de Montanglaust,*

---

[1] This is a contraction of *Ambulance Chirurgicale Automobile,* the official name of the French mobile surgical units which I first saw in Paris May 1, 1915. An interest in the

where No. 7 Evac'n has its headquarters on the ridge overlooking Coulommiers. It's blowing a gale, has turned cold and stormy, while two mournful owls are hooting in the trees near by. I hope our aviators are not out on bombing expeditions in this weather. All the afternoon the sky was humming with them.

It's been a confused day. I've been operating here with first one team, then another, but mostly doing heads with Cutler—two very good ones. Tuffier as a French Consultant here in the morning wishes to see a cranial operation; but no cases in at that time. He was very despondent—just back from Châlons, where he says 3000 French wounded have been waiting three days for operation —much gas infection. Almost as bad at Sézanne, where we visited a large H.O.E. yesterday on the way up here.

A confused day I say—there are about 20 teams at work here and Macrae, the energetic C.O. of this Council Bluffs Unit, says that some 8000 cases have passed through No. 7 Evac'n in the château since the 14th. And there's confusion confounded, I fear, in the line. I just saw a young boy on one of the tables who was wounded Thursday—compound fracture of femur—on the outskirts of Soissons. The Boche came back and overran him and so he lay without food. To-day our people came back—4th Division, I believe—and he was picked up and came in here unsplinted.

There must be a great dearth of splints; and as for medical cards and notes, they're hopeless—mere slips of paper flying everywhere. I saw one American soldier with a *German field card,* and admirable ones they are, written on by a French medical officer!! Account for that if you can! *He* does n't seem to know.

possibilities of these mobile units had been taken by Dr. Joseph Flint while working in a French hospital; and soon after our entry into the war, on his instigation and under the authorization of General Gorgas, $260,000 was raised to purchase one of them from the French Government and have it equipped for the use of a unit from Yale University. It was expected that this unit would serve with the French until needed for our own troops. It consequently came to be given the French enumeration of Auto-chir 39, and it was subsequently known as Mobile Hospital No. 39 when, in March 1918, it was taken over by our Army. This unit had been mobilized in the grounds of the Grand Palais March 1, 1918, when the Chief Surgeon of the A.E.F., fully persuaded of the need of this type of mobile hospital, arranged for the purchase of other units of a somewhat modified type from the French Government. Under this Yale Unit successive mobile hospital groups received their preliminary instruction. The first of them, Mobile Hospital No. 1 (Major Macrae, C.O.), was an Iowa unit from Council Bluffs, Mobile No. 2 (Major St. John, C.O.) was an offshoot of Base Hospital No. 2, the Presbyterian (N.Y.) Hospital Unit, Mobile Hospital No. 3 (Lt. Col. Coe, C.O.); Mobile No. 4 (Major Clopton, C.O.) was organized from Base Hospital 21; Mobile No. 5, an offshoot of Base Hospital No. 4, the Lakeside (Cleveland) Unit; Mobile No. 6 (Major Towne, C.O.) was an offshoot of Base Hospital No. 5, etc.

Over to La Ferté-s.-Juoarre this evening to see Col. Hutton, the Chief Surgeon of the Paris Group. He wants me to go to Crépy-en-Valois to-morrow to look out for Evacuation Hospital No. 5—a new outfit just going up there—a pretty hot place, he says, due to a Boche counter in the direction of Soissons. Stopped in at the divisional F.H. No. 103, where a Major Blanchard, M.R.C., has succeeded Col. Morrow, who goes to Evac'n No. 1. McWilliams has taken over Lee's divisional job and Yates, Bernheim, Lyman, Brennan, and Hetzel were at work there.

The members of this Iowa outfit are early birds and I 'd better turn in. We were routed out at 5.45 this a.m. Breakfast at 6.30. What would they say to this at a British C.C.S.?

.   .   .   .   .   .

"We 're doin' fine." Col. Hutton says we 're in Etrépilly this afternoon and the Boches are moving back. Certainly none are left south of the Marne. The 42nd is to be moved down here from the Châlons region and with it Evac'n No. 4 and Mobile No. 1. Just as well I did n't undertake to go back there.

July 22nd: Séry-Magneval

9 a.m. Times and dates are difficult to figure out. This must be Monday. It 's hot and quiet—the birds chirping—the hornets and flies troublesome. There 's a smell of hay about as I lie on the grass in front of a square U.S. Army tent which is to be shared with Greenwood—two others were evidently here during the night shift.

We 've been operating all night behind the 2nd Division in this newly pitched evacuation hospital which had never seen a battle casualty till forty-eight hours ago and found itself equipped with hospital supplies dating from before the Spanish War—no X-ray —no Dakin's fluid—no nurses, nor desire for any—not a prepared sterile dressing—no sterilizer suitable for field work—and little compressed bundles of ancient gauze and tabloid finger bandages with which to dress the stinking wounds of these poor lads.

But to go back to early yesterday a.m., in the remote past. Colonel Hutton intimated that Fred Murphy must be having his hands full—had not been able to get in touch with him for two days—this new unit sent up in a most chaotic state—completely raw, with new and untried operating teams. Would I go to a place called Crépy-en-Valois south of the Forêt de Compiègne, where I might possibly locate them and be of some service.

My notes *en route* read: "Coulommiers, 7 a.m.—La Ferté-sous-Jouarre—Lizy-sur-Ourcq—up the east side of the Ourcq to Ocquerre—Cruoy—Montigny—Mareuil-sur-Ourcq, loaded with French chasseurs and their supplies—the clouds breaking —across the Ourcq—along a well-camouflaged road to Auteuil about five km. from the recent line—poppies and wheat—wire and gun emplacements—flying men getting out despite the high wind —blue patches of sky above, blue patches of chicory in the fields below, blue *poilus* beyond on a distant hillside—batches of Boche prisoners—Ivors—behind the Forêt Villers-Cotterets—'*pour aller à Crépy tournez à droite près Vaumoise*'—funny little camouflaged French tanks, all gun, chewing their way along the soft side of the country road—caches of ammunition—a British artillery brigade all freshly shaven and very smart—lorries and more lorries till the mud becomes dust—more herds of Boche P.O.W.— at last Crépy, evidently severely bombed of late."

The hastily manned hospital near the station at Crépy had been hard hit and was evidently untenable—obviously necessary to evacuate. For this purpose an ambulance train, No. 54 U.S.A., was drawn up alongside the badly smashed-up station—equipped to transport 360 lying cases; it was about to leave with 622 wounded of all kinds, mostly severe.

Altogether 2000 casualties had been routed through Crépy with the aid of a few surgeons and dentists from Mobile No. 1. With them were Kerr and Trout, who had just reached France and been pitchforked into this mess to do strange operations under stranger circumstances—put into a car and fired up here not knowing what would be expected of them. They began to take in Thursday afternoon—had 604 last night alone, and they're rather done in.

Meanwhile Proust, the Consultant of the French 4th Army, with Fred Murphy and a Captain Crafts, had been struggling to straighten things out. At the station, wounded had been lying out all night in the storm untouched—waiting for the train. Bert Lee in desperation finally wangled some empty lorries and sent a large number of them, thoroughly drenched, to this place, a matter of about five kilometres over narrow, torn-up country roads. F.M. said he never imagined anything so appalling— would I beat it to Séry-Magneval and help this untried outfit get started—nothing to do but route all possible cases there—the situation bad and certainly going to get worse. Gossip has it—confidential like all gossip—that General Pershing was here last night—the corps to be moved out—several divisions very hard hit.

Well, I could tell much more both about Crépy and about this awful place—the utter confusion—the large number of rotting men for whom no possible relief was in sight; my effort to get some order out of the chaos while the C.O.—the poor man had a bad carbuncle on his neck—disappeared for some hours to get a needed rest; his fury at my having ventured in his absence to number the hastily pitched ward tents—a prompt reconciliation—visits later from Hall, from a very haggard Bert Lee, from Murphy, Allison, Salmon, Bevans, the Corps Surgeon, and many more. Persuaded a Red Cross official to get through by telephone to Paris for a lorry of sterile Boston dressings in tins —more wounded and still more, many of them three days old. E. A. Poe's brother (Nat, I believe) found in one of the crowded tents—Redmond Stewart, a judge advocate, there with him; operations all night in a Bessonneau tent we finally managed to get set up—amputations of the thigh—sucking chest wounds— mutilations—German wounded. I recall a young Seaforth Highlander subaltern and a Jock of the Gordons (the 15th Scottish has come down here to back us up) wounded by the air raiders who passed over near midnight—the only two wounds which I saw that were not stinking.

All told it was a bad night. Sometime about dawn, while waiting for the next head to be shaved, I lay down on an empty operating table, went promptly to sleep, and fell off. Morning has now come and it all seems very far away. I 've had coffee, a shave, and will take a nap—the flies permitting—before we go on again.

I suppose these people have done as well as could be expected —like learning to swim by being thrown in the water after hearing a lecture on how to do it. To add to his sleepless troubles the poor C.O. had been ill enough to put him to bed any other

General Gouraud and the Poilu of 1918

time. Their equipment was of an ancient vintage, and they had never opened their boxes. Some of them contained bolo knives, saddles, and bridles, when one wanted sterile gauze! Laid over the supplies in one box, I was told, was a newspaper headlining that Cervera's fleet was expected off New England—but this may have been someone's imagination. · · ·

Wednesday, July 24. La Trousse

7 p.m. At Mobile No. 2, set up 24 hours ago here on the Château-Thierry road 3 km. east of Lizy-sur-Ourcq. A beautiful spot—a large guest room in the château of the Comte de Cruoy, on a hill overlooking a park with lovely vistas and near by a lake and fountain—quite different from some spots I have lately seen.

Since my last notes on Monday morning much has happened difficult to recall; but there was another day and long night operating on head cases with Harry Kerr at No. 5 Evac'n at Séry, where they began to get hold of themselves, though those first two days were a nightmare.

A few Red Cross nurses under a Miss Patterson, sent up by Miss Fitzgerald—old J.H.H. friends—finally arrived and some order grew from the chaos. Supplies also come from Paris—a Bessonneau was put up accommodating ten tables—another for an X-ray plant, and we began to stay the tide of new cases by Monday afternoon, though we never got to the poor fellows waiting in the closely packed hospital tents. They were lucky even to be under shelter.

Fred Murphy finally managed to start evacuation of cases through Crépy, where he had set up some tents, and where yesterday morning, when I came through, were some tired M.O.'s and Y.M.C.A. people asleep on stretchers while German prisoners were being utilized as bearers for the wounded.

After a couple of hours' sleep I got away in the afternoon carrying a report on the situation to Col. Hutton. Séry—Crépy—Betz—Acy, and through Vareddes to Meaux—a wonderful ride, war or no war, with showers and sunshine and such lights and shadows! At Meaux in No. 6 Evac'n it was arranged to have Lt. Hanson given the responsibility for the head cases and I shall hope to send him some proper tools.

Then, after passing miles of the 42nd Division coming up, to

La Ferté-s.-Jouarre again, where I report to the G-4 Paris group and am taken by them to dinner. Afterward on to No. 4 Evac'n, just moved in to a fine place—the *Château La Perreuse*, south of La Ferté, where Col. Edwards put me in bed in his billet and I knew nothing more till this a.m. after nine hours actually in pyjamas.

To-day more of the same. First to No. 103 F.A. in La Ferté —next to No. 4 Evac'n again to see Major Ogden and get him started. Then to Montanglaust for a conference and afterward to the R.C. hospital at Jouy-s.-Morin near La Ferté-Gaucher, where Maj. McCoy was making a rapid turnover of his cases and I got a telephone through to Paris for supplies. Then La Ferté-s.-Jouarre once more via Rebais to find the place packed with "Amex" troops. There I was told to proceed to this place, where many head cases were supposed to have congregated—a false rumor.

G-4 gives out that our casualties from July 16–24 have been heavy; I should judge about 5000 for each division engaged. The 1st Division hard hit: 5300 casualties, 700 killed; the 2nd and 28th possibly even worse.

Thursday, July 25th

From La Trousse, where no pressure of work, to La Ferté to report; lunch with Cols. Hutton, Edwards, Murphy, and others. Rumor that Ouchy is to-day's objective. Col. Hutton having difficulties getting sites for hospitals. With Leopold, the 4th Divisional Psychiatrist, to Cruoy-sur-Ourcq, where is a *Franco-Américaine Groupement d'Ambulances*—the U.S. Unit being No. 19 F.H. with 4 operating teams and 10 nurses acting as an evacuation hospital and forwarding to Meaux. The night spent again at La Trousse.

Friday, 26th

From La Trousse to Lizy, and on to Juilly over a country dotted by the graves of 1914 in the wheat of 1918—Etrepilly, Barcy—new trenches and wire at St. Soupplets, as also our 33rd Engineers. Hall and Shepley both away—the remaining M.O.'s at Evac'n No. 8 found highly critical of the state of the wounded, of the Army and the world in general. To Meaux to pick up young Hanson and get him started as neurosurgeon for No. 8.

Orders received for Evac'n No. 6 to move forward, and yet wounded still coming in.

Saturday, 27th

Yesterday afternoon to Paris for the Research Committee, too late to hear much of the afternoon session by Leriche and Heitz-Boyer. This morning's session on "wastage," most of which I also missed owing to necessary purchases of instruments and the like for neurosurgical teams. General Burtchaell, the new "D.G.," analyzed the British figures for the year past—1,400,000 casualties, 823,000 cases of sickness, only 1298 of them in the typhoid group. This, as I estimate it from his diagram, would give 577,000 wounded and 40,000 deaths, but I was not quite clear whether it referred only to the Base or to the C.C.S.'s as well— he possibly did not intend it to be clear. He paid our "casual" Reserve Corps M.O.'s attached to the British a fine compliment —told how many have received citations and said that the casualties among those serving in forward areas had been 12.74 per cent, and among the R.A.M.C. 12.6 per cent.

The afternoon session given over to the evacuation of wounded; Col. Gallie as usual was informing and amusing in his description of their difficulties of the early days in the B.E.F.—especially when the nurses first came out. He has laughed and joked his way through many a tangle as other Irishmen have before him. He paid a tribute to the way the evacuation from Crépy was handled by Fred Murphy, and probably meant it. He could appreciate the difficulties better than the Congressmen who are over here and who want to know why the wounded can't have notepaper and envelopes in the Evac'n Hospitals. He had established a C.C.S. at Senlis for the British divisions, and had been in and about Crépy during the worst of Fred's troubles.

Sunday, July 28th. Paris

Visits to the hospitals of Paris group; the Univ. of Virginia people with Cabells and Venables a-plenty just moving in. Luncheon with Mrs. MacMonagle, and with her to see the new cemetery for American soldier-dead on the hill at Suresnes overlooking Paris. Her son lies buried at Friancourt-s.-Meuse, near where he was shot down. His body will not be moved; others will probably feel the same way about their boys.

p.m. Having nothing better to do, this is a good chance to review the events of these past ten days during which the last phase of the great German offensive collapsed at Reims and now promises to change hands altogether.

THE OFFENSIVE CHANGES HANDS

This show has been going on a long time—since *Monday the 15th* when the long-awaited German attack was launched. It is said that our divisions held when even some of the French gave way and we are being showered with credit, deserved or undeserved. The enemy got across the Marne to a depth of 5 miles, on the 16th, in the Dormans–Châtillon region halfway between Château-Thierry and Reims, but were held there as well as at other points of attack—indeed were driven back by our troops. In General Gouraud's area east of Reims in the Prosnes–Suippes line no gains were made. Severe fighting—heavy losses—prisoners—probably for both sides. Quentin Roosevelt killed in an aerial engagement.

On the 17th, the day I was at Écury, the great drive which was to engulf Reims and its protecting mountain was definitely checked, though they made some slight progress toward Épernay. East of Reims Gen. Gouraud held fast. A Franco-American counter regained St. Agnan and the region north of the Condé–Dormans road. The Boche plans were doubtless confused thereby.

On the 18th at 4.35 a.m. Foch launched his brilliant counter on a front of 27 miles from Fontenoy to Belleau with Franco-American troops, reaching the Mont de Paris, a mile from Soissons, by early afternoon—the greatest depth eight miles—5000 prisoners—apparently a complete surprise. The performance was not unlike the famous stroke by the French 6th Army under Maunoury along the Ourcq in September 1914 and promises to be of equal importance in compelling the enemy's withdrawal. The American troops took part and did finely. The German lines of communication were under fire and their position became awkward. This was the best day for the Allies on this Western Front for many a month.

On Friday the 19th Ludendorff's offensive ended and the active rôle passed to Foch. The Boche under pressure retreated across the Marne with heavy losses.

On the 20th, the day I was at Montanglaust, the western line was advanced to the plateau dominating Soissons, with 20,000 prisoners; and the Americans, as I learned that night from Col. Hutton, captured the dominating plateau of Etrepilly which the Boche finally evacuated after holding it for 50 days. People began to talk of an Allied victory and bells were rung in the U.S.A. as they were in London after Cambrai.

On Sunday the 21st, the day of the Séry-Magneval mess, Franco-Ameri‾ can troops moved up practically to the Soissons–Château-Thierry road, seriously threatening the enemy's line of communication. Château-Thierry was taken and they were forced to make a complete withdrawal north of the Marne. They began extricating themselves cleverly behind a screen of smoke and machine guns—meanwhile excusing their withdrawal by similar methods in the *communiqués.*

On Monday the 22nd, we got back across the Marne at two points between Passy and Dormans. The Boches were retreating, blowing up ammunition dumps, and had withdrawn five miles north of Château-Thierry. Though their pivotal points at Soissons and Reims unhappily were holding—54 German divisions identified—their position looked critical. The Americans reported 6000 prisoners. These were the Séry-Magneval days and we must confess to many wounded in the German counter-attacks.

On Tuesday the 23rd when we were fretting at La Trousse the Americans took Jaulgonne, the bridgehead of the Fère-en-Tardenois road.

On July the 24th it looked as though our advance were slowing up. At least the Boche resistance was stiffening and he was even countering—it was rumored with a new army. The 26th Division took Epieds.

On July 25th the Boche countered again at Dormans with no effect. Oulchy-la-Ville fell to the Americans. To show how delayed our news may be, the 26th Div. (according to Gen. Edwards's order to his troops) got into the Forêt de Fère and as far as the Jaulgonne–Fère-en-Tardenois road on this date.

By July 26th even the British press began to talk about "the bravery and impetuosity" of our infantry. Oulchy-le-Château, the last point on the Château-Thierry–Soissons road, was taken. Gen. Gouraud recaptured all the strip east of Reims, which the Boche overran the first day. The pressure of the Franco-American troops became so threatening by nightfall that a general withdrawal began which lasted through *Saturday the 27th* and *Sunday the 28th,* on which day Fère-en-Tardenois was reached.

How far they withdrew is not at all clear. Nor is it entirely clear why they withdrew at all. Something must be happening to the Boches. They were outwitted by Gouraud on the first morning; they were soon held south of the Marne; on the morning of the fourth day they were crushingly surprised by Foch's attack. They had poured reënforcements into a "pocket" until it was jam-packed, and suddenly decided on a swift withdrawal. No equal spectacle of German indecision since the war began.

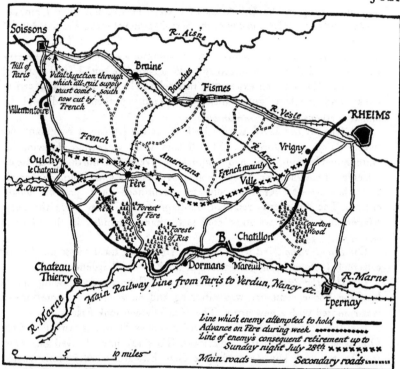

Belloc's Map Showing the Status of the German Retirement from the Tardenois Salient by the End of July 28th. Arrows Indicate the American Thrust at Fère-en-Tardenois, the Important Crossroads for the German Lines of Communication, Where They Made a Desperate Four-Days Resistance along the Ourcq at Sergy, Seringes, and Cierges

Monday, July 29th. Neufchâteau

Returned here to-day from Paris via Lagny, Esternay, St. Dizier, and Joinville. We stopped at Coulommiers, where were a large number of wounded lying about waiting their turn. No. 1 Mobile is moving out to a site near Château-Thierry and the burden will fall on No. 7 Evac'n. The wounded largely from the 42nd, who recently moved into that region—mostly machine-gun wounds. The Boche has taken a heavy toll.

Yesterday they turned and attempted to hold. There was severe fighting, particularly in the districts of Chambrecy and Ville-en-Tardenois. Sergy was the scene of particularly bitter conflicts [cf. page 484], and has changed hands four times, being now held by the 42nd, I believe. The same is true of Seringes.

They were up against the Prussian Guards and a Bavarian Reserve division—it was hand-to-hand fighting with the bayonet and no quarter, according to hearsay.

Thursday, August 1st

Two days passed in getting organized in our new quarters across the Meuse. As Young's department—somehow in possession of their own private motor car—has a way of absorbing most of the information afloat, Bertner is to be G-2 [1] of our group—G.U.-2, as someone suggested. Allison and Greenwood back with much needed information regarding disposition of divisions and evacuation hospitals. Kerr to be attached here to help with formation of neurosurgical teams for each hospital.

.   .   .   .   .   .

There is a pause in the battle—the quietest day since July 14th. For all but ourselves it means the end of four years of war—to celebrate this the German military dictator of the Ukraine has been assassinated; and it is rumored that last night Boulogne was again badly bombed with a direct hit demolishing the R.A.M.C. headquarters. Stirling, on night duty there with some N.C.O.'s, was wounded.

Tuesday, August 6. Neufchâteau

After three days in bed with a N.Y.D.[2] malady which I regarded as the Spanish flu—three days' grippe—or what you will. This came on top of two rackety days around Château-Thierry, getting back home supperless, cold, and wet, in an open Dodge at 1 a.m. I had suddenly aged and our driver had to help me upstairs—teeth chattering and done in. . . .

Greenwood and I were supposed to leave in a National at 5 a.m. Friday morning the 2nd for Chierry, just east of Château-Thierry, where No. 1 Mobile had gone into unwilling liaison with No. 6 Evac'n under a new C.O., and where there was said to be much work—and there was. A borrowed open rackety car came for us at 8 a.m.—about as much as we can expect these fallen times.

The highly illegible jottings in my pocket notebook are: "*Aug. 2.* Neufchâteau, Gondrecourt, Ligny, to Bar-le-Duc, along

---

[1] The General Staff was divided into five sections corresponding to those of the French Army, viz.: G-1, Administration; G-2, Intelligence; G-3, Operations; G-4, Coördination, including hospitalization, evacuation of sick and wounded, G-5, Training and activities pertaining thereto.

[2] Not yet diagnosed.

the old canalized river bed with highlands jutting out from the west. Showers, and the crops are being hustled in. Revigny and to Châlons, 53 km. along a most uninteresting plateau with vast acres of wheat, barley, oats, and patches of scrub pine—a wearying solitude. West at the crossroads of La Grande-Romanie. A blowout near Châlons—luncheon there in a Hôtel Renard with a lot of young French aviators, one of them an ace of aces, Fonck, the centre of a circle, a big bottle of sauterne before him, and a ribbon so elongated with palms it hangs in his pocket. A meeting with John Gibbon and Norris—all quiet these days in their area and they devote themselves to French lessons.

"Across to Épernay—along the Marne Valley—with the forested Montagne de Reims sticking up into the wet clouds. Épernay must have been a handsome place—champagne brings money —fine residences—very badly bombed—shellfire, I should judge. Following the left bank, about 7 km. from Épernay we came to recent battle territory near Œuilly—the farthest east the enemy got after crossing the Marne. The highway thick with French— fresh trenches and wire—shell dumps along road—gun emplacements—many large trees down and craters everywhere— pretty villages perched on the sides of the opposite hills—Châtillon, Verneuil, Treloup—now gaunt and sepulchral—ghosts of their former state.

"A pontoon bridge at Troissy well camouflaged—Boche ammunition everywhere in large amounts—77's in the triple woven baskets of old, but far less well made. The remains of a direct hit on a Boche battery—the 6 horses just being buried—phew!!— entrenching tools, hand grenades, pontoons full of holes that never got to the river's edge, clothes, overcoats, helmets, wire, telephone spools, piles of artillery ammunition, French and German. Not a tree has escaped—many with severe multiples— every now and then one down or uprooted. All the original bridges destroyed—railroad engines blown up and tracks demolished—German signs still up in villages.

"Dormans a holocaust—almost worse than the sepulchral towns of Flanders, pictures in disarray on the walls and the beds hanging out of the second-story level—the work still at the sewing machine, though half the house gone. German graves,

German boots and baskets—a milestone broken in two; putrid smells; gray-green overcoats.

"Courthiezy and Reuilly with Italians—then the curve in the river across which lie Barzy and Jaulgonne, with quite precipitous highlands beyond and where our boys somehow got across. Moulins, where was the 2nd Batt'n of the 3rd Division, and Crezancy; then Fossoy—the present Divisional Hq. for the 3rd; and finally Chierry, where No. 1 Mobile and No. 6 Evac'n are found pitched together in a wet field."

It was an unkempt-looking place, this field—just off the main highway on a level several feet below it so that the wet top-soil had become thoroughly churned up by ambulances and trucks. They had been very busy—had thrown over all attempts to do any special work. Indeed the sight of Consultants staggered them and I don't wonder—more colonels around, of both leaf and chicken variety, than one could count. There was a good deal of indecision as to what to do with the head cases—Cutler had been doing general work at No. 1 with only an occasional head and Harrington of the No. 6 Evac'n group had done none at all. One young captain of infantry whom I ran across in the ward was regarded as inoperable and I persuaded Macrae to let me take him on with Harrington, to show what might be done under such circumstances.

By about 11 work suddenly began to slack up and Cutler put me to bed on a canvas cot in their communal tent. I soon began to feel feverish and to ache—though I did not know what was coming on.

In the morning of the 3rd—still no work—evidently a lull in the fighting—we took Cutler into Château-Thierry across the pontoon bridge to find a *blanchisseuse*—and sure enough he did, in the guise of a returned refugee who could give no address, as her house was down. We stopped at the château near Chierry where Evac. No. 5 with F.H. No. 26 and F.H. 27 were encamped—not a very happy-looking combination.

Then over to La Ferté-Milon, having been asked to report on the hospitals just moved up there. Except that we passed north of Hill 204 we practically followed the old line of July 15th, through battered towns and woods and a shell-pocked countryside much fought over. Keeping Vaux on the left, we take the road to Torcy, passing Boche graves with helmets on them and long formal German inscriptions. Bouresches, and then Belleau and Belleau Wood, which is likely to remain celebrated in American history.

The early Boche trenches along the south side of the road with hand grenades in dumps and each man's allotment in a little cave dug in the bank. Belleau hamlet a sad and tottering wreck. *Poilus* harvesting the patches of oats between shell holes in the fields— poppies and chicory. Then Torcy and Bussiares—also tottering. Gun carriages and baby carriages thrown up by the roadside— nothing more incongruous than an old battered silk hat and an abandoned Boche helmet side by side in the ditch—baby carriages and top hats indicate refugees.

On the side of the hill by Veuilly-la-Poterie—the place where on June 7th our first notable counter-attack was made—were large Boche dugouts—indescribable burrows where men had actually moled themselves into the earth—in one of them a *Leipziger Nachrichten* of May 31st with a leading article: *"Vorwärts zwischen Soissons und Reims. Die Neue Deutsche Offensive. Zur Durchbruch—Schlacht beim Chemin des Dames,"* etc. Alongside of this was a letter of the date "26 mai, 1918"—a rusty gun— a perforated Boche helmet. *May 27* was the day of the opening of the great offensive and presumably this soldier of an unknown regiment came in on the high tide of the invasion, reached Veuilly, and lived there in this hole only 40 miles from Paris until the happenings of July 18th.

Near Veuilly we met a scabetic from the 10th Machine Gun Co., 4th Division, who said he was looking for a hospital— wanted directions how to get back. The two *poilus,* who turned him over to us, were not quite sure of him; their orders are strict about arresting chance people wandering about in American uniforms. So on to Chézy-en-Orxois along a road on which both Boches and Americans have been entrenched—many graves—many penetrated helmets—Boche and French. Finally La Ferté-Milon with its old ruined castle and its newly ruined churches and dwellings, where we found No. 3 Evac'n (Col. Lamson, C.O.) with six teams on hand and St. John's No. 2 Mobile as an appendage—at least the first half of it—under Parsons's tutelage. The other half not yet arrived.

The 2nd Division were in this area on the eventful 15th-18th July, with the French Moroccans on their left, and the 1st still further north, I believe. The Boches never got into La Ferté, though they were about 3 km. away on June 1st and many of the graves are inscribed June 5th or June 6th. Again on June 15th they got to the edge of the town for a day or two, when the 2nd Division came in and drove them back again.

Then south to Lizy along the east side of the Ourcq Canal, passing an extraordinary series of secondary defenses with wire and trenches. Geo. Brewer at La Trousse recovering from a spell of illness and looking very thin. We learn that Mobile No. 2 and No. 3 Evac'n are to be moved to a place near Mézy. We are given lunch and sped on our way. So quiet all the morning we had supposed the line must be getting stabilized; and it was a great surprise to learn that Soissons had been taken (i.e., on Friday, Aug. 2nd, the day previous) and that the enemy were again in full retreat.

At La Ferté-sous-Jouarre find G-4 much bucked up since the advent of Col. Stark, and I learn that since July 15th, 37,241 casualties had been evacuated through the hospitals reporting to their office. Nothing more they want us to do so we gladly turn homeward—and Greenwood being very anxious to go via the north bank of the Marne, I submit.

We stopped at Méry, the Hq. of the 26th Division, to see Gen. Edwards, who was in Paris—his A.D.C., Capt. Hyatt, doing the honors for the Yankee Division. A large 210 howitzer stands in the yard of the château where they are billeted—the biggest gun they had so far captured.

On along the valley of the Marne—very beautiful. Charly-le-Pont—beginning to see signs of American transport—much-abused roads—our first pioneers—F.H. 128 at Azy, the 32nd Division therefore—Essommes—Château-Thierry again—Brasles—Gland, its signboard broken in two—the 3rd Division identified and the 28th going up in lorries. Mont St. Père badly damaged—Chartèves, our cavalry going up. We miss our way by the heights behind Jauglonne and get on the road to Fismes. Barzy, with many German signs pointing to places for crossing the river —signs dating back to July 15th undoubtedly. Marcilly, deserted but for its graves and ruined houses. All the poles along the road carrying the current from a power plant cut down—probably in the French retreat. Passy wrecked and deserted, with the church absolutely collapsed and the roads littered with abandoned Boche ammunition. Courcelles, another cadaverous town, through which a mule-drawn ammunition train of the 32nd Division is passing.

At Treloup and Dormans the valley opens up, and along the road are Boche pontoons riddled with holes—evidently shot to pieces as they were bringing them up. However this is where they finally got across, as the sign which I ripped off from a tree indicates—"*Zur (Schweren) Ponton-Brücke. Tragfähigkeit bis Einschl. 5t.*"—all nicely initialed, though the "Schweren" had been painted out. But there was no crossing for us at Dormans despite this sign, and we had to make a long detour to get across on a pontoon bridge at Verteuil, where a French *pont renforcé* was also going up.

This brought us by twilight to the south bank on our old road, and it began to rain—supperless via Épernay, Châlons, St. Dizier, Ligny, and home at one a.m. in the state I have told.

Office Work at Neufchâteau

Wednesday: Aug. 7th

Up and about but very feeble. . . . The attack which began *July 18th* under Generals Mangin and Degoutte on the German right flank south of the Aisne may be considered over. It is amazing that only three days before Ludendorff still had the initiative. It seems undoubted that the start made by Gen. Gouraud's army in Champagne, saving Épernay and Châlons, was what made possible the shift of the offensive to the Allies—what gave them the ball.

Aug. 8th, Thursday

The grippe or something worse.[1] . . . Rumor that the French and the British 4th Army under Rawlinson have suddenly opened up on the Amiens front—a successful surprise attack in a mist

---

[1] It turned out to be worse.

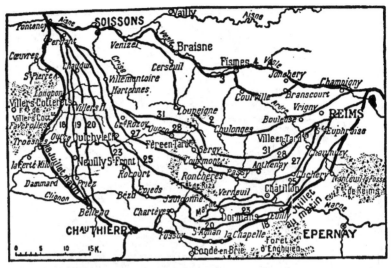

The Successive Stages of the German Second Retreat from the Marne to the Aisne between July 18th and August 3rd, 1918

between Albert and Montdidier. Pearce Bailey from the U.S.A. and Salmon at our mess for supper.

Aug. 9th

Canadians and Australians push forward two miles on a 20-mile front—17,000 prisoners. Montdidier threatened by the French —the maximum advance nearly 12 miles, and they are within a mile of Chaulnes. This with cavalry, armored automobiles, and "whippet" tanks. "One of the greatest and most gratifying surprises of the war, and so far the most serious German defeat."

Aug. 10th

The news from the British front still good. Montdidier taken: 24,000 prisoners. The Canadian cavalry played a brilliant part in the advance—they got in so far and so fast they actually captured a brigade headquarters intact.

The first American Army is formed and Pershing takes command. Corps Commanders are Bullard, Liggett, Bundy, Reid, and Wright.

Sunday, August 11th

Very feeble. To Contrexéville and Vittel with Kerr for the day, seeing heads and peripheral nerve cases.

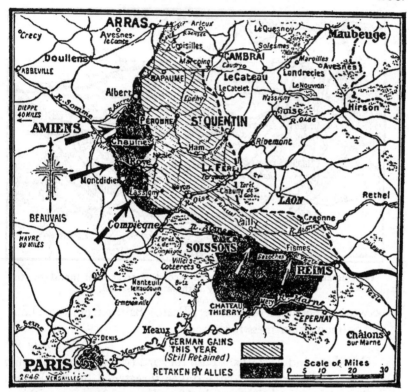

To Show the Situation of the New Anglo-French Offensive in the Amiens Sector Launched on August 8th. The Total Ground Recovered by Allies from July 18th to August 11th Shown in Black

August 18, Sunday. Neufchâteau

Advised by Thayer a week ago to go off to the Riviera for a rest. Got as far as Paris and after five sweltering days in the Continental, restless with fever though sleeping most of the time, am glad to be back here with something to do.

Aug. 19th, Monday

Things are brewing on a large scale. Neufchâteau becomes an army headquarters, the area full of troops—a rumor that with half a million men we are going to stage a show on our own account between Commercy and Toul, with Metz and beyond as our objective. I wonder if we have not lost our heads—or are we really the darlings of the gods and capable of doing things others could not do? We shall see.

Meanwhile the Consultants carry on ignobly as an impatient body of pundits. We can now no longer move. Salmon says it's just as though someone had poisoned the country doctor's horse —it did n't hurt the doctor but he was no longer any use to his patients. Bill Fisher in turn takes to his bed with fever.

Wed., Aug. 21st

Very hot—flies and hornets. The neighborhood stiff with troops. Evacuation hospitals all about us brought down from the Château-Thierry region. Cutler here last night—in surgical charge of Evac'n No. 3, which with much energy he is remaking—what one can't get by proper means one steals. They 've had a bad time, these hospitals, with dysentery, and I believe there has been an investigation following a report by Hans Zinsser, who does not think much of our boasted sanitation.

We 've been much upset by orders to move out—Neufchâteau now the H.Q. of the Army—"Gen. John" at the château—billets wanted for regular officers. Consultants can vamose—who are they anyway? We managed to give up 15 rooms by doubling up and persuading some who should really be at the Base to return where they more properly belong.

. . . . . .

The 10th French Army under Gen. Mangin yesterday followed up Saturday's attack by a further gain of 4 km. between the Oise and the Aisne, taking 8000 prisoners and threatening Roye and Noyon. Meanwhile Gen. Byng let the 3rd British Army loose north of the Ancre and advanced three miles toward Bapaume. The Allies may be said to be alternately attacking on a continuous front from Albert to Reims, or, if we include Gen. Gouraud's steady pressure, from Albert to the Argonne. When *we* are permitted to join forces this front supposedly will spread to—let us say Nancy.

Thursday, Aug. 22

Still very hot, dusty, a cloudless sky and the temperature in the 90's. Many disgruntled M.R.C. officers at the office, and justly so. All the good men pulled out of the base hospitals and sent forward as teams are forever lost to their units, which have to carry on with a heavy service, undermanned and with juniors at best.

Too feeble to walk back here to 51 rue Gohier for lunch, so take a haversack with me and eat at the offices with the wise Salmon. He points out how the regular army has circumvented the Owen Bill, framed to give the National Army its just quota of generals, colonels, etc. This by an act whereby there is no longer a "national army," everyone henceforth being U.S.A.—good thing, I should think.

Saturday, August 24th. Besançon

Sent with Pearce Bailey (over here on a tour of inspection) to visit Gustave Roussy at Besançon and the Centre Neurologique, etc., *la 7ème Région*—a most instructive jaunt. Incidentally it took us into the delightful country of the Département Doubs on the edge of the Jura.

In one of our uncertain Nationals, behind Holbrook, we got away from crowded Neufchâteau at nine on a showery morning. Through Langres, the Dijon road as far as Longeau, then left into the Haute-Saône, passing the Maryland people of the 79th at Champlitte, and on to Gray. There we lunched with a medley in a small French restaurant where tame magpies hopped about and regarded you curiously, doubtless wondering whether it was worth while to chance snatching a metal souvenir off your tunic.

Somewhere below Gray we crossed into the Département, doubtless named from the doubling river which winds through it. Then Besançon, the former capital of the Franche-Comté, a place of historic interest in most picturesque surroundings—a fortress of the first class with a citadel perched high on a tongue of land nearly surrounded by the river, and with other detached Vauban fortresses scattered about. One of them we were to see.

We were lucky enough to find Roussy, who promptly gave to us the rest of his day. He showed us the general plan of organization and then took us to the Besançon Hospital, used as a neurological *triage*. After seeing some of the neurosurgical cases there we departed for Salins, some twenty-five km. to the south, where the psychoneuroses are sent to be treated. Despite the rain, a wonderful trip across country, with charming views, along deep valleys, of the winding Doubs and its tributaries. Salins itself— a healing salt spring, as its name indicates—is a most fascinating village stringing along, with what foothold it can get, in the

to 51 rue Gohier for lunch, so
and eat at the offices with the wise
the regular army has circumvented
the National Army its just quota of
by an act whereby there is no longer
henceforth being U.S.A.—good

Saturday, August 24th. Besançon
over here on a tour of inspection) to
and the Centre Neurologique,
instructive jaunt. Incidentally it took
the Département Doubs on the

Nationals, behind Holbrook, we got
at nine on a showery morning.
road as far as Longeau, then left
the Maryland people of the 79th
There we lunched with a medley
tame magpies hopped about
wondering whether it was
a metal souvenir off your tunic.
crossed into the Département,
river which winds through it.
of the Franche-Comté, a
picturesque surroundings—a
citadel perched high on a tongue
river, and with other detached
One of them we were to see.
Roussy, who promptly gave to
us the general plan of organi-
Besançon Hospital, used as a
some of the neurosurgical cases
twenty-five km. to the south,
to be treated. Despite the rain,
with charming views, along deep
and its tributaries. Salins itself—
indicates—is a most fascinating
what foothold it can get, in the

The Picturesque Site (*above*) of the Century-Old Fortres
(*below*) Its Main Portal

crack between two towering heights, each of them surmounted by one of the subsidiary forts of the Besançon cluster. One of these was our objective, and Holbrook, who had already skidded badly in dodging an ambulance when leaving Besançon, looked at the road askance; but up we went, a most wonderful view unfolding before us.

We finally reached the top, where Fort St. André, now Station Neurologique No. 42, is one of the centres given over to the psychoneurotics—more particularly those with congealed hands (*les mains figées*) and clubbed feet. These, of course, represent the neuroses which are apt to arise in the case of men with trifling wounds—men whose psyche is not satisfied with the magnitude of their injuries and who fear they may get sent back into the line. Many of these *acro-contractures* and *acro-paralysies*, alas, are attributable to the surgeon—and more particularly to the orthopædist, if he is not to be called a surgeon.

An unnecessarily long period of fixation by dressing is bad enough, but a succeeding period of immobilization in apparatus of some kind for a supposed muscle or nerve injury will do the business. And here they were, men with all imaginable types of fixed deformities—the *main d'accoucheur, main en bénitier, main en coup de poing*—a most extraordinary collection. Many of the injuries were two or three years old, the men meanwhile having been nursing their extremities set in the favored posture for all this time, until finally they were drawn into this neurological net.

The whole situation, of course, lent itself admirably to successful therapeutics—just as Lourdes does or Ste. Anne de Beaupré—a picturesque spot, the expectation of recovery (much as it was dreaded), a room littered and lined with the canes and crutches and braces for back and arms and legs of those who have marched out presumably cured. Stress is laid, by those in control, on the fact that no neurological examination of any kind is made after admission to this place—only psychotherapy. The detailed physical examination, which necessarily implies to the patient uncertainty of diagnosis, is done elsewhere and by other people—in the sorting station at Besançon or wherever else. Here treatment alone and no questions asked. One can understand how much its success depends on personality by watching Captain Boisseau,

Roussy's collaborator, take these self-deformed people in hand and after a brief séance disabuse them of their paralyses—men that had come in that very day permanently crippled, to all appearances.

We climbed the embankment to the old fortress wall for a glimpse of the valley and town, with the almost sheer hillside below us. Then back to Salins to see in the *caserne* an important last stage of the treatment—the training battalion—the discharged cases from Station No. 42 divided into three groups: those getting ready to go back to the line, those doubtful, and those probably permanently unfit. They were drawn up on parade, the first group fully equipped for service, under command of a crippled captain wearing an apparatus for a musculo-spiral paralysis. As they marched by us Roussy picked out one probable *récidive* from among the A class. He will doubtless be sent back to Fort St. André for three days' solitary confinement followed by another strenuous therapeutic session—one mind struggling to get control of another that has good reason to resist.

Then back to Besançon in a downpour which flooded the valley, a late supper in Roussy's comfortable billet, and to bed in the last room of the single hotel. . . .

Aug. 26–27. Neufchâteau

Working on organization of neurosurgical consultants for hospitals in base areas.

Wednesday, Aug. 28th

With Longcope to visit the hospital arrangements in our Toul Sector on the basis of information from Col. Stark. Picking up Gibbon and Norris, now Corps Consultants, we begin with the Justice Hospital Group, formerly the French H.O.E. No. 3 in three large *casernes*—a place capable of holding 10,000 beds. It is now occupied by two of our base hospitals and two evac'n hospitals. Lt. Col. Maddux, who has been pulled out of Mesves to have charge here, is not quite sure what his position is—whether Commandant for Toul, or for the area, or where the S.O.S. comes in; and whether the fact that Col. Morrow of Evac. No. 1 outranks him makes any odds, etc., etc.

He will have a large job with Toul alone, even if the others are not included. Base Hosp. No. 45, Stuart McGuire's outfit, is

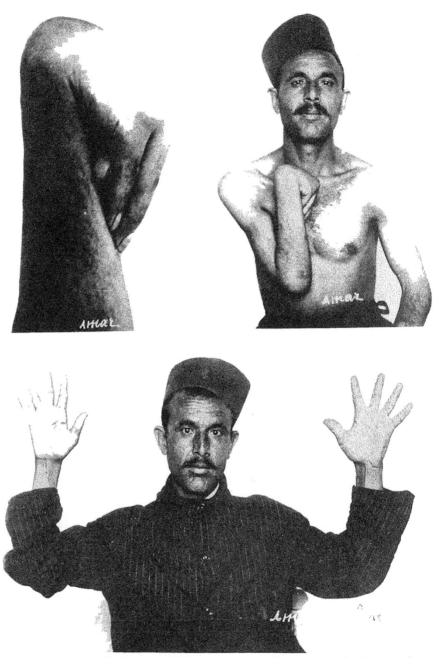

A Moroccan with a *Main Figée* before and after his Psychotherapeutic
Séance

about 60 per cent ready. They will take medical and gas cases—
the surgeons to be scattered. Evac. No. 3, Cutler's group, is about
90 per cent ready and E.C. was fairly bursting with his plans,
having tried out his machinery yesterday, to Gibbon's horror, on
a hernia case! Evac. No. 14 alongside has just arrived in France
—their senior surgeon, Major Meredith, arrived only yesterday
—and they have no equipment whatsoever. Base Hospital No. 51,
a "U.S. at Large" Unit, made up chiefly of Boston M.O.'s, only
landed in France Aug. 18th; they are without nurses and the last
they saw of their equipment was in Hoboken.

We went on to Sebastopol and saw Evac. No. 1 and the new
and unpromising Mobile Unit No. 3. Then on to the field hospitals of the 89th Division now in the area, No. 355 in a fine lot
of Bessonneau tents left by the French in the woods near Minor-
ville. Another, No. 356, in the old abbey buildings of Rangeval,
from which we could see Montsec standing up out of the plain,
in whose attempted capture the French lost so many thousands.
We also visited No. 353 and No. 354 somewhere in the woods.

On the way back we stopped at Lucy, the Divisional H.Q., and
I looked up Col. Kilbourne for a moment and found him very
fit but a bit down owing to the general neglect of the 89th and
the way they have been treated; their General not yet with two
stars and the Division sent in on a front from Montsec to Fey-
en-Haye, where they began cutting enemy wire and taking prisoners on the third night—their predecessors never having taken
any. Hence information of the conditions of the sector was completely wanting when they came up.

Thursday, Aug. 29

Widener's French confidant says that Gen. Pétain was here yesterday and is going up to the Nancy front. There are many rumors of all kinds—of probable actions—of breaking through to
Metz—of spies in the guise of couriers shot on the roads—of
German aviators flying over here in a Caproni machine dressed
as Italian flying men, and of their being brought down by the
British R.F.C. because they did not answer signals.

· · · · · ·

The news continues to be encouraging. Certainly something
unaccountable has happened to the Boches. They seem to be

beating a retreat toward the old Hindenburg Line before the British, who are clinging to their heels. Yesterday, in an advance of 10 km. on a front of 40, Chaulnes and Nesle and 50 lesser vil_ lages fell to them and the French; and now Noyon and Péronne are threatened. The British have even crossed the Hindenburg Line east of Arras and as far south as Croisilles. Can it be that the Boches have cracked?

Friday, Aug. 30th

Very busy offices with many people, constituting teams, coming and going. Most of Fisher's time spent in Chaumont. Lunch as usual, on "bully" and jam plus yellow jackets innumerable, in Salmon's room. Bert Lee and Ruggles from the 2nd Division there. Flint, very large and busy, in this afternoon. His guess is that it will be Monday! May the weather hold. To-day could not have been improved upon.

．　　．　　．　　．　　．　　．

The British still bang away. The New Zealanders have taken Bapaume and Péronne is threatened. Marcel Hutin laconically says: *"Ils ne sont plus à Noyon!"*

Sat., Aug. 31

Most of the young officers out here go booted and spurred— boots often of the drawing-room variety, accompanying thin soles and pointed toes. These are particularly characteristic of new-comers. The story has come with them that someone asked Joe Cannon why so many officers wore spurs—even aviators wear them—and he replied: "To keep their heels from slipping off the desk."

One of our newly arrived "chicken colonels" appeared at break-fast to-day to our great joy with his spurs upside down, and when he went to ride this afternoon—for Webb is giving him riding lessons—he thought it was safer to take his spurs off, though he has worn them continuously as a pedestrian and automobilist.

We're an amusing lot surely. Goldthwait, who has just come back from the much neglected Base, which he has made his own and where he has been doing some excellent work, told at lunch of a soldier just sent home—drafted in June; immediately sent over with a replacement group, absolutely untrained; reached France and was sucked into a division supposedly *en repos;* this division was drawn unexpectedly into the line in the July battles before he had even learned to fire his gun; wounded in the first day's fight; sent home by transport the end of August—all in the space of two months.

It's commonly understood that there were several hundred of these men in the 1st and 2nd Divisions—men who had never learned to put the clips on their rifles, far from learning the manual of arms—the surprising thing is they did very well.

. . . . . .

Yesterday Combles and Bailleul were retaken by the British. The Australians are across the Somme above and below Péronne. An attack by the Canadians toward the angle where the old Hindenburg Line joins the highly fortified switch line Quéant-Drocourt—i.e., the Wotan Line. The French are progressing through difficult country, and the Americans with them entered Juvigny yesterday.

Sunday, Sept. 1st

Discover that my threatened blindness is an acute 2-diopter presbyopia which has rushed on me in a period of ten days—an accompaniment of the muscular enfeeblement of the grippe, according to George Derby. Specs for me henceforth.

Monday, September 2nd. Neufchâteau

Again a perfect day—cool and cloudless. But Neufchâteau is torn up and dust-covered by the incessant passage of transport —everything from lines of *camions* borrowed from the French to processions of clucking motor cycles newly landed and straight from St. Nazaire.

The streets of this small place are really astonishing if one stops to squint through the dusty haze. This afternoon, on the road coming into town from our offices, Russians were piling crushed stone in preparation for the steam roller doing its work farther on. A column of French lorries driven by Annamites —very funny in their tin hats—were going west and another column of heavy U.S.A. cars full of troops were coming in, while motor cycles with or without side cars, decrepit Y.M.C.A. and Red Cross flivvers, pedestrians, and an occasional officer on a loaned horse dodged in and out as best they could.

The motor-transport people—our neighbors—were gathering

for their supper, mess kit in hand, while a big Caproni bombing plane circled overhead. Farther on, a squad of Boche prisoners in their green uniforms—content and well-fed, be it said—were being herded to their cage by a single *poilu*. Loitering on the streets were occasional Italians belonging to an aviation squadron hereabouts, samples of our negro troops, men of the English Flying Corps stationed just north of here, a smattering of blue *poilus*—a kaleidoscope seen through a cloud of dust.

Preferring cows and a narrow path beside the bad-smelling, swampy Meuse to all this, I cut cross-lots to our billet. The fields are spotted with purple colchicums sticking their blossoms out of the grass as much as to say, "Don't take me for a crocus and think this is spring.". . .

Wednesday, Sept. 4th

Our scarcity of transport makes us hunt in couples—even in foursomes at times. Yesterday I joined a traveling X-ray circus behind Sgt. McCormack, with Case and one of his sanitary-corps repair people.

To Pagny-sur-Meuse via Vaucouleurs. Pagny full of guns and *camions*, a scant 200 yards from the railroad and still less from a huge ammunition dump. Evac'n Hosp. No. 12 under Col. Bloomberg, newly arrived in France (*viz.*, Aug. 28), was making its nest as usual in an abandoned H.O.E. The Unit, gathered at large, had Bronson Crothers among them. Clopton, too, was hovering about not knowing where to place his Mobile No. 4— certainly no room in this crowded spot—Trondes a possible solution, for there a so-called "provisional evac'n hosp." is being formed out of unattached field hospitals.

To Toul, and luncheon before reporting to Geo. "High Ranking" Gosman, who sat spurred and booted and covered with eagles in his office. He has ideas of his own concerning Consultants— present company of course excluded—would put 'em at work— with their hands, etc. Not a bad idea on the whole. He gives Case directions about placing X-ray machines in all divisions and we depart to the Justice Group to interview Maddux and Edwards. Cutler, at No. 3 Evac., and his C.O. who follows him around like a puppy dog, are found more than ready and awaiting an inspection from the Chief Surgeon.

So to Nancy, where Case flew about as erratic as a spark from one of his own coils, and where McCormack got tires and Case a uniform, after which we discovered at La Mal Grange another "provisional evac'n hosp." made out of the 163rd F.H. of the 41st Division, under Major Ostrom. Then north along the valley of the Meurthe to Frouard, and very pretty country with surprising towns on the hillsides—thence west along the Moselle and the Marne–Rhine Canal some 10 miles from the line, to Liverdun, an old walled town perched high on a pointed hill with fascinating outlooks of valleys and rivers and distances shadowed by the low sun.

A bad place for a motor car, but McCormack safely negotiated the narrow twisting and precipitous streets. We found Grissinger away and had to satisfy ourselves with Maj. Tenney, my *quondam* classmate who happily discourages Case from doing any business with them. So we returned via Nancy, stopping at Chavigny, where Evac. No. 13, also newly landed in France (Aug. 26th), was found ensconced in a fine H.O.E. and believing themselves ready to take severely wounded to-morrow if necessary.

While Case was being delivered of another apparatus I interviewed the embryo neurosurgeon, and it grew dark and air raids began—the usual picture—searchlights and Archies—so familiar last summer. They followed us, indeed, all the way to Colombey-les-Belles and Autreville before we ventured to use a single headlight, and it was precarious business, as the roads were full of lorries and guns and troops going up in clouds of dust. We got into Neufchâteau about 11 not knowing that bombs had been dropped here, causing great excitement, for the experience was novel to this place.

.   .   .   .   .   .

The British did great business in crossing the Drocourt–Quéant line last Monday, and report 10,000 prisoners. One of the most startling operations of the present interallied offensive. Lens has been evacuated. The French, too, are working further around the western flank of the Chemin des Dames. Some American troops are said to be at last engaged alongside the British in Flanders. The U.S. has recognized the Czechoslovaks as co-belligerents. *La désillusion règne en Allemagne.*

X

REDUCING THE ST. MIHIEL SALIENT

Thursday, Sept. 5th

RAIN. Plans to go to the research meeting in Paris spoiled by the advent of teams requiring instructions. A visit from Jim Perkins, who is in this area on a Red Cross mission—also Hugh Scott. We are green-eyed with envy at sight of the Pierce-Arrow limousine in which they travel. George Brewer back from his tour of the base hospitals, much encouraged by the condition in which the wounded have arrived there.

Arrangements made with Dexter for a combined tour of the Souilly hospital group in anticipation of the attack we have been told would open there to-morrow on the west of the St. Mihiel salient. Fisher, however, has just brought word from Chaumont that only one division of the 5th Corps remains in that area. In fact, they have us guessing, and probably the Boche too. The whole operation may be shifted to the Franco-British sector, where the enemy are rapidly falling back to their old line. Foch presumably knows, but who else?

. . . . . .

The remnant of the Boche's Marne "salient" is caving in. The Vesle was crossed yesterday by Franco-American forces west of Fismes. This largely the result of Gen. Mangin's dogged pressure north of Soissons.

PREPARING FOR CASUALTIES

Friday, 6th. Benoite Vaux

. . . On through Euville, encountering more of the 1st Division—Commercy, scarred by bombs—Lérouville, and along a camouflaged road in view of the distant enemy positions—

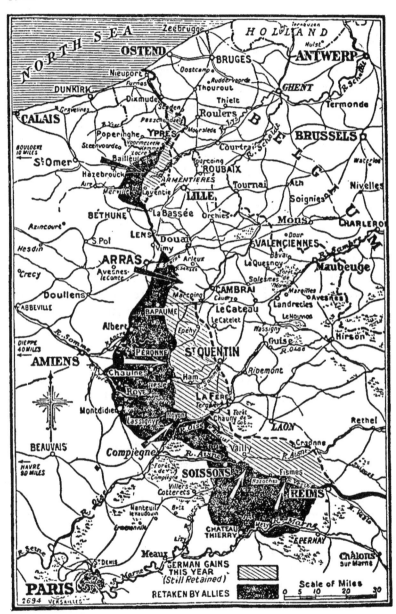

Showing the Changes in the Western Front Since the Great German
Spring Offensive of March 21st. Ground Regained by the Allies in
Black. British Break Hindenburg Line September 2nd

Sampigny, where a French guard warns us that this is our limit, for the Commercy road soon passes dangerously near the tip of the salient and the Boche lines. So to the left to Menil-aux-Bois behind more camouflage of the brush-mat variety, through woods of pine, birch, maple, and oak full of French artillery—to Baudre_ mont past extensive dumps, along a beautiful road now parallel to the lines—past fields purple with colchicum, in which women are cutting and gathering a late crop of sweet-smelling grass— Villotte-dev.-St. Mihiel—Nicey, where are some outposts of the 80th Division and where we miss our turn and proceed east to Rupt-dev.-St. Mihiel, where a French *triage* and *poilu* cemetery make us suspicious of our error—so back to Pierrefitte and across country via Courouvre, and in a sudden downpour we reach our destination.

Salmon's newly established hospital—a *triage* for acute neuroses —is on the road to Issoncourt just west of Benoite Vaux. It is surrounded, wonder of wonders, by an extensive truck garden, and occupies the huts of a former French hospital of small size, with the officers' quarters in cabins on a hillside behind. We plant ourselves there for the night and in the absence of patients find beds, food, and a welcome.

Then to Récourt, where Mobile No. 2 sits in its bones on a hillside—the canvas ready to put up when the show opens and not till then, lest the erection of hospital tents betray the coming operation. There a pot of tea—a pleasant novelty in the A.E.F.— and a conference with Neuhof, who is to do the head cases.

So on to La Morlette just west of Ancemont to locate Mobile No. 1 to which Dowman is attached—our way via Villers-sur-Meuse with lovely views to the east, though much of the roadway was screened. The presence of the 4th Division assures us of four in this area despite the rumors down the line. Then back to Benoite Vaux for a six-o'clock supper with Allison and Salmon's eager youngsters, Lt. Stout the C.O., Cannaday, Leavitt, and Sands. At twilight the rumble of passing guns and transports begins—twilight gives way to darkness and then pitch darkness with heavy rain, out of which emerges one of Allison's capable young divisional people named Grady who had come in a side car from somewhere—the 33rd moving up to Blercourt west of

Verdun to be brigaded out with the French—never in the line before and after only a short British experience—no splints whatsoever and what shall they do? So that accounts for a 5th division in this sector.

Saturday, Sept. 7th

. . . Dexter is easily prevailed upon by Garcia to remain up here and care for the gassed cases, and I leave him happy at the hospital at Rambluzin where they are to be routed. . . . At Souilly—or just west of Souilly—alongside the railway and adjacent to a huge dump with a mountain of fodder in its centre, Evac'n Nos. 6 and 7 sit conspicuously, inviting air raids, on the side of a hill in two old French H.O.E.'s. They are well equipped and well cared for with terraces, dugouts, flower beds, and duckboards indicating long and fond tenancy. Here will go the severely wounded, as is true of Evac'n No. 8 at Petit-Maujouy. (Harrington is at No. 6, Sam Harvey at No. 7, and Hanson at No. 8.) No. 9 at Vaubécourt is for sick and slightly wounded. Nos. 1 and 2 Mobile are for non-transportables, with Dowman and Neuhof for cranial wounds. The psychiatric cases to Benoite Vaux of course, and the gassed to Rambluzin; while all French casualties, so far as sorting permits, go to Fleury, where they retain an H.O.E. It will be a difficult *triage*.

Later to see Lt. Hanson at Evac'n No. 8 on the Génicourt–Ancemont road just west of Macrae's outfit. Hall very well fixed in another H.O.E. with a fine well-lighted operating hut holding 18 tables for which he has too few teams. Lunch there and back to Souilly where Allison and Col. Beeuwkes were struggling to get up and distribute supplies of hip splints for femurs. A few Boche planes over, followed by shrapnel—let's hope they learned little. Nothing more that I can do, so back to Neufchâteau to turn in the car as agreed, via Bar-le-Duc; a French officer just from ruined Reims is picked up, and with him to Ligny. Gondrecourt, where we passed the 91st Division moving up—very fine-looking lot from our Northwest. Finally Neufchâteau in 3.5 hours' fast going.

.   .   .   .   .   .

On Thursday, British troops took "Plug street" and Hill 63 and have passed some of their old positions near Givenchy.

Toward Cambrai they are up to the Canal du Nord and report 16,000 prisoners in the four days since the battle of the switch opened.

Yesterday the enemy withdrew rapidly all along the line toward their positions of March 21st, and late in the day the French took Ham and Chaulny. The Americans are approaching the Aisne and the Boches will probably make a stand on the Chemin des Dames. They meanwhile have begun a "peace offensive" and Hindenburg gives out a manifesto warning the troops against our propaganda—"our bombarding their front with a drum fire of printed paper." The Crown Prince also gives an inspired interview with quite a change of face—so far as his mousy face *can* change.

Sunday, September 8th. Benoite Vaux

They are certainly provident people, the French—so it was not all British talk, after all. The 2nd Division, hustled into French motor trucks, was thrown into the line west of Château-Thierry. The Marines stuck up their flag and refused to retreat—the Boche was checked and probably Paris saved. On the first of the month our government got a bill for 280,000 francs for the use of the trucks for which we had provided the *essence*—the bill was paid. Whether this is truth or fiction I can't presume to say —rumors which often prove false circulate over here amazingly and facts get distorted in the process. After all, a tendency to drive a close bargain is also a Yankee characteristic, and this war is being fought in France, not New England.

It is Sunday afternoon in this Field Neurological Hospital No. 1 on a road over which goes at night an incessant traffic of lorries and artillery and tanks—predatory creatures which conceal themselves in the wood by day. Imagine a tar-paper hut of rustic French pattern perched on the side of a hill at the edge of a beech forest looking down over the cluster of ten or twelve Adrian huts composing the hospital group. This particular cabin, with its two cots, measures about twelve by eight feet, and I am to share it with Dexter. Allison and Salmon are close by in another, and innumerable paths wind in and out of the *forêt* rising up on the hill behind us.

While preparing—each of us in his own line—for something

soon to happen to the St. Mihiel salient, we meanwhile, on getting back here nights when possible, may be regarded as psychiatric patients—all colonels come more or less in that category, anyway. Salmon has pinned over Allison's cot this medical card:—

NAME	N. Allison, K.B. RANK Lt. Col. ORG. M.C.
No. ADM.	1
DIAGNOSIS	Shell shock (severe melancholia with paranoiac tendencies)
PROGNOSIS	Bad
TREATMENT	Disciplinary

A real feeling of autumn in the air, with driving clouds, and before reaching here late this p.m. we passed through a heavy downpour. But the water soaks in fast and the rain helps road making.

. . . . . .

Yesterday the British reached Beauvois, on their way to St. Quentin, and the French crossed the Crozat Canal. The captured Huns are said to be much depressed, and Hindenburg's power wanes. But the 26th Division is much more interested in the fact that the Cubs beat the Sox in the second game of the series. "Boy Howde!"

Monday, September 9th

It's interesting that eight out of the first ten patients admitted to this hospital had widely dilated pupils with hallucinations— a few being actively excited. One of them this morning was clear-headed enough to recall that, in addition to some blackberries, he had eaten about five large ripe berries, which grew on a bush four or five feet high, and they left his mouth puckery. So Dexter and I struck off into the woods this afternoon on a botanizing expedition—and incidentally to find a short cut over the hill to his hospital at Rambluzin. An incomparable beech forest with an occasional mountain ash and white oak, carpeted with delicate wood ivy and blue Canterbury bells in profusion.

There were innumerable crisscrossing paths which were dry despite the downpour this morning, but which were also confusing, and, having no compass, we got well lost. Most of the woods hereabouts are jam-packed with troops, but we saw not a human being—not even a lumberjack, though there were plenty of re_cently felled trees trimmed and ready to go to the mill at Benoite Vaux.

We finally, after about two hours, came to the top of a hill where the ground was badly torn up and the trees all dead within a circle of some one hundred yards across. The place was guarded by a single barbed-wire strand fastened to the trees, and within were eight huge perfectly formed craters about thirty feet across and thirty feet deep. We ventured under the wire and found the ground strewn with rusty Mills' hand grenades, almost all of them exploded. I picked up from the rubble a perfectly formed fossil bivalve which had been blown up out of the chalk—also a fossilized mandible, ape-like in form. The trees above a six-foot level had been so completely riddled they had died—certainly a year or two ago. What is the explanation?

From this place we took another path, and, as luck would have it, encountered a *Chasseur Alpin* sitting on a log. He pointed the way to Rambluzin and casually remarked that the branches with the big black berries we had in our hands were poison— belladonna, as every Frenchman knew. There was only one va- riety, he was sure. Our quest was satisfied, and not three hundred yards away we came to the edge of the woods and found ourselves looking down on the huts of Dexter's place.

Tuesday the 10th. Benoite Vaux

The weather has certainly broken—rain a-plenty. This morning Dexter, Allison, and I in the Dodge to Souilly and beyond, while Salmon and Bailey conspire here. The 5th Corps Hq. is moving up to Ancemont and it is rumored that the 3rd Corps is to come to Souilly.

Nat stops at his splint dump while Dexter and I, with Marshall Clinton, who is acting as 5th Corps Consulting Surgeon, push on in a driving downpour, well soaked, to Robécourt to visit No. 9 Evac'n. They too in a well-planned French H.O.E., though bedraggled as a lot of chickens in a wet henhouse. The C.O., a man named Johnson from the Surg. Gen.'s Office, and a major of the same name from Beverly, Mass., the Senior Surgeon. A very promising outfit, and after lunch we hand over such instructions and information as we think they will absorb and tolerate. As they have just come over we tread cautiously.

Back to Souilly over bad country roads, cheered by patches of sunshine. Pretz—Beauzée-sur-Aire—Amblaincourt, all of which must have been about on the edge of the 1914 German advance, for the hamlets are badly tumbled and many isolated graves dot the fields and line the roads—French with the tricolor—one Boche painted black—"*Allemand inconnu.*" Serancourt—Rignaucourt—Heippes, and again on the wide-sweeping military highway to Souilly. Clinton is dropped, Allison rescued, and we return to Benoite Vaux to find Salmon and Bailey impatiently awaiting their only means of transportation.

I go on with them to locate the *triages*, which we find are not yet established. To Récourt and across the Meuse behind the camouflaged roads. Génicourt-sur-Meuse, a red-roofed intact hamlet in the western lee of a hill—no plans as yet. Then Rupt-en-Woëvre, where the YD has its headquarters—nothing there as yet. So we give up the *triage* business; and since Bailey wishes to see Verdun, though rather late, we go up the east bank of the Meuse along the canal. This full of canal boats, many of them sunk—in all probability cached there since 1914—now occupied only by an occasional cat, a box of geraniums, and a bedraggled old man or woman.

Across the Meuse things are lively—the familiar zone of activity behind the lines when something is coming off. We soon run into another heavy rainstorm and, after completely missing Verdun to our left, find ourselves confronted by a lone French guard at a crossroads on the ridge of a hill, who says we are at Bras, headed for the Boche lines some 4 km. away. So we turn about and go through the outskirts of the tottering and riddled town, but get so confused in the surrounding park full of wire entanglements that we never even located the citadel. All this brought us back late to supper and we are now warming and drying ourselves at a small stove newly installed in Salmon's cabin.

·   ·   ·   ·   ·

During our absence Fisher and Baer appeared on a coat-tail visit to the Evac'n Hospitals. Finney has returned—General Gorgas said to be coming. Finney and Thayer to be generals. How ₛiₗₗy. they will feel—or will they? It may well curtail their ac_ tivities, and mean their sitting on waffle chairs at Tours. Others of us also to be moved up, it is said. This too has its drawbacks. No more operating at Evacuation Hospitals for a Lt. Colonel.

Wednesday, September 11th

9 p.m. Sam is as black as the ace of spades and says if he can only "git one foot on de aidge of the *U*-nited States he 'll sure quick find his way back to *Co*-lumbia, South Ca'lina—jes' one foot, yaas sah!" He 's been sent in here as simple-minded (prob_ ably by some Yank M.O.), whereas he 's just nigger. You should hear Cannaday, a Virginian, draw him out regarding his ex_ periences in the trenches.

"Sam, what did the regimental doctor ask you?"

"Oh, he done ask me who 's de captain ob de *U*-nited States."

"What did you say?"

"Oh, I done said *Washington*, he 's de captain ob de *U*-nited States, an' *Paris*, he 's de captain ob France, an' *Berlin* he 's de captain ob Germany—yaas sah!"

"Sam, who are we fighting in this war?"

Sam, hesitatingly: "Why, we 's fightin' de Germans."

"Who else, Sam?"

"We 's fightin' de Australians, too—yaas sah."

Sam is good at finding bits of wood and we again have a fire in Salmon's leaky hut to-night, hoping to dry our things out, for the rain has kept up all day.

Thursday 12th

7 a.m. "Hullo, Sam, what are you doing in there?" From Sam, evidently proud of his difficult task: "Ise wakin' de colonels, yaas, sah." But why wake the colonels? The 26th Division cap- tured one yesterday in a raid—an evidence, as someone remarked, that they must have gone in very far—for colonels and higher ranks usually remain securely in the rear. A general is said to have accosted a supposedly exhausted but actually drunken soldier lying by the roadside, thus: "Where is your unit, my lad?" The d. s., rousing himself: "Must be a hell of a long way off if you 're up here, old man." This is a story with applications.

THE ST. MIHIEL BATTLE

Sunday afternoon, September 15th

Much has happened since Wednesday night, when, unaware of
its imminence, we are fretting over the delay in the offensive.
The French generously give our troops the credit: *"L'attaque
américaine dans la région de St. Mihiel,"* and so forth. Luck was
certainly with us.

Thursday the 12th opened raw, cold, and rainy. There had
been heavy gunfire during the night, but the strong westerly wind
and storm had completely muffled it from us. Salmon unhappily
had ventured to go down to Neufchâteau, where "the offices" had
grabbed Sullivan and our pilfered Dodge car and we were legless
in consequence. But during breakfast the good Lord sent out of
the rain a flivver containing Cannon, Yates, and Middleton, who
dropped Dexter at his Poison-Gas Station and carried Allison and
me over to Souilly. There, to our astonishment, Garcia, who is
G-4 under Colonel Stark in this area, told us the show had opened.

Dropping Allison at his splint dump, which grows apace, we
went on to No. 1 Mobile at La Morlette. There, about 11 a.m.,
Macrae and his officers, unaware of what was going on, were found
sitting at a practice conference while the first ambulance of
wounded actually stood unannounced at the Admission Hut. Cannon and I then hustled to the F.H. 101 *triage* at Génicourt, expecting to find an overcrowded and busy place full of wounded
—"shocked" from cold, wet, and exposure. But no such thing.
A mere handful were dribbling through, and Captain Taylor had
them well in hand.

Thence on to the headquarters of the 26th, to see the Divisional
Surgeon, but he was away and we learned that the attack had
opened with a heavy barrage at 2 a.m. which kept up till five;
that the boys had gone over at daybreak; that so far very few
wounded had come through; that General Edwards's billet was
just around the corner.

Hyatt, at the headquarters, insisted on our going up to the
Divisional P.C. on the side of the hill just east of the town—the
Bois des Trois Monts, I believe—where we should find the Gen_
eral in one of the dugouts. We did, and passed a most exhilarating

hour—like listening to election returns when things are going one's way. The place was full not only of the General, but of maps and telephones and aides and liaison officers and messengers coming and going—Peter Bowditch; Captain Simpson; Major Pendleton; Colonel Alfonti; Captain Malick, formerly Joffre's A.D.C., and a lot more. The advance on the whole was going well—St. Rémy and Dommartin-le-Montagne taken—but somewhere we were being held up by a machine-gun nest and C.E. became greatly exercised and characteristically profane.

In the midst of all this someone announced that thousands of prisoners were coming in. The General looked skeptical, remarking that prisoners always dwindled in number or else about half of them got away. Still, we went out and stood on the slippery duckboards commanding a view along the valley where masses of Boches were being herded down the road. Soon word came from somewhere that a whole battalion had been captured with its officers, a medical officer among them.

"That means a job for you after lunch," said C.E. "Find out if Hindenburg is in Metz; where their artillery is; what divisions there are—anything you can." He held us to this, and after a brief lunch in his billet Cannon and I were left to interrogate the young M.O. whom Captain Horsman, the Divisional G-2, soon showed in. We gave him food and pumped him in a language somewhat halting from disuse, but he gave forth what he knew. . . .

A young, spectacled, erect, square-headed Prussian named Pick —in 1914 a student of Garré's, at Bonn, now Battalion M.O. in the 13th Landwehr Division—for the last 12 days in the trenches after a rest period at the lazaret in Dompierre. Yes, he had had as good a lunch as this yesterday; possibly the bread was not so good. The offensive a complete surprise—thought the barrage meant only a strong local attack, but it kept up so long they grew suspicious.

The first thing they knew they were surrounded by Americans. No artillery behind them—had been none for a long time—no *Flügers* either—High Command might have known of attack, of course, and withdrawn guns—Austrians in south of his division —no knowledge of other wing—nor of Hindenburg, who still dominates the situation despite our rumors to the contrary—we 'll have peace this autumn because the French and English and Americans will be satisfied with these recent advances.

Get into Germany? Never! There are three strong lines of defense to fall back upon—stronger than the Hindenburg Line by far—if the Allies have any such idea it will be a long war. Knew that Americans were over here, but did not know any were on this side of the salient—had seen them, but thought French were wearing khaki for purposes of deception. Yes, three fourths of the German people wanted peace, but they were well controlled. Give up the Hohenzollerns? Never.

How about the Bavarians and Württembergers? They are very good Germans but not good Prussians. The morale of the troops? Not as good as formerly—the *Stosstruppen* a mistake, as divisions had been weakened—but this would be corrected. Worst trouble due to the reclaimed Germans who had been prisoners in Russia and who refused to go into the front lines again. Bolshevism? *"Das ist möglich."* The U-boat campaign a recognized fizzle and von Tirpitz now discredited. . . .

There was much more that I need scarcely set down; we broke up and, after an exchange of compliments, I presenting him with a cigarette and he me with his peculiar gas mask, which he will no longer need, he was returned to the waiting sergeant.

Then in a heavy downpour back to Génicourt, passing a long column of Austro-Hungarian prisoners. Only 490 wounded through F.H. 101, including wounded Boches. Up the river road to Haudainville to the 28th F.H. behind the 4th Division, which apparently has not yet been in action—no wounded whatsoever. In turn to No. 1 Mobile via Ancemont, where Yates has been wallowing all day in chest cases sorted out and routed there for his benefit. Supper with them, and back to Benoite Vaux by moonlight—a clear night promising well for the morrow.

Pte. Jeremiah Sullivan, cursing picturesquely, has just returned from Neufchâteau with our ramshackle and uncertain Dodge. We thought best to ask no questions regarding the source of two new tires!

Friday the 13th, after a downpour during the night, opened raw and rainy. Cannon appeared in his precious flivver and with him to Pierrefitte, and from there along the recently forbidden road direct to Commercy via Rupt-devant-St. Mihiel with its French *triage*, where they have had but few wounded—Kœur_ la-Grand, much knocked about—and so along the road, camou_ flaged from the heights of St. Mihiel and the sharp hill of the Ft. du Camp-des-Romains, to Sampigny, with a lovely outlook over the Meuse and its canal. This road around the tip of the

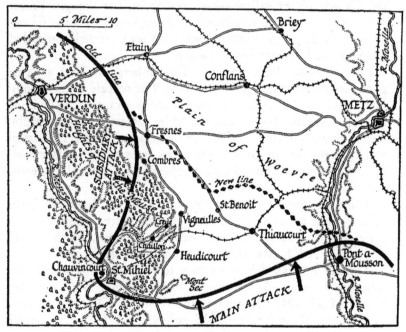

The St. Mihiel Salient Showing the Directions of the Attack of September 12th on Its Southern and Western Flanks

salient must have been under the Huns' view nearly as far down as Commercy, judging from the varied kinds of protections set up to conceal it.

At Aulnois, from 11 a.m. Thursday to 11 a.m. to-day, 201 cases with 170 operations by seven teams. The *triage* at Raulecourt not very effective; nor was it well done at the hospital itself, Kerr having had none of the head work. Flint at Mobile No. 39 very busy having to "mother" No. 11 Evac'n, a new unit just moved in to Sorcy, as well as his own enlarged hospital group. He has already been warned that he may have to move again.

After lunch, on to Sebastopol; and while Cannon investigates conditions of shock I learn that 1100 wounded have passed through Evac'n No. 1, which includes Mobile No. 3, though the latter unit was being dismantled to move to Royaumeix. Later at Toul we find that 3000 casualties have passed through the Justice Group, 2000 of them wounded. Cutler's Evac'n No. 3, with 12 teams, managed to do 190 operations in the first 22 hours out of their 730 cases all told.

An unexpected gathering of people at Col. Maddux's office; George Brewer, who says the outposts from west and south have met at Vigneulles, that Thiaucourt has been taken, and there are rumors of 13,000 prisoners. Thiaucourt fell within the first six hours, the plan having been to reach it on the second day. Finney appears, beaming as usual, glad to be back in this juncture, though confessing that he has lost hold. Gen. Ireland with him. Thayer, Crile, Gibbon, and others also appear.

At 6 p.m. we started back, passing on the way to Pagny a long procession of Boche P.O.W.—two to three thousand at least, and from every side joyful children were pouring down the road from the adjacent villages to see the sight. Then a mile or two of French lorries drawn up beside the road waiting to pick up the 91st Division, one regiment of which, the 363rd, we saw coming up the road from the south and deploying into a big open field spread out at our feet—a fine-looking lot, thrilled at the sight of the Boche prisoners and impatient to get to the Front and join in the fray.

A LOOK WITHIN THE SALIENT

On *Saturday the 14th,* as there promised to be no work, Cannon and I went on a round of the *triages* and found the Corps moving out, the map people gone and—what for us was more serious— no *essence* to be had. We finally wangled some from the forester squad. Through Rupt-en-Woëvre and toward the line through Mouilly, the road much torn up and undergoing repairs by the French "Jennys" (*génie du soldat*). They were also laying a Decauville,[1] meanwhile uncovering the real roadbed a foot or more below its present covering of mud and rocks tossed up by

---

[1] These were narrow-gauge (60 cm.) light railways, known as *voies de soixante,* used by the French for carrying ammunition to the front lines

the barrage. Many old French cemeteries, large and small, along the road. Mouilly on the sheltered side in ruins, with No. 114 F.H. in what is left of its church. Capt. Frank Stevens of Bridge_ port, the C.O., told us that in the first 36 hours, 2160 prisoners were taken by the 26th, and that only 348 casualties came through; but they were no longer coming down, the church was emptied of patients, and a table was set for lunch in the wreck of the chancel.

Stevens accepted our offer to accompany us and we took the much shot-up road toward les Eparges and soon emerged from the fairly well-preserved wood into the strip of No Man's Land —always a staggering spectacle with its stumps of trees, its wire, its trenches and shell holes. "Jenny" was busy here also re_ making the strip of road which during all these sad years had totally disappeared. Now partly repaired, the worst half mile was jammed with every kind of vehicle, horse, mule, and gas-drawn, trying to get through.

The delay gave us time to look into the trenches—what was left of them—for the 26th certainly had put up a devastating barrage. What remained, however, showed how well the Boche trenches had been made—largely of concrete with extensive and intercommunicating dugouts, the names of the officer occupants carefully lettered on the blocks that formed a part of the parapet. Many of our doughboys were wandering about gathering souvenirs of every imaginable kind, those that interested me most, in view of Hindenburg's recent address to the German troops, being the Allied propaganda, many samples of which were being blown about everywhere.

The block finally opened up and the procession moved forward. We left the les Eparges road and turned right on the Grande Tranchée de Calonne which led to Vigneulles, and I may add that the Boche front-line trenches lay west of this crossroads, not east of it as all of our maps have shown. We soon got on to the well-kept highway which served as the enemy's L. of C. and went on through the beautiful Forêt de la Montagne, chiefly of beech, still fairly well preserved. It probably covers many dead, recent and unburied as well as long since buried, for German graves are numerous along the roadside—numerous and ornate, with massive stone or concrete headstones, elaborate in the Boche fashion.

The road crosses several large traps for tanks, great pits with branches thrown over them, out of which a tank would have great difficulty in climbing. German signs, also, everywhere, the one which chiefly interested us being ZUM VERBANDPLATZ with an arrow pointing down the road. On past big gun emplacements, the surroundings littered with green wicker baskets over three feet in length, each containing the brass shell case of a 150 mm. gun—the shell cases filled with long strands of cordite. In the woods were little houses, rustic in style, reminding one of the houses in Grimm's *Fairy Tales,* tucked away here and there in the forest.

The "Verbandplatz" was in the middle of the forest, about opposite Dompierre-aux-Bois—a so-called "Lager Rubezahl." Here Capt. Blair of Providence had already established his field hospital, and they were caring for about 100 men who had just come in, victims of a German bombing raid which had occurred somewhere in the neighborhood of Vigneulles. The German aid station was in an old quarry, extraordinarily well made and protected. There were many underground chambers with all sorts of interesting medical supplies, bandages and equipment of various kinds, all evidently left in a great hurry—possibly by Herr Dr. Pick himself—even the record sheets of recent patients lying about—some of them evidently Hungarians, judging by the Hungarian newspapers among the litter. The conditions within Germany were made apparent by the bed mattresses, which were covered with a very stout paper difficult to tear, out of which they are said also to make clothing.

After a frugal lunch with Col. Hobbs of the Engineer Corps, who is in charge of the road reparation in the area, on along the Grande Tranchée until suddenly we burst out of the forest on the edge of the high plateau of the Côtes de Meuse which shelves off abruptly to the plain, giving, both north and south, most extraordinary views, the ruins of Hattonville lying at the end of the road.

One could see many burning villages to the north; a Boche balloon shot down in flames; Woel burning; a French officer look-

ing through a large stationary binocular pointed out the Lac
Lachaussée behind the Bois des Haudronvilles, with Jonville beyond, which was being shelled, and we could see Chambley and
perhaps also the chimneys of Conflans across the level plain at
our feet. Far to the south the highlands of St. Mihiel stood out,
and possibly Montsec, though we were not sure of it, and farther
west the familiar heights flanking Toul, 30 or more km. away—
an unforgettable spectacle of a promised land.

From Hattonville we wound down the road to Vigneulles,
which is on the level of the plain, the road lined by the peculiar
Boche camouflage resembling latticework strips of cloth woven
obliquely in and out of the wire mesh, as well as kinds made of
rushes, much neater than the French brushwork gabions. Vigneulles, like all the other villages, had been burned in the retreat,
though not to the ground, for French stone houses are gutted by
fire, not burned down. The pungent smell of charred timbers
permeated the place, now occupied by Americans, for it was here
that they met coming from the two sides of the salient.

We delayed briefly to interview the *civils*. One weazened old
woman whom I asked for recent German papers took me into her
ruined house—until yesterday occupied by Boche officers, while
she slept in a little back room and cared for them. She produced
some papers, among them the *Gazette des Ardennes* with its
illustrated weekly supplement, published for distribution among
the French *civils*.

I asked her if she had any German money, and after some
hesitation she closed the outer door to her tumbled combination
of kitchen and bedroom, and in the corner under her bed disclosed
a trapdoor leading into the cellar with a rustic ladder down which
she went, to reappear shortly, burdened with a small trunk simply
filled with paper money, German and French, old and new.
There were all sorts of promissory notes, as well as German paper
money. The promissory notes had been issued, as she explained,
by the local French banks in the captured communities; also that
the French civilians were paid for their services with these notes
"guarantis par les Communes"—certainly an effective way of
getting an indemnity out of a community without actually demanding a cash payment outright from them. I purchased some

of these bills from her and she drove a very close bargain, demanding full price for the French notes, and insisting that the mark was double the franc in value—the poor old thing.

Then on by the aid of very admirable Boche road signs, down between the forested hills leading to St. Mihiel—Creue, well burned, even its *Lichtspielhaus*—Chaillon, also in cinders, the residence of its *Ortskommandant* and all else. Then on along a road which had been thoroughly shelled, now lined by happy *poilus* who waved gayly at us, across many narrow-gauge Decauville roads with their *"Achtung: Feldbahn,"* and so to the edge of the hill leading down to St. Mihiel.

Here a puncture gave us a chance to walk down into the town, at whose outskirts, on the side of a hill, was a beautifully kept Boche cemetery of large size dominated by a huge Hindenburgian concrete monument bearing an Iron Cross at the hill's crest. Almost all of the many graves were marked with more or less elaborate and massive headstones, ornately figured and with well-kept flower beds and ivy—graves dating back to '15 and '16, most of them. The finishing touch to the scene was furnished by groups of *poilus* in their *ciel-bleu* regarding wonderingly the *"Hier ruht im Gott"; "Den Heldentod fürs Vaterland."*

In the town itself an old man told me that there had been about 2000 civilians, and that he himself had lost 26 kilos in weight; he looked well enough, however, as did the many children who were about, though I cannot say they were Mellen's Food babies exactly. He added that, had the attack been made 24 hours earlier, we would have taken many prisoners, for the last of the German troops did not leave until then. As it is, they had sucked the orange dry and really very little of military value appears to have been left in the salient. Flags were out in the town, French and American; and, our car catching up to us, we proceeded up the east bank of the Meuse, crossing again the double line of trenches near Meizey, where also were French "Jennys" filling up the holes in the shell-torn roads and the trenches which crossed them.

To our left, Chauvoncourt across the Meuse lay in ruins, and on the right of the road were the two heights of more than 300 metres which gave the Boche his dominating position so long retained in this area. Such masses of wire, all the way from here up the river, I have never seen, and the Boche trenches themselves were very beautifully made with blocks of concrete as neat as a Roman bath; but they had tumbled wire into the trenches, and probably burned out the dugouts before leaving.

As we crossed the French first line of trenches about half a mile beyond the German first line they were just filling in the road, so we again had to wait. I climbed down into the trench where were some *poilus*, one of whom pulled off from the side a French wooden sign reading VERS P. P. DES ÉTATS-UNIS, with an arrow pointing to the *petite poste de secours* of their advance line. This he presented to me with many smiles and bows.

So on to Rouvrois-sur-Meuse, quite demolished—the road thoroughly camouflaged against the view from the heights to the east. Then Lacroix-sur-Meuse, and Troyon, which must have been a fine place in its heyday, judging from the ruins of its *musée*, before which a colossal though somewhat chipped Jupiter and Minerva still stand with the bare sky above their surprised heads and no longer a portico for them to support. As the road went north it was screened first on one side, then on the other; at Troyon there were Boche and Hungarian prisoners, and we left the French and found the Yankee Division again; then Génicourt, and Rupt, where Capt. Stevens was dropped, Ancemont and No. 1 Mobile, where Cannon in turn was dropped, and I to Rambluzin for supper.

There a long powwow on organization with Dexter and Allison, in the midst of which Salmon and Bailey appeared after a day's survey of the Southern Corps fronts. The 1st Corps, so far as I can judge, did not make as much progress as was expected, the positions probably being stronger and the terrain more difficult. The 4th Corps to their left, and the 5th—the 26th Division being its only unit in action—did better as far as the depth of the advance went.

To-day, *Sunday*, has been a perfect day, warm and cloudless. Sullivan not having appeared with his broken-down Dodge, Bailey's borrowed car supplied our great need and we proceeded in a body to Souilly, where we were warned of a forthcoming movement on a large scale, with 15 divisions. The present operation may therefore be considered to be about over.

Col. Garcia indicated to us where some of the new hospitals that are moving up were to be placed, and we visited Evac'n No. 4 near les Souhesmes, and No. 5 at Ville-sur-Couzances, both of them tumbled into temporary quarters with their supplies in a mess until they could be told where they were finally to go. It's going to be difficult, this hospitalization business.

.   .   .   .   .   .

My impression of these last few days is that the enemy made an extraordinarily good get-away during Wednesday night, and though we are cheering loudly and much elated over regaining the salient, it has not been a great military victory. Though everything went smoothly enough, there is no knowing what would have happened had there been serious resistance and had we received large numbers of wounded. Our Medical Corps has yet to meet the consequences of stubbornly resisting picked troops such as we grew all too familiar with in last autumn's battles at Passchendaele. It will surely come—perhaps south of the Argonne, where we must next lay plans. Meanwhile we gain experience.

XI

THE ARGONNE OFFENSIVE

Tuesday, Sept. 17th. Neufchâteau

"UNCLE" FRANK BILLINGS, fresh from Washington, D.C., is billeting here with us. He tells of the group loitering around a country store in a remote part of the South which the news of the war rarely reached. A newcomer strolled up and someone said: "Jim, did you hear a big battle was going on over there?" "That so?" says Jim. "They 've sut'ney got a fine day for it." He gave us a long account of the reconstruction work they are planning at home.

This morning I drew from Col. Stark his plans for hospitalization during the coming offensive. Three army corps—15 divisions —with a front from Verdun to the west of the Argonne.

The French naturally are loath to give up their long established H.O.E.'s in the area till absolutely necessary; and our Army people don't want us to show any canvas or even a nurse's skirt on the landscape till the last minute. Stark is indigestive and about crazy; and says he never wants to see a Frenchman or a calf again —I fear he 's had too much *veau*.

Wednesday, Sept. 18th

To Bazoilles this a.m. and back in a side car—no joke. Luncheon for Gen. Gorgas and Col. Furbush. Lt. Col. Barclay Parsons of the Engineers and others there. Gen. Walker here to see what can be done with our means of transport, which is reduced to one threadbare Sharon. Elliott Joslin, Joe Capps, and a group of picked medicos from the U.S.A. arrive. Alec Lambert to dinner. Bert Lee in later, bearing trophies and full of his experiences with the 2nd Division, who reached Thiaucourt on the first day, so he moved up there and operated in a cellar, but got shelled out when the 78th moved in—they could n't stand it. The 78th are now digging in so we are about through, though not as far forward as we hoped to be.

Noncombatant Preparations

Sunday, the 22nd. Benoite Vaux

8 p.m. Rain and shine—mostly rain—the usual autumn weather. Thayer and G. Bastianelli, here on a visit, depart after breakfast, dropping me at Souilly. Garcia, Baker, Clinton, and I in a large staff car to a place called Deuxnouds where a 200-bed H.O.E. for eye, ear, and maxillo-facial work has been in operation by the French since March. A château owned by Mlle. de Beye, who is much interested, and do I think it will do for a head hospital? I had thought of trying three centres—perhaps at Villers-Daucourt, Fleury, and Souilly—one for each corps, but this alternative of one centre a little farther back is possibly a good one. Perhaps a favorable place for Towne and the beginnings of Mobile 6 if they can be secured? We shall see.

Then to Vaubecourt, where a medical dump is going in alongside of No. 9. So to Revigny—badly damaged in 1914—where lunch in a French officers' place with nothing to drink but red ink; then a visit to the French H.O.E. into which No. 15 Evac'n has moved and where Base Hospital 83 will come later. A 1670-bed place in Adrian huts made very attractive with an abundance of flower beds and vines; and instead of the ugly sandbag protections against *avions* there are nice fortifications covered by gabions over which nasturtiums bloom profusely. No wonder the French dislike to give these places up.

So back to Souilly via Laheycourt—Villotte, where a puncture and delay in the rain—Rembercourt, all the villages badly damaged in '14 by the French in driving out the resisting Germans—Chaumont-sur-Aire in a downpour and then another puncture with no extra tires, so we ignominiously beg a ride and leave the staff car to its fate and chauffeur.

Allison and Dexter were picked up in Souilly, and we find Salmon here. But Maj. Rhein has come in as C.O. with a new bunch of "nut pickers," our little quartette of lieutenants having moved on—and, what is more, with their negro cook, of griddle-cake and

Virginia-biscuit fame. 'T is now another's place, and we must look
elsewhere.

.   .   .   .   .

Continued British and French pressure reported between Cambrai and St. Quentin—a new offensive on a large scale in Palestine
by Gen. Allenby—the pursuit of the Bulgars progresses around
Lake Dorian with another 5000 prisoners—reports of activity,
too, come from the Archangel and the Murmansk fronts. The
Boche needs to look many ways.

Monday, 23rd Sept. Benoite Vaux

8 p.m. Probably our last night in this quiet place, for to-morrow
we migrate to Fleury to live in R.C. Hosp. 114 with McCoy
rather than in the Deuxnouds hospital as expected. Salmon, Allison, Finney, Dexter, and Rhein are next door discussing medical
education around a stove.

It poured all night and into the morning. Five of us in the
Dodge to Souilly, and there Salmon, Dexter, and I stood from
about 9 till 3, eating a paper of macaroons wangled from the men's
Y.M.C.A. for our lunch. Behind closed doors were deep consul-
tations between Garcia's cabinet and the Divisional Surgeons—
Eastman, Grissinger, Bevans, and several more. About eleven Finney appears and he too waits. Then people one by one were admitted by a six-foot guard—by ticket as it were. I manage to
propound the scheme for a *triage* to Deuxnouds with Towne and
his Mobile 6 as a nucleus, and hope the plan registered. We will
learn later; but meanwhile, on Salmon's suggestion, Sam Harvey,
with a team from No. 7, is taken over and deposited there as a
decoy.

We get away at 3 in Yates's flivver in which Finney now pere-
grinates. To Deuxnouds, which pleases us all much, though the
French occupants are removing things scarcely in the contract. We
find rooms we would like, and I discover a great cache of "Boston
tins," only partly emptied of their dressings, in the storeroom in
the barn.

Then Nubécourt, where we dump Salmon—Fleury, where Cutler and DeForest are fretting because Evac'n 3 is tied to an R.C.
hospital and where Finney decides it 's the best place to take up
our abode. So to Julvécourt to get Dexter at his gas place, and

back to Souilly for ditto Allison and, after a word with Garcia, thence to our home in the beech wood—an extraordinary evening with marvelous cloud effects as we crossed the open country on our way. A crack in the leaden sky to the west through which could be seen great pink cumulus masses against a blue background— to the east swirling masses of milky clouds tossed into fantastic shapes below the almost black sky—so low they seemed to touch the very hills. From the woods on all sides the gray smoke of the campfires of hidden troops curled out of the trees—no danger in this as no possible flying to-day, hence the roads have been full of troops, and huge howitzers were moving west along the Souilly-Ippécourt road.

.   .   .   .   .   .

Allenby has routed the Turks in Palestine—18,000 prisoners— Nazareth occupied—the field of Armageddon crossed—the Sea of Galilee reached.

Tuesday the 24th. Evac'n No. 7. Souilly

2 p.m. He also serves, etc., though it is difficult to believe at all times. Waiting since 9 a.m. again to-day—Finney off in our single car somewhere—Garcia fearing to move on the Deuxnouds proposition until he hears from Wadhams—nothing to do but wait. Maybe we are too late for a head-centre plan. Allison thinks the storm will break to-morrow, but rumor is probably his informant —rumor with the camouflage of authorization. Meanwhile colonels buzz in and out of Garcia's office down this wooden hallway —mostly begging transportation as usual, but otherwise complaining of the number of sick they are having—Baker says 1200 sick here, mostly infectious streptococcus throats out of which come many pneumonias. Hall has just as many and he is mad, and wants it put on paper that Evac'n No. 8 is to take only seriously wounded.

Other people come and go—nurses: "I wish you could see the linen they sent over to us this morning, it's per—fectly aw— ful!"—another from Mobile No. 2: "How can I get my power of attorney attached to these papers; can an officer be authorized to hold a court-martial, etc?" The poor adjutant. The French *central téléphonique* of H.O.E. days is perhaps as amusing as anything, particularly with its effort at concealment:—

"That you, Lakewood?" "Well, we want Col. Eastman."
"What! Is n't 'Lakewood' Ville-sur-Couzances?"

"Hello, West Point. Is Col. Salmon there in Benoite Vaux?"
And so on, with "Podunk," "Waterfall," "Widewing," and other
names—if one listens long enough even at one end of the line he
usually can find out who is at the other and where he is. I just got
Binns at Neufchâteau via "Waterfall," only to learn that Finney's
car is not yet ready to send up, so we five will continue as uncertain Dodgers.

To cheer up the locality the 16th Reg't band has just opened
up—very fine; and the afternoon has become sunny and pleasant.

9 p.m. R.C. Hospital 114, Fleury. Our kits were brought over
here this morning and we find ourselves in a little wooden barrack
—all to ourselves with a cubicle apiece, a stove in the hallway,
pyjamas laid out on cots with sheets on them!

McCoy himself rather sore. When he took this place over the
Médecin Chef with many bows pointed to the nicely planted market garden full of green cabbages and the like, saying, "This
potager militaire is all yours." McCoy accepted the gift—which
really was no gift as it belonged to the hospital—with thanks and
there was much bowing and scraping and saluting. The next day
we learned that the *Médecin Chef* had already sold the garden to
the *Génies* for 1500 francs. McCoy thereupon set a guard around
the garden.

The engineers countered by a complaint to the *Inspecteur
Général* of the district, who told McCoy he could not have the garden, but there was a potato patch near by which he could have for
900 francs. McCoy paid it. We asked him why, and he said he had
a brother in the cavalry, in charge of a remount station. The
French tried to sell them some horses—all old enough to vote and
otherwise broken down—at a prohibitive price. He refused. The
French complained—word finally reaching Gen. Pershing, who
ordered the purchase of the horses at the French price. They were
purchased and all had to be shot in a day or two. The General evidently does not want any bickering with the French on money
matters *pendant la guerre;* but some day we 'll possibly get even
with 'em.

Wednesday, September 25th

After a cold night with incessant rumble of lorries down the Wally road just behind us, we had the usual a.m. mix-up about the disposition of our decrepit Dodge—Salmon, Finney, Allison, Dexter, and I all needing to go in different directions. Learn at Souilly that a message from Colonel Tuttle states Mobile No. 6 ordered to Deuxnouds—now "Doughnuts," in soldier parlance— without waiting for completion of equipment and organization.

So we beat it there and drop Captain Harvey to make an inventory of the things the French are to leave—none too soon, for they were packing up everything, even to the stationary engine. Untidy, but not an unpromising place—chief features a good market garden (already sold by the outgoing French to a native of the village, who will sell it back to us for 200 per cent profit); four good wards of thirty beds each; a pile of coal, with some wood; a hillside where Towne can pitch his Bessonneau tents; and lastly a cache of *essence*. Only serious drawback that water must be carted from the spring at the entrance to the grounds.

Back to Souilly, where Garcia takes me to see Mlle. de Beye, the "Angel of Verdun." She very cordial—may have anything in her stores. Salmon promises ten of his nurses, and Marshall Clinton will help arrange about teams.

Our calculations for the eight divisions, with six in reserve, are 14,000 casualties—that is, 6 per cent of total engaged if there is serious resistance, as there is almost certain to be; of these, 3000 dead and 11,000 wounded, of which we may expect 10 per cent to have head wounds. The C. in C. is reported to have said, "Hell, Heaven, or Hoboken by Christmas."

THE BATTLE OPENS

September 26th. Fleury

9 p.m. The initial artillery preparation—very violent—began about 2 a.m. and continued till six. A cold, misty-clear morning. Finney and Allison to the divisional *triages*. Salmon and Dexter off in the Dodge. I, in a decrepit flivver wangled from Mobile No. 5, in chase of Towne's outfit, which is lost somewhere and must be ready to "take in" to-morrow.

To Souilly, where Garcia shows me a telegram which states: "Mobile 6 leaves Paris to-night at eight. Be on lookout for them to-morrow. Wadhams." So, with instructions to keep in touch with St. Dizier and to corral trucks if possible, I beat it for Deuxnouds over the plateau via St. André, with the Argonne ridge standing up beyond, the haze of the morning's barrage slipping away, the sky full of planes, the row of balloons to the north, the fields, where not being ploughed, simply alive with American soldiers who had emerged from the woods; all need for concealment over, they were being drilled in squads, eager to get forward.

No word of the unit at Deuxnouds, where Sam Harvey and his team were found at work straightening things out. Then to the station at Beauzée, where I find a funny loop of narrow-gauge road far from the town, with a French official who does not think it likely any express from Paris will come here. So back to Deuxnouds and lunch with the hospitable remnant of French Ambulance 225, a dentist educated in Philadelphia and Dr. Lataillade, the eye man. Two trucks had been sent us and it seems best to get rations from Souilly and to find what news, if any, has come. There was none, so I go on to the *triage* at Dombasle, through crowded dusty roads past lorries and tanks and batches of German P.O.W. There F. H. 315 is found under Maj. Harris, a Virginian from Fredericksburg, in an Adrian on a hillside near Mobile No. 1—very few wounded, only about a hundred for the 5th Corps, and possibly 4000 prisoners. The few head cases forwarded to Mobile 1. Gracious, I had expected him to say a thousand wounded at least. . . .

Friday, Sept. 27th. Fleury

8.30 p.m. The "strategy board" sits in Allison's cubicle mostly on his bed and a wooden box, for we do not use chairs, principally because we have n't them. They are reading Count Hertling's speech about the "U.S., whose bellicose ardor has been let loose."

After rushing about most all day to locate Mobile 6, Towne and Goethals suddenly appeared *here!* an hour ago—their whole outfit on some 30 cars have been 48 hours on the way from Paris. We have been trying to send them on to Souilly, where there is a good detraining platform. Here they would in all likelihood smash up their *camions*. We may with good luck be able to "take in" at

Deuxnouds to-morrow and there is much work still to be done, for Finney comes back saying that some 1200 wounded 24 hours old are being brought in to the 3rd Corps *triage*.

This morning in the rain, after dropping Salmon at Nubécourt and Allison at his dump, on once more to Deuxnouds. Find that 20 nurses from Base Hospital No. 5 under the guidance of Lt. Mulligan, Towne's X-ray representative, had arrived during the night via Bar-le-Duc and Beauzée, and had taken over one of the wards for their quarters—no breakfast for them or any sign of any. This defect being supplied with some borrowed loaves from the French officers who were packed and ready to depart, we went through the hospital and made all possible plans to receive the lost unit of whom there was still no trace. Back to pick up Salmon and then to Dexter's gas place—via Fleury on the great highway to Clermont, passing Autrecourt—Froidos, where are Mobile 2 and No. 10 Evac'n, and so Rarécourt. Only some 40 gas cases, all of a mild suffocative type—phosgene.

Ruined Clermont is most picturesquely situated on the side of one of the sugar-loaf elevations at the southern edge of the Argonne plateau. Thence through the forest, passing the 92nd—the Midnight Division—waiting to go in, to los Islettes and northward to the little town of Florent in search of the *triage* of the 77th, which we find had been moved. As we were due at Souilly at two we fled back via Julvécourt, where another of Dexter's places is set up and where we beg a loaf of bread to eat with a box of sardines found under the seat of the car—very good too. Clearing; and Sullivan puts back the top—the roads dry and we stop skidding into every passing vehicle, and they are many. Ippécourt—Souilly.

Dexter and Salmon go on to the St. Mihiel front and report to-night that the 26th made a two-brigade attack Thursday to aid in the general offensive, with some 200 wounded. At Deuxnouds again, this time in Finney's car, find two unexpected teams, but no word or sign from Towne. The 1st Division still in and about Deuxnouds—not called up yet. Back to Souilly, to find Finney away somewhere with Fisher and Col. Keller on "team" business; so Nat and I venture at 6 p.m. to use his car to return here—along the R.R. where across the valley stands Gen. Pershing's private train beside which a U.S.A. band is playing, while a crowd of *poilus* and others are gathered about. On the road itself, humping up under their camouflage of bedclothes, were no less than ten big 14-inch naval guns—a different picture every night.

Saturday, Sept. 28th

6 p.m. Sitting here at Fleury while a borrowed carpenter and sign painter, with a stolen pot of red paint, is making some 36″ × 8″ signboards reading, with directional arrows: —

```
MOBILE HOSPITAL NO. 6
     HEAD CASES
```

It's been a rotten day—racketing all over this area trying to get a hustle on No. 6—trucks—signboards to nail up routing ambu_ lances to Deuxnouds—all in Crile's rattly old Henry of ancient vintage. . . .

The day's peregrinations were somewhat as follows: After an interview with Towne, whose outfit is still here on the siding, to Souilly with Finney, then to Rampont to beg for Crile's car—in it via Ville-s.-Couzances and Froidos to Fleury, again to tell Towne to hustle up and beat it for Deuxnouds. Then via Nubécourt to get a sample sign from Lt. Stout and to Deuxnouds myself, where Harvey is hanging on, having accumulated four unexpected teams, some of them Lt. Colonels!

Four Packard trucks have fallen from heaven and we arrange to have three of them sent to Fleury and one to Souilly for neces- sary rations. Back again to Fleury and manage to steal two large motor trucks which seem to be unattached, and start Goethals fill- ing them "toot sweet." Then Souilly again, where Col. Johnson is found holding down Garcia's job, and I get some thick red paint from No. 6, all the remaining cardboard signs I can find, and to the Medical Dump where a box of boards is pilfered. Then to Dexter's Gas Hospital in Julvécourt to beg the use of their sign painter, but he is sick in bed, and old Henry gets a puncture and it takes an interminable time to reshoe him. So here an hour ago paint, painter, and boards were successfully brought together and this brings me where I started. . . .

We think the war is over. I hear Allison remark through his partition—"The poor miserable boobs!" We've seen lots of prisoners about and there are many German wounded. Last night there was another heavy barrage and the attack was renewed. Montfaucon, where the advance was stoutly resisted, has fallen and we 've gone well beyond—also up along the left bank of the Meuse—so they say.

.   .   .   .   .   .

Meanwhile the French have attacked west of the Argonne and advanced several miles. The Serbs and others "have seized Ishtib," wherever that is, but it 's bad enough to cause rumors of a demand for an armistice from Bulgaria. The progress continues in Palestine and Gen. Allenby has reached the Sea of Galilee, taking Tiberias, founded by Herod. The British press hard on Cambrai in a new attack. The poor boobs!

10 p.m. General Brewster, the Inspector General of the Army, has blown in and asked for a bed. He gets Salmon's and remarks that he 's more afraid of that man than anyone in the A.E.F. He has been all over the front—the 3rd Corps up to Brieulles-sur-Meuse; from there the line drops well back to Cierges, whence our troops have had to withdraw. On the left the conditions are better. There is very stiff resistance—machine guns—the roads are impassable except on foot or horseback, and one of the main roads is blocked by a mine hole and a stalled French tank. A lot of wounded can't be got back. It 's set in to a steady downpour.

11 p.m. Colonel Beeuwkes in to see the General—dripping wet —just back from Béthincourt. The road from there to Esnes impassably blocked—was nearly ten hours in going as many kilometres; cars ditched everywhere—artillery, food, and ammunition trying to get up, empties and others with wounded trying to get down; some fools had double-banked; no lights permitted, even smoking prohibited—a hard regulation to live up to a night like this. . . .

Sunday, Sept. 29th. Fleury

The day largely spent in mothering No. 6 Mobile and endeavoring not to appear to do so. By afternoon Towne was persuaded to let Sam Harvey receive a few patients and Garcia turned the head cases from Souilly in to them—the profane Jerry Sullivan drove me around in the Dodge and I nailed up the signs on the uncertain road corners between Souilly and Beauzée. . . .

George Brewer and Darrach here for dinner—Geo. being sent home much against his will—he 's had many physical hardships and looks it.

Mon. the 30th. Fleury

11 p.m. General Brewster with us again to-night, very pleasant and companionable. Richard Strong also here for dinner, somewhat at a loss to know, now that the trench-fever report is finished, just what his job is to be—a Red Cross position with Murphy, or here with the Army to stem the throat infections—streptococcus pneumonia in particular having become a real menace.

The R.C. hospital here is choked with wounded—500 preoperative cases just sent out and some 400 yet to be sorted; many in very bad shape—wounded last Thursday or Friday. Just like our experience of last summer—after things slacked up at the end of the third day the roads got opened and the wounded of the early days—wet, exhausted, and infected—begin to be brought down, to the despair of all. I 've been over the head cases with E.C. and McCoy and have sent on to Deuxnouds as many as they are likely to be able to handle. The *triage*, I believe, is the most important place in any hospital, and requires the sort of judgment that only comes from long experience with wounded—not the judgment of a blood-pressure apparatus and the laboratory.

To-day much like yesterday—to Rarécourt to drop Dexter—Ville-sur-Couzances, the H.Q. of the 1st Corps, to give Brewer missives home—Souhesmes—Deuxnouds via Ippécourt and St. André (a bad road). Sam Harvey had done good work the night before, seeing through 28 cases. Towne considerably cheered up, though the whole situation is bad for them, with no typewriting machines—no army forms—no transcription, and no much else. Geo. Derby turns up to help and I to Fleury to post more road signs in anticipation of a stream from that direction—luncheon en route at Nubécourt, where I find Salmon. Then Souilly for conference with Garcia, Clinton, Merritt, the X-ray man, Lyle, etc., concerning the threatened withdrawal for service elsewhere of Mobile 6, leaving Deuxnouds stranded with many wounded and insufficient personnel—concerning teams—concerning X-rays—transportation, etc., etc.

Raining again hard. Sent to locate Law, the X-ray man from

B.H. 115; first to Evac'n No. 11 on the road north of Brizeaux, via Ippécourt, Fleury, Waly, and the southern tip of the Forêt d'Argonne with its striking twin mounds. Douglas Duval, C.O., and Ellsworth Eliot, much unshaven, and a lot of major work still to be done, but no Maj. Law. So to Evac'n No. 10 at Froidos, on the Fleury–Clermont highway. Baker there from Evac'n No. 6, endeavoring to bring some order out of the chaos—also Law, with whom I escape, sending him on to Deuxnouds while I drop off here.

Things perhaps are not going so well—the advance hereabouts checked much as were the costly advances of last summer. There certainly have been more casualties than we were led to expect. Rumors of an attack being launched north of Châlons with American divisions thrown in without provision for wounded. This may have accounted for Col. Stark's growls this p.m. He certainly can't stand the strain long. Evac'n 3 and Mobile 5 are said to be going there to back up the 2nd and 36th Divisions—the nucleus of a new army.

. . . . . .

The Boche is certainly getting it on all sides: (1) The British and Belgians have gained since Saturday a.m. more ground than in the entire Ypres affair last fall. (2) The British also are in the outskirts of Cambrai and with the American divisions have breached the supposedly impregnable Hindenburg Line at Bellenglise.

Oct. 1st. Fleury

9 p.m. Cold and raw, especially in an unheated hut. *"Les journées glorieuses,"* with victories of the Allies on all fronts, according to the French papers; but I am not so sure that our own show has been so glorious after all. As I gather from Gen. B., who is still with us, the Boche has plenty of kick left and more or less played the fool with us by withdrawing his troops under our barrage, letting us get well in and then showering us with machine guns, followed yesterday and to-day by a lot of mustard gas. Just the sort of performance so familiar to the much-scorned 5th Army last autumn. We, formerly with the B.E.F., do not dare make the comparison. I wish they could make their attacks with tanks alone and no preliminary barrage, so as to spare the countryside and make transportation easier both for troops and for ambulances.

Here in Fleury our little family has broken up—Finney with a treacherous cold, Fisher, Baer, and Strong back to Neufchâteau in three cars, leaving Dexter and me with the damaged Dodge, which it takes Jerry all day to get repaired with the aid of his friends in the 26th. Finney left me at Deuxnouds, where the day was spent trying to help out Towne and Harvey, who have been swamped with wounded and have been on continuous duty for about 48 hours; but they will soon get on their feet again.

Wounded of all kinds, from some foreigners of the 79th Division with nothing much wrong with them but trifles, to severe head cases many days old, and one man who had been wearing a tourniquet for thrée days on a badly fractured arm. I operated on a head case as a demonstration for one of the new teams and with the help of poor eyes did it very badly. They have very few supplies, but things are improving despite altercations with some French women over the potato patch on the hill, which they still claim to be theirs.

. . . . . .

We have unquestionably been severely handled. The 35th Division on the right of the 1st Corps lost three of its four colonels, all of its lieutenant colonels and majors, and probably most of its captains and subalterns. The 79th came out much bedraggled, and General Brewster says it will probably be broken up or have its number changed, as there's no use trying to build up an *esprit* from a unit with a bad name. The National Army has not made such a good showing as was expected.

Oct. 2nd. Wednesday. Fleury

A fine clear cold day. Dexter and I remain. He now a major, doing great work with his gas hospitals and trying to get Corps Convalescent Camps established. Jerry sick, so no wheels for us, but Col. McGee away with Beeuwkes and loans me his car for the morning. Dexter dropped at Julvécourt and on to Souilly to report conditions at Deuxnouds. Much confusion in the offices at No. 6 Evac'n. Wounded have come in at an appalling rate and everything is choked—20,400 casualties, including 5000 "sick" since Sept. 26th. The chief difficulties and failures evidently lie: (1) in an unsuccessful *triage;* (2) in poor routing; (3) in the failure to send back to their units men slightly gassed or wounded who should not go to the Base. At the present moment evacuation much impeded from lack of trains, ambulances, and trucks—even from lack of engines to-day. Col. Stark tears his hair.

With Marshall Clinton to Mobile No. 1, which has been hard pressed owing to its advanced position on the Dombasle–Souilly road. Macrae highly vociferous about his troubles—late cases—awful wounds—hospital on a hillside—promised an evacuation with 20 ambulances last night—100 severely wounded brought down to the roadside ready to be loaded—no ambulances came till noon the next day, and then only three—dreadful condition of cases brought in, many of them three days old—often from 24 to 30 hours in the ambulance on the way down without food—frequently the ambulances bring in dead.

He gave me to read a copy of a snappy report he proposes to send to G.H.Q. I dissuade him; but do not lessen his troubles by taking away two nurses for Evac. 11, where there are practically none, and by removing Dowman to Deuxnouds. The great pressure of wounded seems to have come via Esnes—Dombasle—Rampont—Souilly, crowding No. 1 Mobile and Souilly; and via Boureuilles—Clermont—Froidos—Fleury, crowding No. 2 Mobile and No. 114 R.C. The other hospitals have largely escaped, possibly as the drivers, if there be any pretext, will take the main arteries of traffic and avoid the side roads if possible. I wonder how many of them voluntarily chose the tortuous way to Deuxnouds.

Then back to Souilly, dropping Clinton, and to Fleury to surrender McGee's car. McCoy provides a driver. Then Deuxnouds once more, encountering Schwab en route—they are doing well, though the place is filled up—212 patients in 187 beds. Fortunately many slight wounds.

Give Schwab a lift to Nubécourt and on before dinner to No. 4 Mobile via Fleury—Froidos—Clermont—los Islettes to La Frange, in the middle of the Forêt d'Argonne. There find to my surprise that Clopton has had practically no wounded. Either the 77th Division has had few casualties or else they have not been routed via their own *triage.*

Bill Darrach and Swift and other 1st Corp Consultants turn up and they are full of rumors, such as that Austria has given Ger_ many two days to state her peace terms—most unlikely. One bat_ talion of the 92nd (Midnight) Division has been tried in the line and they did n't stick—labor for them hereafter. Some more ex_ perienced divisions are being brought in and Beeuwkes says we will have some better news soon. . . .

At the moment Dexter and the General, who is shaving, are discussing the virtues of different varieties of razors. Me for bed. There are two categories of men—those who *do* and those who do *not* use safety razors.

.   .   .   .   .   .

Events march swiftly. The defenses of the Cambrai and St. Quentin line are breaking and the enemy is burning and blowing up both places. The Boche is withdrawing in Flanders. Damascus has fallen—the oldest city of the world—Jerusalem is as yesterday compared to her.

Oct. 3rd. Thursday

A fine cold October day, with hoarfrost covering everything this morning, and dust everything this afternoon. Young and Bert- ner here for the past night. With our borrowed chauffeur, Everett, who has been all night in the operating room on duty, to Julvé- court to drop Dexter, who finds to his great despair that half of his personnel has been ordered away during the night; the three places full of gassed cases and his remaining people about all done in from the week's strain.

To see the 1st Division (lately the 35th) *triage* at Cheppy near Varennes. Julvécourt, Jubecourt, Auzéville and Clermont along east of the Argonne, passing the bedraggled 35th coming out, and to Neuvilly, where a block. All these forward towns much de- stroyed, though at Neuvilly the church, characteristic of the neigh- borhood, still stands despite a huge hole in the side of the steeple. Someone—doubtless a "frog," as the French are universally called—has disobeyed the road signs and tied up the traffic.

The road signs—so familiar one hardly notices them—would make an interesting chapter in the story of the war: "*Route gar- dée*"; "*Fractionnez vos convois*"; "*Laissez 50 met. derrière tout disque rouge*"; "*Défense de stationner*"; "*Observez les con-*

signes"; *"Tenez votre droite"*; *Sens* [or *Circuit*] *obligatoire"*; *"Défense de doubler"*; *"Éteignez vos lumières"*; *"Eau suspecte,"* or *"Non potable,"* etc., etc.—with routings for hospitals, directions of towns, of corps, divisions, brigade or regimental quarters —on stumps of trees, corners of ruined buildings, or chance posts.

From Neuvilly to Boureuilles—or what remains of it, for it stood just about at the old line. A km. or so south of it is a huge crater completely wrecking the road—the result of a mine let off by the French on July 4th or 5th, when I believe the Boche attacked here and the French had to withdraw. The place a great tangle after these seven days, with the French "Jennys" trying to bridge the gap (Query: Why is it always the French engineers?) while the traffic is deviated in a wide semicircle to the west. We finally get through, and then past the lines—masses of wire, and at Boureuilles itself another huge crater wrecking the road, and about a kilometre further on still another—this time a Boche mine, I presume. "No Man's Land" all this, sure enough, and the zone shows clearly as it runs across the distant Argonne highland, for there is a treeless strip plainly to be seen.

To Varennes, where the American Army is eating its lunch— by the road and in the fields, and probably wonders greatly at the ruined town, for it is a new lot, the 82nd, going up to relieve the 28th. We missed the turn to Cheppy and go on almost to Apremont along a road completely screened by German camouflage before we find our error. It becomes warm there for heavies are firing, though the day is quiet enough, and there are flights of planes from seven to thirteen in wild-duck wedges—very high; but we see no air battles.

We finally locate the ruins of Cheppy where two field hospitals are fused—the third under Maj. Wilson and the 12th under a Capt. Black wearing a *Croix de Guerre* with two palms and four wound stripes on the right sleeve. A very admirable *triage*. . . .

There have been interruptions and it 's too late to finish to-day's story except to say that Deuxnouds, visited in the late afternoon, is doing creditably. The hospitals are all choked and Gen. B. has intimated that there would be a fresh attack by new divisions to_ morrow; and considerable distant firing has already started up. Beeuwkes says 12,000 casualties, sick and wounded, have gone through Vaubecourt alone in the seven days; Col. Turnbull has handled the situation well but proper evacuation is difficult, and hundreds of thousands of dollars' worth of salvageable stuff—not human—is also spoiling, as it can't even be covered.

. . . . . .

General Gouraud's army of seven corps with our 2nd Division making an eighth attacked opposite Souain to-day, taking Challe_ range. The 2nd Division did well and took White Hill, while the French on each side lagged, leaving them in a desperate salient for three days.

AN ENFORCED CHANGE OF SCENE

October 4th, Friday

To Bar-le-Duc in the early morning behind Jerry, who has re_ covered, and there is a train to Paris with standing room only. Not being very good on my hind legs these influenzal days, I would have been done in had not a young French aviator insisted on my taking his seat most of the way. The ride via the opened-up Châ_ teau-Thierry road would be a great spectacle for anyone who has not become satiated with the sight of shell craters and ruined villages.

Paris on time, and so the last part of the Research Society meeting. Sir David Bruce—very dreary, on the old subject of tetanus.

Tuesday, Oct. 8th. En Route, Paris–Chaumont

The last four days passed with the kindly Strongs, who are much concerned about my health, and, though poorly themselves, they nevertheless have made their apartment a hospital for me. Something has happened to my hind legs and I wobble like a tabetic and can't feel the floor when I unsteadily get up in the morning. Bastianelli, who has a ready thermometer, has taken my temperature every time he's seen me and finds I have fever; Thayer caught me defenseless last night and could n't elicit my deep reflexes and mumbled something about extrasystoles. They all insist on my going away—the Riviera, Rome, Oxford, all suggested. These places all sound to me like going to the moon. So this is the sequence of the grippe. We may perhaps thank it for helping us win the war if it really hit the German Army thus hard in February last. . . .

A smart young major sits by me, just off the *Leviathan*, fresh from home—clad in thin clothes—on the General Staff—only to be over here a couple of weeks—fears he has caught cold and wants to know if I think he has the grippe, which he hears is prevalent. Complains of being "unseasoned"—the pioneers on his transport were "unseasoned"—only together six months and most of them sick all the way over—great advantage to have been over here for a year so you can get "seasoned."

I quite agree with this and try to interest him in the military situation, but he says he understands everything over here is going fine, also the response to the last Liberty Loan has exceeded all expectations and it 's been a hot summer in Washington. He wears a service web belt outside his overcoat and a pistol hangs from it —doubtless thinks he will meet a Hun at any moment—safety first. . . .

Four days are a long time to catch up in this journal—events move so fast. Most important and significant of all was the news that came to us Sunday of the proposal from Max of Baden, the new Chancellor, for an armistice.

Weary as we all are of the war, the response seems to have been unanimous—unconditional surrender—and we feel that it is but a clever dodge to let the Boche get off with a whole skin and withdraw his troops and stores quietly from France and Belgium rather than to do so with the Allies snapping at his heels. It 's just like the *"Kamerad"* of the machine gunner who has fired till the last minute and then throws up his hands, expecting to be spared. A Prussian squeal, in fact.

On July 31, 1914, they gave France 18 hours to declare that in the event of a Russo-German war she would remain neutral, betray her ally, and as a guarantee give up Toul and Verdun to Germany till the end of the war. No one believes in Germany's honesty of purpose. This is no offer to make Peace. It 's a proposal to halt the present battle, which is going against her, while she discusses President Wilson's peace principles. It 's a matter for Foch, not for Pres. Wilson to decide, and the only possible terms are for her to lay down her arms.

To go back to my story. On Saturday too feeble to do much with the open meetings; and so missed the "streptococcus pneumonias" of the afternoon completely, the session being largely given over to reports from recent arrivals and the experience of home camps. The Committee meeting was better, though too social, and too elaborate a preliminary tea provided for the enjoyment of the British. Sir David Bruce sank into a divan, stretched out his highly polished boots into the middle of the room, inserted his spurs into the rug, drew his John Bull visage deep into his clothes, turtle fashion, and slept profoundly—this was good for the General and also helped the meeting.

General Ireland appeared, probably for the last time, and brought with him Col. McCaw, which probably answers the speculations concerning his successor. He favored the proposed subject of discussion for next time [1] and we had the usual reports of committees, among them that of Joe Blake, Heitz-Boyer, and Sinclair, all of whom were present.

Sunday was largely passed in bed and in breaking engagements, Monday more or less ditto, though I went to St. Cloud in the morning on a goose chase to find out about Towne's missing truck and side car—they having gone forward, it seems, with Mobile No. 7. The lively Miss Nichols of Boston, now serving as a V.A.D. at an H.O.E. in Vitry-le-François, came to lunch, and also one of the Patterson boys of Ann Arbor—a private in the field artillery of the 1st Division, who brought with him a huge sheep dog that had adopted him in Buresches and Belleau Wood days—a French dog captured by the Boches and taken prisoner with them in our counter-attack. Patterson, like many another young private, has had enough of the war and is subdued by the Army.

The afternoon in bed and an examination by Thayer, who solemnly shakes his head—after which I resolve to beat it for Neufchâteau. "No matter how lowly," etc.

Wednesday, Oct. 9. Neufchâteau

In bed with what they call the grippe and a hot-water bottle—not a bad combination. The time passes with Duruy's *History of France* and friendly visitations.

Meanwhile the news is excellent. While awaiting Mr. Wilson's reply the Allies have smashed away all together on several fronts, the best possible answer to the German note. In our 1st Army area

---

[1] I.e., the November meeting: subjects "Triage and Routing."

Last Meeting of the "Conférence Chirurgicale Interalliée" on the Steps
of the Val-de-Grâce. *Central Figures, Standing:* Sir George Makins and
Docteur Tuffier

Medical Research Committee at 12 Place Vendome after Its Last Session,
November 1918. *Standing (Back Row)*: Rose Bradford, Finney, Makins,
Thayer, McCaw, Emerson, Bowlby, Fletcher, Winter, Cummins, Elliott.
(Second Row): Siler, Harris, Cannon, A. Lambert. *Front Row (Seated)*:
Cushing, Wallace, Crile

things have continued to march along. The attack in the Argonne which started Friday morning, the 4th, seems to have been largely a movement east of the Meuse, though there was also pressure toward Exermont, and the Argonne woods and ravines are being slowly relinquished.

There is a remarkable story of a battalion of 500 Americans from the 308th, 77th Division, under a Major Chas. Whittlesey, a N.Y. lawyer before the war. During the attack of Wednesday, Oct. 2nd, they had reached their objectives but got cut off from their contacts in a ravine, some 3 km. east of Binarville. They became surrounded by the Boches, and put up a desperate resistance in the wilderness of wire and underbrush. Without food, water, or shelter, wet and cold, with almost no ammunition, they stuck it for four days and were relieved Monday. The Boches gave them an invitation to surrender, but Whittlesey replied in effect that they could go to hell first.

Thursday, the 10th Oct.

Wilson's answer through Robert Lansing to Max of Baden was in last night's *communiqué*—very skillful—a diplomatic counter-manoeuvre to the peace offensive—as clever and sure as was Foch's military counter on July 18th. In short, do you really mean this, Mr. Max, or for whom are you speaking, the High Command and Prussian militarism, or the German people? We cannot speak of an armistice without the immediate retirement of the Central Powers from all invaded territory.

Meanwhile the British with the American 2nd Corps continue their victorious advance between Cambrai and St. Quentin in the direction of Le Cateau, and yesterday morning Canadians entered Cambrai, which was blown up by the retreating Boche. Poor Cambrai, will it ever again return to its 400 years of muslin-making?

October 11–12

More or less in bed owing to my hind legs, which are in a chronic state of being asleep up to the knees and threaten to leave me in the lurch.

The British have chased the retreating enemy as far as Le Cateau, where was fought one of the most famous of the 1914 battles of the "Contemptible Little Army" in their retreat from

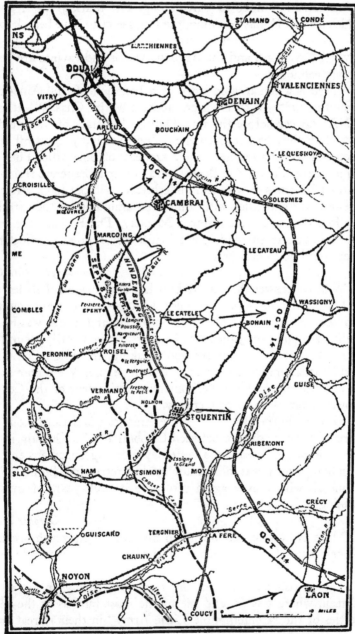

The Bursting Through of the Hindenburg Line and the Capture
by the British of Le Cateau, La Fère, and Laon

Mons—23 kilometres advance in two days—the Hindenburg Line is left far behind. *"Les Allemands, durement bousculés, battent en retraite."* Laon comes next. The enemy are forsaking the Chemin des Dames, leaving the Suippe, and have evacuated the main pass through the Argonne. Gouraud on the 11th advanced five miles, reaching Mont St. Rémy on the way to Rethel.

Sunday, Oct. 13th. Neufchâteau

Pouring, so a trip to Deuxnouds postponed. With Widener alone at our supper of beans and *veau* to-night, when Lee and Pincoffs blew in. Pincoffs carries the same single bar on his shoulders he was wearing when I first encountered him in the prison of Ypres—in short, still a battalion M.O. and alive. The 2nd Division is out *en repos* after a lively time with Gouraud's army. Seven French corps participated in the attack of Oct. 3rd, and the 2nd Division, which made an eighth, had a front of about 5 km. just north of Souain. Their objective was in the direction of Somme-Py and, pushing ahead, they were left for three or four days way out on a salient enfiladed from both sides; for the French failed to come up. From the 3rd to the 9th they had 5000 casualties and 800 dead.

Pincoffs, who is in charge of one of the F.A.'s as well as "director of field evacuation" for the division, was out in all of it getting the wounded back, and he certainly deserves the D.S.C. if anyone ever has. Through Dick Derby, who has been made the divisional surgeon, he has been given the chance to organize the entire ambulance service of the division, and I judge that things are better than they were when he made the notes about the conditions under which the 2nd Division labored last July.

Generals Finney and Thayer, wearing their stars for the first time, came in late with Alec Lambert, having motored from Paris via Suippe, and we managed to scrape up a bully-beef supper for them. A long talk with Pincoffs about the duties and responsibilities of a battalion M.O.—most informing.

Monday the 14th

In response to an appeal from Major Kerr, a trip taken to Deuxnouds, crossing the recovered salient via Hattonville again —a long, tedious trip. No. 6 Mobile has moved out in large part and is to go to Varennes, while No. 8 Mobile, a Philadelphia outfit, will take their place—the present teams to remain. . . . I tried to operate for them on a bad case, but the light was poor and I could not see well enough to do a proper job. All the way home in the car I had spells of diplopia.

Tuesday the 15th. Neufchâteau

Salmon has just related an unsung tale of sacrifice, which he got yesterday from a young lieutenant of the heavies. They were bringing up coast-guard guns and were passing through a French village—a row of caterpillar tractors towing the heavy pieces, also on their caterpillars. He was sitting behind his piece and a jovial gunner had crawled up astride of the gun which he was straddling, whistling "My Girl Back Home." On the side of the road were some doughboys, dealing out bits of chocolate to an eager group of French children. Suddenly a little girl on the opposite side of the road caught sight of them and, oblivious of the traffic, darted across the road to get her share. She thought she could get between the tractor and the gun, not realizing it was being towed, and darted for the spot.

Quick as a flash the gunner swung under the long barrel of which he was astride, caught the child while almost in the air, and threw her back into the road, but before he could recover himself the caterpillar of the gun carriage went over his head. The gunner was buried by the roadside near the village; and when they came out, some weeks later, the grave was covered with flowers and on the wooden cross the villagers had placed a tablet—to the brave American soldier who had given his life for a little French girl.

A cold depressing rain to-day. To the office and back with great effort. Bagley turns up, after some three weeks in working his way by "channels" to these H.Q. from Southampton, where they landed. The usual story. This time Transport 56— i.e., the *Olympic*. He was ship Medical Officer. There had been no grippe in the States(?), but nine cases developed on the boat, with one death from pneumonia. They were held in Southampton Harbor 24 hours before disembarking, and 384 cases developed during this brief time—very severe—temperatures of 105° frequent in men at the very outset. People standing guard would fall in their tracks. They were sent to a rest camp near

The Offices of the Medical Consultants at Neufchâteau

French Lorries Parked on the Road through Neufchâteau with their
Annamite Drivers

The Valley of the Meuse beside Neufchâteau

Southampton and in a week 1900 cases developed, with several hundred pneumonias and 119 deaths before he left. Of the 342 nurses who were left on shipboard after the troops disembarked, 134 developed influenza.

The weekly report of *Oct. 3rd* of the relation of patients to beds in the A.E.F. gave as a grand total:—

	Occupied	Vacant	Normal	Emergency
Base Hospitals	91,740	26,703	109,897	160,286
Camp Hospitals	15,138	2,850	16,264	17,798
Grand Total	106,878	29,553	126,161	178,084

Thus 84.7 per cent of the normal and 60 per cent of the emergency beds were then filled and we were lacking personnel for 35 base hospitals. A few days ago it was reported that we had beds for only two days if wounded and sick continued to come in at the present rate, and the weekly report of *Oct. 10,* just come to-day, gives:—

	Occupied	Vacant	Normal	Emergency
Base Hospitals	119,739	12,906	110,994	162,068
Camp Hospitals	17,719	6,260	21,939	24,289
Grand Total	137,458	19,166	132,933	186,357

In short, our base hospitals are 107.9 per cent full, our camp hospitals 82.5 per cent full, and 73.3 per cent of our emergency beds are occupied.

In regard to the prevailing influenza epidemic, Haven Emerson's Weekly Bulletin of Oct. 9th frankly admits a serious present situation in the A.E.F.

Wed., Oct. 16th

Rain! Bagley reports sick with a chill and temperature of 103.6°. Kerr manages to get an ambulance and takes him to No. 18 in Bazoilles. I had hoped to turn over the affairs of this office to him and then get out myself, as I am growing very tottery and had considerable difficulty in dressing this a.m. Even so, I shirk my job and ignominiously retire to blankets and a cheap novel at our forlorn and smelly billet.

Finney, back from Chaumont and Dijon, says for the first time he finds Col. Wadhams in the dumps—the American Army being still further split up and two divisions now ordered to the Belgian coast—troops scattered from there to Belfort—the French don't want our troops concentrated anywhere—don't want us to get too much credit now that the Boche is on the run—no pinch-hitter business for them. Quite an understandable feeling.

Meanwhile the formation of our 2nd Army is announced—under Gen. Bullard with the 4th, 7th, and 6th Corps. An attack northeast of Nancy is projected and trainloads of tanks are said to be moving up there, though no hospitals as yet. It will lead to an interesting crisis for the enemy if we can close his line of retreat through the valley of the Moselle south of the Ardennes and limit him to the one route further north via the Meuse, where he poured through four years ago! It may bottle him up in Belgium.

. . . . . .

The evening papers give the full text of Wilson's remarkable note, which practically means surrender and a change of government. He has caught the Kaiser with his trousers down, has taken two spanks at him, and now hands the shingle to Foch. Meanwhile the British have taken Menin and crossed the Lys, Lille is being encircled, and our troops have broken the Kriemhilde-Stellung position at several points. *"On les a!"* now replaces *"On ne passe pas."*

Thursday, Oct. 17th

Too poor on my pins to go to Vichy as planned. Marked increase of numbness and unsteadiness with a good deal of involvement of my hands. Schwab comes to the rescue, takes me to his hospital at Priez-la-Fauche as "a guest," and gives up his room to me.

. . . . . .

The Anglo-Franco-Belgian advance continues on a 32-mile front between Dixmude and Douai. Thourout fallen; Courtrai entered. We have taken Grandpré. More than a hundred German slow-fused mines exploded during the day in the region of Laon.

OCCUPYING A BED IN PERSON

Oct. 18. La Fauche

Very kind people here. I am being kept in bed, having little use of my lean and shrunk shanks. Schwab shakes his head and talks about a multiple toxic neuritis with leucopenia. A new set of visitors and acquaintances—notably a vociferous militia colonel who occupies the room next to mine and is strong on things to eat and drink at bizarre hours.

.   .   .   .   .   .

Lille, Douai, Ostend délivrés. La cavalerie aux portes de Bruges. Les Anglais aux bords de Tourcoing. The first person to enter Lille after the German evacuation came out of the air, a young aviator, Captain Delesalle, with a *Croix de Guerre boisée de quatre palmes*—Lille his native city, of which his father is *maire*—he literally flew into his father's arms. Wilson has sent his "separate note to Austria-Hungary." His earlier distinction between the King of Prussia and the Imperial and Royal Government of Austria-Hungary is noticeable.

Oct. 19th, Saturday

In bed getting my sensation tested, and having a female from the Sargent school, built like a football tackle, give me massage. One particular inning which consists in beating my sore and wasted extremities seems to me unnecessary. I call it the barrage—I 'd much prefer to have her go over me with a tank.

.   .   .   .   .   .

Le roi Albert entre dans Ostende et Bruges. The British advance five miles, along a 50-mile front, occupying Tourcoing and Roubaix. The French take Thielt.

Monday, Oct. 21st

Allison here and says everything going on well in our forward area, though we are up against a stiff proposition and are fighting in the almost impassable country of the 1916 Verdun battles. The 29th and 33rd have gone over to the right of the Meuse, and the 26th is in support with their H.Q. at Verdun, Clarence Edwards and his staff living _majestically in the Citadel. The 42nd has replaced the 91st, and I believe the 1st, the 35th. The 91st, with one other (the 37th?), has gone to Flanders. All have done very well—even the 77th has quite redeemed itself, and the story of Whittlesey and his 500 is true "and then some," as Allison expresses it.

.   .   .   .   .   .

More gains in Belgium—Zeebrugge and Bruges left behind. The British 2nd Army in close to the Scheldt, where the enemy

may hold. The 5th Army east of Lille approaches Tournai—
the 1st is nearing Valenciennes. French troops are well across the
Oise, and south of the Serre have penetrated the Hunding Line.

Tuesday, 22nd Oct.

Two Generals to call this afternoon—Thayer and Finney—
La Fauche much excited—far more than I. Thayer perfunctorily
goes over my neurological extremities and looks solemn—remembers cases of neuritis in 1889—necessary that I stay here,
as the only room in France with a fireplace—a good excuse to get
Sir Wm. Osler over, etc. All this interspersed with various stories.
Finney has made new arrangements—*viz.*, Lyle to be C.S. of the
1st Army and Clinton of the 2nd. They are to have Asst. Army
Consultants under them, rather than Corps Consultants—e.g.,
Lyle will have Pool, Darrach, and Lee under him—and thus these
men can supervise the work of the Evac'n Hosps., which they
otherwise, as Corps people, could not do.

Schwab gives a dinner party at the *estaminet* in La Fauche
village run by one Suzanne—Padre Taylor, Col. Rumbolt, the
C.O., Miss Butler the R.C. worker, Miss Johnson a civilian em-
ployee, the head nurse Miss Postum, and another. I was taken
reluctantly in an ambulance, wobbly in mind and body. Walking
is very bad, and one dresses with great difficulty, buttoning being
almost impossible—hands now almost as awkward and stiff as
feet—a good deal of soreness but fortunately no pain.

.   .   .   .   .   .

The Boches have replied to Mr. Wilson saying that they *are*
democratic and have *not* committed atrocities.

Wed. 23rd

A gorgeous warm October day with soft air and a brilliant sky.
The C.O. took me for a half hour's ride before lunch—through
the woods—*chasse réservée*—and over to Leurville, near which
is an astonishing crater, as though the earth's crust had caved in—
an area about a half mile at the top and some 200 feet deep—
le Cul du Cerf. The gorgeously colored trees in the bottom and
at the margins stood out against the gray chalky slopes like the
painted figures against the gray background of a Vermeer.

The woods are superb. There are blood-orange patches made
by sumac, maple, and elder; but the beeches are the glory of all.

They have a rich tinge of yellow and old gold, and the green ivy climbing on their gray trunks gives a brilliant contrast. At a distance the woods suggest a soft Persian shawl spread over the hills.

. . . . . .

The 3rd (Byng) and 4th (Rawlinson) British Armies have jumped ahead to-day between the Scheldt and Sambre–Oise Canal in the direction of Le Quesnoy and threaten to outflank Valenciennes by cutting its L. of C.

Friday, Oct. 25th

What one might call flyable weather. I've just managed to bring down 300—actual count—in individual combat—none counted unless seen to crash or come down in flames. I feel that I am sort of an ace of aces, though I have not yet got the supremacy. There are apparently just as many more in this room—the penalty of having had my window open yesterday, for it was warm and sunny. Mayhap the French fly, which has a persistence and an *élan* all its own, accounts for the reluctance of the human element to keep their windows ajar.

Later. My score reached 500 at supper time—there were others left, chiefly of the *chasse* variety, hovering out of reach.

. . . . . .

Mr. Wilson comes back at 'em somewhat at length. Briefly he offers this dilemma—surrender without mercy or suppress the Hohenzollern rule. Meanwhile the Allies nibble away, the British making further notable gains toward Valenciennes, which is the next important station after Lille in the great lateral railway system of the frontier. To avoid destruction of their large towns it seems to be the intent to manœuvre the enemy out of his position by flanking movements. If the British can get through or around the Forest of Mormal and get Bavay and possibly Maubeuge, commanding the valley of the Sambre, it will seriously threaten the line of the Meuse. The Sambre Valley is vital to the Boche defense.

Saturday the 26th

I begin to question whether late suppers of sardines, cheese, and champagne partaken of by the Padre, the Colonel, and the Psychotherapeutist in the room of the Patient are entirely conducive to his rapid recovery, though they may serve for his amusement.

Sunday, the 27th

I must have touched bottom yesterday—without knowing it, for my soles are devoid of sensation. Distinctly better to-day and able to bathe and dress again. Bishop Brent in for a long call after lunch—then Miss Shepley from the offices in Neufchâteau with mail and papers.

· · · · · ·

It is stated that Ludendorff has resigned and Karl Liebknecht been liberated. Germany has briefly replied to Mr. Wilson's last to the effect that "we will be good" and that a people's government awaits *proposals for an armistice!* It is their business to approach Marshal Foch and Sir David Beatty with a white flag. The Kaiser does not appear. Col. E. M. House has quietly slipped into Europe—pointed toward Versailles! Meanwhile we keep on attending to the war with good purpose. The Americans, British, and French in their several areas are fighting with determination.

Oct. 28th

Dexter here in the p.m. with welcome news of the changes in our forward area. Pershing still at Souilly, which remains the Advanced H.Q. for the army, though Ligny is now the H.Q. 1st Échelon. Preparations have been under way for some time for a large offensive on our Argonne front—nine divisions to participate. It was expected to come off some days ago but was postponed, according to rumor, because of the capture by the Boche of a Lt. Col., who was inspecting the front lines while carrying on his person all the orders and plans of the operation.

I attempt to walk and manage about 200 yards down our roadway. Like walking on a ship's deck in a high sea with both your feet asleep. Was glad to get back safely to my room.

· · · · · ·

We get the day's papers here about 8 p.m. To-day's news is interesting, e.g., Austria-Hungary appears to be breaking up; and according to the Paris *Herald* "all America is saving nutshells and fruit pips." This, I suppose, evidences our determination to win the war.[1]

---

[1] The slogan in America to "Eat More Cocoanuts" and to save nuts and fruit pips was due to the fact that charcoal of the best quality for use in poison-gas respirators could be made from these husks.

La Fauche, Oct. 29th
9 a.m., while anxiously awaiting my enemy the masseuse. Would that I were capable of thumb-sketching this place and some of its inmates. Due to my short tether, acquaintances are somewhat limited, to be sure, even here in the château, which is some distance from the hospital. Still, such as they are, they are unique. The Colonel for example.

He 's been here several weeks with a foot drop—probably due to kicking at the Regular Army, though said to be acquired while walking around the front areas looking for battery positions before the Argonne fight opened. He 's an old National Guardsman— 40 years' experience more or less—from the state where one has to be shown—the ancient and honorable artillery kind—oldest battery in the country, sir—marched all the way to Mexico City and back without the loss of a man.

Then the Colonel himself has a most ancient and honorable lineage, the details of which I have heard several times. It goes back to Thor and thunderbolts, I believe, and comes down through Sir Somebody who was something or other to "Ollie" Cromwell. His immediate forbears went to live in Scotland, so he has an overpowering scorn and hatred for the English, which even surpasses his sentiments *re* the Boche.

I don't see how the Army gets along without him. He has no sense of humor and a deep voice—the voice of command—and with it tells you all about his relations and, when not his relations, the National Guard and its ill-treatment. When he gets home he 'll run for Congress on his National Guard record and when he gets in—well, the Regular Army will get what 's coming to it.

But there 's a far pleasanter side to the Colonel which I enjoy more. He 's a handy man about the house—a natural-born fixer. When Schwab—who decidedly is not—breaks at midnight an irreparable pane out of the window at the head of my bed in a moment of anger and fit of profanity directed against a particularly pestiferous fly, the Colonel, hearing the crash, comes in and repairs it with a combination of yesterday's *Le Matin* and some thumbtacks.

This morning there were cries of fire from the next room, which is an officers' dormitory. The Colonel appears and orders us not

to worry, but to dress, dashing off again. Schwab in great trepida_
tion, with visions of being court-martialed, hastily gets on his
green bathrobe—the gift of an admirer in Chicago, a patient—
"an old lady," of course—also his boots—slings open the huge
French window for a look at the smoke and leaves it open—
then the door ditto, so that I, preferring fire to frost, climb back in
my bed. He disappeared after the Colonel and found him looking
up the chimney—probably between his legs—by the aid of a
large mirror he had ripped from the wall and was using periscope-
fashion. The French housekeeper—relic of other days—says they
normally catch on fire—only way to clean the chimneys.

When our single and treasured oil lamp does not burn square,
and Schwab makes it worse with the aid of a safety pin, the Colonel
comes in, sweeps him aside, and produces the biggest pocket knife
in the world, combined with a variety of corkscrews, gimlets,
saws, etc. He trims the wick admirably and admiringly. And so
it goes.

But the Colonel is at his very best along toward 11 p.m. just
as I am laboriously getting to bed and Schwab is preparing to write
a letter home to his wife, the inspiration for which he apparently
gets from sucking a piece of Q.M.A. stick candy. The Colonel is
heard pussyfooting down the hall. He knocks, and enters bearing
a bottle of wine, boxes of sardines, a tin of cheese, and half a loaf
of bread—his mouth watering. How he gets these things, and
why, I dare not ask—sometimes oxtail soup and other strange
viands.

The Padre is called if he has n't gone to bed, and they go to it.
Schwab promptly breaks off the cork in a violent effort to extract
it. The Colonel brushes him aside, demands a penknife—two
penknives—inserts their blades alongside the cork and, lo and
behold, on the second trial twists out Mr. Cork. Wonderful!
Oh, that 's nothing at all—his father was an inventor—even so
Thor, who invented thunder, I believe—and R. has inherited
these capabilities. A similar episode occurs with the can of sardines.
It refuses to open for Schwab, who with an oath spills most of the
oil on his blotter. The Colonel's complicated knife bears a can
opener, and, presto! The Padre, meanwhile, is burning the toast
and his fingers. The Colonel is especially particular about wood

fires and the way to lay them—his ancestors probably were too. The Padre is brushed aside, the sticks rearranged, the embers exposed and blown upon by a pair of huge National Guard lungs— and, behold! perfect toast in a jiffy.

In short, he's a wonder, the Colonel—about the house—he takes a half inch of butter on his toast, pepper and salt on his cheese, finishes the bottle of wine, and then salvages all the tinfoil from the packages of cigarettes, from the neck of the bottle, from the cheese, from my shaving soap—"Why, this must be saved— a thousand tons of it comes over here a month—ammunition can be made out of it, guns in fact." Quite a goodly sized ball of it sits this morning on the mantel entirely forgotten by the Guardsman, who, since the fire, has probably gone somewhere in quest of cheese, champagne, and sardines for to-night. It's a fine, crisp, sunny October day—good hunting weather. *C'est la guerre.*

9 p.m. McCarthy and Naffziger from B. H. 115 here to-day— also Bagley. We powwow over the establishment of a real Neurological Institute to grow out of the war.

A COMBATANT'S CASE HISTORY

Wednesday, October 30. Priez-la-Fauche

Some days ago Schwab brought in a young officer to be interviewed. I have heard him stuttering around the hallway—stuttering both as to gait and as to voice. What history tells us about war concerns the mass movement of troops, and the victories, or otherwise, of this or that general in command. What meanwhile has happened to the individual foot soldier or his company officers rarely gets recorded. So here is one story at least. It has come out bit by bit in the course of several conversations—its fragments told in a most impersonal manner without a vestige of self-consciousness.

Captain B. of the 47th Infantry was admitted here September 11, 1918, with a sealed letter from B. H. No. 3 stating that from reports he was one of the best of the younger types of officers —brave and resourceful; also that he was blind when admitted to No. 3 and had very marked motor inhibition. Here for six weeks, with the diagnosis of "psychoneurosis in line of duty." He has improved steadily, but still stammers considerably and walks with a peculiar muscle-bound gait; has worked very hard to overcome this and is eager to get back to his regiment.

A clean-cut, fair-haired young fellow, 24 years of age, of medium height, and with the build of a football tackle. German parentage and exemplary habits—no tobacco or alcohol. Was very pro-German before the war, and in consequence has always felt that he had doubly to make good. In the Nat. Guard since 1911 and on the Border with the 1st Indiana troops. Enlisted in the Regular Army Jan. 1917 and was commissioned 2nd Lt. eight months later.

The Division sailed May 11, 1918, to Brest and May 19 to Calais. A lot of ill-feeling between our men and the Tommies—a British N.C.O. was killed—probably stupidity and lack of understanding on both sides. His regiment was billeted at Samer, some of the junior officers, three from each battalion, being sent to the British front for instruction. He saw a good deal of fighting during the Somme retreat and for nine days was constantly under fire—a very confusing time, with the British morale low. Felt terribly green, but tried to keep his eyes open and learn what he could.

Rejoined his regiment and was put in charge of a group of officers who were apportioned to our 2nd Division for experience. Was with them from June 5 to July 9, in the 23rd Infantry—Colonel Malone's outfit—under fire most of the time. Between June 6 and 10 came the taking of Bouresches and next the Belleau Wood affair by the Marines, supported by the 23rd. It was point-blank fighting, as hot as anything could be for a green man, and some places like Lucy were thick with dead. Still they got through, though the casualties were high; one battalion, for example, lost 75 per cent of its men when going through an exposed wheat field. Things were fairly quiet until July 1, when the 3rd Battalion of the 23rd and the 1st Battalion of the 9th took the village of Vaux—a very successful attack, but there were no reserves, and, had the enemy only known, they could have walked through.

Then a couple of quiet days, when the French on the right of the 9th Infantry went over, and, being a reserve liaison officer, he went with them—a fine advance, getting their objective, Hill 204, but they were driven back by a vigorous counter-attack, in which *mêlée* everyone had to take a hand with machine guns and rifles, observers and all. The French had to retreat even behind their former positions, with heavy losses.

On the ninth of July they were relieved by the 102nd (26th Division) and B. rejoined his own unit, the 47th, in reserve near La Ferté Milon, which the French were holding. It being supposedly a quiet sector, a lot of officers were loaned to the French for experience and observation. Here he learned what a real barrage might be, for between July 10 and 14 the enemy made a thrust at La Ferté, with heavy shelling. The French, about ready to quit, would only say, "*Beaucoup de Boches—beaucoup de Boches.*" They dropped behind the barrage, while the attached Americans—company commanders, platoon leaders, and so forth —went forward, got separated, and had heavy losses. Everyone was dumbfounded—some few French went forward with the Americans. In half an hour the French came back—pistol, rifle, and bayonet.

It was a brief episode, and after two days, he again rejoined his regiment, which had moved up to La Ferté. The 4th Division (the 58th, 59th, 39th, and 47th Regiments) had been stationed in a reserve line along the Ourcq from Crouy to Marchiel, and on the morning of July 14 the 39th and 58th attacked at Chézy, B. going with them, the 58th on the right so badly hit that the 59th leapfrogged them—an unsuccessful affair in which the 47th took no part. The next day the Boche offensive opened. B. was recalled to La Ferté and the division had no part in Foch's counter until the end of the first week. Meanwhile, being in charge of the wireless, he knew pretty much what was going on.

On July 25 or 26, he is not quite sure which, his regiment, being fresh and having had no part in the Chézy affair, was sent as shock troops—hustled in trucks through the other formations, first to bolster up the French at Grisolles and La Charme. From there they were rushed forward where the advance had met its chief stumblingblock—Seringes, Sergy, and Cierges. They were all night in going up, made their way through the Forêt de Fère, which was full of gas, and to the open fields beyond. Here the 42nd was holding the line, the Alabamans (167th) to the left and the Iowans (168th) to the right. The 47th was to go in between them toward Seringes and Sergy, but being then only a lieutenant he knew nothing of the plan.

They were just too late in getting through the woods to follow the barrage which had been put up for the attack, and had to go it unprotected in double time to catch up to the 168th and 167th, who had already moved forward. No sooner had they emerged into the open than they met a heavy fire. The lieutenant colonel and one major were severely wounded, and soon the other major and B.'s captain were killed, leaving him senior officer of his battalion.

About this time a general appeared from somewhere and asked B. if he had received any orders, which he had n't, and with a wave of his arm the general said, "You 're to cross a river over there and take a town called Sergy." It was tough work—the men had marched all night—they formed combat groups and went through wheat waist-high under direct fire from the Boche artillery. They carried one day's rations, one hundred rounds of rifle and one bag of *chochant* (automatic) ammunition. In some unaccountable way, Company L had received an order to withdraw, leaving what remained of three full companies, *circa* 700 men. The Ourcq, which proved to be a mere creek, was crossed with a run and jump, and, getting into Sergy, they fought their way through by 10 a.m., finally being brought to a halt beyond the village at a sunken road which was filled with machine gunners.

There was terrific shellfire, both our own and the enemy's, which seemed to be concentrated on Sergy, and finally, after heavy casualties, they had to fall back as far as the Ourcq again. Here they established not only their battalion P.C., but a first-aid station in a battered mill (La Grange au Pont), and did what they could for such of their wounded as they could drag in. Later in the day, after heavy artillery firing, the enemy countered. The dwindling battalion met them in the village and drove them out as far as the road again. The Boches came back with reënforcements, and all night there was house-to-house fighting in the village— the boys standing it very well despite their fatigue and losses.

On the next day, with no artillery aid, they succeeded in getting the village again cleared back to the road and held the Boches there till dark. Then the Boches countered once more and drove

Contours of Allied Advance from the Marne to the Vesle, July 19 to August 14. Note Bulge at Fère-en-Tardenois, Sergy, and Cierges, Where the Advance Was Long Stalled during the Last Week of July Owing to Severe Enemy Attacks Which Covered His Lines of Communication and Permitted His Final Withdrawal them back to the mill, where they again held and spent the whole night in once more clearing the village, which they succeeded in doing by dawn. That day the Boches came back at noon and reached the mill—and so it went, back and forth, the place chang-ing hands nine times between Friday the twenty-sixth and Tuesday the thirtieth, the twenty-eighth being their worst day. They finally held at the road on the thirtieth and were relieved on Wednesday the first.

Practically without sleep, with no medical officer, with only such food, after the first day, as they could get off the dead, with almost incessant shelling and many hours of actual combat every day, it was something of a strain. On Tuesday night B. got over to the 168th, and the colonel wanted an estimate of his strength in view of a possible widespread attack: "18 men and one officer fit for duty"—out of 927 men and 23 officers, these alone were left.

B. admits that he was getting rather fed up. He was acting as gas officer, for many of the men were suffering from bad burns and all had been more or less gassed. Then as intelligence officer —in other words, as a runner, once or twice by day and two or three times by night, always in the open—a necessity, since lines that he got over to the 168th were soon blown to bits and there was no one at the 168th P.C. who could read flash messages; there was no communication at any time with the rear. Also as medical officer, directing the getting in of the wounded, always under fire, back to the mill; he did two leg amputations himself with a mess-kit knife and an old saw found in the mill. One night they had sent back 83 wounded men on improvised litters.

When sufficiently quiet, the nights had to be spent in searching their own and the enemy's dead for food and ammunition. They once got down to as low as twenty rounds of cartridges, and much of the time they used Boche rifles and ammunition—also Boche "potato-masher" hand grenades, which caused at first a good many casualties among the men, for they were timed at three or four seconds instead of four or five like ours. The Boche food was good when they could find it—sausages and bread and Argentine "bully."

The least fatigued men had to be used to get in the wounded, for it was an exhausting process, since they often had to be dragged along a foot or two at a time, as occasion offered. Many men with three or four wounds continued in the fight—had to, in fact—and a sound man and a wounded man often fought together, the latter loading an extra gun even when he might not be able to stand. Their only protection was to get in shell holes.

During these days B. saw for the first time a case of shell shock, though he did not know what was the matter with the man—thought he was yellow. Every time a shell would land near, he would race to shelter, shaking and trembling; but he always came back and got to work. He simply could n't stand the explosions. They were all pretty shaky from the almost constant artillery fire —high explosive alternating with gas of one kind or another. Many of the men still fighting had mustard burns.

But almost the worst was a "rotten-pear" gas which made them sneeze and often vomit in their masks, so they had to throw them away and take a chance. Everyone was more or less affected, and marksmanship was poor from lachrymation.

On Monday, B. was quite badly stunned by a high-explosive fragment which struck his helmet—like getting hit in the temple by a pitched baseball. Men often thought they were wounded—would feel a blow on the leg, perhaps, and see blood and a tear, but on slipping off their trousers would find only a bruise, the blood having come from a neighbor's wound.

On Tuesday afternoon the Boches sent over a terrific barrage —a combination of artillery and machine-gun fire. They had learned by this time that after a barrage the only thing to do was "to beat the Boches to it"—so he and Lieutenant K. with their eighteen men rushed them (there were some two hundred Boches) and succeeded, after a sharp engagement, in getting into their positions along the sunken road just north of the village. It was a case of *"Gott mit uns,"* for not one of the eighteen was killed. They captured some machine guns, and, getting them in favorable positions, held the enemy off.

Not long after, word came by runner from the 168th to hold on, for they were soon to be relieved. B. sent back word that they could n't hold much longer without reënforcements, and fifty men were sent over from the 168th in support. At about 2 a.m., B. and two men with *chochants* and grenades crawled out and put out of commission an Austrian 88 which had been trained on them and from which they had suffered much. They captured the crew and officers. It was the last post holding the sector. The Boches had evidently begun to withdraw.

About this time Seringes was taken by the 1st Battalion of the 47th on their left. They had probably gone through similar ex_periences, but apparently Sergy had been the most difficult nut to crack. Cierges had not yet fallen.

Wednesday, a day of intermittent firing, was spent in collecting the wounded. They were relieved at sundown—two officers and eighteen men—and they marched all night to get back, all very much done in. Lieutenant K. had been hit through the heel—was cursing and swearing, and quite out of his head. The men all appeared low indeed—one chap, Madden by name, had had no sleep the whole time, for he had been acting as runner on the left, three or four times every day under observation and fire.

They went through the Forêt de Fère and met the chow wagons about noon—found a new acting-colonel who knew precisely what to do; gave the men good food and made them go to sleep. Not until they had arrived did B. notice that he was shy of his tunic, in the pocket of which was his artillery code—had left it under the head of one of the men, who was badly hurt, and forgot it when the time came for them to go out. Insisted on going back after having a rest—was afraid someone would find it. Was given a motor cycle and to his great relief found the coat where he had put it, but the man was dead.

On coming out he saw one of his own men who had been wounded and was overlooked near the mill at the far edge of the creek. He went down and tried to get him across the creek to the motor cycle, but the Boches opened up and they could not duck fast enough. B. felt a heavy blow on the top of his helmet, which mashed it in against the back of his head. He fell forward—had a sick feeling—found he was bleeding from the mouth and nose, and the back of his neck was bloody. Started to look for the man and found him all cut up with a huge hole in his side and a glassy stare, so he knew he was a goner and left him—reached the cycle and started off under heavy fire.

As soon as he got back they saw something was the matter and gave him a stiff drink of whiskey—he tried to sit down, but came down heavily with a jar, and began to shake and stammer. He was afraid to go to sleep—had an idea he would be unable to see when he woke up. They threw cold water on him, and he felt that his entire left side had given way and all vision was gone except a yellow fog in front of him. Through all this he still had a feeling that he was O.K.—merely exhausted and needed sleep. He was very sick, vomiting more or less all the rest of the day— ears humming—everything swimming.

They wanted him to go to a hospital, but he remembers fighting them much as a football player sometimes does when he is forced to leave the field after an injury; has strangely vivid memories of this occurrence and subsequent events—patchy, though very acute memory pictures. Knew by the hum of the machine that it was a G.M.C. ambulance; could n't see much except a yellow cloud before his eyes; was taken to a field hospital and a doctor asked him what was the matter. He said "Nothing," he merely wanted a little rest; was talking well enough at the time.

First in a horse-drawn wagon, then in a Ford ambulance, a very rough ride, to No. 7 at Coulommiers, a matter of a good many hours—does not know whether he was alone or not. Terrific headache all the time. His hearing was getting bad—a constant hum in his right ear. When the machine would scrape branches of trees it sounded to him like the whish of a shell—the worst sounds he had ever heard. . . .

"Of course if they had known we were so weak they could have come through at any time. You see, I am now Senior Company Commander and I want to get back because I can have the pick of the companies and can get into some really big push before it 's all over.

"The chief trouble now is the dreams—not exactly dreams, either, but right in the middle of an ordinary conversation the face of a Boche that I have bayoneted, with its horrible gurgle and grimace, comes sharply into view, or I see the man whose head one of our boys took off by a blow on the back of his neck with a bolo knife and the blood spurted high in the air before the body fell. And the horrible smells! You know I can hardly see meat come on the table, and the butcher's shop just under our window here is terribly distressing, but I'm trying every day to get more used to it. Yes, it was unpleasant amputating those men's legs, and we had to sharpen a knife from a man's kit for it, but what could one do otherwise? It was not quite so bad as dragging the wounded men in, hunching along foot by foot, both of us on our backs and under direct fire all the time—that was interminable. But the worst of all are the dying faces that come to me of the men of the command—the men I could not bear to see die—men whose letters I had censored, so I knew all about them and their homes and worries and dependents.". . .

Thursday, Oct. 31st

A "guest" here, a fortnight now—unfortunately missing the last act of the drama. It's a curious business—unquestionably still progressing—purely a sensory affair, fortunately without pain, though with considerable muscular wasting. The paresthesias are chiefly in soles and palms and I have a vague sense of familiarity with the sensation—as though I had met it somewhere in a dream. Like stepping barefoot on a very stiff and prickly doormat—a feeling, too, as though the plantar and palmar fascias had shrunk in the wash and were drawn taut. As Gowers used to say, our sensations transcend our vocabularies. But it's so characteristic someone who has it ought to describe it—preferably a doctor.

Such a one, however, has himself under observation—the fool for a patient idea—well, it does n't work very well and that's possibly why—though there have been exceptions, like Bernhardt and his meralgia—why M.D.'s as a rule don't scrutinize their own maladies too closely or describe them. They traditionally wind up with what they have been chiefly interested in—the examples are many. Accordingly I should properly be in hospital with "G.s.w. skull" rather than with this. It would have been appropriate and more interesting to watch.

. . . . . .

The *Conférence Interalliée* has again assembled in Paris. There have been 4482 deaths from influenza among the civil population of England the past week.

Friday, Nov. 1st

All Saints' Day, and Hallowe'en was celebrated here last evening by a dance for the enlisted men of the Unit and the patients

—very festive, I 'm told by the nurses of my floor. The men, who had spent the day digging the hobnails out of their shoes, are probably far better dancers than the officers, to whom heretofore the privilege of dancing with the nurses has been restricted.

.　.　.　.　.　.　.

The news astonishes. Old World dynasties are tottering, and the Kaiser stands a lone figure in the democratic ferment which is beginning to affect even Germany. L'ARMISTICE EST SIGNÉ AVEC LA TURQUIE!! is heavily headlined in *Le Petit Parisien* which reaches us late in the evening. Among its conditions are the right of passage of the Straits—the occupation of the Dardanelles forts —the immediate repatriation of prisoners. Nothing equal to this since the *dégringolade* of Bulgaria.

Sat., Nov. 2nd

During the past few days the Austrian Army has become little more than a demoralized rabble; and yesterday the Allies opened up again against all the vital points from the Dutch frontier to the Meuse. The Turkish terms are published and Austria will be able to judge what her own may be.

Sunday, Nov. 3

a.m. My hands now have caught up with my feet—so numb and clumsy that shaving 's a danger and buttoning laborious. When the periphery is thus affected the brain too is benumbed and awkward.

Still, there are bright spots. A visit from Kerr this morning with documents from the office—also McLean, with a new novel and the news. This grows more and more amazing every day— the collapse one by one of the props on which Germany has built up her dreams of world domination—Mittel-Europa and the East.

p.m. For the first time since Wednesday from my chair laboriously to one of our Dodge cars. Soft air—soft smoky colors— the foliage almost more beautiful than in its earlier stages of ripening. As far as Reynel and back—the old peasants in their white caps—church bells ringing—even the cows idled about the villages with the air of *permissionnaires,* as though taking a deserved Sunday afternoon off. The French gardener here is planting pansies along the south wall of the L— "so the Americans can send blossoms home in envelopes to their sweethearts."

THE LAST FEW DAYS

Monday, Nov. 4th

The Kaiser's abdication is again officially announced as imminent, and after a statement that he approves of the constitutional amendments he betakes himself to the German H.Q. for the protection of his troops. This via Zurich. The King of Bulgaria has started the abdication fashion.

Since July 15th the Allies have taken 362,355 prisoners. There is a cry in England for a Ministry of Health, and Sir Auckland Geddes tells some "appalling facts about the health of the British nation." The pandemic of influenza may after all have served a worthy purpose. It takes a scourge—or a war which is but a scourge—to rouse nations to constructive acts.

Nancy dedicates a monument at Barthelemont to "the first three American soldiers to give their lives to France during the present war." They were killed on November 3rd, 1917. There are some American noncombatant graves of Sept. 5th among the forest of crosses at Étaples which seemingly are forgotten.

Wed., Nov. 6

It was a year ago to-day that the last desperate attack was made by the British for a few yards more toward Passchendaele, leaving a British Army discouraged and decimated after three months of desperate fighting with gains so slight it was not even necessary to move the hospitals forward. To-day what a different story and what a different type of warfare, with an enemy being pursued at all points despite his rear-guard machine-gun nests!

The Americans have made their way across the Meuse, threatening the pivot of the enemy's retreat. The Austrian terms are made public. The Hun is at bay—Russia, Bulgaria, Turkey, Austria, one by one have abandoned him, and now the Bavarians, their southern border exposed, grow restless and threaten to follow suit.

Nov. 7th, Thursday

M. Clemenceau in a *"vibrante allocution"*—one can see him —makes known to the Chambre the terms of the Austrian armistice whereby she is stripped of her army, navy, and the territory she has invaded. Day by day the victorious Allies sweep on with an ever-shortening front, as one can even appreciate in hospital, unable to follow the receding line except on an official map with pins and a ball of yarn. My only form of amusement; but I 'm no longer able to hold and stick in the pins.

.   .   .   .   .   .

The British on one side of the Ardennes have gone through the Forest of Mormal and progressed along the Sambre toward Maubeuge and Mons. On the other side, the Americans have finally broken through in the direction of Stenay on the Mézières-Metz line. In between these pincers the Boche forces may become trapped, and a second Sedan be the result unless mayhap they can manage to trek through the forest, for they are clever at extricating themselves.

But these occurrences are *outside* of Germany. *Inside*, things also are happening—most significant of all an amazing "proclamation to the people" from a New Government, concerning the transfer of essential rights from the Emperor to their representatives—freedom of the press and the right of meeting. *"Le Gouvernement et, avec lui, les chefs de l'armée et de la marine veulent la paix: ils la veulent loyalement, ils la veulent bientôt."* This unquestionably is to prepare the German people for the terms of an armistice which cannot possibly be any less rigid than those imposed upon and accepted by Austria and Turkey. Mr. Wilson's note of yesterday—probably to be his last—says, "Ask Foch"; and it is stated that a delegation left Berlin instanter for the Western Front for this purpose. But why a delegation and not an officer with a white flag?

It hardly seems possible that these are the same people who a short fourteen weeks ago were sweeping victoriously toward Paris and Amiens and the Channel Ports. Nor the same people McCarthy has just been telling me about—the Berliners of 1916. He was serving with Alonzo Taylor in the Embassy under Gerard at the time, with the unpleasant duty of inspecting prison camps, and was asked on one occasion to go to a meeting of Army medical officers—an invitation he accepted. At the opening of the meeting the assemblage arose and at a signal raised their right hands, roaring in unison, *"Gott strafe England."* With this benediction they resumed their seats and proceeded with their business. McCarthy, having an Irish sense of humor, had great difficulty in concealing his emotions for they were, to say the least, considerably mixed.

He has been here for several days on a visit and his experiences in the Diplomatic Service would make a book. He was more or less mixed up in the Casement affair—in the Fryatt episode, which he fears he precipitated by his search for the four women prisoners. In the officers' prison camps he had many strange encounters, such as the meeting with Christian Denker, late of the J.H.H. and Hull House, Chicago, a prisoner at Maidenhead complaining that they were badly treated by not being given the daily papers from the *Vaterland*; and, what 's more, the roof leaked!

All of our Embassy people, though they were carefully watched, had *laissez-passer's* which gave them freedom of movement and certain powers of inspection—one in particular which they called the "Weer Willy" owing to its *Wir Wilhelm* beginning.

Crile here for the day visiting the hospital and Thayer in for a moment after dinner. To our relief he is able to contradict the depressing rumor to which we had endeavored to adjust ourselves, namely, that Woodrow Wilson has been assassinated. Thayer is off for England with Longcope. To-day almost my worst day so far—the labor of dressing too much for me.   .

Friday, Nov. 8th

My room is changed so that Schwab is no longer afflicted by having to adjust his habits to those of a semi-invalid. With such trifles to emphasize the days, they slip by.

Alec Lambert in at noon. He shares my tray and between the killing of flies makes toast over my wee fire. He brings the news that Foch has notified the German envoys to proceed along the Hirson–La Capelle road to our outposts.

The American advance yesterday with our successful crossing of the Meuse will probably help them to accept the Allies' terms, whatever they may be. After our long steady pressure we have finally burst through to Sedan, and when the story comes to be told it should be a thrilling one. The old home of the de la Marcks and the de la Tour d'Auvergnes, where Turenne was born, which Vauban fortified, where Prussia within living memory struck the most crushing of the blows which laid France at her feet, delivered of its Boche invaders by a despised army of Republicans from beyond the seas—Prussian militarism defeated on the scene of its most brilliant achievement in that war which made Militarism the popular ideal—it is the finger of fate!

. . . . . .

Later. Foch, after an interesting exchange of radio telegrams, received the German plenipotentiaries this morning—they had crossed the lines at Haudroy last night.

The armies are pegging away to the last—the Americans have entered Sedan and cut the railroad connecting the important towns behind the enemy's present front. The British are within eight miles of Mons. There is a revolt under the red flag in Hamburg, another at Kiel, and popular outbreaks are reported at Cologne. Messrs. Erzberger and Oberndorf, Generals von Gündell and von Winterfeldt, may well hasten.

Nov. 9th. Saturday

We have received the news of a possible armistice with a peculiar indifference almost amounting to stupefaction. No shouts or throwing up of hats—we cannot believe it quite yet.

Finney and Salmon in to see me this afternoon. F. still under the weather with his particular kind of grippe. Salmon knocks into a cocked hat my plans to keep on at work here and to organize the nucleus of a National Institute of Neurology in the A.E.F. at Vichy. The war's over—people are tired, God knows—the Army (especially McCaw) will not listen to any new constructive schemes—sick and wounded will be shoved home immediately at the rate of 10,000 a week—America will be much more receptive to such an idea, and an institution transplanted from the A.E.F. won't "take"—first thing necessary is to beat it home and get a gigantic *triage* started at the Staten Island plant where cases can be combed out, sorted, and routed to proper hospitals—for this purpose should have representatives there of all departments, and Schwab, McCarthy, and I are suggested for Neurology.

Salmon is the only man who can put across such a large scheme. Will he be willing to go and do it? He favors a university rather than Red Cross or national auspices for the proposed Institute—possibly with the General Education Board's backing. Above all, avoid any relations with Congress, for if it has any brains it does n't use them—"a Congressman is nothing but a heart and a pants pocket"—just sentiment and cash, in other words.

. . . . . .

The German delegates were belated in getting over the roads Thursday. Whereas Foch ordered a cessation of firing at 3 p.m. to permit their passage, they did not reach Guise until late that night. They stayed at the château of the Marquis de l'Aigle near the Fôret de Compiègne, and apparently were admitted to Foch yesterday morning. He received them in his train at the Rethondes station and gave them 72 hours to reply—i.e., until Monday at 11 a.m. There will probably be tearing of hair at Spa, the Grosse Hauptquartier, *"mais la situation militaire et la situation intérieure parlent un langage singulièrement impérieux."*

The Wittelsbachs after 800 years of rule have been dethroned and a republic has been proclaimed in Bavaria—the Socialist Party has given an ultimatum demanding the abdication of the Kaiser and renunciation of the Crown Prince—the German fleet at Kiel has mutinied—the French approach Hirson and the British are drawing near Mons.

Nov. 10th

Max of Baden dismounts as Chancellor and Friedrich Ebert, a saddler, is in the saddle. The Kaiser, after doubts and hesitations, is finally reported to have signed his abdication last night at the German headquarters in the presence of the Crown Prince and Hindenburg. *L'incroyable est accompli.* There is much talk of what Wilson really means by "the freedom of the seas" among his 14 covenants; and the story is circulating that there was a good deal of difficulty at the Versailles Conference in fully understanding other of the Fourteen Points. Finally Clemenceau in some desperation said, "Why, the Bon Dieu has given us only ten."

Later. It is told that the German envoys on being admitted to Foch asked for an immediate provisional cessation of hostilities "on the grounds of humanity." This was rejected by Foch. The story I have heard through General Glenn is that von Winterfeldt breezed into the compartment with a sort of old-chap-how-are-you air and that Foch looked him in the eye with no sign of recognition. Also that the first demand was not from them but from Foch, for the secret plans for all the traps and delayed mines placed under bridges and in towns in the line of the retreat. It was through this that Ostend was saved. Von W. had been military attaché in Paris at the time of the 1913 manœuvres and was given the *Légion d'Honneur.* I wonder if he wore it last Friday.

Nov. 11th. Monday

La dynastie des Hohenzollerns a été balayée; but in this process some twenty millions of human beings have perished or been mutilated, and who is to be held responsible for this? The terms of the armistice were signed early this morning, though the signal to "cease fire" was not given until the 72 hours were up, *viz.,* at 11 a.m. In these last few hours many poor fellows must have needlessly fallen.

Thus the Great War ends at the eleventh hour on this eleventh day of the eleventh month of 1918; and the Kaiser awakes from his forty years' dream of world dominion. It 's a piteous spectacle. All the king's horses and all the king's men could n't put Humpty Dumpty together again. He came so very near to fulfilling his ambition—the Hohenzollern rule of a Prussianized world. *Weltmacht oder Niedergang.* He gambled and lost, so it is to be downfall.

The past few days have been comparable to the last few minutes of a decisive intercollegiate football game at the end of a season. On one side of the field, alive with color and excitement, an exultant crowd, touched by the last rays of a November sun— an unexpected victory within their grasp through an unlooked-for collapse of the visiting team. Across, on the other side of the darkening field, tense, colorless, shivering, and still, sit the defeated, watching their opponents roll up goal after goal as they smash through an ever-weakening line that shortly before seemed impregnable.

Just so, till the whistle blew, the Allies plunged ahead on the five-yard line of the Western Front. The Americans pushed over at Sedan—a mass play carried the French beyond the Mézières-Hirson line—and the British Guards Division on the left centre went through to Mauberge and Mons, where early in the game they so desperately and hopelessly resisted an apparently unconquerable foe. Surely the Bowmen of Agincourt, the Angel of Mons, and Saint George himself must have appeared yesterday,

even as they are said to have appeared in those tragic days of
August 1914.

It's a trivial comparison,—a world war and a football game,
—but when something is so colossal as to transcend comprehension
one must reduce it to the simple terms of familiar things.

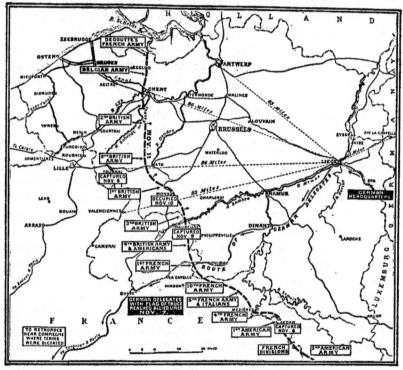

The Final Positions of the Allied Armies on the Morning of November 11th;
also the Route Taken by the German Delegates from Spa to La Capelle

Kerr and Bagley here in the afternoon to discuss plans for a
survey of the peripheral nerve cases and the ways and means of
keeping track of them. Later Pte. Duncan brings me from Neufchâteau a much needed shaving mirror and nail brush. He takes
back with him my tunic for alterations—chickens on the shoulders
and three service stripes on the left sleeve. Almost too much for
one day—the completion of 18 months since our embarkation on
May 11, 1917; a colonelcy; the cessation of hostilities.

How still it must be with the guns silent—they can sleep now "amid the crosses row on row." There will be much celebrating, I presume, and drawing of corks—but perhaps not so much after all. That would have happened after the football game—a large dinner and the theatre—wine and song. This contest has been too appalling for that kind of thing, and there's a lot yet for everyone to do. . . .

We celebrated simply here before a wood fire with tea at 4.30 —the Matron, the Padre, Schwab, and I—and after wondering what the future held in store for us we switched to a serious discussion of religion which was prolonged till dinner time. The Padre admits that Army chaplains have learned much in this war —especially about men. For example: a trench-going Padre makes a church-going battalion. He thinks he will no longer wear clerical garb when he gets home—and he lingered to say that though the Jew was an agnostic he thought him one of the most religious men he ever knew. Wethered said something like this about Capt. Telfer at No. 46 C.C.S. last summer.

Tuesday, Nov. 12th

What an opportunity to redeem himself before his people by facing the music the Kaiser missed, and how ignominious his flight! So far as one can gather from the fragmentary reports, it was before the terms of the armistice reached Spa. The German courier, leaving the French G.Q.G. near Senlis after many vicissitudes, was reported by wireless to have reached the German Headquarters at 10.55 Sunday morning. A message from The Hague states that the ex-Emperor arrived Sunday morning by special train at the Eysden station on the Dutch frontier. He is reported to have signed his letter of abdication Saturday night.

Wednesday morning, Nov. 13th

On ne se bat plus. It's an intoxicating November day which must reflect the gayety, light-heartedness, and thanksgiving of France. What must Paris be like—the boulevards crowded— the Strasbourg statue, after near 50 years of mourning, probably bedecked with banners and flowers—the *Place* filled with captured guns—the blue glass all removed from the street lamps— what would one not give to be there!

It's blowing here and the last yellow leaves from the poplars are joyously zooming and side-slipping and nose-spinning as they leave their hangars and seek somewhere a safe landing place. The leaves indeed are mostly gone, and the fruit trees which I can see from my windows, crucified against the walls of these old farm buildings, are quite naked—only to the chestnuts do leaves still cling, and to some of the lower branches of the beeches unswept by the wind. It blows down my chimney too and sends gusts of wood smoke into the room, and my morning toast made on a pair of tongs smacked of it.

The sun was pouring in when my batman appeared, started the fire, stropped my razor (for that particular gesture is beyond me these ataxic days), and brought my green canvas tub—the very tub that one "Chopsticks" scrounged for me in Lillers, eons ago, and now it in turn begins to leak, a lamentable circumstance, for the like of it comes not with the A.E.F. Then bacon and the smoky toast and a pot of G.W. coffee with the aid of my old friend "Beatrice," faithful since 46 C.C.S. days—and now in bed again enveloped in a blue-gray dressing gown which harks back to Geoffrey Dodge and my first trip to Paris near 18 months ago. *La guerre est finie,* and what a procession of associations these familiar objects serve to recall. It's doubtless why we cling to old things—old books, old friends—an ancient pair of slippers, no matter how shabby, may be rich in memories forever lost on replacement with what is new—and clean.

Thursday the 14th

Another brilliant morning. In the farm courtyard below chanticleer crows, guineas and geese cackle, porcs grunt, and the beagles bark excitedly. Frenchmen of the vintage of 1870 in their velveteens are doubtless making for the *bois* to get a pot at a wild boar or two. The Boches having now been finished by the younger generation, there is ammunition a-plenty for them and the boars. . . .

A last ride this afternoon, taken early, for the sun lies low and cold by three. Through the forest roads again, with a climax on a hilltop overlooking the valley, the horizontal rays of the sun streaming through an open wood of towering silver birches with spruce and hemlock for a background. The leaves nearly all wind-blown by now except the lower branches of oaks and beech, though from a distance one can still recognize the patches of birch, clearly demarcated from the rest of the forest by their striking color of burnt sugar.

Friday the 15th

Yesterday afternoon for the first time well enough to attend the Reclassification Board Meeting—very interesting—conducted like a hospital clinic, each M.O. presenting his own cases for "boarding," with diagnosis and class in which he believed the patient should fall—then, after the man was dismissed, a free discussion. The presentations admirably made by young M.O.'s like Durkin, Thorn, Clymer, and others. Schwab deserves unending credit for the way in which he has built up this school of unconscious instruction and made an interesting daily seminar out of what in most places is regarded as a chore.

All the advantages of a full-time university service—paid by the government—no outside responsibilities—no office hours to keep—merely undivided attention to the work at hand, and the work made interesting and vitalized by the thought that perhaps to-morrow any individual may have to stand on his own feet as psychiatrist to a division or regiment. There is nothing quite like this combination in civil life—no comparable incentive. How can we transfer some of its good features to civil conditions?

Saturday, November 16th

7 *p.m. Adieu, La Fauche.* Four weeks there were somehow passed, under the kind attention of Schwab and his people. So in the old Dodge back to the attic of 57 rue Gohier in Neufchâteau, with its smells and draughts and flapping paper partitions. We huddle about a cylindrical iron stove and envy the deaf Duncan, the mangy "Gamin," and the slatternly Henriette, who together occupy the warm box of a kitchen. Too tired, squalid, and uncomfortable to talk to one another, we scarcely need to do so while familiar shibboleths resound in our ears—that this was to be a war to end all wars, and that the world from now will be made safe for democracy. We wonder. We shall at least see what democracy can make of it—and after all this destruction there is certainly much remaking to be done.

> And these shall be no easy idle years,
> For only by the toil of stubborn men,
> Of women toiling stubbornly with men,
> Shall earth attain her heritage of dreams.

EDITOR'S AFTERWORD

BOTH diary and semi-invalided diarist continued in their appointed orbits long after November 14th. Although the stream of *blessés* had dried at the source, the overseas hospitals remained full of patients who must be cared for until they could be transshipped to the destination all were eager to reach, but to which the sick and wounded supposedly had the right of way. Their number may be gathered from the following Thanksgiving Day entry in which some casualty figures are cited:—

* *Neufchâteau, Nov. 28*

Rainy season in earnest. All day in the office filing peripheral nerve literature and keeping close to a stove. Found in the enemy literature (*Deutsche Med. Wochenschrift*, 1918, p. 854) an article on *Polyneuritis ambulatoria*—"in young and otherwise healthy individuals, with loss of deep reflexes and without signs of cortical disease." So I am not the only one. . . .

All are wondering now that Mr. Wilson—or Mrs. Wilson?—has decided to come over, what particular claim we have to a prominent seat at the Peace Table. Our total casualties are some 326,000, only a little more than half of them representing battle casualties, *viz.*, 179,625. The few thousand American dead are tabulated as follows:—

Killed or died of wounds	36,164
Died of disease	14,601
Died unspecified	2,604
	53,369

Unofficial reports credit the French (excluding the Colonials) with 1,700,000 dead and casualties untold, a large percentage of the *poilus* having of course been wounded more than once. This far exceeds the losses of the British, who have had only 658,704 dead out of something over three and a half million casualties. Indeed someone has stated that the total number of cases (mostly British) treated by each of our six original Base Hospital Units serving with the B.E.F. exceeds the total casualties of the A.E.F. B.H. No. 4, for example, had 67,591 patients.

What an insignificant toll we have paid after all! It is illuminating to compare the Canadian and American lists and to find the figures practically identical. The Canadian Corps with its total of *ca.* 400,000 volunteer troops have been in the thick of it since the second Ypres, while we with something like five times that number in the A.E.F. have had battalions in the line for only a few paltry months.

	Canadian	*American*
Wounded	152,779	179,635
Prisoners	2,860	2,163
Missing	5,394	11,600
Dead	50,334	53,369
TOTAL	211,367	246,767

While we have been prodigal of our regulars and marines, a very small proportion of our *ca.* two million men have been in contact with the enemy; the Canadians, on the other hand, from the outset have been regarded as essentially a fighting corps. To put it another way, approximately two out of every four Canadians who have served in the B.E.F. have been killed or wounded, whereas something less than two out of every sixteen Americans who embarked to the tune of "Over There" were booked for casualties.

An Amsterdam report of the German losses shows that during the past few weeks they have rapidly risen, almost to the level of the French figures, which, as a matter of fact, may never be precisely made known.

		Up to Oct. 31	*Up to Nov. 10*
Germans	killed	1,580,000	1,600,000
"	missing	260,000	103,000 (?)
"	prisoners	290,000	618,000
"	wounded	4,000,000	4,064,000
	TOTAL	6,130,000	6,385,000

At the close of hostilities nearly 18,000 wounded Americans were occupying beds in overcrowded hospitals officered and manned by war-weary people, most of whom were looking for any kind of excuse to get leave and go sightseeing along with the Army of Occupation. Since many of the wounded were still in need of serious secondary operations, the problem was one for which G.H.Q. scarcely knew the answer. It was at first decided that they were to be rushed home; but soon after this programme was set in operation, the ports of embarkation became so jammed that at Savenay, for example, 10,000 patients in 8000 beds, mostly under canvas, were despondently awaiting the long-over-due transports. Ere long came word from Washington that since no more hospital beds were available at home, the remainder must stay in France until provision could be made to receive them. As no one had had any experience with demobilization on a large scale, there were orders and counter orders and unbeliev-able confusion.

Meanwhile, final meetings were being held in Paris of the R.C. Research Committee; also of the *Conférence Chirurgicale Inter-alliée* in which British, French, Belgian, Italian, Portuguese, Japanese, Serbian, and American doctors compared notes. It was even thought that further sessions might profitably be held and plans were laid accordingly; but these things required construc-tive efforts for which there was no longer either enthusiasm or leadership.

Conscientious medical officers, however, had much paper work to do in their several hospitals. Orders were issued by G.H.Q. that reports must be written which could be used later on for an official medical history of the war. This necessitated the accumu-lation of statistical data from as many of the scattered hospitals in the A.E.F. as could be reached and could be persuaded to take the trouble to analyze their case records, which a good many re-fused to do. Elaborate and somewhat humiliating qualification cards for rating had to be filled out before movement orders of any kind could be secured; and there were other masses of red tape to be unraveled by those whose patience was itself fast un-raveling.

On December 22nd came a message from Chaumont stating that the medical headquarters at Neufchâteau were to be closed and that movement orders had been issued for the diarist and three other members of Base Hospital No. 5 still attached there to rejoin their original Unit with the B.E.F. at Boulogne. They

somehow managed to get transportation to Paris, where two days
later the following entry was made:—

Christmas Eve

After a cold damp night in Epernay we had breakfasted, badly enough,
in company with some young British officers who after a period of leave
were making their way across the old battle areas to rejoin their units.
The morning promised fine and we got away, proceeding due north over
the Montagne de Reims, whose southern vine-clad slopes bristle at this
time of year with neatly stacked poles which from a distance give to the
hillsides the appearance of an unshaven chin. A heavy mist shrouded all
the valleys, and the series of hills poked their heads out of it in most en-
chanting fashion.

So on and up into the forest, mostly of oak and birch, the trees green
to their terminal branches with moss and lichen—past the *zones evacuées,
interdit pour civiles*—past countless bypaths with signs innumerable by
"*Ordre d'Armée—Défense absolument d'entrer—Dépôt du munitions
P.A.C.A.*"—past a French military cemetery—past wire and trenches
and *chevaux de frise*. As we begin to descend and the wide views of the
country beyond open out we pass successions of secondary fortifications,
and road screens abound, both lateral and horizontal. By Monchenot,
which must have been under observation from all sides—Champfleury
with still more defenses, and through the screen of mats concealing the
road come the first distant glimpses of the cathedral. Then line after line
of defenses—French cavalry coming out—and so, over a choked and
mossy canal paralleling the river bed of the Vesle, into Reims. . . .

It was an unforgettable picture—the western façade of the cathedral,
the most beautiful product of the greatest of centuries, still magnificent, for
Reims has come through the fire glorified like the soul of Jeanne d'Arc
herself—this as a gray background while in the Place du Parvis the survivors of the 100th Regiment of *Chasseurs*, the defenders of Reims in their
marvelous blue, were drawn up in open square for a *prise d'armes*.

We came upon this unexpected scene just as the sun, low in the south,
burst through the reluctant clouds eager to add light and warmth to the
moving spectacle.

A fanfare of trumpets and drums, followed by some bars of the
"Marseillaise," the regiment presents arms, and General Petit decorates
and embraces in turn three officers as Chevaliers of the Legion of Honor.
Again, and the exploits of eight *poilus*, one after the other, are read out
and, one after the other, tapped on each shoulder by the sabre of *Mon
Général*, each has a *Croix de Guerre* pinned on his left breast. Then the
turn of the regiment itself, and with the same preliminaries—a burst of

martial music, a short stirring address—the presentation of arms—a cross
is pinned on the regimental colors so that henceforth all may wear the
green *fourragère*.

We meanwhile from our pile of crumbling masonry looked on with
awe and reverence mingled with a sense of apology for having stumbled
upon a solemn rite held by its defenders in honor of an edifice—imperish-
able though mutilated, typifying the soul of France.

It was over. Forming columns, they swung around the empty pedestal
on which the Maid's statue once stood and to stirring music marched out
of the square and away into the tumbled wreck of Reims.

On reaching Boulogne, the diarist was taken into Sir Almroth
Wright's billet and there, while marking time for another three
weeks, material was gathered from the hospital records for a
subsequently published account [1] of the Unit, whose personnel
by this time was fretting to know what was in store for them and
when and by whom they would be demobilized, whether by the
B.E.F. or the A.E.F.

On January 17th, the diarist was ordered to proceed to England for the purpose of observing reconstruction work that was
being done in certain Base Hospitals there. This made it possible
for him once more to spend a week-end with his old friends in
Oxford. And so it came about that on the following Sunday, after
dining with Osler by candlelight in Wolsey's Hall at Christ
Church—the first such gathering to be held here for three years
—he was taken home at 9.30 and put to bed at "The Open Arms"
with a hot water bottle at his back, a bed lamp at his side, and
Walt Whitman's *Memoranda* of another war put in his hands to
read.

From these Memoranda of 1862–1865 two excerpts were taken
which might have been written—so it is stated—by a Red Cross
worker, let us say at Evac. No. 7 in Coulommiers during the
autumn of 1918:—

(1) We have undoubtedly in the United States the greatest military
power—an exhaustive, intelligent, brave and reliable rank and file—
in the world, any land, perhaps all lands. The problem is to organize
this in the manner fully appropriate to it, to the principles of the Republic, and to get the best service out of it. In the present struggle as
already seen and reviewed, probably three fourths of the losses, men, lives,

[1] *Cf. The Story of Base Hospital No. 5, Harvard Univ. Press, 1919, anon.*

&c., have been sheer stupidity, extravagance, waste. The body and bulk came out more and more superb—the practical Military system, directing power, crude, illegitimate—worse than deficient, offensive, radically wrong.

(2) Such was the war. It was not a quadrille in a ballroom. Its interior history will not only never be written, its practicality, minutiæ of deeds and passions, will never be even suggested. The active soldier of 1862–'65, North and South, with all his ways, his incredible dauntlessness, habits, practices, tastes, language, his appetite, rankness, his superb strength and animality, lawless gait, and a hundred unnamed lights and shades of camp—I say, will never be written—perhaps must not be and should not be.

The diarist remained in England long enough to appreciate the tragic aftermath of the war for the returning "heroes," most of whom found someone younger and more vigorous than themselves holding down their former jobs. Disillusioned veterans were encountered everywhere openly begging in the streets or clutching at the straws of a possible livelihood by peddling some trifle to the passers-by. In the daily papers were long *Personal* columns with advertisements by relatives requesting information about "the missing"; by former officers and N.C.O.'s who were giving their qualifications and offering themselves for menial jobs. Not the least disillusioned were the middle-aged medical officers entitled to wear four blue service chevrons on their sleeves, perhaps even a wound stripe or two and some pieces of ribbon on the breast. Home again, but broken in spirit after their four wasted years, they must start in once more at the bottom, replace their out-of-date office equipment and try to recapture some of their lost practice if it ever could be recaptured. It was a depressing time, with the menace of strikes to stop railroad traffic and close down industry and, perhaps worst of all, a peace conference sitting in Versailles planning how to humiliate Germany most effectively and to make her pay for all that had happened.

Finally there came, on the last day of January, a movement order for the diarist to proceed to Liverpool, there to embark for home on a transport. And the story may close with some of the entries made on the old *Canopic*, now in use as a troop ship, on which our diarist crossed as the senior medical officer when she brought back the 162nd Infantry.

Wednesday evening, Feb'y 12th

"*Come* seven!" "Once mo', bones!" "Joey, don't you hear me?" "Ten dollars on de side he doan make it." "Come natural!" "An' a seven over-took him." "Two he's wrong." "Dollar he shoots." "Three to two no ten." "Come bones!" "Look at 'em come!"—all this with snapping of fingers, much profanity and no less obscenity.

With one's eyes closed it might be a group of doughboys from the Midnight Division crouched around a ground sheet and a torch; but it's really a flushed group of officers crooning over the throws of the dice as they crowd around a large table in the smoking room. There they "roll the bones" all day and all night, and so do other ranks on levels below this hurricane deck.

Ewers of A Company tells me it pervades the entire force and by a week after pay day the money of each company is in the hands of four or five people—usually, be it said, the same people—and they play it off for heavy stakes till it rests often in the hands of one man. To make it quick in the end, the pack is simply cut for high or low cards at $500 a throw. One of his sergeants has sent home $8000 won at craps since they came over a year ago. It's a vice by no means confined to the South and West for Donovan tells me many of the most successful crap-shooters are New Englanders. Even New York may do better than the surly-looking Major of the 77th whom I just saw leave the table after losing the last of his Express Company checks to the tune of 780 dollars.

I've confessed before that we were a blasphemous and a thieving army but this gambling business never came home to me so acutely as on this voyage home. If it's as widespread as these young men admit, I'm not sure but that wine and women are less serious evils. War, after all, isn't Hell—it's demoralization, which is far worse. Hell, for all one knows, may be very well governed.

Sunday the 16th of Feb'y

It's been a week of winds and what the Captain's bulletin calls a "confused sea." The daily inspection has been kept up with its not unwelcome intermission. The men's quarters are reasonably clean, though I do not particularly envy one or two of the Companies their accommodations; and we have had no special sickness to cause anxiety—one pneumonia, two cases of mumps, and a naval ensign who is dying with tuberculosis, very cheerfully be it said.

Are we naturally a discontented lot or have we had cause to grumble? Troublesome investigations—Congressional and otherwise—are likely to follow if the temper and feelings of these youths aboard represent that of the national army as a whole. The pettiness and incapacity of the regu-

lar officers in most services, which the mask of discipline but feebly concealed, seem to have roused the ire of the rank and file, and from one
point of view it perhaps speaks well of our national characteristics that
during the time of stress there was no movement other than to work with
the machine, much as it obviously needed to be overhauled and put in
new hands to get the best out of it. To have eagles perched on your shoulders when most others have bars does not lead to intimacies or confidences;
but the thing is there, nevertheless, on all sides, without much being
said.

The only ones aboard to whom this does not appertain seem to be
those who have served with the British—the naval officers, some of the
casual M.O.'s, and a few of the flying men. Those who served with the
R.A.F. consider themselves most lucky. One of them is a Minnesota boy
who, every flyable night, has been down the Rhine Valley in a huge
Handley Page to drop bombs on Mannheim or even Cologne. Having come
to love and respect the officers under whom he served, he can't understand
why our young aviators feel as they do. Have they had a particularly raw
deal, or does all this really indicate profound differences in British and
American qualities of leadership?

Monday

"We are holding our own" and a bit more—229 miles. This means
with good luck sometime Wednesday, 15 days out from Liverpool. Whew!
Snow, a northeast gale, a heavy sea, and another case of mumps have
punctuated the morning.

Restraints are beginning to break down more and more—the ship
was badly policed this morning, perhaps due to yesterday's omission of
inspection. Talk in the lounge and smoking room is getting a little more
free. Somewhat mutinous and indignant talk in spots now that the bridle
is off—from casual aviators, ordnance people and National Guard—
particularly National Guard. The few regulars aboard are outnumbered
and though they give orders, which are obeyed, they are not so greatly
feared as when the ocean and the censorship lay between the A.E.F. and
home.

The regular is so constituted that he strains at trifles—at the gnat and
swallows the elephant. Just now it's over the absurd question of what
may be worn when we disembark—as though it much mattered, provided
officers were clean, neat, and had a soldierly bearing. Many a one com-
plies with regulations and yet looks unaccountably sloppy—regulations
concerning the type of boots and whether 4 or 5 inches of lacing exempts
or necessitates the wearing of spurs. No service caps to be worn ashore,
and yet most of us have nothing else. Spiral puttees are taboo, as are trench

coats and also Sam Browne belts! We are all still more or less in terror of the M.P. Be sure and salute him first is common advice. "Why, organ‑ izations have been held up a whole month at Brest because an M.P. re‑ ported an outfit, some doughboy from which was seen with his blouse unbuttoned, etc. etc."

Tuesday, the 18th Feb'y

A little better run yesterday, and we should get in to-morrow. Despite 12 cases of mumps, a bad outbreak of "cooties" in Co. A, and two or three very sick-looking members of the ship's motley crew in the hospital bay, landing papers have been made out with young Capt. Mark, the Transport Surgeon, Capt. Crothers of the 126th, and old Dr. Smilie, for 32 years ship's surgeon on the *Canopic*.

The rotund and imperturbable Smilie! What a chain of associations he brings up—of the *Canopic* in March of 1915 and our little band off for a few weeks to the American Ambulance at Paris. Among them were Cutler, Osgood, and Boothby, who came out again on this second ad- venture. I can see Richard Strong sitting at the very desk over there in this lounge correcting proofs of his South American report—continuously from early morn till 5 p.m. on a glass of water for lunch. And Helen Homans, that bright soul who alone of our party served abroad without intermission until her heroic death.

Curious the repetitions of places visited and of persons encountered in the first and on this second more prolonged episode. It almost merges into a single absence—out on the *Canopic* in March 1915 and now by chance home on the same boat nearly four years later. There are over- lapping memories of the second and third Ypres and of many persons and places in between—Makins, Wallace, Sargent, General Sloggett, Rob- ert Bacon, the Oslers, Col. Gallie, the American Ambulance people, Tuf- fier, the Ypres salient, the Carrels, Dakin, the Casino at Boulogne, the Strongs, the Blisses, Sir Almroth, Keogh, the wounded *poilu*, the wounded Tommy—all these and many more emerge from the background of both episodes.

But somehow there was a break in the story: the *Lusitania* got sunk; submarines became too many to tolerate; and ere long a lot of sturdy youths, vigorous enough though not very trim in appearance, wearing cowboy hats and carrying bolo knives, both of which they were made to discard soon after they came to be identified thereby—these American youths, I say, began to appear, and soon in multitudes, and with them a horde of persons who did n't belong to the first chapter, Red Cross and Y.M.C.A. people and Knights of Columbus and Salvation Army folks with coffee and doughnuts; and docks got built and railroads laid down, and it was too much for the enemy and the taut line frayed, finally broke, and then the end.

So here we are, a very few of us, finding our way home on the *Canopic*, three months after this end came, and we are a fortunate company of 1400, for there are about two hundred times as many as we still to be brought home from France.

In the back of the last volume of these chronicles, one finds pasted a small printed sheet asserting that the diarist had been honorably discharged from the Army. His official *Military Record* on the verso states: "No record. Sailed from U.S. for foreign service May 11, 1917. Arr. port overseas May 21, 1917. Sailed from port overseas for U.S. Feb. 5, 1919. Arr. Hoboken on *Canopic* Feb. 20, 1919. *Remarks:* Discharged per S.O. 1614, S.G.O., Washington, D.C., April 9, 1919."

INDEX

ABBEVILLE, in war time, 299, 300

Acton, Capt., 124, 125

Adami, Dr. J. G., working on Medical History of the War, 75

A.E.F., early tactlessness of officers, 297, 298, 350; first glimpses of, 301–304; to be brigaded with Allies, 322; at Seichprey, 342; scorned by French, 346; many troops at Calais, 370; growing numerous, 372, 389; lack of mobility of its medical personnel, 384, 385; first army formed, 419; enters Juvigny, 427; in Flanders, 429; in Sept. offensive (1918), 434, 461; influenza epidemic in, 473; being split up, 473, 474; second army formed, 474; during final days of war, 492–494, 497; casualty figures of, 502–504; post-war disposition of wounded in hospitals, 504

1st Division, at Montdidier, 351; captures Cantigny, 364; hard hit, 408

2nd Division, en route to the Front, 301, 304; its magnificent counter, 372; at Vaux, 392, 394, 395, 417; at Thiaucourt, 450; at White Hill, 466; with the French, 471; during final days of war, 474, 475

4th Division, 403

26th Division, relieves 2nd, 395; its brilliant offensive, 411; at St. Mihiel, 439, 440, 448, 457; at Verdun, 475

29th Division, 475

33rd Division, 475

35th Division, severely handled, 462, 475

42nd Division, at Baccarat, 348; north of Châlons, 399, 404, 407; pays heavy toll, 412; replaces 91st, 475

77th Division, at the Argonne, 463, 469, 475

78th Division, 451

79th Division, severely handled, 462

82nd Division, at Varennes, 465

89th Division, 396; neglected, 425

91st Division, 475

92nd Division (Midnight), 396; at the Argonne, 457; fails to stick, 464

Marines, cited three times, 392

Alexander, Col., 269

Alfonti, Col., 440

Allenby, Gen., in Palestine, 452, 453, 459

Allison, Lt. Col. N., 301, 303, 432, 448; at Neufchâteau, 386, 413; at Séry-Magneval, 406; at Souilly, 433–437, 439, 451–453; at Fleury, 455–458

Ambulance Américaine, 25, 35; organized, 3; arrival of Harvard Unit at, 11, 12; work of, 40–52; under Univ. of Pa. and Red Cross, 81; overcrowded, 384

American Red Cross. See Red Cross

Ames, Joseph, 89

Amiens, visit of Cushing to sector at, 18–30; the 1918 spring drive on, 310–312, 316–322

Anderson, Dr., surgeon at No. 32, 173, 231

Anderson, Maj., at No. 4 Canadian, 335, 341

Anderson, Mrs. Larz, in France, 278

Andrew, A. Piatt, head of Field Ambulance Service, 82

Anstruther, an English M.P., 322

Antoine, Gen., 216

Arbuthnot, T. S., in Paris, 288

Argonne, thrust at the, 398, 399, 402; offensive at the, 455, 457, 459–462, 464–466, 469

Armour, Dr. Donald, in London, 108

Arras, ruins of, 141; Allied losses at, 308

Ashford, batman for Cushing, 178, 247, 248

Ashford, Col. B. K., at Langres, 346, 347, 386, 387

Astor, Lady, 110; at No. 15 Canadian, 296, 297

Asturias, torpedoed, 291

Atkins, Col., 66, 69, 70, 72

Australian troops, 419, 427

Austrian army, a near rout on Piave, 389; demoralized, 491

Auto-chir, of French army, 52, 53, 216, 402 and *n*.

Azan, Maj. Paul, at Saturday Club, 95, 96

BABINSKI, DR., 37, 388

Bacon, Robert, 3; his plans for 1040-bed hospitals, 47, 48; in Flanders, 65, 69; plans for U.S. medical units, 80; in Paris, 149, 276

Bacot, Dr., of Lister Institute, 258, 267

Baer, Dr., at Neufchâteau, 386, 437, 462

Bagley, Charles, 262; medical officer of *Olympic*, 472; at Neufchâteau, 473; at La Fauche, 481, 498

Baigeant, Maj., 124

Bailey, Pearce, 419, 422, 436, 437, 448

Bailleul, the hospitals at, 66, 69

Bailleul, Jean de, 116

Baker, Dr., at Evac. No. 10, 451, 453, 461

Baker, Newton D., 309, 381, 394

Balfour, Lord, 90, 91, 98

Barcroft, Col. Joseph, 355, 357

Barnes, Maj. James, 353

Bartholomew, A.D.C. to Wilberforce, 309

Barton, L. G., member Harvard Unit, 4; at Steenwerck, 122

Base Hospitals:

No. 2, on *St. Louis*, 106

No. 5, efforts to mobilize on Boston Common, 82–96; prepares to entrain, 97–101; the crossing, 102–107; in England, 107–111; takes over at Camiers, 111; loses its identity, 112; to remain with B.E.F., 320; nurses from, at Fleury, 457. *See also* Cushing, Dr. Harvey; General Hospital No. 11

No. 18, Johns Hopkins Unit at, 302

No. 45, 424, 425

No. 51, 425

No. 83, 451

Bashford, H. H., 145, 152, 154, 160, 204

Bastianelli, G., 202, 451, 466

Bastianelli, R., 218, 219

Batchelor, Maj., 198

Bazett, Dr. Henry, at la Clytte, 69, 70, 76

Beatty, Sir David, 478

Beaujon, the, 53

Beauvais, the cathedral at, 356

Beeuwkes, Col., 433; at Fleury, 459, 462, 464, 465

B.E.F., abbreviations used by, 57; evacuation of wounded in, 67, 68; at Messines Ridge, 116; wastage in, 233, 262, 263; pushes through Hindenburg Line, 263; gives way at Arras, 308; in 1918 spring drive on Amiens, 310–312, 316–322; at end of April (1918), 351; at Chemins des Dames, 366, 367; crosses Hindenburg Line, 426, 427, 429; in Sept. offensive, 433–435, 452; at Cambrai, 459, 461, 469; during the last days of war, 474, 475, 477, 493, 495, 497; casualty figures of, 502, 503

1st Army, research work in area of, 130–132; at end of war, 476

2nd Army, at Messines, 114, 116; "daily intelligence summary" of, 128; before Passchendaele, 166; at Menin Road, 207; south of Ypres, 217–219, 227; at end of war, 475

3rd Army, hospitals of, 133, 134; north of the Ancre, 421; at close of war, 477

4th Army, 166, 217, 418, 477

5th Army, under Gough, 128, 166, 193, 194, 216–219, 226, 233; criticism of, 253 *n.*; in Amiens drive, 311, 318, 319; in closing days of war, 476

Bell, Col., 387

Bell-Irving, "Micky," in hospital, 358

Belmore, Earl of, in Dublin, 361

Benet, Geo., member Harvard Unit, 4

Benet, Mme., 46, 47

Benoîte Vaux, as a hospital centre, 432, 434–437, 451, 452

Bernard, Rev. Dr., Archbishop of Dublin, 362

Bernhardt, Sarah, 33

Bernheim, B. M., at F.H. No. 103, 404

Bernstorff, Count von, 80

Bertner, to be G-2 at Neufchâteau, 413; at Fleury, 464

Besançon, a visit to, 422, 423

Best, Maj., 355, 383

Bethmann-Hollweg, 158

Bevans, Col., at Séry-Magneval, 406; divisional surgeon, 452

Bewley, Col., 140, 141

Beye, Mlle. de, 451, 455

Bigbee, Col., 107, 110

Bigelow, W. Sturgis, 95, 99

Billings, "Uncle" Frank, 450

Binney, Horace, 157

Bird, Maj., C.O. *St. Denis*, 292

Birkett, C.O. No. 3 Canadian, 256

Black, Capt., at Cheppy, 465

Black, Maj., 125, 132, 332, 367

Blackader, Gen., 180, 188, 189

Blair, Capt., at Neufchâteau, 385, 445

Blake, Capt., at No. 46 C.C.S., 269; at No. 4 Canadian, 334

Blake, Dr. Joseph, greets Harvard Unit at Neuilly, 12, 16, 52; at No. 46, 177, 213; at R.C. Hospital No. 2, 266, 290, 384, 385, 468

Blake, Mrs. S. Parkman, 91

Blanchard, Col., 195

Blanchard, Maj., at F.A. No. 103, 404

Blaylock, Col., Canadian Commissioner, 255, 263, 271

Bliss, Robert B., in Paris, 149, 150, 267, 278

Bloomberg, Col., of Evac. No. 12, 428

Bluem, Maj., 398

Boardman, Mabel, 81

Bock, Arlie, 275; at No. 13 General, 376

Bodley, Thomas, founder of Bodleian, 295

Boggs, Thomas, 277, 301, 345

Boisseau, Capt., at Station Neurologique No. 42, 423, 424

Bolling, Col., killed in Amiens, 345

Boothby, Dr. W. M., at Algeciras, 8; at Neuilly, 43, 50, 51; crosses to England, 73; sails home on *St. Paul*, 77, 78; returns to England, 108

Boston City Hospital, 80

Boston Common, question of hospital mobilization on, 83–96; protests of Committee on, 92

"Boston tins," 82

Bouchet, Dr. G. W. du, at American Hospital, Neuilly, 3, 49, 52

Bouchet, Mlle. du, 53

Boulogne, in spring of 1918, 369; badly bombed, 413. *See also* General Hospital No. 13

Bours, the *donjon* at, 342

Bowditch, Peter, 440

Bowen, pilot, 182

Bowlby, Sir Anthony, 64, 66, 69, 72, 269, 348; at Hazebrouck, 115, 117, 118, 121–123, 125, 128–135, 161, 166; inspects No. 46, 175

Bowles, Admiral, 91

Brackett, Col., 386

Bradford, Sir John Rose, 64, 144, 157, 354, 387, 388

Bradley, Col. (later Gen.), 228; Chief Surgeon, A.E.F., 320, 345

Brandt, Capt., 383

Brennan, at F.H. No. 103, 404

Brent, Bishop, 478

Brewer, George, at No. 61, 173, 180,

192, 197; with 42nd Division, 399, 400, 417, 430, 443, 460
Brewster, Gen., at Fleury, 459–461, 464, 465
Briand, Aristide, 150
Briggs, at No. 64, 226, 230
Brigham Hospital, 80; Surgical Dressings Committee established in, 81, 82
Broodseinde, attack on, 218–220
Brown, Percy, 105
Bruay, the Army School at, 284–286
Bruce, Sir David, 109, 466, 468
Bruce, Lieut., of Reserve Ambulance Co. No. 15, 393
Brues, Dr., entomologist, 258
Bryden, Capt., at Abbeville, 299
Bulgaria, demands armistice, 459; abdication of King, 492
Bulkley, Maj., 132
Bullard, Gen., corps commander, 419
Bülow, Gen. von, 312
Bundy, Gen., at Sommedieue, 304; corps commander, 419
Burdon-Turner, Mrs., 216
Burge, Maj., 169
Burlingham, 84
Burr, Allston, 91, 93
Burtchaell, Maj. Gen., succeeds Sloggett as overseas D.G., 363, 367; at Research Meeting, 409
Butler, Cushing's batman, 143
Butler, Miss, at La Fauche, 476
Butler, Rifleman, wounding of, 214
Buttar, Dr. Charles, 205 n.
Buttrick, Mr., 206, 207
Buzzard, Dr., in London, 357, 358
Byng, Gen., 263, 311, 421, 477

Cabot, Hugh, goes to Camiers, 81; at No. 22 General, 143
Cadorna, Gen., 254, 257
Calais, in war time, 298, 299, 309; hospitals remaining in, 369, 370
Call, Cpl., of Base Hospital No. 5, 352
Cambon, 150
Cambrai, the pushes toward, 263, 264, 268–270, 286, 459; Canadians enter, 469

Cameron, Sir Charles, at Royal College of Surgeons, 360, 361
Cameron, M.O. at No. 32 Stationary, 320
Camiers, arrival of Cushing and his unit at, 111; camp life at, 142–147, 150–159; bombed, 200–204. See also General Hospital No. 11
Campbell, Col., at No. 11 General, 113; at No. 4 Canadian, 335
Campbell, Maj. Gen. Lorn, 76, 293
Canadian troops, at Ypres, 70, 71; at Vimy, 136; at Passchendaele, 234 and n., 249 and n.; strongly entrenched (Arras–La Bassée), 339–341; pushing on, 419, 427; casualty figures of, 503
Cannaday, Dr., 432
Cannon, W. B., 102, 106, 345, 354; in England, 107, 108; a trip to Wimereux, 112; in Paris, 287–289; at Béthune, 346; and Tuffier, 388; during St. Mihiel battle, 439–449
Canopic, outward-bound (1915), 3–7, 9; the homeward crossing (1919), 508–511
Cap Trafalgar, 8
Capps, Joseph, 450
Carling, surgeon, at No. 32, 173; at No. 64, 226, 230
Carmania, 8
Carr, Col., at Boulogne, 60, 62, 151
Carr, Gen., 367
Carrel, Dr. Alexis, visits Cushing at Neuilly, 30; in charge of Hôpital Complémentaire 21, 32, 33; inspects Auto-chir, 52
Carroll, Charles, 30–32, 48
Case history, a combatant's, 481–490
Cassel Hill, 65
Castelnau, Gen., commander 2ème Armée, 23, 24, 317 n.
Castle, William R., of Red Cross, 154
Casualty Clearing Stations, a round of the, 128, 129
  No. 1 Australian, 118, 122, 129, 130
  No. 2 Australian, 122, 125, 322
  No. 2 Canadian, 118

No. 3 *Canadian*, 118
No. 4, 173, 174
No. 4 *Canadian*, 326, 334–343
No. 8, 133
No. 10, 118, 119, 129
No. 11, 118, 122, 123, 129
No. 12, 129, 165, 186
No. 14, 133
No. 17, 118, 188
No. 18, 326, 327, 396
No. 19, 133
No. 22, 329
No. 23, 326, 329
No. 26, 152
No. 32, 170, 173
No. 41, 133
No. 44, 173
No. 46, 82, 129; before Passchen-
   daele, 164–175; personnel of,
   167; has close shave, 320, 321.
   See also Cushing, Dr. Harvey
No. 47, 173
No. 51, 152
No. 54, 130, 131
No. 58, 324–330, 333
No. 61, 173, 320, 321
No. 62, 166, 230, 233, 234
No. 63, 166, 229, 230
No. 64, 165–167, 179, 186, 192
No. 66, 386
Casualty figures, of the different armies,
   502–504
Cesare, Jean, operation on, 48
Chamberlain, Col., 89, 90
Chance, Sir Arthur, on the *Leinster*,
   363
Chapin, Mrs. H. B., 295, 296, 358
Chapin, Robert, 295
Chapin, Dr. W. A. R., his *Lost Legion*,
   320 *n.*
Chasseurs d'Afrique, at Janville, 34
Chasseurs Alpins, 216
Château d'Agincourt, 28
Château d'Annel, at Longueil, 34, 35,
   40
Château La Perreuse, 408
Château Lovie, army headquarters at,
   174, 199, 233
Château Marie Louise, 63
Château de Montanglaust, 402

Château d'Offemont, 38–40
Château de Philiomel, Lillers, 324, 330
Château-Thierry, the offensive at, 370,
   398, 399, 402, 410, 411
Chaveau, Dr., 48
Cheever, Dr. David, returns home, 81
Chemin des Dames ridge, Germans
   break through at, 364, 366, 370
Cheyne, Sir W. Watson, 205 *n.*
Chittenden, Prof. R. H., 294, 308
Chopping, Col. Arthur, 115, 123, 219
Christopherson, Dr. J. B., 250 *n.*
Churchill, Lady Randolph, entertains
   Cushing, 110
Churchill, Winston, 110
City of Corinth, torpedoed, 107
Clayton, The Rev. P. T. B., at Talbot
   House, 374
Clemenceau, 395; and Wood, 278; and
   Foch, 317 *n.*; French confidence
   in, 321
Cleveland Unit, organized, 79, 81, 97;
   off to France, 103, 105, 107
Clifford, Pte., 152, 161, 180, 254, 273
Clinton, Marshall, 436, 437; at Souilly,
   451, 455, 460; at Fleury, 463;
   to be C.S. 2nd Army, 476
Clopton, Maj., 230; C.O. Mobile
   No. 4, 403, 428, 463
Cloth Hall (Ypres), ruins of, 211, 219,
   236, 250, 251
"Club, The," 87, 99, 100
Cochrane, Mr. Alexander, 91
Coe, Lt. Col., C.O. Mobile No. 3,
   403 *n.*
Coffey, Padre, 167, 218
Cohn, Alfred E., at Neufchâteau, 385
Colebrook, Dr., 255
Coleridge, anæsthetist, No. 46, 167
Collaran, Sgt. Maj., the army record
   of, 130
College of Physicians, N.Y., 3
Collett, Maj., 322
Columbia Unit, on *St. Louis*, 103
Combatant's case history, 481–490
Compiègne, as a hospital centre, 30–
   37; the palace at, 37; German
   drive on, 377, 381
Conférence Chirurgicale Interalliée, in
   Paris, 258, 490, 504

Congress, U.S., votes for war, 87
Congreve, Gen., wounded at Arras, 133, 141
Connaught, Duke of, receives members of Cushing unit, 107
Coolidge, Algernon, 84
Coplans, Capt. Myer, sanitarian 2nd Army, 124, 219; his trips to Ypres, 241–244, 250–253
Copstick, L./Cpl., batman for Cushing, 326–328
Corps Dressing Stations:
    At Irish Farm, 234–236
    At Solferino Farm, 237, 239
    No. 2, 127
    No. 3, 127, 128
Cotton, Capt., at No. 4 Canadian, 342
Councilman, Prof. W. T., 95
Cowley Hospital, visit to, 295
Crafts, Capt., at Crépy, 405
Crafts, James M., 87
Craig, Dr., 53; at Steenwerck, 122
Crawford, James, at No. 4 Canadian, 335
Crépy, the confusion at, 404–406
Crile, Dr. G. W., 458, 494; director Western Reserve Unit, 3; organizes Base Hospital unit, 79, 81, 97; sails on Orduna, 103, 105; off for France, 107; at Hazebrouck, 123; at No. 10 C.C.S., 129; at No. 17, 188, 194; and death of Revere Osler, 197, 198; in Paris, 288; at No. 9 General, 344, 345; visits Boulogne, 376; 377; visits Justice Group, 443
Crothers, Bronson, at Evac. No. 12, 428
Crothers, Capt., on Canopic, 510
Cummins, Col. Lyle, A.D.M.S. 16th Irish, 168; on British Research Committee, 344; in Paris, 354, 388, 389
Cunningham, Miss, 156, 161
Curley, James M., and question of hospital mobilization on Common, 83, 84, 86–93, 100
Cushing, Dr. Harvey, organizer of Harvard Unit, 3; sails on Canopic

(1915), 3–7; lands at Gibraltar, 7, 8; at Algeciras, 8; at Madrid, 9; at Irun and Hendaye, 9, 10; into France by military back door, 10, 11
With the Ambulance Américaine (1915): arrival at Ambulance Américaine, 11, 12; first days in Neuilly, 12–18; visits 2ème Armée in Amiens sector, 18–30; visits Carrel and Compiègne hospitals, 30–40; further work at Neuilly, 40–52; dinner at Mme. Benet's, 46, 47; at Marne battlefields, 54, 55; to No. 13 General, 56–64; inspects Étaples and Meerut Hospital, 61–63; a tour of Flanders, 64–73; crosses to England, 73; at the Oslers', 74; in London, 74–77; sails on St. Paul, 77, 78
In Boston (1915–1917): urged to organize Base Hospital unit, 79; at Tavern Club, 82, 99; his efforts to mobilize Base Hospitals on Boston Common, 83–96; at Saturday Club, 85, 95, 96; at "The Club," 87, 99, 100; a hasty trip to Washington, 89; and Gen. Wood's visit to Boston, 90–92; receives mobilization orders from Gorgas, 96; completing preparations to entrain, 97–101; in Washington again, 97, 98; departure from New York, 102, 103; on the Saxonia, 103–106; a few days in England, 106–111; the crossing to France, 111
With the B.E.F. (1917–1918). At No. 11 General: taking over at Camiers, 111–113; a trip to Wimereux, 112–114; ordered to Hazebrouck, 115–117; a round-up of hospitals, 117–119; during battle for Messines Ridge, 119–129; on rounds with Bowlby, 128–135; visits Vimy Ridge, 135–141; and camp life at Camiers, 142–147, 150–159; in Paris (July 4–6, 1917); 147–151; inspects St. Omer, 153, 154

At No. 46 C.C.S.: awaiting zero hour, 160–175; during first Passchendaele battle, 175–180; during Westhoek battle, 180–185; during Langemarck attack, 185–189; during Menin Road attacks, 190–193, 207–210; during Inverness Copse attack, 193–200; and death of Revere Osler, 197, 198; to inspect bombing casualties at No. 11 General, 200–204; at conference of surgeon specialists, 204–206; a visit to Ypres, 210–212; during Zonnebeke attack, 212–217; during attack on Broodseinde, 218–220; during Poelcappelle attacks, 221–227, 231–234; a day's operating list, 225; a trip to Paris, 227, 228; a visit to Irish Farm, 234–236; to Duhallow, 236, 237; to Solferino Farm, 237–239; Ypres again, 241–244; dinner with 18th Corps Flying Squadron, 244–246; trials with a batman, 247, 248; during thirteenth battle, 248, 249; a farewell to Ypres, 249–253; farewell to No. 46, 254

At No. 13 General: settling in, 254–256; to Paris for Research Committee Meetings, 258, 259, 266, 267, 275–278, 288–291, 300, 354, 355, 387, 388, 409, 466, 468, 504; routine work, 259–266, 268–272; Thanksgiving Day, 261, 262; gives dinner for Lambert, 271, 272; Christmas 1917, 272, 273; Paris again, 275–278; to take over neurological work, 277; at Bruay Army School, 283–286; ill, and Paris leave, 286, 287; completes head-wound monograph, 291; five days in England, 291–297; visits No. 15 Canadian, 296, 297; in Calais, 298, 299; with Australians at Abbeville, 299, 300; has glimpse of A.E.F., 301–304; at Verdun, 304–307; during advance on Amiens, 308–323; inspects P.O.W. Camp No.

94, 309, 310; his patients at Boulogne, 313–315; to be detached, 320; at C.C.S. No. 58, Lillers, 324–330; at No. 7 General, 330–334; at No. 4 Canadian C.C.S., 334–343; to Paris via Rouen, 343–345; at Neufchâteau, 345–350; a lecture at Langres, 346, 347; censorship difficulties, 351–355; his first flight, 353, 354; Boulogne again, 355, 356; in London to discuss neurosurgical unification, 356–358; a visit to Dublin, 358–363; at Étaples, 364, 368; during third phase of spring offensive, 369–383; appointed Senior Consultant in Neurological Surgery, A.E.F., 381; good-bye to No. 13 General, 383; a few days in Paris, 384–385

With the A.E.F. (1918). At Neufchâteau: getting oriented, 385, 386; silver leaves, 386; another lecture at Langres, 386; in a Paris air raid, 387; visiting old haunts in Paris, 388–395; a round of hospitals, 393, 394; July 4 (1918), 394, 395; Bastille Day, 397, 398; to Châlons, 399–402; at Mobile No. 1, 402, 403; Crépy and Séry-Magneval, 404–407; La Trousse, 407–409; two rackety days, 413–418; three days in bed, 413, 418; very feeble, 418–420, 422; a tour of inspection to Besançon, 422–424; inspection of hospitals in Toul Sector, 424, 425; trouble with his eyes, 427; joins "traveling X-ray circus," 428, 429; a tour of Souilly hospital group, 430, 432–437; to be promoted, 438; during St. Mihiel battle, 439–443; interviewing a German prisoner, 440, 441; a round of the triages, 443–449; preparations for Argonne offensive, 450–455

At R.C. Hospital 114, Fleury: a move to new quarters, 454; during Argonne offensive, 455–466; his illness in Paris, 466–468; back to Neufchâteau, 468

Neufchâteau again: still in poor health, 468, 469, 472–474; in bed at La Fauche, 474–481, 490–494, 498–501; "chickens" and service stripes, 498; celebrates Armistice, 499; at meeting of Reclassification Board, 501; back to Neufchâteau, 501

After the Armistice: paper work, 502–504; ordered back to Boulogne, 504; a glimpse of impressive ceremonies at Reims, 505, 506; three weeks at Boulogne, 506; observing reconstruction work in England, 506, 507; homeward-bound on *Canopic* (Feb. 1919), 508–511; his official military record, 511

Curtis, James, 96

Cutler, Dr. E. C., at the Ambulance Américaine, 14, 42, 50, 51, 53; at Oxford, 108; at No. 13 General, 202, 255, 260, 271, 275, 292, 311; at No. 58 C.C.S., 324; at No. 4 Canadian, 335; at Mobile No. 1, 403, 415; remaking Evac. No. 3, 421, 425, 428, 443, 452, 460

Cutler, George C., 90–93, 98

Czernin, Count, 280

DAKIN, DR. HENRY, 33

Damascus, fall of, 464

Darrach, William, operates on Revere Osler, 197; at Fleury, 460, 464; to be assistant army consultant, 476

Daumale, Lieut., operation on, 46, 49, 53

Davidson, Gen., 183

Davidson, Maj., D.A.D.M.S., 135–141; A.D.M.S. at Lillers, 324

Davies, Capt. Saxon, 280 *n.*

Davis, Lincoln, at Evac. Hosp. No. 2, 349

Dawson, Sir Bertrand, 64, 208, 280; an interesting person, 373, 374

De Forest, at Evac. No. 3, 452

Degoutte, Gen., 402, 418

Dehelly, Dr., at Compiègne, 33

Delaney, Col., 357

Delesalle, Capt., at Lille, 475

Denker, Christian, a prisoner, 494

Denny, George, at Camiers, 146, 157; at No. 46, 170, 177; at No. 13 General, 255, 273

Depage, at La Panne, 278, 292

Depew, Mr. and Mrs., at Château d'Annel, 34, 35

Derby, George, 105, 108; at Camiers, 151, 157, 168; at No. 46, 170, 172, 177; at No. 13 General, 292; at Neufchâteau, 427

Derby, Lord, 395

Derby, Richard, 304; at F.A. No. 1, 393; divisional surgeon, 471

Deuxnouds, the H.O.E. at, 451–453

Dexter, Dr. Richard, at Neufchâteau, 385, 430, 433–436, 439, 448, 451, 452, 478; at Fleury, 455, 457, 458, 460, 462, 464

Dick, Col., C.O. No. 1 Australian, 118

Dillon, Commissioner, 87

Doctors' Club, 94, 95

Dodds, Gen., at McCrae's funeral, 281

Dodge, Geoffrey, 150

Dopter, Prof., paper by, 288

Dorbon, Lucien, his *Essai de Bibliographie Hippique,* 295

Dosinghem, hospitals at, 166

Dowman, C. E., at Mobile No. 1, 432, 433; at Deuxnouds, 463

Doyle, Conan, a story about, 381–383

Draper, Mrs. W. K., 296

Driver, Capt., at No. 30, 370

Dubail, Gen., 395

Dublin, in war time, 358–363; St. Patrick's Cathedral in, 362

Dumont, Dr., and French *Auto-chir,* 52

Duncan (Earl of Camperdown), 99

Duncan, Miss, matron No. 46 C.C.S., 320, 321

Dunkerque, shelled from sea, 309

Dunn, Capt., 131

Dunn, Sister, 180

Duval, Douglas, C.O. at Evac. No. 11, 461
Duval, Pierre, paper by, 289
Dyson, Mrs., at Boulogne, 256

EAMES, COL., at Wimereux, 114; at No. 32 Stationary, 265, 271, 274, 299
Eastman, Divisional Surgeon, 452
Eaton, Dr., at *Château d'Annel,* 34
Ebert, Friedrich, takes helm in Germany, 496
Edward, Prince of Wales, 153, 315, 316
Edwards, Gen. Clarence, 417, 439, 440; offers aid to Cushing, 97, 100; at Verdun, 475
Edwards, Col., at Evac. No. 4, 408; at Justice Group, 428
Edwards, Sgt., at Boulogne, 372
Elder, Col., 256, 263, 274, 280–282
Eliot, Ellsworth, at Evac. No. 11, 461
Eliot, Pres., of Harvard, 85, 94–96
Élise, of Villa St. Joseph, Boulogne, 255, 275, 312, 322, 327
Ellery, Col., C.O. No. 13 C.C.S., 216
Elliott, Col. T. R., 256, 259, 267, 271, 274–277, 291, 370; and the Research Council, 110, 354, 355; at No. 32 Stationary, 265, 267
Ellis, Col., at No. 46 C.C.S., 129, 167
Emerson, Haven, 95, 473
Emmons, R. Van B. ("Bobby"), 74
England, tragic aftermath of the war in, 507. *See also* London
English, Sgt., at Camiers, 202
Erskine, Sir Henry, 298
Erzberger, 495, 496
Estaunié, Edouard, a visit to, 389
Étaples, hospital base at, 61, 62; badly hit, 356, 364, 365
Evacuation Hospitals:
No. *1,* 349, 425, 443
No. *2,* 349
No. *3,* 416, 417, 421, 425, 443, 452, 461
No. *4,* 400, 402, 404, 408, 409
No. *5,* 404, 407, 415, 449

No. *6,* 407, 413, 433, 462, 463
No. *7,* 394, 403, 412, 433
No. *8,* 390, 433, 453
No. *9,* 433, 436
No. *10,* 457, 461
No. *11,* 442, 461
No. *12,* 428
No. *13,* 429
No. *14,* 425
No. *15,* 451
Evans, Capt., C.O., F.A. No. 1, 393

FARLOW, WILLIAM G., 85
Farnen, F. James, batman at No. 4 Canadian, 335, 336, 339, 340
Farquhar, Capt., 383
Fearnsides, Dr., in London, 357
Ferguson, Capt., 383
Ferras, Dr., at Offemont, 39
Ferraton, *Genl. Inspecteur* French army, 209
Fiaschi, at Abbeville, 299
Field Ambulance Service, 82
Field Ambulances, disposition of, 126
No. *1,* 393
No. *3,* 139
No. *8,* 69, 70
No. *9 Australian,* 126, 127
No. *15,* 393
No. *16,* 393
No. *103,* 393, 404
No. *150,* 236, 237
Field Hospitals:
No. *28,* 441
No. *101,* 439, 441
No. *114,* 444
No. *315,* 456
No. *353,* 426
No. *354,* 425
No. *355,* 425
No. *356,* 425
Field Neurological Hosp. No. 1, 434
Finney, Eben, at Neufchâteau, 301, 302, 304
Finney, J. M. T., Chief of Surgery, 262, 277, 286, 288, 345, 348, 350, 384–386, 452, 453, 457; at Neufchâteau, 385, 386, 396, 471, 473; leaving for home, 399; returns, and made a general, 437,

438, 443; at Souilly, 458, 462; at La Fauche, 476, 495

Fisher, Capt., at No. 4 Canadian, 335, 341

Fisher, William, 277; at Neufchâteau, 301, 303, 385, 398, 421, 426, 430, 437, 457, 462

Fitz, 108, 142, 366

Fitzgerald, Miss, Edith Cavell nurse at Boulogne, 256, 260, 407

Fitzsimons, killed at Camiers, 200, 201

Fleming, Dr., 256

Fletcher, Capt., at No. 55, 374, 375

Fletcher, Lieut. Col., at Bruay, 284, 285

Fletcher, Walter Morley, lunches with Cushing, 75; and the Research Council, 110, 111

Fleury, R. C. Hosp. 114 at, 452, 454

Flint, Joseph, 216; and the *Auto-chir*, 403 *n.*; at Mobile No. 39, 442

Flying Squadron, 18th Corps, mess of the, 245–247

Foch, Marshal, in supreme command, 317, 321, 356, 410, 411, 467, 474, 493; and the peace negotiations, 478, 493; receives German plenipotentiaries, 495, 496

Fonck, René, 414

Forbes, W. Cameron, 85, 91

Forbes, Edward W., 85

Forbes, Henry, 99, 155, 183

Forbes, Stewart, liaison officer with the French, 353

Fordham, Private, operation on, 144

Forest, Robert de, 103

Foster, Michael, at Wimereux, 270; in Paris, 287, 291; at No. 55, 374

Fowler, Sir James, 295, 296

Fraser, Capt., 171, 346

Fraser, Forbes, 118

Freeman, Dr., 255

French Ambulance 225, Deuxnouds, 456

French, Lord, 66, 72, 73; and the Sinn Feiners, 357, 359; at Royal College of Surgeons, 360, 361

French army, camaraderie of, 26, 27;

at end of April (1918), 351; resisting stubbornly, 370; in July offensive, 410, 411; at Montdidier, 419; in Aug.-Sept. push, 426, 427, 429, 435, 452; at the Argonne, 459; jealous of A.E.F., 474; during final days of war, 474–476; casualty figures of, 502, 503. *See also* B.E.F.

1st Army, 216

2nd Army, 57; a visit to, 18–31

6th Army, 31, 57

10th Army, between Oise and Aisne, 421

Frere, Dr., at *Château d'Annel*, 34

Friendly Brother House, Dublin, 359

Fries, Col., 355

Frothingham, Paul Revere, 86

Fullerton, Col., 114, 265, 274, 308, 373

Furbush, Col., 450

Gage, Col., Receiving Officer, Boulogne, 315

Gallie, Col., at Boulogne, 61, 66; at Abbeville, 299, 300; at Research Meeting, 409

Galliéni, Gen., 20

Garcia, Col., 433, 439, 449, 451–453, 455, 456, 458–460

Gardiner, of 18th Corps Flying Squadron, 246

Gardner, Mrs., "Queen W.A.A.C.," Boulogne, 315

Garstin, Sir William, 322, 323

Gas, need of military secrecy regarding, 355

Gask, Col. George E., 290; at No. 7 General, 329, 331, 332

Gavin, Maj., 341

Geddes, Sir Auckland, 492

Geddes, Sir Eric, 357

General Hospitals (*See also* Stationary Hospitals):

No. 1 Canadian, suffers greatly, 356, 364, 365

No. 3, 344

No. 7, 329–334

No. 9, under Crile, 344

No. 10, 153

No. 11 (Camiers), Cushing unit takes over, 111–113; bombing of, 200–204. *See also* Camiers

No. 12, St. Louis outfit in, 344

No. 13 (Boulogne), 56–61; arrival of Cushing at, 254–256; bombing near, 271, 272; Christmas at, 272, 273; work slackens, 292; history of its patients, 313–315; very busy, 343; a bad raid, 356; filling up with Americans, 375–377

No. 22 (Camiers), 143, 144, 154; supplied by Harvard, 81; relies on "Boston tins," 82

No. 30, still at Calais, 370

No. 35, still at Calais, 369, 370

George V, of England, 70, 108, 110, 315

Gerard, Ambassador, 92, 493; his *Four Years in Germany*, 199

German army, making stand on New Hindenberg Line, 84; its 1918 spring offensive (Amiens), 310–312, 316–322; on the Lys, 324–331, 334, 335, 337–342; at end of April (1918), 351; in third phase of the attack, 364–372; drives on Compiègne, 377, 381; launches attack from Château-Thierry to Argonne, 398, 399, 402; moving back, 404, 410, 411, 425, 426, 429, 434, 435; at the Argonne, 459, 461; in last days of war, 474, 476, 492–495; casualty figures of, 503

German government, the new, 493, 496, 497

Gerrard, Miss, anæsthetist, 152, 161, 180, 254

Gibb, Capt., at Lillers, 324

Gibbon, John, at Evac. Hospital No. 1, 302, 386, 414, 424, 425, 443

Glenart Castle, torpedoed, 291

Glenn, Gen., 496

Godlee, Sir Rickman, 108, 205 *n*.

Godson, Col., 108

Goethals, Gen., 103, 263, 264, 456, 458

Goldthwait, Joel, arrives in England, 110; to be Chief of Orthopædics, 262, 277, 346, 352, 354; at Neufchâteau, 386, 426

Goode, ambulance driver, 29

Goodrich, Wallace, 94

Goodwill, Maj., 144, 145

Goodwin, Col., 97, 98; C.O. No. 22 C.C.S., 284

Goodwin, Gen., 357

Gordon, Col. M. H., at Research Meeting, 288, 290

Gordon-Lennox, Lady Algernon, at Boulogne, 315

Gordon-Taylor, at No. 53, 129

Gordon-Watson, Col., consultant for 2nd Army, 115, 175, 219

Gorgas, Gen., 403 *n*., 437, 450; proposes Medical Reserve Corps units, 79; and Cushing, 89; orders Cushing unit abroad, 96, 98; visionary, 145

Gosman, Col. George, 428

Gosset, Dr., 52

Gough, Gen., commander 5th Army, 128, 166, 170, 179, 189; in Amiens drive, 311, 318, 319

Gouraud, Gen., 400, 410, 411, 418, 421, 466, 471

Gowlland, Col., C.O. Solferino Farm, 239

Graham, Capt., 112, 142, 143, 145

Grahame, Col., C.O. No. 58 Scottish, 333

Gray, Col., 270

Greeley, Russell, 150

Greene, Warwick, 267, 345

Greenough, Dr. R. B., an organizer of Harvard unit, 3; on the *Canopic*, 4; arrives in Paris, 11; at Ambulance Américaine, 40

Greenwood, Allen, 385, 404, 413, 417

Greer, Maj., A.D.M.S. 4th Canadian, 242

Grissinger, Col., 348, 429; a divisional surgeon, 452

Gros, Dr. E. L., at American Hospital, Neuilly, 3

Groves, Hey, 291

Guillaumat, Gen., 395

Gündell, Gen. von, 495, 496

Gurdleston, Capt., at Oxford, 108, 109

Guthrie, C. G., at Base Hospital No. 18, 302

Guynemer, stunting over Paris, 147

HADFIELD, LADY, 278, 279, 315

Haig, Field Marshal Douglas, 125, 129, 253 n., 317 n., 329; his disquieting Army Order, 333

Haldane, Lord, 65, 68, 108

Haldane, Miss, at Boulogne, 256, 292

Hall, Lt. Col., at Juilly, 390; at Séry-Magneval, 406, 433, 453

Hamerton, Col., at No. 12 C.C.S., 129, 274

Hamilton, Gen., 130

Hanon, brancardier, at Offemont, 39

Hanson, Lieut. A. M., at Evac. No. 6, 407; at Evac. No. 8, 433

Harcourt, Lady, 110

Harjes, Hermann, 28

Harmon, Capt. D. W., adjutant Base Hospital No. 5, 100, 101; at Camiers, 153, 154

Harrington, of Evac. No. 6, 415, 433

Harris, Capt., killed at Brandhoek, 188, 192, 193

Harris, Maj., at F.H. 315, 456

Harte, Richard, 164, 173

Hartley, 160, 204

Hartmann, Dr., 37

Harvard Unit, organized, 3; en route to Neuilly, 3–12. See also Ambulance Américaine

Harvard Univ., supplies No. 22 General, 81. See also Lowell, A. Lawrence

Harvey, Capt. S. C., 152, 263, 264; at Evac. No. 7, 433, 452, 455, 456, 459, 460, 462

Haskins, C. H., 95

Hawkins, Miss, at No. 13 General, 273

Hayes, Dr., 15

Haywood-Farmer, 182

Hazebrouck, before the Messines battle, 115–117; the hospitals around, 117–119

Head, Dr. Henry, of London Hospital, 34, 58, 357; his neurological work, 110, 111

Heitz-Boyer, in Paris, 52, 385, 409, 468

Henry, Capt. Herbert, 267, 279

Hepburn, Sgt., of Base Hospital No. 5, 99; his astonishing career, 377–382

Herrick, Ambassador Myron T., 3

Herringham, Sir Wilmot, 64, 65 and n., 72, 98, 135, 168, 171, 355

Hertling, Count von, 280, 456

Hetzel, at F.H. No. 103, 404

Heuer, G. J., at Evac. Hosp. No. 1, 349; fresh from the U.S., 386

Higginson, Major Henry L., 29, 85, 87, 88, 90, 91, 96, 99

Hill 60: 70, 71, 73; recaptured, 123

Hindenburg, Gen., 434

Hodgson, preparing portable houses for Common mobilization, 90

H.O.E. at Deuxnouds, 451, 453

Holmes, Gordon, at Boulogne, 56–58, 64, 72, 256, 274, 371; at Research Meeting, 388

Homans, Helen, V.A.D. probationer, 53, 510

Horne, Gen., 284, 285

Horrax, Gilbert, 156; at No. 46, 183, 185, 194, 208, 214, 222, 224, 249–253; at No. 13 General, 254, 255, 343, 374

Hospitals, army, relation of patients to beds in (Oct. 1918), 473. See also Base Hospitals; Casualty Clearing Stations; Corps Dressing Stations; Evacuation Hospitals; Field Ambulances; Field Hospitals; General Hospitals; Mobile Hospitals; Stationary Hospitals; Territorial Hospitals

House, Col. Edward M., 47, 85, 478

Howard, Maj. Gen. Sir Francis, 205 n.

Howe, Mark A. De W., 85, 95

Huard Château, 393

Humphries, Col., C.O. No. 11 C.C.S., 123

Hutchinson, James P., 81, 384, 390

Hutier, Gen. von, 312

Hutin, Marcel, 426

Hutton, Col., 404, 407, 408
Hyatt, Capt., of 26th Division, 417, 439

INDIAN TROOPS, 227 and *n.*, 322; a disappointment, 59; in Meerut Hospital, 62, 63
"Indian Village," 38, 40
Inverness Copse, attack on, 194–198
Ireland, Col. M. W. (later Gen.), 267, 278, 355, 396, 399, 443, 468; the real thing, 386
Irish Farm, C.D.S. at, 234–236
Irwin, Gen. Murray, D.M.S. 3rd Army, 116
Italian army, weakness of, 254, 263

JACOBS, CAPT., 277
Janet, Pierre, 75
Jarvis, Maj., of Astoria Hosp., 394
Jeffries, Padre, 273
Joffre, Gen., 30, 35, 90, 98, 287; in New York, 103; at Picpus ceremony, 148; on July 4, 1918, 395
Johns Hopkins Unit, takes undergraduates, 80, 87; at Base Hospital No. 18, 302
Johnson, Peer P., at Evac. No. 9, 436
Johnson, Col., at Souilly, 458
Johnson, Miss, at La Fauche, 476
Jones, Capt. Graham, 171
Jones, Robert, 110, 113
Joslin, Elliott P., 450
Jougeas, Dr., at Neuilly, 41
Juilly, the hospitals at, 390, 391. See also Ambulance Américaine
Jusserand, Ambassador, 9
Justice Hospital Group, 424, 443

Karlsruhe, 5
Kean, Col. J. R., 85, 89, 94, 97, 98, 150, 267
Keller, Col., 345, 384, 386, 402, 457
Kelly, Capt., at No. 30 General, 372, 374
Kelly, Col., C.O. at Westhof, 127
Kennedy, Foster, 204, 205, 388
Keogh, Sir Alfred, 50, 57, 65, 111; at the War Office, 75, 76

Kerensky, Alexander, and Korniloff, 256, 257
Kerr, Maj. Harry, 471, 491, 498; at Crépy, 405; at Séry, 407; at Neufchâteau, 413, 419; at Raubecourt, 442
Kettell, architect for Common mobilization plans, 89, 90, 92–94
Keyes, E. L., at Neufchâteau, 301, 397, 398
Kiggell, Lt. Gen., 125
Kilbourne, Col., 287, 425
Kitchener, Lord, 75, 315
Kitto, Col., 145
Kluck, Gen. von, 19, 20, 49
Kocher, Albert, 50, 51
Kocher, Theodor, 33

LA BADE, COL., 23
La Chapelle, *gare régulatrice*, 43–46, 51, 52, 61
Laënnec, the, 37
Lafayette Escadrille, 53 *n.*, 82
Lafourcode, operation on, 49–51
Lambert, Alexander, 258, 271, 275, 276, 388, 392, 450, 471, 494
La Motte, Ellen, 191
Lamson, Col., C.O. Evac. No. 3, 416
Lance, Capt., at Pernes, 340
Landolt, Dr., at Royallieu, 37
Langemarck, attack on, 186, 188
Langres, the Army School at, 346, 347
Langridge, Capt. (later Maj.), of the Red Cross, 267, 268, 271, 343, 344, 368
Lansing, Robert, 469
La Pitié, 38
Lataillade, Dr., 456
Laughlin, Irwin, 107
Law, Maj., of B.H. 115, 460, 461
Lawley, Sir Arthur, Red Cross Commissioner, 255, 271, 308, 322
Lawrence, Bishop, 100, 146
Leake, Col., at Bailleul, 118, 122, 125, 130
Leavitt, 432
Lee, Burton J., 301, 303, 304, 426; at F.A. No. 103, 393, 394, 404–406; visits Neufchâteau, 450,

471; to be asst. army consultant, 476

Lee, Roger I., 93, 381; in England, 107, 108; a trip to Wimereux, 112; at Camiers, 153–155, 157, 158; in Paris, 266; a wire from, 343; at Juilly, 390, 391

Leek, Capt., at Bailleul, 66

Leinster, 363

Leishman, Sir William, "sanitary boss" of B.E.F., 62, 146, 147, 276, 277, 290, 344

Leitch, Capt., 171

Le Maître, 290

Le Normant, *Médecin Chef,* 216

Leri, at Research Meeting, 388

Leriche, René, at Research Meeting, 409

Lewis, Dean, at American Ambulance, 388

Liebknecht, Karl, 478

Liggett, Gen., corps commander, 419

Lille, evacuation of, 475

Lindsay, Maj., 204

Lindsay, William, 3

Lister, Col. William T., 144, 373

Lloyd George, David, 110, 257, 280, 315–317, 395; opposition to his conscriptive legislation, 359

Lockwood, Maj., 126, 129, 387

Lodge, Henry Cabot, 86

Logan, Maj. James A., 49

London, in 1915, 74–77; depression in (1918), 357, 358. *See also* England

London Hospital, 34, 58

Long, Walter, in Dublin, 361

Longcope, Warfield, 424, 494

Lopp, G. Washington, 41, 42, 51, 52

Lowell, A. Lawrence, 91; his attitude toward preparedness, 80, 81, 85, 95

Lowell, James A., 93

Ludendorff, Gen., 253 *n.,* 311, 410, 418; resigns, 478

Lusitania, sinking of the, 76–78, 80, 105

Lusk, Graham, 294, 308

Lycée Pasteur, 3, 11

Lyle, Maj. H. H. M., C.O. at Evac. Hosp. No. 2, 349, 460; to be C.S. 1st Army, 476

Lyman, Henry, 143, 156, 273; at F.H. No. 103, 404

Lyons, Col., C.O. No. 63, 229

Lys, offensive on the, 324–331, 334, 335, 337–342

Lyster, 277

McCarthy, D. J., of B.H. 115, 481, 495; under Gerard in Berlin, 493, 494

McCaw, Col., 352, 354, 399, 468, 495

McCormack, Sgt., 428, 429

McCormick, at Boulogne Medical Society, 373

McCoy, Capt., of 1st Anzacs, 244

McCoy, Col. Frank, 278

McCoy, Maj. James A., at Jouy-s.-Morin, 408; at R.C. Hosp. No. 114, 452, 454, 460, 463

McCrae, John, 256, 274; death of, 280, 281; and "Windy," 281–283

M'Dougall, William, 109

MacEwan, at No. 4 Canadian, 335

McGee, Col., 462, 463

McGowan, pathologist, at No. 58 Scottish, 333

McGuire, Clarence, wounded at Camiers, 200, 201

McGuire, Col., C.O. 9th Australian F.A., 126, 127

McGuire, Stuart, at Base Hosp. No. 45, 424

McKernon, J. F., 354; at Neufchâteau, 385

McLean, Franklin C., 491

MacLeod, injured at Camiers, 202

MacMonagle, Douglas, 82

MacMonagle, Mrs., in Paris, 409

McNee, John W., at Bailleul, 69, 131; at No. 46, 171, 259, 267; at No. 4 Canadian, 335, 336

Macpherson, Gen., 197, 367; visits N.Z. Stationary, 125; visits No. 11 General, 151, 153; at Hesdin, 153; farewell dinner for, 371

Macrae, Maj., at Mobile No. 1, 394, 402 and *n.*, 403, 415, 439, 463
McWilliams, at Evac. Hosp. No. 1, 349; succeeds Lee at F.A. No. 103, 404
Maddux, Lt. Col., at Justice Hospital Group, 424, 428, 443
Maher, Maj. Gen. Sir James, D.D.M.S., Dublin, 359
Makins, Sir George, 280; at Boulogne, 56, 59, 60, 62; in Flanders, 64–66, 69, 71, 72
Malick, Capt., 440
Malloch, Archibald, of No. 3 Canadian, 262
Malone, Col. P. B., 482
Mangin, Gen., 402, 418, 421, 430
Marie, Pierre, at Offemont, 38; at Research Meeting, 388
Mark, Capt., Transport Surgeon of *Canopic*, 510
Marne, battlefields of the, 54, 55
Marriott, Col., at No. 10 C.C.S., 129
Marshall, Col., 341
Martel, Th. de, 52, 53, 394, 395
Martin, Col., 291; C.O. No. 58 C.C.S., 324
Mary, Princess, of England, 108
Mary, Queen, of England, 108, 110, 153
Mass. General Hospital, 80
Mather, Samuel, 3
Max, of Baden, proposes armistice, 467, 469; no longer Chancellor, 496
Mead, Mrs. F. S., and the "Boston tins," 81, 82
Meakins, Col. J. C., 355, 357
Meath Hospital, Dublin, 362
Meerut Hospital, 62, 63
Mendinghem, hospitals at, 165, 166
Menin Road, attacks on, 190–193, 207–210
Menzies, Lieut., 217
Meredith, Maj., at Evac. No. 14, 425
Merriman, Roger, 74; visits Ambulance Américaine, 15, 16
Merritt, X-ray man at Souilly, 460
Messines Ridge, battle of, 114–117, 119–124, 128, 129

Mewburn, Col. F. H., at No. 15 Canadian, 296
Mignon, Dr., at Neuilly, 41, 48
Miller, Dr., at No. 46, 191, 206, 247
Mills, Capt., 400
Milner, Lord, 317 *n.*
Minot, James J., 94
Mitchem, Col., at Governor's Island, 102
Mixter, Capt. Charles, at Juilly, 391
Mobile Hospitals:
    No. 1, 393, 394, 403 *n.*, 404, 412, 413, 432, 433, 439, 441, 456; hard hit, 463
    No. 2, 402 and *n.*, 407, 416, 417, 432, 433, 457; crowded with wounded, 463
    No. 3, 403 *n.*, 425, 443
    No. 4, 403 *n.*, 428, 463
    No. 5, 403 *n.*, 461
    No. 6, 403 *n.*, 452, 455, 456, 458–460, 471
    No. 8, 471
    No. 39, 403 *n.*, 442
Montfaucon, fall of, 459
Moore, Sir Frederick, president Royal Zoölogical Society, 359
Moore, George F., 85, 87, 99
Moore, Capt. MacLeod, 341
Morgan, Col., 132, 135–141, 272
Morrison, Capt., at No. 26, 152, 160, 171, 204
Morrow, Col., at Sommedieue, 304; Divisional Surgeon, 393; at Evac. No. 1, 404, 424
Morton, John J., at No. 46, 170, 174, 177, 180, 185, 194, 204; at No. 13 General, 255, 273
Mosher, Maj., M.O.R.C., 262
Moshier, Maj., 243, 244, 263; O.C. No. 11 F.A., 338–340
Muhr, Alan, Ambulance Corps driver, 19, 21–31, 56
Mulligan, Lieut., at Fleury, 457
Munie, Dr., 28
Munro, at No. 4 Canadian, 334
Munroe, Mrs. George, 47
Murchie, Guy, 90
Murphy, F. T., 215, 222, 228, 267,

460; at No. 12 General, 344; at Crépy, 404–409

NAFFZIGER, H. C., of B.H. 115, 481
Neufchâteau, American troops in, 301; becomes army headquarters, 420, 421, 427, 428; medical headquarters to be closed, 504, 505
Neuhof, 433
Neuilly. See Ambulance Américaine
Neurological Home Service, at cross-purposes, 357
Neville, Gen., his failure on the Aisne, 253 n.
Newland, Col. H. S., 173
New Zealand troops, take Bapaume, 426
Nichols, Miss, V.A.D., in Paris, 468
Nicolle, M., paper by, 288
Norris, 386, 414, 424
Northcote, Mrs., at Boulogne, 256
Norton, Richard, 150
Norton-Harjes Field Service, 82
Noyes, Lieut. Raymond, 353

OBER, F. R., at No. 13 General, 292
Oberndorf, 495, 496
O'Brien, Sir Ignatius, in Dublin, 361
O'Brien, Robert, 93
Ogden, Maj., at Evac. No. 4, 408
O'Hegan, purser of Canopic, 5, 7
O'Keeffe, Gen., D.M.S. 4th Army, 116
O'Neil, Col., at No. 12 Stationary, 118
Opie, Eugene, 271
Orduna, 103, 105, 106
Osgood, R. B., on the Canopic, 4; at Ambulance Américaine, 13, 47; in England, 107, 110; at Wimereux, 112; at Camiers, 157; preparing to sail for home, 352; at Research Meeting, 354
Osincup, M.O. at No. 32 Stationary, 320
Osler, Revere, 74; death of, 197, 198, 296; his grave, 230
Osler, Sir William, 48, 50, 58; entertains Cushing, 74, 75, 295, 296, 506, 507; proposes U.S. medical units, 80; greets Cushing unit,

107, 108; death of his son, 197, 198
Osler, Lady, 74, 76, 156, 197, 296, 358
Osterhout, Dr. W. J. V., 94
Ostrom, Maj., at La Mal Grange, 429

PAGE, WALTER HINES, 107
Paget, Lady, 110
Painlevé, M., 149
Palestine, Allenby in, 452, 453, 459
Panet, Col., 341
Papen, Franz von, 80
Paris, on July 4, 1917, 147–149; discouragement in, 345; threatened by Boches, 367, 370; an air raid on, 387; on July 4, 1918, 394, 395
Parker, Col., at Oxford, 108
Parkinson, A.D.M.S. Sanitation, Lillers, 324
Parmelee, Miss, her heroism at Camiers, 201, 202, 204
Parsons, Maj., of Engineers, 148, 450
Passchendaele, preparation for offensive at, 166, 174; battles: first, 175–177, 179, 180; second, 180–185; third, 185–189; fourth, 190–193; fifth, 193–198; sixth, 207–210; seventh, 212–215; eighth, 218–220; ninth, 221–223; tenth, 223–226; eleventh, 231, 232; twelfth, 234–240; thirteenth, 248, 249
Patterson, Maj. R. U., in command Base Hospital No. 5, 81, 98–101, 103–105, 107; a trip to Wimereux, 112; at Camiers, 146, 158, 170, 249; at Tours, 352; a colonel, 385
Patterson, Miss, at Séry, 407
Patterson, Pte., in Paris, 468
Pau, Gen., 395
Peabody, Endicott, 100
Peabody, Jacob, 87, 89–91
Peabody, Malcolm, chaplain, 100–102, 104, 158
Peabody, Rose, at Mobile No. 2, 402
Peake, Col., C.O. No. 53 Stationary, 118

Peck, Charles, 265, 277, 345, 384, 385

Penhallow, 110

Perkins, James, with Paris A.R.C., 150, 228, 322, 430

Perkitt, Padre, 167

Perry, Thomas, 50, 99

Pershing, Gen. John, 169, 179, 263, 278, 457; arrives in London, 130; in Paris (July 4, 1917), 147–149; comes up to scratch, 317; takes command first American army, 419, 421; his treatment of the French, 454; at Souilly, 478

Pétain, Gen., 317 n., 425

Peter Bent Brigham Hospital. See Brigham Hospital

Peters, Col., 242; A.D.M.S. 4th Canadians, 339–341

Petit, Gen., decorates officers at Reims, 505

Philadelphia Base Hospital Unit, arrives in England, 110; in France, 164

Pickering, Prof. E. C., 85, 95

Picpus, ceremony at the (July 4, 1917), 148, 149

Pike, Col. (later Gen.), D.M.S. 1st Army, 114, 116

Pilkington, pilot, 182

Pinches, Col., at No. 35, 369, 370

Pinchot, Gifford, turned out of Belgium, 77, 78

Pincoffs, M. C., still a battalion M.O., 471

Plumer, Gen., at Messines, 114; telegram from, 128

Poelcappelle, attacks on, 221–227, 231, 232

Poincaré, Raymond, 47, 395

Ponysigne, Jean, in hospital at Neuilly, 15

Pool, Eugene, at Evac. Hosp. No. 1, 349, 385; army consultant, 476

Poperinghe, a lively place, 164

Porter, Gen., D.M.S. 2nd Army, 115, 116, 126, 135, 188, 219, 272

Portuguese troops, give way at La Bassée, 324

Postum, Miss, at La Fauche, 476

Potter, William, 105; at No. 13 General, 255; at Langres, 386

P.O.W. camp No. 94, 309, 310

Powell, Col., 299; at Abbeville, 299; C.O. No. 2 Australian, 322

Poynton, death of his son, 74

Prince, Norman, 53 and n., 82

Proust, Consultant French 4th Army, 405

Prynne, Maj., at St. Omer, 153

Purdy, Col., C.O. at Abbeville, 299

Quenu, Dr., at La Chapelle, 44, 45, 52

R.A.M.C., overseas hospitals of, 58; status of medical consultants in, 64; high casualties of, 67

Randall, Blanchard, 125

Rawlinson, Gen., 319, 418, 477

R.C. Hospital 114. See Stationary Hospitals

Red Cross, its attitude toward preparedness, 79, 81–83, 86; mix-up between army and, 228. See also Ambulance Américaine

Red Cross Civil Hospital, Neufchâteau, 386

Red Cross Military Hospital No. 3, 384, 385

Reed, Walter, in Cuba, 278

Reford, Lewis, 256

Reid, corps commander, 419

Reid, Mrs. Whitelaw, 110; her hospital, 384

Reims, seriously threatened, 367; a thrust at, 398, 399, 402; an impressive ceremony at, 505, 506

Reinach, Salomon, 50, 51

Research Committee Meetings, Paris, 258, 259, 266, 267, 275–278, 288–290, 300, 354, 355, 387, 388, 409, 466, 468, 504

Reserve Ambulance Co. No. 15, 393

Reynolds, Capt., volunteer quartermaster of Base Hospital No. 5 Unit, 84, 85, 90, 92, 98–100, 103

Reynolds, Maj., at Luzancy, 393

Rhea, Lawrence, 274, 280, 283

Rhein, Maj., at Souilly, 451, 452

Rhodes, James Ford, 85, 99
Rhodes, Mrs., *auxiliaire*, in Paris, 148
Rice, F. B., 89
Richards, Theodore, 95
Richardson, surgeon at No. 46, 167
Riddoch, George, at Empire Hospital, 357
Rist, Dr. Edouard, at Complègne, 37, 290
Robertson, O. H., at No. 11 General, 152, 155, 156, 158; at No. 13 General, 268, 270
Robinson, Padre, 162, 167
Rodway, Col., at Wimereux, 270
Rohan, Duc de, 30–32
Romando, Maj., 209
Roosevelt, Archibald, in hospital, 385, 392
Roosevelt, Nicholas, 49
Roper, Capt., at No. 46, 109, 110, 167, 218
Ross, Pipe Major, 182, 183, 217, 229
Ross, Quartermaster, 181, 182, 217, 229, 230
Rossignoli, Lieut., 36, 38
Roussy, Gustave, 422, 424
Royal College of Surgeons, Dublin, honors Cushing, 359–361
Royal College of Surgeons, England, 294
Royal Welsh Fusileers, mess of the, 188, 189
Royal Zoölogical Society, Dublin, 359
Rubino, Pte., killed, at Camiers, 202
Ruggles, A. H., with 2nd Division, 426
Rukke, Col., 349
Rumbolt, Col., C.O. at La Fauche, 476
Rund, Capt., quartermaster Base Hospital No. 5, 100
Russell, Sir Charles, 308, 315, 316
Russell, Col., at Abbeville, 299
Russell, Sgt., of Base Hospital No. 5, 352
Russia, desperate situation in, 254, 256, 257, 263

Sage, Lieut., killed at No. 3 Canadian, 367
St. Denis, *Hospital Ship*, 292

St. John, Maj. F. B., C.O. Mobile No. 2, 403 *n*.
St. John's Hospital, Étaples, badly hit, 364, 366, 368
St. Louis, first U.S. armed merchantman, 85, 106
St. Louis Base Hospital Unit, arrives in England, 110
St. Martin's Cathedral (Ypres), ruins of, 250, 251
St. Mihiel, battle of, 439–443
St. Omer, to be large hospital centre, 153, 154; a war-time view of, 332, 333
St. Paul, 75, 77, 78
St. Quentin, German break-through at, 319
St. Thomas's Hospital, 68
Salmon, Thos. W., 347, 348, 419, 448, 472, 495; at Neufchâteau, 385, 399, 421, 422, 426, 439; lectures at Langres, 386, 387; at Research Meeting, 388; his *triage* for acute neuroses, 432, 434–437; at Souilly, 451, 452; at Fleury, 455, 457, 459
Saltonstall, John L., 87, 91
Sampson, surgeon at No. 32, 173
Samson, Capt., 133
Sanatorium pour les Enfants, Hendaye, 10
Sanford, at Evac. Hosp. No. 2, 349
Santos, dos, 265, 266
Sargent, Percy, at Boulogne, 56, 57, 61, 64, 69, 72, 98, 113, 114, 256, 265; in London, 357
Saturday Club, 85, 95, 96
Sawyer, Gen., 265, 272, 274
Saxonia, crossing on the, 102–106
Scherpenberg Hill, the battle from, 70
Schott, Mr., M.P., in Dublin, 361
Schwab, Sidney I., at Nubécourt, 463; at La Fauche, 474, 476, 480, 481, 494, 495, 499, 501
Schweinitz, Maj. de, M.O.R.C., 262
Scot-Skirving, Maj., at No. 58 Scottish, 333
Scots Guards, mess of the, 182, 183, 217, 229, 230; at Cambrai, 269
Scott, Gen. Hugh, 269, 430

Scottish troops, in Lys offensive, 326, 329; their unserviceable uniforms, 329

Sears, Mrs. J. M., 91

Sedgwick, Ellery, 95

Senlis, the ruins of, 19–21

Service de Santé, summary of, 36; author's views of, 76; absorbs Field Ambulance Service, 82; Tuffier's account of, 228 and *n*.

Séry-Magneval, confusion at, 404, 406, 407, 411

Sharp, Ambassador William, 47, 395; at Picpus ceremonies, 148

Shattuck, Frederick C., 95

Shaw, Col. Kennedy, at Lillers, 324

Shelton, anæsthetist, No. 46, 167

Shepley, Miss Julia, 478

Sherrington, Sir Charles, 108, 109, 295

Shine, Col., at St. Omer, 331

Shurly, Maj., 350

Siler, Col. J. F., 267; Chief of Pathology, 277, 290

Simpson, Capt., 440

Simpson, Col., C.O. No. 8 Stationary, 113

Sinclair, Maj., 113, 265, 468

Singer, Charles, 295

Singh, Sir Pertab, 227 *n*.

Sinn Feiners, 357, 359, 360

Skinner, Gen. Bruce, D.M.S. 5th Army, 116, 166, 167, 171, 183, 191–194, 199, 204, 206, 209, 249, 272

Slater, Col., at Mont des Cats, 194

Slater, Mrs. H. N., 156

Sleeper, Henry D., and Field Ambulance Service, 82

Sloggett, Sir Arthur, overseas D.G., 50, 57, 65, 72, 111, 153, 177, 208, 227, 281, 289, 356; retired from active list, 363; his elaborate send-off, 367, 368

Smilie, Dr., ship's surgeon of *Canopic*, 510

Smith, Capt., at Baccarat, 348, 349

Smith, Col. Maynard, 172, 173, 234

Soissons, falls to Brandenburgers, 367

Solferino Farm, C.D.S. at, 237, 239

Soltau, Col., 115, 218, 219, 221, 284, 332, 387

Souilly, the hospital group at, 430, 432–437, 450–453

Souli, Mr., 6, 7

Spooner, Rev. W. A., 296

Stanley, Dr., at *Château d'Annel*, 34

Stanton, Col., at Picpus, 148

Stark, Col., 402, 417, 424, 439, 450, 461, 463

Station Neurologique No. 42, at Salins, 423, 424

Stationary Hospitals (*see also* General Hospitals):

No. 2 (*Bailleul*), 118, 122, 130

No. 3 *Canadian*, a direct hit at, 367

No. 4, 153, 201

No. 7 *Canadian*, 153

No. 8, 113

No. 12 (*New Zealand*), 117, 118, 124, 125, 128; closed, 188

No. 15 *Canadian* (*Cliveden*), 296

No. 32, 113

No. 53, 118, 122, 125, 126, 129, 130

R.C. *Hosp.* 114, 452, 454; choked with wounded, 460, 463

Steele, Col., C.O. No. 4, 160

Stevens, Capt. Frank, at F.H. No. 114, 444, 448

Stewart, Sir Edward, 263

Stewart, Redmond, 406

Stiles, Lieut. Col. H. J., 205 and *n*.

Stimson, Henry L., 276

Stirling, Capt. A. D., 115, 119, 121, 128, 219, 272; wounded at Boulogne, 413

Stoddard, James, 105, 202, 275

Stokes, Adrian, 118, 119, 129

Stokes, Henry, 118, 119, 129, 269

Stone, at Base Hospital No. 18, 302

Storey, Moorfield, 85, 99

Storrow, James M., 97

Story of Base Hospital No. 5, 506 and *n*.

Stout, Lieut., 432, 458

Strong, Richard P., on the *Canopic*, 4, 6; at Algeciras, 8; at Madrid, 9; visits 2ème *Armée*, 18–30; off to

Serbia, 30; in Boston, 86; returns to France, 89; in Paris, 147, 258, 267, 271, 278, 300, 301, 344, 385, 388, 390, 466; at Fleury, 460; at Neufchâteau, 462
Sullivan, Corpn. Counsel, 90
Sullivan, Pte. Jeremiah, 441, 457, 459, 462, 466
Sutcliffe, Col., at No. 32, 173
Sutton, Maj., C.O. 18th Corps Flying Squadron, 245, 293
Swift, at No. 46, 180; on Research Committee, 258; at Fleury, 464

TANKS, British, a glimpse of, 238, 239
Tavern Club, 82, 94, 99
Taylor, Alonzo, 493
Taylor, Capt., of F.H. No. 101, 439
Taylor, Capt., pilot, at Tours, 353, 354
Taylor, Dr., 94, 267, 274, 362
Taylor, Sir Frederick, 205 n.
Taylor, Padre, at La Fauche, 476
Tefft, Col., at Evac. No. 7, 394
Telfer, Capt., 499; evacuation officer, No. 46, 167, 172, 196, 209, 233; last to leave, 321
Tenney, Maj., 429
Terhune, William B., at Neufchâteau, 386
Territorial Hospitals:
  No. 7, 153
  No. 58, 153
  No. 59, 153
Tetanus, treatment of, 276
Thaxter, L. T., 295
Thayer, W. S., at Neufchâteau, 301, 345, 385, 399, 420, 451, 471; to be a general, 437, 438, 443; in Paris, 466, 468; at La Fauche, 476; off for England, 494
Thayer, William Roscoe, 85, 94, 95
Thenault, Georges, Story of the Lafayette Escadrille, 53 n.
Thomas, at No. 53, 129
Thompson, Gen., D.M.S. 1st Army, 267, 277, 283–285, 330, 332, 386
Thompson, intelligence officer 18th Corps Flying Squadron, 244, 246

Thorburn, Col. William, 271, 299
Thursday Evening Club, 94
Thurston, Col., C.O. Abbeville district, 299, 323, 383
Toul, military importance of, 302
Toussaint, Dr., 52
Towne, E. B., 152, 157, 161, 169, 177; C.O. Mobile No. 6, 403 n.; at Fleury, 451, 452, 455–460, 462, 468
Towse, Sir Beachcroft, 114, 274
Tredwell, Miss, auxiliaire, 216
Trench-fever research, instituted, 258, 259, 267, 300, 301; at American Hospital, 390
Trimble, Col., in raid on Étaples, 366, 368
Trotter, Capt. Wilfred, 357
Trout, Hugh H., at Crépy, 405
Tuffier, Dr., 42, 43, 53, 228 and n., 388, 403
Tugo, Pte., killed at Camiers, 201, 202
Turberville, pilot, 180, 181, 199
Turnbull, Mr., in Paris, 148
Turnbull, Col., 466
Tuttle, Col., 455

VANDERBILT, MRS., in Paris, 150
Van Gorder, G. W., 295
Vaucher, Dr., 289, 290
Vennison, Capt., of Saxonia, 104–106
Verdun, in 1918, 304–307
Viallet, Dr., 29
Villaret, Lieut., 99, 101–103, 377, 380
Vimy Ridge, a visit to, 136–140
Vipond, Charles N., 138
Vlamertynghe, ruins of, 242
Von Bissing, Gen., 242

W.A.A.C.'s, 279, 280
Wadhams, Col. S. H., 399, 453, 456; at Juilly, 390; discouraged, 473
Wadsworth, Eliot, 87, 88, 97, 103
Wagstaffe, W. W., at No. 4 Canadian, 308, 334, 335
Walcott, Dr. H. P., 85, 87, 95, 96
Walker, at No. 4 Canadian, 335, 342
Walker, Capt. Gideon, M.O. Scots Guards, 217, 224, 229, 230;

killed in attack on Cambrai, 269
Walker, Dr. Norman, 205 n.
Walker, Gen., 450
Wall, Capt. J. P., at Boulogne, 261, 262
Wall, Col., at Meerut Hospital, 62, 63, 280, 292
Wallace, Col. Cuthbert (later Maj. General, Sir), at Boulogne, 56, 60, 114, 183, 267, 284, 332; at No. 58 C.C.S., 323, 324
Walloert, Dr. L., at Lillers, 324, 328
Ward, Lady, 110
Waring, Col., at No. 7 General, 331
Warren, John Collins, 94
Warren, John, Quartermaster, at No. 46, 167
Watson, Sir David, G.O.C. 4th Canadians, 340, 341
Webb, Col., C.O. at Steenwerck, 122, 130, 426
Webb, Gerald, 386
Webb-Johnson, Col., at No. 32 Stationary, 265, 271, 272; at Calais with Cushing, 369, 370
Weed, C. F., 87
Welch, Dr. William H., 258, 267
Welpley, "Tiny," surgeon, at No. 46, 167, 190
Wendell, Mrs. Barrett, 99
Western Reserve Univ., medical unit of, 3
Westhoek, attack on, 180, 183
Westminster, Duchess of, her hospital at Le Touquet, 369
Wetherell, Maj., 152
Wetherill, Padre, 167
White, J. William, at Neuilly, 81
Whitlock, Brand, at Picpus, 148
Whitman, Walt, his Memoranda quoted, 506, 507
Whitney, Mrs. Harry Payne, 3, 390
Whittlesey, Maj. Charles, the remarkable story of, 469, 475
Widener, Lieut., at Neufchâteau, 345, 471
Wilberforce, Gen., inspects No. 94 P.O.W., 309, 310; and Prince of Wales, 316

William II, of Germany, 478, 491, 497; abdicates, 492, 496; his flight, 499
Williams, Capt., aid to Gen. Wood, 276, 278, 287
Williams, Col. Frank, 86, 87, 93
Williams, James T., Jr., 90
Wilson, Capt., at No. 4 Canadian, 335
Wilson, Sir Henry, 317 n.
Wilson, Maj., at Cheppy, 465
Wilson, Woodrow, 85, 280; reëlected on peace platform, 79; declares war, 86; French reception of his notes, 149, 150; his reply to Pope's peace proposals, 197, 199; and Wood, 396; his peace negotiations, 467–469, 474–478, 493; to attend Peace Conference, 502
Wingate, Col., C.O. No. 17 C.C.S., 118
Winsor, Robert, 91
Winterfeldt, Gen. von, 495–497
Woerner, Lieut., 26, 27
Wolfenden, 113
Wolstenholme, C.O. No. 64, 161, 167, 171, 192, 226
Wood, Gen. Leonard, 49, 97; his herculean efforts for preparedness, 79; demoted, 85; in Boston, 90–92; in Paris, 276, 278, 286, 287, 291; home again, 317, 396
Wood, Mrs. Leonard, 103
Woods, bugler, killed at Camiers, 202
Wright, corps commander, 419
Wright, surgeon at No. 46, 167
Wright, Sir Almroth, 59; in charge of laboratory, Boulogne Casino, 64, 131, 154, 255, 256, 265, 269, 270, 273, 274, 278, 279, 292, 300, 315, 364, 383, 506
Wright, Mrs. H. P., 296
Wright, Phœbe, 255

YATES, JOHN L., at F.H. No. 103, 288, 301, 404, 439, 441, 452
Yellowlees, Capt., 204
Young, Capt., at Lillers, 324
Young, Lt. Col. Taylor, 165, 169; at No. 46, 263; to be Chief of Vene-

real Diseases, 262, 277, 300, 301; at Neufchâteau, 386, 413; at Fleury, 462

Ypres, a glimpse of, 69–73; the ruins of, 211, 212, 219, 243, 244, 250–253

ZINKHAN, LIEUT., 213; adventures of, 178–180; at Ypres, 210–212

Zinsser, Hans, investigates sanitary conditions of army, 421

Zonnebeke, the attack on, 212–215; wreckage around, 241

WS - #0051 - 030624 - C0 - 229/152/33 - PB - 9780364280225 - Gloss Lamination